*f*P

BROKEN

The Troubled Past and Uncertain Future of the FBI

★

RICHARD GID POWERS

FREE PRESS

NEW YORK · LONDON · TORONTO · SYDNEY

FREE PRESS
A Division of Simon & Schuster, Inc.
1230 Avenue of the Americas
New York, NY 10020

FREE PRESS and colophon are
trademarks of Simon & Schuster, Inc.

For information about special discounts for bulk purchases,
please contact Simon & Schuster Special Sales:
1-800-456-6798 or business@simonandschuster.com

Designed by Dana Sloan

Illustration credits appear on pages 493–494

Manufactured in the United States of America

1   3   5   7   9   10   8   6   4   2

Library of Congress Cataloging-in-Publication Data
Powers, Richard Gid.
Broken: the troubled past and uncertain future of the FBI / Richard Gid Powers.
p.   cm.
Includes bibliographical references and index.
1. United States, Federal Bureau of Investigation—History.
2. Law enforcement—United States—History—20th century.
3. Criminal investigation—United States—History—20th century.   I. Title.
HV8144.F43 P68   2004
363.25'0973—dc22   2004053349

ISBN 0-684-83371-9

TO THE VICTIMS OF 9/11

CONTENTS

BROKEN

A Shadow of Itself

THIS IS THE HISTORY of an American tragedy. The story of how as great an American institution as the FBI could become so traumatized by its past that it failed its duty to the nation it was sworn to protect.

The morning of September 11, 2001. I was in my car on the Gowanus Expressway along the Brooklyn waterfront. Just before nine o'clock, sirens. Traffic slowing. Fire trucks sped toward Manhattan. Over the car radio, word that a plane had crashed into one of the World Trade Center towers.

When the planes hit, this history of the Bureau was well under way. I knew that the FBI was, by law and presidential directives, the country's lead agency against terrorism. For years the FBI had been "rendering" terrorists from overseas back to the United States to stand trial for attacks against the United States. Where the Marines would once have landed, Presidents Reagan, Bush, and Clinton had ordered the FBI to investigate embassy bombings, barracks explosions, and assaults on American warships. Under Clinton, law enforcement had emerged as the country's preferred weapon against terror. The architects of this doctrine may never have meant for law enforcement actually to replace military action or diplomacy, but during the 1990s FBI law enforcement had effectively taken their place. Then came 9/11. The dream of bringing terror under the rule of law through arrests, prosecutions, and punishment suddenly seemed the tragic and failed relic of an impossibly idealistic era.

I had recently interviewed the FBI's top official on counterterrorism, Neil Gallagher, assistant director in charge of the National Security Division. When I asked him what the Bureau was doing about terrorism, he took me to their high-tech Strategic Intelligence and Operations Center, where government leaders could stay in touch with a terrorist attack site by means of banks of computers and monitors. He briefed me on the Bureau doctrine of joint operations command and joint information facilities, used to coordinate the efforts of first responders. The FBI's planning for a terrorist attack focused on establishing order at the "crime scene" to preserve evidence and organize it for the eventual trial. The Bureau's famed Hostage Rescue Team—the guys who slither down ropes from black helicopters–had been embedded in a "Critical Incident Response Group" who were to take charge at violent crime scenes. The team rehearsed "close quarters battle" against the "Tangos" (aviation lingo for the letter *T,* meaning terrorists) in mazelike shooting ranges at the FBI Academy in Quantico, Virginia, preparing themselves to fight barricaded terrorists. In field drills and "tabletop" exercises at headquarters the Bureau had practiced restoring order as a panicked population tried to flee an urban center (one scenario was a biological attack on Wall Street) while emergency personnel—police, fire department, military personnel, government leaders—made their way through the crowds. The Bureau had spent the better part of a decade studying how to shape the chaos of a terrorist attack into investigative order for an eventual trial. The focus was on response, not prevention. FBI Director Louis Freeh liked to reassure critics disturbed by memories of the Hoover era that *his* FBI was and always would be reactive, never proactive.

The first few hours after the 9/11 attack would make that planning seem irrelevant, almost bizarrely misguided. As for preserving evidence, getting ready for a trial, everyone in the world had seen the crime, and the terrorists were all dead along with their victims. There would be no trial. There was no evidence in any real sense, only the recovery of what remained of the victims for burial. And although the FBI succeeded in identifying the nineteen hijackers with startling speed, that was cold comfort.

The question we were asking was not who had done it, and whether they could have been convicted. It was why the FBI (and the CIA) hadn't kept it from happening. But when I had asked the FBI's National Security Division what they were doing to stop terrorist attacks, they had replied, again and again, with the mantra "We aren't violating anybody's civil liberties."

That hadn't impressed me then. It was going to impress other people even less after 9/11.

Pearl Harbor, the only intelligence disaster in American history comparable to 9/11, ushered in years of finger-pointing, with Democrats and Republicans each trying to assign the other guilt for the intelligence failure, and for over half a century conspiracy buffs have promoted the idea that only colossal incompetence or treason could explain how clues to Japanese intentions were ignored by FDR, the Navy . . . or the FBI. But all responsible historical examinations of Pearl Harbor found that those few meaningful "signals" pointing to an attack were drowned out before December 7, 1941, by the meaningless "noise" of conflicting messages.

I had no doubt that after 9/11, too, all manner of "signals" would surface that supposedly should have tipped off the FBI and other agencies about the impending attack, had those signals been interpreted correctly. I expected that this time, too, careful investigation and sober reflection would reveal that those meaningful signals were distinguishable only in hindsight from the static of meaningless noise. There would be no smoking guns. There would be no really damning answer to the question, What did the Bureau know and when did it know it?

・・・

I was wrong.

This time there were more than a few signals lost in the static. This time there actually would be, in a figurative sense at least, smoking guns, and the full picture of how the FBI had mishandled the pre-9/11 investigation would be so devastating as to raise the question of whether the FBI would—or should—be allowed to continue in its role as the nation's primary defender against the threat of terrorist attack.

The FBI—and the CIA and many other intelligence agencies—had come tantalizingly close to cracking the 9/11 conspiracy during the summer of 2001. No one can say for sure that even if the Bureau had pursued all its leads vigorously and effectively, it could have spared the country the 9/11 attack. But the fact is that the FBI did not pursue those leads—and it had *good* leads—vigorously or effectively. The 9/11 failures of the Bureau were the result of decisions so wrongheaded as to seem almost incredible to anyone hearing about them for the first time—decisions, however, that were not only predictable but almost inevitable, when viewed against the turbulent history of the FBI.

・・・

By 9:30 A.M. on September 11, when the president told the country it was under terrorist attack, Bush, his top advisers, and key officials in the FBI knew exactly who was responsible. Like a persistent and unshakable stalker, Osama bin Laden had been following America, in his thoughts at least, long before America or the FBI had any thought of him. Sometime around 1989 bin Laden assembled his top lieutenants and told them he was founding a new organization that would be "focused on jihad" both in Afghanistan and elsewhere in the world. Driving the American military out of the Arabian peninsula was (and still is) his primary objective. Soon after that, the United States began to come under ever more frequent terrorist attacks at home and abroad. The first World Trade Center bombing in 1993 has not been directly linked to bin Laden, but Ramzi Yousef, who planned the 1993 attack, and several of the other bombers had trained in Afghanistan at al Qaeda camps. Ramzi Yousef himself is the nephew of al Qaeda's Khalid Shaykh Mohammed (Mukhtar, or "the brain"), the mastermind of the 9/11 attacks (and currently in U.S. custody—somewhere). Bin Laden's brother-in-law, Mohammed Jamal Khalifa, probably provided the financing for Yousef's failed plot in 1995 to blow up twelve American airliners flying Pacific routes. When Yousef was arrested in 1995 by the FBI's Brad Garrett, he was staying at a bin Laden guesthouse in Pakistan.

Preventing an attack like 9/11 should have been the Bureau's most pressing objective after its earlier investigations of fundamentalist Islamic terrorism. The FBI had been collecting information on bin Laden since its investigation of the October 1993 attack in Somalia that killed eighteen U.S. Marines and became the movie *Black Hawk Down*. The Bureau concluded that bin Laden's organization was behind the attack, and this led to a June 1998 sealed indictment against him for a "conspiracy to attack defense installations of the United States." On June 7, 1999, bin Laden was put on the Bureau's Ten Most Wanted fugitives list. The Bureau (along with other intelligence agencies) collected enough evidence that bin Laden and al Qaeda were responsible for the 1998 attacks on the American Embassies in Nairobi and Dar es Salaam for an unsealed indictment of bin Laden on November 4, 1999, for conspiring to "murder United States nationals anywhere in the world, including in the United States."

The FBI foiled the "Millennium" plot to bomb Los Angeles International Airport on January 1, 2000, when it picked up an al Qaeda operative carrying explosives near the Canadian border. The FBI had more proof that bin Laden planned and financed the October 2000 bombing of the USS *Cole* in Yemen, evidence gathered by an army of FBI agents sent to the crime scene. On the morning of September 11, the FBI was investigating no fewer than three major al Qaeda attacks abroad: the 1998 bombings of the U.S. Embassies in Tanzania and Kenya and the attack on the USS *Cole* in 2000, to say nothing of the Iranian-inspired Khobar Towers bombing in Saudi Arabia in 1995, which had become something of a personal obsession for Louis Freeh, who was working that case like a street agent.

The CIA had also been warning about the danger bin Laden and al Qaeda posed to American lives and interests. On January 8, 1996, the CIA set up a bin Laden unit within its Counterterrorism Center, and in 1998 the agency declared that bin Laden and al Qaeda were *the* most dangerous current threats to the United States. That year the director of Central Intelligence, George Tenet, told his agency that it was "at war" with al Qaeda, and that "I want no resources or people spared, in this effort, either inside CIA or the [intelligence] community." Tenet testified to Congress on June 24, 1999, that bin Laden was planning attacks within the United States. On February 21, 2001, the CIA's annual worldwide threat analysis reported that "UBL [the CIA and FBI use the spelling "Usama" for bin Laden's name, hence "UBL"] and his associates remain most immediate and serious threat. UBL's commitment of striking against the U.S. undiminished . . . strong indications planning new operations . . . capable of mounting multiple attacks with little or no warning."

For two years the intelligence community—the FBI, CIA, and Defense Department intelligence agencies—had been receiving reports that bin Laden was planning to strike targets within the United States at an unspecified time and an unspecified place. Soon after bin Laden's February 23, 1998, *fatwa* calling for attacks on American military and civilian targets everywhere in the world, he began hinting that the war would be brought home to America. As early as August 1998, intelligence agents told the FBI and the Federal Aviation Administration that a group with ties to al Qaeda was talking about flying an explosives-laden plane into the World Trade Center. Throughout 1998 and 1999 the intelligence community had reports on other al Qaeda plans to utilize aircraft in attacks within the United States. One report, not shared with the FBI, had bin Laden thinking about using commercial pilots in a "spectacular and traumatic" attack on the country.

During the spring and summer of 2001 the intelligence community was getting more signals than ever that there might be an al Qaeda attack on American interests, though these were unspecific as to time, place, or method. On June 25, 2001, the intelligence community warned government leaders of an upcoming "spectacular" strike. On June 30 senior government officials were told that bin Laden's organization was telling its followers to expect an imminent attack on the U.S. with dramatic consequences. At the beginning of July a memo circulated to senior government officials warning that,

> *based on a review of all-source reporting over the last five months, we believe that UBL will launch a significant terrorist attack against U.S. and/or Israeli interests in the coming months. The attack will be spectacular and designed to inflict mass casualties against U.S. facilities or interests. Attack preparations have been made. Attack will occur with little or no warning!*

Meanwhile, George Tenet was all over town warning of an imminent attack, though he could not say where or when. But the FBI was telling the law enforcement community that it had no credible information of an imminent attack *within* the United States.

■ ■ ■

A week after that July 2 warning, FBI agent Kenneth Williams of the Phoenix field office sent Washington headquarters an "electronic communication" that pointed directly to the unfolding 9/11 conspiracy.

Williams had been watching several Middle Eastern men in his area for more than a year. He had noticed that several of them were taking flight instruction at a Prescott, Arizona, branch of the well-known Embry-Riddle Aeronautical University.

When Williams interviewed the Middle Eastern students, they made it clear that they hated the United States. One of them had a poster of bin Laden in his room. Another, who was taking expensive aviation training although he was from a poor Middle Eastern country and had not studied aviation before his arrival in the United States, was in touch with Abu Zubayda, chief of bin Laden's training camps in Afghanistan. Several of the other students had also been involved with al Qaeda. All this led Williams to suspect a coordinated campaign by Muslim extremists to use civil aviation to attack the United States.

While conducting physical surveillance of his primary subject, Williams learned that he was using a vehicle registered to another Middle Eastern individual who had been detained in 1999 when he and a friend tried to enter the cockpit of a commercial airliner. They claimed they had mistaken the cockpit for the bathroom and "accused the Bureau of racism" for questioning them. They were released for lack of evidence and the case was closed. In November 2000, the owner of the car was placed on the State Department's watch list on the basis of a report that he may have gotten training in explosives and car bombs in Afghanistan. In August 2001 he was denied reentry into the United States.

In his July 10 memo, Williams also told headquarters he thought al Qaeda had an active presence in Arizona. Several members of bin Laden's organization had lived in or traveled to Phoenix recently. One of them was Wadih el-Hage, a bin Laden lieutenant, who was later convicted for his role in the 1998 U.S. Embassy bombings in East Africa. Williams believed it was el-Hage who had established the bin Laden network in Arizona (and Williams believed it was still in place when he testified before Congress in 2002).

Williams's communication named ten individuals, all subjects of FBI investigations. They were Sunni Muslims from Kenya, Pakistan, Algeria, the United Arab Emirates, India, and Saudi Arabia. Some were in flight training, others studying aeronautical engineering and international aviation security.

Williams concluded with a list of recommendations for the Bureau:

- Headquarters should accumulate a list of civil aviation universities and colleges around the country;
- FBI offices should establish liaison with these schools;
- Headquarters should discuss the theories in the EC [electronic communication] with the Intelligence Community; and
- Headquarters should consider seeking authority to obtain visa information on persons seeking to attend flight schools.

Along with his memo to Washington headquarters, Williams also forwarded the names of eight of the suspected al Qaeda sympathizers to the CIA.

Williams had outlined a plan of action for the Bureau to follow that, had it been implemented across the country, would have had a very good chance of uncovering several, maybe all, of the strands of the plot. He had given headquarters something else just as good. One of the people he named was in contact with hijacker Hani Hanjour. The Bureau now believes that the individual in Williams's memo took flight training with Hanjour beginning in 1997 and may have belonged to the same mosque. The FBI also learned after September 11, 2001, that another of the individuals mentioned in Williams's memo as connected to the al Qaeda network was arrested in 2002 in Pakistan, where he was meeting with prominent al Qaeda figures.

■ ■ ■

A month after Williams's electronic communication, headquarters got another clue just as good as Williams's, maybe even better. Tipped off by alert flight instructors at Pan American International Flight School near Minneapolis, FBI agents from that field office had arrested a student pilot named Zacarias Moussaoui.

Moussaoui had begun flight lessons at the Airman Flight School in Norman, Oklahoma, on February 26. His reason for transferring to the Minnesota flight school was suspicious in itself. With only fifty hours' flying experience and as yet no license, Moussaoui had shown little interest in the Cessna 152s and 172s that were the standard training aircraft at Airman and most flight schools.

Pan American, unlike the flight school at Norman, catered primarily to advanced pilots working for the airlines. Moussaoui wanted time on Pan American's Boeing 747 flight simulator, used primarily by newly hired airline pilots, who would have had the highest rating awarded by the FAA—an Air Transport

Pilot license—and more than a thousand hours of flight time, or by veteran airline pilots refreshing their skills. For a pilot at Moussaoui's level of training to ask to use that particular simulator was so strange that it immediately raised the suspicions of his instructors. They also thought it odd that Moussaoui had paid $6,800 in cash in advance for the simulator training, when most student pilots working toward a career as professional pilots lived hand-to-mouth, supporting themselves by giving lessons to beginning student pilots. And, despite his interest in advanced flying, when Moussaoui started his simulator training he was unable to grasp the most elementary lessons on aircraft systems, yet showed a strange curiosity in how the plane's doors operated and how the control panel was arranged. He also asked to fly a simulated flight from London's Heathrow to JFK.

Two days after Moussaoui began his classes on August 13, a suspicious flight instructor called the FBI's Minneapolis field office. When the agents arrived to take a look at Moussaoui, they thought there was something peculiar and even threatening about him. They thought he might be a potential terrorist and so opened a case file on him.

The agents soon learned, from immigration agents working on a Joint Terrorism Task Force with the Bureau in Minneapolis, that Moussaoui's visa had expired on May 22, 2001, meaning he was subject to detention and deportation. The Minneapolis office asked headquarters for advice. A supervisory agent in the Counterterrorism Division in Washington suggested that Minneapolis put Moussaoui under surveillance.

The lead case agent later said:

> The decision on whether or not we were going to put Mr. Moussaoui under surveillance rested with me. And I made the decision that he was going to be arrested because we had a violation. The INS [Immigration and Naturalization Service] was participating as a member, a full member of our joint terrorism task force. My background in the criminal arena suggests that when a violation occurs and you can stop further or potential criminal activity, you act on that. So that is exactly what I instructed the agents to do. If we had the possibility of arresting him, we were going to arrest him. If we needed to surveil him, we certainly could have instituted a surveillance plan. . . . It was not appropriate to do [so] in this case.
>
> I didn't want him to get any additional time on a flight simulator that would allow him to have the knowledge that we could no longer take back from him to operate an aircraft. This provided us the opportunity to freeze the situation as it was going on right there, prevent him from gaining the knowledge

that he could use at some point in the future. And, if ultimately we determined all we could do, after interviewing him and doing some other investigative steps, if all we could do was deport him, then we would be sensitized to the fact that he was interested in doing something else and he could be put in the Tip-off System. He would be put in—the appropriate notifications could have been made if he attempted to reenter the United States. But our focus was on preventing him getting the knowledge that he would have needed. . . .

On August 16, FBI agents accompanied by INS officers confronted Moussaoui at his residence and determined that he did not have a valid passport. When they asked him if they could search his belongings and his laptop computer, he refused.

The agents suspected that the laptop might contain vital leads, so they asked the Minneapolis office's legal counsel (FBI Agent Coleen Rowley) to find out if they could legally search the computer without Moussaoui's consent. She told them they would need a search warrant. They had three options: to get a criminal search warrant, to ask for a Foreign Intelligence Surveillance Act (FISA) search warrant, or, failing that, to turn him over to the French, who had agreed to search the computer and report back to the FBI. There was not much time, because the INS does not customarily hold foreigners in Moussaoui's situation for more than twenty-four hours, though in this case they were willing to stretch that to a week or so.

At this point another Middle Eastern individual attempted to post bond for Moussaoui's roommate. The roommate's friend, it later developed, had been the subject of a full-field FBI international terrorism investigation at the Oklahoma City field office. He was, in fact, in charge of overseas operations and recruiting for the Palestinian al-Fatah and a member of the Muslim Brotherhood. He was also a close associate of the imam at the Islamic center that hijackers Nawaf al-Hazmi and Khalid al-Mihdhar attended. And this imam was an associate of another imam in San Diego who, it turned out, was the hijackers' spiritual adviser.

By this time the Minneapolis agents were frantic to get a look at Moussaoui's computer, and were pleading with headquarters to get them a FISA warrant to examine it. A FISA warrant could be obtained only from a special panel of judges in Washington, and could be granted even if there was no probable cause for supposing that a crime had been committed, if the purpose of the warrant was an intelligence investigation of individuals working for a foreign power or group. In response to the request from Minneapolis, the supervisor of the Radical Fundamentalist Unit in the Counterterrorism Division at headquarters criticized the lead agent in Minneapolis for getting people "spun up" over Moussaoui. The Minneapolis agent replied—in these exact words—that he was trying to get people at FBI Headquarters "spun up" because he was trying to make sure that Moussaoui "did not take control of a plane and fly it into the World Trade Center." The headquarters agent responded, "[T]hat's not going to happen. We don't know he's a terrorist. You don't have enough to show he is a terrorist. You have a guy interested in this type of aircraft—that is it."

Shortly thereafter, French intelligence told the Minneapolis office (through the FBI's legal attaché, or "Legat," in Paris) that Moussaoui was affiliated with a Chechen radical Islamic group in turn tied to Osama bin Laden. The Minneapolis agents now believed that Moussaoui was in some way involved with al Qaeda, and so they felt they had to get into his computer. They redoubled their efforts to get headquarters to approve a FISA warrant.

Moussaoui was not simply involved with al Qaeda—he was, as he would later admit, a full-fledged member. One theory is that Moussaoui was supposed to be the pilot of a fifth plane, targeting the White House. An alternative and more likely conjecture is that Moussaoui was intended as a substitute for hijacker pilot Mohammed Atta's roommate in Hamburg, Ramzi bin al-Shibh, who was, however, refused entry into the United States. Al-Shibh himself was supposed to learn how to fly in the United States so that he could take the controls of the plane eventually flown by Hani Hanjour, whose piloting skills were so negligible as to raise doubts among his superiors about whether he could hit his target. Unfortunately, Hanjour turned out to know how to fly well enough to fly his plane into the Pentagon.

If the Bureau had mounted a full-scale investigation of Moussaoui, they would have learned what they quickly did after 9/11. After he graduated from South Bank University in England with a master's degree in international business, he joined the same mosque as Richard Reid, later arrested for trying to set off a shoe bomb on a transatlantic flight. In April 1998 Moussaoui traveled to the Khalden terrorist training camp in Afghanistan, where he became close friends with Flight 175 hijacker Hamza Alghamdi. He may also have fought for al Qaeda in Chechnya. In 1999 French intelligence discovered Moussaoui's name in an address book of a Muslim fighter killed in Bosnia. Moussaoui moved to Malaysia by September 2000, where Yazid Sufaat, who was present at a Kuala Lumpur meeting with two of the 9/11 hijackers in January 2000, furnished him with false business credentials from a legitimate firm called Infocus Tech.

That same year Moussaoui began writing to one of the same flight schools (Airman Flight School in Norman, Oklahoma) that hijacker pilots Mohammed Atta and Marwan al-Shehhi visited in July 2000. Moussaoui arrived in

Norman on February 23, 2001, and began lessons. In May, like almost all the hijackers, he prepared for the physical aspects of the takeovers by working out in a gym in Norman.

The Phoenix and Minneapolis offices had actually given the FBI leads better than it had in any of the classic cases of its history.

• • •

While the Bureau was deciding what to do with this information, the 9/11 plotters were making final preparations for their attacks on Washington and New York. Most of them had arrived in the United States between spring 2000 and summer 2001, although one of the hijack pilots, Hanjour, had been in and out of the United States since 1991.

Atta, al-Shehhi, and Ziad Jarrah, along with Hanjour who would eventually be the four hijacker pilots, entered the United States in May or June 2000. All three were fast learners. Atta and al-Shehhi did especially well and got their commercial pilot licenses on December 21, 2000. They then left the country in January: Atta to Spain, Germany, and an unknown third country, and al-Shehhi to Morocco. They presumably reported to al Qaeda on their progress.

While he was getting his pilot's license at flight school, Mohammed Atta, who would be assigned to lead the plot, acted in a reckless, almost ostentatious, manner. He was so antagonistic toward other fliers that his nickname at his Florida flight school was "the little terrorist." He flew to small airports in Georgia, rudely demanding information about what could have been interpreted as terrorist targets—chemical factories and hydroelectric dams. Throughout July and August 2001, Atta and several other Middle Eastern men visited a crop-dusting firm in Florida, where they insistently questioned the owner about crop-dusting operations and demanded that he let them sit in the plane. Atta got a traffic ticket for reckless driving and driving without a license, and failed to appear for his hearing.

The full complement of hijackers was finally assembled in the United States by July 2001, the so-called muscle or strong-arm men arriving in April, May, and June. Atta, al-Shehhi, and Jarrah each took command of a four- or five-member team. Nawaf al-Hazmi seems to have been in command of Hanjour's team. Most were working out in gyms to prepare for physical combat.

Elementary intelligence tradecraft would dictate that an operation like the 9/11 plot be highly compartmentalized, so if one hijacker were arrested, he could not reveal the entire plan. The 9/11 hijackers either didn't know this or didn't care. Al-Shehhi gave Atta's address when asked for a residence on returning to the U.S. from his frequent trips abroad. Other hijackers gave the motel rooms where they were all staying as addresses when applying for driver's licenses. Groups of hijackers made use of the same sources (known to the authorities) to get false affidavits of address for their driver's license applications.

Alone or in groups, sometimes all four together, the pilots began to take flights on the same routes as the planes they would hijack, always sitting in first class close to the cabin doors to observe security procedures. Actor James Woods spotted four Middle Eastern men acting suspiciously on a Boston–San Francisco flight, and two of them later proved to have been the hijackers. The four pilots seem to have gotten together frequently, several times in Las Vegas to discuss plans, the last time on August 13 to go over the final details. Any investigation that therefore led the Bureau to one of the hijackers might have led to them all.

There was still more activity that would have looked suspicious if the FBI had been looking. The key to stopping the plot would have been to put together the Phoenix and the Minneapolis leads, that is, to look at Moussaoui's activities in the light of Ken Williams's theory that there might be a widespread plan by al Qaeda involving commercial or civil aviation, and to investigate the names on Williams's list.

■ ■ ■

With all these leads, and with the government buzzing with warnings that a big attack might be coming, what went wrong? Why wasn't the FBI, with the new Counterterrorism Division that Director Louis Freeh had set up a year earlier to track terrorists, its new Investigative Services Division (devoted to nothing but analysis of intelligence gathered from across division lines), and its dozens of counterterrorism task forces, all over these leads?

In a phrase that would come up repeatedly in the post-mortems, the reason was "an excess of caution." Kenneth Williams's electronic communication to headquarters was routed to the Radical Fundamentalist Unit (RFU) and the Usama bin Laden Unit of the Counterterrorism Division. The memo was first scanned by an intelligence operations specialist in the RFU, who focused particularly on Williams's request for visa information on Middle Eastern students seeking flight instruction. According to congressional investigation, the ensuing "discussion centered on the legality of the proposal and whether it raised profiling issues." Since one of the suspects named in Williams's memo had previously been in the Northwest, the memo was also forwarded to the Portland FBI office, but without any request for action—for informational purposes only.

With that, the counterterrorism specialists at FBI Headquarters decided to close the investigation. One of them later said that she had intended to take another look at the memo when she had time, but she never did get the time—at least not before September 11. She and another specialist both claimed that they had briefly considered turning the memo over to an analytic unit at headquarters but decided against it. The memo died. The only interest it had stirred at headquarters was concern that Phoenix might be asking the Bureau to do something that might appear to unfriendly observers to be racial profiling.

Later, after 9/11, the head of the International Terrorism Operations Section at FBI Headquarters said that since the memo mentioned planes, it should have been shared with the FAA. It mentioned intelligence, so it should have gone to the CIA. The mention of visas should have routed it to the State Department. The FAA official in charge of intelligence felt that if he had gotten the memo it would have sparked action there, because whenever the agency gets word of a potential threat to aviation, it immediately opens a top-priority case file.

The Phoenix memo *was* sent to two counterterrorism agents in the New York field office, since New York was the office of origin for Osama bin Laden cases. These agents said they paid little attention to it because they had long known that al Qaeda sent pilots to the U.S. for training. Since nothing had been done about this in the past, it needed no attention now.

If headquarters' treatment of Williams's Phoenix memo was incomprehensibly obtuse, its handling of the Minneapolis field office's arrest of Moussaoui was so perverse as to arouse suspicions in Minnesota (only half whimsical) that the Counterterrorism Division in Washington was infiltrated by al Qaeda moles.

Minneapolis had wanted to get legal authority to search Moussaoui's computer hard drive, and so it sent its request to the same Radical Fundamentalism Unit that had waved off Williams's electronic communication. The unit first refused to let the Minneapolis office apply to the local U.S. attorney for a criminal warrant, claiming it might prejudice any later application for a Foreign Intelligence Surveillance Act warrant. The FBI lawyers were afraid that the FISA court would reject the application if it could not pass a so-called "smell test" showing it was not tainted by any possible interest in an eventual criminal investigation. Minneapolis understood this to mean that headquarters would consider only a FISA request, and so proceeded on that basis.

But then the Radical Fundamentalist Unit took what appear to have been deliberate steps to sabotage Minneapolis's application for the FISA warrant, to ensure that no FISA warrant would be granted—for that matter, to make sure the application would never even be seen by the FISA court.

When Minneapolis asked what it would need to get a FISA warrant, headquarters said they would have to connect Moussaoui to a "recognized foreign power" that appeared on a list of recognized terrorist organizations for which the FISA court had previously granted warrants. This sent Minneapolis on several weeks of a wild-goose chase to see if a Chechen group linked to Moussaoui qualified. Headquarters consistently told Minneapolis that it did not, and that they would have to somehow connect the Chechen group to al Qaeda, which *was* on the list.

Headquarters then scolded Minneapolis for notifying the CIA's Counterterrorism Center about Moussaoui's arrest. This had gotten the CIA alarmed enough to begin referring to Moussaoui and Hussein al-Attas (Moussaoui's fellow flight student and roommate) as "suspect 747 airline attackers" and "suspect airline suicide attacker[s]" who might be "involved in a larger plot to target airlines traveling from Europe to the U.S." Minneapolis was ordered not to contact anyone except through headquarters.

All this time, the Minneapolis agents should have been developing leads based on an examination of Moussaoui's belongings—and interrogating him after confronting him with their findings. Instead, the agents had to try to accomplish what was for them—in Minnesota—almost impossible: establishing a link between Moussaoui's Chechen group and al Qaeda. In fact, the supervisor advising Minneapolis was totally mistaken, as were the FBI attorneys he consulted: The Chechen group certainly *did* qualify as a "recognized" foreign power for purposes of FISA.

Minneapolis finally submitted a FISA application to headquarters that linked Moussaoui's Chechen group to al Qaeda. But before passing the request on to the FBI's deputy general counsel for his approval, the supervisor removed the laboriously acquired information about the links between the Chechen group and al Qaeda, which he had previously insisted upon. Without the information about the Chechen groups, the FBI lawyer consulted by the Radical Fundamentalist Unit (again mistakenly) ruled that there was insufficient evidence that Moussaoui was connected to a foreign power, and so he refused to forward the application to the FISA court.

At their wits' end, the Minneapolis agents now prepared to deport Moussaoui to France, where the French authorities had promised to examine the computer and to inform the FBI of its contents. The deportation was scheduled for September 14, but, of course, events intervened.

Had the Minneapolis agents been able to pursue their Moussaoui leads before 9/11 (as they hastened to do after the September 11 attacks), they would have quickly discovered a highly interesting connection between Moussaoui and bin Laden's personal pilot, who had trained at the Norman, Oklahoma, flight school where Moussaoui had started his training, and who had begun cooperating with the Bureau after the East African embassy bombings. They would also have learned that Moussaoui was receiving large sums of money, perhaps for the hijack team he would lead.

If headquarters had ordered an investigation of the names in Williams's electronic communication, the Bureau would have been led to the imam who was the hijackers' spiritual leader in San Diego, and to the imam of the mosque where al-Hazmi and al-Mihdhar worshipped. On August 27, 2001, the FBI got a tip from the CIA that two of the hijackers, al-Mihdhar and al-Hazmi, recent additions to the terrorist watch list, were now in the country. Their names and addresses could have been found on their VISA credit card records—which both had used, in their own names, to buy tickets on the hijack planes. That same day, most of the hijackers bought electronic one-way tickets on the planes they were going to take over. After 9/11, in fact, the Bureau *was* able to discover their addresses from their VISA records in just a few hours. And al-Hazmi, who had earlier been living in San Diego with al-Mihdhar, had had many contacts with a longtime FBI informant in that city, though these contacts were not revealed to the Bureau until after 9/11.

If al-Hazmi and al-Mihdhar had been put on a watch list by the CIA earlier, as the CIA's own rules had dictated, the FBI could have asked their informant if he could find out anything about them. This was characterized later by the congressional Joint Inquiry into 9/11 as missing an opportunity "to task a uniquely well positioned informant" to collect information about the hijackers and their plans, and to follow leads that might have led them to Hanjour, who would flunk out of flight school again just before the hijacking.

Hanjour, who must have been in a state of panic about his flying abilities, tried to check out a rental plane near Bowie, Maryland, but after going up with three different instructors, not one of them would fly with him again—even though he had a pilot's license and six hundred hours' flight time. If the Bureau had put Hanjour under surveillance as a result of the Phoenix leads, his unusual requests for primary training despite his experience might have aroused further suspicion.

But instead of moving against the plotters as 9/11 approached, and even while the rest of the intelligence community escalated its warnings of an impending al Qaeda attack, the FBI again reported that it had no evidence that there was a threat within the United States. It even asserted that "[w]hile international terrorists have conducted attacks on U.S. soil, these acts represent anomalies in their traditional targeting, which focuses on U.S. interests overseas." On July 26, 2001, the FBI's deputy assistant director for counterterrorism, Terry Turchie, told the House Subcommittee on National Security, "FBI investigation and analysis indicates that the threat of terrorism in the United States is low."

■ ■ ■

As I was driving across the Verrazano Bridge watching the towers burn, Minneapolis special agent and chief division counsel Coleen M. Rowley also was getting first word of the 9/11 attack. She immediately contacted that same supervisory special agent (SSA) at the RFU who had been stalling Minneapolis on the Moussaoui warrants. She told him that in light of the attacks, which were still under way, Minneapolis should immediately get a criminal warrant to search Moussaoui's laptop and belongings. It would have to be the "hugest coincidence," she said, if Moussaoui were not involved with the 9/11 attackers. "The SSA stated something to the effect that I had used the right term, 'coincidence' and that this was probably all just a coincidence and we were to do nothing in Minneapolis until we got their Headquarter's permission because we might 'screw up' something else going on elsewhere in the country."

Minneapolis was still being ignored a few days after the 9/11 attacks, when FBI Director Robert Mueller put out a statement that the FBI had had no advance warning, but if it had, the FBI might have been able to take some action to prevent it. The Minneapolis office was amazed: Had no one told Mueller about Moussaoui? (Minnesota still had not been told about the Phoenix electronic communication.) Coleen Rowley and other Minneapolis agents tried to warn Mueller that his statement was far from accurate. They were worried that Mueller's statement, in Rowley's words, "could easily come back to haunt the FBI" when news of the Moussaoui case inevitably surfaced when he was indicted, if not sooner.

Minneapolis was again ignored. Counterterrorism Division Assistant Director James T. Caruso went before Congress and repeated that the FBI had had no good leads before September 11, had done everything it could, and would accept no blame for the 9/11 attacks. Rowley and the other Minneapolis agents finally faced, she said, "the sad realization that the remarks indicated someone had decided to circle the wagons at FBIHQ in an apparent effort to protect the FBI from embarrassment."

Minneapolis's frustration with headquarters' treatment of the Moussaoui case might have faded away unnoticed outside that office, except that eight months later, Rowley was summoned to Washington to testify before the Senate and House Joint Inquiry. To prepare for her testimony, Rowley wrote a thirteen-page memo that constituted a nearly unprecedented revolt by an FBI agent against the high command. Since Rowley was her family's sole breadwinner and expected to retire in less than three years, she added a few sentences at the end requesting protection under the federal whistle-blower law.

Rowley didn't pull any punches. She accused Director Mueller and the top officials of the Bureau of attempting to "shade/skew" the facts concerning the FBI's mishandling of the case.

> *Although I agree that it's very doubtful that the full scope of the tragedy could have been prevented, it's at least possible that we could have gotten lucky and uncovered one or two more of the terrorists in flight training prior to September 11th, just as Moussaoui was discovered, after making contact with his flight instructors.*

With ill-concealed sarcasm, she observed that although "your conclusion otherwise has to be very reassuring for some in the FBI to hear being repeated so often (as if saying it's so may make it so), I think your statements demonstrate a rush to judgment to protect the FBI at all costs."

She told Mueller she had been infuriated to learn that the supervisory special agent in the Counterterrorism Division who had blocked Minneapolis's attempts to investigate Moussaoui had actually been promoted after 9/11. Nobody "ought to be burned at the stake," but she noted that a "lowly field office agent" who "committed such errors of judgment" would have been severely disciplined.

She accused the headquarters agent who had blocked the Moussaoui investigation of trying to avoid "what he may have perceived as an unnecessary career risk." She noted that the SSA who "seemed to have been consistently, almost deliberately thwarting the Minneapolis FBI agents' efforts" had not only been retained in his position but was given an important role during the 9/11 crisis. "During the early aftermath of September 11th, when I happened to be recounting the pre-September 11th events concerning the Moussaoui investigation to other FBI personnel in other divisions or in FBIHQ, almost everyone's first question was 'Why?—Why would an FBI agent(s) deliberately sabotage a case?' "

She wrote,

> *The fact is that key FBIHQ personnel . . . continued to, almost inexplicably, throw up roadblocks and undermine Minneapolis's by-now desperate efforts to obtain a FISA search warrant, long after the French intelligence service pro-*

vided its information and probable cause became clear. In all of their conversations and correspondence, HQ personnel never disclosed to the Minneapolis agents that the Phoenix Division had, only approximately three weeks earlier, warned of Al Qaeda operatives in flight schools seeking flight training for terrorist purposes!

Mueller's newly-announced plans for a headquarters "Super Squad" to handle terrorism cases, she said, "simply fly in the face of an honest appraisal of the FBI's pre-September 11 failures." In fact, she wrote, "I'm hard pressed to think of any case which has been solved by FBIHQ personnel and I can name several that have been screwed up! Decision-making is inherently more effective and timely when decentralized instead of concentrated." The Phoenix, Minneapolis, and Paris offices

reacted remarkably exhibiting keen perception and prioritization skills regarding the terrorist threats they uncovered or were made aware of pre-September 11. The same cannot be said for the FBI Headquarters bureaucracy and you want to expand that?! Should we put the counterterrorism unit chief and SSA who previously handled the Moussaoui matter in charge of the new "Super Squad"?

Rowley offered her own theory about why headquarters' performance in the 9/11 cases had been so miserable, why, in fact, it had been so perverse that some agents had wondered if the Counterterrorism Division was deliberately sabotaging the investigation. She pointed to the past decade when high-ranking FBI officials whose decisions "in hindsight, turned out to be mistaken or just turned out badly (i.e., Ruby Ridge, Waco, etc.) have seen their careers plummet and end." As a result, "in most cases avoidance of all 'unnecessary' actions/decisions by FBIHQ managers (and maybe to some extent field managers as well) has, in recent years, been seen as the safest FBI career choice." In the pre-9/11 FBI a

climate of fear . . . has chilled aggressive FBI law enforcement action/decisions. In a large hierarchal bureaucracy such as the FBI, with the requirements for numerous superiors' approvals/oversight, the premium on career-enhancement, and interjecting a chilling factor brought on by recent extreme public and congressional criticism/oversight, and I think you will see at least the makings of the most likely explanation.

Headquarters' policy of "writing up" agents for intelligence oversight board "errors," that is, for having begun intelligence investigation that later proved not to have been fully justified (although such an error can be discovered only after performing the investigation, a true catch-22), had come to have a "chilling effect upon all levels of FBI agents assigned to intelligence cases." This prevented "aggressive investigations of terrorists."

But this was all that could be expected from an FBI management filled with "short-term careerists who, like the SSA in question, must only serve an 18 months-just-time-to-get-your-ticket-punched minimum (And no wonder why FBIHQ is mired in mediocrity!)."

Rowley's memo to Mueller was released to the press, which hailed her as a hero. She was named one of *Time* magazine's "People of the Year," along with the female whistle-blowers in the Enron and WorldCom corporate accounting scandals. Within the Bureau, however, it was a different story. She was informed that high-level FBI officials in Washington were considering filing criminal charges against her. Retired agents were particularly brutal. Charles George, then president of the Society of Former Special Agents of the FBI, said that she was no better than convicted spy Robert Hanssen. In the society newsletter he called her action "unthinkable"; "instead of going to the Russians, she went to Congress." Some other retired agents sent her copies of the Elbert Hubbard essay on loyalty that J. Edgar Hoover used to keep posted in all Bureau offices: "If you work for a man, in heaven's name work for him; speak well of him and stand by the institution he represents. Remember—an ounce of loyalty is worth a pound of cleverness . . . If you must growl, condemn, and eternally find fault, why—resign your position and when you are on the outside, damn to your heart's content."

■ ■ ■

Throughout the year 2002, a House and Senate Joint Inquiry Committee had been looking into the run-up to 9/11. It was this Joint Inquiry that had solicited Rowley's testimony and so had prompted her letter to Mueller. In December 2002 the Joint Inquiry issued its classified report to Congress.

The Joint Inquiry examined the FBI's handling of the Phoenix electronic communication and the Moussaoui case, and in both cases found the Bureau's performance wanting. The Joint Inquiry argued that a vigorous FBI investigation of its leads might have uncovered at least part of the plot. The Joint Inquiry Summary (JIS) charged that the intelligence community, the FBI included, *missed opportunities to disrupt the September 11th plot by denying entry to or detaining would-be hijackers; to at least try to unravel the plot through surveillance and other investigative work within the United States; and, finally, to generate a heightened state of alert and thus harden the homeland against attack.*

The Joint Inquiry's critique of the FBI was devastating. But since the Joint Inquiry's official report had to reflect a consensus between members of the two houses of Congress and, of course, the two political parties, it was restrained in comparison with the findings of individual members of the inquiry.

Senator Richard Shelby, Republican of Alabama, the vice chair of the Senate Intelligence Committee and so a member of the Joint Inquiry, attached his personal addendum to the report ("Additional Views") stating that the inquiry did not go far enough in assessing the institutional and individual blame for 9/11. Shelby argued that the FBI had so discredited itself by its pre-9/11 performance that it could no longer be trusted with the nation's security. He called for abolishing the Bureau as it now stood, taking away its responsibility for collecting and analyzing domestic intelligence about foreign terrorist or espionage threats and handing it over to a new agency.

Shelby rested his case for taking intelligence-gathering away from the FBI on five specific failures by the Bureau:

- that the FBI had acquiesced in permitting FISA to serve as a wall of "no coordination" between criminal and intelligence investigations so that, at a moment in American history of unique peril, it had left the country with no one at the barricades to guard against terrorist attacks;

- that it had, to suit its own institutional interests, created rules where they did not exist that allowed it to refuse to share the results of criminal investigations, specifically grand jury investigations, with the rest of the intelligence community;

- that "the tyranny of the case file" rendered the FBI incapable of the synthesis of disparate information necessary to understand and prevent terrorist threats;

- that as an institution it had developed a positive resistance to engaging in real analysis of intelligence;

- and that the FBI had proven incapable of keeping abreast of developments in modern information technology, leaving it with an obsolete computer infrastructure that agents have had to avoid to accomplish their jobs.

A great deal of "the blame for the dysfunctional nature of pre-September 11" coordination between law enforcement and the intelligence community, Shelby claimed,

> *can be traced to a series of misconceptions and mythologies that grew up in connection with the implementation of domestic intelligence surveillance (and physical searches) under the Foreign Intelligence Surveillance Act (FISA). Rigid and restrictive readings of FISA in the early and mid-1990s acquired with time the apparent legitimacy of long-presumed acceptance, and created a sterile and ultimately fallacious conventional wisdom that effectively—but unnecessarily—prevented meaningful LEA/IC [law enforcement agency/ intelligence community] coordination.*

The result of "this organizational allergy even to the most common-sense forms of counterterrorist cooperation [that] became infamous after September 11 [was that] a 'Wall' had been built between intelligence and law enforcement." The "wall" meant that no information could be shared between agents conducting intelligence investigations of terrorists and other agents trying to build a legal case against them. It was to maintain the integrity of the "wall" that headquarters had placed so many barriers in the way of the Minneapolis agents trying to investigate Moussaoui.

The FBI might have claimed it was an innocent victim of rules promulgated by the courts and by "timorous" lawyers within the Justice Department, except that these rules made effective intelligence operations so patently impossible that the Bureau's lawyers should have pressed vigorously for their modification or abolition. And, in fact, they would have had the literal language of FISA and its legislative history on their side had they attempted to demolish the "Wall, as the post-9/11 decision by the FISA appeals court made clear." But it is also clear that Louis Freeh, for his own motives—demonstrating that the FBI was primarily dedicated to protecting civil liberties, and that it was, in all ways, dramatically different from the Hoover-era FBI—all but gloried in those restrictions and even built the "wall" higher than required by the Justice Department.

As Shelby put it,

> *Perceiving there to be an unbridgeable gap between law enforcement and intelligence work, the FBI thus refused even to talk to itself in order to prevent mayhem by known Al-Qa'ida terrorists in the United States. Meanwhile, al-Mihdhar and al-Hazmi were in the final stages of their preparations for the September 11 attacks.*

These bizarre maneuvers of trying (and failing) to pass information over the FISA "wall" were actually based on "years of timorous lawyering in the Justice Department and Intelligence Community reticence" that "had created an institutional culture hostile to coordination." As FBI official Michael Rolince put it, procedures for information sharing became so baroque and restrictive that sharing was essentially prohibited: "In terrorism cases, this became so complex and convoluted that in some FBI field offices agents perceived 'walls' where none actually existed."

Shelby then pointed to the FBI refusal to share the results of its criminal investigations with other intelligence agencies. Shelby argued that this was based on another myth, this time an exaggeration of Rule 6(e) of the Federal Rules of Criminal Procedure. Rule 6(e) "really did" prohibit grand jury information from being lawfully shared with intelligence analysts. But "[l]ike the mythology of the coordination 'Wall' in the years before September 11 the 'Rule 6(e) excuse' acquired an unwarranted mythological dimension of its own."

The FBI had "sadly" turned 6(e) into an "excuse for not sharing information"—leaving vital collections of shareable information about international terrorist groups off-limits to intelligence community analysts. For years, it was routine FBI and Justice Department practice to respond to virtually any intelligence community requests for information with the answer that Rule 6(e) prevented any response. As two frustrated National Security Council veterans recalled it, "Rule 6E [*sic*] is much more than a procedural matter: it is the bulwark of an institutional culture. . . . It is one of the Bureau's foremost tools for maintaining the independence that the FBI views as its birthright." And in fact when Attorney General Janet Reno tried to get the FBI to curtail its overuse of the Rule 6(e) excuse, even though Reno was "Louis Freeh's boss, [she] could never bring him around."

Shelby then examined what he called the "tyranny of the case file" as another example of the FBI's inadequacy as an intelligence agency. In the FBI, Shelby wrote, "information is stored, retrieved, and simply understood principally through the conceptual prism of a 'case'—a discrete bundle of information—the fundamental purpose of which is to prove elements of crimes against specific potential defendants in a court of law." But although the "case file" approach is in large part responsible for the Bureau's status as the "world's premier law enforcement organization," it almost disqualifies the FBI as an intelligence agency.

The tyranny of the case file presents a fundamental obstacle to national security work, for the simple reason that law enforcement organizations handle in-

formation, reach conclusions, and ultimately just think differently than intelligence organizations. Intelligence analysts would doubtless make poor policemen, and it has become very clear that policemen make poor intelligence analysts.

Despite the FBI's claim that it had totally revamped itself into an analytic organization in 1999, Shelby said it had paid mere lip service to the concept of intelligence analysis. The FBI had created an analytic division (the Investigative Services Division), but it was perceived in the Bureau as not really a place for "players," and its analysts (and it had very few) were systematically misused by detailing them to operational units engaged in case work. As the Joint Inquiry staff put it,

> *at the FBI, our review found that, prior to September 11, 2001, support for ongoing investigations and operations was favored, in terms of allocating resources, over long-term, strategic analysis. We were told, during the course of our FBI interviews, that crime prevention occurs in the operational units, not through strategic analysis, and that, prior to September 11, the FBI had insufficient resources to do both.*

Shelby argued that

> *on top of a general lack of emphasis upon national security work within the organization as a whole, the FBI suffered in particular from a positive aversion to long-term strategic analysis of the sort routinely expected of intelligence agencies. CT [counterterrorism] investigations, after all, were at least investigations—and bore at least some resemblance to ordinary law enforcement work. Analysis, however, was apparently anathema. Even as the FBI received ever-greater amounts of CT money and personnel during the late 1990s, therefore, it showed little interest in devoting more effort to strategic intelligence or to analytical efforts aimed at al-Qa'ida cells in the United States. According to the JIS [Joint Inquiry staff], the FBI's disinterest in analysis work led managers systematically to reassign good analysts from doing strategic analysis to supporting operational (i.e., investigative) units.*

This had a very specific bearing on the FBI's failure to protect the country against the 9/11 attacks:

> *JIS investigators were "told that the FBI's al-Qa'ida–related analytic expertise had been 'gutted' by transfers to operational units and that, as a result, the*

FBI's [international terrorism] analytic unit had only one individual working on al-Qa'ida at the time of the September 11.

Only one analyst was working on al Qaeda on September 11!

The FBI's failure to emphasize intelligence analysis, despite its 1999 reorganization for that purpose, was, Shelby said, profoundly "discouraging." Because of the Bureau's "aversion" to analysis, he lamented, the FBI was totally deficient in

the fundamental prerequisite for any organization that seeks to undertake even the most rudimentary intelligence analysis. The FBI, however, has repeatedly shown that it is unable to do this. It does not know what it knows, it has enormous difficulty analyzing information when it can find it, and it refuses to disseminate whatever analytical products its analysts might, nonetheless, happen to produce.

All the officials who led the American intelligence community in the decade before 9/11, Shelby insisted, should be held accountable.

The U.S. Intelligence Community would have been far better prepared for September 11 but for the failure of successive agency leaders to work wholeheartedly to overcome the institutional and cultural obstacles to interagency cooperation and coordination that bedeviled counterterrorism efforts before the attacks: DCIs [directors of Central Intelligence] George Tenet and John Deutch, FBI Director Louis Freeh, and NSA [National Security Agency] Directors Michael Hayden and Kenneth Minnihan, and NSA Deputy Director Barbara McNamara. These individuals are not responsible for the disaster of September 11, of course, for that infamy belongs to al-Qa'ida's 19 suicide hijackers and the terrorist infrastructure that supported them. As the leaders of the United States Intelligence Community, however, these officials failed in significant ways to ensure that this country was as prepared as it could have been.

In his own "Additional Views" appendix to the JIS, Senator Pat Roberts of Kansas charged that the FBI was permeated with a culture of "risk aversion." While agent Coleen Rowley blamed this risk-aversive culture on headquarters mediocrity and careerism, Roberts argued it had historical roots. He recounted instances in which FBI agents were asked about the Bureau's timidity in intelligence investigations. For instance, Roberts recalled *at the September 24, 2002 JIS open hearing, a cloaked "Minneapolis FBI Agent" testified about risk aversion in the FBI. He was asked if he thought previous disciplinary actions involving agents making erroneous applications to the Foreign Intelligence Court of Review (the court set up under the Foreign Intelligence Surveillance Act, or FISA) had made agents reluctant to file FISA applications. He responded that these did indeed have a chilling effect.*

Roberts also recalled incidents that suggested the FBI was, in many instances, paralyzed by fear of being accused of racial profiling. These fears were

acknowledged by a Phoenix special agent who attempted to alert FBI headquarters about suspicious individuals seeking pilot training. The special agent's now-famous electronic communication to headquarters recommended that it consider seeking authority to obtain visa information from the State Department on individuals who got visas to attend flight school. The intelligence operations specialists at FBI headquarters who reviewed the "Phoenix Memorandum" told the JIS that they had decided among themselves that seeking that authority raised profiling concerns. FBI qualms in this regard were stimulated by public allegations of racial profiling that were made against FBI agents who questioned two Middle Eastern men who had acted suspiciously on an Air West flight from Phoenix to Washington, D.C. in 1999.

Pat Roberts noticed that "many comments on risk aversion alluded to congressional oversight and/or investigations dating back to the Church and Pike investigations of the 1970s." These investigations of the CIA and the FBI, led by Representative Otis Pike of New York and Senator Frank Church of Idaho, exposed the worst of J. Edgar Hoover's efforts to repress political dissent and, certainly by implication and possibly by intention, convinced many that *any* FBI investigations of domestic political groups were presumptively both illegitimate and unconstitutional. According to Roberts, the 1980s congressional investigation and litigation involving the FBI's investigation of the Committees in Solidarity with the People of El Salvador led indirectly to newer agents being "warned to be careful that they do not violate religious groups' First Amendment rights." "It is quite possible," Roberts suggested, "though this theme was not fully explored by the JIS—that a legacy of caution left by these historical episodes contributed to timidity in tackling the Al Qaeda problem before Al Qaeda struck on 9/11." If there was a smoking gun in 9/11, according to Roberts, it went off back in the 1970s.

Testimony before the Joint Inquiry Committee by past and present FBI directors reinforced the image of a politically correct Bureau fearful of pursuing logical leads involving a plot by members of one ethnic group. Louis Freeh told the Joint Inquiry: "But I think the intelligence has to come from some place. We can't come up with an invalid profile or stereotype . . . that becomes the focus of what we do. We don't do that in America. We don't do it well and we don't do it at all." The current director, Robert Mueller, told the Senate Judiciary Committee in June 2002 that fear of political punishment over concerns about "profiling" may have hindered the FBI's investigations of terrorism: "I think I've seen indications of concerns about taking certain action, because that action may be perceived as profiling." For the record, Mueller made it clear, "The bureau is against, has been and will be against any form of profiling." This FBI director, like the last, evidently preferred political correctness to recognizing the fact that al Qaeda terrorists are recruited among Islamic radicals, specifically young Middle Eastern Islamic radicals.

■ ■ ■

After a decade of ever-more-urgent warnings that al Qaeda intended to bring terrorism home to America, after a decade during which the FBI had been handed the assignment of protecting America from terrorism and had had billions of dollars showered on it to fight terrorism, after the Bureau had loudly and proudly reorganized itself to make its highest priority the prevention of terrorist attacks, it turned out that the country had unknowingly placed its faith in:

A risk-aversive FBI that reflexively avoided tough investigations if it thought they were too complex or too difficult.

A politically correct FBI that scrapped promising investigations rather than risk accusations that by tracking suspicious Middle Eastern men they were racial-profiling everyone from the Middle East.

An FBI so ignorant of the legal procedures it was supposed to follow that it abandoned perfectly legitimate investigations under the misimpression that they were prohibited by rules the Bureau and the Justice Department had drawn up themselves.

An FBI that had erected impenetrable walls blocking cooperation between parallel investigations, so that there were teams of "clean" and "dirty" agents tracking the same terrorists, forbidden to discuss their cases with each other.

An FBI whose headquarters supervisors, instead of ensuring that investigating agents were kept informed about one another's investigations, hoarded that information and then forgot about it.

An FBI that had fallen so far behind the computer revolution that agents had to flee its e-mail and automated case file systems and do their work on paper if they were to have any hope of communicating with one another.

■ ■ ■

But what happened to the two-fisted, square-jawed FBI agent of the gangbusting era, the G-man who always got his man? For that matter, what happened to the FBI agent who, critics claimed, trampled on civil liberties to get his Nazi saboteur, his communist spy, his KKK lynch mob?

What happened to the Bureau that put the science into scientific crime fighting?

What happened to the FBI that generations of Americans had relied on for protection against bank robbers, kidnappers, spies, and saboteurs? The Bureau that for a century had told Americans that they could "leave it to the FBI"?

What happened to that FBI? The answer to that question of what went wrong begins long, long ago, when the FBI began.

TWO

A New Force
(1902–1908)

A HUNDRED YEARS AGO a crime was committed high on the slopes of Oregon's Mount Jefferson, a snow-capped, 14,000-foot peak surrounded by miles of wilderness preserve that juts dramatically above deep green forests and the blue lakes of the Cascade National Forest, eighty miles by air southeast of Portland, two hundred miles by road. The crime would lead to jail and disgrace for some of the most powerful politicians in the country. It would turn the detectives who solved it into national heroes, and would lead to the force of detectives that would become today's FBI.

A hundred years ago Mount Jefferson was just as remote, its summit just as steep and rugged, just as beautiful. Something about it persuaded several farmers, perhaps moved by aesthetic impulse, to try to raise crops on its high peaks—strawberries, no less. An unlikely dream, perhaps, but Americans, God bless them, dream many strange dreams.

In October 1902, papers were filed in the Eugene District Land Office affirming that twelve indomitable sons of the pioneers had carved out strawberry farms in Township 11-7 on the high slopes of Mount Jefferson. They swore they had been raising berries on those farms for the past five years, precisely long enough to warrant them compensation for their property, now that the government had announced it was going to seize their lofty homesteads for the new Cascade National Forest Reserve.

The Forest Reservation Act of 1897 had authorized the Interior Department to set aside land for forest reserves. It also directed the department to compensate qualified homesteaders for their loss by issuing "lieu lands" scrip. This scrip could then be exchanged, acre for acre, for other public lands, perhaps without the same fine view enjoyed by the owners of those lofty strawberry patches, but perhaps more conveniently situated with respect to railroads, timber, and good water. If the mountaineers did not care to try lowland farming, they might find brokers willing to relieve them of their land at an agreeable price. In short, a benevolent government had prepared a bonanza for these upland strawberry farmers, and so they carried their land claims to a helpful lady named Mrs. Emma Watson.

Emma, who registered the strawberry farmers' claims for scrip at the Eugene land office, was in on the plot, along with two timber speculators with the inspirational names of Horace Greeley McKinley and Stephen A. Douglas Puter (the latter enjoying amorous relations with the amiable Mrs. Watson). They had plans to sell the scrip to timber broker Frederick A. Kribs, their profit to be $6,280. Kribs's intention was to exchange the scrip for prime timberlands in the public domain on behalf of his lumber company clients. Thousands of similar transactions had been taking place for years across the West, many of them organized by the team of McKinley and Puter. Nothing special about the 11-7 transaction. Rather routine, in fact.

It so happened, however, that at this moment in Washington, D.C., the General Land Office at the Interior Department received a letter from a Joost H. Schneider of Tucson, Arizona, who informed the folks in Washington that for the past twenty-three years he had been part of a California-Oregon land-fraud ring. As evidence of his bona fides, he provided the names of the principals, John A. Benson and F. A. Hyde. Schneider's motive for coming forward, he said, was revenge.

The commissioner of the Land Office in Washington was a prominent Oregon politician named Binger Hermann, who served under Interior Secretary Ethan Allan Hitchcock, who was a man of uncommon and, in Hermann's eyes, inconvenient integrity. Hermann saw no point in annoying Hitchcock with Schneider's revelations, so he filed the letter without courtesy of reply.

More letters followed from Schneider and his attorney. These met a similar fate. Then Hermann went on vacation, forgetting, perhaps, that while an honest man can on occasion refresh himself with a few hours of relaxation away from the job, success as a thief demands eternal vigilance. While Hermann was diverting himself elsewhere, one of Schneider's letters fell into the hands of a political rival, Assistant Commissioner W. A. Richards, who had his eye on Hermann's job. Richards sent a Land Office special agent to interview Schneider in Arizona.

When Hermann returned from his vacation, he was shocked to find that Schneider's story was being investigated. He tried to recall the agent, but it was too late. Schneider was interviewed in September 1902, and claimed that "about three-fourths of the . . . entries in the Cascade Forest Reserve in Oregon were bogus. All the . . . entries in the Lake Tahoe Forest Reserve were bogus, as were most of those in Zaca Lake, Pine Mountain and the addition to the San Jacinto Forest Reserve." The Benson-Hyde ring, according to Schneider, had bribed clerks, agents, and officials in the state and federal land offices. When the interview report arrived in Washington, Hermann buried it in the files, as Richards had expected he would.

After waiting a decent interval, Richards carried the transcript of Schneider's interview to Interior Secretary Hitchcock. Hitchcock was outraged. He demanded an explanation from Hermann, judged it unpersuasive, and sacked him. Through the intercession of Hermann's senatorial sponsor, John H. Mitchell of Oregon, Hermann was allowed a few weeks to tidy up his office, which he accomplished through the efficient expedient of burning his day-books and other files.

As Richards had hoped, Secretary Hitchcock gave him Hermann's job. With Hitchcock now paying close attention to the alleged frauds, Richards sent special agents and attorneys to Oregon and California to investigate Schneider's charges.

The investigators sent to Oregon, two Interior Department special agents named Greene and Linnen, had the good luck to arrive just as acrimony was dissolving the partnership of Mrs. Watson, Puter, and McKinley. Puter had held back money he owed McKinley for the strawberry fields. This left McKinley in desperate financial straits, so he raised cash by selling property the partners had just acquired in a new fraud (Township 24-1, also in the Cascade Reserve) before either he or his partner had recorded the deeds. Puter raced to the Land Office to protect his interest by recording the property in his own name before McKinley's customer, a Clyde D. Lloyd, could register the claims he had just purchased from McKinley. When Lloyd discovered he had been swindled, he complained to Agents Greene and Linnen. They took the evidence about the 24-1 conspiracy to Oregon U.S. Attorney John Hall, who indicted Puter, McKinley, their attorney Dan Tarpley (Daniel Webster Tarpley, no less), and Miss Marie Ware (Marie Antoinette Ware), who supplemented her day job as the commissioner of the Eugene Land Office by moonlighting as McKinley's mistress.

The investigators sent to California—a Land Office special agent named Steece, and Arthur Pugh, a law clerk for Assistant Attorney General Willis Van Devanter—had a less productive trip. When they arrived in Tucson to depose

Schneider, they found he was no longer inclined to talk, thus rendering his earlier letters to the department worthless as evidence.

Nor were the investigators able to corroborate Schneider's account of the conspiracy when they got to California. Nobody was talking. The case seemed dead. The Mount Jefferson strawberry-field affair seemed destined to remain a run-of-the-mill swindle involving four small-time operators, with nothing linking them to any higher-ups. Now that Schneider had retracted his charges, the government had nothing against Benson and Hyde—or anybody else of any consequence.

But one of the California investigators was not ready to give up. When Arthur Pugh returned to Washington, he told Secretary Hitchcock that the department would never learn the truth about Schneider's story until it sent an experienced detective there to investigate. Hitchcock was eager to get to the bottom of the mystery, because the Oregon congressional delegation's efforts to protect Binger Hermann made him suspect that the Oregon scandals reached all the way to Washington. Hitchcock passed Pugh's recommendation along to President Theodore Roosevelt. They needed a detective. Roosevelt, who was passionately dedicated to preserving the natural heritage of the West, agreed. But where were they to get one?

With so many of the potential targets of the investigation working for the Interior Department—a department special agent, a forest supervisor, and a Land Office commissioner—it seemed inappropriate and probably counterproductive to use the Interior Department's own investigators. The detective would have to come from outside the Interior Department. But from where?

Since the case, when and if it ever went to court, would be prosecuted by Justice Department attorneys, why not use the Justice Department? The problem was that the Justice Department had no detectives available for that kind of investigation. It did have a "general agent" supervising ten "examiners" who audited the accounts of the federal courts and marshals. There were also two "special agents," but they were fully occupied with crimes on Indian reservations and Spanish-American War claims.

When the attorney general needed additional detectives—for antitrust work, peonage cases in the South, or, as now, land frauds—he, like the heads of all the other executive departments, borrowed them from the Treasury Department's Secret Service, which had, since its founding in 1865, evolved into a central detective bureau for the entire government. Sometimes the Secret Service chief would dispatch a special agent from his own permanent staff of ten. More often he would choose one from a civil service "eligible list" of approved investigators available on a per diem basis. During the land-fraud investigations that were about to commence, there were as many as thirty-two agents over the course of a year on detached duty from the Secret Service to the Justice Department and the Interior Department. A smaller but significant number worked for the Army, Navy, Post Office, State Department, and the other cabinet offices.

And so Secretary Hitchcock requested a detective from Secret Service Chief John Wilkie, a former Chicago newspaperman who had raised the already well-regarded force to new heights of professionalism since taking over in 1898. Since the Oregon congressional delegation was a potential target of the investigation, it could be expected to defend itself with all the political and legal pressure it could bring to bear on the investigation. The job would demand a detective of courage as well as experience. Wilkie sent Hitchcock his best man, Special Agent William J. Burns.

William James Burns—"Billy Burns" as he was known in the press—was the most famous detective in the country. In 1903 he was forty-four years old, red-haired with a bristling mustache, stocky, usually decked out in a three-piece suit with a gold watch chain, topped off by a bowler hat. He had a talent for blending into his surroundings, and could pass himself off as anything from a barroom loafer to a prosperous businessman. He had recently solved a counterfeiting case in Pennsylvania and a theft at the San Francisco Mint. He had been just as effective when on detached service to other departments.

Burns showed up at the Interior Department on May 1, 1903, introducing himself as a law professor researching the history of the public lands laws. Those laws, he learned, had been intended to convey public lands in small parcels to settlers for their own homes and farms, but most of these so-called homesteads wound up being assembled into large tracts through sales of lieu-lands scrip and other schemes. Railroads and timber companies used agents like Benson and Hyde to acquire the enormous tracts of land that were essential to their corporate operations but were denied to them by the spirit (and letter) of the land laws.

Burns noted that some names, among them the "F. A. Hyde" of the Benson-Hyde ring, appeared so often on the lieu-lands records that any honest Land Office official should have been suspicious. He went to Secretary Hitchcock and told him that the personnel of the Land Office—all of them—were either fools or crooks, and "I don't think they're all fools." The General Land Office, Burns told Hitchcock, "is corrupt at every level. Corrupt to the very core."

Hitchcock hoped Burns was exaggerating. He demanded evidence. Burns produced it. In Schneider's letters there were references to an agent "B" in the

Washington office who was being paid off by Benson and Hyde. Burns suspected that "B" was J. J. Barnes, a respected forty-year veteran in the school lands division of the Land Office, and he used a bluff to scare him into confessing. Barnes told Burns everything he knew about the conspiracy. Barnes said that Hyde had studied the Land Office's procedures for processing lieu-lands scrip, and thereupon had systematically corrupted every person along the paper trail.

Burns suspected that the key to the fraud on the West Coast was B. F. Allen, the forest superintendent in Los Angeles. Burns found evidence in Washington that Allen had been padding his expense vouchers. He confronted Allen with what he knew about the expense account chiseling, and this convinced Allen that Burns knew everything, including Allen's corrupt arrangements with Benson and Hyde. Allen gave Burns a point-by-point confirmation of Schneider's original charges. Burns learned that Allen, who was responsible for picking out land for new forest reserves, had let Hyde lay out the boundaries, draw up the maps, and even write Allen's reports to Washington. Hyde once bragged that a report he had written for Allen was so good that Allen should have gotten an official commendation. Allen went on to reveal that his immediate superior in Washington, H. H. Jones, the head of the Forestry Division, was also working for Benson and Hyde.

By now Burns had figured out why Schneider had backed off from his original charges against Benson and Hyde. His real motive had been blackmail, not revenge. He had been trying to stir up an investigation so that Benson and Hyde would pay him to keep quiet. They paid, so he stopped talking.

Burns was now ready to interview Schneider. This time he used a different, but well-practiced technique. He would first hit Schneider with a wildly inaccurate accusation. Schneider would indignantly deny it. Burns would offer to accept Schneider's denial, but in return he would entice Schneider into admitting something else just as incriminating. By the end of the interview Burns had gotten Schneider to confirm everything he had written in his letters to the Interior Department.

With Schneider's and Allen's confessions in hand, Burns got confessions from all the other officials Benson and Hyde had bribed. These included Grant I. Taggart, Interior Department forest supervisor for Northern California; Major Harlan, head of the Interior Department's force of special agents; and William Valk, head of the lieu-lands division.

The California land-fraud case against Benson and Hyde seemed just about wrapped up. Hitchcock took Burns to the White House, where the detective related the whole story to Roosevelt, who was delighted, slapped Burns on the back, and urged him to keep going, to get the men at the top of the land-fraud ring, no matter how high and mighty they might be.

But the key to exposing the entire conspiracy was finding something to connect Benson and Hyde's California frauds with the McKinley and Puter ring, whose case was just coming to trial, and so far, Burns had nothing. That would change in October 1903, when U.S. Attorney for Oregon John Hall asked Attorney General Philander C. Knox for an assistant United States attorney to help him with the trial. He asked Knox to appoint an attorney associated with the Oregon Republican machine, one who came furnished with the endorsement of the Oregon senators, John Mitchell and Charles Fulton.

By now Knox shared Hitchcock's suspicions that something was rotten in Oregon. He approved Hall's request for an assistant, but instead of appointing the man Hall wanted, he sent San Francisco attorney Francis J. Heney to Portland to work with him.

In an era of tough westerners, Heney was one of the toughest, though with his slicked-down hair parted in the middle, his clean-shaven face, and his rimless eyeglasses he hardly looked a match for the mustachioed land pirates he was going up against. (That is, the younger suspects wore mustaches; the older ones, like Oregon Senators Mitchell and Fulton, favored the long full beards that served to remind voters they belonged to the Civil War generation of heroes.)

Heney had grown up in the rough "South of the Slot" district of San Francisco and had run with street gangs as a kid. He had started college at Berkeley, but had been expelled for fighting, then spent years drifting, drinking, and gambling around the Northwest before he put himself through law school and moved to New Mexico. There he ranched, ran a trading post, fought Geronimo, and killed a man in a Main Street gunfight, Western-style.

His Tucson law practice flourished. In 1892 he became the territorial attorney general, and expected to be sent to the Senate when Arizona became a state. He came out on the wrong side of a political battle between rival machines, however, and was forced out of office. He moved to San Francisco and became one of the most successful lawyers in town, with a reputation for being willing to battle one of the most corrupt (and violent) city governments in the country.

In early 1903 Heney had represented a federal judge in Alaska who was being removed from office (deservedly, as it turned out) and had carried a character reference for the judge to Attorney General Knox. Although the attorney general was not persuaded that Heney's client deserved any special attention, Heney made a strong and favorable impression on Knox, who made inquiries about him and then tried to get Heney to accept an appointment as an assistant attorney general. Heney did not want to take time from his law practice, and so he declined, but when Knox asked him to take the Oregon job, Heney felt he ought not to refuse twice, and accepted the offer.

Heney showed up at John Hall's Portland office expecting, as the personal representative of the attorney general, that he would be in charge of the case. Instead, he found himself treated as a mere assistant. Heney was also puzzled by Hall's legal strategy: Instead of basing the case against Puter *et al.* on the Mount Jefferson strawberry fields in the 11-7 township, which Heney thought was a strong and winnable case, Hall insisted on going to trial with the 24-1 case, the one that had set McKinley and Puter against each other, and which Heney considered much the weaker of the two.

Heney carried his complaints about Hall to Washington, where Attorney General Knox, to give Heney more standing in Portland, changed his title to special assistant to the attorney general, and told Hall that Heney was in charge of the cases. While Heney was in Washington, he paid a visit to the office of Interior Secretary Hitchcock. There he met William Burns for the first time, although their meeting did not go beyond introductions. They would get to know each other much better before long.

Burns was still working on the California case against Benson and Hyde, and when he met Heney he was working on a ruse to lure them to Washington, where, he hoped, he could catch them passing more bribes to their accomplices in the Land Office. About two weeks later, Benson did in fact turn up in Washington and he did try to bribe Harlan and Valk to head off Burns's investigation. By now Harlan and Valk were cooperating with Burns. They turned the money over to Burns. This was enough to let the Justice Department get indictments against Benson and Hyde.

When Benson and Hyde resisted their extraditions from New York and San Francisco to Washington, where the trial was to be held, the United States attorney entrusted with the extraditions botched the proceedings so badly that it looked as though the land-fraud cases might never get to trial. Knox therefore pressed Heney into service to get the extraditions back on track. Heney had to consult with Burns about the California aspects of the cases. He found the detective's insights into the cases so impressive that after the Circuit Court of Appeals ordered Hyde and Benson removed to Washington (on September 2, 1904), Heney asked Burns to bring his team of detectives (which included

Burns's son George, also a Secret Service agent) to Oregon. He issued a challenge to Burns: "Let us see," he said, "who is behind the Puter-McKinley-Tarpley land thieves of Oregon."

Burns and Heney now began to wonder why Hall was so intent on prosecuting the weaker 24-1 fraud instead of the stronger 11-7 case. They had different theories. Heney attributed it to professional jealousy: Perhaps Hall wanted Heney to lose the 24-1 case, so that Hall could save the day with the 11-7 case. This, Heney speculated, might improve Hall's chances for reappointment as U.S. attorney. To test his theory, Heney had Hall reappointed so that he could stop worrying about his job. He then ordered Hall to forget about 24-1 and use the 11-7 indictment against Puter and McKinley.

Burns's explanation was a lot simpler: Hall was a crook. "I tell you," Burns told Heney, "he is protecting somebody."

Meanwhile Burns's son George was up on the slopes of Mount Jefferson with a photographer, and the pictures they brought back were revealing—and even hilarious. There were vertical cliff faces, ravines filled with rocks and fallen timber, and steep pinnacles, precisely at the locations where Puter and McKinley's pioneers were supposed to have been raising strawberries for half a decade.

Soon after the trial began in late November 1904, events convinced Heney that Burns had been right about Hall. Burns was on the verge of getting superintendent of the Cascade Forest Reserve Salmon B. Ormsby to "open up" about the land frauds. Hall demanded that he be allowed to speak to Ormsby privately. After meeting with Hall, Ormsby refused to talk. That was enough for Heney. He removed Hall from the case and argued it himself. On December 6, 1904, the jury found Puter, McKinley, and Tarpley guilty of a conspiracy to defraud the government in the matter of the 11-7 strawberry fields.

By now President Roosevelt, Attorney General Knox, and Interior Secretary Hitchcock were all urging Heney and Burns to find out why Oregon's senators and congressmen had been so quick to intervene whenever Interior Department officials implicated in the land frauds fell under suspicion. Binger Hermann was not the only one they had tried to save. When Forest Superintendent Ormsby had come under suspicion of corruption, Senator Mitchell had gotten Hall to end the investigation. This looked bad, and yet there were innocent (or at least semi-innocent) explanations: Senators often put in a word for constituents in trouble; United States attorneys often listen to senators; United States attorneys do have broad discretion in deciding which cases to prosecute.

Burns felt that if there was a wider conspiracy, Puter would be the key to unlocking it. On December 15, 1904, Burns had finally broken Ormsby, who confessed that when he worked with the Puter ring to create the Blue Mountain Forest Reserve, Oregon State Senator F. P. May had been in on the plot. So Burns now knew that Puter had had help from at least one higher-up. He did not think, however, that a mere Oregon state senator had the political clout to pull off such an impressive coup. Ormsby and May must have had more powerful political help, probably unknown to Ormsby. Puter was the key. How would Burns get him to talk?

Puter was an outdoorsman who had an unholy horror of being locked up. Puter's brother, who was an attorney, was now desperately seeking a deal that would let his brother avoid jail. Burns had Heney put out word that Puter was going to "get the limit" when it came time to set his sentence, and had the judge tell Puter's brother the same thing. Burns also leaked word to State Senator F. P. May and the other unindicted conspirators that they were under suspicion, which made them avoid any contact with Puter. When Puter asked for bail money, they turned him down. He felt abandoned and isolated.

Giving Puter time to reflect on his plight, Burns visited him in his cell to offer a deal. He would get Puter out of jail if he would testify. Puter said he hated the idea of "squealing" on his friends. Burns sympathized, but asked Puter whether his friends were really his friends. They were looking out for themselves; it was time for Puter to look out for himself, too. Puter began to talk; even better, he turned over ledger books and diaries that implicated nearly every important figure in the Oregon Republican Party, with additional leads pointing to national politicians from California, Wyoming, and Arizona.

When Puter had registered his 11-7 claims for Mount Jefferson, a clerk in the Interior Department had held up processing. Since the twelve claims were still in the name of Emma Watson, Puter brought her to see Mitchell. He introduced her as a poor widow who would be destitute if the claims were not approved. Puter hoped that Mitchell's heart might be softened by her plight or melted by her beauty, but, leaving nothing to chance, he pushed two $1,000 bills across the table to reinforce his argument. Evidently the little melodrama did appeal to Mitchell's sensitive nature. "Mr. Puter, you cannot afford to pay me such a sum as this," Mitchell murmured, and pushed one of the bills back to Puter. But just one. A kind-hearted grafter, but still a grafter. Mitchell then spoke to Binger Hermann about Puter's land claims, and they were quickly approved. Mitchell was doomed when Burns got his hands on a letter from the senator to a confederate in which Mitchell explained his efforts to wriggle out of trouble, a letter which ended, "burn this without fail." When Heney produced the letter during Mitchell's trial, the newspapers began calling the senator "Burn Without Fail" Mitchell.

By now Burns's investigations had netted Heney thirty-four Oregon politicians, including Congressman John Williamson, Binger Hermann, three state senators, and John Hall, who had been removed from office by Attorney General Knox on Heney's recommendation. Burns also had evidence, unusable in court, that Senator Fulton was as corrupt as the rest.

The Oregon political establishment did not give up without a fight. Underworld sources told Burns that gunmen had been hired to kill Heney. That could not be dismissed as a hollow threat: In Colorado a Secret Service agent working on a land-fraud case had been murdered, so Burns provided Heney with an armed guard. There was more. Hall persuaded Marie Ware to testify that Heney had taken her to a hotel room for the obvious purpose. Heney hauled Ware before the grand jury, where she confessed that Hall had her "put up this job" with the knowledge and approval of Hall's political allies. Heney obtained an additional indictment against Hall for a "conspiracy to defeat the administration of justice."

By the time Mitchell's trial began in June 1905, the evidence was overwhelming. Mitchell's defense amounted to the claim that he had often done what he had done for Puter and Ware without taking bribes, a little like the Irishman who countered the twenty witnesses who had seen him steal a ham with twenty others who had not seen him take it. In any event, the jury was not swayed. On July 3, 1905, after eight hours of deliberation, Mitchell was found guilty. He was fined, sentenced to six months in jail, and banned from public office. On December 8, 1905, he died from an infection following surgery while the verdict was still under appeal. By that time Heney was prosecuting most of the leading figures of the Oregon Republican Party. On September 28, 1905, after two mistrials, Heney convicted Congressman Williamson on perjury charges stemming from another land fraud. A few years later Heney convicted Hall on similar charges. All told, Heney won thirty-three cases against the Oregon land-fraud ring. Only Binger Hermann escaped conviction.

■ ■ ■

Theodore Roosevelt and his supporters were delighted at the outcome of the Mitchell case. To Roosevelt's progressive reformers, Mitchell represented everything wrong with America, the type of senator who was supposed to have answered, when he was asked why he didn't work for the people, "I work for the people the people work for." For progressives, Mitchell had become a symbol of the corrupt alliance between crooked businessmen and crooked politicians and of the corrupt political machines that dominated state and local government. His conviction encouraged them to hope it was possible to defeat the prosecutors and judges who protected the wealthy and powerful who were looting the country. Muckraking progressive journalists like Lincoln Steffens turned Burns into the hero of the land-fraud cases, Steffens titling his *American Magazine* story about the investigation "A Detective Story."

Roosevelt's political enemies, the regulars of the Republican Party, did not see it that way. To them it was a declaration of war by a president intent on overturning what Woodrow Wilson, when he was a university professor, had called Congressional Government, which the regulars considered to be the only form of government sanctioned by the Constitution. And they had a good deal of history on their side: Since the Civil War, Congress had controlled the government. The president and the courts executed and enforced the wishes of a Congress ruled by the Republican Old Guard. And that Old Guard saw itself as the divinely appointed protector of the free economy that was enriching the country against attacks by misbegotten political movements—populists, socialists, and, yes, progressives—bent on destroying the free market system with regulations born out of a pious but impractical notion of social justice.

Roosevelt's enemies could see as clearly as Steffens that the Oregon land-fraud case had in fact been "A Detective Story," because without the work of Burns and his associates from the Secret Service, the cozy workings of the land-fraud rings would have gone on forever, and Mitchell and his associates would have retired rich and loaded with honors. And so Roosevelt's detectives became the target of their counterattack. Where had he gotten those detectives? Was he supposed to have them? And had he broken any laws in getting them?

The Old Guard leadership of Congress—spearheaded by the House Appropriations Committee under Republican James A. Tawney of Minnesota—launched an inquiry into the history of the Secret Service with the goal of proving that Roosevelt had connived with Secret Service Chief John Wilkie to escape the strict limits Congress had—repeatedly—set on the activities of the Treasury Department detectives. This inquiry touched off a war between Theodore Roosevelt and Congress over the Secret Service that lasted from 1906 until 1909, a struggle that finally produced the force of detectives that would become today's FBI.

■ ■ ■

This controversy over the Secret Service was the latest chapter in a battle over the role and scope of federal law enforcement that had been raging since the beginning of the Republic.

The federal government began its life under the Constitution without any department specifically charged with investigating violations of federal laws.

The Judiciary Act of 1789 created the post of attorney general, but without a department of its own. Instead the attorney general headed an "office," which was what we would today call a "virtual" office—he was, an early attorney general complained, "expected to furnish his own quarters, fuel, stationery and clerk" out of his compensation of $1,500 a year.

The first attorneys general all complained they could not do their job without assistance, but not until 1818 did Congress relent and give the attorney general a clerk. The next year, he got some money for office rent and stationery. In 1822 the attorney general finally was given a one-room office of his own in the old War Department building and in 1839 that lonely clerk got a messenger to keep him company, and they all moved to the second floor of the Treasury building.

It would take an excess of credulity to believe that it was by an oversight that Congress kept the government's chief law enforcement officer in such helpless straits. If it was an oversight, that error was called to Congress's attention by, among others, an exasperated Supreme Court justice, who observed sarcastically that Congress seems "to have forgotten that such a thing as internal police or organization is necessary. I believe in my conscience many members imagine that the laws will execute themselves."

An even more cynical observer might have noted that without the annoyance of enforcement, inconvenient federal laws could safely be ignored; by keeping federal law enforcement poor and (presumably) honest, the congressmen and their economic accomplices could happily and safely be rich and dishonest. Less cynically, by the states'-rights theories of the day, federal laws delving into the internal affairs of the states were presumptively illegitimate as well as unwelcome and inconvenient. Not that the states were doing much of a job of policing themselves: In fact, there is a rather persuasive theory that the American national character has been significantly shaped by the fact that we have been an underpoliced country throughout our history, at least by the standards of European countries or our own neighbors to the north. But whether by design or historical accident, there was actually little work for the attorney general before the Civil War, especially since each federal department had its own lawyer (generally called a solicitor) to handle its legal business.

The Civil War changed all that, producing a vast increase in legal work for the government—most urgently, policing the nation's currency. The Union paid for the war by printing large quantities of paper money, and counterfeiters promptly exploited the public's unfamiliarity with the new "greenbacks" and flooded the country with bogus currency. Unless the government could stop this counterfeiting, the public's confidence in the currency would collapse, and with it the Union's ability to finance the war. The Treasury Department had to do something about it.

It is a well-known and long-standing constitutional principle that the executive branch can employ whatever means it finds necessary to accomplish its constitutional duties, as long as the means do not violate the Constitution or the law, and as long as Congress has appropriated money for the ends that, so to speak, justify the means. In this manner presidents and cabinet officers have regularly established executive agencies without specific legislation merely on the authority of an appropriation. This does not mean Congress gives up its authority: If Congress—in fact, if any single congressman—objects to an agency created by the executive branch, a point of order during the debate over the appropriation bill will be enough to suspend the operation of the new agency, at least until Congress decides on a permanent arrangement.

And that was how the Secret Service was born. Congress appropriated money to the Treasury Department to suppress counterfeiting and on July 5, 1865, on the authority of that appropriation, the secretary of the treasury organized the Secret Service. The federal government now had its first, and, until the FBI was established, its only force of detectives.

Congress went along with this because the government was clearly faced with an emergency that threatened government operations. It could even be called a war emergency, since the counterfeiting crisis was caused by the war, and because the money used to create the Secret Service was appropriated before the end of hostilities, although the service began its work after the war was over. (Lee's surrender was April 9, 1865; the war in the West ended May 26; the appropriation that gave birth to the Secret Service went into effect on July 1.)

Congress did not object to this augmentation of executive power because the target of expanded law enforcement—in this instance, counterfeiters— obviously had no supporters in Congress, and no supporters among the interests whose influence Congress habitually took into account. Just the opposite: The country's most powerful private interests were precisely those most harmed by the fake greenbacks. Congress would not be so passive if federal law enforcement began to bother people who did have sponsors on Capitol Hill.

But in allowing the Treasury Department to establish the Secret Service, Congress had certainly not abandoned its reflexive antipathy to federal law enforcement. The Secret Service was emphatically not authorized to function as a general detective agency investigating all violations of federal law. It was specifically directed to investigate counterfeiting, and counterfeiting only. Other federal laws were left, as before, to enforce themselves.

Nevertheless, it was not long before Congress legislated another expansion of federal law enforcement when a new crisis challenged Washington's ability to govern the country. This was the South's violent resistance (by way of the Ku Klux Klan) to Reconstruction era efforts to protect the civil rights granted freed slaves by the Reconstruction amendments to the Constitution (the Thirteenth, outlawing slavery; the Fourteenth, granting blacks citizenship and guaranteeing equal protection under the laws; and the Fifteenth, guaranteeing freed slaves the right to vote), along with Reconstruction civil rights laws and the enforcement acts aimed at dismantling the Klan.

To provide the manpower to investigate the Ku Klux Klan cases, Congress looked to the newly formed Secret Service, and expanded the scope of the Treasury Department's 1867 appropriation to let the service detect "persons perpetrating frauds against the government." Congress specified to Treasury that it should include the Klan in that rather elastic category, along with bootleggers, smugglers, mail train thieves, and public land swindlers.

The crisis over the Klan also led Congress to search for ways to reorganize the attorney general's office, since he now had to prosecute the Klan cases as well as handle the enormous increase in legal work left in the aftermath of the war, such as war claims, disputes over wartime procurement contracts, and requests for amnesty. The attorney general had the legal responsibility of representing the government in all these cases, but their sheer volume made it impossible for him to supervise the solicitors of the different departments who were actually bringing the cases to court. This situation produced a proliferation of federal legal opinions without any coordination, which, in the words of one senator, "murdered" the law. Congress's solution was to turn the office of the attorney general into a federal "department" of law headed by the attorney general. And so, on July 1, 1870, the Department of Justice came into being.

Initially Congress said nothing about giving the new Justice Department any men or money to investigate crime, but in 1871 the chair of the House Appropriations Committee asked Attorney General Amos T. Akerman if "he could use a special appropriation for detective purposes." The congressman specifically had in mind enforcement of laws passed in 1870 and 1871 to combat the Ku Klux Klan. Akerman accepted the offer, and in 1871 the department received the sum of $50,000 for "the detection and prosecution of crimes against the United States," an appropriation thereafter renewed annually. And so the Justice Department's first appropriation for law enforcement originated in an effort to protect the civil rights of black Americans. That same appropriation was what the attorney general would use to establish the detective force that eventually became the FBI.

Akerman hired a single "special agent," a detective reporting directly to him, and then regularly asked the Treasury Department to lend him Secret Service agents, since they were the only federal investigators Akerman considered "capable and trusty." While they were working for the Justice Department Akerman paid the agents out of his appropriation "for the detection and prosecution of crime."

The federal commitment to the civil rights of black Americans during Reconstruction had led to the first real expansion of federal law enforcement. But before very long that commitment began to weaken, and the country, and with it the federal government, grew tired of the constant and only marginally successful struggle to protect blacks against the white South's persistent (and violent) campaign to regain control of its state and local governments. When the presidential election of 1876 between the Republican Rutherford B. Hayes and the Democrat Samuel J. Tilden ended inconclusively, there was wheeling and dealing between the two parties and a compromise that let the Republicans keep control of the White House, while in exchange federal troops were withdrawn from the South. As soon as the last Republican Reconstruction governments fell to Democratic "Redeemers," and blacks were disenfranchised, their votes no longer figured in Republican hopes for capturing the presidency or control of Congress. Without the Republicans' partisan interest in black votes, federal concern for protecting their civil rights vanished, not to revive until the middle of the twentieth century. With the Reconstruction law enforcement crisis resolved at the expense of Southern blacks, the traditional congressional opposition to federal law enforcement—which in practice meant keeping the Secret Service from investigating anything except the laws against counterfeiting and prohibiting it from working outside the Treasury Department—reasserted itself.

Two powerful groups in the country were particularly opposed to investigations of federal crimes by the Secret Service or anyone else, and they were groups who would grow ever more powerful for the rest of the nineteenth century: Southern Democrats and big business. And so in 1880, responding to the demands of Old Guard Republicans representing the business interests and of Southern Democrats defending the "Southern way of life," meaning white supremacy, Congress ordered the Secret Service to restrict the use of its appropriations to investigations of counterfeiting and related offenses, and "for no other purpose whatever."

This deprived the Justice Department of the only detectives (except for its lone special agent) it had to enforce the law. But federal laws were still being broken, and the Justice Department still had its appropriation for the "detection and prosecution" of federal crimes, so Attorney General Benjamin H. Brewster (1881–1884) had to turn to private detective bureaus for investigators. In a short time the largest and most famous private detective bureau, the Pinkerton Agency, became the Justice Department's semiofficial bureau of investigation.

The Pinkerton Agency was, in fact, a formidable law enforcement force, with many of the crime-fighting resources and skills that later became trademarks of the FBI, including a terrific public relations machine.

After the Civil War, Allan Pinkerton's agency became the most famous, as well as the best, detective organization in the country, its trademark a wide-open eye with the motto "We Never Sleep" (hence the nickname "private eye"). In an era of rampant police corruption, the Pinkertons were honest and efficient. They also could—and did—conduct nationwide investigations when no other police force could: The Pinkertons' resources included mug shot galleries, modus operandi files, and networks of underworld informants.

Pinkerton learned, as would J. Edgar Hoover, that publicity was good for business and maybe even for crime fighting. He published eighteen volumes of ghostwritten casebooks from 1875 until 1886. Pinkerton was, in fact, something of a public relations genius. But fame, as the FBI would also discover, is a two-edged sword. When violent industrial strikes swept across the country between 1877 and 1892, detective agencies became strikebreaking armies for employers. The Pinkerton Agency worked on seventy strikes, including some of the bloodiest, most notoriously the strike at the Carnegie Steel Corporation's mills at Homestead, Pennsylvania, in which three guards and ten strikers were killed by gunfire. All detective agencies acted as strikebreakers, guards, and labor spies, but because the Pinkertons were the most famous, they were especially hated as symbols of management violence. There was even a popular song about them in 1892: "Hear the poor orphans tell their sad story / Father was killed by the Pinkerton men."

The Pinkertons' involvement in that Homestead strike led to congressional investigations of the use of private detectives in labor conflicts. These investigations focused on the Pinkertons and particularly on the federal government's use of them to conduct official investigations. In 1892, with the Pinkerton Agency in mind, Congress outlawed the use of private detectives by the federal government, even though Pinkerton's Investigative Division, which contained the most highly trained and effective detectives in the country, was a separate operation from its Protective Services, which supplied strikebreakers and industrial guards.

But the Justice Department still needed investigators, especially after passage of the Sherman Antitrust Act in 1890. That gave the Justice Department the responsibility of policing, with no resources of its own, the country's richest, most powerful corporations, led by men who knew all about defending themselves in the courtroom, in the statehouses, and in Washington. The situation was ludicrous to anyone who took the antitrust laws seriously, and delicious to those who didn't. In 1896, Attorney General Judson Harmon told Congress that if it would not give him detectives to collect evidence in antitrust cases, those investigations ought to be farmed out to another department with more adequate resources (that would be, presumably, the Treasury Department and its Secret Service), so that Justice could concentrate on the prosecutions. Doubtless the great corporations and their congressional allies, many on corporate retainers, were not distressed by the attorney general's lament that "the small, unorganized forces of the Justice Department were utterly insufficient" in their legal struggles against the trusts and their superb legal defense teams. Nor would it be overly cynical to suspect that congressional conservatives thought they had worked out a satisfactory compromise: Reformers got the regulation of industry they wanted, while business got a federal law enforcement system utterly incapable of enforcing those regulations.

When Theodore Roosevelt became president in 1901, he brought a new energy to Washington, and much of that energy was directed to vigorous enforcement of the law. Roosevelt's brand of progressivism—the New Nationalism, he would later call it—saw a country corrupted by wealth and power, its natural resources despoiled, food, land, and air poisoned, workers reduced to wage slavery in factories and mines that menaced life and limb, local governments controlled by corrupt political machines that sold out their immigrant workers to business interests. Roosevelt's appeal to reformers was his willingness to recognize that the day of limited government had passed and that for democracy to survive in an era of gigantic business enterprises, government had to be powerful enough to defend the public interest against special interests. But unlike other reformers, who yearned somehow to bring back an earlier age of small business and small farms (an industrial age version of Jefferson's agrarian democracy), or socialists or anarchists who proposed a revolutionary transformation of society, Roosevelt would rely on regulations based on a scientific approach to the problems of modern society: scientific land management, scientific forestry, scientific water management; utility commissions; food and drug administrations; child labor laws; public health. He counted on the vigorous application of antitrust laws to tame the arrogance and power of the financiers who increasingly controlled the nation's economy, and he looked to criminal investigations to root out corruption from government.

But Roosevelt and his attorney general had almost no means of enforcing the laws and regulations that were to be his tools for reform. The Justice Department by now had a general agent with ten "examiners" who reviewed the accounts of U.S. attorneys, marshals, and clerks. There was one special agent who investigated claims before the Spanish Treaty Claims Commission, and another who handled criminal investigations. Without anyone to investigate violations, federal laws were little more than dead letters. In 1905, William H. Moody complained in his Attorney General's Report that with the resources he had, he could manage only an occasional antitrust prosecution. And for that, he had to rely on the complainants themselves to prepare antitrust cases for the department. Any more would require a remedy "deeper than any law now upon the statute books."

There was nowhere Roosevelt could get detectives except from the Secret Service. But Congress had very specifically, and repeatedly, prohibited the Treasury Department from spending its investigative appropriation on anything besides currency-related cases (and protecting the president). And so the Justice and Treasury departments worked out a legal subterfuge, one that put Secret Service agents to work on Justice Department cases without, Roosevelt felt, being in technical violation of congressional prohibitions.

Here was the routine: The Justice Department would notify the chief of the Secret Service that it needed a certain number of detectives. The chief would then detail some of his detectives over to Justice. While they were working for the Justice Department, they would be considered legally separated from the Treasury, although they would still report to the chief of the Secret Service and would submit their expense vouchers to him. The Secret Service chief would then forward the agents' reports, along with a bill for the agents' services, to the attorney general, who would pay the Secret Service out of the Justice Department's Sundry Appropriations for the Detection and Prosecution of Crimes. The Treasury Department felt that this procedure was technically in compliance with the limits placed on its investigations.

To make sure he had the manpower to lend to the other departments, the Secret Service chief would keep on his rolls some twenty detectives over the number authorized by his budget. If other departments requested more investigators than that, the chief would dip into an "eligible list," maintained by the Civil Service Commission, of men with investigative experience, mostly former policemen or railroad claims agents. In short order, the Secret Service under Theodore Roosevelt became what one attorney general called "a central pool of detective manpower."

By the time of the Oregon land-fraud cases, most of the Justice Department's investigative work was being done by detectives detached from the Secret Service to the Justice Department, or detectives recommended by the Secret Service, and so the Justice Department's enforcement of the antitrust laws, civil rights, and anti-peonage laws, and, of course, the investigation of the Western land frauds all depended on the attorney general's ability to borrow detectives from the Treasury Department.

The work was getting done, but the arrangement defied principles of efficient management, and to Congress's unfriendly eye the procedure seemed a substantial violation of the law. As the Appropriations Committee noted, with ill-concealed sarcasm, "there was a situation of agents from one department [Treasury] loaned to another [Justice] to investigate violations of laws under still another Department [Interior] and reporting back to the Secret Service Division which had nothing to do with the administration of the laws violated or the prosecution of the violators."

■ ■ ■

The Oregon land-fraud investigations and Mitchell's conviction called Congress's attention once again to the use of Secret Service agents outside the Treasury Department. Roosevelt's enemies hoped this might be a political and perhaps legal weakness in the president's case against Congress. In 1906, when the cabinet secretaries presented their appropriations requests, the chairman of the House Appropriations Committee, James A. Tawney of Minnesota, demanded a complete roster of the detectives working in all their departments, and to put this in the worst light, the committee adopted the commonplace, but inaccurate, usage of referring to *all* federal detectives as "Secret Service agents," whether or not they worked for the Treasury Department. Tawney claimed he was only trying to force the administration to obey the law, but it was clear he was really trying to switch the discussion from land fraud and political corruption by Congress to lawbreaking by the president and attorney general.

During Tawney's grilling of Justice and Treasury department witnesses, he made clear his suspicions of all federal law enforcement. Other Old Guard Republicans and Southern Democrats were even more blatantly hostile. They chimed in with denunciations of antitrust investigations of corporations, anti-peonage investigations of Southern plantation owners, and the land-fraud investigations, which many Westerners saw as criminalizing a legitimate means of getting federal land into the hands of Westerners, where it belonged. Through it all, they painted Secret Service Chief John Wilkie as a master conspirator, plotting with the president to infiltrate the Secret Service throughout the government to destroy the Constitution's system of checks and balances.

The Roosevelt administration, for its part, refused to buckle under congressional pressure, or to admit it had done anything wrong in its use of the Secret Service, although it admitted that employing Secret Service agents outside the Treasury Department was not particularly efficient (which hardly mollified those congressmen who thought that the investigations [of them] had been *too* efficient). What the administration really wanted, Attorney General William H. Moody (who succeeded Knox) declared in his 1906 Attorney General's Report, was for the Justice Department to have its own "organization for the investigation of suspected offenses."

Moody was not a particularly energetic attorney general, and he did not share Theodore Roosevelt's enthusiasm for exposing political corruption. His resignation late in 1906 therefore gave Roosevelt the chance to appoint a fellow spirit to head the Justice Department: Roosevelt's longtime friend, Maryland lawyer Charles Bonaparte, a grandson of Napoleon's brother Jerome and a grandnephew of Napoleon himself, a circumstance that encouraged witticisms from those who saw in Bonaparte's family heritage positive proof of malign, and possibly dictatorial, intent.

Bonaparte was an all-purpose reformer. He had battled for twenty years to pry Maryland loose from corrupt political machines, and had defeated a "grandfather clause" that would have disenfranchised Maryland blacks. Bonaparte was also a cofounder of the National Civil Service League, which campaigned to make competitive examinations instead of political connections the qualification for government jobs, the key element in the progressive program of replacing corrupt politics with rational, scientific solutions to social problems.

Soon after he became president, Roosevelt gave Bonaparte a chance to apply such solutions to the government itself. First Bonaparte went on the Board of Indian Commissioners, where he helped reform Indian policy. Then Roosevelt appointed him secretary of the Navy, telling him he would go to the Justice Department as soon as it could be arranged. And arranged it was, on December 17, 1906.

In his first *Attorney General's Report,* Bonaparte began pressing Congress to permit the Justice Department to organize "a small, carefully selected, and experienced force under its immediate orders," so that it would be spared the inconvenience and inefficiency of "suddenly" having to borrow Secret Service agents. "A Department of Justice with no force of permanent police in any form under its control," he reported, "is assuredly not fully equipped for its work." Instead of responding directly to Bonaparte's request, Tawney and the Appropriations Committee continued to attack any use of Secret Service detectives outside the Treasury Department.

On April 2, 1908, Bonaparte appeared before the House Appropriations Committee and again suggested that Justice should be allowed to have its own detective force. Instead, Tawney proposed that

> *when the necessity arises . . . the Department of Justice [get] the eligible roll in the Treasury Department and simply [select] a man from that roll and [employ] him for the particular work the Department desires him to do. . . . And then when he has completed the work he was employed to do, his service ends and he is no longer a Government employee.*

Bonaparte pointed out the problem with Tawney's suggestion. These temporary employees, who knew that they would be going back to the Treasury Department list after their detail at Justice was over, would never develop the discipline and loyalty of a permanent force. Moreover, Bonaparte warned, "If you pay him by the job and make his continued employment dependent on his finding more jobs, you run the danger . . . of making him what they call abroad an 'agent provocateur,' a person who creates the crime in order that he may get the credit for detecting and punishing the criminal."

A few weeks later, Tawney reported to the House on his exchanges with Bonaparte. He explained that "there is no question of [the Justice Department's] right to pay secret-service men out of the general appropriation for United States Courts. There is no question about that." Tawney said what he opposed was the control that Secret Service Chief Wilkie, and through him the president, retained over the agents no matter where they were dispatched, thus in effect making Wilkie a spymaster reporting back to Roosevelt on all branches of the government. The real issue, Tawney claimed, was that Roosevelt had turned the Secret Service into a general detective force he could use to police the entire government. Unless the Secret Service were reined in, it would soon become in law what it was in fact, a general investigative agency spying on the entire government. The administration's supporters replied that perhaps a general police force (letting pass the loaded reference to a "secret police") for the federal government was just what was needed. Pointing to recent antitrust prosecutions in New York, they said that it was only by using the Secret Service that the prosecutors had been able "to procure evidence and procure the attendance of witnesses and if this limitation goes through they will be cut out of all that sort of thing and [the prosecutors] will be left in New York, against some of the smoothest, brightest lawyers," "some of the 'slickest' men God ever let live." Without the Secret Service working on antitrust for the Justice Department, the government would be "absolutely defenseless."

Tawney had by now made an historical study of the legal basis for the administration's expanded use of the Secret Service. He reported that the use of the Secret Service outside the Treasury Department, or for that matter their use within the Treasury Department on any investigations not involving counterfeiting or threats to the president, had been specifically and repeatedly prohibited by Congress. It was illegal. And so whatever crimes the Secret Service may have discovered while working for the Justice and Interior departments, they paled in comparison to the Roosevelt administration's own violations of the law and the constitutional system of checks and balances.

Encouraged by Tawney's report, Roosevelt-haters in Congress went on a political rampage. They claimed the administration had turned John Wilkie's Secret Service into a presidential spy system to attack, intimidate, and humiliate the president's enemies in Congress. They claimed (falsely) that there had been a vast growth in the number of "secret service agents" in government under Roosevelt, padding their figures by counting as "secret agents" any investigators anywhere in the government—and there were thousands (including meat inspectors, lighthouse inspectors, and dozens of others who were hardly doing anything in secret).

Roosevelt's enemies hoped to convince the public that there was a secret pattern behind every controversial act by this most controversial of presidents. That pattern, they claimed, was Roosevelt's use (or rather misuse) of the Secret Service to expand his power, in defiance of the limits placed on his authority by the Constitution. If the public accepted this premise, then the merest hint of any involvement by the Secret Service in an investigation might be enough to discredit it. Congressmen began to use the Secret Service to smear Roosevelt's investigations of peonage cases in the South, land-fraud cases in the West, antitrust cases throughout the country, and, of course, the recent political corruption cases in the House and Senate. Roosevelt's critics claimed that the real issue ought to be Roosevelt's illegal and unconstitutional use of Secret Service detectives (the term "secret service detective" had by now been expanded to include anyone conducting an investigation for the executive branch).

Tawney's investigation of the Secret Service encouraged Roosevelt's enemies to recycle all their old complaints against the president. For instance, the Secret Service controversy let the president's foes launch a new attack on his harsh treatment of the black soldiers involved in a race riot in Brownsville, Texas, on August 12, 1906, which had left a bartender dead and a policeman wounded. Unable to identify the soldiers responsible, Roosevelt had dishonorably discharged more than 160 of them, including six Medal of Honor holders. Ohio Senator Joseph B. Foraker, who had his eye on a run for the presidency in 1908, had championed the Brownsville soldiers to appeal to the Republican Old Guard, which still responded to the bloody shirt of the Civil War. So now Foraker charged that Roosevelt had sent Secret Service agents to Texas to harass the soldiers.

Roosevelt's enemies in the Secret Service controversy also made much of a recent revelation that the secretary of the Navy had borrowed an agent from the Secret Service to "shadow" a naval officer engaged in an extramarital love affair. Roosevelt's "spy system," his enemies claimed, had stooped to the blackmail tricks of divorce lawyers to dig up dirt on his enemies. Roosevelt's defenders insisted that the facts hardly supported that conclusion. The secretary of the Navy had been hounded by an indignant and socially prominent Washington husband who complained that his wife had disappeared in the company of a naval ensign. The secretary had first ordered naval investigators to locate the spouse-snatching sailor and his smitten siren. When they failed, the Navy secretary asked the secretary of the Treasury to see if Secret Service agents could find the amorous mariner and the wayward wife, and indeed they did locate them in a New York hotel. The Secret Service notified the Navy where they were, and terminated its involvement in the case. Southern congressmen, ever sensitive to federal violations of states' rights—by which they meant the right of white southerners to do what they liked to blacks without any meddling by outside agitators—seized on the Secret Service controversy to blast the president and the attorney general for investigating anti-peonage law violations in Florida and Mississippi. In this case no Secret Service agents were actually involved, but there *were* federal investigators, which was close enough.

The Roosevelt administration had sent investigators to investigate charges (from the foreign offices of Italy and Austria) that Italian immigrants were being forced to work under conditions of peonage on plantations in Mississippi and Florida. Both countries were so concerned that they had warned potential immigrants to stay out of the South, and to avoid Mississippi in particular. Bonaparte sent a Charles W. Russell to investigate, accompanied by Assistant to the Attorney General Mary Quackenbos (whose name southerners found almost as hilarious as Bonaparte's), together with an Italian-speaking labor agent named Pettek to serve as translator. The investigation produced only one indictment, and afterward Russell stated that conditions in the labor camps were far better than he had expected. Nevertheless, Southern congressmen claimed that the investigation had violated their precious states' rights, and so they took advantage of the Secret Service controversy to lambaste Roosevelt and Bonaparte ("this transplanted bud of alleged French nobility") for insulting the honor of the South. For the sake of the argument, Russell, Quackenbos and Pettek were all stuffed into the infinitely expandable category of "Secret Service agents."

Ironically, Tawney's historical research unearthed a rather surprising fact, unknown to both sides at the start of the controversy, that in some ways made the entire discussion somewhat moot: Throughout its entire history the Justice Department had always had the power simply to create a detective force on its own, without any explicit authorization from Congress. The attorney general could have simply relied on his appropriation for the investigation of crimes against the United States, which appropriation had been renewed annually since 1871. He needed no further permission from Congress. In the course of his research, Tawney became aware of something everyone had forgotten: The Treasury Department had created the Secret Service on its own, without an authorizing act of Congress, relying on its appropriation for the detection of counterfeiting. Even Roosevelt's opponents had to concede, however grudgingly, that there was no reason the attorney general could not do the same. But at the beginning Bonaparte and his supporters were all laboring under the same misapprehension as his enemies, that only an act of Congress could give Bonaparte the legal authority to organize his own bureau of investigation in the Justice Department.

At the end of the hearings there was no meeting of minds, no knowing what Tawney would tell Bonaparte to do: to organize his own force, as the attorney general had asked, or just to keep borrowing agents from the Treasury Department, perhaps with some new restrictions.

But what Tawney actually did was altogether different and completely unexpected. He attached an amendment to the Sundry Appropriations bill that read (in its final form), "No part of any money appropriated by this act shall be used in payment of compensation or expenses of any person detailed or transferred from the Secret Service Division of the Treasury Department, or who may at any time during the fiscal year 1909 have been employed in or under said Secret Service Division." With that he abruptly deprived the Justice Department of any means of investigating its cases, effective July 1, 1908. Evidently, all else failing, Tawney had decided he would prove that a Roosevelt-Wilkie plot existed by passing a law against it.

What resources did the Justice Department have at this moment for the investigation of crimes? There were twelve "examiners" authorized by statute and charged with investigating the accounts, acts, and records of the U.S. attorney, marshals, and clerks, which was a responsibility transferred from Treasury to Justice in 1894. (The examiners had until recently been under the direction of a "General Agent" and an "Assistant General Agent" who also audited the construction and accounts of federal prisons, but those posts had been abolished the previous October.) The department had six special agents assigned to peonage cases and seven more assigned to the land-fraud cases. Since all of these twenty-five investigators had specific assignments that absorbed all their time, the department had to rely completely on the Secret Service agents detailed to the Justice Department (numbering thirty-two at that time) to investigate any other violations of the law, particularly antitrust cases. Without the help of the Secret Service, therefore, the most serious federal crimes, the ones that most concerned Roosevelt's progressives, would remain undetected and unprosecuted.

Roosevelt and Bonaparte, joined by United States attorneys around the country, protested that Tawney's amendment would leave the government with no means of enforcing the law. The *New York Times* editorialized, "The Representatives have, however unwittingly, become the tools of thieves. The Senators are duly warned." Ignoring the warning, the Senate followed the House's lead by passing Tawney's amendment on May 27, to take effect on July 1.

Roosevelt and Bonaparte had by now learned the history of the Secret Service's birth through executive order, thanks to Tawney's research. They moved rapidly to employ the same means to remedy the current impasse. On June 24, 1908, Bonaparte appointed Stanley W. Finch, a former examiner of the department, to be "Chief Examiner." Finch then selected nine Secret Service agents who had previously worked for the Justice Department (plus one additional agent who had not worked for the Secret Service) and on July 1, Bonaparte commissioned them special agents of the Justice Department. In addition to the nine new recruits, Finch was given the thirteen special agents detailed to Southern peonage and Western land-fraud cases, and the department's force of twelve examiners.

The transfer of these agents was fully agreeable to Secret Service chief Wilkie for two reasons. The Secret Service, deprived of the funds it had been getting from other departments for its agents, was going to have to let go of the extra agents it had been carrying on its roster for that purpose. Second, it was Roosevelt's intention to move all government investigators, including the Secret Service, into the Justice Department to be merged into the new force, and Roosevelt intended to name Wilkie to command the entire operation. Wilkie expected that in a few months he would be rejoining his old subordinates in the Justice Department, bringing the rest of the Secret Service with him. Roosevelt had in fact written his friends proposing that "Chief Wilkie should be transferred to the Department of Justice and placed at the head of the force therein organized."

But the Secret Service, and Wilkie in particular, had taken so much fire from Roosevelt's opponents that giving Wilkie a bigger job than he already had would have been foolhardy. It would have goaded Wilkie's enemies into an attack on the Justice Department, and so, despite Roosevelt's admiration for him, Wilkie had to stay in the Treasury Department leading a sadly diminished agency.

When July 1 arrived, the Justice Department had a new force, born in a clash between the political parties and the branches of government. It had as yet no official name, but was informally called the "Special Agent Force," consisting of thirty-five investigators, under the command of Chief Examiner Stanley Finch. On July 26, 1908, Bonaparte ordered that all investigations with the exception of bank examinations and naturalization matters be referred to Finch, and so, somewhat arbitrarily, the FBI has designated July 26 as its birthday, celebrated with varying degrees of festivity down to the present day.

Stanley Wellington Finch thus stands in history as the first director of what is now the FBI. He was born on July 20, 1872, in Monticello, New York, and was not quite thirty-six when he assumed command of the Special Agent Force. He had graduated from Baker University in Baldwin, Kansas, and then attended the Corcoran Scientific School in Washington, D.C., with further training at business colleges in Albany, New York, and Washington. He had joined the Justice Department in 1893, first as a bookkeeper, then examiner, special examiner, and finally chief examiner. In 1908 he got his law degree from National University (later George Washington University), where J. Edgar Hoover would study just a few years later.

■ ■ ■

Congress was in no position to protest the creation of the new bureau without seeming to be trying to cover up misdeeds of malefactors in its ranks. There matters might have rested. But Roosevelt was nothing if not pugnacious, and never left his vanquished enemies in the dust without giving them a farewell kick. On December 8, 1908, he sent a gratuitously insulting message to Congress in which he charged that "the chief argument in favor of the provision [barring the departments' use of Secret Service agents] was that Congressmen did not themselves want to be investigated. . . . I do not believe that it is in the public interest to protect criminals in any branch of the public service." He suggested that Congress might solve its problem by authorizing Secret Service agents to investigate any crimes *except* those committed by members of Congress.

Roosevelt's letter touched off one of the most entertaining debates in congressional history, one mined for years by enemies of the FBI to prove that Congress had been suspicious of the Bureau from the beginning and had been opposed to its founding. But the uproar had almost nothing to do with the Bureau itself. It was actually a wild scramble by congressmen, thrown on the defensive by Roosevelt, who were trying to demonstrate that Wilkie and the Secret Service had been a danger to the Republic. They were trying to show that by placing restrictions on the Secret Service, Congress had nipped Roosevelt's and Wilkie's ambitions in the bud. The issue was never Bonaparte's creation of a Justice Department bureau of investigation. The fight was over the Secret Service, and whether the Secret Service had been a force for good, or whether it had been a threat to American liberty. At the end, both sides conceded that Bonaparte had every right to set up his own bureau. Roosevelt's enemies even applauded the founding of the Bureau as if it had been their idea all along, a fortuitous means of halting the dangerous growth of the Secret Service.

During this debate one of Roosevelt's congressional enemies set a standard for political insult that would be hard to top:

It is unfortunate not only for President Roosevelt, but for the citizens of the Republic, that he has not a legal mind and equipoise of executive reason, riding through and around the arena of political action on his bronco of arrogant, egotistical impulse, pretending to throw his lariat of execution at the heels and broad horns of capital, for the delectation of voting labor, and ending the scene with the cunning catch of a prairie wolf or a gopher. In all of this fuss and feathers of the whole administration, he and his pliant Attorney General have not sent a single plutocrat to the penitentiary. Such a keen political speculator, and political and financial strenuosity has never been seen before in this Republic, and let us fervently hope that his like shall never be seen again.

Then, in an abrupt shift of allusion, he ended with a classical flourish:

The liberty of the people is gradually and secretly stolen by sneaking executive encroachments. . . . While imitating Rienzi and Cromwell in fooling the people he is practicing the hypocrisy and dictatorship of Cleon and Dionysius and has built up a Roosevelt ring in the army, navy, and civil service, all for his per-

sonal and political glory, supreme in his impudence, vanity, arrogance and imperial egotism.

Congressmen may not have made much more sense then than now, but at least they had style.

Congress had taken particular umbrage at Roosevelt's suggestion that Congress had hobbled the Secret Service to help congressional criminals escape justice. The president had not helped matters by offering to exempt congressional felons from Secret Service investigation. One congressman, who evidently fancied himself a wit, said he

> *would welcome a presidential shadow as amusing company at all times, and . . . I am going to ask leave to have inserted this proviso: . . . that nothing in this law contained shall be so construed as to prevent the President of the United States from appointing a corps of secret-service agents, not exceeding 489-odd in number, the sole function of whom and the sole duty of whom shall be to shadow, espy upon, and report to the President of the United States concerning the conduct of each member of the House of Representatives and of the Senate.*

One remark by Congressman Walter I. Smith of Iowa has been frequently taken as a prophetic allusion to the abuses of the Hoover era of the Bureau: "Nothing is more opposed to our race than a belief that a general system of espionage is being conducted by the General Government." But Smith was referring not to the just-created Bureau of Investigation, but rather to the Secret Service, which had, in his view, become a "general spy system" under John Wilkie. Smith boasted that by stopping the Secret Service from conducting any more investigations outside the Treasury Department, he had eliminated the "general system of espionage" he was denouncing. Besides, Smith's defense of civil liberty has to be taken with a grain of salt. One of his closest political allies was implicated in the frauds uncovered by the Secret Service.

Another frequently quoted passage, this by Congressman William F. Waldo of New York, has also been misconstrued as an attack on the Bureau:

> *The only question here before the House is whether we believe in a central secret-service bureau, such as there is in Russia to-day, or whether we believe the separate departments should investigate the violations of law in those departments by a trained force of their own. . . . I believe it would be a grave blow to freedom and to free institutions if there should arise in this country any such*

*great central secret-service bureau as there is in Russia. We do not need it here
in this country and there ought not to be any such bureau. Crimes are amply
prosecuted. They are much better investigated and detected by the several departments of the Government which have trained men who understand the
business of their different departments.*

Once again, this congressman was actually defending the Justice Department's bureau, since it had kept Wilkie's Secret Service from continuing to
function as a "central secret-service bureau." Even Tawney claimed that all he
had been doing was trying to keep Wilkie from building up a "large central secret-service bureau under no limitations, under no restrictions, and responsible to nobody but himself."

It was remarkable, amazing even, that when the dust had settled, the same
congressmen and senators, Smith and Waldo among them, who had fulmi-
nated against Wilkie's machinations and who had compared his Secret Service
to Fouché's spies under Napoleon and to the tsar's Black Cabinet in St. Peters-
burg, now enthusiastically endorsed the new detective bureau in the Justice Department. There was general agreement that Bonaparte had done nothing
wrong in setting up the bureau on the authority of his appropriation. As Congressman George Norris of Nebraska reminded the House, "The authority to
create what was created in the Department of Justice existed before this limitation was ever put on the statute books, and the Attorney General had the authority then, as he has had since, to organize [his own bureau of investigators]."
Tawney chimed in, "But he did not know it."

Even more remarkably, in Congress's haste to clear itself of any charge that
it had interfered with law enforcement by shackling the Secret Service, Congress provided the new Justice Department bureau of investigation with a
mandate far more wide-ranging than Wilkie at his most ambitious, by his enemies' estimates, had ever contemplated. A Senate select committee under James
A. Hemenway of Indiana had been instructed to look into Roosevelt's charges
against Congress. When Hemenway issued his report on February 11, 1909, he
triumphantly quoted Wilkie's testimony the preceding spring that the proper
place for a detective bureau with general investigative authority was in the Department of Justice. Wilkie had said,

*I grant you that the ideal situation would be to have under the direction of the
Attorney-General in the Department of Justice a well-trained force that could
be used for the purpose of gathering evidence in all these cases. That is where*

investigating forces really belong, in my opinion. They should be in the Department of Justice. The cases have to go there eventually. All our cases go to the department of prosecution.

Hemenway happily endorsed Wilkie's suggestion, which he saw as a complete refutation of the charge that Congress had blocked Wilkie from investigating crime, and he declared that Congress had done exactly what Wilkie had recommended:

> *Congress has made an appropriation for the employment of secret-service agents by the Department of Justice, and that department has at present such a force organized; and it is the opinion of . . . [this] committee, that with the exception of a small force in the Treasury Department for use in investigating counterfeiting and protecting the person of the President of the United States, the Department of Justice is the proper place for the employment of secret service agents, as it is the department to which finally all violations of the law must be reported and which must conduct the prosecutions and trials.*

Hemenway then stated that it was the judgment of his committee that the new force in the Justice Department had the authority to investigate *all* federal crimes, with one exception:

> *The Department of Justice, to which ultimately all prosecutions for violations of law must be referred, should have secret-service agents to enable that department to properly conduct such prosecutions. It has not appeared to your committee that there are any violations of federal laws that the Department of Justice has not the authority to investigate, including lotteries, trusts, customs frauds, and all others, except, perhaps, counterfeiting. That department now has a secret service force of its own which will no doubt be increased as future needs demand it.*

Lest there be any mistake, Hemenway repeated his view that the new force had the authority to investigate *all* federal crimes not reserved to the Treasury Department:

> *I make this statement, and I make it upon the authority of evidence from the Department of Justice, that they have complete power to investigate every crime against the Government, with the possible exception of counterfeiting, and that is because we make a specific appropriation to investigate counterfeit-*

ing. They have power to investigate every crime for which investigation a spe-
cific appropriation is not otherwise made.

That expansive statement of the new Bureau's jurisdiction was seconded by
the same Congressman Smith whose rants against Wilkie were still ringing in
congressional ears. Smith boasted that through his efforts the government now
had a general detective force located where it should have been all along, and he
invited the rest of the government to make use of it.

Now we have organized in the Department of Justice a general detective force.
Let that force do what it was created for . . . If some special thing exists, where
it is necessary to call in some of these men [meaning detectives] in one of those
branches or departments which has not a special distinctive inspections service,
the Department of Justice charged with the enforcement of all the laws should
furnish the men, and they should not be furnished from the counterfeiting sec-
tion of the Treasury Department. [Applause.]

Coming from Smith, this was rather astonishing. One of his colleagues, evidently remembering how Smith had attacked the Secret Service for acting as a
general detective bureau, asked Smith whether he agreed that "the committee
had provided a secret service in the department of Justice which would be used
in the prosecution by the Attorney-General of crimes against the Government,
without respect to the department in which the crime was committed." Smith
replied, "I say that that force can be used for the enforcement of the laws of the
United States anywhere; yes sir." Still smarting from the president's offer to exempt congressmen from investigations, he even specifically invited, even challenged the new bureau to investigate the lawmakers: "Not only has the
Department of Justice a right to use this force in seeking violations of the laws
of the United States, but if it is deemed advisable to pay out of the Treasury of
the United States men to follow Congressmen or Members of the Senate,
whether suspected of crime or not, this force can be used now for that purpose
without any legal impediment whatever; that there is absolutely no restraint
whatever upon the following of Senators and members of the House by the
secret-service force in the Department of Justice." Roosevelt must have loved
that.

Completely vanquished, Roosevelt's enemies were now reduced to pretending that their only intent had been to block the ambitions of John Wilkie, and
in doing so they deserved the gratitude of a nation they had rescued from dire
peril.

Roosevelt had won almost everything he wanted. He now had a detective force within the Justice Department available for the antitrust and political corruption cases that progressives wanted investigated. With the aid of Bonaparte's detectives and the Secret Service, he soon had evidence that three of the congressmen who led the attacks on him during the controversy, Senators Foraker and Ben Tillman, and Representative Walter Smith of Iowa, were implicated in antitrust or land-fraud crimes. These revelations shattered the careers of all three. The land-fraud investigations ended the influence of Tillman of South Carolina, who had long strayed from his populist roots to become a racist menace. Tawney went down to defeat in the next election, with Roosevelt's reminder to the voters of Tawney's opposition to the Secret Service no small reason for his defeat. Finally, Congress was forced to concede that almost any investigation by the Justice Department's new detective bureau was legitimate as long as it was not conducted by Secret Service agents on loan. Congress came away with the cold comfort of having insulted Roosevelt in return, having voted overwhelmingly to table that portion of the president's message that contained the insulting reference to criminals in Congress.

■ ■ ■

The formal establishment of the "Special Agent Force" was completed on March 16, 1909, when Bonaparte's successor in the Taft administration, Attorney General George W. Wickersham, issued an order formally designating the force as the "Bureau of Investigation of the Department of Justice." He also named Stanley Finch, who was still the chief examiner, to be Chief of the Bureau.

Finch commanded his Bureau from an office in the Justice Department, located from 1908 until 1917 in the Baltic Hotel on K Street in northwest Washington. His second in command was A. Bruce Bielaski, who had been serving under Finch as an examiner. Bielaski ran the office when Finch was in the field, and he also led squads of special agents on cases himself. Finch ran his Bureau with the same discipline and attention to detail that would later come to be associated with J. Edgar Hoover. Agents reported to Finch daily on their progress, and every month Finch sent the attorney general a report on the work done by each of his thirty-six agents. Finch's men had to detail all their expenses and submit vouchers with their daily reports, ensuring a stream of intelligence back to Washington. More pressing communications were handled by means of coded telegrams. (Sometimes Finch or his agents could not figure out what the messages meant, and had to beg that they be re-sent using as few coded terms as possible.)

Finch was an innovative reformer in his leadership of the Bureau. The reforms J. Edgar Hoover instituted when he took over the Bureau in 1924 might better be described as a return to the original progressive principles of the Finch regime after straying from them in the early 1920s. One of Hoover's most celebrated measures, his requirement (which was in practice more of a goal) that his agents have training in law or accounting, was simply an enforcement of one of Finch's standards.

■ ■ ■

The Justice Department now had a detective bureau—a monument to the progressive spirit of idealism and reform that had led to its creation. Indirectly, its origins in reform went back even farther, to the Reconstruction-era crusade for the civil rights of freed slaves. The Bureau was born out of the progressive struggle to end corruption in government and bring to justice malefactors of wealth. The president and the attorney general who founded the Bureau expected it to enforce the law against the rich and powerful, against senators and congressmen, against judges and lawyers, against corporate tycoons and their industrial empires. Teddy Roosevelt founded the Bureau because the federal government, and only the federal government, had the power to bring criminals of power and wealth to justice.

But now, in 1909, Roosevelt was out of the White House, slaughtering big game in Africa. Without continued leadership from the president and attorney general, would the Bureau keep investigating the most serious "crimes against the United States"? How long would its progressive legacy survive?

THREE

The First Decade (1909–1918)

O N DECEMBER 26, 1908, Jack Johnson beat Tommy Burns in Sydney, Australia, to win the world heavyweight boxing championship. America liked to call itself a white man's country, but it now had a black man lording it over the manliest of sports. An African-American paper chortled that "no event in forty years has given more genuine satisfaction to the colored people of this country than has the signal victory of Jack Johnson." Novelist Jack London covered the fight in Australia and called Johnson's victory a defeat for the Caucasian race. "The White Man must be rescued," he wrote.

Coming to the rescue would be the new Bureau of Investigation. The Johnson case would signal a dramatic and ominous reorientation of the Bureau's mission: From the investigation of high-level crime by the politically powerful and well connected to the punishment of high-profile offenses by politically powerless outcasts who challenged American values. Less than half a decade after its founding, the Bureau would begin to veer from its founders' vision of a force of investigators concentrating on the most serious and significant "crimes against the United States" to a new role as the nation's agent of vengeance against whoever might be the public enemy of the day.

Johnson's triumph over Burns sent fight promoters on a frantic (and financially rewarding) hunt for a Great White Hope to restore the Great Race's stolen prestige. Then Johnson demolished former champion Jim Jeffries, who had come out of retirement in 1910 as the most hopeful of the White Hopes. It was clear that the man did not live, white or black, who could survive a day in the ring with Jack Johnson. Someone had to punish Johnson for private behavior that the public and, it turned out, President William Howard Taft's Justice Department now considered to be a "crime against the United States."

What was Johnson's crime? It was not just that Johnson had beaten white boxers, but how he beat them. He mocked them, he taunted them with racial epithets, and he kept them on their feet after they had lost the ability to defend themselves, so that he could prolong their pain with lasting injuries.

Johnson's personality also drove white America nuts, and Johnson loved driving white people nuts. That, obviously, could be dangerous at a time when African-Americans were being lynched for far lesser breaches of racial conventions. Johnson piled up arrests for driving fast cars. He spent staggering sums of money, lavishly and ostentatiously. And there were his women. His white women. He ran through them like sparring partners. He generally traveled with a retinue of white women—Etta Terry Duryea, his white wife, along with an entourage of white prostitutes. He liked posing for photographers with himself in their midst, a carnal smirk on his face. It was all good for business, which for Johnson was boxing, vaudeville, and anything else that paid; but it was a dangerous business.

Most of all, the country hated the racial pride he aroused in black Americans. A black Chicagoan said, "Johnson's victory demonstrates the physical superiority of the black over the Caucasian. The basis of mental superiority in most men is physical superiority. If the Negro can raise his mental standard to his physical eminence, some day he will be a leader among men."

But by 1912 it was becoming evident that boxing's search for a Great White Hope was hopeless. If Johnson were ever to be beaten, it would have to be outside the ring.

One way would be to outlaw professional boxing altogether. Theodore Roosevelt, an amateur boxer himself, endorsed the idea. Another strategy would be to eliminate boxing movies, which were a principal source of income for Johnson. Late in 1912 Congress passed such a law, prohibiting the interstate distribution of boxing films.

On September 11, 1912, something happened that pointed Johnson's enemies toward a more promising strategy. Johnson's wife, Etta, who was being neglected by her husband, except for the occasional beating, committed suicide. That focused white attention once again on Johnson's outrageous relations with white women. It did not escape notice that he soon took up with another young woman, a white and comely eighteen-year-old whore named Lucille Cameron.

Acting on a charge of abduction lodged by Lucille's mother, the Chicago police arrested Johnson on October 18, 1912. He immediately put up bail, but the case had attracted the attention of the United States attorney for Chicago, James H. Wilkerson. Wilkerson announced that his office would try Johnson on federal charges and he ordered agents at the Bureau of Investigation's Chicago division to begin gathering evidence.

It did not matter that there were no federal laws prohibiting interracial sexual activities—for that matter, there were precious few federal laws at the time prohibiting *any* kind of private activity by individuals. And so Wilkerson decided to charge Johnson with violating a law passed in 1910 to combat large-scale organized prostitution—known, in the parlance of the day, as "white slavery." It did not matter that Congress had never intended this law, the Mann Act, to regulate the sexual behavior of private individuals. It was a legal weapon that could be used against Johnson and it was close at hand.

■ ■ ■

By 1902, when an international assembly met in Paris to study the problem, "white slavery" had come to mean the coerced employment of women as prostitutes. Out of this meeting came the 1904 International Agreement for the Suppression of the White Slave Traffic, ratified by the Senate on March 1, 1905, and incorporated into the 1907 Immigration Act (section 3), strengthening a prohibition on the immigration of prostitutes that had been law since 1875. The new treaty obligated the United States and the other signatories to collect information about the immigration of prostitutes, to keep watch over train depots and ports to stop the entry of prostitutes, and to rescue and send home the victims of the international sex trade. Theodore Roosevelt announced American adherence to the treaty on June 15, 1908, which was only a formality since the treaty had already been ratified. The next year, Representative James R. Mann from the Hyde Park suburb of Chicago met with President Taft and Chicago U.S. Attorney Edward Timm to discuss forced prostitution in Chicago and elsewhere. Mann was chair of the Interstate and Foreign Commerce Committee, and he had used the commerce clause of the Constitution, which gave the federal government authority to regulate interstate trade, to draw up federal railroad rate regulations (the Mann-Elkins Act) and the Pure Food and Drug Act. With those laws as precedents, Mann introduced a bill on December 6, 1909, to regulate interstate commerce in prostitution, calling his bill the "White Slave Traffic Act."

When the Mann Act was debated in 1910, popular concern over white slavery had risen to what can fairly be called an hysteria. Reginald Kauffman published a best-selling white-slavery novel, *House of Bondage.* Clifford Roe published the results of his investigations of prostitution he had conducted for the Chicago state's attorney's office as *Panders and Their White Slaves.* Roe claimed he had first seen the word "slave" applied to prostitutes when a girl in a brothel threw him a note: "Help me—I am held captive as a slave."

Mann claimed that his bill was needed because white slavery was even worse than the black slavery of the past century: "All of the horrors," he said, "which have ever been urged, either truthfully or fancifully, against the black-slave traffic pale into insignificance as compared with the horrors of the so-called 'white-slave traffic.' " Unless his bill was passed, he said, there would continue to be "conscripted" each year "65,000 daughters of American homes" into "the great army of prostitutes." As it happened, the white-slave trafficker found few defenders in Congress, and so on June 25, 1910, the Mann Act was passed by Congress, and signed into law by President Taft.

With the enthusiastic backing of Attorney General George W. Wickersham, Chief Stanley W. Finch mobilized the Bureau to enforce the new law. He opened field offices in Chicago and New York, and soon afterward in San Francisco and San Antonio. Agents fanned out across the country, attaching themselves to the offices of the United States attorneys.

The organizations that had pressed the United States to enforce the 1904 white-slave treaty now lobbied the Justice Department to enforce the Mann Act. The World Purity Association and its American branch, the American Vigilance Association, called on "all organizations that stand for higher things" to urge Congress to support "Mr. Finch and his work." In 1911 and 1912, petition drives backed Finch's efforts. For his part, Finch urged Congress to continue to fund the drive against white slavery. He warned that without the protection of federal officers, "No one could tell when his daughter or his wife or his mother would be selected as a victim."

The Bureau was soon devoting so much time to Mann Act enforcement that in April 1912, Wickersham gave Finch a new title, Commissioner for the Suppression of White Slave Traffic, while Finch's assistant, A. Bruce Bielaski, ran the Bureau. The precise relationship between Finch and Bielaski is unclear: Years later another attorney general concluded that "for a while the Bureau and its chief are said to have been under the general supervision of the Commissioner." It was hard to tell which special agents were working for Finch and which for Bielaski. One estimate was that in February 1913 there were 220 white-slave officers in the Justice Department and 40 regular agents in the Bureau.

Historians sometimes refer to Mann Act enforcement during the white-slave scare as the Bureau's "first big assignment," which "gave the Bureau of Investigation its first big push toward an important place in the detective world."

Actually, its Mann Act enforcement really gave the Bureau its first "big push" *away* from the important, but difficult and sensitive, economic and political investigations of 1908 toward splashy investigations with big publicity payoffs that did not annoy any important political or economic interests. There were still monopolies violating the antitrust laws. Congressmen were still selling their services to special interests, and those special interests had not stopped looting the public treasury. Southern plantation owners were still keeping black and immigrant farm workers in a state of peonage, and the South was still violating the constitutional rights of African-Americans under color of the law. The Mann Act was actually the Bureau's first *small* assignment, since it directed federal law enforcement away from genuine "crimes against the United States" and set it off in pursuit of symbolic criminals who represented the fears and hatreds of the masses or the classes.

Finch developed a systematic approach to enforcement of the Mann Act that led to a swift expansion in the number of Bureau field offices across the country. From the original two field offices in Chicago and New York he had opened in 1910, Finch added two more, in California and Texas. Agents were stationed in all the country's largest cities. There they conducted mail polls of local officials to determine the location of brothels in their districts, and then the agent in the field office assigned to white-slave cases would hire a local lawyer as an assistant. Together they would visit brothels to create a registry of women at each establishment, listing where each had come from and whether she was being held by force. Upon the arrival of a new girl, the madam was supposed to fill out a biographical form and forward it to the Bureau so that the registry could be updated. Very few of the cases turned out to involve interstate "commerce," and so in most instances the agent would urge the police to make arrests under the pertinent state laws.

Attorney General Wickersham ordered the Justice Department to "refrain from instituting technical or trivial cases, or cases which more properly belong to the state courts, and . . . [restrict] itself to the class of cases at which the act was primarily directed." In fact about 98 percent of the department's Mann Act cases (there were only 2,801 convictions between 1910 and 1920) did involve commercialized traffic in sex. The Johnson case was an exception to this rule, but in 1912 a black man in America as successful as Johnson was an exception to many rules.

■ ■ ■

At first Wickersham thought U.S. Attorney Wilkerson in Chicago had made a mistake in bringing Mann Act charges against Johnson. He asked Wilkerson whether this was not a "mere question of abduction or anything not within [the] general scope of evils to be reached by [the] white slave act." But Wilkerson's arrest of Johnson had focused national attention on the case. After Johnson made bail, white mobs gathered in Chicago calling for him to be lynched. Unless Wilkerson made the case stick, those mobs might start thinking about lynching *him*. And so Wickersham's scruples were quickly swept away by the press of events.

Initially the case against Johnson did not look promising. Although Lucille Cameron's mother claimed that Johnson had lured her daughter from her home in Minneapolis to work for him as a prostitute, Lucille told the grand jury she had been a prostitute for at least three months in Chicago before she met Johnson. She denied that Johnson had played any part in her choice of profession. And so Wilkerson had the Chicago field office of the Bureau look for more evidence to use against Johnson, but although they found witnesses who would swear that Johnson had paid Lucille for sex, there was nothing to indicate any interstate aspect to the case. The acting special agent in charge in Chicago, M. L. Lins, met with Wilkerson's assistant who was going to try the case in court, Harry A. Parkin, and they agreed that they had nothing against Johnson for a Mann Act violation with Lucille. They decided to park her in jail while they debated what to do.

By now the Justice Department was so deeply committed to convicting Johnson that Attorney General Wickersham and Bureau Chief Bielaski decided to work up a completely new Mann Act charge against the boxer. The attorney general ordered the Bureau's Chicago office to help Wilkerson come up with something, anything, on Johnson. And so Special Agent Bert Meyer got a tip from a safecracker in the Chicago tenderloin district about a white prostitute who had lived with Johnson and harbored a grudge against him for dumping her. Her name was Belle Schreiber. The Bureau traced her to a brothel in Washington.

Special Agent T. S. Marshall brought Belle to Bielaski's office at the Bureau's Washington headquarters, and she gave the agents the colorful details of her affair with Johnson. But Bielaski was discouraged when he learned, as he informed the new special agent in charge of the Chicago office, Charles DeWoody, that Belle and Johnson had spent most of their time together before the Mann Act became law. Nor had she worked as a prostitute during their travels together after the Act. Nevertheless, the department decided to see if a grand jury would indict Johnson on the basis of this new testimony. After listening to Belle's stimulating account of her activities with Johnson (she had a nearly photographic, not to say pornographic memory), with special reference to the "crimes against nature" she and Johnson had committed together, the grand jury voted, on November 7, 1912, to indict Johnson. The charge was that Johnson had violated the Mann Act on August 10, 1910, by bringing Belle Schreiber to Chicago from Pittsburgh for the purpose of setting her up as a prostitute. In doing so Johnson had committed, the indictment affirmed, a crime "against the peace and dignity of the United States."

As soon as he made bail, Johnson repaired to his Chicago home and married Lucille Cameron. Whatever his motives, and they may have been to eliminate her as a witness against him, it is hard to imagine anything better calculated to inflame a white public that already thought sending him to jail was letting him off way too easy. The governor of Virginia called the marriage "a desecration of one of our most sacred rights." There was almost as much outrage north of the Mason-Dixon Line. New York's governor called it a "blot on our civilization."

The department's case against Johnson—a case now personally supervised by Wickersham and Bielaski in Washington as well as Wilkerson and DeWoody in Chicago—would depend almost completely on Belle's testimony. She was, however, proving to be a difficult witness, so difficult that Bielaski decided to keep her in the custody of the Bureau until the trial. First he sent her to a home for wayward women in New York. She was unhappy there, since she was accustomed to regular doses of narcotics and alcohol, and her keeper, New York Special Agent in Charge William Offley, failed to provide her with the requisite supplies. Her evident dissatisfaction made Offley apprehensive that she would try to escape, and so Bielaski suggested that Offley divert her with trips to the theater. These recreations made her somewhat more tractable. Bielaski also tried to scare her by warning that in other white-slave cases the white slavers had murdered women who had refused "the protection they would have had from attack" in government custody. He reminded her she was in danger from Johnson, who was in fact looking for her. Finally Belle became so unruly and unmanageable that Offley begged Bielaski to take her off his hands. Bielaski had her put on a train to Washington, but she met some old friends on the way and insisted on getting off in Baltimore. She proved to be too much for J. J. Grgurevich, the agent assigned to her in Baltimore, who had to spend days and nights catering to her whims. Indeed, for the six months before the trial, the care and feeding of their star witness seems to have been the major preoccupation of Bielaski and the Bureau.

Bielaski finally sent Belle to Chicago for the trial in April 1913. Things looked good from the government perspective. DeWoody wrote Bielaski: "If the attitude of the grand jury can be taken as any criterion to the jury trial, there will be no difficulty in convicting Johnson." The Bureau had carefully investigated the jury pool, and helped prosecutor Parkin empanel an all-white jury that was, agents reported, "strongly prejudiced against Negroes."

The Bureau's parade of witnesses gave abundant testimony about Johnson's prodigious sexual appetites, and verified that Johnson had indeed sent money to Belle, that he had paid for her passage from Pittsburgh to Chicago, and that she had practiced prostitution in an apartment he had rented for her. Belle's testimony about her many sexual meetings with Johnson, together with the testimony of other prostitutes, madams, and pimps who corroborated her story, consumed five days. In his testimony, Johnson admitted that he had sent Belle money and paid her living expenses, but said that he did not know she had plied her trade while living on his largesse. He claimed that Belle had said the money he gave her was for the care of her pregnant sister, and that she had performed stenography and other secretarial services for him in exchange for the money he had paid her, and nothing else.

The judge instructed the jury, however, that they simply had to decide whether Johnson expected to receive sexual favors from Belle when he paid for her passage from Pittsburgh to Chicago; it did not matter, he told them, whether she was an untouched virgin or a hardened prostitute. If money had changed hands, if the woman had crossed state lines, and if a sexual act had occurred, the law had been violated. It didn't matter that the government could not prove whether Johnson had made any money off Belle, since it was not the concern of the government whether or not a "white slaver" was a good businessman. Those instructions made it easy for the jury to return a verdict of guilty after only two hours of deliberation. On June 4, 1913, Johnson was sentenced to a year and a day in federal prison and a fine of $1,000.

By any measure, the use of the Mann Act against Jack Johnson by the United States attorney, the attorney general, and the Bureau was a travesty of justice. A law enacted to combat interstate criminal enterprises had been redirected to punish the personal behavior of an unpopular individual. Nor did the prosecution bother to conceal that the Mann Act was merely a pretext for punishing Jack Johnson for violating popular prejudices. During the trial, prosecutor Parkin admitted that while Johnson the "individual" may have been unfairly singled out for prosecution, "it was his misfortune to be the foremost example of the evil in permitting the intermarriage of whites and blacks . . . he has violated the law. Now it is his function to teach others the law must be respected." Johnson's fate, according to Parkin, proved that blacks were better off "penniless and happy."

By the standards of the time, Jack Johnson *had* committed a "crime against the United States" by refusing to submit to the racial conventions of his day, though it was hardly the sort of crime envisioned in the 1871 appropriation that was the basis of the Bureau's authority. Seventy years later, Johnson's biographer wrote that "the Bureau of Investigation and the Department of Justice did not so much consciously conspire to get Johnson as express the more general attitude of white society toward blacks who threatened the social order. Johnson had unwillingly become a symbol of disorder and therefore a real threat."

Just before Johnson was due to report to jail, he fled to Canada, and from there to Paris. He had hardly bothered to hide his plans for escape, nor was it his first attempt. He had rearranged his bail to spare his mother any loss if he escaped. He shipped his automobiles to Germany. He even visited DeWoody to find out if he could legally leave the country. But DeWoody and the Chicago field office paid no attention to these signals, not even when Johnson told them he was going on a fishing trip to Indiana. It almost seemed as if DeWoody's office wanted Johnson to escape.

And that was Johnson's explanation later. In a newspaper interview in Paris, Johnson claimed he had paid $50,000 to, among others, Parkin, DeWoody, and Meyer to let him escape. Bielaski questioned them all, and they of course denied the charges. Johnson's mother and sister, on the other hand, corroborated Johnson's story, and said that Parkin's share had been $5,000. A woman in the prosecutor's office also claimed that DeWoody and Parkin had extorted money from Johnson.

There is no doubt that Johnson had provided large sums to two bagmen to fix the case or facilitate his escape. There is also no doubt that the bagmen kept most of the money for themselves. It is possible that Johnson had been the victim of a not entirely original scam by confidence men who lied to him about their contacts with the Bureau and the United States attorney—although checks from one of Johnson's confederates did wind up in the hands of Parkin's brother, who claimed it had been a "loan." For whatever reason, the government showed little interest in getting Johnson back from Europe.

Johnson finally ended his exile in 1920, and returned to the United States via Mexico. Upon his return, Assistant Director Frank Burke asked him if he had bribed DeWoody, Parkin, or Meyer. Johnson was hoping to win an early release from prison, and so did not want to make any enemies in high places. He refused to answer without the advice of an attorney. The matter was dropped. Thus, in some measure at least, Johnson did avenge himself against the Bureau for railroading him: The cloud he cast over the Bureau's reputation by his escape was never removed.

. . .

The Johnson case was only the first in a long history of redirections *away* from the heavy responsibilities envisioned for the Bureau by its founders. Early attorneys general stressed high-level investigations of corporate crime in their messages to Congress in the months immediately after the establishment of the Bureau of Investigation. Bonaparte and Wickersham (despite Wickersham's departure from this principle in the Jack Johnson case) emphasized that the Bureau was founded to detect those crimes that had the most serious impact on the nation, meaning high-level white-collar crimes, particularly antitrust violations and political corruption. Bonaparte had told Congress just before he left office that

> we have one [antitrust case] against the Standard Oil Company which is going to be tried below on the 23rd of March. We have one against the Tobacco Trust, which is in the Supreme Court. We have one against the Powder trust in which the Government's testimony has been taken. . . . We have a case against the Union Pacific and the Central Pacific, against the Harriman system generally, in which they are taking testimony. . . . The testimony is very voluminous. Then we have one against the anthracite coal carriers in Pennsylvania in which they're taking testimony. . . . There are seven or eight very large cases, and there are a certain number of small ones.

Wickersham brought even more antitrust cases against business than had the Roosevelt administration.

Nevertheless, from the start the Bureau was pushed and pulled away from these sensitive and difficult investigations of high-level economic and political crimes in favor of low-level crimes against persons and property, and the Johnson case was a particularly egregious example of this. Many, even most, of the new responsibilities Congress began heaping on the Bureau soon after its founding were in effect distractions that consumed the resources of the Bureau and made it impossible, even had the Bureau been willing, to hunt the elusive, well-heeled, and well-protected white-collar criminals pursued by Roosevelt and Bonaparte. And the Bureau and its directors may not have minded immersing themselves in trivia, because any official with a tender regard for his job would rather avoid tangling with wealthy and powerful suspects if he could instead pursue public enemies of the day who were unprotected by anyone powerful or wealthy enough to make trouble.

Even in its early years, the Bureau showed a compulsion to move into those areas of traditional derring-do that could adorn it with the heroic image of the action detective hero. Agents began to participate in manhunts for fugitives, usually teamed with deputy U.S. marshals and local police. Agents did not receive federal authority to carry weapons without reference to local laws until 1934, but two months after the Bureau was founded, Finch established a weapons armory for his special agents, and dispatched Special Agent J. W. Green to purchase four twenty-inch carbines, a 30-30 rifle, four leather scabbards, four web belts, and two hundred rounds of smokeless cartridges. The media took notice: In 1910 the *Boston Post* called Chief Finch a "King Detective."

Finch's first reports suggested that even as early as the Taft administration, the Bureau, if left to its own devices, would drift into pedestrian areas of law enforcement, to routine offenses against persons and property. Part of the problem was the scope of the Bureau's jurisdiction, which covered all federal crimes not specifically reserved to another agency. Of the two dozen or so categories of cases Finch mentioned in his reports to his superiors in 1909, most were local crimes that could have been handled by detectives hired by local federal attorneys, since the cases required no national coordination or supervision. Few rose to the level of "crimes against the United States," the crimes of national importance that Roosevelt and Bonaparte had created the Bureau to investigate.

Even if the Bureau had focused properly on federal crimes, it faced a fundamental trade-off of quality vs. quantity. Should the Bureau investigate all federal crimes, or only the most serious? If the Bureau tried to spread its limited resources to cover all federal crimes, it would not have the manpower or the money to investigate the most serious of them. It would by default begin to specialize in the relatively petty crimes against persons and property that furnished the bulk of its work, and which produced plenty of quantifiable results in the form of convictions. To investigate only the most serious crimes—quality investigations—would mean ignoring lesser federal crimes. Only the president and the attorney general could determine which level of crime the Bureau should pursue. The decision involved national law enforcement policy and hence was inherently too political to be decided by civil servants such as Bureau directors. Without strong leadership from above, the Bureau's priorities would be chosen for it either by United States attorneys responding to local pressures, or by special agents in charge intent on running up impressive numbers of closed cases. Either way, the Bureau would avoid difficult cases, particularly ones involving powerful suspects with political connections, and would concentrate on unpopular individuals or groups who, in the course of doing whatever made them unpopular, coincidentally ran afoul of federal laws. Like Jack Johnson.

■ ■ ■

In its original intent, however, the Mann Act really had directed the Bureau toward an unquestionably serious form of crime: the international (and national) sex trade—in other words, international and national organized crime. Why didn't the Bureau set its sights on the kingpins of the international and national prostitution rings, the original targets of the Mann Act? The trouble was, those masters of crime were worse than elusive. They did not even seem to exist. Nor did there really seem to be any national, let alone international, prostitution rings. And while the Bureau was devoting most of its resources to low-level Mann Act enforcement, the public began to lose interest.

From the beginning there had been skeptics who looked at the white-slave scare as a typical example of American Puritanism gone berserk, a "hysteria," a "joke of huge proportions perpetrated on the American public." The *New York World* called it "a new witchcraft mania." A. W. Elliott, president of the Southern Rescue Mission and editor of the *Young Women's Magazine,* claimed in 1913 that after six years working among prostitutes he had not yet found a single instance of the "over advertised" white slave. In March 1910, Chicago organized a "Vice Commission" to study the problem. A year later the commission reported it had not been able to find any white slavers, any white slaves, or any white-slave conspiracy. Dozens of other cities and states organized their own vice commissions modeled on Chicago's, and they all reported the same results: As far as they could see, there was no such conspiracy. The panic turned out to have been over precisely nothing.

By 1913 the white-slave scare was clearly over. Finch resigned and in 1914 the Wilson administration abolished the Justice Department's White Slave Commission, which Finch had led. Bielaski stayed on as head of the Bureau. Every now and then Bielaski tried to reassure the old anti-white-slavery coalition that the Bureau had not given up the fight. But it had.

In a trivial sense, the Bureau had for the first time investigated organized crime—international organized crime at that—but in reality the Bureau was looking for a form of organized crime that did not exist, where years later it would fail to look for the kind of organized crime that *did* exist. Less trivially, perhaps, during the white-slave scare Bureau agents for the first time worked with local police in what were, in effect, anticrime task forces. From those investigations the Bureau did acquire a certain amount of intelligence about organized crime, although this intelligence was peripheral and even unrelated to what they were supposed to be investigating. Many years later the task force approach would be the key to the success of the Bureau's investigative strategy against organized crime.

If the good that came out of the white-slave scare was soon buried, the evil lived on. The Bureau had transformed itself into a force large enough to investigate national and international white-slave rings, and now the Bureau found it had, as far as its original mission was concerned, absolutely nothing to do. But doing nothing would have been better than what the Bureau actually did with its Mann Act enforcement over the next few years.

During the debate over the Mann Act, the legislative intent had been clear. Representative Mann stressed that the law was not intended to apply to individual prostitutes, whether new recruits or hardened veterans. Nor was Congress concerned with the sex industry as such, but only with the coercion of women into prostitution. But two words, "immoral purposes," added during the drafting of the bill to the forms of prohibited interstate commerce eventually changed the effect of the legislation. The phrase was derived from Immigration Bureau testimony during the hearings that seduction, drugs, and trickery were often used to lure innocent women into prostitution. "Immoral purposes" was added to the bill to cover those less violent forms of coercion. But "immoral purposes" proved to be an elastic clause permitting the prosecution of private, noncommercial sexual activities the Mann Act's sponsors had exempted from the law.

The courts quickly began to use "immoral purposes" to create an expansive interpretation of the Mann Act as prohibiting any sort of sexual immorality— defined as extramarital sex—when it crossed a state line. In *Athansaw v. U.S.* (1913) the Supreme Court ruled that a theater owner could be prosecuted under the Mann Act for having furnished a railroad ticket to a prospective chorus girl when he propositioned her after she arrived at his theater. In 1915 the Supreme Court ruled that a prostitute (or, indeed, any other woman) involved in a Mann Act case could be prosecuted as a coconspirator.

The most important expansion of Mann Act jurisdiction was in *Caminetti v. U.S.* (1917), in which the Supreme Court ruled that any unmarried couple who crossed state lines "for immoral purposes" could be prosecuted. The defendants in *Caminetti* were two prominent married men from Sacramento, California, who were in the habit of taking out-of-town pleasure trips with their girlfriends. The men decided to move the women (ages nineteen and twenty) to Reno, Nevada, and set up housekeeping in contemplation of getting divorces and then marrying them. At the instigation of the men's wives, police arrested the two couples on Mann Act charges. Since one of the unlucky lovers

(Drew Caminetti) was the son of Woodrow Wilson's commissioner of immigration, Republicans tried to embarrass the administration by claiming that young Caminetti was being shielded from prosecution because of his father's influence. The U.S. attorney, to avoid charges of conflict of interest, had to appoint a special prosecutor, who convinced the jury that Caminetti's romantic escapades not only were immoral but were federal crimes.

Even though the Justice Department sometimes tried to restrict prosecution to "the class of cases at which the act was primarily directed," the Mann Act became a bludgeon that could come down on anyone who ran afoul of popular notions of moral behavior. U.S. attorneys in the field had almost complete discretion in deciding which instances of "immoral purposes" would be prosecuted, and they used the Bureau agents in their districts to conduct their investigations. And so a law originally drafted to combat the national and international commercialized sex industry accustomed the Bureau to the notion that investigations of ordinary crimes by ordinary people should be its normal routine. Extraordinary threats to the nation, while never shirked and investigated bravely and sometimes effectively, were, well, extraordinary, and afterward the Bureau could return to its ordinary routine, pursuing individual criminals who had committed crimes against private persons and property.

■ ■ ■

But if the Bureau characteristically shied away from taking on the political and economic elite, there was one kind of powerful enemy that the Bureau, from its earliest days to the present, has never backed away from. And that is any rival investigative force that has the temerity to try to intrude on turf the Bureau considers its own.

The new Bureau's sweeping jurisdiction over all crimes against the United States almost immediately drew it into conflict with a wounded, yet still powerful and increasingly jealous rival, the Secret Service. The struggle was over the most prestigious of all fields of investigation, national security.

Just a few years before, the Secret Service had conducted *all* investigations for the government. The struggle with Congress in 1908 had left the service with the truncated responsibility of chasing counterfeiters and protecting the president. It could use its appropriations "for no other purposes whatsoever." And yet the public still regarded the Secret Service as the nation's premier counterespionage agency. It was, in fact, the only federal agency that had ever actually caught a spy, a distinction it had won ten years earlier in the Spanish-American War.

During the buildup to that war, American newspapers filled their pages with reports that the country was teeming with Spanish spies. It had fallen to Secret Service Chief John Wilkie to reassure the country that the threat was under control.

But in 1898 the Secret Service had only a dozen or so permanent agents. If the spy menace was as dangerous as the public believed, that was too few to provide an impression of credible security. The solution Wilkie hit upon was to organize an auxiliary force funded by a special grant from President William McKinley. He enlisted thousands of civilians as "emergency men," and put them to work running down rumors and shadowing "suspicious characters." Wilkie called reporters in to show how he could stay in touch with his counter-spy network by means of a large wall map studded with steel pins that located every man on the force, a prop later employed to dramatic effect by generations of FBI directors. His operatives reported to him with coded daily telegraph messages addressed to "John Ehlen," a name he had registered with telegraph companies as a cover for the service's counterespionage activities. This system, Wilkie claimed, let him maintain "close surveillance" over some six hundred men and women "of many occupations and widely varied social status." The press was dazzled.

He dazzled them some more by breaking up a Spanish spy operation in Montreal headed by Spanish naval attaché Ramon de Carranza and by disrupt-ing enemy espionage rings in New Orleans and the Gulf Coast. He even set up a spy network in Spain itself. The Secret Service developed an intimate working relationship with British intelligence officers, probably the best in the world, which had helped Wilkie roll up that Montreal ring. Wilkie emerged from the war with an enormous reputation as a spy catcher, and so even after Congress pulled the Secret Service out of the spy game, everyone—the public, the press, and the popular entertainment industry—associated spy hunting with the Se-cret Service.

And the Secret Service wanted back in the game. Catching spies was far more glamorous than chasing counterfeiters ("chasing the queer," they called it then), and counterespionage's obvious importance—its supreme importance, in times of crisis—meant that the agency assigned to spy work was *ipso facto* re-garded as *the* premier federal investigative agency.

Friction between the Bureau of Investigation and the Secret Service was in-evitable once the young Bureau assumed jurisdiction over those few federal laws dealing with national security—chiefly neutrality regulations that prohib-ited raising foreign armies in America or staging attacks on another country from American soil. So the Secret Service watched with amusement flavored with resentment as the Bureau took its first faltering steps learning how to run down spies along the Mexican border.

During the last years of Porfirio Diaz's dictatorship, just before the revolution of 1910, political unrest in Mexico filled the border regions of Texas and New Mexico with Mexican rebels trying to raise money and men. To keep an eye on all this, which would have been handled by the Secret Service in the old days, the Bureau opened one of its first offices outside Washington in San Antonio, Texas. (Because of the sheer number of neutrality law cases Mexico generated during the Bureau's early years, the Bureau's oldest national security files are titled the "Mexican files.")

In October 1909, Diaz had been president of Mexico almost continuously since 1877. He had just defeated a rebellion by General Bernardo Reyes and was planning to run for the presidency again at age eighty. To demonstrate his stature as an international statesman, he wanted to meet President Taft. A meeting was scheduled on the border between Ciudad Juarez and El Paso, Texas. The site was risky: Ciudad Juarez and El Paso were filled with Diaz's enemies, supporters of General Reyes, along with other Mexican nationalists angry at the Americans who dominated the Mexican economy. So when the American Embassy in Mexico City heard rumors in September of an assassination plot against Diaz timed for the October 16 meeting, the reports seemed credible. The embassy notified the State Department, which passed along the report to Chief Wilkie, since the Secret Service had the job of protecting the president. Wilkie recommended the two presidents be guarded by a military escort.

The State Department now began to receive more warnings of threats to the presidents. The Bureau of Investigation claimed that one of its agents had learned of a plot to assassinate Taft and Diaz. But when the State Department sent the Bureau's reports to Wilkie, he thought they read too much like the "blood and thunder dime novels of the period." There were so many inconsistencies that Wilkie concluded the plot was almost surely a hoax concocted by the Bureau's informant. "I became satisfied before halfway through the stuff," Wilkie said, "that this man [the Bureau's informant] was discovering this revolutionary talk for revenue only. It is fair to assume that if he reported there was no conspiracy he would lose his job."

Wilkie took a train to Texas to review the situation personally. When he arrived in El Paso he met with the chief of the Mexican Secret Service, who said he was at a loss to understand who the Bureau's "prominent revolutionaries" were. He suspected they did not exist. Wilkie agreed. When the Bureau agent claimed that he had the supposed assassins under surveillance (by the informant), but was strangely reluctant to arrest them, Wilkie insisted that they be brought in for questioning. Once he had the alleged conspirators in front of him, he was able to demonstrate that none of them even remotely resembled the informant's descriptions in his earlier reports. He was also able to discover that none of them could have been where the informant placed them during the previous few days. The entire conspiracy had, as Wilkie suspected, been a transparent fraud concocted by the Bureau's informant to get money from the Justice Department. Wilkie's son, a Secret Service agent who had also worked on the land-fraud cases, bragged that the Secret Service "stood alone in their insistence that the affair was a hoax." The Mexican border affair proved, Wilkie said complacently, that "when the various departments in Washington confront a really difficult case they can rely upon the Secret Service."

■ ■ ■

Conflict with the Secret Service would soon escalate. In August 1914 war broke out in Europe, with Germany, Austria-Hungary, and Turkey in battle against Britain, France, Russia, Italy, and Japan. For two and a half years America maintained neutrality, an invitation for both sides to launch propaganda, espionage, and sabotage activities in the United States, all under the generic term of "intrigues." The result was an eruption of indignation among Americans who favored one side—usually the British—or the other, and who therefore regarded the other side's intrigues as something warranting investigation by the government.

The question was, which detectives would do the investigating? Would it be the Secret Service, despite the congressional restrictions on its operations? Would it be the ambitious intelligence arms of the Army (the Military Intelligence Division) or the Navy (the Office of Naval Intelligence), eager to gain control over all counterintelligence, at home and abroad? Or would it be the fledgling Bureau of Investigation, still busily engaged in spurious battle against the white-slave conspiracy?

The FBI's national security responsibilities, which would define its role for the rest of the century, emerged out of this battle over bureaucratic turf. But the Bureau's motive for throwing itself into this fight had little to do with any belief that enemy intrigues posed a real threat to the country. Rather it was the determination of a civil libertarian attorney general, Thomas Gregory, to keep rival agencies—unrestrained by any commitment to constitutional procedures—out of law enforcement.

The Bureau entered late in the race to satisfy the public's demands to hang spies, round up traitors, and generally be edified by public pageants of loyalty.

The problem was that there were very few federal laws covering the sort of propaganda and espionage campaigns the British and Germans were engaged in after 1914, and so the Secret Service, not restricted to investigating violations of federal law (in fact, barred from such investigations), could operate freely where the Justice Department feared—or rather, refused—to tread.

The applicable federal legislation included a 1911 law that outlawed disclosing "national defense secrets." The Articles of War prohibited spies from "lurking" around defense installations. The neutrality laws made it a crime to recruit Americans into foreign armies, or to plan attacks on other countries from American soil. Since these were federal crimes, they did fall within the jurisdiction of the Bureau, which therefore began to spend an increasing portion of its appropriations on national defense. In 1915, for example, the Bureau was already spending $14,000 investigating violations of the neutrality laws.

But the propaganda activities by foreign agents that were disturbing the country—such as German efforts to stir up Irish and East Indian immigrants against the British—did not, in the opinion of Attorney General Gregory, violate any existing federal laws, and he felt those federal laws that did exist would have to be stretched to the breaking point to deal with them, as when the government indicted Illinois Congressman Frank Buchanan for speaking out against munitions manufacturing. (The Buchanan case involved a creative application of the antitrust laws, calling Buchanan's speeches an illegal conspiracy in restraint of trade.)

With the Bureau, according to Gregory's interpretation of the law, relegated to the sidelines, Gregory looked on resentfully as the Treasury Department's Secret Service got credit for one headline-grabbing intelligence coup after another during the early months of the neutrality period (August 1914–April 1917). He watched as Secret Service Chief William Flynn and Frank Burke, the head of the service's New York City office, emerged as national heroes after rounding up a few spies and propagandists. Gregory complained that the Bureau could launch an investigation only when a federal law had been violated, and he could see no prosecutable offenses being committed by the German "intriguers." Congress rebuffed Gregory's request in December 1915 for a sedition statute against "foreign intrigues" on American soil, and so Gregory decided he had no legal basis for investigating them. He groused that the Secret Service and the military were acting without legal authorization in their energetic counterespionage operations, and that if there were any legal basis for investigation and prosecution, the job belonged to Justice.

Woodrow Wilson's ambitious secretary of the treasury, William McAdoo, did not share Gregory's legal scruples. Eager to restore the lost glory of the Secret Service, and perhaps ride that glory to the White House, McAdoo persuaded President Wilson to give the Secret Service back its authority to conduct investigations upon the request of the secretary of state. When Secretary of State William Jennings Bryan asked McAdoo to find out whether German diplomats were engaged in espionage, Flynn sent ten Secret Service agents under Frank Burke to work with the New York Police Department to gather evidence to expose their activities.

Bryan's pro-British successor as secretary of state, Robert Lansing, was even more determined to expose German propaganda. He encouraged McAdoo and the Secret Service to continue to investigate German intrigues, and on July 24, 1915, Frank Burke purloined a diplomatic briefcase that contained a detailed description of a German propaganda and sabotage ring directed by Franz von Papen and Heinrich Albert. The most sensational revelation was that German Chancellor Theobald von Bethmann-Hollweg was actively involved in the plotting. McAdoo consulted with President Wilson and then turned the incriminating documents over to the *New York World*. The uproar convinced Americans that there was a dangerous German underground at large in the United States.

The Secret Service's coup outraged Gregory and Bielaski and made them look incompetent and uninformed. Bielaski had no idea where the *World* had gotten the documents. He ordered the newspaper to name its sources. The paper refused. Gregory further damaged the Bureau's reputation when he lamely told reporters that the Bureau investigated only violations of federal law and that no federal laws were being violated. The Secret Service's role in all this was only suspected by Gregory and Bielaski. It was, of course, familiar to Secretary of State Lansing and the president, and confirmed them in their judgment that the Secret Service was the detective service of choice in national security matters. Meanwhile the Justice Department and the Bureau were being ridiculed for being unable or unwilling to defend the country.

On July 30, 1916, an enormous explosion at a munitions stockpile, a disaster generally assumed to be the work of German saboteurs, leveled Black Tom Island in New York Harbor (now the site of the New Jersey Museum of Science, near the Statue of Liberty). Congress wanted every available federal investigator working on the case, so it gave the Bureau the same authority as the Secret Service to conduct investigations unrelated to federal crimes if so requested by the State Department.

The Bureau suffered another defeat when the Secret Service got credit for the most sensational intelligence coup of the era, the "Zimmermann telegram." In January 1917, British Naval Intelligence intercepted a coded message from

German Foreign Secretary Arthur Zimmermann to the German ambassador to Mexico, Heinrich von Eckhardt. The telegram read, in part,

> *We intend to begin on the first of February unrestricted submarine warfare. We shall endeavor in spite of this to keep the United States neutral. In the event of this not succeeding, we make Mexico a proposal of alliance on the following basis: make war together, make peace together, generous financial support and an understanding on our part that Mexico is to reconquer the lost territory in Texas, New Mexico and Arizona.*

By using American diplomats as intermediaries, the British adroitly concealed that it had been they who had filched the telegram. They had the American Embassy in London forward it to Wilson on February 24, 1917, and four days later, Wilson released it to the press. In his war message to Congress Wilson cited the telegram, along with the German resumption of submarine warfare, as a reason he was asking for a declaration of war against Germany. Some reporters suspected the telegram was a British plant, and asked Secretary of State Lansing how he had gotten the message. Lansing replied that he could give no information without endangering the agent responsible. The press, at least that portion willing to give Lansing the benefit of the doubt, assumed that the nameless hero was an American agent, and so most likely a Secret Service agent.

The British soon worked up a scenario to explain how that mysterious American agent had gotten the telegram. British authorities in Halifax, Nova Scotia, had confiscated the steamer trunks of the German ambassador to the United States, who was on his way back to Germany after the break in relations with America. The British announced that the seals on the ambassador's trunks had been broken between February 9, when the ambassador had left New York, and February 16, when he had arrived in Halifax. Who could have done it? Presumably that courageous and still anonymous American agent. Since the only secret agents the country knew about were in the Secret Service, the Zimmermann telegram, which was from start to finish a British operation, added more glory to the reputation of the Secret Service.

The Zimmermann telegram encouraged journalists, limited only by the power of their imaginations, to assure Americans that the telegram was the blueprint for Germany's actual invasion plans: The declaration of war would quickly be followed by an armed uprising of the 350,000 German aliens in the country, joining forces with millions of German-Americans to blow up bridges, tunnels, railroads, and factories. Hordes of Mexicans would sweep across the borders of Texas, New Mexico, Arizona, and California, pillaging, raping, and killing. Since the coast of California provided another obvious invasion route, it was postulated that Japan would swap sides, ally itself with Germany and Mexico, and pour into Los Angeles and San Francisco. Meanwhile, German submarines would be lobbing shells at eastern seaboard cities, their targets relayed to them by radio from German spies who were, it was feared, everywhere. And so America snapped to attention. Soldiers were quickly dispatched to guard railroad tunnels in the Sierras. The president of Stanford University contemplated arming himself with a revolver. Cecil B. DeMille proposed defending Los Angeles with an armed detachment from his movie studio—perhaps costumed as cowboys and Indians.

Government leaders did nothing to calm the panic over spies, saboteurs, and enemy invasions. In his war message on April 2, Wilson fanned the flames: "From the very start of the present war," he told Congress, Germany

> *has filled our unsuspecting communities and even our offices of government with spies and set criminal intrigues everywhere afoot against our national unity of counsel, our peace within and without, our industries and our commerce . . . it is now evident that its spies were here even before the war began . . . that it meant to stir up enemies against us at our very doors the intercepted note of the German minister to Mexico City is eloquent evidence.*

■ ■ ■

With the country howling for protection against spies and saboteurs and groups mobilizing for freelance spy hunting, the Bureau could not stand by. Attorney General Gregory responded to the furor by authorizing the Bureau to investigate rumors of espionage and sabotage. The Secret Service struck back, protesting that its own "ancient lineage and experience was sufficient license to catch spies," and that the Bureau's involvement was unneeded and unwanted.

The declaration of war on April 6, 1917, gave the Bureau new authority to combat espionage. It immediately rounded up sixty-three German agents already under surveillance. Over the next few months the Bureau would arrest some nine hundred more on suspicion of furthering the interests of Germany.

The Bureau gained even more authority on April 6, when Wilson invoked the 1798 Alien Act. This made German nationals, now legally defined as "alien enemies," subject to internment. It excluded them from sensitive areas like ports or defense plants, and strictly regulated their movements. Enforcing the Alien Act vastly increased the Bureau's workload, since the 480,000 German nationals in the United States tended to live in the same major cities now proclaimed defense zones, and they tended to have skills needed by defense industries. Another complication was the fact that many alien enemies were parents or spouses of naturalized German-Americans who could not humanely be separated from their families. All this meant the Bureau had to handle thousands of appeals for exemption from internment and requests for permission to remain in war zones and work in war industries. The Bureau's solution was to emphasize surveillance rather than arrest and internment to cut down on work and expense. The Bureau would investigate over sixty thousand enemy aliens by the war's end, but it interned only two to three thousand.

Each month the war brought more work for the Bureau. On May 18, Wilson signed the Selective Service Act, which required males between twenty-one and thirty-one to register for the draft on June 5. The government and the public expected (mistakenly) that there would be widespread resistance, so the Bureau got ready to investigate mass violations. On June 15, the Espionage Act gave the Bureau still more responsibilities, since the act not only criminalized spying, but also outlawed words or deeds that could be construed as interfering with the war effort.

But the public, urged on by the press, wanted something more satisfying than new laws. It wanted spies. And it wanted the spies executed. Since the Germans had been spending money before the war to influence American opinion, it was logical to suppose that Germany "is still spending money and for the same purpose. The thing needs no proof. She is paying every man who will accept pay for the same purpose for which, before the war began, she was paying every man who would accept pay, to handicap and weaken the arm of the American Government." "AMERICA INFESTED WITH GERMAN SPIES" ran one headline. The *New York Tribune* claimed German spies were "everywhere." Theodore Roosevelt organized a countersubversive American Defense Society, which claimed (falsely) that the War Department had already executed fourteen spies. The *Providence Journal* proposed that "every German or Austrian in the United States unless known by years of association, should be treated as a spy." Former President William Howard Taft recommended firing squads for spies and "plotters." For months Americans had been hearing that the country was teeming with spies. Now the country was at war. It had laws against spying, and detectives were supposedly at work looking for spies. So where were they?

Americans seemed to have caught a dose of execution envy. When they looked overseas, they could see that their allies and enemies had plenty of spies to execute. Early in the war, the British hanged Carl Hans Lody for sabotage. In October 1915 the Germans had executed nurse Edith Cavell. The French executed Mata Hari in 1917, and early in 1918 they executed the Egyptian Paul-

Marie Bolo, known as Bolo Pasha, for fostering antiwar sentiment. (*Boloism* became a synonym for disloyalty.) Americans wondered when they would get some executions of their own, as Representative Julius Kahn of California demanded "a few prompt trials and a few quick hangings."

Some thought the way to close the spy gap was to turn spy hunting over to the military. Other nations had assigned counterespionage and countersubversion to the soldiers, and so the American Army and Navy demanded that they too be given jurisdiction over the home front. Assistant Attorney General Charles Warren agreed. He drafted a bill that would make counterespionage a military responsibility. Without notifying Attorney General Gregory, Warren submitted his bill to Congress, saying that "one man shot, after court-martial, is worth a hundred arrests by this department." He argued that although the Articles of War limited military jurisdiction to war zones, in the modern era the entire nation was a war zone, and should be so declared.

John Lord O'Brian, whom Gregory had put in charge of the Justice Department's war work, strenuously opposed the bill, and it was withdrawn. But the Army did not give up. Its Military Intelligence Division under Lieutenant Colonel Ralph Van Deman said it was impatient with Justice's "leniency" toward traitors, and became openly contemptuous of its civilian counterparts. There was a Washington theatrical farce called *Why Worry* that had a Military Intelligence Division operative being chased by Bureau of Investigation agents who think the MID man is a spy. At the end the military operative outwits the special agents, catches the real spy, and gets the girl.

Van Deman lobbied for complete authority to handle national security on the home front so that he could arrest suspected spies, saboteurs, and subversives, and try them in military courts. He promised that if he got his way, there would be plenty of executions. Without the knowledge of his superiors in the War Department, Van Deman organized a Plant Protection Section to protect factories from spies and saboteurs. In July 1917, Gregory discovered that Van Deman's agents were arresting civilians. He protested and Secretary of War Newton C. Baker ordered Van Deman to cease operations and refer all leads to the Bureau for investigation and arrests.

But there was no end to Van Deman's ambitions or his ingenuity. He organized a Volunteer Intelligence Corps with a thousand members, largely in the Western states, to gather intelligence about spies and saboteurs. When Secretary Baker heard about this, he transferred Van Deman overseas, and placed General Marlborough Churchill in charge of Military Intelligence, with orders to curb the division's home front operations. But instead of disbanding the Volunteer Intelligence Corps, Churchill merely had it operate with greater secrecy.

Gregory protested to Baker that "the Office of Military Intelligence has definitely decided to supplant the investigation services of the Department of Justice throughout the country." Baker agreed with Gregory that the Army had no business investigating civilians, and turned the Volunteer Corps and its rosters over to the Justice Department.

Military Intelligence had one more card to play in its campaign to take over counterintelligence. It managed to get its hands on an actual spy, Pablo Waberski, a German agent who was actually a German naval officer named Lothar Witzke, who had been working in Mexico for Kurt Jancke, head of German intelligence there. He was dragged across the border by two undercover operatives, one belonging to the British Secret Service, the other to American Military Intelligence. The Army wanted to execute him. He had not been doing his spying near their installations, however, and so, according to military regulations, it was not clear they had any right to hold him, let alone shoot him. That privilege belonged to, if anyone, the Justice Department.

The Army tried to turn Waberski into a test of its authority to investigate, arrest, and execute spies at home. During congressional hearings over Warren's bill there had been testimony that some twenty thousand aliens in the country who had been judged as security risks were actually spies, and should be shot. One witness said, "I know of no objection or reason why there should be any further delay in organizing the squad, or why they should not, when organized, work overtime in order to make up for lost time." Encouraged, on August 25, 1918, the Army decided to resolve the Waberski case. They tried him in a secret court-martial, and sentenced him to death. The case was to be appealed directly to the president rather than the federal courts. If the president upheld the execution, it would constitute formal presidential approval for the Army to take over espionage investigations and prosecutions. In November, Witzke's appeal reached Wilson, who, evidently persuaded by Gregory of the dangers in giving authority over United States security to the military, commuted Witzke's sentence on May 27, 1920, to life at hard labor in Leavenworth Federal Penitentiary. After the war the Germans lobbied for Witzke's release. In November 1923 he was sent back to Germany, where he was greeted as a hero and awarded the Iron Cross First and Second Class. He may well have resumed his role in German intelligence during the 1930s, spying in China for Germany.

■ ■ ■

But the Secret Service's challenge to the Bureau's authority was still alive. Secretary of the Treasury William McAdoo was talking up a plan to set up a Central Intelligence Agency in the State Department to oversee the activities of the Secret Service, the Bureau of Investigation, the Military Intelligence Division, the Office of Naval Intelligence, the Post Office, and all the other federal detectives. Since the Secret Service had staked out a quasi-official position as the State Department's primary investigative agency even though it was still housed in the Treasury Department, this bureaucratic reshuffling would have restored the Secret Service's preeminence over the other spy-hunting agencies.

Gregory could make a strong legal case against allowing the Army or the Secret Service to muscle in on national security investigations, since these cases would eventually land in civilian courts and only the Bureau could prepare cases that would stand up in court. But even though Woodrow Wilson trusted Gregory, the public, encouraged by the Bureau's rivals and by the press, believed there was an immediate danger from spies, saboteurs, enemy sympathizers, disloyal immigrants, political radicals, and other opponents of the war. Until Gregory and Bielaski could convince skeptics that the Justice Department had the resources and the ability to cope with a threat of that magnitude, the Bureau would continue to be threatened by rivals who could claim that the Bureau, by itself, could not do the job.

The Bureau was now a force of about three hundred agents soon to become four hundred, but this was clearly not enough to cope with what the public perceived as an enormous threat. Neither Gregory nor Bielaski wanted the Bureau to grow much larger, fearing that it would then be impossible to control. Nor did they think that so many agents would be needed after the war. But if they did not demonstrate that the Bureau was big enough to fight the supposed army of spies, they risked losing control of home-front security to the Secret Service, the Army, and the Navy. They needed to find a way to rapidly expand the Bureau's numbers and just as rapidly reduce them once the war was over. And at that moment the answer seemed to appear at the Chicago office of the Bureau.

The special agent in charge of the Bureau's Chicago office was a remarkably energetic detective named Hinton D. Clabaugh, perhaps a little too energetic for his own good or that of the Bureau. Like any good detective, Clabaugh had managed to establish sources of information around town, with particularly good contacts inside the Chicago Police Department and the local business community. These relationships had served him well during the white-slave crusade, when he had developed a network of informants to provide him with information about Chicago vice operations.

On February 2, 1917, the day after Germany's announcement that it had resumed unrestricted submarine warfare sent the country into violent war jitters,

Clabaugh was approached by a Chicago advertising man named Albert M. Briggs. Briggs had already persuaded friends in the business community to lend the Bureau a dozen automobiles to help Clabaugh's shorthanded office investigate violations of the neutrality laws. Clabaugh had complained to Briggs that the Chicago office was being swamped with complaints about German activities. Briggs now said he could organize a force of volunteers to help Clabaugh and the Bureau with its national security investigations.

On March 14, Briggs visited Clabaugh with a more elaborate proposal. He told Clabaugh he would organize "a volunteer organization to aid the Bureau of Investigation of the Department of Justice. Purpose: to work with and under the direction of the Chief of the Bureau of Investigation, of the Department of Justice, or such attorney or persons as he may direct, rendering such service as may be required from time to time." Clabaugh relayed Briggs's proposal to Washington, and on March 20, Bielaski accepted it. He put Clabaugh in charge of making the confidential arrangements, and on March 22 sent orders to the field offices notifying them of Briggs's organization. He described it as "a volunteer committee or organization of citizens for the purpose of co-operating with the department in securing information of activities of agents of foreign governments or persons unfriendly to this Government, for the protection of public property, etc."

Briggs established his headquarters in a Chicago office lent by financier Samuel Insull. He contacted friends across the country and set up a division in each major city, each headed by a leading businessman. He named the new organization the American Protective League (APL).

The APL was being organized on April 2, when Wilson charged in his war message that Germans in America were plotting espionage and sabotage. A hundred branches of the APL were in business by the April 6 declaration of war. Two months later there were 100,000 members in six hundred cities. A year later it numbered a quarter of a million.

The Bureau's most pressing task at the outset of the war was supervising the upcoming draft registration scheduled for June 5, when all ten million draft-age men were to show up at their local election districts. The Bureau needed a presence at all conscription centers to see that the law was being enforced, that assistance was available to confused registrants, and to guard against any organized opposition to the draft. The job was assigned to the APL, and so APL members wearing badges bearing the words "Secret Service" fanned out across the country. The day passed without incident, and no organized protests.

The APL was a sensational public relations success. Volunteers flocked to the league offices. Women clamored to be admitted to the APL as "spies," but the policy was to reject female applicants. One APL official hoped to recruit the entire nation into the mighty legion:

> *I have often thought it would be a wise move on the part of the President to issue a proclamation calling on all loyal citizens of the United States, both men and women, and even boys and girls, to constitute themselves Secret Agents of the Government and report to the authorities every suspicious circumstance and disloyal remark or conversation coming to their notice.*

The APL took over the Bureau's investigations of applicants for overseas duty in the Red Cross, Knights of Columbus, and YMCA. It also handled security clearances for the armed forces, and enforced liquor and prostitution laws around bases. It even collected domestic intelligence for the War Department. The 250,000 APL auxiliaries of the Bureau were powerful allies in Gregory's battle against the military for control of domestic security. To make the Bureau's strength seem even more impressive, Gregory combined the APL's numbers with those of all the other loyalty organizations and police forces at his disposal, claiming that his resources now numbered 400,000.

The media suddenly discovered new virtues in Bielaski and the Bureau of Investigation, now that it had seemingly grown into a truly massive force. Its size offered reassurance to the public that wherever German spies might lurk, the government was in position, eye at the keyhole.

The press turned Bielaski into a celebrity. Newspaper readers learned that "Mr. Bielaski lives in Chevy Chase, Md. He is married. Every morning he arises at an unearthly hour and works in his garden or takes a long walk before breakfast. . . . He is never nervous, never irritable, and apparently doesn't know the meaning of fatigue." "It is his constant application and his unending, everlasting persistence that make him the most feared man in America by the German spies." Reporters gushed over Bielaski's "fighting smile," his "low crisp voice." He was now working "round the clock," but before the war "he played third base in a Washington church baseball league, then after dinner would show up at the YMCA for a boxing work-out with one of the pros." He rowed, he ran, he was the live wire of the Justice Department, a "young man with a steady eye, a square, fighting jaw, and a short, upturned nose."

The press reported that Bielaski had tested his strategy for leveraging the Bureau's investigative resources during the white-slavery campaign, when he had also enlisted the help of other agencies, police forces, and individuals. The *Springfield* (Massachusetts) *Union* reported, "In every city in the United States there are 'shadows,' young men who are indistinguishable from hundreds of other men. They haunt the various railway depots. Some of them are there on assignments. Others are 'free lances' commissioned to follow strangers of whom they have suspicions."

Angry that the Justice Department had left it in the dust, the Treasury Department protested that by calling its members *Secret Service* agents, the APL was stealing the identity of the real Secret Service. President Wilson, goaded by Treasury Secretary McAdoo, asked Gregory to reach some accommodation with the Treasury Department. Bielaski responded by regularizing the relationship between the Bureau and the APL. He ordered Briggs to halt distribution of "Secret Service" badges and to inform his agents that they were not affiliated in any way with the United States Secret Service. He had Briggs make his agents take an oath to uphold the Constitution, and he asked for a roster of the APL's officers. In return, Bielaski closely associated the Bureau with the APL, conferring official status on the league. Bielaski notified the Bureau that the APL would be "co-operating with the department in securing information of activities of agents of foreign governments or persons unfriendly to this government." APL chiefs in major cities were commissioned as special agents in the Bureau. These APL chiefs were ordered to organize investigative divisions within each APL office that would then report to the Bureau. In Los Angeles, for example, the special agent in charge had the APL members report directly to him rather than to the APL superintendent. In May 1918, Gregory allowed the APL to replace "Secret Service" with the inscription "Auxiliary to the Justice Department" on their badges.

■ ■ ■

As the War Department, the Justice Department, and the draft boards began to plan roundups of "slackers" (draft evaders), they soon realized that the APL had no power to arrest anyone. They decided to rely on ambiguity, to have the APL apprehend and detain slackers, but not to call them arrests. The selective service chief notified draft boards that "the Department of Justice and the American Protective League which is auxiliary to the Department of Justice are the only investigating bodies to be recognized by the boards." Then Bielaski and Gregory arrived at a formulation where APL members would "cause" recalcitrants to present themselves to the draft boards or to special agents of the Bureau.

The roundups began on March 26, 1918. The Bureau and its APL auxiliaries rounded up the first one hundred suspected slackers in Minneapolis. That summer the Bureau picked up 36,000 in Cleveland. On July 11, some 150,000 were interviewed in Chicago. Bureau agents were soon dragged along by head-strong APL units that had freed themselves from the control of Chief Bielaski or the local United States attorneys. The Bureau had become in effect auxil-iaries of its auxiliaries. The APL had its own agenda, and local Bureau agents had become so dependent on the APL's help that they adopted the league's view of events. Bielaski might flood his local offices with the warning that "agents shall take particular care that their conduct shall be at all times in accordance with the law," but there was no way of ensuring, due to the press of caseloads, that his orders would have any impact. Across the country, every man who could not produce his selective service card was rounded up and herded into a makeshift bullpen, where some had to wait for days before they could arrange to have their draft cards delivered. Only a pitiful few were slackers; the great majority were simply men who, like most Americans, were unfamiliar with the concept of carrying personal identification.

The most notorious slacker raid was in New York City just before the end of the war, when Selective Service Chief Enoch Crowder realized that all available lists of registrants would be exhausted by October 1918. He needed more bod-ies and asked the Bureau for a mass roundup in New York City. Until then the Bureau had curtailed its New York City operations because the APL had fewer volunteers there than in other cities, but the special agent in charge, Charles DeWoody, was working hard to recruit more agents for the local APL.

On August 15, 1918, Bielaski ordered DeWoody to draw up plans for a slacker raid in New York. Albert Briggs moved his headquarters to DeWoody's office for the duration. On Tuesday, September 3, the roundups began, marred by confusion caused by lack of manpower. The Bureau had been counting on the help of the Army and the Navy, and that was not available. The Bureau and the APL went ahead anyway, even though they had not worked out the logistics for the giant raid. The result was that thousands of men were roughly rounded up and held for days without being able to communicate with their families. By Thursday the Bureau realized it had a major fiasco on its hands, and President Wilson himself was asking questions. The head of the Justice Department's War Emergency Division, John Lord O'Brian, visited New York, made a cursory investigation, and whitewashed the raids. Gregory reported to Wilson that there might have been abuses, but they were unauthorized, and that large num-bers of slackers had been discovered. Overcoming his doubts, Wilson used Gregory's report to generate support for the fourth great draft registration, held on September 12.

. . .

Without the APL, the Bureau could not have given the appearance of being able to handle the supposedly enormous job of protecting the country from slackers, spies, saboteurs, and subversives, and so it might not have been able to protect itself from poaching by agents from the Treasury, War, and Navy departments. But there was really not much legitimate work for the Bureau or the APL to do. Of the two thousand indictments during the war under the Espionage Act, none were for espionage; all were for criticizing or opposing the war effort, and only half resulted in convictions. There just weren't any spies and almost no slackers—but the Bureau had a quarter of a million eager spy chasers looking for something to do. That "something" turned out to be the Bureau's most ambitious and consequential wartime operation, its destruction of the largest radical labor union in the nation's history, the IWW, the Industrial Workers of the World, known by the nickname of "The Wobblies."

The Justice Department was coming under increasing pressure from Western governors even before the war to intervene in labor disturbances in their states. The governors blamed the unrest on the IWW, which claimed to represent the masses of unskilled workers in the forests of the Northwest, the mines of the Rockies, the textile mills of the East, and the hobo jungles along the rail line. Once the war began, the Bureau, by now less the leader than the follower, teamed up with the APL to destroy the IWW.

The IWW had been organized in 1905 in Chicago by William D. "Big Bill" Haywood, a one-eyed ex-miner. Its preamble defiantly stated,

> *The working class and the employing class have nothing in common. There can be no peace so long as hunger and want are found among millions of working people and the few, who make up the employing class, have all the good things of life. . . . Between these two classes a struggle must go on. . . . It is the historic mission of the working class to do away with capitalism.*

In 1909 the IWW launched a nationwide "Free Speech Movement" that goaded local authorities into repression as the IWW wrapped itself in the Bill of Rights. In 1912 the IWW shut down the textile mills in Lawrence, Massachusetts, in a strike drenched in revolutionary rhetoric pitting "human rights" against "property rights."

In practice, the IWW more often behaved like an ordinary labor union working to secure better pay and working conditions for its members, but its style was anything but ordinary. Its rhetoric was of militant "direct action" (slowdowns and sabotage), and it dreamed of a general strike that would overthrow the capitalist order. The Wobblies' flamboyant propaganda made it easy for industrial leaders to use the IWW to terrify the security-loving American middle class. Long before the start of the war, management propaganda had turned the IWW, with its self-proclaimed hatred of religion and patriotism, its red flag symbol, and its never-achieved goal of "one big union," into—most inaccurately—the face of American labor. The IWW became so unpopular that the rest of the American labor movement had to shun it in self-defense. The principal political party on the left, the American Socialist Party, expelled its IWW members in 1912 by outlawing "the advocacy of crime, sabotage or other methods of violence."

■ ■ ■

Before the war there were few signs that the Bureau had any particular interest in the IWW. In fact, the evidence is to the contrary, as the Bureau did its best to avoid being drawn into what appeared to be local labor disputes. In October 1915 the governors of California, Oregon, Washington, and Utah petitioned the Wilson administration to investigate the IWW to see if it merited federal prosecution. Wilson agreed, and ordered Attorney General Gregory to look into the situation. The Bureau sent a special agent west to gather evidence, but his report disappointed the governors. He discovered no violations of federal laws by the IWW, and pointed out that the IWW's real numbers were far less alarming than claimed by the governors. He was able to find only about four thousand members in all of California and Washington. But as the Wilson administration moved closer toward war in 1916 and 1917, the Wobblies' rhetoric became more provocative and more objectionable to the administration and to Wilson himself. "Capitalists of America," the IWW threatened, "we will fight against you, not for you." Once war was declared, local authorities could claim that the IWW's strikes and organizational drives were impeding the war effort and so were, in the terminology of the day, "pro-German." When a mine accident in Butte, Montana, in June 1917 led to an upsurge of union agitation for better pay and safer conditions, the IWW quickly moved in to capitalize on the unrest. The Pacific Northwest saw a wave of lumber strikes. In Everett, Washington, middle-class vigilantes battled the IWW, and a Wobbly organizer was lynched. In June 1917 an IWW-led general strike shut down the timber industry.

At first Attorney General Gregory responded to howls for the IWW's blood by pointing out that there were no federal laws prohibiting IWW activities. Conservatives turned to the Immigration Bureau, urging it to use administrative procedures to deport alien Wobblies. Secretary of Labor William B. Wilson, however, ordered investigators to establish that an individual had knowingly violated immigration laws before deportation, thus blocking the mass deportations employers wanted. They then turned to the Army, which proved more tractable. The Army authorized local commanders to "sternly repress" seditious insurrections, leaving it up to local commanders to ask local business leaders on whether a strike constituted sedition. It is not hard to imagine an employer's reply. This placed platoons of soldiers under junior officers at the disposal of the local business establishment, and soon the Army had moved into the lumberyards of the Northwest and the mining areas of the West, breaking strikes and occupying the minefields. In Butte, Montana, the local APL worked with Military Intelligence in union spying and strikebreaking. The local Bureau of Investigation agent reported to the Justice Department that if the APL and Military Intelligence Division continued on this course, the result would be widespread labor violence.

The APL was, in terms of personnel and corporate affiliations, indistinguishable from the business interests that had been clamoring for federal action against the IWW for years. Now that the IWW's enemies were in the APL, they were—in their own estimation at least—federal agents, able to do pretty much what they wanted to the Wobblies. And so the APL went on a nationwide rampage against labor radicals and socialists, with special attention to the IWW. In Chicago the APL organized a "flying squad" that followed IWW leaders, infiltrated their ranks, broke up meetings, provoked riots, and then arrested the Wobblies for disturbing the peace (half the APL flying squad members were local police). In rural areas the APL stood guard over harvests to prevent IWW interference. Later on in the summer of 1917 the Arizona APL, which reported "one thousand" APL investigations, rounded up eighty-five IWW members, locked them in boxcars and shoved them across the California border. This was followed by another expulsion of twelve hundred Wobblies, also in locked boxcars, across the New Mexico border.

At this point Gregory made a decision that encouraged more APL violence against the IWW. Across the country independent volunteer loyalty organizations were springing up, many engaged in vigilante action against the Wobblies. To gain control over the loyalty movement, Gregory had the APL, supposedly under his control, absorb these freelance loyalty groups, which were particularly strong in New England. In Massachusetts, for example, U.S. Attorney George Anderson had attached one to his office. But the worst problem was in the rabidly anti-IWW and antisocialist state of Washington, where the Army had set up a Loyal Legion of Loggers and Lumbermen, which was then taken over by the private group, the Minute Men. After Gregory's order, this became the Minute Men division of the APL and carried out a campaign of arrests against the IWW.

The wave of IWW arrests caught the attention of President Wilson, who asked Gregory for a report on the IWW. At the cabinet meeting of July 13, 1917, Gregory told him that in actuality the IWW was not "an imminent danger" and that no federal laws were being broken. But Wilson's questions warned Gregory that he had better take action. There was always the Treasury Department and Secretary McAdoo lurking, ready to volunteer the Secret Service should the Justice Department seem less than enthusiastic in the performance of its duties. On July 14, Bielaski notified his agents that the IWW was "taking advantage of the needs of the country occasioned by the war to advance its own interests utterly without regard for the welfare of the people as a whole." He ordered his agents to collect information on them. Meanwhile, there were more and more complaints about the Wobblies. A California official came to Washington demanding that all IWW members be placed in concentration camps until the end of the war. His proposal was endorsed by Secretary of the Interior Franklin K. Lane. The president rejected the idea, but this encouraged Gregory to redouble his investigations of the IWW.

At this point Hinton Clabaugh of the Bureau's Chicago office again emerged as a key player. John Lind, former governor of Minnesota, now the state commissioner of public safety, summoned Clabaugh to Minneapolis. He demanded mass arrests of IWW leaders. Clabaugh shared his APL reports on the IWW with Lind, and they decided that the leaders could be charged with conspiracy to impede the war effort. Alien members could be deported as anarchists. Clabaugh discussed the idea with Gregory. At first Gregory resisted, holding that actual violations of the law should be dealt with by local authorities. Then Bill Haywood telegrammed the president, threatening a miners' strike unless the IWW's strike demands were met. Wilson was furious, and this changed Gregory's mind about the IWW. He now decided on immediate arrests of IWW leaders, whether or not there was any likelihood of conviction. Bielaski ordered Bureau agents across the country to forward information on the IWW to Clabaugh, whose Chicago office would coordinate the investigation. Clabaugh set up a secret office where Bureau agents could work with their APL counterparts.

Meanwhile, vigilante action against the IWW was spreading. Oklahoma arrested thousands of Wobblies for resisting the draft and impeding the war, accusing radical farmers of being part of an IWW conspiracy, and threatened them with the death penalty. Western governors claimed their economies were being destroyed by the panic over the IWW.

Clabaugh now had a complete list of the leaders of the IWW. He ordered his agents, including the APL, to prepare for raids across the country at exactly 2:00 P.M. on September 5, 1917. At that hour Bureau and APL agents raided IWW headquarters and homes in Chicago and twenty other cities. IWW leaders Bill Haywood and Ralph Chapin were handcuffed and jailed. The Bureau announced that the raids had smashed a "country-wide" plot to destroy the economy and disrupt the war effort. On September 28, 166 leaders of the IWW were indicted on charges of conspiracy to prevent by force the execution of the laws, particularly the draft laws. The Wobblies' defenders protested that their constitutional rights had been violated. The president asked Gregory for the facts and Bielaski queried Clabaugh, who told him that IWW meetings had in fact been broken up by the APL against his wishes, but that he could not afford to offend the APL since he depended on their help.

The APL helped the Bureau gather evidence for the IWW leaders' trials and all of them were convicted and sentenced to prison. Years later J. Edgar Hoover bragged that

> the IWW case was inaugurated by a simultaneous national move against every IWW headquarters throughout the United States. All national and local leaders of the IWW were indicted and over one hundred sentenced to long prison terms. As a result of this joint national action the IWW was crushed and has never revived.

The Bureau also used the APL to build its cases against other antiwar radicals. In June 1917 the Bureau raided the offices of Emma Goldman and Alexander Berkman's Nonconscription League and arrested them for violating the Selective Service Act. An APL operative who posed as a handyman for two of Goldman's friends provided evidence against her. Both Goldman and Berkman were convicted and spent the war in prison. Socialist publishing houses and presses were also raided by APL and Bureau teams, which shut down the country's radical press.

At the end of 1917, there were twelve hundred city units of the APL cooperating with the Bureau, with seventy-five hundred members in Chicago alone, but this was the peak of the Bureau's cooperation with the APL. John Lord O'Brian persuaded the Justice Department to end what he was beginning to feel was an unhealthily close relationship between the Bureau and the APL.

Early in 1918, O'Brian tried to loosen the APL's organizational links to the Bureau so that no longer would members of the APL be given commissions as special agents, and special agents would not be allowed to head APL units. APL members were instructed not to make arrests. They were told that their responsibility was simply to transmit information to the Bureau of Investigation. Clabaugh notified the APL of the new order of things, but that did not fully end the freewheeling activities of the APL. The Bureau simply needed the APL too much to risk alienating it. To take up the slack, Bielaski tried to reduce his dependence on the APL by recruiting agents with legal or linguistic qualifications.

McAdoo launched one final attack on the Bureau and the APL when William Flynn resigned as head of the Secret Service to protest what he claimed was a lack of cooperation from the Bureau. The Treasury Department claimed that *it* had done all the work in the IWW raids, and that the Bureau had stolen the credit. McAdoo claimed that the APL could serve as a cover for German spies, and once again publicly urged President Wilson to create a national central intelligence agency led by the Secret Service. Flynn gave a newspaper interview in which he blasted the Bureau and urged centralization of intelligence. The paper backed him in an editorial: "the evident laxity of the Department of Justice in dealing with the enemy is, we believe, another subject of grave concern, especially in view of what the enemy is doing abroad."

But the Bureau, with the help of the APL, had demonstrated that no assignment was too large for it to handle, and McAdoo's initiative went nowhere. On March 6, 1918, O'Brian set up a Justice Department clearinghouse for intelligence, with the participation of the Army, Navy, Post Office, Labor, Justice, and Treasury. The Treasury Department again protested its diminished role, but was rebuffed; its representative began to absent himself from the meetings. The Secret Service was finally out of the spy-catching business, never again to challenge the Bureau's monopoly over national security.

■ ■ ■

At the end of the war in November 1918, O'Brian and Bielaski had regained control over loyalty investigations. They ordered local agents not to start prosecutions without consulting the U.S. attorney. The Bureau began to pull back from labor investigations and to begin to think about the postwar status of the APL. Gregory and Bielaski favored disbanding it altogether. Fearing that, some units of the APL, particularly in Chicago, began to work out arrangements to come under the protection of the Labor Department and Military Intelligence. In December 1918, Military Intelligence began to use the APL to investigate radicals. The Justice Department complained, and on January 24, 1919, the War Department reversed the policy, although Military Intelligence did continue to get reports from the APL.

On December 21, 1918, Bielaski announced his resignation from the Bureau. He ordered his field offices to reduce the roster of special agents to prewar numbers. He told the APL that the government would no longer have any use for them after January 1. He also ordered the Chicago field office, which had grown enormously during its antiradical drives, to cut its agent force from fifty to twenty-five immediately, and to fifteen by the first of the year.

In the fall of 1918, Gregory had sent Bielaski to Congress to testify about the department's wartime activities: "We prepared for eventualities that did not materialize." The real function of the Bureau during the war, he said, was to give the public a feeling of security. That would not be the last time the Bureau would be called upon to offer "a feeling of security" to a public terrified by threats that were as vague as they were unsettling.

■ ■ ■

The Bureau was only ten years old in 1918, but that was enough time for disturbing patterns of behavior to have emerged, patterns that would become only more pronounced and more disturbing in the future.

The Bureau had already begun to lower its sights from the serious "crimes against the United States" that were its original mission. Law enforcement at that high level is possible only with leadership and support from a correspondingly high level of government—that is, from the president and attorney general. It is rare, however, for administrations to look for fights with the country's political and economic elite. Presidents belong to that class, and can govern only with its support. Theodore Roosevelt's uniquely confrontational style was unlikely to become a permanent feature of the American presidency. Indeed, it vanished with his departure from the White House.

Without Roosevelt's encouragement of high-level investigations of political and economic corruption, the Bureau of Investigation was left with no mission, at least none as significant as the investigations of senators, congressmen, and industrialists that had led to its founding. But the Bureau could always find plenty of work that needed no support or direction from above. It began to concern itself more and more with low-level crimes against persons and property. Some of these crimes were within the jurisdiction of the Bureau from the start—crimes on Indian and other government reservations, for example. Others were local crimes that became federal once state lines were crossed. Finally, others were crimes assigned to the Bureau by Congress, as in the Mann

Act or, in a few years, the Dyer Act, which made interstate auto theft a federal crime.

There would always be enough work at the lower levels of law enforcement to keep the Bureau busy, but there would never be work of real significance—high-level crimes against the United States—without the leadership and support of the president. That would rarely be forthcoming.

Even during those early years, when the Bureau was small and almost unknown, it was being drawn into the often pernicious pageantry of symbolic politics. In ordinary times, the Bureau could devote itself to ordinary crimes in uncontroversial areas of law enforcement unlikely to annoy anyone who might make trouble for the Bureau. But even in ordinary times, extraordinary events could produce irresistible demands for government action. The Jack Johnson case would teach the government how useful the Bureau could be when a symbolic threat—a black challenge to white supremacy—demanded a symbolic response. The Bureau was, after all, the federal government's premier detective agency, the closest the government could come to calling out the troops without actually calling out the troops. And when the Bureau was sent out in pursuit of a symbol, well, the Bureau always got its symbol. It is not exactly justice according to the lawbooks, but it is probably an unavoidable part of democracy. It is, however, somewhat harsh on the unfortunate individual whose bad luck it is to be designated a symbol of whatever is alarming the public. In extraordinary times, wartime for instance, the pressure on the government to provide symbolic reassurance never lets up, the symbolic enemies now being dissenters from the national solidarity produced by war.

Another unsettling pattern was the Bureau's struggle with bureaucratic rivals over control of national security investigations. During World War I the struggle was over whether control would be in the hands of the Bureau or vigilante groups, the military, or the traditional spy-catchers in the Treasury Department's Secret Service. These turf battles were a factor in almost everything the Bureau did during the war, and would shape the Bureau's national security strategy forever after.

Given Gregory and Bielaski's civil libertarian scruples, it is unlikely the wartime Bureau by itself would have done much more than pursue the few individuals who violated the espionage laws had Justice not been goaded into action by threats from the military, from local loyalty groups, and from the Secret Service. The Justice Department would have lost control over this vital area of law enforcement, one emphatically within its proper jurisdiction, unless it had responded to every call for dramatic action no matter how unwise or unnecessary. As officers of the law, Gregory and Bielaski realized that they had an obligation to maintain, as best they could, the rule of law within the field of national security, and they felt that not only the Bureau but the rule of law itself was threatened by rivals demonstrably willing to jettison due process in favor of quick, dramatic, and supposedly effective action. The Army would have introduced courts-martial as the routine response to security violations. The loyalty groups would have instituted vigilante justice. The Secret Service would have gone about gathering intelligence unfettered by any legal restrictions at all, since its authority came from a request for "information" from the secretary of state rather than from any obligation to build a case admissible in a court of law.

Competition with rival agencies emerged early as characteristic of the Bureau. The Bureau would also learn early on that cooperation could also be dangerous. And so the Bureau began to develop its much-criticized reluctance to cooperate with other investigative agencies. The Bureau found that the price of its alliance with the American Protective League was conforming to the APL's antilabor and antiradical agenda. The alternative—not cooperating with the APL—might have been just as bad, since the proliferation of grassroots loyalty organizations clearly reflected the public's conviction that the home front was in danger and that only a massive drive against spies, saboteurs, subversives, and slackers could save it. The fact that the threat was largely a delusion did not free the government from the need to respond somehow in a manner commensurate with the supposed problem. Since the Bureau was tiny and the country was huge, Gregory and Bielaski had to bulk up the Bureau quickly to a size that could persuade the public it was adequately protected. And so the Bureau found itself in a situation where it was controlled by, rather than controlling, its alliance. Since the Bureau was the link between the APL and the government, the Bureau found itself, and not the APL, blamed for the league's gross abuses of civil liberties. In the future the Bureau would look back at the APL experience as a permanently valid lesson of what was likely to happen whenever the Bureau was forced to cooperate with another agency—and so such cooperation should be avoided at all costs. The only way in the long run to escape the need to cooperate with other law enforcement or intelligence agencies was to grow—to grow great or die.

The Bureau's experience during its first ten years would shape its development as it grew from the tiny agency of 1908 to its mammoth presence today: a tendency to devote resources to low-level crimes rather than significant "crimes against the United States," a leading role in national pageants of symbolic battles against symbolic enemies, a rush to battle stations whenever challenged by rivals poaching on the Bureau's national security turf. The Bureau of

Investigation's true enemy during the war was not the spy or the slacker, but the Secret Service agent. Forever after, the Bureau would be more on the alert for threats from bureaucratic rivals than from enemy spies, subversives, or terror- ists. Forever after, it would be nervous about cooperating with other agencies, having learned that it, not its allies, would be blamed when things went wrong, as is often the case in the affairs of men—or of G-men.

FOUR

Red Webs and Normalcy (1919–1933)

L ATE ON THE NIGHT of June 2, 1919, a bomb exploded in front of the northwest Washington, D.C. home of A. Mitchell Palmer, the attorney general of the United States. That same night the homes of nine other prominent Americans in eight different cities were also bombed. With those attacks the FBI began its battle with communism, one that would consume the Bureau for most of a century. The bombings, as perhaps their most important consequence, also launched the career of J. Edgar Hoover, the face of the FBI, it seems, forever.

● ● ●

A politically motivated attack like the June 2 bombing—a classic act of terrorism—on a national official of Palmer's rank would have produced a violent response from any government in the best of circumstances. But 1919 was the worst of times, with international upheavals and political reversals of fortune that ranked the year with other great watersheds of history, like the fall of Rome, the Protestant Reformation, the French Revolution.

The Great War had provoked the pivotal event of the twentieth century, the Bolshevik Revolution in Russia and had also destroyed four empires—the Austro-Hungarian, German, Russian, and Ottoman—and greatly weakened two others, the British and the French. Then the armistice of November 11, 1918, touched off a new wave of communist revolutions, first in Germany and Hungary, then across the rest of Europe and into Asia. Most failed, but everywhere there was political violence.

During 1919 the chaos—violent strikes, demonstrations, and bombings—would reach America. And casting a grim shadow over these events was the November 1917 revolution in Russia led by Lenin and his Bolsheviks. The Bolshevik Revolution had shocked America twice, first by taking Russia out of the war and its alliance with the United States, and then by casting doubt on President Wilson's justification for the war. Lenin's "Decree on Peace" challenged Wilson's rationale for the war—to make the world safe for democracy—and proclaimed that only a worldwide revolution could eliminate the fundamental causes of war: capitalism, imperialism, and militarism. From the start, Americans saw Bolshevism as hostile, even "pro-German," since its consequences had been so favorable to the enemy. Many Americans were even convinced, based on the logic that identifies results with intentions (and on some documentary evidence later proved to be forged), that the Bolshevik Revolution was a German plot against America and its allies.

The Bolshevik Revolution not only realigned world, but also American, politics, particularly the radical political parties. Around the world socialist parties had warned that if war came, workers would stay out of a rich man's fight. But when the shooting began in August 1914, all the socialist parties of Europe forgot their scruples, and joined their nations' war efforts, often entering coalitions of national unity. But during the two and a half years before America entered the conflict in April 1917, American socialists and their allies became even more opposed to the war. When the American Socialist Party voted to oppose the war, it was branded as unpatriotic, even pro-German, and was targeted by the Bureau and the APL loyalty brigades for violating the selective service and espionage laws.

If their refusal to support the war was not enough to damn radicals, their enthusiastic applause for the Bolsheviks's withdrawal of Russia from the war finished them off. While the rest of the country was reeling from the news of Russia's defection and howling for revenge, the socialists and their radical friends, battered by the blows of government repression, loudly applauded the great news from Russia, and pledged their loyalty to Lenin and the Bolsheviks. Eugene Debs gushed that "from the crown of my head to the soles of my feet I am a Bolshevik and proud of it." The IWW's Bill Haywood, jailed during the Bureau's campaign against the Wobblies, exulted that the Russian Revolution was "the greatest event of our lives. It represents all that we have been dreaming of and fighting for all our lives. It's the dawn of freedom and industrial democracy." Anarchist Emma Goldman, who had also been jailed and was now free appealing her conviction for interfering with the draft, said she had "set my face toward the red glow on the social horizon; after all that is the only real and worthwhile love." John Reed had been in Petrograd during the November revolution, and returned to write his monumental *Ten Days That Shook the World*.

He reported that his American audiences "would weep with joy to know that there is something like dreams-come-true in Russia." It was not just the revolutionary radicals of the socialist movement who felt this way about the Bolsheviks. Congregationalist minister A. J. Muste, head of the antiwar Fellowship of Reconciliation, wrote that "revolutionary Russia, with all its faults and excesses, is the promised land, the father land of the spirit to multitudes of radical workers throughout the world."

As the Bolsheviks struggled to maintain their foothold in Russia, there were uprisings throughout Germany and across the shattered Austro-Hungarian Empire, and general strikes and mutinies in Britain, France, and Italy. Leon Trotsky predicted that the center of the revolution would soon shift to Germany, and that communist Latvia, Poland, Finland, and the Ukraine would soon connect Russia to a communist Europe.

The Bolsheviks did not ignore the United States. On August 20, 1918, Lenin published his "Letter to American Workers," inviting them to join the revolution. In January 1919 he again called on American workers to support the "powerful 'Soviet movement' " spreading across Europe. The IWW responded by declaring that "every strike is a small revolution and a dress rehearsal for the big one." When the Seattle Central Labor Council called a general strike in January 1919, a frightened American public thought Lenin's and Trotsky's commands were being obeyed: "REDS DIRECTING SEATTLE STRIKE—TO TEST CHANCE FOR REVOLUTION" ran the headlines. Although the strike was soon defeated by Mayor Ole Hanson riding into town at the head of a column of federal troops, the Seattle general strike taught Americans to see the seeds of a communist revolution in every strike, and in 1919 there were thousands of strikes as the wartime ban on work stoppages was relaxed, and employers tried to reverse workers' wartime gains by rolling back wages.

Pressure mounted on the government to do something. Attorney General Thomas Gregory promised he would deport seven or eight thousand "alien anarchists and trouble makers." On February 6 thirty-six alien Wobblies were loaded onto a train in Seattle, the "Red Special," and sent to Ellis Island in New York to await deportation.

Meanwhile the Left Wing of the American Socialist Party was looking for ways to ally itself with the Bolsheviks, while overseas, revolutionaries from all countries were racing to Moscow for a conference of what the Bolsheviks called the "now well-defined and existing revolutionary International," to lend aid to the "tremendously swift pace of world revolution." On March 4, 1919, that conference proclaimed the Third Communist International (the Comintern). Its manifesto announced that the Comintern was to be "the international of open mass action of revolutionary realization. Socialist criticism has sufficiently stigmatized the bourgeois world order. The aim of the International Communist Party is to overthrow it and raise in its place the structure of the socialist order." The enthusiasm at the closing session was almost giddy: "The Movement advances at such dizzy speed that it may be said with confidence: Within a year we will already begin to forget there was a struggle for communism in Europe, because within a year all Europe will be Communist." Two weeks later, as if to lend proof to the Comintern's boasts, a communist regime took over in Hungary under Béla Kun.

And then bombs began to explode. A month before the explosion at Palmer's house there was a salvo of bomb attacks against three dozen government and civic leaders across America. One target was the antiradical mayor of Seattle; another exploded at the home of Senator Thomas Hardwick of Georgia, maiming his maid and injuring his wife. The other bombs, intercepted by the postal authorities, were addressed to, among others, John D. Rockefeller, J. P. Morgan, and A. Mitchell Palmer. On June 2, besides the bomb at Palmer's house, there were explosions at the homes of the mayor of Cleveland, Ohio; a Massachusetts state legislator; a textile factory owner and a judge in Paterson, New Jersey; another judge in Boston; federal judges in New York City and Pittsburgh; and a jeweler and a Catholic priest in Philadelphia.

There was intense pressure on Palmer to respond to the bombings in a convincing and dramatic way. "I was shouted at," he later said,

> from every editorial sanctum in America from sea to sea; I was preached upon from every pulpit; I was urged—I could feel it dinned into my ears—throughout the country to do something and do it now and do it quick, and do it in a way that would bring results to stop this sort of thing in the United States.

Palmer shared the general belief that the bomber—identified by his pamphlets as an anarchist—was almost certainly an immigrant, since almost all of the anarchists whom the public knew about had been foreign-born. The country's two most famous anarchists were Alexander Berkman, who had tried to kill steel magnate Henry Clay Frick in 1892, and Emma Goldman, editor of the anarchist journal *Mother Earth*. Both were immigrants. The noisiest of the many anarchist societies in the United States was an Italian immigrant faction. The Industrial Workers of the World, by far the largest anarchist organization in the country, had a sizable foreign-born contingent, although its leaders and most of its members were native-born. And the most notorious American anarchist in history was Leon Czolgosz, who had assassinated President McKinley in 1901. Czolgosz was inconveniently native-born, but his name certainly sounded alien to the public's ear, and so, despite the facts, he too confirmed the common belief that anarchism's political violence was a foreign import.

Palmer was correct in his assumption that the bomber who had blown himself up in front of his house was a foreigner. From the few surviving scraps of evidence—a polka-dot tie traced to its manufacturer, a shoe to its cobbler, an overcoat to its tailor—the Bureau of Investigation concluded that the bomber had been Carlo Valdinoci, publisher of *Cronaca Sovversiva,* the journal of a small group faithful to the doctrines of Italian anarchist Luigi Galliani. Valdinoci probably belonged to the Gruppo Autonomo of East Boston, whose fifty members included Nicola Sacco and Bartolomeo Vanzetti, who had probably helped with the June bombings. The Bureau was able to trace a defective letter *S* appearing in the text of a leaflet left by the bomber at Palmer's house to a New York City print shop, where evidence suggested to the Bureau that the Gruppo Autonomo may well have been responsible for *all* of the bombings of 1919 and others in 1920, and that the bombings may have been intended as revenge for the government's repression of anarchists during the war.

But not for a moment did Palmer think of limiting his investigation to those immediately responsible for the bombings of the past two months. With radicals everywhere calling for the overthrow of their governments, and American radicals swelling the chorus, the public demanded nothing less than a war against the entire radical movement. Palmer would give it to them.

There was some question as to the Bureau's jurisdiction, however, since it was not clear that the bombings had violated any federal law. Murder, attempted murder, and conspiracy to commit murder were all local offenses. Nor at that time was it a federal offense to deliver a bomb through the mails. To cover himself, Palmer asked Congress for a special appropriation for a comprehensive investigation of revolutionary violence. The country was facing, he said, a plot to "rise up and destroy the government at one fell swoop."

While he was waiting for authority from Congress, Palmer began to assemble a team to lead the investigation. The attorney general had spent the war as the alien property custodian, charged with confiscating German-owned enterprises. His chief investigator and right-hand man had been Francis P. Garvan. On June 4 Palmer named Garvan assistant attorney general in charge of investigating the radical movement. Palmer also named William J. Flynn, the former chief of the Secret Service (1912–1917), to lead the Bureau of Investigation, which had been run by William E. Allen (as acting chief) since Bielaski's resignation on February 10. Finally, Palmer appointed Frank Burke, who had led the Secret Service's New York office and headed its Russian Division, to serve as Flynn's assistant director (or "Chief").

Flynn and Burke brought with them their wartime fame as the engineers of several sensational counterintelligence coups against the Germans, most notably purloining the German documents that had first detailed the German "intrigues." The appointments of Flynn and Burke transferred to the Bureau the prestige they had earned in the Secret Service, and reminded the public that the Bureau had assumed the national security responsibilities that had made the Secret Service famous.

On June 12, Congress gave Palmer an appropriation of $500,000 to investigate the bombings. He convened an all-day meeting with Garvan and Flynn on June 17 at the Justice Department to plan their strategy. The decision: a campaign to round up and deport alien radicals.

There were practical prosecutorial reasons to concentrate on aliens, since their lack of citizenship solved the problem of what to do with them after their arrest. Their offense would simply be their advocacy of political violence or their membership in anarchist organizations that advocated violence. Neither advocacy nor membership was, in the case of citizens, a crime.

On the other hand, immigration law did prohibit immigrants from advocating the overthrow of the government, or belonging to organizations with such goals. In either case, they could be deported. More importantly, immigration law treated deportation as an administrative remedy, not a criminal punishment. This meant that few, if any, of the constitutional safeguards that protected criminal defendants applied to deportation hearings. Moreover, mass roundups of citizens were legally impractical if not impossible. Dragnet arrests of aliens, however, were quite feasible if the offense was violation of immigration regulations. As a technicality, however, the Justice Department was authorized to investigate only crimes, and so immigration investigations belonged to the Labor Department, which administered the immigration laws. But with Congress pressing money on Justice to do something about the bombings, Palmer had little to worry about on that score.

To plan and direct this campaign, which promised to be the most ambitious and extensive roundup in American law enforcement history, Palmer reached deep into the ranks of the Justice Department. On July 1 he announced he had selected a twenty-four-year-old lawyer who had spent the war years classifying and processing Germans and Austro-Hungarians for internment to lead the government's drive against radicalism. This young man, now with the title of special assistant to the attorney general, was J. Edgar Hoover.

Hoover's youth and rank within the Justice Department made him an unexpected choice for such an important post. But Hoover's background and experience made his selection, if not quite inevitable, at least thoroughly plausible.

John Edgar Hoover, known even as a child as "Edgar," was born in southeast Washington, D.C., on January 1, 1895, just three blocks behind the Capitol Building. It was an all-white neighborhood of civil servants and their families, their lives centering on the federal agencies and the segregated schools and churches of Washington. Hoover's father, Dickerson, was a platemaker in the United States Coast and Geodetic Survey, where Hoover's grandfather had also worked as a printer. Through his mother's side of the family Hoover was related to the prominent District of Columbia Judge John Hitz and to United States Supreme Court Justice Harold Burton.

Hoover was the pet of the household, doted on by his parents and cherished by his older brother and sister. It was a close and loving family, but troubled: Hoover's father was subject to periods of psychological distress that sound like episodes of depression, and several times he had to be hospitalized.

As a boy, Edgar actively involved himself in activities at the neighborhood Lutheran Church of the Redemption, serving as secretary of his Sunday school class and corresponding secretary of the entire school. When his brother joined a more historic and prestigious church, Old First Presbyterian near Judiciary Square, which included presidents, Supreme Court justices, and congressmen among its congregation, Edgar followed him.

Hoover generally joined the most prestigious organizations available to a youth of his background, and this determined his choice of high school, the city's most distinguished, Central High. During Hoover's day Washington's public schools had reached a peak of academic excellence, and attracted tuition-paying students from the suburbs in search of a more challenging and prestigious education. The school had a student body of 1,060 and a demanding curriculum: Hoover studied Latin, French, physics, and four years of mathematics. He joined the debate team at the end of his freshman year. During his junior year his team went undefeated, and during his senior year he was the leading speaker on a team that claimed the city championship.

Even more important than debate in training Hoover to be a leader was Central's High School Cadet Corps. Students wore their military uniforms to class on their twice-a-week drill days, when they prepared for drill competitions leading up to the citywide competition held in the spring on the White House Ellipse. There were parties and dances for each company and a citywide regimental ball. (This was for the white schools only; black schools had their own cadet corps and competitions, but they were ignored by official Washington and the white press.) During his freshman and sophomore years Hoover drilled under the command of the upperclassmen. During his junior year he was second sergeant in Central's Company B. During his senior year Captain Hoover commanded Company A, a six-squad company that placed second in the citywide competition to an eight-squad company from another school.

Hoover graduated from Central in June 1913. He had by now the sense of confidence and lack of self-doubt evident in his graduation picture: rail-thin, clench-jawed, and intense. He carried away from Central not merely a fine education, but a firm sense of who he was and what he stood for—and what he was against. He had enlisted in the institutions of order that white, middle-class, Protestant America had erected to guard its way of life against forces of turmoil and change. He had discovered leadership abilities in himself that carried him to the top of those institutions. He had won approval and applause as a leader and had trained the men under him until they could compete against the finest and be recognized as the best.

Coming from a family of civil servants, Hoover probably had his sights set on a government job from the beginning. He enrolled in George Washington University Law School, where it was possible to skip the undergraduate degree and pursue a three-year bachelor of laws. It was possible to get his degree after work, as a "late afternoon" student. To support himself, Hoover took an entry-level job as a messenger at the Library of Congress, just a few steps from his home at Seward Square.

The spring of 1917, while he studied for his master's in law, was a tumultuous time for the nation—and for Hoover. On April 2, Woodrow Wilson had delivered his war message, and on June 5, Hoover, like all young men his age, had to register for the draft. But Hoover's father, who had been under medical care for his psychiatric problems, now had what family members called a "nervous breakdown" and he had to retire from the Interior Department, leaving Edgar and his brother to support their mother and ailing father. Since Dick had a wife and three children, the burden would mostly be Edgar's. He passed the bar exam for the District of Columbia on July 3, and on July 26, 1917, secured a job as a clerk in the Justice Department at a salary of $990 a year, just $150 more than he had been making at the Library of Congress. Within a year he was promoted to the rank of "attorney" with a salary of $1,800, just about what was needed to replace his father's income.

The press of war work soon proved so overwhelming and disruptive to the department's operations that Attorney General Gregory recruited Attorney John Lord O'Brian from Buffalo, New York, to take charge of war work. Around December 4, O'Brian organized a new War Emergency Division that included an Alien Enemy Bureau headed by Charles W. Storey. Hoover was assigned to the Alien Enemy Bureau either immediately or soon after he joined the Justice Department, and was given the task of processing arrested alien enemies for internment or parole.

Initially Hoover's cases were interned German seamen, and he reported to Storey's assistant. Somewhat puzzlingly, Hoover is referred to in a December 14 table of organization as a "special agent," raising the possibility that he was initially engaged in Bureau of Investigation work. This is unlikely, however, since Hoover was signing documents as "Permit Officer" and was soon promoted (June 8, 1918) to the rank of attorney. But though he was probably not actually housed within the Bureau of Investigation, Hoover worked closely with the Bureau, which had to perform the investigations Hoover needed for his recommendations to O'Brian. He was in a position to observe the Bureau as the war transformed it into the government's chosen instrument for policing the home front.

He also gained experience processing aliens, determining who should be interned, who turned over to the Immigration Bureau for deportation, and who should be freed. The grounds for holding or deporting aliens tended to be political, based on their membership in anarchist or other antiwar groups. By the end of the war Hoover had an expertise on radical aliens that was probably unmatched in the Justice Department, particularly after there was a mass exodus of attorneys seeking the greener pastures of private practice in peacetime.

• • •

Having appointed Hoover to head what was soon called the Radical Division of the Justice Department, Palmer left its organization up to him while he turned his own attention to more pressing concerns: a political crisis over inflation ("the high cost of living"), labor disturbances, and his hopes in the forthcoming presidential race.

This Radical Division (Hoover would rename it the General Intelligence Division, or GID, in 1920) was in effect an interdivisional task force within the Bureau, able to draw on the resources of the Bureau and the other divisions of the Justice Department. Hoover's pay as special assistant to the attorney general initially ranked him third in the Bureau, after Flynn and Assistant Director Frank Burke, but within a year he would be making more than anyone except Flynn. He got his orders directly from Garvan, and issued orders to Bureau agents in Burke's or Flynn's name.

Initially the Radical Division was a research operation gathering "general intelligence," meaning information not directly connected to a criminal investigation. But within a few months the expertise Hoover was gathering on the radical movement would also equip him to take operational command of the antiradical campaign.

To man his new division Hoover hired and trained a pool of forty translators and readers to monitor some 500 radical publications, and collected files on more than 60,000 "radically inclined" individuals. Within a year the division was reviewing 625 newspapers and its card catalog of supposed radicals numbered about 200,000.

Hoover's experience enforcing the immigration statutes suggested to him the possibility of mass deportations of radical aliens, if he could get a ruling from the Labor Department that membership in the radical organizations they belonged to violated the immigration law. All he would then have to do was secure the membership rolls of the organizations, or capture individuals with membership cards, and they all could be deported without the government having to prove anything about their personal political beliefs.

As Hoover accumulated information about the radical movement, he began to draw up plans for what would be the largest dragnet in American history to date. Nor was that all he hoped to accomplish. His ultimate goal was to use the campaign against radical aliens to build public support for a law that would extend to peacetime the same prohibition against "sedition" (by aliens *or* citizens) as in wartime. There were several such bills being considered by Congress late in 1919, some with a definition of sedition broad enough to include almost any citizen popularly stigmatized as a troublemaker:

> *Whoever, with the intent to levy war against the United States, or to cause the change, overthrow, or destruction of the Government or of any of the laws or authority thereof, or to cause the overthrow or destruction of all forms of law or organized government, or to oppose, prevent, hinder or delay the execution of any law of the United States, or the free performance by the United States Government or any one of its officers, agents, or employees, of its or his public duty, commits, or attempts or threatens to commit, any act of force against any person or any property, or any act of terrorism, hate, revenge, or injury against the person or property of any officer, agent, or employee of the United States, shall be deemed guilty of sedition.*

A second section of this proposal, which defined the offense of "promoting sedition," was even more drastic:

Whoever makes, displays, writes, prints, or circulates . . . any sign, word, speech . . . or teaching, which advises, advocates, teaches, or justifies any act of sedition . . . or organizes, assists, or joins in the organization of . . . any society . . . which has for its object . . . the advising, advocating, teaching, or justifying any act of sedition . . . shall be deemed guilty of promoting sedition.

These bills did not pass in 1919, but Hoover hoped his antiradical drive would turn them into law in 1920.

In the summer of 1919 Hoover was in the awkward position of being poised to attack any revolutionary organizations he could find that contained large numbers of aliens, but as he knew all too well, such organizations did not yet exist, or rather existed as yet only in the dreams of radicals intoxicated by the Bolsheviks' success in Russia. The Left Wing of the Socialist Party, one candidate for Hoover's little list, was actually drawing up plans to affiliate with the Comintern, but had not yet done so because it was still hoping to capture the whole party to bring it into the Soviet orbit.

Hoover had to hunt for an organization that would give him a test case. He told Flynn to order his agents to make a "vigorous and comprehensive investigation of anarchistic and similar classes, Bolshevism, and kindred agitations advocating change in the present form of government by force or violence, the promotion of sedition and revolution, bomb throwing, and similar activities." He ordered agents to confine their inquiries particularly to "persons not citizens of the United States," but also told them to keep their eyes on citizen radicals who might be arrested "under legislation of that nature which may hereafter be enacted."

Flynn confessed unhappily to Hoover that he was not having much luck: "Real anarchists are usually associated together, if at all," he explained, "simply in groups or gatherings which have no constitution or by-laws and no officers other than a secretary-treasurer."

Despite the anarchists' failure to fall in with his plans, Hoover located three suitable targets. One was El Ariete, a Spanish anarchist group in Buffalo; another was l'Era Nuova, a Paterson, New Jersey–based group of Italian anarchists. But between them they had only thirty-six members, hardly enough to pose what the department claimed was a monumental anarchist threat. Moreover, the department had already used El Ariete to test a Civil War–era seditious conspiracy statute, and the case had been thrown out by a judge who ruled the law required actual use of force: The law did not forbid overthrow of the government "by the use of propaganda."

The third organization, however, was perfect, the Union of Russian Workers, with a membership of between four thousand and seven thousand Russian immigrants. Even better, the Labor Department had already determined that membership in the UORW rendered a member subject to deportation, since its constitution proclaimed that the masses should "take possession by forcible social revolution of all the wealth of the world," and that "having destroyed at the same time all institutions of state and authority, the class of the disinherited will have to proclaim a society of free producers." It made no difference that the constitution, written prior to 1911, was aimed at the tsarist regime in Russia rather than the American government.

By the end of October pressure was mounting on Palmer and Hoover to show some results from the antiradical investigations they had been bragging about to the press and Congress. On October 14 the Senate unanimously demanded from Palmer a report on his progress with the June bomb attacks and his investigation of radicals. The press echoed Congress's impatience, and criticized Palmer for not acting more swiftly.

But Hoover was just about ready. He satisfied himself that immigration authorities would accept a UORW membership card as sufficient evidence to merit deportation. He then gave the Immigration Bureau a list of six hundred members of the UORW, requesting that they prepare warrants for the aliens' arrest.

On November 7, 1919, the second anniversary of the Bolshevik Revolution, Bureau of Investigation agents reinforced by local police raided UORW meeting halls in twelve cities. At the national headquarters of the union at the Russian People's House in New York, raiders, commanded by the head of the New York Police Department's "bomb squad" (the antiradical unit), destroyed the office and its equipment, and arrested 650 individuals, releasing all but 39 after interrogation. The next day the New York State Assembly's committee investigating radicalism (the "Lusk Committee"), chaired by Assemblyman Clayton R. Lusk with the ferociously anticommunist Archibald Stevenson as chief counsel, raided seventy-three more radical meeting places, arresting five hundred. Similar raids across the country lodged hundreds of aliens in makeshift holding pens. In Hartford, Connecticut, ninety-seven aliens were held incommunicado for five months before being transferred to a federal prison.

The November raids turned Palmer into a national hero. The public—or at least the press and many politicians—demanded that he expand the raids to include the Wobblies, communists, and even the American Federation of Labor. Palmer took advantage of his new fame to press for passage of a peacetime sedition law, and the *New York Times* agreed, endorsing one such bill. Meanwhile as many detainees as could be managed were herded together at Ellis Island in New York harbor, awaiting final processing for deportation.

Showing a quickly developing flair for public relations, Hoover now made sure his first group of deportees included some celebrities. He fixed his attention on Emma Goldman and Alexander Berkman. Goldman, known to the public as Red Emma, had arrived in America from Russia in 1889 at the age of sixteen. She was one of the best-known political activists in the country—a feminist, a birth control reformer, and an anarchist, promoting her beliefs in her magazine, *Mother Earth*. Although she claimed to be a citizen, there was a technical flaw in her naturalization and Hoover picked it up: Her marriage to an American citizen had been performed by a Jewish functionary (a ritual slaughterer) whose authority to perform marriages was recognized by neither Jewish nor American law. Berkman, notorious because of his attempted murder of Carnegie Steel executive Henry Clay Frick during the 1892 Homestead steel strike, and who had been, like Goldman, imprisoned during the war for obstructing the draft, had admitted he was an alien. No problem there.

Hoover took personal charge of the Goldman and Berkman investigations. He even wrote the deportation briefs himself. A few years later a magazine story on Hoover, probably based on interviews, claimed that he

> *went to their place of living; read and studied Emma Goldman's books and writings; attended her lectures and talked over her philosophy with her and sounded out the feelings and sentiments of those gathered about her until after six months of thought and investigation he had thoroughly established the fact that they were really enemies of our established government and worked out the legal way of deportation.*

On October 27, Hoover presented the case against Goldman, and on November 29 the Immigration Bureau ordered her deportation. On December 9 the government quashed Goldman's writ of habeas corpus, and Hoover appeared at this hearing too. When the judge inquired about the arrangements for their deportation, Hoover assured the judge that their passage had been booked to "Red Russia," as specified in the deportation order.

Hoover had already gotten a boat from the War Department, the USS *Buford*, capable of carrying the deportees to Russia. On December 21 the Justice Department released Hoover's brief against Goldman to front-page headlines, and 249 aliens were loaded aboard the *Buford*. Of these, 184 were members of the UORW, another 51 were anarchists being deported under the 1918 immigration law, and the rest deported for criminal activity, for pauperism, or for illegal entry. Hoover chatted with Goldman as they waited for the barge to take them to the ship. He also told reporters Goldman and Berkman were the brains behind the revolution, and assured them that there were enough soldiers on board—some two hundred—to prevent mutiny, since the department expected Berkman to cause trouble. "The Department of Justice is not through yet by any means," Hoover promised. "Other 'soviet arks' will sail for Europe, just as often as is necessary to rid the country of dangerous radicals."

Yet, as is frequently the case, flaws invisible in the prototype become disastrously clear after the shift to mass production. First, beyond an assumed general allegiance to shared principles of anarchism, no one deported on the *Buford* was connected even remotely to the bombings that had led to congressional demands for action. Second, though the physical mistreatment of prisoners and denial of due process were initially ignored, the abuses were widespread. Should the Bureau move on to arrest thousands instead of hundreds, that kind of official misconduct would unleash a flood of complaints about what would surely seem a deliberate pattern of abuse.

Meanwhile, alien radicals were coalescing into the kind of targets for which Hoover had been hoping. In November 1918 the Left Wing caucus of the Socialist Party organized itself into the Communist Propaganda League in Chicago. This Left Wing had some American citizens swept up by enthusiasm for the Bolshevik Revolution, but even greater numbers of recent immigrants from the tsarist empire whose imaginations had been stirred by the events in Russia.

In the Socialist Party elections during the spring of 1919 the Left Wing, organized behind reporter John Reed, defeated the national leadership of the party and placed twelve of its members on the national executive committee. The old leadership, fearing a peacetime sedition law would make criminals out of members of an organization that advocated violence, refused to leave office, and expelled the Left Wing. Some forty thousand, about two thirds of the membership, were forced out of the party for espousing violence.

The Left Wing decided to attend the national meeting of the Socialist Party, scheduled for the end of August in Chicago, to try once again to capture the party. Its manifesto stated:

> *Revolutionary Socialism must use these mass industrial revolts to broaden the strike to make it general and militant; use the strike for political objectives, and finally develop the mass political strike against capitalism and the state . . . revolutionary Socialism does not propose to "capture" the bourgeois political state but to conquer and destroy it.*

On August 31 the Left Wing formally seceded from the Socialist Party, and the next day the foreign language groups within the Left Wing formed an American "Communist Party." The English-speaking radicals thereupon organized the Communist Labor Party under John Reed, Ben Gitlow, and William Bross Lloyd.

Now Hoover had what he needed: two political parties openly espousing revolution, with perhaps 40,000–70,000 members, fully 90 percent of them aliens subject to deportation for exactly the beliefs proclaimed by the two new communist parties. Hoover threw himself into the study of communism with what would come to be his trademark intensity and energy.

Hoover's introduction to communism during the fall of 1919 came at a unique moment in the history of the movement. There was never (and never again would be) a time when communists the world over were more sure that their time was at hand, that their triumph was not decades or years away, but merely a matter of months or days—even hours. Had Hoover first encountered the movement a year or two earlier, he would have heard communists gamely but vaguely predict their triumph "sometime" in the future. A few years later, and they would once again be viewing their expectations as hopeful eventualities with no set timetable. In 1919, however, the first of what the Italians call the *biennio rosso,* the two red years, communists vied with one another predicting the timetable of their victory. Revolutions were breaking out all over Europe; the Comintern had just been organized as the nerve center of the revolution, and it was firmly installed in the seat of a mighty empire, with Moscow as its secure command post.

Hoover read communist classics, devoured radical periodicals, interviewed communists and their sympathizers. The fruit of his labor was a set of three legal briefs, one arguing that aliens' membership in the Communist Party was a deportable offense; the second a similar argument directed at the Communist Labor Party; the third an argument that the self-styled Bolshevik ambassador to the United States, Ludwig C. A. K. Martens, should be deported.

On December 15, Hoover sent his brief on the Communist Party to Anthony Caminetti, the Immigration Bureau's commissioner-general. On December 22 he forwarded Caminetti the names of 2,280 party members, requesting warrants for their arrest; 441 more names, he promised, would be sent the next day. On December 24 he sent Caminetti his Communist Labor Party brief, along with a list of forty-seven names for warrants.

Labor Department Solicitor General John Abercrombie had already used Hoover's Communist Party brief to deport one of the aliens arrested in the November raids. Now, faced with 2,768 requests for warrants, he realized that something extraordinary was afoot, and he decided that any further decision to proceed with something so important had to come from his boss, Secretary of Labor William Wilson. On December 24, Wilson met with Abercrombie in a conference also attended by Assistant Secretary of Labor Louis B. Post. Wilson approved the arrests of the alien members of the Communist Party, and he may have also approved the Communist Labor arrests. Hoover acted on the assumption that both briefs had been approved, and he asked Abercrombie to sign the warrants—some three thousand in all. Each day he forwarded more names to Abercrombie. Through Chief Frank Burke, orders were sent to Bureau agents to prepare for raids to take place January 2.

Hoover foresaw that the number of arrests he was planning would have an enormous impact on public opinion and hoped they would be devastating to the radicals' morale, so he ordered that preparations for the raids be secret and synchronized. There were going to be hundreds of roundups in thirty-three cities in twenty-three states across the country. Since the Bureau had only 579 agents, Hoover had to call on allies from local police and volunteers from the just-disbanded American Protective League. The sensational nature of the raids and Hoover's reliance on non-Bureau personnel would prove to be a disastrous combination. Not only would the arrests be news, but attention would be directed to their very irregular manner and the inevitably harsh treatment of the detainees.

On the night of January 2, 1920, Hoover ordered clerks to be ready for duty all night. Hoover manned the telephones in the Bureau's offices in the Justice Department himself with his close friend and assistant Frank Baughman, directing the far-flung operation. Informants had been ordered to convene meetings that evening, and most were successful in assembling their radical comrades. As Bureau agents fanned out across the country with their APL auxiliaries, communist meeting halls were packed. That night and over the next few days between four thousand and six thousand radicals were dragged to detention centers. Those with names already listed on warrants were arrested. Some of those not named on warrants were released, but most were held while field agents sent their names to Hoover. He forwarded these lists to Caminetti with an affidavit, based on nothing except the arresting agent's say-so, that the person named was a communist, requesting that a telegraphic warrant be sent by Caminetti to the detention center. For the rest of the month a blizzard of these telegraphic warrants flowed out of Hoover's office, all dictated by him or Baughman. In all they sent 291 memos to Caminetti with 2,705 requests for warrants.

Treatment of the radicals, many of them old enemies of their APL captors, was very harsh. Hundreds of detainees were crammed into holding pens without beds or restroom facilities. No opportunity was given the aliens to communicate with friends, relatives, or lawyers. Soon word got out: First fellow radicals began to protest their treatment; then they were joined by members of the clergy and liberals allied with the radicals before the war; and then, of course, the press. Finally judges, charged with administering jails and prisons, began to notice, too. Out of a combination of inexperience and overconfidence bred by his success in November, Hoover had failed to organize a command system adequate to the scale of the raids. Events were now out of control.

But for the moment, Hoover and Palmer basked in applause, while papers trumpeted, "ALL ABOARD FOR THE NEXT SOVIET ARK." Papers reprinted Hoover's briefs on the two parties.

In January 1920, Hoover launched a newsletter, the *Bulletin of Radical Activities,* to help coordinate the campaign, at first biweekly, then weekly, the name changing in August to the *Bureau of Investigation General Intelligence Bulletin.* He also published monographs on radicalism, which he sent to public figures and members of Congress. One of them was *The Red Radical Movement,* with a foreword signed by Palmer (who said "it is not good reading late at night when you are at home in your own house. It gives you the creeps a little").

Hoover's most ambitious propaganda effort was a "popular survey" called *The Revolution in America.* In it he charged that the strikes, bomb plots, and political turmoil were the work of an array of radical groups all inspired and motivated by the revolution in Russia. His conclusion:

Civilization faces its most terrible menace of danger since the barbarian hordes overran West Europe and opened the dark ages. We have furnished a picture now of the revolutionary thought and of the revolutionary presence. It remains to see the social-industrial problem as it is, apart from our hopes and fears, and to win sight of the ways and means of preventing international collapse.

The "ways and means" Hoover mentioned probably referred to the peacetime sedition bills—at one point there were seventy such measures working their way through Congress. On January 10 the Senate passed the Sterling Sedition Bill. The House was considering the even more repressive Graham Bill. When both bills came under attack from organized labor, Palmer recommended that a third, slightly less repressive, sedition bill be substituted, and threw his support behind one introduced by Martin L. Davey of Ohio. It would have allowed for even more dramatic roundups, this time of radical citizens.

Hoover was now contemplating a systematic campaign of arrests of IWW members, five hundred at a clip.

But Hoover was becoming aware of a rising number of protests. He wrote Assistant Director Burke that

> there is an extensive propaganda on foot that many ignorant Russians were taken in the raid who knew nothing of the organization. While this is not entirely true, yet it has proven meat for propaganda and as the deportation policy must be supported solely by public opinion, I feel that a dragnet raid would be detrimental.

Labor Secretary Wilson, himself an immigrant from Great Britain, now began having second thoughts about the raids. He decided to hold a formal hearing over whether the communist parties actually did fall within the provisions of the 1918 immigration law. Hoover presented the Justice Department case, which focused on Englebert Preis, one of the arrested communist aliens facing deportation for party membership. Evidently swayed by Hoover's arguments, which the press described as confident, brash, and flamboyant, Wilson ruled that Preis could indeed be deported for belonging to the Communist Party.

On March 5, Assistant Labor Secretary Post took over Abercrombie's responsibilities for the deportation cases. Post was seventy-one years old, and before joining the Labor Department had been deeply involved in radical and reform politics. He knew Emma Goldman and had friendly relations with many of the other radicals now under attack. Since Wilson had twice ruled that members of the Communist Party were subject to deportation, Post felt it was his duty to apply the policy, but he decided he would do so only after determining whether each individual alien had in fact voluntarily and knowingly joined the party.

Post began to examine the deportation cases for members of the Communist Party individually. He reported, with some satisfaction, that out of the 6,328 warrants, there had been 4,000 arrests, and that he himself had been able to cancel 3,000. He defended himself against charges he had done so without regard to the facts by pointing out that of "1,000 deportations ordered after hearings, more than 500 were ordered by me."

In Boston there was more trouble. Federal Judge George Anderson had begun to look into the confinement of eighteen radicals held in Boston's Deer Island prison. He ordered a hearing on two British subjects, a married couple named Colyer. Hoover hurried to Boston to help the United States attorney present the case.

Hoover predicted more violence on May Day if measures were not taken. The first of May passed without incident. Doubts began to circulate about the seriousness of the revolutionary threat.

On May 5, Secretary Wilson ruled that membership in the Communist Labor Party was not a deportable offense. The final blow came on June 23. Judge Anderson ruled in Boston that membership in either the Communist Party or the Communist Labor Party was not a deportable offense. His decision was immediately overturned on appeal, but until the Supreme Court issued a ruling, nothing could be done.

Louis Post was releasing alien after alien, finding that there was "no lawful proof" to warrant arrest. Hoover and Palmer responded by encouraging their allies in Congress to call for Post's impeachment. Post demanded a congressional hearing in which he impressively refuted his opponents. The committee voted to suspend any further hearings, not only on Post but also on all other radical matters, including the sedition bill. The Bureau's campaign against the so-called "revolutionary movement" had collapsed in shambles, ending Palmer's political ambitions. It appeared Hoover might be a casualty as well.

But Hoover survived, and so did something else: an enduring hatred of Hoover and the Bureau that would live on in the soul of the American left. That hatred would become a permanent fixture in American life through the actions of the American Civil Liberties Union. The National Civil Liberties Bureau, the immediate ancestor of the modern ACLU (which took that name on January 20, 1920), had in fact been organized in 1918 specifically to protect radicals targeted by the Bureau and the APL during the war. Then during the Red Scare it continued to defend the anarchists and communists rounded up during Palmer and Hoover's antiradical raids.

The ACLU, along with the National Popular Government League, assembled twelve prominent lawyers (among them Felix Frankfurter and Roscoe Pound) who investigated the antiradical activities of the Justice Department and the Bureau during the Palmer raids, and released their findings in the enormously influential *Report Upon the Illegal Practices of the United States Department of Justice.* They concluded that the real threat to liberty in 1920 was not the communist movement but the "present assault" by Palmer and Hoover "upon the most sacred principles of our Constitutional liberty."

The ACLU would evolve into a powerful organization, which gradually acquired an image as an apolitical institution dedicated to protecting all victims of government repression of civil liberties, regardless of the victims' political beliefs. In fact the ACLU was born during the Red Scare to defend communists from the Bureau of Investigation, and its early board included communists and others who regarded themselves as "comrades" of their communist allies. Over the years, particularly during the Cold War, the ACLU broke its few remaining ties to the Party and even tried to cozy up to J. Edgar Hoover at the height of his power, but it really never shed that hereditary hostility to the Bureau and Hoover, which even now seems to survive as a reflexive skepticism about the Bureau's actions, which it believes threaten to send the nation down a slippery slope to assaults on civil liberties, attacks on dissent, and repression of the American left.

There were other reasons the Bureau's campaign against communism in 1920 collapsed besides the counterattack by civil libertarians. The world situation had changed during the course of 1920. What had seemed to be a dire emergency now appeared to have been an overblown and somewhat embarrassing case of the nerves. The revolution had entrenched itself in Russia, but had lost all its other footholds in Europe. In Russia the Bolsheviks had their hands full trying to avoid starvation at home. Lenin saw clearly how his fortunes had fallen, and denounced terrorist activity as harmful to the cause in his 1920 *"Left Wing" Communism: An Infantile Disorder.*

The Bureau's drive against radicalism in 1919 and 1920 did demoralize the communist movement, as Hoover and Palmer had intended. It demonstrated to aliens that it was dangerous to belong to revolutionary parties, and to citizens that it might be dangerous for them, too, in the future. The result was a precipitous drop in the membership of the two communist parties.

But the harsh hand of the Soviets, who were just then enforcing discipline on the national communist parties, might have had the same effect on the fortunes of the American movement. During the Second Congress of the Comintern in 1920, the Soviets began a campaign of "Bolshevizing" the foreign parties along strict guidelines set down in the so-called "21 Theses." There was no longer any place in the American communist parties for anyone unwilling to subordinate himself completely to Russian foreign policy. That in itself might have been enough to marginalize the Communist Party until the Depression of the thirties once again created new hopes for a global revolution.

Despite the collapse of his anticommunist drive, Hoover kept the General Intelligence Division busy gathering information on communist activities. He was as aware as anyone that the communists' factionalism was destroying the noncommunist radical left. And yet he persisted in warning that there was still an immanent threat of communist-directed revolution in the United States.

This encouraged irresponsible American anticommunists to conjure up fantasies of Red Webs linking all of American reform to communist plots supported by Moscow gold.

• • •

Palmer had hoped that by the spring of 1920 he would be the leading contender for the Democratic nomination for president. Instead he found himself drowning in political disaster. He soon found himself before Congress defending himself against charges that he and the Bureau had trampled on the Bill of Rights. On June 1, Palmer appeared before the House Rules Committee: Hoover prepared Palmer for his testimony and was at his side. Hoover told Palmer the hearing was

> *an excellent opportunity not only to answer these specific charges but also to tell the committee and the country the real story of the red menace, both the International and national phase of the same, the efforts of the Department of Justice to specifically curb the spread of Bolshevism, and the results obtained from these efforts and finally the consequences following the action of the Assistant Secretary of Labor in canceling the warrants.*

But the charges against the department and the Bureau were specific and detailed, while Hoover's defense amounted to little more than a gory picture of what might have happened had the Bureau not acted—in other words, Hoover had to try to refute a "what happened" with a "what might have happened," shaky grounds for a winning argument. Palmer's performance was generally panned. The failure of the Red Scare campaign, along with labor's hostility toward Palmer because of the drive, pretty much did in his candidacy. The eventual winner of the Democratic nomination, James M. Cox, found it politically expedient to repudiate and denounce the Bureau's campaign against radicals.

After the 1920 election Senator Tom Walsh of Montana dragged Hoover and Palmer to appear before the Judiciary Committee to answer more charges against the Bureau. Conservative members of the committee, led by Chairman Thomas Sterling of South Dakota, the author of one of the sedition bills of the previous autumn, kept Walsh from issuing his report, and so it was not until 1923, during the Teapot Dome investigation, that Walsh was finally able to read his findings into the Congressional Record. Walsh's scathing report stands as the definitive indictment of the Bureau's conduct during the Red Scare.

Even after the demise of his Red Scare campaign, Hoover kept watching the communist parties as they declined from perhaps 60,000–88,000 members in

September 1919 (a figure that included many members of socialist locals who had had their names transferred when their officers joined the Communist Party) to less than 6,000 at the end of 1920. The public was not as aware as Hoover of the sorry state of radicalism after the raids, but the country was no longer worried about communism.

Even though there was one final bombing in the wave of political violence that had begun the previous spring, the public no longer seemed to be listening to the Bureau's warnings. On September 16, 1920, a blast outside the Morgan Bank in lower Manhattan killed thirty-three people and injured two hundred. Like the earlier bombings, the Wall Street bombing was probably the work of Italian anarchists, not communists. The motive may have been revenge for the arrests of Sacco and Vanzetti earlier that year. Yet, even faced with a new, very real case of terrorism, Hoover was unable to revive his anticommunist campaign.

■ ■ ■

Palmer stayed on as attorney general until Warren G. Harding's inauguration as president, and on March 4, 1921, Harding's campaign manager and confidant, Harry M. Daugherty, was named attorney general. Daugherty, up to his armpits in politics, was well aware of his unfitness to run the nation's law office, but paradoxically thought that he was ideally suited to protect his friend Harding from other crooks: "I know Harding, and I know who the crooks are and I want to stand between Harding and them." Daugherty presided over the spoliation of the government from the infamous "Little House on H Street," lent to him by the owner of the *Washington Post,* Ned McLean. There were so many scandals involving Daugherty, as well as Interior Secretary Albert Fall, and Navy Secretary Edward L. Doheny that Daugherty's Justice Department became known as the "Department of Easy Virtue." Harding's biographer Francis Russell points out, however, that Daugherty's appointees as assistant attorneys general were men and women of high integrity, and that even after Daugherty's disgrace they vouched for his honesty as attorney general. But among historians, however, Daugherty has few defenders.

Daugherty kept Flynn on as director until he could persuade William J. Burns, Daugherty's boyhood friend from Ohio and our old friend from the land-fraud investigation, to take the job. On August 22, 1921, Daugherty appointed Burns to run the Bureau, that same day naming the twenty-six-year-old J. Edgar Hoover to serve as Burns's second in command, with the title of assistant director and chief.

The two directors who led the Bureau between the end of World War I and

Hoover's appointment as director in 1924, William Flynn and William Burns, had national reputations as master detectives. They both showed the same flair for self-promotion that Hoover would later display in the thirties. Flynn edited a crime magazine called *Flynn's Weekly,* while Burns was a notable figure in New York City's nightclub scene, acted on the Broadway stage, and wrote a series of novels and stories based on his more celebrated cases.

The *New York Times* called Burns "the only detective of genius whom this country has produced." He had been running his own detective agency since leaving the Secret Service in 1909, and as a private detective Burns was as successful as he had been as a government investigator: In 1910 he solved the bombing of the *Los Angeles Times* building by uncovering evidence implicating the chief suspects, a pair of American Federation of Labor officials. They confessed when they saw Burns's proof, flabbergasting the labor movement and its friends, who had assumed that the case was an antilabor frame-up by "Burns and his bloodhounds," in the words of Samuel Gompers. Burns also collected evidence that Leo Frank, the Jewish superintendent of an Atlanta pencil factory, was innocent of raping and murdering a girl in his factory, a crime for which Frank was subsequently lynched. Burns narrowly escaped the same fate. During the neutrality period Burns worked with equal efficiency uncovering German intrigues for the British and exposing British shenanigans for the Germans.

While he was employed by the British, Burns made the acquaintance of a gentleman whom J. Edgar Hoover would later refer to as the "Amazing Mr. Means." Gaston B. Means worked for the Germans during the war as their Agent E-13. Before that he had had a career that included insurance fraud (against the Pullman Company for an accident, probably self-inflicted, while in one of their sleeper cars) and the probable murder of a wealthy widow whose accounts he had looted. Burns installed Means in the Bureau as a temporary special agent, where he advertised himself as an all-purpose fixer, claiming to be able to rig federal trials, quash indictments, arrange for federal pardons, and obtain "B" permits that granted permission to withdraw impounded liquor from government warehouses supposedly for sale overseas, permits naturally much sought after during the Prohibition era. Means actually performed none of these services, but he pocketed the fees and bribe money all the same. The circumstances naturally made it difficult for his victims to complain through any legitimate channels. Gaston Means ran his rackets out of the Bureau until August 1922, and when he left he took with him an ample supply of official Justice Department legal forms that he continued to sell to his clients.

Years later Hoover shared his recollections of Means with his ghostwriter

Courtney Ryley Cooper: "I knew him first in 1921 when, as a newly appointed Special Agent of the Bureau of Investigation, he lumbered into the Department of Justice where I then was a subordinate, and immediately began to investigate everything within reach." He was, Hoover remembered, "a bulky man, with a heavy body and long, gorillalike arms." Once established in the Bureau, Hoover went on, "the word went through the underworld that there was a man in the Department of Justice who could 'fix things.' "

> *"You see, it's this way. I'm a great friend of the President. As a high official of the Department of Justice, I know everybody in the Cabinet. And I'm on close terms with the National Committee. Now the Committee is a little short of funds, so if you'll just pay me so much a barrel, I'll see that you get all the whiskey you want. To be perfectly frank with you, I've got so much power in Washington, that I can take care of anything in Government departments except murder."*

Hoover added, "No one wanted murder; whiskey was the desired commodity." Hoover observed that all those who bribed Means waited for their whiskey until realizing they had been duped, but that since they were equally guilty of a law infraction, they were "loath to make a complaint against him."

Means became for Hoover a vivid symbol of the Bureau before he took charge in 1924:

> *The man had always disgusted me. A subordinate at that time, I had determined that if ever I became Director, I would end all possibility of the Bureau again being sullied by such a person. That became my first big endeavor when I received my appointment. Investigations were instituted into the entire lives of candidates for Special Agents. Impeccability of character was made a prime requisite. Other than the contribution of being a horrible example, the life of Gaston Means presents little that is high minded.*

The Bureau under William Burns may or may not have been as corrupt as Hoover claimed, but about its political partisanship there can be no dispute. The war years and the Red Scare saw the Bureau squarely on the side of management in repressing the militant labor movement: the IWW, the antiwar socialists, and the new communist parties. During the Harding administration the Bureau became even more aggressive in working against labor in its struggles with capital, and it regularly engaged in red-smearing to brand the labor disturbances of the early twenties as communist-inspired.

The labor wars of the twenties began when the coal mine owners and the railroad barons decided to roll their workers' wages back to prewar levels. John L. Lewis of the United Mine Workers was told by President Harding that his men would have to take the same wage cut imposed on nonunion workers; their high pay "imposed a burden on the consuming public and the whole industry." Lewis was unmoved by the president's appeal and unpersuaded by his logic; if nonunion miners were being forced to cough up their wage gains, their proper recourse, he thought, was to join his union and keep their pay. On April 1, 1922, Lewis pulled his workers out of the mines. On July 1 the Railroad Shopmen's Union, ordered by the Railroad Labor Board to accept a wage reduction, also went out on strike.

During the summer of 1922 the coal strike turned bloody. In Herrin, Illinois, strikebreakers were imported by a strip mine operator. The strikebreakers were surrounded by union members and forced to surrender. They were attacked by the furious strikers; twenty-one of the strikebreakers died in what the press called the Herrin Massacre, which had the effect of turning public opinion against all the strikers, railroad workers as well as miners.

The railroad strike also turned violent. Encouraged by the Railroad Labor Board, the owners began to replace union workers with strikebreakers and to surround the yards with guards. The railroad owners announced that since the workers had disobeyed the Railroad Labor Board, they too would reject any nationwide settlement, and would accept workers back only upon individual application. The strikers began destroying bridges, tracks, and switches and attacking the strikebreakers. On August 18, Harding addressed a joint session of Congress vowing to "use the power of government to maintain transportation and sustain the right of the men to work."

At this moment Attorney General Daugherty decided that the strike was a red plot. On September 1, 1922, he obtained an injunction from Chicago federal Judge James H. Wilkerson that prohibited strikers from loitering or congregating near railroad property, from picketing, or "in letters, circulars, telegrams, telephones, or word of mouth, or through interviews in the papers, [to] encourage or direct anyone to leave or enter the service of the railroad companies." The rest of Harding's cabinet was outraged that the Justice Department should intevene in a labor dispute with such blatant partisanship. Samuel Gompers of the AFL had Illinois Congressman Oscar E. Keller introduce a bill of impeachment against Daugherty for "abridging freedom of speech, freedom of the press, the right of the people peaceably to assemble." Keller charged that Daugherty had conducted himself "in a manner arbitrary, oppressive, unjust and illegal" by appointing "untrustworthy, dangerous, and corrupt persons" and "using the funds of his office illegally and without warrant for certain lawful acts which under the law he was specifically forbidden to prosecute." The Judiciary Committee, however, rejected the charges against Daugherty and was sustained by the full House.

Daugherty by now was becoming paranoid. He was convinced the communists were plotting to kill him. At one point he claimed he noticed a smell coming from what he was convinced was a "deadly gas trap in the flowers" beside a speaker's stand while he was orating. Burns backed up his boss by swearing to Congress that Moscow was behind the strikes.

Meanwhile Daugherty's injunction had broken the strike. Any union action was noted down by Bureau agents as evidence workers were violating the injunction. By November the strike was over.

There was no truth to Daugherty's claim that communists were responsible for the labor struggles of 1922, but it was not for lack of effort on their part. The communists were trying to organize a left-labor political coalition and had set up even in these early years "front" organizations secretly controlled by the Communist Party. Many more would be founded over the years, among them the Society for Technical Aid to Soviet Russia, the National Defense Committee (which helped communists rounded up in the Palmer Raids), the Friends of Soviet Russia, the Women's Bureau, and the National Council for the Protection of the Foreign Born. But the communists defeated their own efforts by attacking socialists and other leftists who remained outside the Comintern fold as "class enemies," more dangerous than the capitalists themselves.

But while the American Communist Party, obeying the ever-shifting party line dictated by Moscow, was sabotaging American radicalism, the Bureau of Investigation was spinning theories of red plots and leaking them to cooperative newsmen. In August 1922, Special Agent Jacob Spolansky, who had gained a reputation shadowing Reds, heard that the party had scheduled a national meeting somewhere near St. Joseph, Michigan. Nosing about, he discovered that eighty-six members of a "singing society" had rented a farm in nearby Bridgman, Michigan, for a retreat. Spolansky managed to plant an informant in the group, and then lurked about the meeting until William Z. Foster spotted him. The communists hurriedly buried their records in potato barrels and fled. Spolansky's informant led him to the buried records. He turned them over to Michigan authorities, who used them to put the communist leadership on trial for violating the state's sedition law.

After the trial, Hoover, who was still running the Bureau's General Intelligence Division as well as handling the day-to-day operations of the Bureau as Burns's deputy, turned the records over to newspaper reporter Richard Whitney, who was also head of the countersubversive American Defense Society. Based on information furnished to him by Hoover, Whitney wrote one of the original "Red Web" books, *Reds in America*. Whitney used a theory of "interlocking directorates" to demonstrate how the communists maintained control of the left through a "spider web" of shared board memberships. If a communist served on the board of one organization, Whitney argued that the communist was able to control not only that group, but any other group whose board shared directors with it, even if the individuals were not communists themselves. For countersubversives like Whitney, communist dreams were the same as deeds, with proof constructed from a paper chain of names on organization letterheads.

In 1924, Hoover placed the authority of the Bureau behind a report submitted at the request of the Senate Foreign Relations Committee. It consisted of four hundred pages of documents on communist intrigues in the United States. The committee used the report to block diplomatic recognition of the Soviet regime (which did not actually take place until 1933).

Warren G. Harding died of coronary thrombosis on August 2, 1923. Three months later, on October 22, the Senate opened hearings on the Interior Department's leases of the naval oil reserves at Wyoming's Teapot Dome. Congressional investigation exposed Interior Secretary Albert Fall's role in awarding oil reserve leases to oilmen in exchange for loans that looked like bribes. There followed an investigation of Daugherty by a select committee chaired by Senator Smith W. Brookhart, but led by the junior senator from Montana, Burton K. Wheeler. Wheeler charged Daugherty with nonfeasance for failing to investigate corruption in the administration. Daugherty retaliated by sending Bureau of Investigation agents to look for incriminating evidence on his accusers to be used to intimidate or discredit them.

One of the most damaging witnesses against Daugherty was Gaston Means, who told stories of lurid goings-on at the Little House on H Street and at a Little Green House on K Street, of bags of bribe money, and of his own corrupt carryings-on at the Bureau of Investigation, made possible, he made clear, by his friendship with William Burns. When Daugherty refused to turn over Justice Department files requested by the Senate committee, President Calvin Coolidge fired him. Daugherty blamed his misfortunes on a plot by the communists to get rid of him because he had blocked their plans to subvert the country.

When Coolidge appointed former Senator Atlee Pomerene of Ohio and future Supreme Court Justice Owen J. Roberts as special counsels to investigate Teapot Dome, they were warned by Senator Tom Walsh "not to use agents from the Department of Justice because Attorney General Harry M. Daugherty was under investigation by another Senate committee and Senator Walsh was convinced that Daugherty's agents could not be trusted." Pomerene and Roberts turned to the Secret Service, whose chief, William H. Moran, warned the Secret Service agent investigating the scandal that "we have learned that you are being followed by agents of the Bureau of Investigation and the Burns Detective Agency, who seek to ascertain the progress and scope of your investigation. I suggest you avoid keeping written notes and that you submit all reports via registered mail."

For the Democrats, Teapot Dome and the Bureau of Investigation's corruption seemed to have given them a winning issue in the 1924 presidential elections. Their chances were ruined, however, by the legendary 103-ballot fight between William McAdoo and Al Smith that finally produced a relatively unknown Democratic candidate in John W. Davis. Meanwhile Coolidge reinforced his image of rectitude by surrounding himself with cabinet appointees of stalwart integrity like Daugherty's successor as attorney general, Harlan F. Stone of the Columbia Law School, who took over on March 28, 1924. Two weeks later, Bureau Director William Burns admitted to the Senate Committee that he failed to speak up when Daugherty falsely denied he had sent Bureau agents to investigate Senator Wheeler. Stone decided that Burns had to go. He began looking for someone to succeed Burns. He asked for advice from his fellow cabinet members. Commerce Secretary Herbert Hoover asked his confidential assistant, Larry Richey, if he knew of anyone who could run the Bureau. Richey had been in the Secret Service before going to work for Herbert Hoover, and had been in the squad assigned to guarding the president. Richey knew J. Edgar Hoover from those days and recommended him for the job, as did Mabel Willebrandt, the assistant attorney general in charge of Prohibition enforcement. Willebrandt told Stone that J. Edgar Hoover was "honest and informed and one who operated like an electric wire, with almost a trigger response." That was enough to give Hoover the edge over his chief rival, Internal Revenue investigator Elmer Irey. On May 9, Stone asked for Burns's resignation, and the next day he named J. Edgar Hoover, now twenty-nine years old, acting director of the Bureau of Investigation.

By now the Justice Department was so discredited that the press was calling it not only the "Department of Easy Virtue" but the "Department of Hysteria and Intolerance." Harlan F. Stone was so highly respected, however, that everything he did was looked upon as a clean break with the past, and so even though Hoover had had his hand in everything the Bureau did during the Palmer and Daugherty years, the press saw in Hoover's appointment a repudiation of William Burns's policies and a fresh start for the Bureau.

This was partly due to a belief that Hoover's appointment represented a sort of salutary ethnic cleansing. Billy Burns was everyone's image of the corrupt Irish flatfoot, the silent movie Keystone Cop. In fact Burns had been smart and honest, but he was certainly old-school, or, as the papers put it, "the reincarnation of Old Sleuth," a man "who knew the ways and wiles of criminals as well as any man in the world. He had been brought up with his nose to the ground." That is, Burns had subscribed to the "it takes a crook to catch a crook" school of criminology. Hoover, on the other hand, projected an image of straight-laced WASP respectability of the most earnest and upwardly striving variety. He was the first non-Catholic director in years, which was greeted with approval in some circles. Hoover was a lawyer, which Burns was not, and so he was praised because he had gotten rid of "the 'old gum shoe, dark lantern and false moustache' tradition of the Bureau and substituted business methods of procedure." Hoover was "the disciple of Blackstone," an expert in "the new school of crime-detection" and "as clean as a hound's tooth . . . furthermore he plays golf. Whoever could picture an 'Old Sleuth' doing that?"

In fact, there is no reason to suppose that Hoover disagreed with any of Palmer's or Daugherty's ideas about the communist threat or the need to take forcible action against it or any organizations infiltrated by it. After all, it was Hoover who had supplied Palmer and Daugherty with their information about the supposed threat. Nor is there any reason to suppose that he disagreed with Daugherty's belief that the labor disturbances of 1922–1923 were caused, at least in part, by the activities of communists. It had been Hoover who gathered the evidence Daugherty used to get his injunction against the strikes. In fact, Hoover was probably more convinced and certainly more sincere in this regard than either Palmer or Daugherty, who were political opportunists and who probably saw the issue of communism first and foremost as a convenient weapon to use against their enemies and to promote their political careers. And, as events would prove, it was actually not such a bad idea for the government to keep its eye on the communists, who would in a few years form the nucleus of Stalin's underground in America.

But some of the contrast between Hoover and Burns was not far off the mark. Burns was just what he seemed, an old-time detective who knew from experience that crimes were solved by following the trail of ill-gotten money, by locating the weak links in conspiracies, and by turning suspects into informants. He had no illusions about the honesty of politicians, judges, congressmen, and cabinet officials. He had helped convict more than a few himself, and he understood that in the nature of things political, almost all politicians operated on the edge of the law when it came to servicing important constituents, and that they lived in the constant vicinity of conflicts of interest. Burns was used to going after big crimes, and that meant big criminals.

Hoover was used to something else completely. His antiradical campaign in 1920 had attacked an unpopular movement by targeting relatively insignificant individuals who could be dramatized as symbols of the threat. His experience with politically powerful individuals was that they had better be left alone. Angering some of them had in fact destroyed his mentor, A. Mitchell Palmer, and had come close to destroying him as well. Hoover seems to have emerged from the Red Scare having learned an enduring lesson: senators, congressmen, and anyone else important enough to have powerful allies should never be openly investigated by the Bureau—and as long as Hoover was in charge, they never were. Information on powerful Bureau enemies that might come in handy when released to the Bureau's friends might be collected secretly, but under Hoover the Bureau would never launch criminal investigations of the wealthy or politically prominent, precisely the kinds of investigations Burns had never shied from.

And, unlike Burns, who was none too choosy about means if they would accomplish his ends, Hoover tended to think of processes rather than results, and this reflex was reinforced by his disastrous experience with the Palmer Raids, where procedural irregularities and his failure to control his agents let his enemies derail the drive. Teapot Dome taught Hoover to see success in law enforcement as a matter of preventing scandal. In a maxim that would become all too familiar under his leadership, he would make sure that agents did nothing that could embarrass the Bureau or him. Hoover wanted his Bureau to convey an image of respectability in what it did, how it did it, and the character of men that it employed. In other words, left to his own devices, Hoover would opt for a Bureau that did not do much, if anything, and so could not get into any trouble doing it.

Which was just about what Harlan Stone wanted. Stone had been one of the leading critics of the Palmer Raids, and at the time had called for a congressional probe of the Bureau. After Teapot Dome there was even talk of abolishing the Bureau and handing its duties back to the Secret Service. Instead, Stone called Hoover in and gave him strict guidelines. He ordered him to reduce the size of the Bureau, removing those deemed "incompetent and unreliable" and hiring only "men of known good character and ability, giving preference to men who have had some legal training." The Bureau was to confine itself "strictly to investigations of violations of law, under my direction or under the direction of an Assistant Attorney General regularly conducting the work of the Department of Justice." That meant an end to the information-gathering activities of the General Intelligence Division, and in fact meant an end to the General Intelligence Division itself. Stone stressed to Hoover that "the Bureau of Investigation is not concerned with political or other opinions of individuals. It is concerned only with their conduct and then only with such conduct as is forbidden by the laws of the United States."

The American Civil Liberties Union, wondering about the wisdom of placing Palmer and Daugherty's top lieutenant in charge of the Bureau, visited Hoover and Stone in 1924 to make sure the Bureau had really halted its surveillance of radicals and reformers, and happily reported back that "we were wrong in our estimate of . . . [Hoover's] attitude." They were pleased when Hoover claimed he had carried out all of Stone's instructions to end the Bureau's anti-labor and antiradical activities.

Was Hoover telling the truth? Did he really end the Bureau's intelligence gathering on radical groups and individuals? Later historians, incensed at Hoover's repressive campaigns against radicals during the Cold War and Vietnam eras and his sorry record in civil rights, have pored over the files of the Bureau during the twenties, looking for evidence that Hoover disobeyed Stone's edicts, secretly continuing to gather information on radicals. They have been able to find some instances, triumphantly trumpeted as proof that the Bureau was forever and always bent on political repression, in the twenties as well as later. But while the Bureau did, in a handful of cases, gather information on individuals not under any investigation for federal offenses, it was always when ordered to do so by the White House. Generally this was to provide the president with information on people whom he was going to meet. This may have been better done by the Secret Service than the Bureau of Investigation, but vetting the president's visitors, potential appointees, and critics was a service the Bureau continued to provide presidents since Herbert Hoover's administration, until it was carried to notoriously abusive extremes under Lyndon Johnson and Richard Nixon.

One group dismayed by the Bureau's withdrawal from general intelligence gathering on radicals was the countersubversive anticommunist community. Prone to conspiracy theories, the belief took hold among countersubversives that the communists' ultimate goal during the early twenties was to defang the Justice Department. With Stone's imposition of the new guidelines on the Bureau, the Reds had succeeded, and now could run wild. This weird theory spread throughout the far-right anticommunist movement during the thirties, and became a permanent fixture in the grand conspiracy theories still believed (and expanded) by paranoid groups like the remnants of the John Birch Society.

Six days after taking charge, Hoover wrote Stone that he had begun reviewing the personnel files "and [I] have already recommended a number of Special Agents whose services may be discontinued for the best interests of the service." When Hoover took over there were 650 employees, including 441 agents. By the end of the first year, 61 agents had been terminated, and 5 out of the 53 field offices closed. By the end of the decade, there were 581 employees, 339 agents, and 30 field offices, a drastic decline from the peak year of 1920, when the Bureau had 1,127 employees and 579 agents. In 1932 the number of field offices would reach an historic low of 22.

With the Bureau rapidly shrinking, and Stone showing far more interest in what the Bureau was not doing than what it was doing, what actually was there for Hoover to do? No longer was the Bureau watching for subversives, and the business-oriented administrations of Calvin Coolidge and Herbert Hoover were uninterested, to put it mildly, in any investigations directed against big business or big business's allies in the ruling Republican Party.

Under Stone the Justice Department was far more interested in avoiding criticism than in pursuing high-level political or economic crime, investigations which would spark just the sort of criticism Stone and Hoover wanted to avoid. But the question might be asked whether an obsessive concern for civil liberties might not finally smother effective law enforcement. An unintended consequence of the Bureau's reform during the twenties was that it abetted the government's turning a blind eye on the pervasive lawlessness in the financial community that would topple the economy at the end of the decade.

Hoover was directing a Bureau that had little to do. The political surveillance responsible for the expansion of the Bureau had been abolished. The Justice Department had withdrawn from the labor wars. The Republican administrations of Coolidge and Herbert Hoover were notably uninterested in aggressive law enforcement against political and economic crime. And so the imaginative and energetic Hoover transformed himself into—a reformer.

Historians have a word for the sort of earnest, white Anglo-Saxon Protestants who appeared during the late nineteenth and early twentieth centuries determined to end the rule of corrupt machines over local, state, and national government by substituting honest, efficient public administration guided by scientific research and staffed, not surprisingly, by people like themselves. The word was *progressive,* and it exactly fits J. Edgar Hoover during the 1920s, and for that matter, with decreasing conviction, perhaps, for the rest of his life.

The progressives' goal was to replace political influence with professional ability as qualification for public office. Their chosen instrument was the civil service examination. Not coincidentally, this put a premium on educational background rather than political connections and it ensured the triumph of

the old-stock elites over the immigrant masses and the political machines supported by their votes.

Hoover realized, however, that civil service gave employees a modicum of
protection from their superiors, and so he wanted nothing to do with it per se.
But by requiring a college education of his agents, he achieved the benefits of
civil service without accepting the limits it would impose on his total control
over his agents.

Since the public perception of an elite organization at the time was that it
should be exclusively white, Hoover's Bureau embraced that kind of exclusiv-
ity. There were a few black special agents in the Bureau when Hoover took over,
and these few continued to serve, in some instances for decades. But Hoover
hired almost no new black agents until near the end of his career, and then only
because of irresistible pressure from Attorney General Robert F. Kennedy. The
most noticeable blacks who worked in the Bureau under Hoover in later years
were his personal servants: his doorman and his drivers, since the employment
of black servants was a mark of gentility among white Washingtonians of
Hoover's background.

Progressives understood professionalism to mean the pursuit of efficiency
through the application of scientific standards to organizational activity. The
federal government should lead not by coercion but by example. It should encourage voluntary cooperation with the states by making itself indispensable
to them.

Hoover adopted that very strategy. By recruiting agents with professional
degrees and founding the FBI Academy, eventually located at Quantico, Virginia, Hoover made the Bureau the leading force in the professionalization of
American law enforcement. Beginning with the fingerprint collection that
soon became the signature of Bureau publicity, he also succeeded in making
the Bureau synonymous with scientific crime detection. He set up crime laboratories, and produced, for the first time, uniform national crime statistics. The
FBI now symbolized the dream (or illusion) that law enforcement could be
made a science, a vision that even today continues to inspire the Bureau and
fascinate the media and the public. "Before science," Hoover liked to say, "all
must fall, including the power of crime."

As a scientific manager, J. Edgar Hoover immediately adopted strategies for
improving his agents' efficiency. He reemphasized the preference, in place since
Stanley W. Finch but hardly enforced, that new agents have training in law or
accounting. In 1925 he set up a training school in the Bureau's New York field
office, but found that this was too much of a strain on the resources of his
shrinking Bureau, and so he substituted a policy of sending new agents to the

field, where their training was supervised by the special agents in charge. He soon realized, however, that the public expected members of a progressive force to have formal training from recognized educational institutions with a rigorous course of study, and so in November 1928 he reestablished a training school in Washington that eventually moved to Quantico, Virginia. In 1931 Agent Charles Appel urged Hoover to set up a crime lab within the Bureau, and, on November 24, 1932, the Technical Lab opened in a converted lounge, chosen because it had a sink. Appel was the entire staff.

The number of agents kept diminishing, but Hoover's system of controls over them expanded and was refined. The FBI's complex and elaborate system of supervision (onerous and counterproductive, it seemed to many disaffected agents) dates back to those early days. He devised controls that would let him know what every agent was doing every day, every hour, even every minute. In 1924 he established the Bureau's legendary system of regular field visits by the Inspection Division from Washington, which included a regular six-month inventory of Bureau property. On July 12, 1925, Hoover established a strict system of controls over the Bureau's files, permitting withdrawal only by agents working on a case, and then only with the approval of the special agent in charge and a written record of the approval. In September 1927 he began to equip each agent with a loose-leaf manual of instructions that covered standard investigatory and reporting procedures. This was revised in 1929 and again in July 1930.

When Hoover took over there were nine field divisions, each with a division superintendent. Each of these supervisors had complete authority over his field offices. On February 29, 1925, Hoover reorganized the Bureau, setting up six administrative divisions in Washington, each with responsibility for a specific class of investigation or administrative function. This put Washington in direct control over each special agent in charge, while Hoover oversaw the division heads.

■ ■ ■

Hoover's major accomplishment during the twenties was to turn himself and his Bureau into the symbols of police professionalism. He and his Bureau became famous and admired within the law enforcement community years before the general public heard of them. Hoover did this by managing to have the Bureau assume a role that already existed, as yet unfilled, but ready to be filled: leadership of the national movement for police professionalism. The law enforcement community, events would show, had already created this movement for the Bureau, and all but invited Hoover and his Bureau to take it over.

The movement to professionalize the police was a reaction to the sorry history of early law enforcement in the United States. From the earliest days, foreign observers had judged the United States to be an underpoliced—almost an unpoliced—country. In the opinion of some, that lack of policing had shaped the American national character in some unfortunate ways, breeding a casual attitude toward the law. But despite the obvious inadequacy of American law enforcement, few called for the centralization that was proving so effective in Europe and Canada. In fact, so strong was the tradition of local control that for a politician even to think about federalization of the police would have been political suicide—so no one did. When America thought about such things, it believed that centralization of law enforcement in the national government would spell death to local liberty and personal freedom. It made no difference that there was plenty of evidence to the contrary in London or Paris, where efficient, centralized law enforcement had, if anything, improved the police forces' respect for civil liberties.

Beginning in the 1890s, this decentralized, inefficient, and often corrupt American law enforcement system produced, in reaction, a movement to turn policing into a recognized profession. This drive became an important part of the progressive program. These reforms began at the local level, and then moved up to the state police forces, a sequence characteristic of the progressive movement. The progressives, in fact, referred to the states as the "laboratories" of government reform. Only after the police professionalism movement had evolved, and even matured, within local and state police forces did the FBI assume leadership of it.

The International Association of Chiefs of Police (IACP) was founded in 1893, and given its present name in 1902. It was by far the most important force in police professionalization. It called for civil service rules for police, uniform procedures for arresting fugitives on telegraphic notification, a uniform system of identification, and a Central Bureau of Identification. Its national meetings discussed the effect of technology on law enforcement, condemned torture and the third degree, and criticized entertainment's stock character of the comedy cop.

By the 1890s the progressives generally believed that the best way to achieve police professionalism was to adopt a military model of administration. The goal was to have a scientifically trained police professional in total control of a scientifically trained force. Under closer examination, however, this model allowed only the chief to act as a true professional—independent of political pressure, guided only by professional standards—while under him his officers' activities were controlled in minutest detail by departmental policy. The chief was the professional, while the force was a bureaucracy.

Police academies were an indispensable part of the professionalization movement. St. Louis and Cincinnati were the first cities to set up police training institutes. Berkeley, California, and New York City established theirs in 1908 and 1909. In 1916 the University of California at Berkeley began the first university-based police training program.

The IACP was quick to see the advantages of a fingerprint identification system over the then-accepted Bertillon system of collecting a complex series of skull and skeletal measurements. A demonstration of the new system at the 1904 IACP convention led the St. Louis Police Department to set up the country's first fingerprint bureau. As soon as the Bureau of Investigation was founded in 1908, the IACP began to lobby to have the Bureau assume management of the collection, which was a heavy financial burden on the association. A proposal for the Justice Department to take over the Bureau failed in Congress in 1922, but finally, in 1923, Attorney General Daugherty ordered the federal prison system's fingerprint collection at Leavenworth, Kansas, and the IACP fingerprint bureau records moved to the Justice Department.

The IACP, in fact, pioneered and developed almost all the innovations that became FBI trademarks. The IACP had begun to collect crime statistics in 1922 and in 1930 published a *Manual on Uniform Crime Reporting*. Hoover was a member of the IACP committee that set up these reporting standards. When the Bureau set up its National Academy in 1935 for training local police officers, it was with the full cooperation of the IACP. In 1916, August Vollmer, chief of the Berkeley, California, police force, set up the first crime detection laboratory employing a full-time criminologist. When Hoover set up the Bureau's first crime laboratory, perhaps the most important step in making the Bureau the national symbol of scientific law enforcement, he was once again adopting an innovation pioneered by local police forces.

In fact, when Hoover began to turn the Bureau into the symbol of police professionalism in the United States in the 1920s, August Vollmer was universally regarded as the leader, even the founder, of the police professionalization movement. Vollmer stressed the need for the police to cooperate with the community, but Vollmer's idea of professionalism meant the independence of the police from political influence, which in practice meant isolation from the community. In this sense, Vollmer's idea of professionalization meant an impersonal standard of police work, which makes close ties to the community difficult or impossible. This somewhat contradictory definition of police professionalism would be adopted by Hoover, putting him at odds with the rest of the profession when it began to pay more attention to the social and economic roots of crime in the 1960s and 1970s.

Hoover and the Bureau were actually latecomers to police professionalism. Nevertheless they emerged as leaders of a movement so clearly pioneered by innovators like August Vollmer and other progressive chiefs. But it was the Bureau, and not the IACP or one of the leading police departments, that finally emerged as the symbol of police professionalism.

Much of the credit belongs to Hoover, but chiefly for recognizing that *only* a federal law enforcement agency like his could give the professionalism movement what it needed. Weaving through the concerns expressed by the chiefs about the poor image of policing in the United States were complaints about the lack of prestige of the profession and the popular image of the police officer as comical, corrupt, and incompetent. Although the law enforcement community needed to improve its standing with the public, no individual police department had sufficient stature to improve the status of the profession, now that the image of the police was so thoroughly shaped by the national news and entertainment networks. Only a law enforcement agency on the national level could change the image of the police community. And so it was with relief and gratitude that the nation's police, and particularly the chiefs, welcomed Hoover's assumption of the mantle of leadership of the profession. They were quite willing to ignore the fact that the Bureau's scientific facilities—its labs in particular—were actually *less* advanced and capable than those of departments like Vollmer's. Hoover's success in taking over the leadership of police professionalism was due, essentially, to the police community's willingness to be led. There was a potential for leadership, and Hoover adroitly fit the Bureau into that role.

By the late 1920s, Hoover had emerged as the leading figure, in fact the symbol, of police professionalism in the United States. He had turned the Bureau into an indispensable resource for local police forces, providing them with the technical assistance they needed to carry out modern criminal investigations. He and his agents gave local police a model admired by the nation and they had become, as far as the law enforcement community was concerned, the public image of professional, scientific law enforcement.

Hoover's success in turning the Bureau into the symbol of professional law enforcement was the foundation for the FBI's even greater successes during the gangster era of the thirties and the national security era of the forties and fifties. But that scientific image subjected the Bureau to an impossible standard in the later decades of the century. The Bureau's failings in scientific crime detection and lapses in organization would be judged against the reputation Hoover created during the twenties and thirties, when it became a symbol of infallible and omnipotent law enforcement professionalism.

The Bureau spent the 1920s consolidating its position as leader of the

American law enforcement community. But the Bureau's retreat from politically sensitive investigations during that decade did not mean that it had lived down the bitter legacy of the Red Scare raids. Just because the Bureau did nothing to arouse the wrath of its enemies during the 1920s did not mean that those enemies had forgiven or forgotten.

After the Palmer Raids and the FBI's antiunion campaigns of the early twenties, the left's hatred of the Bureau had hardened into a basic fact of American political life. This anger toward the Bureau and Hoover stemmed not just from suspicion of the Bureau's motives in domestic surveillance, but also from a bitter determination to settle scores for injuries inflicted on radicals whose only fault, many felt, was fighting for justice. To the extent that the Bureau's effectiveness in law enforcement depended on public cooperation, after 1920 it had to contend with an articulate segment of American public opinion that saw the Bureau as its enemy as well as an enemy of civil rights and civil liberties.

The intensity of this hatred meant that the Bureau could mollify its enemies only by doing nothing that might anger them, which meant doing almost nothing at all. During the 1920s the Bureau veered from violent political controversy to seek a safe place where it could avoid any investigations that might raise political hackles. This strategy established a pattern for future occasions when it would again have to lay low after being laid low by scandal: a retreat into apolitical scientific crime detection, law enforcement professionalism, and ostentatious displays of agent ethics. But if the Bureau was doing nothing about political corruption, financial fraud, or, during the 1920s, American communism's cooperation with Soviet espionage, then nothing at all was being done about them.

The hostility toward the Bureau born during the 1920s was never going to completely disappear. Even in the best of times for the Bureau, its enemies would bide their time, pointing out the Bureau's failures and scoffing at its successes. And if the Bureau fell on hard times again, as it had in the twenties, through bad fortune or its own transgressions, that hostility could once again swell to a level that could prevent the Bureau from functioning at all. And then the Bureau might revert to the strategy of avoiding controversy, which had worked during the 1920s. Because the public might once again demand that the FBI do nothing, perhaps even at a moment when nothing but the Bureau's very best could save the nation.

FIVE

Hollywood (1933–1945)

SPECIAL AGENT James "Brick" Davis joined the Bureau of Investigation at an exciting moment in its history. The Bureau's hunts for the Midwestern bank robbers and kidnappers—Machine Gun Kelly, Pretty Boy Floyd, and John Dillinger—were turning J. Edgar Hoover's obscure little outfit into world-famous gangbusters, with a new name—the Federal Bureau of Investigation—and sensational new nickname—the G-men.

Davis had the law degree that was usual for a special agent in the Hoover-era Bureau. He also had a Ph.D. and a Phi Beta Kappa key, which were not so usual. His background was very unusual. He was a street tough from New York City, with an education financed by a racketeer with headquarters in a nightclub speakeasy where Davis's girlfriend was a dancer.

Before he joined the Bureau, Davis had been trying to make it as a lawyer, but in his part of New York, you either worked for the mob or you didn't work at all. Then one day he was rehearsing make-believe jury summations as his law school roommate—now a special agent—dropped in, and urged him to apply to the Bureau. He refused. When his friend was killed making an arrest, Davis changed his mind.

Davis's experience in the streets came in handy during new-agent training. His boxing instructor challenged Brick to put up his dukes, and Brick promptly knocked him out. At the target range (instructors explained that while agents could not yet carry guns, they were going to be ready "just in case") Brick turned out to be a crack shot. The martial arts were different. Putting his head down and bulling straight ahead nearly got him killed.

Normally, as a new agent, Brick would have soldiered away for years on routine cases, but his background got him sent to the Midwestern front in the Bureau's war against the bank robbery gangs. In Kansas City a team of special agents and local police had gotten ambushed escorting a gangster from Union Station. By coincidence that gangster was someone Brick had known back in New York. Headquarters decided Brick was the right man to find the killers.

In FBI lore that shootout was the "Kansas City Massacre," the start of the Bureau's war on crime in the thirties. The audacity of the gangsters' attack on federal agents shocked the nation. Congress asked the director what the Bureau needed to fight back. He responded:

> *The state police cannot combat these criminals . . . neither can city police! The law prevents them from following criminals across state lines! With the automobile and aeroplane, these gangs can get from one state to another in a few hours. The Department of Justice is handicapped! . . . A Federal agent can't carry a gun! He can't even make an arrest without getting a local warrant first! Gentlemen, . . . if you will back us by national laws with teeth in them . . . that cover the whole field of interstate crime, . . . that let us work to full effect with state police agencies, . . . these gangs will be wiped out.*

Congress asked him to be more specific: "Make bank robbery and kidnapping federal crimes," the director told them.

> *Make it a federal crime to kill a Governmental Agent . . . to flee across the State Line to escape arrest or to escape testifying as a witness. Arm Governmental Agents . . . and not just with revolvers! If these gangsters want to use machine guns—give the Special Agents machine guns, . . . shotguns . . . tear gas and everything else! This is war! Understand . . . I don't want to make them a group of quick-trigger men, but I do want the underworld to know that when a Special Agent draws his gun, he is ready and equipped to shoot to kill with the least possible waste of bullets!*

Congress gave him everything he wanted.

Brick learned from an old girlfriend that the gang was hiding out at a Wisconsin resort owned by the New York mobster who had sent Brick to law school. Davis and a squad of agents flew from Chicago to the Wisconsin resort, surrounded the lodge and began closing in. A dog barked and the gangsters opened fire. It was like something out of the movies. Brick's men lobbed tear gas into the building and the gangsters made a run for it, using Brick's old friend as a human shield. By the time the shooting was over, all but one of the gangsters were dead, among them Brick's gangster friend. Brick saw that his friend's hands were bound. For all he knew, his bullets had killed him. It was enough to make Brick want to quit the Bureau, but his bosses convinced him that he had to finish the job, to track down the one surviving gangster who was morally responsible for his friend's death.

Before Davis could catch him, though, the gangster killed the girl who had given Davis the tip about the gang's hideout. He also put a bullet in Davis and grabbed the sister of Brick's squad leader as a hostage. Brick staggered out of his hospital bed, killed the gangster (the last surviving public enemy), and rescued the girl. And married her.

Actually, Brick Davis's adventures were not just *like* something out of the movies, they *were* something out of the movies: the most important FBI film ever made, Warner Brothers' 1935 *G-Men,* starring James Cagney as Special Agent Brick Davis.

That movie not only reflected but also shaped a crucial moment in the history of the FBI. The Bureau was being transformed from an obscure government agency hardly known outside the law enforcement community to a fantastically popular symbol of national law enforcement—a symbol, in fact, of the nation itself.

Popularity of the kind the Bureau achieved between 1933 and 1935, during the first two years of Roosevelt's New Deal, has rarely been seen before or since. G-men were American heroes on the order of Sergeant York or Lindbergh or the Mercury astronauts. More remarkably, the Bureau's popularity from the thirties became institutionalized, providing the FBI with an unassailably heroic image that lasted until Hoover's death in 1972. It was an image largely responsible for Hoover's amazing ability to deflect, even demolish, any criticism of the Bureau's sensitive—and controversial—Cold War domestic intelligence operations. When the Bureau's reputation did collapse after Hoover's death, one reason the country turned so violently against the FBI when Hoover's abuses of his power were revealed may have been a sense of betrayal that a venerated national symbol had shamed itself and in doing so had shamed the nation. The Bureau's place in American history, in short, cannot be grasped without understanding how the Bureau went Hollywood during the thirties.

■ ■ ■

One of the Bureau officials most responsible for crafting the G-man image during the thirties, Assistant Director Louis B. Nichols, told me it was simply that "we did the job. We got the Dillingers and the Machine Gun Kellys." But nothing is that simple. In the scales of history, a few petty criminals, no matter how colorful, don't amount to very much. If the Bureau's gangbusting of the thirties had the hefty consequence of laying the foundation for the Bureau's power over the next three decades, something else must have made those cases so important.

The Depression had changed the way Americans thought about crime and criminals. Take the Brooklyn-born Al Capone. By the end of the twenties he was the unchallenged master of the Chicago rackets, controlling gambling, prostitution, drugs, and bootlegging, protecting his interests by thoroughly corrupting the Chicago press, police, and government.

It was certainly not true that Capone was universally admired, but there is no denying that he had become a popular celebrity during the twenties, thanks to Prohibition. "They say I violate the prohibition law," he would say. "Who doesn't?" Compared to the all-but-open corruption of the Prohibition Bureau, which tried to enforce the law, Capone seemed almost, well, honest.

Moralists lamented the rise of the gangster as a sorry sign of the times. With the country as rich and confident as it was during the twenties, it was hard to take those sermons very seriously. But then the Roaring Twenties whimpered to an end with the Black Thursday stock market crash of October 24, 1929, the country took a second look at the public enemy—and didn't like what it saw. Now the rise of underworld empires seemed a grim foreshadowing of a possible future for a beleaguered country.

During the early years of the Depression, the gangsters' contempt for the law seemed to be growing, and the law's ability to do anything about them was declining. Dutch Schultz's main rival for control of the New York City beer racket was Legs Diamond. After being cut, shot, and bombed by Schultz's boys, Diamond decided to take a European vacation. Country after country refused to admit him. The press pointed out that foreign governments could at least keep Diamond off their soil. American authorities seemed unable to put him in jail where he belonged.

In 1931, Vincent "Mad Dog" Coll, another racketeer trying to take over Schultz's business, ambushed members of Schultz's gang. In the crossfire four children were wounded, a five-year-old boy killed. Coll went on trial, but the state's case fell apart when prosecutors put a perjured witness on the stand. Coll walked away unconvicted and unpunished. His lawyer, Samuel Liebowitz, became the personification of the criminal "mouthpieces" who were making a mockery of the law. Dutch Schultz announced that if the law couldn't do the job, he would give Coll what he deserved. His men cornered Coll in a telephone booth and machine-gunned him to death. His gang also took care of Legs Diamond. An editorialist thought that gangland executions like Diamond's and

Coll's were "crime's most daring gestures, and fairly make the entire social fabric of the land tremble in anticipation of a possible extension of gang rule to wider and still wider areas of life." And then Hollywood began to turn out films that suggested Americans were also beginning to see crime as a preview of the future if the Depression continued to eat away at the nation's values.

The most powerful gangster picture of all combined the mythic power of the gangster formula with the raw energy of one of the most dynamic performers ever to appear on film, James Cagney. This was *Public Enemy,* in which Cagney, yes, the same Brick Davis who would win the crime wars in *G-Men,* played gangster Tommy Powers, the untamed criminal as the new American hero. Cagney played Tommy Powers as the classic American good-bad boy, Tom Sawyer with a snap-brim hat and a cigarette instead of a straw hat and a corncob pipe. Tom Sawyer was only a make-believe bad boy. Tommy Powers was the real thing—a thief, a bully . . . and a killer. He laughed at all the symbols of conventional morality like patriotism, education, and romance.

The formula in detective stories had always been crime, then punishment. In the early Depression the formula was just crime, followed by more crime. At the end of *Public Enemy* Tommy Powers dies, of course, as dramatic conventions far older than the movies decreed he must, but it is a triumph for the rule of the jungle, not the rule of law, since he is eliminated only by more powerful gangsters. Warner Brothers recognized how subversive the film was and tacked a nervous message to the film's final frames: "The end of Tom Powers is the end of every hoodlum. 'The Public Enemy' is not a man, it is not a character, it is a problem we all must face."

The Hoover administration was doing nothing to show that the government was facing up to the new challenge of crime. President Hoover, yielding to Chicago businessmen, did unleash the Treasury Department against Al Capone, and managed the not inconsiderable feat of putting him behind bars for good. But when Capone finally went to jail, the country was disgusted that it was only for income tax evasion.

The most discouraging demonstration of the government's inability to uphold the rule of law was the "Crime of the Century," the kidnapping of the infant son of Charles Lindbergh on March 1, 1932. Instead of taking charge of the investigation, President Hoover gave the country a lecture on states' rights and the constitutional limits on federal jurisdiction. The most he would do was make the Bureau available to local authorities if they asked for federal help. Attorney General William D. Mitchell was reluctant to offer even that, saying, "Although there is no development to suggest that the case is within federal jurisdiction, agents of the department will keep in close touch with state authorities on the chance that the perpetrators of the crime in this or in some other activity may have touched federal authority."

The administration disappointed the country again by saying that because of "budgetary limitations" the Justice Department was not able to endorse legislation that would make interstate kidnapping a federal crime, although Mitchell said he would not object if Congress decided to enact such a law. He even cautioned the public not to expect much from new federal laws. President Hoover explained that "every state has ample laws that cover such criminality. What is needed is the enforcement of those laws, and not new laws. Any suggestion of increasing Federal criminal laws in general is a reflection on the sovereignty and the standing of state government."

With Washington failing to provide leadership in the Lindbergh case, the whole country threw itself into the hunt for the kidnappers. Police everywhere claimed that they were pursuing leads. Civic groups sent out patrols. Flying clubs volunteered for the search. Editorials demanded that private crime-fighting forces be organized. Frank Loesch of the Chicago Crime Commission called for nationwide versions of Chicago's "Secret Six," a group of businessmen who financed anticrime measures. "You have to fight this business in a different way. Private individuals could band together to find out who is back of these rings. The organization should be perfected in each state and then organized into a national body." The *Washington Post* said, "The people must be their own law enforcement system or be subject to the crime enforcement system. So long as they fail to organize for the common defense, they are assisting the crime system to flourish and destroy all."

What was taking shape was a grassroots anticrime movement, at this point leaderless and disorganized, some of its proposals clearly hysterical. There were demands for the reinstitution of public whippings and hangings. Some called for the restoration of the old common law concept of outlawry, that a criminal was outside the protection of the law and could be hunted and killed by any citizen. There were even appeals for martial law.

But amid this clamor there was something of a consensus on three specific proposals. First, the public demanded new federal laws that would make the most abhorrent crimes, kidnapping in particular, federal offenses. Second, the public wanted new high-security prisons as a punishment for the new breed of public enemies. Finally, and most insistently, the public demanded a federal police force, based in Washington, that would bring the might of the entire country down on public enemies. The Lindbergh kidnapping, wrote the *Camden* (New Jersey) *Courier-Post*, "shows that America needs a system of state 'Scotland Yards' with a central organization at Washington." The *Philadelphia*

Record urged that the police systems of all the states be unified into "one incorruptible central agency [that] can supervise our national battle against organized crime." Only one thing would turn back the criminal assault, said Senator John J. Cochran of Missouri: "the fear of Uncle Sam." And once these measures were in place, the public demanded that they be harnessed into a coordinated war on crime led by the federal government.

Franklin D. Roosevelt won the presidency in 1932 unencumbered by any promises except a pledge to legalize beer and a vague promise of "action." Certainly he had no detailed plans to expand federal law enforcement or the Bureau.

Roosevelt's election actually seemed to be bad news for the Bureau, or at least for Hoover. FDR's choice for attorney general, Senator Tom Walsh of Montana, was known to have no use for Hoover. During the Teapot Dome scandals, Walsh had chaired an investigation of the Justice Department's misdeeds and he had locked horns with Hoover. Walsh had also defended his senatorial colleague from Montana, Burton Wheeler, against false charges by Attorney General Daugherty that Wheeler had illegally represented a constituent in federal court. During the trial he and Wheeler had both been shadowed by Bureau agents. Walsh believed the case against Wheeler had been a Bureau frame-up, and thought Hoover was as much to blame as Hoover's boss, William Burns. The press was even floating the names of possible replacements for Hoover.

But on March 2, Walsh expired in his Pullman car on the way to the inauguration. It was generally believed that the elderly senator, who had recently married a much younger bride, had succumbed to the rigors of the honeymoon. There was no time to give much thought to Walsh's replacement. Roosevelt had plans to shut down the nation's beleaguered banking system immediately after the March 4 inauguration ceremony. He had to have a legal opinion ready that he had the authority to do this, which meant he needed a nominee for attorney general in place on inauguration day. And so, on the advice of Secretary of State–designate Cordell Hull, he named Homer Stillé Cummings as a stand-in until he could decide on a permanent replacement for Walsh.

Cummings was a Roosevelt loyalist from Connecticut who worked as a floor manager for Roosevelt at the Democratic convention. He had already gotten his reward: governorship of the Philippines. But despite the lack of thought given to his nomination, he would prove to be one of Roosevelt's most successful appointments.

There was nothing in Cummings's or Roosevelt's backgrounds that hinted that under Cummings the Justice Department would become one of the New

Deal's most dynamic agencies. Roosevelt did have some crime-fighting credentials. He had served on a crime commission in New York during the twenties, and had urged the prosecution of New York City Mayor Jimmy Walker. But he had been more concerned with reforming some of the harsher features of the state's criminal code—and attacking political corruption—than crusading against crime. Cummings had been district attorney and mayor of Stamford, Connecticut, but had a reputation more as a civil libertarian than as a crime fighter. Nevertheless, beneath the political surface there was something that (in retrospect) made a New Deal crime crusade under Cummings almost inevitable: the grassroots anticrime movement.

Almost instinctively Cummings moved to take over leadership of that movement. Throughout the spring of 1933, he made himself available to any civic group dealing with the crime problem—the International Association of Chiefs of Police, the American Legion, the Daughters of the American Revolution. Anticrime rallies before Roosevelt's inauguration had been protests against the federal government's inactivity. Cummings's appearances now allied the New Deal with the call for federal action and demands for new laws, new federal police, and new prisons.

By the late spring of 1933, Cummings had taken his position at the head of the previously leaderless grassroots anticrime movement. It was now time to move beyond hints and suggestions to something concrete. Cummings needed to be able to point to something that could pass for the "super police force" he had been promising. His solution was to have Roosevelt sign an executive order on June 10 combining the Prohibition Bureau, the Bureau of Identification (the fingerprint files), and the Bureau of Investigation into a "new" Division of Investigation within the Justice Department. Since this would combine the Prohibition Bureau's 1,200 "dry agents" with Hoover's 326 special agents, he hoped it would entitle him to claim the new "Division" had achieved "super" status without any new outlay of funds. In addition, since Prohibition was obviously on the way out, the new division would solve the problem of what to do with the dry agents once the dry laws were repealed.

Who would run the new division had not yet been decided, so Cummings had the order dated to take effect two months later, on August 10. Hoover was adamantly opposed to any real merger between his Bureau and the Prohibition Bureau, which was widely and accurately considered to be hopelessly corrupt. (The Identification Bureau was already within Hoover's domain, and was not field operational, so it did not present any similar difficulties.) Hoover told Cummings that a merger would swamp the Bureau and undo "all the work we had done to make the bureau honest, sound, and efficient." He even promised to report to the new division head if Cummings kept the two Bureaus separate.

Cummings obviously wanted time to carefully consider his options, but events forced his hand. On June 17, 1933, Bureau agents taking bank robber Frank "Jelly" Nash to Leavenworth prison were ambushed at Kansas City's Union Station, the incident later dramatized in Cagney's *G-Men.* One of the agents (Raymond J. Caffrey) was killed, and two others wounded. Cummings reacted just as the grassroots anticrime movement expected—and as Hollywood would have scripted. He told reporters that he "accepted the murder of a Department of Justice agent among the victims as a challenge to the government." The country had been attacked by the "army of crime." The Kansas City Massacre, he said, was the underworld's "declaration of war" against the United States, and the United States would respond as it would to an enemy attack, with a war against crime.

For the rest of June and most of July, the merger of the three Justice Department bureaus into the new Division of Investigation not yet having been announced, Cummings kept the press guessing about the specifics of that declaration of war. He kept dropping phrases like a "national police force" and an "American Scotland Yard," which could mean anything from a federal takeover of the country's police system to a small flying squad of detectives to assist the local authorities. The national police force was probably more in keeping with what the public was imagining, but it was clearly out of the question, not only from a practical standpoint of managing a force of the size needed to police a continent, but also on constitutional and political grounds: A federal takeover of law enforcement would be impossible without rewriting the federal Constitution into a unitary system of government, which was not going to happen then or ever.

Far less grandiose in conception, the alternative of an "American Scotland Yard" to reinforce the efforts of local police had compelling advantages. It could be constructed without any new resources. Second, a specialized "Scotland Yard" with jurisdiction restricted to federal crimes would allow—if a way were found to add a "federal dimension" to what had been up until now strictly local offenses—the new federal investigators to cherry-pick crimes, focusing only on those that had captured the public imagination. Since the federal agents could concentrate overwhelming force on just a few crimes, they could almost certainly solve them. Cummings began to warm to this solution to his problem.

Then Oklahoma oilman Charles Urschel was snatched on July 23 while the Bureau was still trying to catch Caffrey's Kansas City killers, who the Bureau had concluded were Vernon C. Miller, Adam C. Richetti, and Charles "Pretty Boy" Floyd, though there remain persistent doubts about Floyd. Cummings gamely pronounced the Urschel kidnapping another battle in his new war on crime, and ordered his agents to solve it.

And so events had raised public interest in federal crime fighting to a fever pitch when Cummings finally unveiled plans for his long-promised "super police force." On July 30 he announced that the Prohibition Bureau's Major E. V. Dalrymple was out and a new "Division of Investigation" would be headed by none other than J. Edgar Hoover. To keep the dry agents from contaminating his men, Hoover set up a new Alcoholic Beverage Unit within the division, led by the Prohibition Bureau's second-in-command, John S. Hurley.

Cummings had actually done little more than rename the Bureau of Investigation a "Division." Theoretically this represented an upgrade within the Department of Justice's table of organization, but was hardly anything earth-shaking. But Cummings promised that this reorganization was the beginning of the coordinated anticrime program he would be unveiling shortly.

Then Cummings moved on to the next demand of the grassroots anticrime movement. He announced he was establishing a new "super" prison at a former Army prison in San Francisco Bay called Alcatraz. It would be an escape-proof jail where the new breed of super-criminals would be domiciled after capture by the new super-police. One of its first tenants, Cummings promised, would be Al Capone. Whatever its merits as a prison, Alcatraz was an immediate public relations success, instant folklore, the new symbol of the ultimate penalty short of death.

Meanwhile, out in Oklahoma, the Bureau was on its way to giving Cummings his first victory in the new crime war. Within a matter of hours after Urschel was kidnapped from his Oklahoma City home, the Bureau had a pretty good idea who had done it. Just before Urschel was snatched, Kathryn Kelly, wife of Midwest bandit George "Machine Gun" Kelly, had gone to two Forth Worth, Texas, detectives to see if they would help kidnap a wealthy Texas banker. The detectives turned her down and took their strange tale to the Bureau. Knowing this, the FBI made the Kellys their primary suspects when Urschel was kidnapped.

Almost all crimes, even FBI cases, are solved by informants and lucky breaks. A few days after the kidnapping the FBI got another one. Kathryn Kelly visited those same Fort Worth detectives again and asked them if they could find out if anyone suspected her and her husband in the Urschel case. Once again they reported the contact to the Bureau. That was enough for the Bureau to put the Kelly's Fort Worth house under surveillance. They also began watching Kathryn's mother's farm in Paradise, Texas, near Fort Worth.

Meanwhile, Urschel had been turned loose after his family had paid a $200,000 ransom to the Kellys. While in captivity Urschel had gathered so many clues that a mystery writer would have worried that he was making things too easy. The Bureau fitted them together in a textbook demonstration of the detective mind at work, but of course the scientific razzle-dazzle was somewhat redundant, since the Bureau's informants had already told them who they were after.

Urschel told the Bureau special agents that he had been blindfolded, but from noises and smells he was sure that the car had passed through two oil fields, the first an hour after his kidnapping, the second half an hour later. He had then been taken into what he thought was a garage, where he was transferred from a Chevrolet to a seven-year-old Cadillac or Buick. After another three-hour drive they stopped at a gas station, where he heard the woman attendant tell the kidnappers, "The crops around here are burned up, although we may make some broom corn." Urschel also reported that they finally reached a farm where he could hear barnyard animals. There the two men who had kidnapped him were joined by a man and a woman who talked with the others for a short time and then left. He was able to report that on the farm there were chickens, hogs, and four milk cows. He had drunk water with a rusty taste, drawn from a well with a noisy crank and pulley. He had also noted that a plane passed over the farm every morning at nine forty-five and in the evening at five forty-five, except for Sunday, July 30, when it had rained.

The Bureau determined that the most valuable clues were the planes Urschel had heard overhead, since agents were quickly able to determine that Urschel's schedule fit that of the Fort Worth–Amarillo route, and that the times Urschel had given them would have placed the planes exactly over Paradise, Texas. The diversion of the planes on Sunday due to rain also pointed to Paradise. Following the leads provided by the Forth Worth detectives, the Bureau already knew that Kathryn Kelly's mother owned a farm in that town. On August 12 the Bureau raided the farm, arresting Harvey Bailey, an escapee from a Kansas state prison who was also wanted in connection with the Kansas City Massacre. Some of the ransom money was recovered, as was a machine gun that had been bought in Fort Worth for Bailey by Kathryn Kelly.

Agents took Urschel to the farm, where he was able to point out things he had described to the Bureau during his interrogation. Kathryn's mother, her current husband, and his son admitted their role in the kidnapping and told them that the other kidnappers were Albert Bates and George Kelly. Bates was arrested on August 12 in Denver, Colorado, with more of the ransom money on his person. George and Kathryn escaped, but all those in custody, twelve in all, went on trial and on September 30, seven of them, including Bates and Bailey and the Kelly in-laws, were convicted of a federal kidnapping conspiracy.

Meanwhile the Bureau was still hunting for Kelly, who had been making threats against Urschel and against Assistant Attorney General Joseph B. Keenan, who was arguing the gangster cases for the government. On September 23, responding to a tip that Kelly and his wife were in Memphis, Tennessee, Bureau agents from the Birmingham, Alabama, field office conducted a morning raid, accompanied by Memphis police. According to some accounts, a "sheepish" Kelly woke up, grinned, and told the officers, "Okay, boys, I've been waiting for you all night." But the story popularized by the Bureau and its publicists claimed that when the police and special agents entered, Kelly panicked and shouted "Don't shoot, G-men, don't shoot." That, the story goes, was how FBI agents got their name as well as their man.

The grassroots anticrime movement wanted not just a new super-police force, or new super-prisons; it also wanted new (super?) laws. Over the next year Cummings would skillfully use another Bureau case, the most famous in its history, to push an ambitious new anticrime program through Congress.

John Dillinger—whose death mask would be the featured exhibit on the FBI Headquarters tour as long as J. Edgar Hoover was director—was born in 1903, son of an Indianapolis grocer. After a semester of high school he began to crave excitement. He joined the Navy, deserted, and got married. In September 1924 the twenty-one-year-old Dillinger teamed up with the umpire of a local baseball league to rob a grocery store in Mooresville, Indiana. They panicked, beat up the grocer, and ran off without a cent. Dillinger was captured almost immediately. He believed a prosecutor's promise of leniency if he confessed. Instead he got ten to twenty years and wound up serving nine of them. (The umpire hired a lawyer, was tried before a different judge, and got a two-year sentence.)

In jail Dillinger met professional bank robbers Harry Pierpont and Homer Van Meter. He had found his calling. When his new friends were shifted to the Michigan City, Indiana, jail, he got a transfer with them, and there met two more members of his future gang, John Hamilton and Charles Makley. Pierpont was the smartest and the most experienced; he was the leader, and spun them tales of the banks they could rob when they got out.

It was Dillinger who got them out. His behavior suddenly improved and the parole board was impressed. They released him on May 22, 1933. He robbed a couple of banks, bought some guns, and threw them to his friends over the wall of the jail, but another inmate found them and turned them over to the warden. He packed the next batch of guns into barrels of thread addressed to the prison shirt factory, and this time they made their way to Pierpont, who armed the rest of the gang and broke out on September 26, 1933. By this time Dillinger was behind bars again, picked up while visiting a girlfriend. On October 12 the gang broke into the Lima, Ohio, jail, killed the sheriff, and set Dillinger free.

Then they began to rob banks, and the way they robbed them intrigued the public. Mostly it was Dillinger: jaunty white boater on his head, wise-guy quips to customers and tellers, and a signature leap over the tellers' barrier, even if there was an open gate nearby. Before long the detective pulps were stuffing their pages with the exploits of the Dillinger gang. They were being compared to Jesse and Frank James's gang, a comparison meant as a compliment both ways. By December 1933 both Chicago and Indiana had special "Dillinger squads" working the case.

Dillinger's original run didn't last long. Tucson fireman William Benedict recognized Dillinger from a photograph in *True Detective* magazine, and tipped off the police, who arrested him. Pierpont was sent to Ohio, where he was executed for the death of the sheriff during the Lima jailbreak. Dillinger was packed off to Indiana to face murder charges for killing a policeman during an East Chicago bank job.

Already famous, Dillinger was about to become a legend. Dillinger's arrival turned the Crown Point, Indiana, jail into a media madhouse. The sheriff, a woman named Lillian Holley, obliged the press by providing what turned out to be a photo op for the ages: Prosecutor Robert Eskill, his arm wrapped in comradely fashion around the shoulders of the man he fondly expected to execute, Dillinger's elbow resting casually on Eskill, Eskill leering delightedly at Sheriff Holley, who is nursing her own smug expression of self-satisfaction. And Dillinger, in shirtsleeves and a vest, a sardonic grin teasing at his lips, with his right hand on Eskill's shoulder and his forefinger extended, thumb straight up, fingers curled around what?—an imaginary pistol? That night, producing a wooden gun carved from a broken washboard, Dillinger bluffed his guards into releasing him, and made his getaway in Sheriff Holley's car.

The country—and much of the world—went Dillinger-crazy and began seeing him everywhere—Chicago, Omaha, New York, Montreal, Mexico, even England, where an innkeeper listened to the "strange slang" of some American students on their way to Oxford and notified the police, "I have Dillinger here. His whole gang."

On March 6, Dillinger, now with a new gang, pulled off a bank robbery in

Sioux Falls, South Dakota, and it was a beauty. Dillinger sent gangster John Hamilton ahead to tell residents he was a Hollywood producer and was going to shoot a gangster movie right there tomorrow. The next day witnesses saw a "cast of gangsters" hold the police at gunpoint while the rest of the cast looted the bank and raced away. Dillinger had made fools of the police again.

But the FBI, fresh from its triumph in the Machine Gun Kelly case, had now joined the hunt. In his getaway from Crown Point, Dillinger had driven Sheriff Holley's car across the state line into Illinois, a violation of the 1919 Dyer Act. The stakes were high. Attorney General Cummings pointed to Dillinger's escape as a reason Congress should pass the attorney general's Twelve Point Anticrime Program he had submitted March 20. Cummings proposed making federal crimes out of the murder of federal agents, robberies of banks belonging to the Federal Reserve System, and interstate racketeering, and would strengthen the Lindbergh law. As the Dillinger hunt proceeded, Cummings added measures to arm FBI agents (without having to submit to local firearms laws) and let them make arrests without relying on local police.

Meanwhile the real Dillinger was not being as cooperative as the gangsters in Cagney's *G-Men*. Two agents trapped him in a St. Paul, Minnesota, apartment, but he slipped out a rear door. Worse was to follow. On April 22 the special agent in charge of the Chicago office, Melvin Purvis, got a tip that the elusive outlaw was holed up at a rural resort in Wisconsin called Little Bohemia. He filled a chartered plane with agents and took off for Wisconsin, where he rendezvoused with another squad of agents under Assistant Director Hugh Clegg flown in from St. Paul. In Washington Hoover summoned newsmen to headquarters and informed them Dillinger was trapped.

Purvis and Clegg, to preserve the element of surprise, decided to raid the resort in the middle of the night as soon as they arrived, without any chance to reconnoiter. As they blundered through the trees and underbrush, the agents roused the dogs. Dillinger's men heard the barking and opened fire. This wasn't the movies. Agents and gangsters were firing blindly, and a hotel guest died in the crossfire. A new member of Dillinger's gang, Baby Face Nelson, ran into two agents and killed one of them. Dillinger and the entire gang except for some of their girls had gotten away again.

There were public demands that Hoover be fired, Purvis as well. But Cummings was savvy enough to argue that the fiasco proved the need for his Anticrime Program, and he raised the ante by demanding funds for two hundred more agents (that would make six hundred in all), armored cars, and planes. The chairman of the House Judiciary Committee said that although the bills violated states' rights, "a wrath like that which kindled the frontier when the vigilantes cleaned out the gunmen is sweeping America" and these laws were needed to "make another Dillinger impossible." On May 19, with Cummings and Hoover at his side, President Roosevelt signed six of the bills into law, calling on the public to join the war on the underworld. More bills would follow. "Law enforcement and gangster extermination," he said, "cannot be made completely effective so long as a substantial part of the public looks with tolerance upon known criminals . . . or applauds efforts to romanticize crime. Federal men are constantly facing machine gun fire in the pursuit of gangsters."

The FBI's hunt for Dillinger ended in a showdown as much a part of American legend as the gunfight at the O.K. Corral or Pat Garrett's shooting of Billy the Kid. On July 21, 1934, an East Chicago, Indiana, detective brought the famous "Woman in Red," brothel keeper Anna Sage, to see Melvin Purvis. In exchange for a reward and help at her deportation hearings, she would deliver Dillinger. She was going to the movies with Dillinger and his girlfriend the next night. She would call Purvis when she knew where they were going.

The next night the call came through: It would be either at Chicago's Biograph or the Marbro. Purvis called his men together and told them, "if . . . we locate him and he makes his escape it will be a disgrace to our Bureau." Inspector Sam Cowley led one squad to the Marbro. Purvis took another to the Biograph, where he spotted Sage, Dillinger, and the other woman entering to see Clark Gable in *Manhattan Melodrama*.

While Hoover paced the floor in his home behind the Capitol in Washington following developments by telephone, Purvis entered the theater to see if he could spot Dillinger, but he could not. He positioned his men to cover all angles of the entrance. At 10:30 the movie let out. Purvis spotted Dillinger and signaled with his cigar to his men. Purvis walked up behind Dillinger and said, "OK, Johnnie, drop your gun." Dillinger ran toward an alley, his hand digging in his pocket for his pistol. The agents opened fire and in a split second the most famous outlaw in American history lay dead in a spreading pool of blood, which souvenir collectors soaked up with their handkerchiefs.

The Bureau had been on the verge of being laughed back into the obscurity from which it had emerged. Now it was the talk of the country, its agents national idols. The country couldn't get enough of the FBI. But what kind of FBI? The public and the press wanted to talk only about "Little Mel" Purvis, hailed as "the man who got Dillinger," so would it be Melvin Purvis's FBI? Or would it be Homer Cummings's, the attorney general the *Washington Post* was calling "the superpoliceman for [the] nation"?

Despite the initial prominence of Purvis and Cummings in the Dillinger case, the FBI that would emerge streaming a trail of glory would not be a Bureau of ace agents like Purvis, nor would it be a Bureau subordinate to the greater splendor of Cummings's Justice Department or Roosevelt's New Deal. It would be J. Edgar Hoover's FBI, a well-oiled machine of faceless cogs except for one bulldog countenance, that of J. Edgar Hoover. Quite a feat. How did Hoover pull it off?

Getting rid of Purvis was the easy part. The days following Dillinger's death found Hoover chasing Purvis to get in front of the cameras. A widely circulated picture showed a self-possessed Purvis striding along, Hoover reaching over to help carry his briefcase. Cummings, too, made sure he got his share of photos with Purvis.

Purvis's reputation continued to grow during the next few months. In October, Purvis tracked Pretty Boy Floyd down and killed him. "AND AGAIN MELVIN PURVIS TRIUMPHS," ran the headlines. Next Purvis set his sights on Baby Face Nelson, who had already killed an agent in the Little Bohemia shootout. As the agents closed in, Nelson killed Special Agent Herman Hollis and mortally wounded Purvis's partner in the Dillinger hunt, Sam Cowley, who now headed a roving public enemy squad. Purvis got an identification of Nelson from the dying Cowley, and announced to the press he had taken "an oath in Cowley's blood" to get him. "If it's the last thing I do, I'll get Baby Face Nelson." In Washington, Hoover and Cummings edged into the act by issuing a "shoot on sight order," but within a few hours Nelson was found, dead, mortally wounded in the fight with Hollis and Cowley. Hoover had had enough of Purvis's grandstanding. He pulled Purvis off the public enemies cases, and sent Inspector Hugh Clegg to take over the gangster squad.

Purvis was still enormously popular with the public, but Hoover acted quickly to destroy him within the Bureau. He flooded Purvis's Chicago field office with inspectors, who wrote him up for violating regulations. These rules were so numerous (and so difficult for an agent to obey if he had anything else to do) that, according to Bureau legend, inspectors would ask their bosses how many violations they were supposed to find before they left Washington.

The grass outside the Bureau began to look a lot greener to Purvis, since he was being begged to lend his name to product endorsements, and to sell his charisma to show business. During the summer of 1935 Purvis finally resigned to write a memoir, *American Agent,* and then left for Hollywood. He was hired to head the "Post Toasties Law and Order Patrol" and to be the voice of an unofficial radio adventure, *Top Secrets of the FBI,* where he was introduced as "the man who got Dillinger."

It became Bureau policy that Purvis was a nonperson. Bureau publicists insisted that it had been Sam Cowley, not Purvis, who had led the hunt for

Dillinger. Hoover's publicity chief Louis B. Nichols told me that "Purvis was doing a lot of free-wheeling on his own and he was in water over his head. Sam Cowley was the guy who actually handled the Dillinger case and Purvis was a figurehead." For the rest of Purvis's life, the Bureau quietly sabotaged his efforts to build a second career either in entertainment or in the security field. Even after his death, the Bureau insisted that as a price for its cooperation the entertainment industry either omit Purvis from the Dillinger story or make it clear that Sam Cowley was in charge. When Purvis committed suicide in 1960 with his Bureau revolver, Hoover's executive council debated and then rejected the idea of sending a letter to the widow. The Purvis family telegraphed Hoover, "We are honored that you ignored Melvin's death. Your jealousy hurt him very much, but until the end I think he loved you." But Hoover certainly didn't love him.

Meanwhile Hoover and his publicists, principally Louis B. Nichols, who headed what would be known as the Crime Records Division, the Bureau's public relations outfit, began working with a number of sympathetic journalists to put a special Bureau spin on the great FBI cases. The two reporters who did the most at the time to create the Bureau legend were Rex Collier and Courtney Ryley Cooper.

When I talked to Rex Collier in the mid-1970s, he remembered meeting Hoover for the first time in 1929, when Collier headed a delegation of Justice Department reporters to complain to Hoover that a Bureau spokesman had misled the press about a murder case in the District of Columbia. Collier told Hoover that by helping reporters write their stories instead of making problems for them, he could ensure favorable treatment of the Bureau. The two became fast friends, and their relationship paid off, professionally for Collier and politically for Hoover.

It was Collier who first put a headquarters stamp on the Dillinger story. Since he was based in Washington, Collier needed a new lead on the Dillinger case that would make his stories fresher, more insightful, and more comprehensive than the stories datelined from Chicago. His solution was a formula— the "FBI formula" (the Bureau would finally be renamed the "Federal Bureau of Investigation" in 1935)—which said the *real* story in every FBI case was that the entire FBI organization, fueled by science and teamwork, coordinated and led by J. Edgar Hoover, and *never* an individual agent, was the true hero in every FBI case. With that Collier established the pattern all Bureau-approved stories about its cases would follow forever after.

The formula was unveiled in a series of syndicated pieces that started running on July 26, 1934. As Collier told the story, "Hoover himself had directed the nationwide search [for Dillinger] by long-distance telephone from his office at the Department of Justice." According to Collier, the FBI was so omnipotent and omniscient that once it entered a case, success was inevitable. The FBI's scientific crime-fighting skills were so highly evolved that once the decision was made (by Hoover) for the FBI to get Dillinger, he was as good as dead. It didn't matter which agent had actually gotten Dillinger—in fact, it was even irrelevant which clue had led to his capture. If one clue had not materialized, the FBI's scientific methods would have turned up another.

By that standard, the Lady in Red was really not all that important in the FBI version of the Dillinger case. Anna Sage was an embarrassment to Hoover since she seemed to underscore the importance of old-fashioned detective work by individual investigators with years of experience and personal connections in the underworld and the law enforcement community. According to Collier's scenario—one which he followed in a radio show and a comic strip—if Sage had not turned up, another clue would have, produced by FBI scientific techniques such as Bureau artists' impressions of what Dillinger would look like after his plastic surgery. According to Collier, the real break in the case came when Dillinger stole Sheriff Holley's car, since until that time, Hoover's Bureau had been waiting impatiently for Dillinger "to knock the chip off their shoulders by violating some federal law." According to Collier, that had been Dillinger's great fear: "Dillinger always had a wholesome respect for the G-men—those college-bred agents marshaled by J. Edgar Hoover into the government's far-flung undercover agency. The federals . . . were not open to 'propositions,' they used brains as well as brawn, and state lines meant nothing to them. And most important of all, they never gave up on a case."

A year later, the hottest radio producer of the day, Phillips H. Lord, got Hoover's approval for a 1935 FBI adventure series called *G-Men*, with Rex Collier forced on Lord as a collaborator as the price for Bureau cooperation. The two writers invented a new solution to the Dillinger case. In Collier and Lord's version, there was no Lady in Red. The break came when agents in Chicago found a fingerprint that scientists at the Washington headquarters identified as being from one of Dillinger's girlfriend's. Sam Cowley—the designated hero—ordered agents to follow her to her room. They searched it, and found movie ticket stubs, which gave Cowley the idea of watching the movie theaters, after briefing his men—using a (then) high-tech slide show—about how Dillinger would look after plastic surgery. Their first draft of the shootout at the Biograph did not even include Purvis, but perhaps because Purvis, or at least his cigar, was such a central element of the Dillinger story, Collier and Lord did let Cowley say, "I just put Nellis [that is, Purvis] up against the door to smoke a cigar. The only way to identify Dillinger is by the back of his head—and being by the door, Nellis will get the first look. As soon as he sees him, he will lower his cigar." Then: "Nellis has spotted Dillinger. See—he has lowered his cigar . . . Watch him . . . he's looking around . . . he's wise something is up . . . He's got his gun—duck." A yell. A shot, and Cowley walks over to the corpse: "Dillinger's dead—He had it coming to him." The announcer signed off,

> *The Chevrolet Motor Company offers this series of radio programs in the hope of extending entertaining knowledge about the work of the Federal Bureau of Investigation of the Department of Justice and in the belief that it may increase by spreading that knowledge, the effectiveness of this arm of the federal government service. England has its Scotland Yard, Canada its Northwest Mounties, but never has there been a crime detection organization to compare with that of our own G-men . . . Crime doesn't pay—the G-men never give up the hunt.*

Courtney Ryley Cooper may have been even more important than Collier in creating the FBI formula. Cooper was a flamboyant crime reporter from Kansas City sent by *American Magazine* to Washington in the summer of 1933 to see if there was a story in Homer Cummings's Justice Department. By the time Cooper had finished, he had become J. Edgar Hoover's informal public relations partner. Cooper wrote twenty-four stories about the Bureau between 1933 and 1940, all but one in *American Magazine,* under either his own name or Hoover's. He wrote three books about the Bureau: *Ten Thousand Public Enemies* (1935), *Here's to Crime* (1937), and *Persons in Hiding* (1938; under Hoover's name). He also wrote the scripts for four movies: *Persons in Hiding* (1939), *Undercover Doctor* (1939), *Parole Fixer* (1940), and *Queen of the Mob* (1940), all billed as based on "Hoover's" *Persons in Hiding.*

Behind each of Cooper's individual stories was his big story, and, remarkably, that story in effect became the Bureau's strategic plan for crime fighting as well as publicity for the rest of Hoover's days. Cooper told his readers that Hoover's FBI, through the power of its leadership and example, was turning the country's fragmented, disorganized, untrained, and corrupt police forces into a cohesive, professional, and modern law enforcement system. In Cooper's stories, every FBI case was a test of strength between the legions of crime and a newly invigorated criminal justice system guided by the spirit and intelligence of J. Edgar Hoover. Hoover's FBI agent was a new kind of American hero, one who was "not an individual. Every officer of the Bureau of Investigation represented the full power of American Justice in 'getting his man.' "

Throughout 1933 and 1934 Cooper's stories about the Bureau appeared regularly in *American Magazine,* some with Hoover listed as author, although Cooper did all the writing. Early in 1935 Cooper tied them all together in *Ten Thousand Public Enemies,* the first important book ever written about the FBI.

Ten Thousand Public Enemies took the time-tested formula of true-crime stories and manipulated it into what was, for all intents and purposes, a plan of action for the post-Dillinger FBI. Cooper painted a portrait of the FBI as a modern, irresistible crime detection machine, an army of expert scientific investigators gathering evidence for evaluation by the most advanced crime laboratories in the world, a law enforcement agency led by "the most feared man the underworld has ever known," J. Edgar Hoover. Along the way, Cooper provided an analysis of the crime problem confronting the United States in a way that reinvented the FBI's mission.

Historically, the kind of crime that led to the birth of the FBI in 1908 had been unchecked political corruption at the highest levels of the American government, financial lawlessness in the wealthiest American corporations, and a few years later, the somewhat illusory challenge of international organized crime in the form of white-slave rings.

According to Cooper, the real crime problem that should concern the FBI was not at the highest levels of American society, but at the lowest. Instead of those top-level "crimes against the United States," Cooper pointed the Bureau toward "the roots of crime," on the local level, since he said crime

> thrives because it has a foundation . . . composed of the fences, the bond sales-men, the doctors, the lawyers, the merchants, the automobile salesmen, the women confederates, the hideout owners, and a hundred and one other forms of a supporting background which lives on crime while crime thrives upon it.

As for the notion that the FBI, at the pinnacle of American law enforcement, should concentrate on the highest levels of crime, Cooper turned it on its head:

> Organized crime, as imagined by the average person, with a super criminal at its head, and underlings taking orders, is largely a myth. . . . [T]he American citizen seems to possess a childlike faith in the theory that all crime is run by a guiding genius, and that if the brains of a plot be put in prison, then the problem of law enforcement is solved. The view is idiotic.

In Cooper's scheme, when the FBI entered a case, it served two obvious functions, and one less obvious. First, its entry exposed a failure of the local police and local authorities, since the FBI had to step in to mop up their messes.

Second, FBI investigations provided local police with an example of how professional crime fighting was really done.

Third, by publicizing its gangbusting campaigns, the Bureau was also proclaiming to Americans that the crimes that should concern them—and therefore the FBI—were those familiar crimes against persons and property. Hardly anyone noticed that this was a devolution in the Bureau's responsibilities: Gone was the Bureau's original mission of confronting crimes that threatened the nation in the upper reaches of government and the economy. Now the Bureau measured its performance by its success in killing or capturing those ordinary criminals designated—generally by the media—as public enemies.

Cooper provided a justification for exactly the course Hoover and the Bureau had been following since Harlan F. Stone's reforms in 1924. The Bureau, Cooper argued, should be responsible for facilities that were beyond the capability of any local force, such as fingerprint files and crime labs. The FBI should provide statistical services to help local police understand their problems in the context of the national crime situation, and should direct nationwide manhunts once a criminal had escaped local jurisdiction. But most of all, Hoover's Bureau should hold itself up as an example and inspiration for the American law enforcement community.

The FBI would provide national leadership for local law enforcement, and would help it out in big cases (though local police would complain that the cooperation ran only in one direction, that they gave and the Bureau took). Part of the bargain was that the FBI would not seek authority to investigate the local police, although Hoover would never stop preaching against police corruption. That was because the Bureau's prestige, and Hoover's security, depended on the FBI's alliance with the local police both on the grassroots level and through the International Association of Chiefs of Police. And so under Hoover the Bureau avoided doing anything to upset the police community that provided him with professional and political support.

This notion of the Bureau's leadership did not merely justify FBI publicity, but made it essential. America's ultimate weapon against crime was the FBI's image as a model for American law enforcement, a force for reforming it, and an engine for generating public support for the police. Since the FBI's ultimate role was to lead the American war against crime, the Bureau was doing its job only when it was in the news, when it was making headlines.

■ ■ ■

What happened next ensured that the FBI would be in the headlines even when it was not solving big cases. It went to Hollywood.

Ever since the film industry began, producers had been defending themselves against efforts to censor the industry. Each time the public—or, more accurately, pressure groups—raised demands that the government step in to do something about Hollywood's glorification of sex and violence, the industry had set up a sham machinery for self-regulation. In 1921 the studios had set up Will Hays's Motion Picture Producers and Distributors Association of America censorship office, and in 1927, responding to another wave of indignation over objectionable movies, Hays had issued a list of thirty-eight "don'ts" and "be carefuls" that were supposed to clean up Hollywood's act. In 1930 the Catholic bishops pressured the industry to write a code of ethics for the movies, the Motion Picture Production Code, and to appoint a Catholic to administer it. But for the filmmakers, "the code and the Hays office were tidy bits of camouflage behind which they could continue to do what they wished," and what they particularly wished was to be allowed to continue to make the gangster movies that had been some of their most profitable products since 1930.

Until 1933 there had been no scientific research that could be called on to buttress the conventional wisdom that sex and crime in the movies must have something to do with the apparent collapse of national values. But in 1933 twelve volumes of studies on the impact of movies, commissioned by a research foundation, were published, and two of these, Herbert Blumer and Philip Hauser's *Movies, Delinquency, and Crime* and Henry James Forman's *Our Movie Made Children,* gave Hollywood's enemies exactly the ammunition they needed. Armed with these studies, two influential groups mounted separate campaigns to reform Hollywood: the Roman Catholic bishops and the International Association of Chiefs of Police.

In April 1934 the bishops began their campaign to clean up the movies by founding the Legion of Decency. Millions of Catholics would take an oath at Mass that

> *I shall do all that I can to arouse public opinion against the portrayal of vice as a normal condition of affairs and against presenting criminals of any class as heroes and heroines, presenting their filthy philosophy of life as something acceptable to men and women.*

With this Catholics pledged to boycott films condemned by the legion.

Other religious and civic groups rushed to support the bishops in their drive. The producers surrendered with surprising speed and agreed to abide by the 1930 Code, which they had been ignoring, and to place themselves under a censor, Joseph I. Breen, who had authority to demand changes in scripts and in production that violated the Code. Some of these provisions were so specific that it was clear Hollywood would find it difficult to get gangster films past the censors: "The intent of the Code is . . . to insure above all that crime will be shown to be wrong and that the criminal life will be loathed and that the law will at all times prevail." If that were not enough to gut the gangster movies, the Code also outlawed the use of firearms. The "flaunting of weapons by gangsters and other criminals" was forbidden, and machine guns were completely banned: "There must be no display, at any time, of machine guns, sub-machine guns, or other weapons generally classified as illegal, in the hands of gangsters or other criminals." The police could not be shown dying at the hands of criminals, there could be no more "wholesale slaughter of human beings," nor could there be battles between rival criminal gangs. There could be no more kidnapping, details of crimes could not be shown, and revenge, the chief motivation of gangster films, was specifically banned: "revenge in modern times shall not be justified."

When the studios vowed to abide by the Code late in 1934, the gangster movie was dead.

But Hollywood is nothing if not resourceful. There had been a second influential group pushing for an end to the gangster film, and by appealing to their interests, which were quite different from the bishops', the studios found a loophole that let them produce one last wave of gangster films.

In their 1934 convention, the chiefs of police had also denounced the gangster films, but their wrath was directed mainly at the movies' contemptuous attitude toward the police. The chiefs instructed a committee to go to Hollywood to ensure that "the screen should not be contributory to crime and, second, that the treatment of police characters and stories on the screen should be handled in a true light." When they arrived in Hollywood, the chiefs found the studios understanding—perhaps even suspiciously understanding—of their concerns. Had movies done damage to the image of the police? Well, then, maybe the movies could make amends. If the old gangster pictures had hurt the police, how about some new ones to repair the police's public image? As a sample of what they had in mind, MGM put together a series of short subjects called *Crime Does Not Pay*. The first episode was called *Buried Loot*. Its announcer, the MGM Reporter, began by informing the audience that he was "a man with a message . . . the message that crime does not pay. You can't beat the law. The cards are stacked against you."

Buried Loot, the first of two dozen installments, was shown to the chiefs as an example of what the studios could do. But the chiefs would have to let the studios have a short exemption from the Code's anti-gangster-movie provisions for the specific purpose of making anti-gangster movies.

The chiefs were enthusiastic. The committee chairman reported that he had been

> *agreeably surprised to find that the industry has gone much further in these regards than I had suspected. They have not been satisfied with a negative attitude but are keying all crime stories to emphasize the lesson that crime does not pay . . . The details and Code principles used in this attempt are exhaustive and, in my opinion, highly effective.*

Hollywood's gamble was that if it created a new type of gangster movie focusing on the exploits of idealized and heroic cops, the law enforcement profession's applause would drown out protests of critics outside law enforcement, like the bishops. And the hero the studios chose to lead their breakout from the confinement of the Code was the G-man.

The reputation of the FBI was now so high within the law enforcement community that the chiefs were more than happy to see Hollywood use the G-man as an idealized symbol of all law enforcement. It was just what the police wanted. The chiefs later bragged that the IACP had "brought about a definite change in the sentiment induced by the movies. Gangster pictures, with sentiment definitely in favor of the criminal, were replaced by the 'G' men pictures which induced the public to applaud the efforts of the police."

In all, eight movies glorifying the FBI came out in 1935, with *G-Men* followed by *Public Enemy's Wife; Public Hero Number One; Whipsaw; Mary Burns, Fugitive; Let 'Em Have It;* and *Show Them No Mercy.* The films were advertised as weapons in the patriotic war on crime. Ad campaigns encouraged the public to "SEE UNCLE SAM DRAW HIS GUNS TO HALT THE MARCH OF CRIME." An ad for *Public Hero Number One* had a picture of its star, Pat O'Brien, shaking hands with the real Public Hero Number One, J. Edgar Hoover. Publicity for the G-men pictures explicitly stated that by buying a ticket, the moviegoer was somehow supporting the FBI, the police, and the country in their war on crime: At some showings fingerprinting equipment was set up in the lobby, with audience members encouraged to contribute their prints to police files.

But all good things, even something so good for Hollywood and the FBI, must come to an end. In September 1935, after a complaint from the British Board of Censors, the Production Code office decided enough was enough and notified the studios that "crime stories are not to be approved when they portray the activities of American gangsters, armed and in violent conflict with the law or law enforcement officers." And so the country's last memory of its beloved movie gangsters would be their extermination at the hands of Hoover's FBI.

The 1935 wave of G-men movies helped erode the distinction between the real and the screen FBI in the minds of the Depression generation. For Americans who had been kids during the Depression, with their G-men comics, pulp magazines, bubble gum cards, or toys, or adults watching G-men movies in the theater, J. Edgar Hoover and his G-men would forever be stars, figments of the popular imagination as well as the headlines.

The G-men movies, and the amazing flood of entertainment featuring FBI heroes that followed it, transformed the FBI cases of 1933 and 1934 into American legends and J. Edgar Hoover into a national hero. He then existed on a different level from mere mortal politicians and bureaucrats, and that was a factor in making him invulnerable to the political constraints that had inhibited him before. Later, Hoover's enemies would claim that fear of his files was what intimidated his political enemies and critics. There is certainly some truth to that. But if fear of Hoover's retaliation was one reason for his storied longevity and power, another was the residue of popular entertainment's glamorization of the Bureau and its director during the thirties.

The problem with the FBI's formula of crime fighting through science and organization was that Americans still needed heroes who had faces, and Hoover was promoting his Bureau as a tightly controlled machine of anonymous, faceless agents. But if the public demanded a G-man with a face, a hero, by default that was going to be Hoover. But a hero has to be, well, a hero, and Hoover had never personally even made an arrest, as he was forced to admit in a March 1936 Senate Appropriations Subcommittee hearing, which left the questioner, Senator Kenneth McKellar, in high humor and Hoover in high wrath. Hoover stormed out and passed the word that the highest-ranking public enemy at that moment, Alvin "Creepy" Karpis, was "his." The Bureau insisted that it was not McKellar's taunting that had aroused Hoover. The Bureau claimed Karpis had "sent word to Hoover that he intended to kill him" to avenge the Bureau's killing of "Ma" Barker, the leader of the so-called Karpis-Barker gang, which the Bureau had wiped out on January 16, 1936, with Karpis the sole survivor.

In March 1936, Hoover got word that Karpis was in Hot Springs, Arkansas. He loaded a chartered plane with some assistants, including Clyde Tolson and chief publicist Louis B. Nichols, but when they arrived, Karpis had departed, probably alerted by the local police. A few weeks later Hoover got another chance. His agents had spotted Karpis in New Orleans. Rounding up his posse, and once again accompanied by Tolson and Nichols, Hoover flew to New Orleans's Lakefront Airport. Hoover was not particularly fond of small planes, and when he needed one, he was piloted by Special Agent Murry Falkner (the brother of novelist William Faulkner who retained the original spelling of the family name). As Hoover later recounted the story, "I had told the boys how desperate he [Karpis] was and had given them all a chance to back out if they wished to. Not one made a move. Then I told them they could put on bullet-proof vests if they wished to. Not one made a move." Hoover and his men positioned themselves around Karpis's apartment. Karpis and a friend came out and got into their car. Hoover, waiting in a Bureau car, went into action.

> *I told the special agent who was driving to step on the gas, but just as we started a mounted policeman came galumphing down the street on a big white horse, floppity-floppity-flop. We had to let him go by. He might not have understood what all the shooting was about and charged in on the wrong side. Then, as we started again, a child on a bicycle crossed our bow. We couldn't risk injuring the child, so we stopped again. Finally, we closed in on the gangsters and made the capture. At last, we had in our hands the most dangerous public enemy in the United States. "Put the cuffs on him boys," I said.*

Pretty dramatic stuff, though the public seemed amused by the fact that none of Hoover's men had handcuffs, and they had to bind Karpis's hands with a necktie. There were also some who also found it funny that the G-men did not know their way around the narrow streets of the French Quarter, and Karpis had to volunteer directions. Nevertheless, this was a fantastic story. There were front-page headlines screaming "HOOVER ORDERS STICK 'EM UP." Hoover later allowed loftily that this was "the man who said he'd never be captured." Sounding a little like Cagney himself, he said that Karpis had "quit like the yellow rat he is and the rest of gangland is at heart." Kate Smith told her audience to send congratulations to Hoover, and the National Archives still has the thousands of letters that flooded the top G-man's office.

Once Hoover had gotten a taste for that sort of thing you couldn't keep him in the office. On May 7, 1936, he led a predawn raid on the Toledo hideout of Harry Campbell, a Barker-Karpis gang associate. When reporters asked Hoover if it had been he who had led the raid, he confessed, "I did," but modestly added that "it was a 'we' job, not an 'I' job." In December 1936, Hoover was in New York City when a squad of agents trapped bank robber Harry Brunette and his wife in a West Side apartment. Hoover and Tolson rushed to the scene. Hoover took over, and ordered his men to shoot. In the course of the gunfight the building caught fire from a tear gas bomb. Hoover's men had to hold off firemen who insisted on putting out the fire. Hoover made the arrest himself, and the headlines ran "25 G-MEN LED BY HOOVER CAPTURE BANDIT ON WEST 102ND STREET."

Hoover's most famous arrest was Louis "Lepke" Buchalter, head of the New York City garment rackets and chief of the execution service known as Murder Inc. When Lepke, who was wanted for murder, went into hiding, the police began to close down the operations of the organized crime families of New York, the so-called "Big Heat." Lepke was afraid that other gangsters would kill him to get the police off their backs, and let himself believe a deal had been struck with the FBI to keep him out of the hands of New York State Attorney General Thomas Dewey, who wanted to bring a capital murder charge against him.

When columnist and broadcaster Walter Winchell relayed an appeal to Lepke to turn himself in, Lepke replied that he was willing, but only to Winchell and Hoover personally. Winchell arranged for Hoover to wait alone on the corner of Fifth Avenue and Twenty-eighth Street, a few blocks downtown from the Empire State Building. At 10:15 on August 24, 1939, Winchell pulled up in a borrowed car. Hoover got in. Winchell introduced him to the other passenger: "Mr. Hoover, this is Lepke." "Glad to meet you," said Lepke, hopefully. There had been no deal. After Lepke was convicted on federal narcotics charges, he was turned over to Dewey, who convicted him of murder and electrocuted him in 1944.

Now that Hoover was a star, he began to act like one. He started regularly appearing in the Hollywood gossip columns, sometimes mentioned in (bogus) romances with Hollywood semicelebrities like Ginger Rogers's mother. Bureau publicists divulged his favorite recipes, his favorite songs, even his sleepwear. He and Tolson began to frequent nightspots like New York's Stork Club, which would later give rise to malicious stories (never substantiated and almost certainly untrue) that he had struck up friendships with the mobsters who frequented the clubs.

And, as stars are wont to do, Hoover now began to favor his fellow citizens with his opinions on subjects high and low. Whether the topic was Sunday school or mother love, Hoover shared his ideas with the public, and increasingly used his speeches and articles on crime, which began to number yearly in the dozens, as opportunities to denounce the declining values of the nation.

Crime was, Hoover informed his audiences, a dramatization of the eternal warfare between good and evil: "We will have crime so long as the basic passions and instincts of human nature survive." He claimed that

> none of us can hope that lawlessness can be completely eradicated from the fabric of civilization. The warfare between crime and the forces of law and order has been the topic of narration and writing since prehistoric man learned to speak and write. Philosophies and religions center upon a basic theory concerning the struggle between the forces of good and evil.

The only way to keep these eternal forces of evil in check was "a return to the God of our fathers and a most vigorous defense against the minions of godlessness and atheism, which are allied with the powers of destruction that today threaten America's future." He was tired, he said,

> of the maundering of fanatics and tuffet-heads, who believe that the way to educate the new youth is to allow the new youth to do anything it pleases. . . . We need a rebuilding of the foundations which made this Nation the greatest in all history, bulwarks formed of more stable materials than those of apathy, selfishness or indulgence.

But rarely did Hoover's denunciations of crime include any mention of offenses rising above the level of offenses against persons and property. Hoover was now hobnobbing with top politicians, Hollywood stars, and captains of industry and finance. If he were ever, which seems unlikely, tempted to investigate high-level financial crimes in the business community, now he had another reason to resist the urge. They were all pals.

The Bureau now enjoyed overwhelming support in Congress. Part of this was due to the expanded crime-fighting responsibilities granted the Bureau by the new laws of 1934, and part was the media adulation of Hoover and his G-men. It was suspected, accurately or not, that Hoover's files contained plenty of dirt on just about everyone in Congress. But another reason Congress gave him just about anything he wanted was that he regularly promised none of the new resources the congressmen and senators were giving him would ever be used against them. He would never investigate Congress, if they would never investigate him, and he kept his end of the bargain. Agents following suspects were under orders to break off surveillance if their targets entered congressional offices or the Capitol. And Congress responded with ever-bigger appropriations: From a Depression low of 353 agents in 1933, the number of special agents rose to 658 in 1938; there was an even larger growth in support staff, from 422 in 1933 to 1,141 in 1938. This in the depths of the Depression!

Nor did Hoover's FBI do anything that might disturb his adoring supporters among state and local politicians. Once Hoover had solidified his political base, politicians high and low could do just about anything short of murdering an FBI agent (or criticizing the Bureau—that was even riskier) before the Bureau would take notice. The political investigations that had led to the establishment of the Bureau were now taboo. Hoover's only mention of politics was to denounce any outside interference with the operations of the police—or the FBI. Corrupt politics, for Hoover, now meant purely and simply political interference with the police—and particularly with the Bureau. Nothing more.

■ ■ ■

While the FBI's astounding, media-nourished popularity was, in effect, redefining the Bureau's role in American law enforcement, elevating its sights lower, as the old artillery saying ran, behind the scenes the Bureau was getting a new assignment from the president, one that would remain secret until late in the decade. Between 1933 and 1939 the FBI was leading two lives: Onstage it was the action detective, chasing down colorful criminals, posing for the cameras, and strutting its stuff in the headlines. But backstage it had reentered the field of political investigation with a vengeance.

It began gradually. At the start of the New Deal the Bureau was still operating under Attorney General Stone's restrictions that limited it to investigations of federal crimes, a mandate that, with a few rather unimportant exceptions, it had been faithfully obeying since 1924.

In March 1933, Secretary of State Cordell Hull, relying on that pre–World War I appropriation provision of 1916, asked Hoover to look into a complaint by the German Embassy that it was receiving threats against Hitler. A year later, on March 9, 1934, President Roosevelt, on his own authority, asked Hoover to gather evidence on "Nazi groups, with particular reference to the antiracial activities and any anti-American activities having any possible connection with official representatives of the German government in the United States." This also fell loosely within the Stone guidelines, since any such activities by the Germans would be in violation of the espionage laws.

By 1936 the international situation had become much more dangerous. There was the civil war in Spain (with the indirect participation of the Soviet Union and Germany), Japanese aggression in Asia, and Italy's invasion of Ethiopia. Roosevelt needed systematic and comprehensive information on domestic subversion, specifically activities by American supporters of the Soviet

Union and Germany. In addition to information about threats of violence by American communists and fascists, the president needed information about isolationist propaganda campaigns that might inhibit his diplomatic maneuvers. On August 24, 1936, Hoover reported to Roosevelt that the communists had penetrated the shipping, mining, and newspaper industries to the extent that they could shut down those areas of the economy if they wished. He added that the communists were also making headway in infiltrating the federal bureaucracy.

Roosevelt responded by telling Hoover he wanted systematic intelligence about "subversive activities in the United States, particularly Fascism and Communism . . . a broad picture of the general movement and its activities as may affect the economic and political life of the country as a whole." Even by Hoover's increasingly elastic understanding of Stone's restrictions, this was a major expansion of FBI responsibilities. It went far beyond investigations of violations of federal law, particularly since Roosevelt wanted information about subversion whether or not there was a foreign government nexus. He was also far more interested in getting warnings about prospective threats than investigating past violations of the law.

Neither Hoover nor Roosevelt wanted to stir up a left still haunted by memories of its battles with the Bureau during the early twenties. Moreover, since the American left was trying to unite in the antifascist Popular Front, the communists would probably be supported by their noncommunist allies if the administration cracked down on the Party. For these reasons Hoover and Roosevelt preferred not to go to Congress for a new appropriations authorization for investigations not related to federal crimes. But they did need a plausible defense if they were caught spending money appropriated for the detection of crimes on noncriminal investigations.

Hoover was rarely at a loss when a president he trusted asked him to solve a problem. He told Roosevelt that in his opinion the administration could rely on the venerable 1916 congressional authorization for the Bureau to "investigate any matters referred to it by the Department of State" and "that if the State Department should ask for us to conduct such an investigation we could do so under our present authority in the appropriation already granted."

The next day, FDR called Hoover to the White House. He had already summoned Secretary of State Hull. FDR explained to Hull that Hoover needed a State Department request before he could begin a general intelligence investigation of communists and fascists. Hull reportedly turned to Hoover and said, "Go ahead and investigate the cock-suckers."

The original 1916 authorization previously had been used for Bureau investigations only of specific and limited matters brought to its attention by the State Department. In this case, Hull had issued a blanket permission empowering the Bureau to investigate communists and fascists no matter what they had done or not done, whenever and wherever Hoover or the president wanted. But history is filled with major expansions of federal authority based on little more than a redefinition of a single word, in this case the word "any," from meaning "any single matter" to "any and all matters."

Hull's request of August 25, 1936, remained the basic authority for FBI domestic intelligence operations for the next four decades, although that authorization was considerably augmented by additional presidential directives over the next few years. Hoover returned to his office, and wrote a memo to his aides explaining his understanding of Hull and Roosevelt's directive: The Bureau now had authority, he wrote, to collect information on communist and fascist activities "for intelligence purposes only, and not the type of investigation required in collecting evidence to be presented to a court."

Hoover informed Cummings that he was reestablishing the General Intelligence Division to "collect through investigative activity and other contact and to correlate for ready reference information dealing with various forms of activities of either a subversive or a so-called intelligence type." In a follow-up to Cummings and Roosevelt, Hoover reiterated that the new intelligence section should be financed as a continuation of Hull's request without any new authorization from Congress "to avoid criticisms or objections which might be raised to such an expansion by either ill-informed persons or individuals having some ulterior motive."

■ ■ ■

The situation in Europe grew even more tense in the late thirties as the probability of war increased after Germany's unification with Austria in March 1938. Many Americans demanded that the country declare itself neutral. Others called for the country to prepare for war. And there was mounting alarm that the country was undefended against fifth columnists of all types and persuasions. Pressure was mounting on the government to do something about the supposed spy threat. Roosevelt decided that the time had come to end the secrecy surrounding the Bureau's domestic intelligence operations. He ordered the Army, the Navy, and the FBI to announce that they were engaged in "the greatest spy hunt ever" and that suspected spies were "undergoing a severe grilling by the FBI." Once again, the FBI's intelligence-gathering operations were in the headlines.

On May 9, 1938, the American Legion announced that it too was going into the spy-hunting business. Then on May 10, Congressman Martin Dies of Texas proposed a special committee be authorized to investigate foreign "isms." This led to the establishment of the House Un-American Activities Committee (HUAC) on May 26. It looked like the country was on the verge of another counterspy free-for-all à la 1917. To head this off, the administration had the Bureau announce on May 12 it had just finished a twelve-volume report on Nazi espionage which it had begun in 1935, and on June 20 the Justice Department used that FBI investigation to indict eighteen American members of the Nazi espionage underground, accusing them of running "the greatest peacetime spy ring in history."

By the time of the Munich crisis in September 1938, the Bureau had greatly expanded its domestic intelligence network. The Bureau had a security specialist in each of the forty-five field offices, and had set up new facilities for "specialized training in general intelligence work." With the military also ratcheting up their intelligence operations, Roosevelt decided to define specific areas of responsibility for the competing intelligence services. On June 26, 1939, the president issued a directive giving the Army responsibility for gathering intelligence in Europe, the Navy the Pacific and Asia, and the FBI the Western Hemisphere, including Hawaii.

The full dimensions of the government's new domestic security apparatus were still unknown to the public when Germany invaded Poland on September 1, 1939. England and France declared war. The secrecy surrounding the Bureau's domestic security operations was no longer required, or even useful. Publicity was the thing now, because the relentlessly bad news from Europe had the public on the verge of panic. The country needed reassurance that the government was ready for the emergency. When Hoover discovered the New York City Police Department had established a fifty-man countersabotage unit, he sent an urgent message to the attorney general, warning that the security situation was getting out of hand. He asked Roosevelt to order local police to turn any information they had on "espionage, counterespionage, sabotage and violations of the neutrality regulations" over to the FBI. That same day, September 6, 1939, the president released a statement to the press that expanded on the words of Hoover's memo:

> *The Attorney General has been requested by me to instruct the Federal Bureau of Investigation of the Department of Justice to take charge of investigative work in matters relating to espionage, sabotage, and violations of the neutrality regulations. . . .*
>
> *To this end I request all police officers, sheriffs, and other law enforcement*

officers in the United States promptly to turn over to the nearest representative of the Federal Bureau of Investigation any information obtained by them relating to espionage, sabotage, subversive activities and violations of the neutrality laws.

Three days later President Roosevelt proclaimed a state of emergency.

On November 30, Hoover appeared before the House Appropriations Committee and revealed that the Bureau once again had a "General Intelligence Division." He cited the presidential Proclamation of Emergency as authority for its revival. He told Congress that the GID had "compiled extensive indices of individuals, groups, and organizations engaged in . . . subversive activities, in espionage activities, or any activities that are possibly detrimental to the internal security of the United States." The FBI now had files, he said, on individuals "who may become potential enemies to our internal security, such as known espionage agents, known saboteurs, leading members of the Communist party, and the [German-American] Bund."

In later years the FBI has been often accused of going far beyond any reasonable interpretation of its authority when it investigated the political activities of dissidents. Yet Hoover gave Congress full notice in his testimony on November 30 that along with his investigations of "espionage, sabotage, and violations of the neutrality regulations and any other subversive activities," he was going to be investigating propaganda "opposed to the American way of life" and agitators stirring up "class hatreds." No objections were raised.

Since the Bureau was relying on a State Department request as justification for its general intelligence investigations, State had one last chance to reassert the authority over domestic intelligence it had lost during World War I. Operating on the reasonable assumption that since the Bureau was, in theory at least, acting at State's behest when it investigated domestic subversion, Assistant Secretary of State George Messersmith convened a State Department committee to oversee the Bureau's investigations. Hoover complained to Attorney General Frank Murphy, who passed Hoover's concerns along to the president. Roosevelt promptly slapped the State Department down and dissolved Messersmith's committee. He issued a secret order dated June 26, 1939, that only the Military Intelligence Division, the Office of Naval Intelligence, and the FBI were to handle "espionage, counterespionage, and related matters" and that all other agencies were to defer to the FBI.

It is important to understand the specific details of how the Bureau revived its domestic intelligence operations in the thirties, because over the years—reaching a crescendo in the 1960s and 1970s—Bureau critics used the lack of any specific authorization from Congress permitting investigations other than those involving violations of federal law as a point of attack against the FBI. Certainly, taken out of the historical context, the route by which the Bureau obtained such authority was so labyrinthian—devious even—that it looked as if Hoover had simply made it all up. But he had not. In essence, Roosevelt and Hoover had gotten the State Department—as permitted by a 1916 appropriation—to request occasional domestic intelligence investigations by the FBI, and then interpreted that request to authorize a comprehensive program of domestic intelligence surveillance. Then the president had slid those investigations out from any review by the State Department.

At the time, however, there were pressing reasons of national security for taking such a circuitous route. As for congressional oversight, key members of the Appropriations Committee knew what was going on, as did the secretary of state, although that knowledge was confined to those who needed to know.

In June 1940 the Bureau began a "Custodial Detention Program" to select "dangerous" individuals to arrest in time of emergency. This list was so sensitive that Hoover's superiors insisted that the Justice Department maintain control over the program, and the department took over its administration in April 1941. This program effectively gave the Bureau the authority to investigate any group or person in the country to discover whether the organization was infiltrated by subversives, or if an individual's "liberty in this country in time of war or national emergency would constitute a menace to the public peace and safety of the United States government." Maintaining and updating these lists also provided a legal basis, however tenuous, over the next three decades for the Bureau to investigate almost anyone—generally on the left—to see whether he or she deserved to be included on that roster of potential detainees.

Hoover was well aware of the danger to the Bureau as it moved beyond "investigations," which Hoover defined as "conducted when there is a specific violation of a Criminal Statute," which "always presuppose an overt act and [are] proceeded upon with the very definite intention of developing facts and information that will enable prosecution under such legislation." Events were now moving the Bureau, he recognized, into "intelligence activities" that were based on "an entirely different premise," since the activities by communists and other "subversive elements" that the Bureau was now looking into did not,

in the original state, involve an overt act or violation of a specific statute. These subversive groups direct their attention to the dissemination of propaganda and to the boring from within processes, much of which is not a violation of a

*Federal statute at the time it is indulged in, but which may become a very defi-
nite violation of the law in the event of a declaration of war or the declaration
of a national emergency.*

Roosevelt and Hoover were secretly acting in ways that skirted and perhaps
violated the law because, in peacetime at least, subversion of foreign policy, in
the sense of opposing it and working to frustrate it by almost any means necessary, is what an opposition does, and as such has to be vigorously protected
from the chilling effect of government surveillance. Nevertheless, FDR felt he
had to know, as a matter of national security, what communists and fascists
were doing to subvert, in the strictest sense of the word, the administration's
foreign policy of helping Great Britain in its fight against Hitler and arming the
United States for a war Roosevelt thought was inevitable.

There was no opposition in Congress to the Bureau's new domestic intelligence operations in 1938, and little in the popular press. The left *was* becoming
alarmed, but since the thrust of the Bureau's investigations was against the far
right, that is, against the German-American Bund and native American fascists, criticism from that quarter was also muted.

That changed on February 3, 1940, when the Bureau arrested twelve
Detroit-area veterans of the Abraham Lincoln Brigade on charges of violating the law against recruiting Americans to fight in foreign wars. The Abraham
Lincoln Brigade was regarded by much of the left—despite numerous eye-
witness accounts that in Spain the brigade often acted as an instrument of
Stalin's bloody purge of noncommunist leftists—as a pristine symbol of the
Popular Front solidarity against fascism that united the whole progressive left
until the Hitler-Stalin pact of August 24, 1939. The left was outraged to learn
that these venerated figures had been rounded up by the Justice Department,
especially since the war they had fought was now over. The surge of protest over
the raids was so noisy, in fact, that after a week the attorney general gave in, dismissed the charges, and said that he could "see no good to come from reviving
in America at this late date the animosities of the Spanish conflict so long as the
struggle had ended and some degree of amnesty at least is being extended in
Spain."

The Lincoln Brigade raids made the left take another look at what the Bureau and "G-man Hoover" were doing, and what they saw astonished and
frightened them. Reviewing Hoover's testimony before the House the previous
November and again on January 5, 1940, they learned about the reestablish-
ment of the General Intelligence Division and the institution of the Custodial
Detention Program. The leftist and liberal press now began to equate the

"new" Hoover and his "new" FBI with the old Hoover and his Bureau of the Palmer Raids days.

But on March 16, 1940, at the height of the furor, Roosevelt made a point of ostentatiously calling out to Hoover at a White House Press Club dinner, "Edgar, what are they trying to do to you on the Hill?" Hoover replied, "I don't know, Mr. President," whereupon Roosevelt conspicuously gave the "thumbs-down" gesture, announcing, "That's for them." On June 14, 1940, Roosevelt sent Hoover a "Dear Edgar" letter, thanking him for "the many interesting and valuable reports that you have made to me regarding the fast moving situations of the last few months. You have done and are doing a wonderful job, and I want you to know of my gratification and appreciation."

Hoover replied in a letter that gushed with gratitude. He should have been grateful. Since 1936 he had been skating on thin ice in quietly organizing an entire division of the Bureau—a division publicly announced disbanded by a previous attorney general—on the basis of no more than an oral communication from the president. Many of the reports the Bureau had been forwarding to the White House could not be justified even by the most expansive definition of "subversive." To an unfriendly eye, the Bureau could be charged with having become a private political police force at the beck and call of the president, just what Congress had feared in John Wilkie's Secret Service before the Bureau was established. A misuse of appropriated funds might have been the least of the charges against Hoover if the political winds had shifted and Roosevelt had disavowed him, as political leaders are wont to do to their subordinates when the going gets tough. But with Roosevelt's letter in his office safe, Hoover was off the hook.

The next year liberals were alarmed to learn that the Bureau was using wiretapping in its domestic security investigation. The federal government had been prohibited from tapping phones since the Federal Communications Act of 1934, and this had been reaffirmed by the Supreme Court's Nardone decision of 1939, but Roosevelt told the Justice Department that he was "convinced that the Supreme Court never intended any dictum . . . to apply to grave matters involving the defense of the nation." Roosevelt "authorized and directed" the attorney general to use "listening devices" against "persons suspected of subversive activities against the Government of the United States, including suspected spies," requesting that these taps be limited in number and restricted, as far as possible, to aliens.

For the left wiretapping was a symbol of all governmental disregard for civil liberties. The general public, however, seemed to approve. And so the Bureau's wiretapping authority, like its fingerprinting and its crime labs, became part of

Roosevelt's formula for maintaining home-front morale in his new role as Dr. Win the War.

Whenever the Bureau ran into trouble under Roosevelt, the FBI could be sure the president would back them up. When a squad of special agents was spotted tapping the phone of Harry Bridges, head of the International Longshoremen's and Warehousemen's Union and a suspected communist, hence subject to deportation, the left raised a howl. But at a White House meeting, Roosevelt made a point of referring to the Bureau's embarrassment, teasing Hoover that "that is the first time you've been caught with your pants down."

In return for Roosevelt's unwavering support, Hoover gave the president his complete and enthusiastic loyalty. He placed at Roosevelt's disposal not only his limitless energy and willingness to carry out the most sensitive assignments, competently and silently, but also his immense popularity with the public. In his speeches he began to follow the president's lead in calling foreign dictators "international gangsters," comparing their criminality with the leadership Roosevelt was furnishing America. And in a private letter to Roosevelt, Hoover wrote, "In noting the vast contrast between the Leader of our Nation and those of other less fortunate nations, I feel deeply thankful that we have at the head of our Government one who possesses such sterling, sincere, and altogether humane qualities."

The close partnership between Hoover and FDR had certainly had an impact on the Bureau's relationship with the Justice Department. During the national emergency period between September 9, 1939, and Pearl Harbor, Hoover's personal relationship with FDR gave the Bureau independence from the attorney general whenever conflicts arose between the Bureau and the department. When Hoover complained that Attorney General Francis Biddle had refused to seek indictments against leading critics of Roosevelt's foreign policy, Roosevelt ordered Biddle to go along with Hoover's demands for prosecution of "seditious publications." Roosevelt made requests for background checks on his critics directly to Hoover, and the Bureau funneled them directly back to the White House, thus bypassing the attorney general in both directions.

The FBI's willingness to tailor its crime fighting and spy hunting to suit the immediate needs of the administration limited its effectiveness in dealing with the communist espionage apparatus taking shape during the late thirties. The Bureau's covert surveillance of the Communist Party made it well aware that while many of the rank-and-file communists, and probably almost all of its fellow travelers, simply saw the communists as "reformers in a hurry" or the most militant and effective fighters against Hitler (at least until the Hitler-Stalin pact of August 1939), in its higher echelons the Party was, as one of its informants said in a report passed on to FDR, "nothing but a network of Stalin's agents and spies." But there was little the Bureau could do with this secretly acquired knowledge. To have revealed what it knew about communist espionage and subversion would have stirred up the Bureau's (for the most part) dormant enemies on the left. And, even more importantly, raising the alarm about Red spies would have undercut the Bureau's real job of reassuring the public that there was no danger from fifth columns of the right or of the left, and that the FBI had everything under control. And so the Bureau, for the time being, had to sit on what it knew about Stalin's underground in America.

Actually the Smith Act of June 28, 1940, did give the Bureau a plausible legal pretext for investigating and prosecuting leaders and members of the Communist Party, since the law made it illegal to advocate the overthrow of the government by force, or to organize or belong to a group with that goal. But during the late thirties, with the Communist Party supporting the New Deal, and the first lady herself enjoying close relationships with Popular Front organizations closely affiliated with the Party, communists hardly appeared to be overthrowing anything, despite their rhetoric. And the Bureau knew that judges had been ruling for decades that sedition could be prosecuted only if it went beyond words.

When ex-communist Whittaker Chambers went to the State Department in 1939 with reports that the department was infiltrated by communists, he discovered how reluctant the administration was to act against the Communist Party, even when confronted with the most serious and credible allegations of communist espionage. The administration was not interested. Nor did Hoover take much notice when Chambers went to him a few years later. Hoover shared Roosevelt's conviction before and during the war that American and foreign fascists were the real danger, and that anything that might distract the public, like a hunt for Red spies, was counterproductive.

By the late thirties Roosevelt had a set routine for using the Bureau as a national security blanket: Whenever international tensions threatened to unleash home-front hysteria between the outbreak of the European war and Pearl Harbor, Hoover would be trotted out to announce that he had thwarted another attempt by the Germans to infiltrate, spy, or commit sabotage.

The Bureau was able to back up Hoover's pronouncements because it had penetrated the German underground in America and probably knew more about what their spies were up to than their spymasters in Germany. The Bureau got the break it needed in 1940, when a naturalized German-American named William Sebold went to the FBI after a trip to Germany, where he had gone for medical treatment after a botched operation in New York's Bellevue

Hospital. While he was in Germany, he had been warned that his German relatives would be in danger if he did not agree to spy for the *Abwehr* (the German military intelligence service) when he got back to America. The Germans ordered him to gather information on his own and from other German spies, and broadcast it back to Germany over a clandestine shortwave radio station in Centerville, Long Island. The Bureau told Sebold to pretend to follow his orders, and began giving him disinformation from the State, War, and Navy departments to broadcast to Germany. The return messages from Berlin revealed the identities and activities of German agents working in the United States. One important fact the Bureau learned from the Sebold operation was that the Germans had stolen the plans for the Norden bombsight, then considered the country's most valuable military secret. Sebold was even able to furnish the FBI with the identity of Hermann Lang, the spy who had stolen the blueprints.

On July 30, 1941, the Bureau used Sebold's information to organize a series of spectacular raids that rounded up a German spy ring headed by Fritz Duquesne. Thirty-three German agents, including Hermann Lang, were arrested along with their network of support personnel. These arrests, according to historian Joseph Persico, "practically shut down German intelligence in the United States overnight." The full story of Nazi espionage in America was revealed during Duquesne's trial in September 1941, and the Bureau's investigation was celebrated in a Bureau-endorsed film of 1945, *The House on 92nd Street.*

■ ■ ■

A generation of Americans would always remember what they were doing and what they were thinking when they heard that Pearl Harbor had been attacked. What Hoover was thinking can be guessed in that he almost immediately began working to ensure that no blame would fall on him or the FBI for what would surely be seen as a catastrophic intelligence failure. And after all, he was in the intelligence business, and he was not alone in wondering who would be the eventual scapegoat. Assistant Secretary of State Adolf Berle wrote in his diary the evening of December 7 that it had been a bad day all around, but at least he was not in charge of Naval Intelligence. And Hoover was vulnerable because, technically, the FBI *was* in charge of intelligence in Hawaii. Roosevelt had assigned responsibility for Pacific intelligence to the Navy, Europe to the Army, and the entire Western Hemisphere, including Hawaii, to the FBI. Luckily Hoover had gone on the record asking the Navy to retain responsibility for Hawaii until the Bureau could expand its operations there.

Hoover's reaction to December 7 was typical of his reflexive response whenever the Bureau faced a crisis: to clear the Bureau of any culpability, while pointing the blame in another direction, in the direction, in fact, of his enemies. Before he went to bed that night Hoover sent two memos to the president. The first recounted thirteen war measures he had put into effect, including a roundup of the 770 Japanese agents whose identities the Bureau had learned from a series of burglaries at Japanese consulates; an embargo on travel and communications to Japan; and a watch on all Japanese government facilities in the United States. He also told Roosevelt he had put the Bureau on twenty-four-hour alert and canceled all leaves.

The second memo informed Roosevelt that the FBI had acquired and passed along information that in retrospect might have prevented Pearl Harbor from being surprised by the Japanese attack. The Bureau had been wiretapping a suspected Japanese spy in Honolulu named Mori. During an apparently innocuous conversation with a relative in Japan, Mori had provided information about the location of the fleet at Pearl and details about the Army's searchlights at the airfields. Mori had then been asked, in a seeming non sequitur, what flowers were in bloom in Hawaii, and had replied "hibiscus and poinsettia." Hoover pointed out to the president that these might have been code phrases, and that "the information sought in this conversation with Japan might have been a prelude to the proposed bombing of the Hawaiian Islands today." Hoover told the president he had made this information available to the Military Intelligence Division and the Office of Naval Intelligence just before the attack.

A few days later Hoover weighed in with another self-serving memo to the president that suggested the military intelligence agencies had failed, as we now say, to connect the dots. After bragging again about the Mori intercept, Hoover told the president that Naval Intelligence had intercepted and decoded a message from Japan ten days before the attack that "contained substantially the complete plans for the attack on Pearl Harbor as it was subsequently carried out." The message had specified a code word that would be broadcast three times as a signal for the attack. Hoover claimed that the code word was intercepted on December 5, and that this should have been understood to mean that

the attack was to be made on Saturday or Sunday . . . this information was sent by Military radio to the Hawaiian Islands . . . At this time it is impossible to determine whether there was a breakdown in the Military radio and a failure of the messages to reach their destination, or whether the messages were delivered but not acted upon by the Military authorities.

Hoover was alluding in a garbled way, probably relying only on rumors, to a story that has since become a standby of Pearl Harbor conspiracy theory, the so-called "winds messages." On November 26 the Navy *had* intercepted a message from Tokyo to the Japanese Embassy in Washington that if normal communications were cut off, the embassy should listen for one of three coded messages about the weather that would be inserted into the regular shortwave news broadcasts. The weather messages would contain a reference to the direction of the winds, and one such wind direction would indicate a possible breakdown of diplomatic relations with the United States. This intercepted message became known as the "winds warning" message. If the embassy were to hear the follow-up broadcast (the "winds execute" message) it was to burn its codebooks and secret documents.

Between December 5 and Pearl Harbor, Navy and Army communications units were listening intently for the execute message, and after the attack there were reports, largely from one Navy communications officer, Captain L. S. Safford, that the "execute" message had in fact been intercepted by military communications, but had not been passed along to the command at Pearl. The most extreme version of this story held that Roosevelt and his high command had themselves blocked the warning from going to Pearl because they wanted the attack to succeed as part of a plot to get the country involved in the European war.

After the war the "winds execute" matter was scrutinized intently by a joint congressional committee. The conclusion was that "no genuine message, in execution of the code, and applying to the United States, was received in the War or Navy Department prior to December 7, 1941." The commission also pointed out that the original winds message, with or without the "execute," could not have been considered, by any stretch of the imagination, to have been, as Hoover had claimed, "substantially the complete plans for the attack on Pearl Harbor." The committee even argued that, "granting for purposes of discussion that a genuine execute message applying to the winds code was intercepted before December 7, it is concluded that such fact would have added nothing to what was already known concerning the critical character of our relations with the Empire of Japan." The winds code simply informed the embassy that the ongoing negotiations with the United States were breaking off, a fact known to anyone reading the newspapers, and certainly to the Japanese.

Hoover's December 12 memo is also revealing in that it was one of hundreds, thousands even, of unexamined scraps of information or misinformation that the Bureau sent to the White House during the war, batches arriving on a daily basis. The accumulation of this (for the most part useless) information must have resulted in Hoover's "intelligence reports" eventually being simply filed unread by the president's staff. The poor quality of these FBI reports may also have contributed to an impression in the White House that Hoover, while he had his uses within the limits of his abilities, was nothing more than a glorified cop incapable of appreciating the subtleties of foreign intelligence, and thus disqualified from any serious consideration as postwar director of intelligence.

For the rest of December 1941, everyone of any importance in Washington was sweating to see who was finally going to take the fall for Pearl Harbor. Would the blame travel up the ranks, perhaps all the way to the White House? Or would it be shunted down to the junior officers who manned the radios and flew the picket planes in the Pacific? Roosevelt sent Navy Secretary Frank Knox to Pearl, supposedly to assess the damage. Hoover and the other intelligence chiefs must have suspected that the real reason for Knox's visit was to decide what heads, and how many, would have to roll to slake the public's thirst for scapegoats.

While it would have been unlikely for Hoover's head to be selected for the chopping block, it was within the realm of possibility. An anonymous memo was circulating recalling that the FBI was supposed to "deal with the fifth column in our territory," and Hawaii was certainly "our territory." The *Washington Times-Herald* reported on December 29 that

> the nation's super Dick Tracy, FBI Director J. Edgar Hoover, is directly under the gun . . . [the] preliminary report . . . places the Pearl Harbor Fifth Column blame directly in Hoover's lap. Army and Navy Intelligence are not primarily responsible for the detection of enemy civilians operating as Fifth Columnists. By order of the President, this has become Hoover's direct responsibility. Longtime Capitol Hill foes of FBI Chief Hoover have been whetting up their snickersnees, itching to take a crack at the detective hero as far back as the days of kidnappers and gangsters. Leaders are holding them back with the promise that the report of the Roberts Board of Inquiry will provide the ammunition for an all-out drive to oust Hoover from his seat of tremendous power.

When he read the *Times-Herald* story, Hoover immediately let out a howl that the story was "without a scintilla of foundation," and that "jurisdiction over Hawaiian matters was vested principally in the naval authorities and not in the FBI." Hoover was right to be alarmed. The public was in an ugly mood. The military commanders at Pearl, Admiral Husband E. Kimmel and General Walter C. Short (and their families), were receiving death threats. Some editorials were recommending the firing squad for them, or the traditional revolver and a single bullet. With the Japanese (for all anyone knew) racing toward California, the public was demanding vengeance, and the president might well be scanning the federal roster for sacrifices to throw to the mob.

Eventually, the president concluded that the full responsibility for the disaster could be assigned to the unlucky Kimmel and Short, who were court-martialed. Hoover was happy to go along with this, since his position was that the FBI had provided the military so many warnings based on documents stolen from the Japanese Consulate in Honolulu that it was inexplicable why the Army and the Navy had not figured out what was coming. The FBI, Hoover's memos suggested, had all but spelled it out for them.

The Pearl Harbor aftermath revealed Hoover at his most ruthless and dangerous. Once Hoover was assured he was in the clear, he lashed out at his enemies. He denounced the writer of the *Times-Herald* story as kin to a mule, "without pride of ancestry or hope of posterity." He also lashed out at a rival bureaucrat, claiming that his wiretaps in Hawaii would have been even more productive if Federal Communications Commission Chairman James L. Fly had not refused him permission to tap all wire messages between the U.S. and Tokyo, Rome, Berlin, and Moscow. The FBI might then have been able to give the military even more precise warning of the attack. Hoover had pleaded with Fly, and "in fact" had made "entreaties" for more wiretaps, but the FCC chief had refused on the basis of "existing statutes." Sixty years later the FBI would itself be using the "existing statutes" excuse as a reason for not pursuing leads that might have led to the plotters of the 9/11 attacks.

Many years later, Hoover was on the receiving end of the same sort of unfounded charges he had been leveling against his enemies. His accuser was a British and German double agent named Dusko Popov, who in a book published after Hoover's death, claimed he had told the FBI in 1940 that German intelligence had sent him to gather information about American military facilities. The Germans had given him a questionnaire to fill out with the results of his investigation; part of it, he later claimed, had dealt with Pearl Harbor.

Popov claimed Hoover took an immediate dislike to him and threw him out of his office, the reason being Popov's notorious reputation as a gambler and womanizer. He was supposedly the model for Ian Fleming's 007, and, it has been said, had been given the code name of Tricycle by the Germans based on Popov's fondness for bedding two women at the same time. In his postwar memoirs Popov claimed that the questionnaire amounted to a "detailed plan of the Japanese air raid," and that the disaster at Pearl could have been averted except for this "irrational, ranting man." Hoover, Popov charged, was "the person responsible for the disaster at Pearl Harbor." Some historians not particularly fond of Hoover (there have been a few) have believed, or claimed to believe, Popov's tale. But the FBI actually did bring Popov's questionnaire to the attention of the White House, albeit to demonstrate how the Bureau had figured out the microdot system the Germans used for secret messages. But if the German questionnaire, which Popov claimed the Germans intended to send to the Japanese (although after the war the Japanese denied they had gotten any intelligence assistance from the Germans), had been seriously analyzed by the FBI, they would have been more likely to think the Germans (or the Japanese) were considering sabotage operations against Pearl rather than an air attack. It might therefore have confirmed Kimmel and Short in their disastrous conclusion that sabotage was the real threat to their commands.

But the FBI earned a spectacular reputation for guarding the home front during the war, and it was not just by evading the blame for intelligence disasters. The Bureau had some spectacular intelligence triumphs, none more dramatic than its capture of eight Nazi saboteurs who landed by submarine on the shores of Long Island and Florida in June 1942. Germany intended this small detachment of specially trained agents as the first of a wave of sabotage attacks against American war production, code-named Operation Pastorius by *Abwehr*'s spymaster Admiral Wilhelm Canaris. The initial eight had all lived in the United States and had been sent to a German espionage school for training in American popular culture and current events so they could blend in when they landed. They were taught how to blow up bridges and railroad crossings, Ohio Canal locks, water systems and hydroelectric stations. Then they were loaded on two submarines, one bound for New York, the other for Florida.

On the night of June 13, 1942, four saboteurs, led by a George Dasch, landed on the coast of Long Island at Amagansett. They were still burying their equipment when they were spotted by Coast Guardsman John C. Cullen. He challenged them to identify themselves. Dasch pulled a gun, but, violating instructions as well as common sense, instead of using it he offered Cullen $260 to leave them alone. Cullen agreed, but returned to his station and reported the strange encounter to his superiors. They notified the FBI.

Dasch led his men to New York City, where he and a member of his team named Ernest Burger checked into a hotel. They spent their first day enjoying New York. Then Dasch began to think about their predicament and the slim chance that they would manage to do anything except get caught and executed. He talked it over with Burger, and found that Burger, an American citizen, had come to the same conclusion. Burger, in fact, had intended to steal their money—$84,000—and disappear. They decided to turn themselves in.

For a century, the Federal Bureau of Investigation had been telling Americans that, when it came to national security, the country could "leave it to the FBI" (left, the cover of *G-Men* magazine epitomized this image in the 1930s), and on September 11, 2001, the FBI was the nation's lead agency working against terror, having claimed that fighting terrorism was its number one priority.

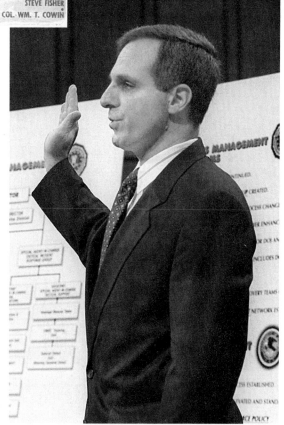

But official inquiries after the 9/11 attacks revealed that although the Bureau had promising leads that might have uncovered the 9/11 plots, they were ignored at headquarters because Louis Freeh's Bureau had become "timorous," "risk aversive," and "politically correct," too fearful of criticism to investigate what needed investigating (right, Louis Freeh being sworn in before testimony to the 9/11 Commission).

What happened to the FBI that left it cowering behind self-erected "walls," unwilling to come out to fight as Islamic terror took root in America? What happened to the two-fisted, square-jawed G-man who once chased headlines and hoodlums, saboteurs and spies, always getting his man? Whatever happened to *that* FBI?

The original idea of a federal investigative force was for Washington to be able to protect the country against the most serious threats to its security—which exceeded the means, abilities, or inclination of any local police force. In 1871, the threat was Ku Klux Klan terror against freed slaves in the South (left). In response the Justice Department applied a $50,000 appropriation to ending the Klan's reign of terror.

By concentrating only on major threats to the nation, the Justice Department was able to get by until the end of the century by hiring Secret Service agents from the Treasury Department or private detectives from the Pinkerton Nationwide Detective Agency (above, agency head Allan Pinkerton in his Philadelphia headquarters).

The twentieth century ushered in another threat that local and state governments were powerless to control: conspiracies by wealthy, powerful interest groups and corrupt politicians to pillage the natural environment. President Theodore Roosevelt ordered his Interior and Justice departments to borrow Secret Service Agent William Burns, whose investigations led to the prosecution and conviction of much of the Oregon political establishment, including Senator John Mitchell (left, above), for processing fraudulent land-fraud claims. Retaliating against Roosevelt's investigation of its members, Congress prohibited the use of Secret Service agents outside the Treasury Department, and so, in 1908, Attorney General Charles Bonaparte appointed Stanley Finch (left) to head a small force of Justice Department agents to investigate continuing political and financial corruption. Thus the FBI was born, to detect and prosecute crimes against the United States by its wealthiest and most powerful criminals.

Almost immediately, the new Bureau lowered its sights from investigating the powerful and wealthy to pursuing unpopular individuals who had become targets of public wrath. Instead of using the 1910 Mann Act to track down the heads of vice rings, the Bureau prosecuted individual prostitutes and their patrons, like the controversial black heavyweight champion Jack Johnson (left).

During World War I, the Bureau took over security for the home front primarily to keep out rival agencies like the Secret Service and Military Intelligence. Bureau Chief A. Bruce Bielaski (right) registered hundreds of thousands of auxiliaries from the violently anti-labor American Protective League (below) to assist the Bureau. In the absence of any real threat from German espionage or sabotage, the Bureau targeted and effectively destroyed the radical antiwar union the Industrial Workers of the World. Such actions gave rise to suspicions forever after that the Bureau would manipulate public alarm to suppress legitimate political reform.

Within ten years of its inception, the Bureau had already established an enduring pattern of allowing bureaucratic rivalries to set the direction of its national security investigations, and of emphasizing dramatic arrests of individual suspects rather than an accurate intelligence analysis of real threats to national security.

Application for Enrollment as a Volunteer in the
American Protective League

Organized with Approval and Operating under Direction of
United States Department of Justice, Bureau of Investigation

A. M. BRIGGS, General Supt.
AMERICAN PROTECTIVE LEAGUE
Chicago, Illinois

Oct 23rd   1917

Dear Sir:—I beg to make application for enrollment as a Volunteer in the   Division American Protective League and for your records in connection therewith, the following information is respectfully submitted:

1. Name in full
2. Residence Address 42/ w 3rd
3. City Abilene State Kans
4. Business Phone 34 Residence Phone 6/5
5. Business Address Merchant - Broadway
6. City State
7. Occupation
8. Age 39
9. Place of birth Abilene Kan
10. Were you ever in the service of the U. S.? Yes
11. If so, when, how long, and in what department of the service were you employed?

12. Are you married? Yes Have you any objection to leaving the city in the interests of the work in an emergency? Yes
13. What foreign languages do you speak or understand?
14. Do you understand that you are to receive no compensation or expense allowances for any services rendered this organization. Yes
15. I reserve the right to resign from this organization at any time, and agree to hand in my badge and commission card at any time upon request of the Chief.

Signed

When a wave of political bombings terrorized the country in the spring of 1919, Attorney General A. Mitchell Palmer (left) appointed the 24-year-old J. Edgar Hoover to lead a campaign against radicalism. The excesses of Hoover's Red Scare raids of 1919 and 1920 mobilized liberals and civil libertarians against the Bureau. The American Civil Liberties Union was created, more or less, specifically to defend the left against the Bureau.

During the Harding administration, Bureau Director William Burns and Attorney General Harry Daugherty put the FBI at the disposal of employers in the nationwide strikes of the early 1920s; that and its involvement in the Teapot Dome scandals led to calls for the Bureau's abolition. Instead Attorney General Harlan Stone called on J. Edgar Hoover (below), by then the Bureau's assistant director, to take over, ordering him to end domestic intelligence gathering and investigate only violations of federal laws.

Besieged by its critics, the Bureau sought refuge in avoiding any controversial investigations, no matter how important, instead focusing on supplying technical services to local police.

Franklin D. Roosevelt's New Deal was, according to Attorney General Homer Cummings, "government in action," and the FBI was at the center of the action. Cummings called the killing of a Bureau agent at Kansas City's Union Station (above, in a scene from the 1959 *FBI Story*) the underworld's "declaration of war" against the United States, and he threw the FBI into that war as the government's army against crime.

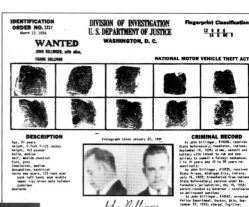

The Bureau's spectacular successes against John Dillinger (above right, his wanted poster) and other Midwest bank robbers led to an expansion of the Bureau's authority, but the new laws, by giving the FBI jurisdiction over local crimes that had attracted national attention, allowed the Bureau to avoid more sensitive and controversial matters, such as organized crime, political corruption, white collar crime, and civil rights (left, Hoover marks a map detailing bank robbery investigations).

Hollywood turned the FBI into American legend through movies about the Bureau's gangbusting cases, beginning with James Cagney's *G-Men* in 1935 (right). There was FBI entertainment in every media: radio shows, pulp magazines, and even bubble gum cards. Hoover's ghostwritten books persuaded the public that all crime was local and the Bureau's job was to take over cases that were too difficult for the local police.

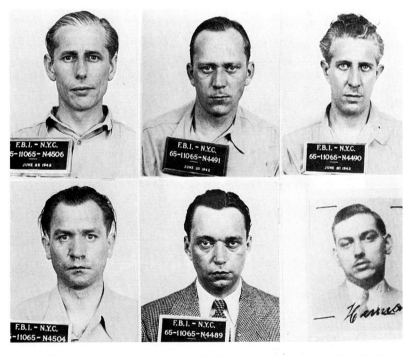

As World War II neared, President Roosevelt used the Bureau's prestige to reassure the public that the home front, which the Bureau called "The FBI Front," was protected. The Bureau functioned as a national security blanket during the war, publicizing its file and fingerprint collections. After a few spectacular arrests of Nazi saboteurs and spies (above), the country was persuaded that it could "leave it to the FBI." Meanwhile the Bureau, instead of analyzing and evaluating legitimate national security intelligence, sent the White House every rumor it collected, in a transparent effort to ensure that, whatever happened, no one could ever say the Bureau had not given warning.

Harry S. Truman shared liberals' distrust of Hoover and the FBI, and so was skeptical of Hoover's warnings about Soviet espionage networks and atomic weapons program. Hoover broke with the president over the issue of communism, allying himself with the rabidly anti-administration House Un-American Activities Committee, making the Bureau even more hated by liberals. Hoover was forced to keep secret the best evidence that his investigators, led by Special Agent Robert Lamphere (above right) had gathered against Julius and Ethel Rosenberg (right), Alger Hiss, and others, because it was based on the ultrasecret Venona Project, which had cracked the codes the Soviet underground in America used to communicate with the Kremlin. And so Americans, already suspicious of the Bureau, began to suspect that the FBI's communist spy cases were little more than elaborate frauds, and that FBI domestic surveillance was always politically motivated, dangerous, and to be resisted.

J. EDGAR HOOVER
Director, Federal Bureau of Investigation

MASTERS OF DECEIT

The Story of Communism in America
and How to Fight It

A GIANT CARDINAL EDITION published by
POCKET BOOKS, INC. • NEW YORK

Hoover's close friendship with Senator Joseph McCarthy (above, McCarthy with Tolson, a friend, and Hoover) created even more enemies for the Bureau. So did his continued warnings about the threat posed by the American Communist Party (left) even as the number of communists in the United States dwindled to the point of extinction. Frustrated by the courts' refusal to enforce emergency laws against the Communist Party, Hoover began to resort to covert, extra-legal means to bring down the Party on his own.

Meanwhile, through such films as *The FBI Story* (1959) (right) and television's *The FBI* (1965–1974), Hoover used popular culture to promote a respectable, apolitical image of the 1950s and 1960s G-man as an all-American family man, with the Bureau as a nonpartisan symbol of national unity. All this as the real Bureau was more partisan and divisive than ever and more committed to a secret life far removed from its image in popular culture.

In the 1960s, Hoover and Assistant Director William C. Sullivan, head of the powerful Intelligence Division (right, above), extended the Bureau's secret campaigns of harassment against the Communist Party to other political dissidents. One COINTELPRO (counterintelligence program) operation was a secret campaign to destroy Martin Luther King Jr. (right, below), whom they suspected of being influenced by communist advisers and knew was no friend of the Bureau.

The Bureau also seriously mishandled its surveillance of Lee Harvey Oswald (left) before the JFK assassination. Its concealment of these blunders contributed to suspicions that the truth about the assassination had also been covered up. As the nation's faith in government crumbled during the Vietnam War, the divergence between the revelations of secret FBI criminality and the Bureau's public pose of rectitude made it for many a prime symbol of governmental hypocrisy and contempt for the liberties of its citizens.

After Hoover died in 1972, the FBI began to self-destruct. Hoover's successor, L. Patrick Gray, quit after admitting he had destroyed evidence during the Watergate investigation. The Bureau was now so hated and distrusted that Clarence Kelley, Gray's successor, all but discontinued surveillance efforts against even the most violent extremist groups. Although Kelley tried to restore faith in the Bureau, initiating the first investigations of political corruption since the land-fraud cases, the counterculture shunned the Bureau, compromising its ability to solve such politically charged cases as the Patty Hearst kidnapping (left).

After the FBI's standoff with American Indian activists at Wounded Knee on the Pine Ridge Sioux reservation (right), hostility toward the Bureau ran so deep that many sympathized with an activist's murder of two FBI agents on the reservation two years later.

In 1975, the Senate Select Committee on Intelligence exposed the Bureau's harassment of Martin Luther King, Jr. and similar COINTELPRO operations against other dissidents. The FBI increasingly became regarded as an organization engaged in a secret war against civil liberties and political freedom. Many believed that the Bureau could never be trusted to investigate anyone fairly (left, *Time* magazine cover story about Hoover's troubled Bureau).

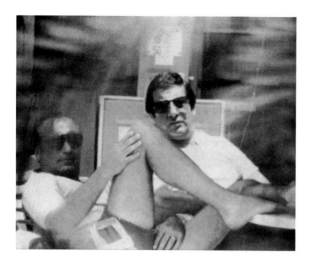

William Webster, who succeeded Kelley in 1978, took advantage of federal statutes such as the Title III wiretap authority gained in 1968 and the 1970 Racketeer Influence and Corrupt Organization (RICO) Act, and launched a comprehensive war on organized crime, targeting entire criminal enterprises and holding the dons liable for the crimes of their families, instead of simply prosecuting low-level members. Using evidence acquired by aggressive undercover agents like Joe Pistone (top), the Bureau prevailed in landmark cases against the Mafia—the Pizza Connection and Commission cases—launching the careers of Rudy Giuliani and Louis Freeh, and sending the godfathers of all five New York City Mafia families, including Fat Tony Salerno (above left), to jail for the rest of their lives.

But the Bureau failed to rethink its counterterrorism strategy in the light of the comprehensive intelligence gathering that had worked so well against organized crime and political corruption (the ABSCAM investigation of bribe-taking congressmen, right). The Bureau instead relied on its elite, semimilitary Hostage Rescue Team (right, below) as its first response against terror attacks. Instead of gathering intelligence on entire terrorist organizations, the Bureau assumed its role was to preserve evidence, investigate, arrest, prosecute, and convict after an attack. The Bureau was content with *not* knowing what was going on in communities likely to shelter terrorism, proof that it was not violating anyone's civil liberties.

08-22-79   12: 43: 25

Preventing terror attacks would have meant reviving domestic intelligence, which would have been interpreted as an attempt to bring Hoover back from the dead (left).

Louis Freeh vastly expanded the Bureau's overseas capabilities and relationships with foreign law enforcement. Armed with new laws, the Bureau "rendered" fugitive terrorists back to the United States in dramatic investigations such as Special Agent Brad Garrett's arrest of Mir Aimal Kansi, who had attacked CIA employees at Langley in 1993 (above left). The Bureau gained supreme authority over counterintelligence after Special Agent Les Wiser unmasked CIA mole Aldrich Ames (below), who had sent scores of CIA informants in the Soviet Union to jail or death.

By now the Bureau had internalized the public's repugnance for domestic intelligence gathering. In cooperation with Justice Department lawyers, the FBI hedged domestic intelligence investigations with so many restrictions that agents believed it was dangerous to work on them at all. Moreover, under Freeh, the Bureau's historic refusal to cooperate with other intelligence agencies was now buttressed by rigid rules and policies that erected walls between criminal and intelligence investigations.

While television's *X-Files* (right, Gillian Anderson and David Duchovny as special agents Sculley and Mulder) presented the Bureau as a snakepit of conspiracy, Freeh tried to restore the public image of the Bureau by focusing on agent ethics and an ostentatious commitment to civil liberties.

During Freeh's tenure, his image of the ethical G-man was undercut by recurrent blunders that created new suspicions that the Bureau was incompetent and dishonest: The mishandling of the postmortem examinations of the Hostage Rescue Team's disastrous operations at Waco (right) and Ruby Ridge (right, below) led to unfounded but widely believed charges that the Bureau had covered up wrongdoing by its agents and officials. The Bureau's reputation was further eroded by the Wen Ho Lee espionage and Olympic Park bombing cases, in which Freeh personally intervened. An FBI specialist in foreign counter-intelligence, Special Agent Robert Hanssen, was arrested for spying for the Soviets for two decades. The Bureau's dysfunctional computer systems resulted in tardy discovery of documents that were supposed to have been furnished to Oklahoma City bomber Timothy McVeigh's defense team, marring what had been a successful FBI investigation. Despite the billions of dollars Congress had given the Bureau for counterterrorism, Freeh's politically correct Bureau refused to revive domestic intelligence gathering and analysis that could have given the Bureau the ability to prevent, and not just prosecute, terror attacks.

Stung by Minneapolis Special Agent Coleen Rowley's revelations (above) that FBI headquarters had sabotaged her office's promising investigation of a student pilot who might have been the twentieth hijacker, and by official investigations into the 9/11 attacks that blasted the Bureau as institutionally incapable of gathering and analyzing intelligence, FBI Director Robert Mueller (below) has tried to transform the Bureau from a law enforcement organization into an intelligence agency that actively prevents terror attacks. This objective has changed agent recruitment, training, and criteria for promotion to emphasize intelligence gathering and analysis.

The question, however, goes beyond the FBI. Will we let it, or any agency, fight terrorism? Can the Bureau overcome the country's ingrained hostility to domestic intelligence gathering? Can a country that does not seem to want to be protected, be protected?

That night Dasch called FBI headquarters in New York, and asked to speak to Hoover. The agent manning the phone filed a report. It was read the next day by his superior and ignored, and so Dasch decided to go to Washington to talk to Hoover personally. He checked into the Mayflower Hotel there, which, by coincidence, was where Hoover and Tolson lunched nearly every day. This time he reached Donald M. Ladd, the assistant director in charge of the Bureau's Domestic Intelligence Division. By now Ladd knew of Cullen's encounter with the Germans, and had been briefed on the sabotage equipment the Coast Guard had recovered from its hiding place on the beach. The Coast Guard had told the Bureau that one of the saboteurs had a white streak in his hair. Ladd assigned Agent Duane L. Traynor, head of the Sabotage Unit, to talk to Dasch. Traynor later recalled that when he saw the streak in Dasch's hair, "I knew he was the real thing." Hoover immediately called Biddle with the news, and Biddle excitedly informed the president on June 19 that German saboteurs had landed in America, with the FBI in hot pursuit. Within two days the Bureau had arrested the remaining two members of Dasch's team; a week later the Bureau had three of the Florida saboteurs in custody and was on the trail of the last.

The Bureau told Roosevelt it had learned the Germans planned to send more saboteurs to America at six-week intervals to terrorize the country. Roosevelt decided that the saboteurs had to die to impress on Berlin that any future saboteurs would be dealt with just as mercilessly. All eight were condemned to death by an ad hoc military tribunal. Dasch and Burger had their sentences commuted to thirty years and life, respectively, were pardoned after the war, and returned to Germany, where they were treated as traitors. When the Supreme Court refused to intervene, the six others were electrocuted.

The FBI's capture of the Nazi saboteurs, following on the William Sebold–Fritz Duquesne trial of the previous September, reassured the country that the FBI had the security of the home front well in hand. These two FBI cases did much to keep the home front calm during the war, unlike during the First World War, when a panicky public had forced the Bureau to expend prodigious amounts of energy and do prodigious amounts of harm hunting a spy threat that simply did not exist. This time, thanks to the FBI, the government—and the public—could concentrate on the real enemy and the real war.

The Nazi saboteur case was such a triumph for the Bureau that afterward enemies of Hoover and the Bureau examined it for flaws, and claimed they had discovered a cover-up. The Bureau, critics claimed, had concealed the role of the Coast Guard, and had created the false impression that the Bureau had cracked the case on its own, concealing the fact that Dasch and the Coast Guard had solved the case for them.

But every criminal case, every intelligence investigation, contains elements that can be exploited by defense attorneys and, when it comes to the FBI, by the Bureau's many enemies. During its glory years the Bureau *was* able to maintain a tight control over its cases, which let it conceal the cases' weaknesses and reveal only the strengths. And so eventually, every important FBI case—which, like all cases in the raw can be something of a mess—has the potential to be turned against the Bureau when, as has become inevitable, all of the facts of the investigation are revealed: loose ends, unconfirmed tips, contradictions never resolved because they have no bearing on the arguments presented in court. In recent years that has happened to almost all the great cases in Bureau history at the hands of hostile historians and sensationalistic writers. As a general rule—applicable not only to the Bureau—the better a case is packaged for the public or for a jury (and the Bureau packaged its cases very well during its great days), the greater the number of inconvenient and inconsistent details that wait to be exploited if someone has the urge—and with the Bureau, it seems that someone always has that urge.

But at the time the Nazi spy case was unfolding, everybody knew that the Bureau had not solved the case on its own. The Coast Guard's role was widely reported, and during Dasch's trial it became well known that he had turned himself in to the Bureau. If in its later retellings of the story the Bureau played up only its own part in the case—well, the Bureau may have thought that the Coast Guard could blow its own horn, and probably would.

The Bureau had so many public relations triumphs during the war that it was frustrating to Hoover that in the one arena where its agents had gone toe to toe with an entrenched and formidable Nazi opponent, the Bureau's victories went largely unnoticed and unappreciated by the public. This was South America, which had been given to the FBI under the demarcation agreement with the Army and Navy. The Bureau's fight in South America was, Hoover complained, "a great piece of work" whose story had never been told.

Of course, getting the American public interested in South America has defeated even greater public relations talents than Hoover's, and despite his best efforts, he never managed to convince the public that his South American operations were anything but a sideshow. Hoover began planning his "Special Intelligence Service" (SIS) for South America in May 1940, immediately after Roosevelt formally apportioned intelligence responsibilities between the FBI, the Office of Naval Intelligence, and the Military Intelligence Division and gave South America to the FBI. Within a month the Bureau had begun sending agents to Central and South America. Some went as undercover agents, others as legal attachés to embassies or liaison officers with South American police forces.

The FBI's mission in South America was to provide Washington with information on Axis activities and to destroy enemy intelligence and propaganda networks. There was vast potential for trouble in the South American republics and colonies. There were 360,000 Germans in Brazil, 194,000 in Argentina, and 129,000 in Chile, many of them in Nazi-controlled nationalist organizations. There was an enormous colony of 280,000 Japanese in Brazil, and another 60,000 in Peru. The Germans controlled a continent-wide radio propaganda network, had great influence in South American governments (particularly Argentina and Chile), and had built up enormous commercial interests that provided the *Wehrmacht* with strategic raw materials. The Bureau's ally in this fight was Nelson Rockefeller's Office of the Coordinator of Inter-American Affairs, which had responsibility for commercial warfare against German interests.

At any one time the Bureau had as many as 360 agents in South America. The SIS identified 887 Axis intelligence agents in Latin America; of these 389 were arrested and 105 convicted. The Bureau identified 281 propaganda agents, leading to 60 arrests. The FBI also located 30 saboteurs, with 20 arrests, as well as 222 smugglers, of whom 75 were arrested and 11 convicted. The Bureau managed to have 7,064 enemy aliens in South America relocated, 2,172 interned, and 5,893 deported. SIS investigations led to the capture of thirty radio transmitters and the shutdown of twenty-four radio stations. Four SIS agents lost their lives, including SIS Chief Percy Foxworth, who had earlier led the Bureau's New York field office. The Bureau's most significant operation on this front was probably its exposure of the Nazi activities of South American government officials, particularly in Chile and Argentina, where FBI investigations helped check these countries' support for Germany and, in the case of Chile, led to the termination of its relations with the Axis.

Hoover's failure to get credit for his good work in Latin America may have tempered his enthusiasm for expanding FBI operations overseas after the war. He did propose using the FBI's legal attachés at American embassies overseas as the nucleus of a postwar intelligence system, but he did not fight as hard for his plan as might have been expected. One reason may have been the puny payoff for his South American operations, compared to his evaluation of its worth and expectation that such valuable work would bring the Bureau new prestige and responsibilities.

■ ■ ■

Throughout the war the Bureau's first concern was to prevent the mass hysteria that had disrupted the home front during World War I. That was the constant

theme of all the Bureau's wartime publicity, and there was a *lot* of Bureau publicity during the war. FBI public relations during World War II followed a predictable formula: First the audience would be reminded that President
Roosevelt had given the FBI jurisdiction over "all investigative work in matters
involving espionage, sabotage, subversive activities, and violations of our neutrality regulations." Then the narrator would urge the public to "leave it to the
FBI," telling them that "if you know of any un-American activities, report them
to the FBI and then say nothing more." In the publicity of the thirties each FBI
case was turned into an argument for making the Bureau the model for all law
enforcement. In a similar way, publicity about the Bureau's Nazi saboteur and
Japanese spy cases were offered as proof that the country was so well protected
by the Bureau that there was absolutely no need for the public to concern itself
about homeland security. As the Bureau's authorized historian of the 1950s,
Don Whitehead, explained,

> *The untold story back of the FBI's anti-sabotage and anti-espionage precau-*
> *tions was that Hoover had two primary motives in initiating them: first, there*
> *must not be any enemy espionage and sabotage such as there had been in World*
> *War I; and second, there must not be permitted to develop any vigilante system*
> *of wartime law enforcement. The records of the FBI reveal Hoover's motives to*
> *be that simple.*

The Bureau's wartime publicity actually began even before Pearl Harbor,
with a January 1940 article in *American Magazine* written by Hoover "with"
Courtney Ryley Cooper: "The citizen should consider his particular task to be
fulfilled when he reports his suspicions to the nearest F.B.I. office." An accom-
panying cartoon showed Uncle Sam raising a giant boot, labeled "The F.B.I.," to
crush the "Spy Menace" snake. A flashlight beam that lit the way was "Public
Cooperation."

Movie audiences got the same message in *The F.B.I. Front,* a Bureau-assisted
March of Time documentary released in 1942. Producers said the purpose of
the film was to "calm the ambitions of any amateur sleuth who fancies himself
an adequate substitute for the trained, scientific, and, above all, humane agents
of the F.B.I."

As he had during the thirties, Hoover saw FBI wartime publicity as an inte-
gral part of his strategy for reassuring the public that the FBI had any potential
threats fully under control. In 1944 Hoover assigned Louis B. Nichols to work
with Louis De Rochemont on a movie account of the Bureau's wartime cases.

This was *The House on 92nd Street,* which came out early in 1945 and ranks as one of the three classic Hoover-era FBI movies (along with *G-Men* and the Jimmy Stewart film of 1959, *The FBI Story*). The star G-man of *92nd Street* was Lloyd Nolan, who had been Cagney's on-screen gym instructor in the 1935 *G-Men. The House on 92nd Street* was filmed in an earnestly journalistic, pseudo-documentary style with the by-now-obligatory fingerprint file and crime laboratory scenes. It made counterespionage work seem dauntingly complicated, best left to professionals. Like *Ten Thousand Public Enemies* and *G-Men,* the film wove together several different investigations (including the William Sebold–Fritz Duquesne case) into an epic showing how the weapons that the Bureau had perfected against the gangsters of the thirties—science and organization—were just as effective against the new international enemies threatening the country then, or that might in the future.

But Hoover would not have been able to convince the public to "leave it to the FBI" if military plants and bases had started to blow up right after Pearl Harbor. One Black Tom explosion and he could have forgotten about "Leave It to the FBI." But there were no proven acts of sabotage during World War II (out of 19,396 investigated reports). Between 1938 and 1945, FBI investigations resulted in ninety-one spying convictions, most of the arrests coming the first few months after Pearl Harbor. By any measure, German and Japanese undercover operations were a miserable failure, and by that standard, the FBI's performance was a brilliant success. It was Hoover's confidence that he had eliminated any possibility of Japanese espionage or sabotage that led him to oppose the internment of West Coast Japanese-Americans. He protested that the Bureau had already rounded up everyone who could be considered a danger. When he was ordered to report on law enforcement problems within the internment camps, he took advantage of the opportunity to repeat his objections to the internment. He evidently felt that the internment reflected a lack of confidence that he and the Bureau could do the job without resorting to such unprofessional measures.

To handle the Bureau's enormously expanded responsibilities during the war, Hoover adapted his peacetime concept of a coordinated, FBI-led law enforcement movement to the wartime conditions. Even though the Bureau expanded during the war, from 1,596 agents in fiscal 1941 to 4,886 in 1944, these numbers were obviously inadequate to supervise security throughout the entire defense industry and to guard the entire country against "sabotage, espionage, and subversion," as FDR had ordered. Hoover's solution was to use the same strategy he and Cummings had developed to deflect calls for a "national police force" in 1933. He relied on cooperative efforts with local police and carefully selected (because of his fears of a repetition of the APL fiasco) civilians to maintain adequate security coverage.

This coordinated domestic security network depended on three large-scale outreach programs. The FBI formalized its ties to local police with the "FBI Law Enforcement Officers Mobilization Plan for National Defense," which sent FBI executives into the field for quarterly training sessions with police executives in major cities. By 1942, there were 73,164 police officers who had participated in these conferences.

The Bureau also had to maintain security in the defense industry. It established a system of informants in defense plants to bring any reports of sabotage to the attention of the FBI. By July 1942 the FBI had a network of 20,718 informants in nearly four thousand industrial plants.

Late in 1940 the Bureau organized a third informant network. This was the "American Legion Contact Program," and its purpose was actually to head off a plan the legion developed during the summer of 1940 to organize its own counterespionage force with its own badges, manuals, and credentials (in effect, a reincarnation of the World War I APL). Hoover was also worried by the legion's growing enthusiasm for HUAC's antiradical investigations chaired by Congressman Martin Dies, who was attacking the Bureau as well as Roosevelt for being soft on communists. By October 1943 the Bureau had recruited about 60,000 legion members into this program, who could be relied on to reassure the legion's leaders that whatever security issues worried them were under control.

The Bureau's success during the war was in part the residue of its record during the thirties. It entered the war with a broad and deep reservoir of public affection and gratitude, with the trust and confidence of the president, and perhaps most important, with a well-honed expertise at turning the often resistant facts of an investigative case into a streamlined demonstration of its prowess. At the end of the thirties the Bureau had learned how to take a case, almost any case, and shape or alter it to fit a predetermined conclusion, highlighting whatever redounded to the FBI's credit while silently burying anything that embarrassed the Bureau. A cynic might call that spin; an enemy might call it a cover-up; but during World War II, as during the Depression, FBI public relations and entertainment gave the country what it wanted and probably needed. The Bureau entered World War II popular, powerful, and proud, and finished it more popular, more powerful, and prouder than ever: Its agent ranks grew from 713 in 1939 to a peak of 4,886 in 1944, while its support staff increased from 1,199 to 8,305.

At the end of the war Hoover had achieved control over American law enforcement, at least as much of it as he wanted, as well as absolute control over domestic security. This was reinforced by complete control over the FBI's public image. Hoover molded and jealously guarded that image, as Frederick Collins discovered when he tried to turn his FBI-endorsed history of the Bureau, *The FBI in Peace and War,* into a radio series in 1943 (with the same name) without Hoover's permission. Hoover was furious and countered with a show of his own, *This Is Your FBI,* which ran for almost nine years, with its memorable "Love for Three Oranges" theme. Its slogan, intoned by veteran movie G-man Frank Lovejoy, was that to "your F.B.I. you look for national security . . . and to the Equitable Society for financial security. These two great institutions are dedicated to the protection of you . . . your home and your country." "In this country," Lovejoy would sign off each week, "espionage is under control."

■ ■ ■

The FBI's greatest contribution to the war effort was building national confidence that the home front was safe and secure, in the same way that the Bureau had restored morale during the thirties with the pageantry of its war on crime. The Bureau had defined success on its own terms: capturing or killing public enemies; putting a few saboteurs or spies on trial to demonstrate that the home front was safe from espionage, sabotage, and subversion. Agents put their lives on the line to achieve that success, and some of them died. And so the Bureau fully deserved the nation's gratitude.

From the beginning of the New Deal until the end of the war, the Bureau rode the crest of an unprecedented wave of popularity. It was adored by the public and invulnerable within the government. You could say that everybody loved the G-men—that is, almost everybody. There were still the Bureau's old enemies from the Red Scare years, who gritted their teeth and bit their tongues when they saw Hoover strutting in the limelight. But as long as he lavished his attentions on the right—Nazi spies and American fascists—and left the left alone—well, the left left *him* alone.

Examined from another perspective, in the Bureau's successes of the Depression and the war could be seen the seeds of future failures. Those successes had been too easy. Statistics prove there had really been no crime wave during the thirties. There had been a media-created illusion of a crime wave, which had really been a wave of overblown stories about a few criminals turned into celebrities by the sensationalist press. Ending a crime wave that had never been was not too hard: All the Bureau had to do was capture or kill those few criminals whom the media had puffed up as symbols of crime.

The national security threat during the thirties and the war years was not a complete illusion: There was a Nazi underground; there were Japanese spies; and, of course, Stalin's underground in America was not only spying but infiltrating itself into the government, unions, and cultural institutions. But once again, from an investigative standpoint it was a very manageable threat. There were only a few German and Japanese spies—a few embassy burglaries, a few walk-ins from informants, and the Bureau knew whom to go after before hostilities began. The danger from a Nazi fifth column was as overblown as the threat from the public enemies: a few pathetic blowhards feeding their private demons by dressing up in brown shirts and goose-stepping in country hideaways like farmyard führers. All the Bureau had to do was round them up and put them on trial, and it could announce that the Nazi underground was kaput.

Even though the Bureau's national security investigations before and during World War II exhibited bravery and skill, the lesson the Bureau learned was that national security was mostly a matter of adroit public relations. The Bureau's real job during the lead-up to war and the war itself was to use its cases to demonstrate that the threat, such as it was, was well in hand. This was a dangerous lesson, since it taught the Bureau that the hard investigative work of gathering, analyzing, and acting on hard-to-get intelligence was less important than the muscle flexing that impressed the public. And so years later it might conclude that, for example, slithering down ropes from helicopters was the answer to terrorism, instead of the hard work of infiltrating Islamic fundamentalist groups, developing informants, and collecting and analyzing reports from its files and from other agencies.

Hoover's evident contempt for intelligence analysis—demonstrated during the war in the unfiltered gossip he forwarded to the White House—may have become institutionalized in the Bureau. In Hoover's FBI, intelligence was valued only if it could be used in a court case, or used to protect Hoover and the Bureau from their enemies. He insisted that the Bureau simply collected facts, and it was up to policymakers to analyze them. Of course it is precisely by fitting the facts into a pattern that high-level crimes and high-level security threats are discovered. But Hoover was not interested in that kind of intelligence, unless it could be used somehow to make the argument that the American Communist Party, no matter how small it might become, was nevertheless always and eternally dangerous.

The Bureau also learned another lesson: that it was always safer to pursue right-wing extremist groups than those on the left, despite Hoover's obvious preference for pursuing the latter. But he learned—for instance, from his arrests of the Abraham Lincoln Brigade veterans—that when investigating the left or issues they supported, one never knew when he might brush up against hidden tripwires that would set the entire left barking, snapping, and sometimes biting. This was a lesson impressed on the Bureau repeatedly, until finally during the 1990s, while terror cells were sinking roots into the Islamic community, the Bureau shied away from any investigations that might have subjected it to criticism for ethnic profiling, maintaining—plausibly, it must be conceded after Oklahoma City—that the real terror threat came from right-wing extremists and militias out in the boondocks, who had few defenders in Washington.

Hoover was right when he said, as he often did, that effective law enforcement and national security investigations depended on cooperation between the Bureau, the entire law enforcement community, and the public. To a great extent that claim was simply public relations, since during the thirties and forties only the image of cooperation, rather than the real thing, was needed to deal with what were not much more than disturbances in the public imagination. Throughout the thirties and forties, whenever the Bureau reached out to the public with its wars on crime or its wartime citizen informant programs, its real goal was to *prevent* unwanted public involvement in law enforcement or national security. The real message was always "Leave It to the FBI." The Bureau wanted the public to join its crusades, but only vicariously.

Given the Bureau's reputation during these years, the Bureau *could* have put together a coordinated nationwide law enforcement or national security system with a high level of citizen involvement, but only if the Bureau remained strictly apolitical, out of the political fray. Needless to say, that was not Hoover's style. Within a few years the Bureau would be so politicized that anything it did would be seen as suspect and fiercely to be resisted. If the time came when the Bureau had to reach out to the public for help in fighting crime or terrorism— as has been the case for the last two decades—rather than producing cooperation, the Bureau's efforts would stir up the old suspicions that the FBI was more dangerous than anything it might be investigating.

The FBI's spectacular success during the Depression and World War II would, in ways hardly noticeable at the time, contribute to its decline as the only investigative agency able to pursue the most serious "crimes against the United States." At the end of the war the FBI was more committed than ever to a philosophy of law enforcement that treated the low-level individual criminal as the only real crime threat, even as Americans (and their leaders) began to call for a more sophisticated, comprehensive approach to civil rights violations, to organized crime, and to political and police corruption. But the Bureau's unassailable position within the government rested, in part, on Hoover's refusal to investigate political corruption, police misconduct, or high-level economic crime. As times changed, Hoover's Bureau would be missing in action in the fight against wealthy, powerful, and politically protected lawbreakers.

The FBI's power and prestige rested on maintaining, at all costs, its close relationship with the public. It nourished that relationship with publicity, and during the Depression and the war that publicity was spectacularly successful.

That success created, however, expectations about the FBI so high as to be unsustainable by any organization, even one as good as the Bureau. FBI publicity portrayed the Bureau as always successful, always getting its man, always thwarting the spy and the saboteur. The Bureau's continued success in dealing with public alarms through public relations fed its conviction that whether the crisis of the moment was law enforcement or national security, the real crisis was public confidence, and that with one spectacular arrest the Bureau could reassure once again the public that with the FBI on the job, the nation was safe.

That strategy could work only if the threat to the public's peace of mind really was symbolic, and so could be dealt with through the symbolism of arrest and trial. It also depended on a public that wanted to believe in the FBI, as the public in fact wanted to believe during the Depression and the war. If the public ever lost that will to believe—and some temporarily mute segments of the public never had believed—and if the threat was not of the sort to be defused by the symbolism of public relations, the FBI would be left weaponless—and defenseless.

SIX

The Cold War FBI
(1945–1961)

I N 1947, SPECIAL AGENT Robert J. Lamphere was a just-married twenty-nine-year-old. The Communist Party's *Daily Worker* described him as "baby-faced but hard-lipped," and one of their most dangerous enemies. Add a prominent, aggressive jaw, a stocky, muscular build, and the requisite G-man attire of double-breasted suit topped by a snap-brimmed fedora, and he looked like a man who would not find a fight—legal or physical—a thing disagreeable to contemplate.

I got to know Lamphere fifty years later. I found that his pugnacity, his most striking feature as a young counterespionage specialist, masked a thoughtful and penetrating curiosity: just what was needed, it turned out, to track down some of the Soviet Union's cleverest and most productive spies during the perilous first years of the Cold War.

Lamphere was detailed to the Washington FBI Headquarters in September 1947. He had distinguished himself as a Soviet espionage specialist at the New York City field office in Manhattan, where he had shadowed and questioned some of the most important operatives in the Soviet Union's global espionage network.

Generally speaking, the Bureau knew what the Soviets were after—the secrets of the atomic bomb—and they knew the Soviets were trying hard to penetrate the Manhattan Project. Trying to stop them was the job of Lamphere's squad. They had been trailing Arthur Alexandrovich Adams, who had gotten classified scientific data from a Manhattan Project employee in Chicago. They watched Amtorg, the Russian trading company, which was a cover for spies, and

Andrei Shevchenko, a Soviet agent operating out of Amtorg, who was after aircraft specifications and procedures.

While on surveillance stakeouts, Lamphere had picked the brains of more experienced counterespionage agents. He learned more about the history of Soviet espionage in this country from them, about the spy networks set up by Robert Switz in the thirties for the KGB, and about the rings established by two other professional KGB spymasters, Vassili Zubilin and Gaik Ovakimian. One of the men Lamphere followed around New York was Anatoli Yakovlev, who was, Lamphere later learned, the KGB controller for the Soviet atom spy rings.

But until the end of the war, the Bureau had little more than tantalizing, usually unverifiable, scraps of information about what the Soviets were up to. The Bureau needed a break, and then in September 1945, Igor Gouzenko, a GRU (Soviet Army Intelligence) cipher clerk stationed in the Soviet Embassy in Ottawa, Canada, defected to the Royal Canadian Mounted Police. He brought the Mounties official papers with the names of Soviet spies in the Canadian government, including the security branches. One document revealed that Alan Nunn May, a British scientist working on the Manhattan Project in Canada, had turned over technical papers on the bomb to the Soviets, as well as an actual sample of U-235 from an American lab. As a result of Gouzenko's defection, Nunn May and dozens of other Soviet spies, both Canadians and Russians, were exposed. Nunn May himself was convicted of espionage.

Besides proving that Soviet espionage had penetrated the Manhattan Project, the Gouzenko transcripts revealed something even more explosive: that the Soviets had agents highly placed in the American government. One Gouzenko document stated that an aide to one of Secretary of State Edward R. Stettinius's assistant secretaries was a Soviet spy. Hoover immediately notified President Harry Truman.

In 1945 another Soviet agent defected to the Bureau. This was Elizabeth Bentley, a Vassar-educated brunette the newspapers would colorize into the "Blond Spy Queen." She walked into the FBI's New Haven offices with a story about a government spy ring organized by Nathan Gregory Silvermaster, a Russian-born official with the Farm Security Administration. Members included Assistant Treasury Secretary Harry Dexter White and White House counselor Laughlin Currie. Bentley had also gotten secret information from Major Duncan C. Lee, an assistant to Office of Strategic Services chief William Donovan; from William Walter Remington of the War Production Board; OSS consultant Louis Adamic; Victor Perlo of the War Production Board; John Abt; and Harold Glasser. Bentley had joined the Party in the early thirties, and had fallen in love with Jacob Golos, Stalin's inspector general over the American

Communist Party and an intermediary between American communist spies and the Soviets. After Golos was exposed by HUAC, Bentley became his courier, collecting documents from his American contacts in New York and Washington. When Golos died in 1943, Bentley took over his spy network. She also told the Bureau one of Golos's agents was tall, thin, with horn-rimmed glasses, a spy named "Julius."

After a month of interviews Bentley provided the Bureau with the names of more than eighty Soviet agents in all. As one agent said, the Bureau had "hit gold on this one." Hoover sent the White House a memo detailing what the Bureau had learned from Bentley—referred to as "Gregory" in FBI documents sent outside the Bureau. The FBI immediately launched a massive investigation of all the agents named by Bentley. This gave the Bureau a detailed picture of Soviet espionage networks in the New York and Washington areas, complete with names of spies, where they worked, and what they had been doing. But when Hoover told the chief of British intelligence in the United States about Bentley's defection and what she was saying, he relayed the information to his deputy in charge of Soviet counterintelligence, who happened to be Kim Philby, a Russian spy himself, and the Soviets began rolling up the Bentley network. "In this intense but nearly invisible combat," Lamphere later wrote, the FBI "was playing catch-up ball; the Soviets had built up an early lead and the FBI, new to the endeavor, was not as knowledgeable or as sophisticated as the enemy."

Lamphere's first assignment at headquarters was designing counterespionage coverage against Soviet satellite countries. After a few months, he recalled, "I longed to get back into fighting the main threat, Soviet intelligence, and I believed that in a locked safe in our espionage unit at headquarters was a means of doing so."

In that safe were a few pieces of paper with fragments of decrypted messages between the Soviet consulate in New York and KGB headquarters in Moscow. "The KGB messages were to change my life. More important, they were to affect the course of history: in the coming years their revelations would lead directly to decisive actions that the FBI took against KGB operations in the United States." When fully decrypted and properly interpreted, they would give Lamphere a detailed map of the Soviet Union's espionage web in America. The effort to decode them was named the Venona Project. Lamphere reasoned that if the Venona experts had access to the information the FBI had gathered about the spy networks and agents that were presumably the subjects of the transmissions, it might help them in their work. He was right. By the summer of 1948, Army code breaker Meredith Gardner was able to give Lamphere almost complete texts of some of the messages. Said Lamphere, "I stood in the vestibule of the enemy's house, having entered by stealth. I held in my hands a set of keys. Each one would fit one of the doors of the place and lead us, I hoped, to matters of importance to our country."

But as the FBI began to build its cases against agents named by Gouzenko, Bentley, and another defector, Whittaker Chambers, the Bureau's past came back to haunt it. Its revelations about Soviet spy networks were seen, by those who remembered the Bureau's indiscriminate Red smearing in the early twenties, as more of the same. "I could hardly believe my ears," Lamphere said, when famed news broadcaster Edward R. Murrow and others began to charge that the State Department's Laurence Duggan and the Treasury Department's Harry Dexter White were innocent public servants hounded to their deaths by anticommunist persecution. In the case of Duggan, Lamphere himself had interviewed another Soviet spy, Hede Massing, who had told him that it was she who had recruited Duggan to work for the Soviets.

What was particularly frustrating to the FBI was that the Bureau's best evidence against Soviet agents like the State Department's Alger Hiss, Duggan, and White came from the Venona documents, and that information could not be revealed for fear of letting the Soviets know that their codes had been broken. (The Soviets already knew. The secret was blown by a spy at the Venona Project, William Weisband, and by Kim Philby.)

In December 1948, Lamphere discovered that a Soviet agent mentioned in the decrypted files as "SIMA" and described as working for the Justice Department in New York but being transferred to Washington, was in fact a young woman by the name of Judith Coplon. Lamphere had learned that Coplon's routine included regular trips to New York to visit her family. On these trips she usually had a meeting with an individual who turned out to be Valentin Alekseevich Gubitchev, a Soviet agent working at the United Nations. Lamphere ordered that official papers be steered to her at the Justice Department. One of these gave the name of an employee at Amtorg who was an FBI double agent. He felt that Coplon would think this information was so important that she would want to deliver it immediately to Gubitchev. Sure enough, on March 4, 1949, Coplon took the bait and headed for New York, where despite Coplon's attempts to evade surveillance, she and Gubitchev were arrested together. Her handbag contained the secret documents, Gubitchev's wallet had $125 in small bills. Coplon was convicted twice, the first time for stealing government documents vital to national security for the benefit of a foreign nation, the second for conspiracy with Gubitchev to commit espionage.

But the two cases actually hurt the Bureau. Both were overturned on appeal because of investigative illegalities involving wiretaps and warrantless arrests. Both errors could have been easily prevented if not for bad legal advice given the Bureau by the Justice Department. Even worse, another procedural blunder by Hoover and the attorney general led to raw FBI files being read in court, which subjected the Bureau to more criticism and ridicule. The Bureau was learning that intelligence and criminal investigations did not mix. In the short run that would lead the Bureau to adopt complex and deceptive file-keeping procedures to conceal the use of illegal intelligence techniques in national security cases that might go to court. In the long run the Bureau would adopt the disastrous remedy of separating its criminal from its intelligence investigations and both from the investigations of other agencies like the CIA.

While the Coplon case was still under way, the Soviet Union had exploded its first atomic bomb. The FBI needed to know whether Russian research on their bomb had been materially aided by espionage at the Manhattan Project. All the Bureau knew for sure was that a Soviet agent had tried to get information from Manhattan Project scientific director J. Robert Oppenheimer and his associates, that another agent had recruited a scientist to spy at a Manhattan Project laboratory in Chicago, and that Allan Nunn May had sent back some atom project information from Canada. None of this seemed all that significant scientifically. According to Lamphere, "It wasn't possible for us to assess accurately how much direct help these penetrations had been to Soviet scientists who had fashioned the Russian A-Bomb."

Lamphere got his answer in a decrypted KGB file from 1944 that described the gaseous diffusion process of weapons material manufacture. The report had originated within the Manhattan Project and also revealed that the source had been a spy among the British scientists at the project. Lamphere requested a copy of the gaseous diffusion report from the Atomic Energy Commission, learned that it had been written by a Klaus Fuchs, and learned that Fuchs was a scientist on the British mission to the project. Now Lamphere had a suspect. Further research in the files revealed that the British had captured a Gestapo document stating that Fuchs had been a communist before he fled Germany for England. Fuchs's name had also been in an address book found in the apartment of Israel Halperin, named in Igor Gouzenko's documents as a GRU agent.

Fuchs was back in England, so Lamphere wrote a memo to MI5 and 6 that Fuchs was now an FBI suspect in the atomic espionage case. The British launched their own investigation and concluded that Lamphere was right. However, the need to keep the Venona Project a secret prevented the Bureau from telling the British all they knew about Fuchs, even though, they later discovered, the British had learned about Venona from their *own* spies. Finally, in

December 1949, under interrogation by MI5 agent William Skardon, Fuchs confessed.

In Fuchs's confession to Skardon, he said that the conduit for atomic information from Fuchs to Soviet intelligence had been a man he knew only as "Raymond." The whole FBI was now sent out to hunt for Raymond. Lamphere and the Bureau believed Raymond would be the key link between Fuchs and the rest of the Soviet espionage network in America.

The one clue Lamphere had to Raymond's identity, after all the others had failed, was that Fuchs thought Raymond had some training as a chemical engineer or chemist. Lamphere recalled that when Bentley testified in 1947, she had mentioned chemist Abraham Brothman as one of her contacts. Brothman had testified before a grand jury that he had known Bentley and Jacob Golos, but beyond that had provided only minor and useless information. But Brothman had made one slip, saying that he had been introduced to Golos by another chemist, someone named Harry Gold. Nothing had resulted from Brothman's grand jury testimony about Gold at the time, but now it came back to haunt them. Lamphere sent Brothman's and Gold's photographs to Fuchs, who failed to recognize either. But Lamphere was gathering more information about Gold that showed his movements were consistent with Fuchs's testimony about Raymond. Lamphere decided, "The photo itself might be the cause of the difficulty . . . since often a witness will be unable to identify a file photo of a man, but will later readily identify a better photo." Gold lived in Philadelphia, so Lamphere ordered the Philadelphia field office to get a better picture.

In May 1950, Lamphere traveled to England to question Fuchs. Lamphere told Fuchs that the purpose of the visit was to identify Raymond, and he played on Fuchs's concern for his sister, who was confined to a mental hospital in the United States: Fuchs assumed that if he did not cooperate the FBI would retaliate against his sister. Lamphere did not disabuse him of this notion. Lamphere gave Fuchs pictures of Gold. Looking through them one by one, Fuchs said he could not recognize Gold from the photos. But when Fuchs saw the most recent pictures, he said, "I cannot reject them." Two days later Lamphere set up equipment to show Fuchs surveillance motion pictures of Gold. Now Fuchs said, "I cannot be absolutely positive, but I think it is very likely him. There are certain mannerisms I seem to recognize, such as the too-obvious way he has of looking around and looking back."

That same day, May 22, 1950, agents in Philadelphia were searching Gold's apartment. Gold had denied he had ever been west of the Mississippi, or had ever traveled to Boston. He was unnerved when the agents retrieved a Boston railroad timetable tucked into one of his books. When they discovered a

Chamber of Commerce brochure for Santa Fe, New Mexico, containing a street map, Gold crumbled. "I am the man to whom Fuchs gave the information." Two days later in London, on May 24, Lamphere got a new shipment of still and motion pictures of Gold. As soon as Lamphere showed Fuchs the new pictures, his response "was almost instantaneous. 'Yes, he said, 'that is my American contact.' "

> *An unbelievably great weight seemed to lift from my shoulders. The essence of my mission to London was already accomplished: the FBI had located "Raymond," and now Fuchs had identified the man as well. The Director had charged us to find Fuchs's American contact, and we had fulfilled that assignment.*

On May 26, Fuchs wrote on the back of two photos of Gold, "I identify this photograph as the likeness of the man whom I knew under the name of Raymond—Klaus Fuchs—26th May, 1950." And now, Lamphere wrote, "We were on the verge of learning, in detail, what the KGB had been doing inside our country during the war years and immediately thereafter."

Soon Lamphere was running some forty-nine investigations based on Gold's confessions. Some involved backtracking to Gold's initial recruitment into Soviet espionage; others stemmed from the Brothman connection. A third line of investigation, which still resonates with the public, led to Julius and Ethel Rosenberg.

One of the Venona decrypts had revealed that there had been an "UNSUB" (an UNknown SUBject) in a "lower level position at Los Alamos" spying for the KGB. The decrypts also revealed that the UNSUB was going to be on furlough in late 1944 and early 1945. Lamphere learned that these clues fit a David Greenglass, who then lived in Albuquerque with his wife, Ruth. When Gold was shown still photos and motion pictures of Greenglass, he thought that Greenglass was his contact. Greenglass's Army file showed that he had been on furlough at almost exactly the same time as the KGB UNSUB. Agents questioned Greenglass, and got his permission to borrow photos of himself and his wife. When Gold saw a picture of them together at the Albuquerque apartment, he immediately identified Greenglass and wrote on the back of one photo, "This is the man I contacted in Albuquerque, N.M. in June, 1945, on instructions from my Soviet Espionage Superior, 'JOHN.' The man in the picture gave me information relative to his work at Los Alamos, New Mexico, which information I later gave to JOHN." That same day agents picked up Greenglass at his apartment in New York and took him to the Foley Square field office. There he confessed to giving classified information to Gold. He also revealed he had been recruited into espionage by his sister Ethel's husband, Julius Rosenberg.

On June 25, 1950, North Korean forces crossed the border into South Korea. The next day President Truman ordered General Douglas MacArthur to stop the invasion. Everyone feared, Lamphere recalled, that this might be the beginning of another world war. David Greenglass was told by his attorney that he and Ruth should make a deal before wartime passions made any bargains impossible. On July 14, having been assured that Ruth would not be charged and that David would get consideration for cooperation, the Greenglasses began to talk.

Now, with the information he was getting from Greenglass, Lamphere could interpret those references in the Venona documents to an agent named Julius who had approached suspected spy Max Elitcher. He could also identify that other reference to an agent's wife named Ethel. And now Elizabeth Bentley's testimony about a cell of engineers organized by Jacob Golos made sense. "The FBI had been taking various glances into the lives of these men for several years, but had never put together the fact that they were all interrelated, and that the linchpin had been Julius Rosenberg," Lamphere remembered. Now the Bureau understood that the individual engineers suspected of spying for the Soviets—Joel Barr, Al Sarant, Max Elitcher, Morton Sobell, and William Perl—were all members of Julius Rosenberg's espionage group.

Barr and Sarant fled overseas, eventually gaining sanctuary behind the Iron Curtain, where they were given prestigious posts in the East European scientific establishment. Morton Sobell fled to Mexico, was arrested, and returned to New York to stand trial for espionage with the Rosenbergs. The Bureau was never able to collect enough evidence to indict Perl or Elitcher. Meanwhile the Greenglasses had told the Bureau they had seen Ethel retype David's stolen documents at the Rosenberg home in New York's Knickerbocker Village. This was enough for the government to charge Ethel Rosenberg as a coconspirator with her husband.

Lamphere expected that once the Rosenbergs had been tried, convicted, and sentenced for treason, Julius would cooperate to save his wife. He was wrong. They were both sentenced to death, yet refused to talk. Without information from the Rosenbergs, Lamphere's investigation was at a dead end. He had heard of another network run by Julius, and felt that if he began to talk, the Bureau could roll up the remaining Soviet spy rings in the country.

But it was not to be. At the end, hoping that at the final moment Julius might crack, the Bureau sent Al Belmont, the assistant director in charge of domestic intelligence, to the death chamber to be ready to bargain if the Rosenbergs decided to talk. Neither did. And Morton Sobell, after serving a thirty-year sentence, is still proclaiming his innocence. "On the whole, though," Lamphere later wrote, "I was pleased with our progress. Four deciphered KGB messages had led us toward members of the Rosenberg family and network—pieces of information that we had been following up since the summer of 1948 were now fulfilled."

Recently some critics of the FBI have claimed that the Bureau's preoccupation with the American Communist Party's political activities distracted it from combating Soviet espionage. They have also argued that any notion that the Roosevelt administration discouraged the Bureau from investigating Soviet espionage rings is "pure speculation."

Lamphere's experience refutes both charges, reinforcing a wealth of evidence from other sources. Despite the tantalizing hints the Bureau got from ex-communist Whittaker Chambers, from Bentley, and from anonymous tips, it took the Venona documents to give the Bureau the information it needed to launch effective and productive investigations of Soviet espionage. And if the history of FBI counterespionage in subsequent decades proves anything, it is that enemy spying has almost never been rooted out without a defection from the enemy, or from captured documents. Rarely, if ever, does cold coverage—so to speak—of possible targets of espionage or possible espionage agents yield useful results.

There is also a wealth of evidence that the Roosevelt administration, quite properly, thought it more important to keep the seriously paranoid Stalin fighting as an American ally than to risk annoying him by rooting out his spies, who were seen as a nuisance at worst. Secretary of State Edward Stettinius returned to the Russians a KGB codebook Bill Donovan had purchased from the Finns. Attorney General Francis Biddle recalled that Secretary of State Cordell Hull was "very much against our doing anything [regarding Soviet defector Victor Kravchenko's offer of information about Russian espionage], being nervous about the effect it might have on Russia." Hull even extracted a promise from Biddle to "take no criminal action against any Russian connected with the Russian Government without first obtaining [the Secretary of State's] approval."

In some ways the Bureau had become a captive of its self-generated reputation as masters of scientific crime detection. With all that science, it would seem, the Bureau should have been able to know just about everything, do just about anything. But history shows that in almost all the FBI's criminal and national security investigations, its successes over the years from Dillinger to the Unabomber to Robert Hanssen have depended on getting a break, whether through luck or design, and not from its scientific wizardry. With the atomic bomb spy rings, the Bureau's break—Robert Lamphere's hunch about how to figure out the Venona documents—came late in the game.

The FBI's postwar counterespionage successes came at a difficult time for J. Edgar Hoover, who was now working for Harry Truman, a president who did not like him and did not trust the Bureau. Hoover had been a loyal subordinate to every president he had served, but he may have known that Truman often referred to the Bureau as a "Gestapo," as in one note to the first lady:

> *I am sure glad the Secret Service is doing a better job. I was worried about that situation. Edgar Hoover would give his right eye to take over, and all Congressmen and Senators are afraid of him. I'm not and he knows it. If I can prevent it, there'll be no NKVD [Soviet Secret Police] or Gestapo in this country. Edgar Hoover's organization would make a good start towards a citizen spy system. Not for me.*

Another aide wrote a note to himself, "Pres. Feels very down, afraid of 'Gestapo.'" Since Washington insiders love to regale each other with sensational gossip, it is unlikely Hoover did not hear about Truman's remarks.

Hoover was also disappointed and worried when Truman fired Attorney General Francis Biddle on June 30, 1945—Hoover and Biddle had clashed over policy on occasion, but the two men respected each other. When Hoover had gotten into trouble (as he had while wiretapping union leader Harry Bridges), Biddle had protected him. And Biddle was a serious law enforcement man. By contrast, Hoover had no respect for Tom Clark, who had unsavory political associates and, according to Eisenhower's attorney general Herbert Brownell, was personally corrupt and had been involved in a pardon-buying ring while he was in the Justice Department. Then too, Clark seemed frightened of Hoover, and for someone of Hoover's bulldog-like personality, the scent of fear touched off a hardwired response of ferocious aggression. In these perilous circumstances, Hoover felt he was on his own. He would have to cement his alliances with conservatives inside Congress and out, his natural allies and constituents.

■ ■ ■

Only someone with a memory in which reverberated the echoes of the past would have known what to expect when the Cold War began. Stalin was on the move in Europe, Truman was remobilizing the military, and civil wars were breaking out in Greece and China. The White House was too distracted to evaluate the domestic consequences of world events. But Hoover had been through all this before. With history as his guide, he thought he knew what he had to do.

Once again Bolshevism was pouring out of Russia. Once again American radicals and their defenders were lending support to Moscow. To Hoover it must have seemed like 1919 all over again. Once again there was going to be a drive to suppress the radical defenders of communist revolution. This time Hoover would not repeat the mistakes of 1920 that had derailed his first assault on the Communist Party and had nearly ended his career.

Hoover at first shared the common assumption that the Russian-American wartime alliance would survive the end of the war. In December 1945 he spoke as though he did not yet think a collision between the two great allies was inevitable. He told the chiefs of police that "we must not let the antics of the American Communists prejudice us against this great nation which has the right to any form of government she desires, nor must we judge the great Russian people by the lunatic fringe which represents the great majority of American Communists."

Wondering what they might mean for him and the Bureau, Hoover watched the events that would unleash the Cold War in 1945 and 1946: the breakdown of the London Foreign Ministers' Conference held to implement the Yalta accords (September 1945); Stalin's February 1945 speech on the permanent rivalry between communism and capitalism; Winston Churchill's Iron Curtain speech at Fulton, Missouri (March 5, 1946); America's coming to the aid of Greek anticommunist forces in March 1947; the Marshall Plan in June 1947; and George Kennan's enunciation of the policy of containment in his July 1947 "Mr. X" essay in *Foreign Affairs.* Hoover interpreted these events as a professional who would have to deal with their political impact on domestic security and as a lifelong anticommunist who saw communism as the enemy that threatened his most cherished values. Hoover's performance during the Truman administration can be understood only by understanding the dual aspects of his personality: He was the domestic security professional, acutely aware of the hazards of neglecting any sign of danger, and he was the moralist, always prone to turn his operations into dramatizations of right and wrong, particularly when the conflict involved communism.

In 1946 Hoover began to flood the White House with information he had come across that might mean the Soviets were planning war. He reported the communists were expecting an "approaching crisis in international affairs, which is expected to reach a crisis prior to Easter of 1946 . . . something which will surmount any situation thus far existing." In February 1946 he told Truman he had heard from American communist sources that communist uprisings were scheduled in France within six weeks; these would be "followed by a Civil War in Spain . . . [then] Soviet Armies in Hungary would move across Austria, Italy and Germany through the French occupation zones and would then intervene in the disturbances in France thereby placing Soviet troops on the Atlantic Coast and on the Mediterranean." The Russians wanted information on the atomic bomb by January 1, 1946, and had a deadline of February 1, 1946, to buy strategic equipment from the United States. Hoover and many others in the government believed that the world was in the midst of a prewar crisis. Soon, he believed, the FBI would be called upon to police the home front, which meant rounding up enemy sympathizers—fellow travelers and communists—who might oppose the mobilization.

Early in 1947 Hoover reported to the White House that American communist officials were discussing the Soviet Union's "firm belief" that in "a few short years" communists would be in control of every country in Europe. The communists were developing plans for sabotage and slowdowns in defense plants in the event of war between the United States and Russia.

Hoover tended to believe anything he heard from communist or ex-communist sources, so he was disturbed when he learned in April 1945 of an abrupt change in the Party line. A French communist official close to Stalin, Jacques Duclos, denounced American Communist Party Chairman Earl Browder for Browder's wartime policy of collaboration with capitalism. Then Browder was replaced in July as national chairman by thoroughgoing Stalinist William Foster. The party resumed its old name, dispensing with its wartime alias of the "Communist Political Association." This was followed by an immediate reversal of the Popular Front program of cooperation with the American government, along with an increase in communist propaganda and agitation. Hoover sent the White House a series of urgent warnings about this rise in American communist militancy. One of Hoover's memos reported that a "generally reliable" source had said that Browder's removal meant that Stalin had been deposed, and that Foreign Minister Vyacheslav Molotov was now probably in charge. Hoover took the threat of war with the Soviet Union seriously enough to make preparation for that event the guiding principle of FBI policy for the rest of the Truman administration.

Behind all this was what might be called a Pearl Harbor syndrome: Hoover was determined that, if there was another surprise attack, he would have a documentary record that he had not been caught napping. The movements of Japanese diplomats might have warned of Pearl Harbor, if anyone had interpreted them properly, so Hoover kept the White House informed of the travel plans of Soviet diplomats and their families. Because of his "no evaluation" policy,

Hoover could claim he had done his duty if he simply passed along every conceivable signal of danger; it was his superiors' job to separate the signals from the noise. This might be viewed simply as a cynical exercise in self-protection, but it was also a serious dereliction of duty. An intelligence agency must analyze, interpret, and offer policy choices. But Congress would repeatedly chastise intelligence agencies when they strayed into policymaking, as during the Iran-Contra affair. Finally, they all would invoke the defense "we don't do policy" as they provided information without context to the White House before 9/11.

· · ·

For years countersubversives had charged the New Deal was infested with communist spies and subversives. Now evidence began to surface that there was something to the charges. On June 6, 1945, John Stewart Service, a State Department China expert, was arrested for passing hundreds of classified State Department documents to a left-wing diplomatic journal, *Amerasia*. The "espionage" here could have been considered an extreme instance of the "document leaks" that support the mainstream news industry, except that the editor of *Amerasia*, Philip Jaffe, was probably a communist, certainly a fellow traveler. After an FBI investigation, the Justice Department charged Service, Jaffe, and four others with espionage. The case was settled with reduced charges after the government found its case had been tainted by illegal FBI and OSS searches of the magazine's offices.

Truman's neglect of these warnings and his promotion of Harry Dexter White to a post in the International Monetary Fund despite Hoover's reports that White was a spy provided the Republicans with what they claimed was proof of Truman's incompetence (the most charitable interpretation) or else a sinister willingness to tolerate communists in government. Hoover himself seems to have wavered between these two explanations. The warnings, however clear they seemed in retrospect (for example, when Hoover gave a detailed account of them to the Senate Internal Security Subcommittee in 1953), were obscured by a high ratio of noise to signal. And Truman knew that nearly every member of the New Deal had been accused of being a communist by the New Deal–hating anticommunist right, and that the FBI had relayed many of these charges to the White House. Why should these new charges be any different? If the public were not already so hysterical, and therefore so likely to believe the worst, Truman could have defended himself by declassifying some of Hoover's more absurd war warnings and internal security memos.

But Hoover had sound reasons for so persistently warning about spies in late 1945. The FBI had statutory authority to enforce the espionage acts and the Hatch Act; it was the Bureau's duty to be on the lookout for espionage. Furthermore, in 1945 he began to get multiple reports from independent sources always naming the same government employees as underground communists. But the most important reason Hoover was so alarmed was his experience that in the past international tensions had almost always provoked spy scares, and that in the past the FBI had been able to calm the public only by serving up spectacular spy cases to prove the situation was under control. By now, however, the White House suspected the spy scare was being concocted by its political enemies, Hoover included. The administration was inclined to consider the source and then ignore Hoover's warnings.

And some of the reports Truman was getting from the FBI were frankly incredible. For example, on May 29, 1946, Hoover sent the White House a report that a "source believed to be reliable" said there was "an enormous Soviet espionage ring in Washington" trying to get secret information about atomic energy. He listed the people involved, claiming that all of them were "noted for their pro-Soviet leaning." The hodgepodge of names included Dean Acheson, Herbert Marks, John J. McCloy, Howard C. Peterson, Henry A. Wallace, Paul Appleby, George Schwartzwalder, Edward U. Condon, Alger Hiss, Abe Feller, and James R. Newman. He called special attention to Hiss, Appleby, Condon, Schwartzwalder, and McCloy. Condon, Hoover reported, was "nothing more or less than an espionage agent in disguise." The FBI's informant also claimed that Senator Brian McMahon's investigation of the Atomic Energy Commission was going to give these spies a chance to pick up an enormous haul of atomic secrets, particularly since Hoover had (in another memo) accused McMahon's secretary of being a communist. The Bureau had learned "through various sources" of the "pro-Russian" political views of Acheson, Peterson, and Wallace, so "it is not beyond the realm of conjecture that they would fit into a scheme as set out above." He reminded the White House that Hiss "has been reported to this Bureau as a former member of the Communist underground organization."

But now the FBI was building a far more accurate picture of Soviet espionage, and its warnings about spies—which were at first circulated only at the highest levels of the executive branch—began to reach the public. The source was a militantly anticommunist segment of the Catholic community, which had been roused to a fever pitch by the Soviet takeover of Catholic Poland. The conduit was a Baltimore priest with long experience in fighting communism in the labor movement. This was Father John F. Cronin, a professor of economics at St. Mary's Seminary. In December 1944, Cronin's superiors told him to take a year off to study the problem of communism in the United States. When he began his research, his contacts in the FBI made Bureau reports available to him. Among them was an FBI memo on Elizabeth Bentley's testimony about spy rings in the government. He submitted his report to the bishops on November 12, 1945. From the bishops, what the FBI had learned about the Washington spy ring made its way to the public through leaks to the press and through a widely distributed booklet also written by Cronin and published by the Chamber of Commerce.

■ ■ ■

Hoover's highest priority at the beginning of the Cold War was that the FBI have a workable and legally viable plan for mass roundups of enemy sympathizers in the event of an emergency. Out of its historical context, Hoover's Custodial Detention Program appears bizarre as well as ominous. In view of Hoover's expectation that he would soon be forced to deal with war hysteria, it is perhaps no less ominous, but hardly irrational. As head of the FBI, Hoover would have been expected to have detailed detention plans ready for instant implementation in the case of attack by the Soviets. The nature of this war with Russia, since its sympathizers would have been motivated by ideology rather than nationality, would have created problems of unprecedented complexity for the Bureau.

Plans for this detention program, with lists of those to be arrested, were an important aspect of the Bureau's intelligence work during the 1940s and 1950s. The only way to round up a convincing number of subversives in the type of emergency that seemed most likely was on the basis of beliefs and associations. The FBI would need to have the names of such persons (with documentation), as well as workable plans for handling the logistics of arrest and incarceration. Hoover's Palmer Raids had eventually collapsed because Hoover had not worked out every detail of the dragnets ahead of time. Hoover had no difficulty recalling the reasons for that disaster.

Hoover stepped up his surveillance of the Communist Party in February 1946 to be ready, he said, for a roundup of communists "in the event of a conflict with the Soviet Union." He advised Attorney General Clark in March 1946 that he was going to "intensify [the Bureau's] investigation of Communist Party activities and Soviet espionage cases," and was compiling a complete list of "all members of the Communist Party and any others who would be dangerous in the event of a break in diplomatic relations with the Soviet Union, or any other serious crisis involving the United States and the U.S.S.R." (Previously the Bureau had only the names of the leaders of the Party.) Since large numbers of those detained would be American citizens, he requested that the Justice Department survey available legislation to see what additional authority should be sought from Congress.

Friction soon developed between Hoover and the administration over the Custodial Detention Program, which added to the White House's rejection of his reports on communist infiltration of the government, made Hoover fear he could not count on any support in an emergency from Truman. Recalling how attacks from liberals and civil libertarians like Louis Post, Judge George Anderson, Tom Walsh, and others had nearly destroyed him and the Bureau during the Palmer days, he must have felt he had no alternative but to treat the administration as a potential enemy and to seek new political allies.

Hoover's 1919–1920 experience had taught him how important public support had been to his success at the beginning of his anticommunist drive under Palmer, and how the collapse of public support brought on by criticism of Justice Department violations of civil liberties had eventually destroyed it. This time Hoover would keep the public on the Bureau's side by undercutting its critics. In February 1946, Hoover approved a recommendation from the Bureau Executive Conference that "an effort should be made now to prepare educational material which can be released through available channels so that in the event of an emergency we will have an informed public opinion." The aim was to counter the "flood of propaganda" that would be unleashed "in the event of extensive arrests of Communists."

This became the Bureau's "Mass Media Program," a coordinated effort by the Crime Records Division and the Bureau's top executives and special agents in charge in the field to shape public opinion to support the FBI campaign against communism. Field agents were trained to work with the local media to develop anticommunist public opinion. Hoover's own speeches were now intended to reach a mass audience, even when addressing groups like the House Un-American Activities Committee about the operational aspects of exposing communists. To gain public support for the Bureau's anticommunist campaign, the Bureau increased its presence in popular entertainment to the levels of the mid-thirties. The public now had a new G-man hero, the undercover informant inside the Communist Party. On the radio, movie screen, and, soon, television, there were now G-men "Leading Three Lives: Citizen, Communist, Counterspy" or going undercover to become "A Communist for the FBI."

During the 1946 congressional election campaign, the Republican National Committee announced that its campaign theme would be the voters' choice between "Communism and Republicanism." Republican Representative

Joseph Martin (soon to be House majority leader) said that the issue was between "chaos, confusion, bankruptcy, state socialism or communism, and the preservation of the American way of life." Congressional Democrats feared the Republicans were monopolizing the loyalty issue. Nervous about the volatile state of public opinion, they too demanded the administration start a drive against subversives in government. In July a House Civil Service subcommittee called for a commission to create a "complete and unified" program to root out government employees "whose primary loyalty is to governments other than our own." Congress busied itself passing laws empowering existing departments to summarily dismiss disloyal employees, and to make sure that any new agencies (such as the Atomic Energy Commission) had this authority. In October 1946 the Chamber of Commerce joined the battle against communists in government with its report (written by Father Cronin with FBI assistance) claiming that communists and fellow travelers had penetrated the government, especially the State Department, and had infiltrated labor unions. The chamber called for a drive to expel "subversives" from any positions they could use to influence public opinion, direct government policy, or control the economy.

The Republicans' Red-baiting campaign gave them victory in November, and control of the House and Senate for the first time in more than a decade. Truman finally realized that his enemies had captured the most explosive political issue of the day, and that they were not going to let it go. In a desperate effort to capture the initiative in the internal security controversy, on November 25 he accepted the recommendation of the House Civil Service subcommittee and appointed a Temporary Commission on Employee Loyalty to deal with the problem of loyalty among government employees. This was chaired by A. Devitt Vanech, whom Hoover had nominated.

Hoover submitted his views to the Temporary Commission on January 3. He warned that "subversive or disloyal persons" in the government were a threat to security because they might commit espionage, might influence government policies to suit the interest of a foreign power, might clothe enemy propaganda with the cloak of "official sanction," or might recruit others in subversive conspiracies. Hoover recommended that a Loyalty Review Board be established with the power to "approve or overrule" departmental decisions regarding loyalty of employees. The FBI should continue to have the responsibility of investigating subversion among incumbent employees. He also insisted, against demands that accused employees be able to confront their accusers, that the FBI be allowed to keep its files confidential.

Many of Hoover's ideas were accepted (the Loyalty Board itself, for one). He was nonetheless profoundly dissatisfied with the commission's recommendations. The commission's report on February 20 reflected Truman's conviction that there was no real loyalty "problem" (as opposed to a loyalty "issue"). The commission's proposals were, in Hoover's eyes, only a cosmetic reorganization of existing loyalty programs. Nevertheless, Truman ignored Hoover's objections and issued his Loyalty Program, Executive Order 9835 of March 22. The Truman program limited FBI investigations to incumbent employees, handed the investigation of new employees and those on temporary duty to the Civil Service Commission, left the decision on firing employees who had received unfavorable reports to the heads of agencies, and gave departments discretion on whether to call on the FBI.

In the midst of the Greek and Turkish communist insurgencies, Harry Truman announced the anticommunist "Truman Doctrine" in March 1947, pledging American power to contain communist expansion. But while Truman was outlining the anticommunist principles that would guide Cold War America for the next half century, Hoover decided that Truman's commitment to anti-communism on the home front could not be relied on. Hoover signaled his break with the administration in a spectacular appearance before the House Un-American Activities Committee on March 26, 1947. His appearance before such a rabidly anti–New Deal and anti-Truman forum proclaimed that he had renounced his historic allegiance to the chief executive and was joining Congress on the loyalty issue.

A week before Truman issued his Loyalty Program, the new Republican chairman of HUAC, J. Parnell Thomas, had invited Hoover to appear before the committee to "submit any recommendations or proposals touching upon any aspects of Communism." Hoover declined to appear, as always when invited to testify before any congressional committees except the House and Senate Appropriations Committees. But once Hoover saw Truman's Loyalty Program, he changed his mind. He ordered his aides to draw up a statement on communism for his testimony.

Like everyone else in the country (except Truman, who would win re-election in 1948), Hoover probably saw the Republican victory in the 1946 congressional elections as a sure sign that the Republicans were going to win the presidency in 1948. Hoover was moving over to the expected winning (Republican) side. He certainly realized the audacity and danger of abandoning his traditional power base within the executive branch of government.

Hoover's March 26, 1947, appearance before the House Un-American Activities Committee was an open declaration of his new alliance with the anti-administration Red-hunters. It was also a bid for recognition as the leading figure on the anticommunist right, and in exchange he gave HUAC's strategy in its fight against subversives his endorsement: to destroy them by means of "prescriptive publicity." The FBI and the committee, Hoover told the congressmen, both had the same goal, "protection of the internal security of the nation." Their methods, however, were different: While the FBI had to produce evidence acceptable in a court of law, HUAC's "greatest contribution," he said, was "the public disclosure of the forces that menace America—Communist and Fascist. . . . This Committee renders a distinct service when it publicly reveals the diabolic machinations of sinister figures engaged in un-American activities."

Hoover's statement before the committee was an updated version of the briefs against the Communist Party he had written in 1919. As in those earlier briefs, Hoover used the communists' own predictions of success to provide an interpretive context for the recent history of American communism. He drew on Attorney General Biddle's finding in the Harry Bridges deportation case for the precise formulation of his thesis, which was that the Communist Party "believes in, advises, advocates, and teaches the overthrow by force and violence of the Government of the United States." Despite recent changes in the Party line, he said, the "American communist, like the leopard, cannot change his spots . . . the one cardinal rule . . . [is] that the support of Soviet Russia is the duty of Communists of all nations."

He painted a picture for the congressmen of a Communist Party of formidable size (some 74,000, with ten additional sympathizers, he claimed, for every member) and vigor. ("They know it is a fight to the finish and that their backs are against the wall.") In this fight "the size of the Party is relatively unimportant because of the enthusiasm and iron-clad discipline under which they operate." He trotted out one of his favorite statistics: "In this connection, it might be of interest to observe that in 1917 when the Communists overthrew the Russian government there was one Communist for every 2,277 persons in Russia. In the United States today there is one Communist for every 1,814 persons in the country."

The raw meat was Hoover's endorsement of HUAC's crusade to keep "Communists and sympathizers out of government services," which was necessary because government agencies had failed to take the Bureau's warnings seriously. Out of the 6,193 cases the Bureau had investigated under the Hatch Act, he said, "there had been only 101 firings, 21 resignations, and 75 cases of administrative action." He told HUAC about one employee of the Federal Security Agency who had been retained even after the Bureau submitted a fifty-seven-page report on his Communist Party activities. After the suspect had voluntarily left the government, he had turned up on the National Committee of the Communist Party. It was a Party requirement, Hoover added, that committeemen had to have been Party members for at least four years before becoming eligible for the office.

This kind of nonfeasance made his own and HUAC's anticommunist drives vital to the security of the nation. "I do fear," he said,

> *for the liberal and progressive who has been hoodwinked and duped into joining hands with the Communists. . . . [for the] school boards and parents [who] tolerate conditions whereby Communists and fellow travelers under the guise of academic freedom can teach our youth a way of life that eventually will destroy the sanctity of the home, that undermines faith in God, that causes them to scorn respect for constituted authority and sabotage our revered Constitution.*

The Communist Party, he said, was a "Fifth Column if there ever was one. It is far better organized than were the Nazis in occupied countries prior to their capitulation. . . . There is no doubt as to where a real Communist's loyalty rests. Their allegiance is to Russia, not the United States."

The committee gave Hoover an enraptured reception. Members called him a "great American," and hailed his testimony as "the most masterful and conclusive statement of your career on the subject of this very definite menace." This encouraged him to escalate his defiance of the administration and, by implication, the president. When Harry B. Mitchell, president of the Civil Service Commission, tried to perform his duties under Truman's Loyalty Program (the Civil Service Commission was charged with looking into the records of new job applicants and temporary employees), Hoover threatened to pull the FBI out of loyalty work altogether unless the Civil Service Commission withdrew and left all investigations to the Bureau. He wrote Attorney General Tom Clark that he was willing to give the Civil Service Commission

> *the full, complete, entire and exclusive responsibility for conducting all investigations of Government employees about whose loyalty there is any question whatsoever. I want you to know that this Bureau is perfectly willing to withdraw from this field of investigation rather than to engage in a tug of war with the Civil Service Commission over the investigative jurisdiction of subversive employees of the Federal government.*

Truman's last attempt to defeat the FBI's monopoly over the Loyalty Program was trying to let the Civil Service Commission keep investigations of new employees, but he realized that this was a futile gesture. He resigned himself to the fact that Congress would not tolerate anything that seemed to hobble the FBI, lamenting that "J. Edgar will in all probability get this backward looking Congress to give him all he wants. It's dangerous." As Truman had foreseen, instead of giving the Civil Service Commission the $16 million and the FBI the $8.7 million the administration had originally proposed, Congress provided the FBI with $7.4 million and the Civil Service Commission with only $3 million. This effectively turned the program over to the FBI.

Once Hoover had broken with the administration over the loyalty issue, the popular press looked to him and not Truman for authoritative and official enlightenment on the communist menace. When *Newsweek* ran a feature on "Communism and its influence in America" it turned to Hoover, "the one responsible Federal official most directly concerned with Communism and Communists."

Hoover told *Newsweek*'s readers that "we effectively protected ourselves against spies and saboteurs during the late world war without sacrificing the civil rights of a single citizen. We can protect ourselves against the infiltration of Communists by the same defensive, democratic means in the American way." He made it clear, however, that the "defensive, democratic means" he meant included congressional hearings to expose communists. When HUAC

> *fulfills its obligation of public disclosure of facts it is worthy of the support of loyal, patriotic Americans. This committee has for its purpose the exposure of un-American forces and as such its files contain voluminous information which, when used with discretion, provide an excellent source of information. The FBI, unlike this committee, must of necessity keep the contents of its files confidential.*

The "slogan in the fight against Communism" should be "Uncover, expose and spotlight their activities. Once this is done, the American people will do the rest—quarantine them from effectively weakening our country."

■ ■ ■

Hoover saw the communist spy cases, like the great gangster cases of the thirties, as a way for the FBI to mobilize a national grassroots movement, this time an anticommunist crusade. The FBI would play a role in this movement similar to what it had done during the twenties. The Bureau would supply research for the movement (through informants, wiretaps, and surveillance), maintain technical facilities (its files), and provide professional training and advice.

There would be training conferences, speeches by Hoover and other FBI officials, FBI publications on communism, and staff assistance to HUAC, the Senate Internal Security Subcommittee, and other anticommunist investigators. Unlike more politically opportunistic anticommunist conservatives, Hoover viewed anticommunism as a comprehensive, cooperative, and national movement, which he cast in the mold of his anticrime drive of the thirties. And never forgotten was his institutional need to have a workable plan ready for the custodial detention of communists and their sympathizers in the war emergency he saw on the horizon.

When the Justice Department rejected Hoover's request for new legislation authorizing detention of dangerous citizens during hostilities (which the Justice Department thought was politically impossible; Hoover disagreed), Hoover endorsed a Bureau recommendation that the department prosecute a test case under the Smith Act (which prohibited organizing or belonging to a group dedicated to the violent overthrow of the government) to obtain a judicial precedent. Then in an emergency the FBI could arrest communists as "substantive violators [of the Smith Act]. This in turn has an important bearing on the Bureau's position should there be no legislative or administrative authority available at the time of the outbreak of hostilities which would permit the immediate apprehension of both aliens and citizens of the dangerous category."

Hoover's preparations for the Smith Act prosecution of Communist Party leaders retraced the path he had followed as the young director of Palmer's Research Division in 1919. First he compiled a historical study of the American Communist Party aimed at demonstrating its legal vulnerability. This was a massive "brief" submitted to the Internal Security section of the Justice Department bulking to 1,350 pages with 546 exhibits. In 1919, Hoover's purpose had been to convince the secretary of labor to deport alien communists; now he had the more difficult task of persuading a hostile Justice Department to indict the Party's leaders, who were citizens. Yet this time Hoover had the Smith Act, precisely the peacetime sedition act he and Palmer had hoped for. In broad design and even in particular details Hoover was replaying the 1919–1929 assault on the American communists, intent on avoiding the mistakes that had defeated him before.

In 1919 congressional pressure (the Poindexter Resolution) had been an important reason why Palmer had taken action against the alien communists. In 1948, shortly after Hoover urged Clark to seek prosecution of the Party leadership to "obtain . . . judicial recognition of the aims and purposes of the Communist party," HUAC demanded that Clark explain why he had not begun any Smith Act prosecutions. The committee had been holding up its own inquiry so as not to interfere with a New York federal grand jury looking into subversion.

Despite the doubts of Clark's assistants that the FBI's case was strong enough, the Justice Department sent it to the grand jury, which voted on June 29 to indict the twelve members of the Communist National Board for conspiring to organize the Party in 1945 (when it resumed its original name after spending the war as the "Communist Political Association"). On July 20, FBI agents arrested five of the Party's top leaders at its New York headquarters; the remaining seven were arrested over the next two weeks.

The Justice Department's decision to restrict initial prosecution to the twelve members of the Communist National Committee disappointed Hoover, who had wanted to arrest all fifty-five members of the National Committee, leaving only the roundup of the rank and file for the beginning of hostilities. In an internal memo a week before the arrests, Hoover complained that the administration was "insincere" in its anticommunism.

> *It had been hoped that the Grand Jury investigation would be carried out in much the same way as the investigation of the Industrial Workers of the World (IWW) in 1917 during World War I. The IWW case was inaugurated by a simultaneous national move against every IWW headquarters throughout the United States. All national and local leaders of the IWW were indicted and over one hundred sentenced to long prison terms. As a result of this joint national action the IWW was crushed and has never revived. Similar action at this time would have been as effective against the Communist Party and its subsidiary organizations.*

Practically speaking, however, the New York trial of the "Eleven" (Earl Browder's case had to be separated from the others' due to his ill health) was probably more devastating to the Party than the larger roundup Hoover had wanted. The government was able to disconcert the defendants by producing a prosecution witness who had been one of their most trusted colleagues. This was Herbert Philbrick, a middle-level official of the Party who had been secretly informing for the FBI since 1940. Following Philbrick on the stand was another FBI informant, Angela Calomiris, who had stayed active in the Party until the minute of her testimony. (In later trials Philbrick and Calomiris would be joined as government witnesses by John Lautner, who had set up much of the Party's underground in the United States. Lautner defected to the FBI when he was falsely accused of being a double agent and expelled from the Party, after a beating, in January 1950.)

The testimony of Philbrick and Calomiris demoralized the Party's leadership by making them begin to suspect one another. The Bureau made it worse by placing "snitch jackets" on unsuspecting members of the Party: planting false evidence that they were working for the Bureau, a strategy that dated back to 1920, when a Bureau of Investigation agent had planted false accusations that Party leader Louis Fraina was an informer.

The government devoted most of its case to proving the guilt of the Communist Party itself, not the defendants. The government relied on quotations from communist classics dating back to the *Manifesto* and the testimony of Louis Francis Budenz, former managing editor of the *Daily Worker.* Federal Judge Harold Medina allowed Budenz incredible latitude to show how, whatever the actual words in the communist classics seemed to say, American Communists understood them to mean that "the Communist Party of the United States is basically committed to the overthrow of the Government of the United States as set up by the Constitution of the United States."

The strategy was a huge success for the Bureau. The jury found all eleven defendants guilty. Judge Medina even sentenced some of the defense lawyers to prison terms for their disorderly conduct during the trial, an action that made it difficult, in some cases impossible, for later Smith Act defendants to secure legal counsel. All the defendants except a heavily decorated war veteran received the maximum five-year sentence permitted for conspiracy under the new federal code (the veteran received three years). The defendants appealed their convictions, but both the New York Court of Appeals and the Supreme Court turned them down. Seven of the communist leaders reported to prison; the five others went underground to continue their Party activities.

Over the next few months the FBI rounded up the remaining members of the Communist Party hierarchy. These were prosecuted in the so-called "second echelon" trials. In all, 126 communist leaders were indicted, 93 were convicted, and only 10 acquitted (the remaining defendants were excused for ill health, died, or had trials end in hung juries). The drive finally slowed in 1954 only when Hoover complained that having to reveal his informants during the trials was reducing "the highly essential intelligence coverage which this Bureau must maintain in the internal security field." He urged the Justice Department to make a careful evaluation before a trial whether the greater benefit would come through prosecution or by continuing to maintain the informants in place.

■ ■ ■

The most important espionage investigation of the Cold War would not belong to the FBI, but to the House Un-American Activities Committee under Congressman Richard Nixon. In 1948, HUAC finally managed to find what frustrated countersubversives had been searching for since 1919: proof, legal proof, of treason in Washington on behalf of the Kremlin. It was the case of Alger Hiss.

Alger Hiss—from 1939 to 1944 a political adviser in the State Department's Far Eastern Division—had many character witnesses on his side. And Harry Truman, in a disastrous blunder, agreed with a reporter's characterization of "the Capitol Hill spy scare" as a "red herring to divert the public's attention from inflation." But if Truman was initially unable to take the charges against Hiss seriously, the FBI had originally felt the same way. The FBI first investigated Hiss when his name appeared among eleven hundred others that HUAC gave President Roosevelt in 1942. When Whittaker Chambers told the FBI in May 1942 that Alger Hiss and his brother Donald were undercover communists while they were in the Agriculture Department, Hoover dismissed the resulting eight-page memo as "either history, hypothesis or deduction."

Chambers had his second interview with the FBI on May 10, 1945. This time Hoover took the twenty-two-page memo on the interview seriously and began leaking its contents to his allies in the anticommunist movement. In October 1945 the FBI got corroborating information from Elizabeth Bentley and from the Canadian interrogation of Igor Gouzenko, and requested permission from Clark to place a tap on Hiss's phone. Secretary of State Acheson asked Hoover about the Gouzenko revelations, but Hoover, while confidentially telling him about the charges against Hiss, told Acheson "that he did not feel it was the time to make any accusations as he lacked direct proof."

Hoover first warned Truman about Hiss on November 27, 1945, in a memo on "Soviet Espionage in the United States" based on the Elizabeth Bentley interviews. In March 1946 he advised the State Department to ease Hiss out without bringing formal charges against him, since that would have unmasked some of Hoover's confidential sources and would have "alert[ed] him and ruin[ed] an important investigation." He recommended informing key people in Congress, and then telling Hiss that Congress was the source of the stories against him, thus concealing the FBI's role in the investigation. For the remainder of 1946 the FBI kept sending reports on Hiss to Truman, Secretary of State James F. Byrnes and Attorney General Clark. By the end of the year Hiss's advancement in the State Department was blocked on Byrnes's orders, and Hiss had learned of the probe of his loyalty. This may have been why he left the State Department on December 10.

The Hiss-Chambers case finally became public on August 3, 1948, when Whittaker Chambers, now a *Time* magazine writer and editor, appeared before

HUAC and repeated his accusations that Hiss had been part of an underground Communist Party group of government employees headed by Harold Ware, son of a Communist Party leader, the famous "Mother" Bloor. Hiss was by far the most important government official yet accused of being a communist. Reporters' ears perked up when Chambers mentioned that Hiss had organized the Dumbarton Oaks conference that planned the United Nations Conference at San Francisco and that he had been with Roosevelt at Yalta.

Hiss's refutation of Chambers's charges was so convincing and effective that it seemed for a while that the investigation of communists in the government *had* been a hoax, and that Truman's red-herring remark was going to be the drive's epitaph. Hiss denied that he had ever even known Chambers. One member of HUAC moaned, "We've been had! We're ruined!" Richard Nixon, however, saw a way out: "[A]lthough the committee could not determine who was lying on the issue of whether or not Hiss was a Communist, we could at least determine which was lying on the issue of whether or not Chambers knew Hiss." And so it was on a charge of perjury that Hiss was eventually indicted, tried, and convicted: on one count of having lied when he said he had not known Chambers, and (the statute of limitations having expired on the more serious charge of espionage) on a second of having falsely denied turning over classified documents to Chambers (among them the notorious "pumpkin papers" Chambers briefly hid in his garden).

After all these years, Hoover finally had the legally unchallengeable proof he had needed in 1919 that the communist enemy was capable of treason, and had committed treason. At last one of the endless and amorphous charges about treachery in government had been proven. But the FBI had not been able to introduce the one piece of evidence, the Venona documents, that might have convinced all of liberal America that the Hiss case, like the other spy cases, was not simply public hysteria, a witch trial.

Truman had bet the prestige of his presidency on the spy scare's being a red herring, and he had lost. He had ceded to the FBI, HUAC, and the conservative anticommunists the role of defending internal security that should have been his by right of office. Truman's inability to master the politics of the internal security issue created a power vacuum in Washington that a host of ambitious politicians—notably Hoover, Nixon, and McCarthy—hastened to fill.

The man who had gained the most from the Hiss case, Richard Nixon, may have worried about the FBI feeling slighted, and paid Hoover an extraordinary tribute on the floor of the House. On January 26, 1950, Nixon gave Congress his report on the Hiss trial and its significance. Nixon insisted on sharing credit with the FBI for the success of the case—but he pointedly excluded Truman's

Justice Department from the love fest. He blamed them for having "failed or refused to institute an investigation which would lead to prosecution and conviction of those involved." Above all, Nixon said,

> *we must give complete and unqualified support to the FBI and J. Edgar Hoover, its chief. Mr. Hoover recognized the Communist threat long before other top officials recognized its existence. The FBI in this trial did an amazingly effective job of running down trails over 10 years old and in developing the evidence which made the prosecution successful.*

The final lesson of the Hiss case, according to Nixon, was that the Bureau must be protected from anyone who would compromise its independence.

With the convictions of the Party's leaders, and now Hiss and (in 1951) the Rosenbergs, and with Lamphere's successes in uncovering Klaus Fuchs and other atom spies, Hoover was riding high. He published his own account of the atomic spying in the May 1951 issue of *Reader's Digest*, written, presumably, immediately after the guilty verdict in the Rosenberg case. "In all the history of the FBI," he wrote, "there never was a more important problem than this one, never another case where we felt under such pressure." The moral was that only the FBI possessed the scope, skills, and experience to protect the country from spies so clever and dangers so great. The spy case was a

> *staggering revelation of how a foreign power, espousing a doctrine of hate, frightfulness and slavery, can unfasten the loyalties of free men and women and turn them into traitors. . . . In them we see the tragic horror of communism: it blights the moral strength of man, leaving him only a puppet to be manipulated at will.*

■ ■ ■

Truman really had no weapons left to use against Hoover. He had painted himself into a corner where any criticism of Hoover would only confirm suspicion that the administration was blocking the FBI's drive against domestic communists. Truman was pathetically reduced to taking private satisfaction in Hoover's anger at Max Lowenthal, a friend Truman encouraged to write what Hoover would have called a "brief" against the FBI and its director. This was Lowenthal's *Federal Bureau of Investigation*, a full-length history of the FBI that appeared in the fall of 1950 to the consternation of Truman's aides, who feared that the president would be blamed for Lowenthal's attack on one of American politics' most powerful figures. Hoover's prestige by late 1950 was so much greater than Truman's that the president even had to deny he had read the book when questioned at a press conference.

The counterattack against Lowenthal showed how powerful Hoover had become. HUAC investigators visited Lowenthal's publisher, William Sloan; they called on Lowenthal at his home and subpoenaed him to appear before the committee. The Society of Former Special Agents reprinted a *Reader's Digest* article by the American Civil Liberties Union's Morris Ernst, an unlikely but longtime ally of Hoover's ("Why I No Longer Fear the FBI"), and distributed it as a rebuttal to Lowenthal. The head of the society sent a copy to Truman.

The FBI's attack on Lowenthal echoed Hoover's battles against critics of the Palmer Raids, since Lowenthal posed much the same danger to Hoover now as Post and the authors of the 1920 *Lawyers' Report* had during the first Red Scare. The FBI's anticommunist drive, and, for that matter, Hoover's career, could be jeopardized if the public's attention shifted from the ultimate purpose of the Bureau's operations (an attack on unpopular groups and ideas) to the abuses of individual rights that occurred (almost inevitably) in any such proceedings. Hoover had learned from his experience in 1920 how important it was to discredit his critics, and so he made it Bureau policy to counterattack vigorously and effectively whenever the FBI came under attack.

■ ■ ■

The motives of Hoover and the anticommunist right were so baffling to Truman that he decided they were simply irrational—crazy. A measure of his bewilderment was that he actually commissioned a study that traced "hysteria and witch-hunting" from the Salem witch trials to the new Red Scare. Truman thought that the similarities between these earlier outbursts of intolerance and the current one utterly discredited the Red hunt as an exercise in irrationality.

Theories that stressed the irrational components of Cold War anticommunism might have seemed plausible within liberal circles, but they now ran up against the inconvenient facts of Hiss, Remington, Coplon, and the Rosenbergs. The Bureau's enemies could complain about red herrings and witch hunts, but all Hoover and his allies had to do to prove that the specter of communism was real was to point to the guilty verdicts.

Liberals dismissed Hoover and his like as "pseudo-conservatives." For his part Hoover worked out his own theory of "pseudo-liberalism," the willful toleration of communism that masked a toleration (perhaps even enthusiasm) for other violations of respectability and traditional standards that led to social disintegration. Once the lines were drawn between "pseudo-conservatives" and "pseudo-liberals" (to use their characterizations of each other), the FBI's great anticommunist cases of the Truman administration became tests between opposing philosophies in which Hoover's enemies had failed to perform the most elementary function of government: to provide for the common defense.

Now Hoover felt free to present the spy cases as a test of strength between those who would abandon traditional American values and those who—like the FBI—defended them. The Harry Dexter White case was more

> *than the charges against one man. This situation has a background of some 35 years of infiltration of an alien way of life into what we have been proud to call our Constitutional Republic. Our American way of life, which has flourished under our Republic and has nurtured the blessings of a democracy, has been brought into conflict with the godless forces of communism. These Red Fascists distort, conceal, misrepresent, and lie to gain their point. Deceit is their very essence. This can never be understood until we face the realization that to a Communist there are no morals except those which further the world revolution directed by Moscow.*

During the Truman administration Hoover had accomplished what he had tried, and failed, to do during the Palmer Raids. Armed with the Smith Act (the peacetime sedition law he had lacked in 1920), his now irresistible prestige, spectacular loyalty cases, an international emergency, and a demand for action against the disloyal, he set out on a course of action that would eventually, by the mid-fifties, crush the American Communist Party as a viable political organization. He had turned the battle against communism into a crusade to determine the values that would prevail as the national morality. In truth, for Hoover communism was the sin as well as the crime of the century.

■ ■ ■

Hoover's power had increased mightily during the Truman administration, but battling with the president was not natural or congenial to him. He was by temperament an insider, most comfortable as the lieutenant of a powerful leader he could trust and respect, who trusted and respected him. Dwight D. Eisenhower was such a man. Eisenhower exerted himself to let Hoover know he wanted him to play an important part in his administration. Seven years of Truman's mutterings about "Gestapos" and "witch hunts" and "red herrings" had wounded Hoover. Not only was the lack of personal respect from the president humiliating; the president's distrust was also a rejection of Hoover's credentials as the country's foremost expert on domestic communism, and Hoover felt he had earned the right to have his authority in that area unquestioned by anyone.

Hoover was once again working for a president who, like Franklin D. Roosevelt, solicited his opinions, took his advice, and acted on his recommendations. Truman's appointees as attorney general did not seem to be serious law enforcement professionals, particularly by contrast to Roosevelt's. With Herbert Brownell and William Rogers, Hoover could once again feel he was working for men who were serious.

Even before the inauguration, Eisenhower made sure Hoover felt he was an insider again. "There had come to my ears," Eisenhower later explained,

> *a story to the effect that J. Edgar Hoover . . . had been out of favor in Washington. Such was my respect for him that I invited him to a meeting, my only purpose being to assure him that I wanted him in government as long as I might be there and that in the performance of his duties he would have the complete support of my office.*

Eisenhower would ask Hoover's advice whenever government policy touched on internal security, whether or not he intended to follow Hoover's suggestions. Eisenhower's self-conscious air of naïveté flattered Hoover and contrasted with the Truman White House's tendency to think it knew more than Hoover about internal security. Eisenhower had to fight the popular impression that the executive branch was congenitally soft on communism. Having Hoover as a visible supporter of his policies was the most effective way of accomplishing that.

Eisenhower managed his office through a strict staff system, so Hoover did not have the informal lines of communication with the president he had enjoyed under Roosevelt. This was compensated for by his close relationships with Attorney General Herbert Brownell and Deputy Attorney General William Rogers (attorney general after 1957). Rogers was Hoover's principal liaison with the administration, and Hoover became closer to Rogers professionally and socially than to any of his previous superiors in the Justice Department.

Rogers got the administration off to a good start with Hoover by letting him know that the FBI's loyalty reports, which the Truman administration had often disregarded, now had the force of law. During the first year of the administration, the attorney general refused to endorse thirty-three persons for presidential appointment solely on the basis of their FBI reports. "There could be no more convincing proof of the value of the FBI investigations," Rogers assured Hoover.

The loyalty issue had destroyed the Truman administration, and for Eisenhower to govern effectively he had to seize the initiative from the congressional investigators. Early in 1953, Eisenhower scrapped Truman's Loyalty Program and set up a system of security officers in each department. The State Department was the target of the Eisenhower administration's most ruthless drive against "security risks." Secretary of State John Foster Dulles hired ex-FBI agent Scott McLeod as security officer, and McLeod put together a security staff of fellow former agents. Before long McLeod announced he had fired five hundred State Department employees without hearings. In October 1953, Eisenhower claimed 1,456 "subversives" had been dismissed, although most of these had been let go for reasons other than disloyalty. Under the new "security risk" classification, J. Robert Oppenheimer, and State Department China experts John Carter Vincent and John Paton Davies, whose continued government employment had angered the radical right, were finally fired, on the basis of their associations and activities, not because of any proof of disloyalty.

The Eisenhower administration's loyalty program was not by itself enough to quiet the congressional loyalty investigators. With Nixon's example before them, senators and congressmen aspired to national visibility by exposing their own spy rings. When the new Congress organized itself under Republican leadership, there were three committees ready to investigate the executive branch: the House Un-American Activities Committee, now chaired by ex-FBI agent Representative Harold Velde; the Senate Judiciary Committee's Internal Security Subcommittee, chaired by William Jenner; and Joseph McCarthy's Permanent Investigations Subcommittee of the Committee on Government Operations (whose chief investigator was ex-agent Don Surine and later Frank Carr, former head of the Bureau's New York field office).

Hiring an ex–FBI agent to run a security program was, in fact, the best demonstration of seriousness. This gave the Bureau additional influence throughout the government, because the ex-agents were of no use to their employers unless they preserved their access to FBI reports by staying on good terms with Hoover. Hoover had become not only the country's leading communist hunter, but the leading trainer of other communist hunters.

Hoover's appearance before HUAC in 1947 had been the signal of his break with Truman. In 1953 he made another sensational appearance before Congress, even more unmistakably partisan than before, to signal his loyalty to the new administration. In November 1953, Attorney General Brownell had decided to contrast the Eisenhower security program with the previous administration's rejection of spy stories as "red herrings." After clearing his plans with the president, Brownell charged that Truman had promoted Assistant Treasury Secretary Harry Dexter White to "a more important position" as executive director of the International Monetary Fund despite Hoover's reports about White's "spying activities for the Soviet Government." The new Republican chairman of HUAC, Harold Velde, followed up on Brownell's charges by subpoenaing Truman. Truman rejected the subpoena on the grounds of the separation of powers, but went on national television to deny Brownell's story. He claimed that he had seen Hoover's report on White, but too late to stop the Senate from confirming the nomination. Truman went further and said he had promoted White only because he had an understanding with Hoover that this would help the FBI with its investigation.

Truman had left himself open to devastating counterattack. On November 17, Brownell and Hoover appeared before Senator Jenner's Internal Security Subcommittee. Hoover denied there had been any arrangement between him and Truman; he claimed White's promotion had even hampered his investigation. He also contradicted Truman's statement that White had been surrounded with persons of proven loyalty, noting that one of White's close associates at the IMF had been removed as a security risk in December 1952. Although Hoover later denied that he had impugned Truman's loyalty ("[I never implied] that President Truman was disloyal or pro-Communist. He was blind to the Communist menace and used very bad judgment"), he had done just that.

Brownell's attack on White and Truman, combined with the truce in Korea and the death of Stalin, eased some of the fears of rabid anticommunists. Perhaps nothing did more to defuse the communist issue than the execution of the Rosenbergs on June 16, 1953. The public began losing interest in the communist issue even as Joseph McCarthy was gearing up for operations as chairman of his own investigating committee, his reward for the Republicans' congressional victory in the 1952 election.

Early in his administration Eisenhower, who had taken heat during the campaign for not denouncing McCarthy's preposterous charges that General George C. Marshall was a communist, resolved to destroy McCarthy. Eisenhower's strategy was not to denounce or disavow McCarthy, but rather to use the FBI to give him "sensational competition."

Hoover and McCarthy had a friendship that dated back to McCarthy's early days in Washington after he arrived in the Senate in 1946. The first investigator McCarthy hired, ten-year FBI veteran Donald Surine, was on Hoover's recommendation, and Surine acted as a liaison between the two men. When McCarthy took over the chair of the Investigations Subcommittee of the Committee on Government Operations in 1953, his staff was stocked with other ex–FBI agents, and his chief counsel was Roy Cohn, who had developed a working relationship with Hoover's all-purpose go-to man, Lou Nichols, when Cohn worked in the Justice Department as a special assistant. When McCarthy fired veteran Red-lister J. B. Matthews as his staff director after Matthews charged that the Protestant ministry was communist-infiltrated, he hired yet another ex–FBI agent, Frank Carr. Later, McCarthy took on another former agent, Jim Juliana, as chief investigator.

Hoover and McCarthy were not just ideological allies, they were close socially. They often went to the track together in Washington, and Hoover and his inseparable companion and second in command, Clyde Tolson, were frequent dinner guests at the home of McCarthy and his assistant, later his wife, Jean Kerr. In August 1953, McCarthy stayed at the same La Jolla, California, hotel with Hoover and Tolson during their summer vacation. On that occasion, Hoover told a reporter for the *San Diego Evening Tribune* that

> *McCarthy is a former Marine. He was an amateur boxer. He's Irish. Combine those, and you're going to have a vigorous individual, who is not going to be pushed around. . . . The investigating committees do a valuable job. They have subpoena rights without which some vital investigations could not be accomplished. . . . I view him as a friend and believe he so views me. Certainly, he is a controversial man. He is earnest and he is honest. He has enemies. Whenever you attack subversives of any kind, Communists, Fascists, even the Ku Klux Klan, you are going to be the victim of the most extremely vicious criticism that can be made.*

Through Lou Nichols, Hoover made information from FBI files available to McCarthy and his staff (probably in the form of "reports" based on the files, and not the raw files themselves), all very confidentially. Hoover was careful about divulging files to congressional committees, since much of the FBI's intelligence had been obtained by illegal means like wiretapping. And even by the indulgent Justice Department theory that circulation of wiretap information in the department was not "divulging" (and hence did not violate the law against "intercepting *and* divulging"), giving the information to Congress would have been a prima facie violation of the law. Hoover did give information *from* the files to friendly reporters and congressmen, but he and the Justice Department made a careful semantic distinction when they said that the "files" themselves were strictly confidential. Nonetheless information from the files was the lifeblood of Washington's anticommunist establishment.

Despite their friendship, Hoover finally had to choose between McCarthy and Eisenhower, and it was at a time when McCarthy needed him most. To

Hoover the evil of both communism and crime was that they were both attacks on authority. Eisenhower had made the presidency the national symbol of authority once again, and so Hoover could not support attacks on it, even when the attacks came from friends and allies like McCarthy.

The Army-McCarthy hearings that began on April 22, 1954, developed out of an earlier McCarthy investigation of subversion at the Signal Corps research center at Fort Monmouth, when McCarthy charged that the Army had tried to block his investigation. The hearings became a national sensation, carried on all three television networks. On the ninth day it was apparent the hearings were going badly for McCarthy. He tried to get back on the offensive by claiming that he had a "carbon copy" of a "personal and confidential" letter from J. Edgar Hoover to the Army warning about thirty-four security risks at Fort Monmouth. Had McCarthy been able to force the Army to explain its failure to follow up on Hoover's allegations, he might have been able to capture the initiative and force the Army once again to respond to his charges instead of his having to answer accusations against him.

The Army's chief counsel, Joseph Welch, objected to the introduction of a copy of a letter as evidence and demanded a statement from Hoover as to whether he had actually written it. Hoover responded that McCarthy's letter had *not* come from the Bureau, although a memorandum from the Bureau had been sent to the Army the same day as the "purported" letter, and much of the information and language in the letter was identical to that in the fifteen-page memorandum. But that was enough for Welch to get a devastating admission from McCarthy's staff that the letter was in fact "a carbon copy of precisely nothing."

Hoover must have realized how disastrous his response would be to McCarthy. Instead of focusing attention on McCarthy's accurate statement that the contents were a faithful summary of the FBI memo, Hoover's reply called attention to what was fraudulent about the letter, its format. Hoover's reply let it be concluded that McCarthy had tried to foist a forged document off on the Senate and that he had been conspiring with disloyal Army employees who had given him classified information without proper authorization.

The "letter" memo so unnerved McCarthy that he tried to excuse his possession of it by publicly congratulating all the officials who had been passing him documents against presidential directives. "As far as I am concerned," he said, "I would like to notify those 2 million employees that I feel it is their duty to give us any information they have." Eisenhower at long last felt that McCarthy, by advocating "a wholesale subversion of public service," had so discredited himself that he could be safely attacked, and so he now openly threw the influence of the presidency into the battle against McCarthy, which finally led to the Senate censure that destroyed him.

■ ■ ■

In popular entertainment of the forties and the fifties, the gangbusting G-man gave way, as might have been expected, to the spy-smashing FBI agent, or, more accurately, the undercover FBI informant because under Hoover actual FBI agents almost never went undercover. FBI undercover informant Matt Cvetic's "I Posed as a Communist for the F.B.I.," edited by Pete Martin, appeared in the *Saturday Evening Post* in July 1950, then was turned into a movie, *I Was a Communist for the FBI,* in 1951, and also a syndicated radio show, beginning in 1952.

Walk East on Beacon (1951) was very loosely based on Hoover's *Reader's Digest* article "Crime of the Century," and got so much assistance from the Bureau that it was practically an official FBI production. The film began by informing the audience that the "FBI's responsibility is to protect the American people against the communist world conspiracy which seeks to overthrow free government everywhere. Nothing is more important to the FBI's efforts than the support of alert Americans," while stock footage showed J. Edgar Hoover working in his office. The picture ended with a warning from Hoover that "there are other hidden enemies and they can only be exposed by Americans armed with the Bureau's motto: Fidelity, Bravery, Integrity."

On television, there were 117 episodes of the show *I Led Three Lives* between 1953 and 1956. Each episode began, "This is the story, the fantastically true story, of Herbert A. Philbrick, who for nine frightening years did lead three lives—average citizen, high-level member of the Communist Party, and counterspy for the Federal Bureau of Investigation." The show cast all government agencies in such a favorable light that many of them used it for indoctrination and enlistment purposes.

J. Edgar Hoover himself worked hard to transform anticommunism into popular culture. He delivered speeches on an almost weekly basis that stressed the religious dimension of the battle with communism. Communism, he said, was the ultimate expression of secularism: "The danger of Communism in America lies not in the fact that it is a political philosophy but in the awesome fact that it is a materialistic religion, inflaming in its adherents a destructive fanaticism. Communism is secularism on the march. It is a moral foe of Christianity. Either it will survive or Christianity will triumph because in this land of ours the two cannot live side by side." The Bureau mined its vast library of radical publications to issue a series of monographs to demonstrate how communist documents "openly attack, vilify, or attempt to vilify, any aspect of the

United States, its officials or representatives; and which openly advocate revolt against the laws of the United States and directly, by implication or inference, endeavor to wield insolent sway over public opinion."

These FBI publications tried to show how the Communist Party had "steadfastly tried to drive a wedge between the American people and the American way of life." The Bureau denounced the tendency "to minimize the revolutionary intent of the Party and to ignore the viciously anti-American statements that are preserved in communist archives." The Bureau's publication of terrifying quotations from communism's glory days would be, Hoover hoped, "an irrefragable and infamous monument" that would "provide all persons combating communism with a handy reference."

■ ■ ■

The civil rights movement was a clear case of justice to many Americans, but to Hoover it was first of all a challenge to authority—the authority of the police, the government and, in many cases, the FBI—a challenge he was bound to resent. It aroused in him the same alarm as any other kind of rebellion. The civil rights movement also challenged the secure life he had created for himself, because much of his comfort depended on personal services rendered to him by blacks.

Hoover had surrounded himself with blacks in menial positions: his driver and gardener, James Crawford; his doorman, Sam Noisette; and his messenger, Worthington Smith. He depended on Crawford and Noisette so much that he made them special agents in 1947 and 1957, respectively. Another black driver was attached to the Miami field office to be available during Hoover's winter vacation, another in California to drive him during his stay at La Jolla. These five were the only black agents in the FBI until the early sixties. Finally, there was Hoover's live-in maid, Annie Fields.

Hoover publicly denounced the racial murders of the fifties, and condemned the refusal of Southern justice to punish the murderers. His accounts of these murders, however, usually carried the imputation that the victims had brought their troubles on themselves by outraging local standards.

Hoover had another reason to look askance at black protest. From his earliest days with the Radical Division, black civil rights organizations were for Hoover first and foremost targets for communist infiltration. With his condescending attitude toward blacks, he was inclined to see them as easy prey for the skilled propagandists of the Communist Party. They could hardly help being infiltrated. The more effective civil rights organizations were, the more tempting they were to the communists. As far as Hoover could see, the country would be better off without an organized black civil rights movement and, by implication, without effective black leadership.

FBI memos to Eisenhower about the black movement discussed it primarily in terms of its susceptibility to communist subversion. In early 1953 the Bureau gave the president a study of "The Communist Party and the Negro" in which it reported that although the Party had devoted an "inordinate" amount of its time to recruiting Negro members, "its efforts had been a failure." In 1956, Hoover sent the White House a detailed report on the national conference of the National Association for the Advancement of Colored People in Washington from March 4 through March 6. Although he reported that the NAACP was anticommunist and free of communist domination, he worried about the Party's efforts to infiltrate it. The report focused so much on the activities of communists at the NAACP conference that the conference seemed hardly distinguishable from a communist cell meeting.

Attorney General Brownell's efforts to have the Justice Department support the civil rights movement were undercut by Hoover's unconcealed opposition to the department's civil rights initiative. When forced to justify his reluctance to take an aggressive stance against civil rights violations, Hoover would point to the difficulty, indeed impossibility, of getting Southern juries to convict whites for crimes committed against blacks, and so the uselessness of trying.

Hoover had twenty-five years of experience with the failure of Southern prosecutors to prosecute and Southern juries to convict whites of crimes against blacks. Ever since Frank Murphy established the Civil Rights Section of the Justice Department in 1939, Hoover had seen nearly every one of his civil rights investigations fail either because of the Southern code against convicting whites for crimes against blacks or else because his superiors in Washington abandoned him when the political heat was on. (In 1947 he reported that out of 1,570 investigations there had been only 27 convictions in twenty years.) By the late forties Hoover's discouragement in this area was so profound that he tried to avoid civil rights cases whenever he could. By the fifties this had become fixed Bureau policy.

Hoover's resistance to FBI civil rights enforcement created a vicious cycle of controversy with civil rights leaders. They would criticize FBI inaction, and then he would respond, as he did to all criticism of the Bureau, denouncing them for attacking an organization as important to the national security as the FBI. This pattern was of such long standing that by the fifties Hoover's principal experience with the civil rights movement was defending the Bureau against civil rights leaders' criticism of its performance. Since Hoover's habitual response to any attack was to question the motives and patriotism of his critics, he was programmed to react with hostility whenever a civil rights leader crossed his sights.

Civil rights investigations also created morale problems for the Bureau, since agents resented having to conduct unpopular investigations with little chance of success, particularly when the suspects were often the same local police officers with whom they had to work every day. The agents sometimes explained to local police that the whole thing was a political charade Hoover had to perform for the benefit of the Justice Department. When he heard of this, Hoover had to lecture his agents to give civil rights investigations their "most meticulous attention." He told them, "I am well aware of the problems which Civil Rights cases frequently create with regard to relations with the police and the public. If the Bureau is to avoid criticism from all sides in the Civil Rights field, the challenge made by these problems must be met by judicious and careful handling of each case." In 1952, Hoover told agents that he had heard a friendly chief of police remark that "the FBI has the unhappy duty of investigating Civil Rights violations. They don't like it but they are good policemen and they carry out their orders." Hoover commented that he was "very much concerned over the fact that some of our personnel have apparently expressed themselves to the effect that the FBI does not favor Civil Rights investigations. I want it clearly understood that all Bureau personnel should be most careful not to indicate any views or expressions of opinion regarding any matters over which this Bureau has investigative jurisdiction."

Once school segregation was outlawed by the May 17, 1954, *Brown v. Board of Education* decision, Hoover had to order his agents not to lend moral support to the white South's "massive resistance" to the decision. His personal racial preferences as a native of old Washington were now in conflict with his progressive commitment to professional standards. He insisted that his agents, at the very least, not openly encourage their Southern communities' defiance of the Supreme Court. He warned them that "recently allegations have been made by individuals representing organizations that Bureau Agents have expressed themselves as being opposed to integration of races in public schools." He said he had not been able to substantiate this, but that "the matter of racial segregation in public schools has been reviewed and passed on by the Supreme Court of the United States. There is no occasion for any agent . . . to express his views on this question. . . . The expression of personal opinions by Agents cannot be disassociated from their official status."

After decades of seeing FBI investigations of civil rights cases rejected by white Southern juries, Hoover instinctively sidestepped cases like the Emmett Till murder in 1955. Till, a black youth from Chicago, was kidnapped and murdered in Money, Mississippi, for wolf-whistling at a white girl. Hoover told a national radio audience:

> We had no right to investigate because there was no violation of federal law. Three days later, we received word that the body of the boy had been found in the Tallahatchie River. . . . The Department ruled that there was, on the facts, no violation of federal civil rights statutes, and, accordingly, the FBI was to conduct no investigation.

To many, Hoover's explanation seemed less than convincing. The FBI's reputation as the national symbol of justice was partly responsible, because the public had come to expect the dispatch of FBI agents as proof of government concern. Refusal to send the FBI meant for many that the federal government was not taking a case seriously. The country knew instinctively, and the informed more specifically, that Hoover had always found a federal angle to justify FBI involvement when it suited him (a federal car-theft angle in the Dillinger case; a white-slave law violation in the Klan investigation of the twenties; fraud in deporting black naturalist Marcus Garvey in the 1920s). On the legalities, Hoover was right; on the basis of practical experience, he was right. As a political leader, he had begun to misjudge his public.

Despite a new Civil Rights Act in 1957 and the mobilization of the civil rights movement, Hoover still did not feel there was enough of a public consensus or enough political support to outweigh the risk for the Bureau if it pursued civil rights violations more aggressively in the South. In effect, Hoover felt his critics were urging the Bureau to take a position in advance of the national consensus. Throughout his career, even when he agreed with an action urged on him (for instance, when anticommunists begged him to move against the Communist Party in 1924–1933), he would never take a vulnerable advance position without overwhelming political and public support. It was going to take massive pressure, including unmistakable presidential leadership, to get Hoover to move on civil rights, and that would not be until Lyndon B. Johnson's administration.

■ ■ ■

Hoover's sense of order and security during the fifties rested on the national consensus he had helped build that nothing was more important than domestic security, and that the Communist Party was the most dangerous threat to that security. That battle won, he had absolute confidence in his ability to deal with his responsibilities as long as they continued to center on the Communist

Party. If he knew anything, he knew American communism and how to control it. But the security he had acquired from his success against communism gave him a personal motive to resist calls for new federal law enforcement responsibilities, since they introduced an element of uncertainty into his tightly organized routine. In other areas his preeminence was not so unassailable. He knew domestic security, and he wanted to stay there. As long as the country continued to believe its most dangerous threat came from communism, his position was safe.

Another unwanted issue the fifties placed on Hoover's agenda was organized crime. Once again Hoover rejected suggestions that he modify his exclusive emphasis on domestic security. Hoover resented demands that the Bureau make a new commitment to organized crime investigations as an implicit challenge to his authority and competence, since he had been on record for years saying that organized crime, as a nationwide entity, did not exist. That put him in an embarrassing position when, on November 14, 1957, New York State Police Sergeant Edgar L. Croswell discovered a conference of more than sixty Mafia dons in the upstate New York town of Apalachin. In the ensuing uproar, the country wanted to know why Hoover, America's foremost law enforcement expert, had not known that organized crime had grown to the extent revealed by the Apalachin conference. Hoover's critics quoted him over the years denying the existence of any such national crime syndicate. He sounded either foolish or deliberately obtuse. There was even some muttering about corrupt bargains between Hoover and organized crime to keep out of each other's bailiwick.

Actually, organized crime, even after the discovery of the Apalachin conference, could have with equal accuracy been described as a loose confederation of locally independent mobs or a truly centralized system. Each perspective had its own implication for federal law enforcement. The first corresponded to Hoover's view of the national law enforcement community as a cooperative federation of independent local police forces, unified informally by the FBI's example and professional standards. The second moved in the direction of a far more tightly integrated law enforcement system demanding a real unification of local, state, and federal agencies.

Preserving (and expanding) the FBI's independence of action, even at the cost of limiting the Bureau's growth and responsibilities, was an absolute priority for Hoover. James Q. Wilson has argued that the principal reason for Hoover's success was that "throughout his rule, Hoover acted so as to protect the autonomy of the FBI by resisting any effort to change or add to the central tasks his agents were performing and by opposing collaborative ventures with other agencies that were or might become rivals."

Hoover's unwillingness to investigate organized crime when it became a national issue during the fifties perplexed many of his supporters because it was so obviously destructive to his own reputation and that of the Bureau. Once again, as in the case of civil rights, Hoover's behavior is less puzzling when it is understood in the light of Bureau history, but since Hoover could not readily explain the bureaucratic reasons for his inaction, his denial of the problem made him look old-fashioned and out of touch.

Attorney General Rogers, who tried to engage the Justice Department in organized crime prosecutions, recalled that Hoover had to be dragged "kicking and screaming" into organized crime investigations. When the Senate Rackets Committee, under John McClellan (with John F. Kennedy a member and Robert F. Kennedy committee counsel), revived the perennial idea of a federal national crime commission, the Justice Department responded by setting up a Special Group on Organized Crime. Instead of cooperating, however, Hoover reacted to this affront in 1957 by instituting an FBI "Top Hoodlum Program" that required every field office to draw up a list of the ten most important underworld figures to target for intensive surveillance. Despite the real accomplishments of the Justice Department's organized crime group, Hoover told the House Appropriations Committee that it accomplished nothing except "nest feathering publicity" and "speculative ventures." His opposition doomed the Special Group, which died after two years. In 1959 there were still four hundred agents in the New York office assigned to investigating the Communists, only four to organized crime.

At the end of the decade the FBI had begun to look completely out of touch about organized crime. Hoover had to work hard to keep the usually docile International Association of Chiefs of Police from supporting a federal central clearinghouse on organized crime, which would have created a rival to the FBI's law enforcement leadership. By 1960 the pressure for action against organized crime was so great that Hoover finally caved in and decided to accept the arguments of his aides, notably William C. Sullivan of the Domestic Intelligence Division, that something along the lines of nationwide organized crime actually did exist.

To make up for lost time in expanding the Bureau's knowledge of organized crime, Hoover decided to approve the use of illegal warrantless microphone surveillance in organized crime cases. In mid-1959 the Chicago field office requested permission to plant a bug at a mob meetingplace on Chicago's North Michigan Avenue. In a radical departure from his past policies, Hoover gave his approval. In doing so he relied on a memorandum from Brownell that had given him permission to plant microphones in cases of "internal security and the national safety." The wording seemed to exclude criminal investigations, but Brownell did later explain that he intended "national safety" to include federal crimes. The Chicago microphone surveillance was enormously productive, and in 1960 provided the Bureau with a complete list of the names of the members of the Mafia's "national commission."

■ ■ ■

The FBI seemed to compensate for its reluctance to move into civil rights and organized crime during the fifties by redoubling its efforts in domestic security. Throughout the fifties, despite the complete collapse of American communism, Hoover never relaxed his efforts to persuade the president and the public that, all appearances to the contrary, the threat from communism was greater than ever. There was a weekly FBI "Current Intelligence Summary," largely a digest of rhetoric emanating from the Communist Party and front groups, together with advance warning about Party activities (no bomb plots—just fund-raising campaigns, marches, petition drives). There was also an annual analysis of the "Communist Party Line" and summaries of "Communist Party Activities."

By the mid-fifties Cold War tensions were decidedly less nerve wracking than five or ten years before. The Soviets evacuated their troops from Austria in May 1955. In July 1955, Eisenhower met with the leaders of Britain, France, and the Soviet Union in Geneva. In 1956 the U.S. government abandoned the detention camps set up under the Internal Security Act of 1950. Hoover's reaction to all this was to complain about a "growing public complacency toward the threat of subversion."

One result of the relaxation of tensions at home and abroad was the demise of the Smith Act. On October 17, 1955, the Supreme Court agreed to hear an appeal of a Smith Act case (*Yates*). In response, on March 15, 1956, the department notified the Bureau that all future Smith Act cases must include evidence of "an actual plan for a violent revolution" before the department would prosecute them.

Hoover's domestic security program needed an overhaul. The Smith Act, in conjunction with the Custodial Detention Program, had given direction and focus to the FBI's surveillance against the Party. The demise of the Smith Act as a viable prosecutorial weapon was a blow to the FBI as much for its use as an operational compass as for its worth as a legal weapon.

Hoover was worried. He sent a memo to cabinet members and other top officials on the "Reaction of Communist Party, USA, To Recent Supreme Court Decisions." He complained that the "Party as a whole is jubilant over these decisions." He quoted one communist who had said "this decision will mark a rejuvenation of the Party in America. We've lost some members in the last few years but now we're on our way again. The people are sick and tired of witch hunts."

At the end of 1955 the Communist Party was leaderless, directionless, reduced to 22,000 members. Then came news of Nikita Khrushchev's speech on the crimes of Stalin before the Twentieth Congress of the Soviet Communist Party in February 1956 (a speech obtained and published by the State Department), followed by authoritative accounts of Soviet anti-Semitism. In June 1956 communist authorities in Poznan, Poland, killed more than one hundred protesters and wounded hundreds more. Soviet tanks then rolled into Hungary in October, crushing the last illusions of American communists and emptying the already depleted ranks of the Party.

The demoralization of the American Communist Party pointed Hoover toward a momentous change in his approach to domestic intelligence. Sensing a historic opportunity to administer the coup de grâce to the bewildered remnants of the Party, but deprived of the weapon of the Smith Act, he and his aides decided to use FBI informants in the Party to stir up dissension by asking embarrassing questions about Hungary, and by stimulating discussions about Khrushchev's speech and Soviet anti-Semitism.

In 1956 Hoover summoned his domestic intelligence agents to a meeting to decide on a new strategy against the Party now that they no longer had the Smith Act. The plan that emerged from Bureau field conferences about a replacement for the Smith Act as a rationale for Bureau domestic security investigations was formally known as COINTELPRO (COunter INtelligence PROgram), a concerted and aggressive campaign to destroy the Party by circulating disruptive rumors and reports about individual members, and by employing other "dirty tricks" to keep the Party from functioning.

COINTELPRO expanded greatly during the sixties, but during the Eisenhower administration the only such program was COINTELPRO-CPUSA. This was the longest-lived of the programs (1956 to 1971) and accounted for more than half—1,388 out of 2,370—of all the Bureau's reported COINTELPRO actions. (Some critics have charged, however, that reported incidents were only a fraction of the actual number of COINTELPRO operations.)

The goal of COINTELPRO was "keeping the pot boiling" within the Party. The Bureau soon saw that the technique offered the additional opportunity "to direct our disruptive tactics toward a specific goal," thus manipulating the Party in desired directions. Soon FBI informants were becoming so influential in Party feuds that Hoover and his top aides seriously discussed whether the

Bureau should support their informants' factions and gain control of the Party. (Eventually, the FBI decided to maintain a "middle of the road" position out of fear of backing a losing faction and thus having the informants expelled from the Party.)

Some of the techniques the Bureau employed in COINTELPRO might be considered legitimate, such as having informants in the Communist Party raise the issue of Khrushchev's denunciation of Stalin. Some were more offensive: Upon learning that a Party official was a homosexual, the FBI arranged with the police to have him arrested to "embarrass the party." Others were pointlessly cruel, such as provoking neighbors' complaints that resulted in the ouster of a communist mother as a Cub Scout den leader. Another was the "snitch jacket": planting false evidence that a Party member was an FBI informant. The Bureau also made anonymous phone calls to keep the Party from renting meeting halls, and it sent anonymous reprints of anticommunist publications to Party members. The only limit on the Bureau's ingenuity was fear of getting caught.

The shock of world events in 1956 might have been too much for the American Communist Party to survive even without the added punishment inflicted by COINTELPRO, but from the Bureau's perspective the program was an incredible success. At the end of the year the Party was a ghost of its former self, with a membership of between 3,000 and 6,000, many of them FBI informants. In December 1957 the paid-up membership sank to a low of 3,474. American Communists had gone the way of the buffalo; now Hoover and his domestic security agents had to worry about going the way of the buffalo hunters.

Hoover recognized how damaging it would be to the Bureau if knowledge of COINTELPRO's existence ever leaked out. For this reason, and because of the legal and moral sensitivity of COINTELPRO operations (being that they were illegal and sometimes immoral), they all had to be approved by Bureau headquarters in Washington. The lowest level at which they could be approved was that of the assistant director in charge of domestic intelligence. Most were approved by Hoover himself.

But with COINTELPRO the FBI became more of a conspiracy than the Bureau's "subversive" Communist target. The Party was, for the most part, operating unapologetically and openly. The FBI, on the other hand, was working in secret, using methods so illegal and often so repugnant that the Bureau's survival depended on keeping them hidden from view. Worse yet, the success of COINTELPRO encouraged the Bureau to expand these techniques to targets other than the Party, should the need or opportunity arise, as it would during the sixties.

In March 1960, the Bureau expanded COINTELPRO-CPUSA by adding a

COMINFIL (COMmunist INFILtration) component. There had been previous COMINFIL operations, but they had been intended only to discover communist infiltration. Now COMINFIL was aimed at actively preventing communist infiltration of mass organizations. The standard disruptive technique was to release information about communist participants in marches and rallies, without admitting the FBI source. The intent (and often the effect) was to discredit the organizations sponsoring each event, the event itself, and, inevitably, the goals of the event as well. This COMINFIL extension of COINTELPRO (like COINTELPRO itself) represented a new form of intrusion by the FBI into the political process. The Bureau had done this before, but such activities in the past had been isolated and infrequent. Now they were systematized as official policy.

COINTELPRO can be seen as a rational, ingenious, and successful effort to capitalize on a unique situation within the communist movement in 1956. But then why did Hoover not only maintain the program after 1956, but, even after the collapse of the Party, expand it? It seemed so clear to Attorney General Brownell, for one, that the Party had been crushed for good, that he retired back to Wall Street at the end of 1957 with the satisfaction of having accomplished his two goals in office: destroying the Communist Party and passing the first civil rights laws since Reconstruction.

But Hoover was the captive of his memories of Bureau history. He had thought he had destroyed the Party once before. The Palmer Raids, the raid on the Bridgman convention, and the state sedition trials of communist leadership had reduced its membership to about 5,000 in the early twenties. The party had been as weak then as it was now in 1957. Yet it had rebounded to 80,000 members during World War II. Others could look at the Party in 1956 and see only its collapse. Hoover saw only the low point of a recurrent cycle of increase and decline. On November 6, 1958, Hoover gave the cabinet a special briefing on Russian intentions, intelligence techniques, and counterintelligence activities. He told them that "the loss of CP membership makes no difference—size has little relation to the importance of the CP's mission."

In the same vein, in 1958 Hoover made one of those remarks that a totally humorless person will make, that leaves you wondering if he is pulling your leg: "[The Communist Party is] well on its way to achieving its current objective, which is to make you believe that it is shattered, ineffective and dying . . . When it has fully achieved this first objective . . . it will then proceed inflexibly toward its final goal." But Hoover probably meant every word.

As the world situation changed and the American Communist Party collapsed (making less credible the threat to national security from a communist fifth column), Hoover shifted the focus of his anticommunism from the Party's infiltration of institutions to its supposed responsibility for the subversion of American values. He charged the Party with trying to "drive a wedge between the American people and the American way of life" and he decried the tendency "to ignore the anti-American statements that are preserved in communist archives." He now claimed the duty and responsibility of separating the "authentic" from the "subversive" in American reform movements. For Hoover the specter of communism was more than just the shadow of the real-life communist. He saw communism as "the latest form of the eternal rebellion against authority," so it represented a tendency rooted in the fallen nature of man. There would never be a moment when the serious anticommunist could beat his sword into a plowshare or his files into papier-mâché.

■ ■ ■

Hoover's tremendous success and power now gave him confidence to seek a more effective forum to deliver moral instruction to the nation. While the Bureau was, with COINTELPRO, becoming more and more a secret society, Hoover's Domestic Intelligence Division was starting work on a project to create a new public image for the Bureau. The book that finally emerged, *Masters of Deceit,* was Hoover's effort to interpret the world for Americans in terms of the struggle with communism. It was his primer for Americans, instruction in the "stern reality" of the world.

The initial draft of the book was produced in the Research and Analysis Section of the Domestic Intelligence Division under the supervision of its chief, William C. Sullivan. Even though *Masters of Deceit* (like Hoover's earlier book, *Persons in Hiding*) was ghostwritten, it was as much a reflection of Hoover's ideas and feelings as if he had actually written it himself. Hoover's style of thought and expression so permeated the Bureau that the FBI's writers could emote in a manner indistinguishable from Hoover's, complete with his characteristic patterns of speech and thought. Moreover, Hoover's editing was vigorous and rigorous and nothing got out of the Bureau without Hoover or his assistants making absolutely sure it met with his approval. They all, and Lou Nichols in particular, bore the scars of Hoover's wrath when he discovered "J. Edgar Hoover" had said or written something the real Hoover did not like.

Masters of Deceit was published in 1958 by Henry Holt, a publishing firm owned by Clint Murchison, the Texas oilman who put Hoover and Tolson up each summer at his Del Charro Hotel during their La Jolla trip. (Holt also published Hoover's *Study of Communism* in 1962.) The financial arrangements show Hoover had come to regard the Bureau as an extension of himself. Even though the book was written on government time by government employees, Hoover and his associates split the money among themselves. *Masters of Deceit* sold 250,000 copies in hardback, 2 million in paper (twenty-nine printings by 1970). Proceeds were divided evenly between Hoover, Tolson, Lou Nichols, *This Week* magazine editor William I. Nichols, and the FBI Recreation Fund.

Masters of Deceit was intended, as its first purpose, to support Hoover's call to continue the anticommunist crusade no matter how weak the American Communist Party might appear. Despite the American Communist Party's infirm state, *Masters* claimed there were proportionately more communists (counting their "sympathizers") in America than in Russia on the eve of the revolution. The Party might seem too small to worry about, but Hoover turned that too into a reason for keeping it under surveillance: "[T]he present menace of the Communist Party in the United States grows in direct ratio to the rising feeling that it is a small, dissident element and need not be feared." Finally, Hoover argued that the size of the Party in the United States was irrelevant as long as Moscow was running the international movement: "[N]ight after night, week after week, these men and women are plotting against America, working out smears, seeking to discredit free government, and planning for revolution. They form the base of a gigantic pyramid of treason, stretching from the little gray house with green shutters to the towers of the Kremlin."

Without totally abandoning the thesis that there was a real danger that the communist fifth column, supported by the Soviets, could overthrow the government, *Masters* argued that the actual danger posed by communism was the "destruction of the American way of life" by spreading "a communist mentality representing a systematic, purposive, and conscious attempt to destroy Western civilization and roll history back to the age of barbaric cruelty and despotism, all in the name of 'progress.' " Although the communists might be only "a few men and women," by means of "thought control" their spiritual "infection" has spread "to most phases of American life." And since communism was a false religion, the only defense against it was a return to the true religion. "In our tolerance for religious freedom, for separation of church and state, we sometimes lose sight of the historical fact that Western civilization has deep religious roots. The very essence of our faith in democracy and our fellow man is rooted in a belief in a Supreme Being." The religious underpinnings of Americanism, Hoover explained,

> *consisted of a belief in the dignity of the individual, in mutual responsibility, in the concept of life as having a meaning that transcends political systems, in a*

sense of stewardship, in an intrinsic morality rooted in the nature of things. To meet this challenge no hesitant, indifferent, half-apologetic acts on our own part can suffice. Out of the deep roots of religion flows something warm and good, the affirmation of love and justice; here is the source of strength for our land if we are to remain free.

Masters of Deceit was only superficially a book about communism. It was really an attempt to repair and restore the kind of Americanism Hoover had known as a boy in the days of William McKinley and Teddy Roosevelt.

■ ■ ■

Hoover's reversion to type as the earnest Christian soldier defending church, school, and home was nowhere more evident than in the film version of Don Whitehead's authorized history of the Bureau, *The FBI Story*. The movie showed the FBI itself as an idealized version of Hoover's home in Washington's Seward Square, the Bureau as the family Hoover had never had himself as an adult.

Don Whitehead was twice winner of the Pulitzer Prize and chief of the *New York Herald Tribune*'s Washington Bureau. He began *The FBI Story* in 1955 with the close cooperation of Lou Nichols and the Crime Records Division. The book appeared in 1956, stayed on the best-seller lists for thirty-eight weeks, and was serialized in 170 papers.

Whitehead was a talented professional who wove almost every issue and event in Bureau history into a single narrative, for the most part in chronological sequence. As might be expected from Whitehead's close relationship with Nichols, who doled out only the information he wanted included, the book is wholly favorable to the Bureau. On the other hand, the point of view is Whitehead's. Nichols was probably telling the truth when he said "you don't edit Don Whitehead." But Nichols didn't have to: Whitehead was as much a believer in the Bureau and its patriotic mission as Hoover.

Most of the book is a readable, engaging history of the Bureau, with plenty of anecdotes and human interest and some previously unknown facts on the Bureau's undercover work, but Whitehead brought his story to a close by deciding that the real significance of the FBI lay not in the crimes it fought, the laws it upheld, but the values it symbolized: "The history of the FBI, in reality, is the story of America itself and the struggle for an ideal. . . . In the whole struggle, the FBI represents the people's effort to achieve government by law . . . And the FBI in the future will be as strong or as weak as the people demand it to be. No more. No less."

The transformation of the FBI into a microcosm of traditional America was carried to its ultimate extreme in Warner Brothers' 1959 film version of *The FBI Story*. The movie turned Whitehead's book into something the *Saturday Review* called "One G-Man's Family." The fireworks were not the gunfights with gangsters or suspense over spies, but the conflicts between its FBI hero and his wife (James Stewart and Vera Miles) as their domestic life was disrupted, time and again, by Stewart's FBI career.

Audiences who went to see *The FBI Story* expecting something like the old G-man movies would have been a little puzzled by Warner Brothers' new breed of family-oriented G-men. The *New York Times* complained the movie was more concerned with "the joys and sorrows of the American home and the bliss of domestic security than the historic details of crime." The film seemed to treat the Bureau's great cases as "occupational hazards" that were sandwiched between such domestic obligations as getting the kids off to school and sitting down to a bowl of breakfast cereal.

Hoover had turned the FBI into a substitute family, and now Hollywood had given him a dramatization of the fantasy. That made his first viewing of the film an emotional experience. Mervyn LeRoy, the film's director, recalled that on that occasion "I was never so nervous in my whole life. . . . So when . . . Edgar stood up and he motioned for me to come over to him and he put his arms around me and he said, 'Mervyn, that's one of the greatest jobs I've ever seen,' and they all started to applaud, I guess they were all waiting to see how he liked it. . . . Because you're doing a man's life . . . Well, it was a beautiful story, it was the story of the FBI."

■ ■ ■

Had LeRoy done the story of Hoover's life, his audiences would have been even more amazed. Hoover's own domestic arrangements were far less conventional than those portrayed by Jimmy Stewart and Vera Miles. The intimate secrets of Hoover's private life died with him, but the least that can be said is that in his emotional attachments he was certainly not heterosexual. His closest relationships, other than with his mother, with whom he lived until her death when he was forty-three, were with two subordinates in the Bureau: first Frank Baughman, who joined Hoover's Radical Division in 1919 and worked by his side during the Red Scare raids, and then Clyde Tolson, who joined the Bureau in 1928 and then, just two years later, was named assistant director.

For the rest of their lives, Tolson functioned as Hoover's right-hand man, the number two man in the FBI, and the Bureau disciplinarian. Whether or not Hoover and Tolson had a homosexual relationship will probably never be known, despite the lurid stories that have spiced up sensationalistic exposés. The most famous of these tales, that Hoover was a cross-dresser and participated in group orgies, are demonstrably false. Hoover and Tolson never lived together, except for a brief period late in their lives when Tolson was an invalid and needed constant care. But they were otherwise inseparable, eating lunch and dinner together every day, vacationing together, and attending Washington social events together. From the White House on down, hosts knew that an invitation to the FBI director should also include Tolson.

In my biography of Hoover I called theirs a "spousal relationship," a deliberately equivocal characterization. The only real evidence I know that their relationship might have gone beyond a very close friendship is a series of snapshots I found among Hoover's papers of Tolson sleeping in his pajamas. All indications are that they were taken by Hoover, and he kept them with his intimate family and private records. Most men would find it an inexcusable invasion of privacy to have another man photograph him while asleep—unless there were a relationship more intimate than a conventional male friendship.

On his death, except for a few souvenirs to close associates, Hoover willed his considerable property to Tolson. During Hoover's funeral Tolson sat in the front right-hand pew, where one often sees the widow, and Tolson was given the flag that lay on Hoover's casket. Today they lie, side by side, in graves in Washington's Congressional Cemetery.

■ ■ ■

Toward the end of the Eisenhower administration, Attorney General Herbert Brownell, who had left office in 1957, had a final conversation with Hoover. "Edgar," he told him, "it is time to retire." He had had a great career, Brownell told him, and had done great things, but it was time to leave. If he stayed on he was putting at risk everything he had done. Hoover thanked him for the advice, and ignored it.

He should have paid attention. A new generation was rising that would be a mystery to Hoover, one that would reject Hoover, Hoover's FBI, and the values of the America that Hoover dedicated his life—and his Bureau—to protecting.

The FBI ended the decade of the fifties on top of the world—or at least on top of Washington, much the same thing. Whether regarded with fear, admiration, or some more complex mixture of emotions, the FBI was a massive presence on the American scene, dominating domestic security and law enforcement, a factor to be reckoned with in any political calculation. The Bureau and its director were American icons, legendary figures.

And yet, in retrospect, for it is only in retrospect that the moment when strength begins to decline into weakness becomes clear, the FBI's moment had already passed, unnoticed behind the swelling panoply of FBI power.

The Bureau's public image, youthful vitality in the era of James Cagney and "G-men," now reflected the comfortable middle age of suburban America, concerned with conformity, respectability, and family values more than the spirit of adventure. When the placid surface of American culture began to crack under the pressure of youthful rebellion at the end of the decade, the FBI and J. Edgar Hoover were almost inevitably two of the most prominent and available symbols of the past for youthful protest.

The FBI had always been loathed on the left. That hatred had done nothing but fester since 1919. To all appearances the left's moment had also come and gone. The old unity of the left that had been destroyed in the twenties, but had reemerged during the thirties, had been shattered again by the Cold War. The Communist Party's complicity with Stalin had tarred radicals with guilt for being part of Stalin's killing machine. The Cold War had split the left between supporters and critics of a foreign policy of containing the spread of communism.

The indiscriminate Red-smearing attacks of McCarthyites had made no such fine distinctions. Liberals felt the same fears that McCarthy was visiting on communists and fellow travelers. Since the FBI was visibly and actively implicated in McCarthyism, even anticommunist liberals had a score to settle with the FBI should the occasion arise.

At the end of the 1950s national security issues, while still important, increasingly had to share public attention with the more usual social and economic issues. Hoover's continued focus on the supposed threat of domestic communism was not only unpersuasive but also made him seem a relic. And his politicization of the Bureau was becoming an ever greater obstacle to its effectiveness. His political alliances made it all but impossible for him to redirect the Bureau's priorities against the will of his sponsors. For example, to have enforced civil rights laws aggressively would have pitted him against his conservative southern allies.

Hoover's dysfunctional relationship with the Truman administration underscores the importance of the FBI's cooperating with the president and the attorney general if it is to operate responsibly and effectively. The FBI's responsibility for potentially explosive domestic security investigations always makes a close working relationship with the administration critical to the Bureau's effectiveness—and the administration's. Let that relationship break down, as it did during Truman's presidency, and almost anything can happen, most of it bad for all concerned.

The Bureau's domestic intelligence investigations are by their nature so sensitive that no FBI director can take the risk of carrying them out unless assured of political support at the highest level. If he does not have confidence that the president will back him, or if he judges the president too weak to protect him, the Bureau will cast about for other allies, and these may well be found among the president's political enemies. The result will be a politicized Bureau. And an ineffective one.

Let the Bureau have confidence in a president, and let the president demonstrate his loyalty to the Bureau when mistakes are made, and there is not much the Bureau cannot do. But even in those happy circumstances, the FBI director will very likely make his own assessment of the political situation, and will be reluctant to carry out the president's wishes if the director does not think that, on any particular issue, the president cannot deliver on his promises of support, as was the situation regarding civil rights and organized crime investigations during the forties and fifties.

The Bureau's disloyalty to Harry Truman was the direct result of Hoover's feeling that he needed more reliable and more powerful political protection than he could count on from the president. By contrast, Hoover's willingness to fight for Eisenhower against McCarthy, which certainly went against Hoover's instincts, reflected his (or any director's) willingness to take risks for a president he trusts. But then an FBI director may feel obligated to do anything such a president wants, and presidents have a way of wanting some things they shouldn't. This may be the price the Bureau has to pay to maintain the presidential support that alone enables it to carry out the sensitive assignments national security sometimes requires.

The Bureau's enormous power and prestige during the Truman and Eisenhower presidencies also made it arrogantly dismissive of its critics. The Bureau had become more divisive than ever, hated and loathed by more Americans than ever, who were repelled by the excesses of its anticommunism and by its refusal to protect the civil rights of black Americans. Only the political weakness of its enemies allowed the FBI to ignore its responsibility to serve the entire public, and not just the (temporarily) dominant majority. The Bureau's critics, while restive and angry, were still powerless at the end of the sixties, and it must have seemed to the Bureau they could safely be ignored. But the only safe prediction in politics is that times can change.

SEVEN

A Secret Society
(1961–1972)

L ATE AT NIGHT ON November 20, 1964, William C. Sullivan, FBI assistant director in charge of the Domestic Intelligence Division, slipped a piece of untraceable unwatermarked paper into an old untraceable typewriter and composed a letter to Martin Luther King Jr.

Fifteen months before, on August 28, 1963, King had made his "I Have a Dream" speech at the March on Washington. It had woven King's own dream of racial equality into the American imagination and made it part of the American dream. The speech had also made King *Time* magazine's Man of the Year for 1963. On October 14, 1964, King had been honored again when he was named winner of that year's Nobel Peace Prize.

Sullivan was fifty-two years old in November 1964, a twenty-three-year veteran of the Bureau. Since June 1961 he had headed the Bureau's key Division Five, the Domestic Intelligence Division. With the rank of assistant director, he was, in effect, the number four man in the Bureau, behind Hoover, Associate Director Clyde Tolson, and Assistant to the Director Alan Belmont. Since he directed all national security investigations—including surveillance of groups suspected of being influenced by communists or being potential targets for such influence, as well as violence-prone groups like black or white hate groups—he was arguably the most important man in the Bureau, after Hoover.

This was what Sullivan typed that night:

> *King, look into your heart. You know, you are a complete fraud and a greater liability to all of us Negroes. White people in this country have enough frauds of their own but I am sure they don't have one at this time that is anywhere near*

your equal. You are no clergyman and you know it. I repeat that you are a colossal fraud and an evil, vicious one at that. . . .

King, like all frauds your end is approaching. You could have been our greatest leader . . . But you are done. Your "honorary" degrees, your Nobel Prize (what a grim farce) and other awards will not save you. King, I repeat you are done . . .

The American public, the church organizations that have been helping— Protestants, Catholics and Jews will know you for what you are—an evil beast. So will others who have backed you. You are done.

King, there is only one thing left for you to do. You know what it is. You have just 34 days in which to do it (this exact number has been selected for a specific reason, it has definite practical significance). You are done. There is but one way out for you. You better take it before your filthy fraudulent self is bared to the nation.

Sullivan earlier had had John Matter of the FBI labs prepare a composite tape that day of the most salacious episodes from months of recordings made from microphones hidden in King's hotel rooms as the civil rights leader moved from city to city encouraging civil rights demonstrations. The tapes contained bawdy conversations between King and his friends, sexual conversations between King and several different female partners, and the sounds—mattress creaking, groans, and cries—associated with sexual intercourse. When he had finished typing, Sullivan packed the note in a package with the reel of tape. The next morning Sullivan handed it to Special Agent Lish Whitson, telling him to fly to Miami and call when he got there. When he got Whitson's call, Sullivan instructed him to address the package to King care of the Atlanta office of the Southern Christian Leadership Conference, and mail it from the Miami Post Office.

When it arrived in Atlanta, King was in Norway getting his Nobel Peace Prize. The package was set aside, where Coretta King found it on January 5. She liked to listen to recordings of King's speeches, and assumed that this was one of them. She soon realized it was something different. When she read the threatening note she called King. Then she, King, Ralph Abernathy, Andrew Young, and Joseph Lowery listened to it all.

They immediately concluded that the source had to be the FBI: The combination of the surreptitious recording, mostly of a stay at Washington's Willard Hotel, along with the postmark from Miami, suggested resources possessed by few except the Bureau. "They are out to break me," King said. "They are out to get me, harass me, break my spirit." Some of King's friends thought the purpose had been to blackmail King into declining the Nobel Prize. Others thought it was to goad King's wife into divorcing him. Or maybe the plan was to put the thought of suicide in King's mind. How could the FBI have sunk so low?

■ ■ ■

King had first come to the notice of the FBI a few years after the 1955 Montgomery, Alabama, bus boycott, when, in September 1958, the Bureau learned that King had been introduced to Benjamin Davis, a black Communist Party leader.

That discovery would have set off an alarm in Hoover's mind, and in the minds of those subordinates whose job security depended on their ability to read his. From Hoover's earliest days in the Radical Division in 1919, the civil rights movement's primary significance for him was as a target for communist subversion. His background, a white in a segregated city, probably made him deaf to calls for racial justice. And he would have seen civil rights confrontations as a dangerous weakening of national solidarity. But it was as an anticommunist, first and foremost, that he judged the civil rights movement, as he judged everything else. He had been reading communists' writings all his life, and so he knew that from the time of Lenin, communists had believed that black Americans constituted a true revolutionary class. From the beginning, Hoover had his agents scrutinize all civil rights groups for any signs of communist infiltration. Now those fishing expeditions had netted a big one, and Hoover watched, probably with a fighter's anticipation of battle, as King's star rose in the national black community.

When King took part in the Freedom Rider campaign in May 1961, Hoover ordered an investigation. Hoover reported to Attorney General Robert Kennedy on January 8, 1962, the Bureau had learned that one of King's most trusted advisers was a New York attorney named Stanley Levison, who had been identified in the early fifties as a key financial backer and adviser to the Communist Party. Levison was of particular interest to the Bureau because one of the FBI's most important informants in the American Communist Party, Jack Childs (who, with his brother Morris, was given the Bureau code name "Solo"), had told the Bureau that Levison managed the Party's finances in the late forties and early fifties. Over the next seven years, Levison's continued contact with King would be Hoover's principal pretext for the Bureau's merciless persecution of the civil rights leader, a persecution that continued even after King's assassination.

Until Levison turned up as King's adviser, the FBI thought that Levison had quit the Party in late 1955. Agents had even tried unsuccessfully to recruit Levison as an informant in February 1960. Now the Bureau changed its mind and decided Levison must have been a "sleeper," a passive undercover communist trying to gain control of the civil rights movement by manipulating King. After 1961, the Bureau subjected Levison to almost continuous surveillance, but never discovered any hint that Levison was other than what he represented himself to be: an ardent supporter of the civil rights movement and of King in particular. In the FBI's reports to the White House, to the attorney general, and to Congress, and in its leaks to the news media, the Bureau never let on that its suspicions that Levison was still active in the Party were simply conjectures. By circular logic, Hoover and the Bureau used Levison's supposed continued membership in the Party as evidence of King's subversive intent.

Attorney General Kennedy, President John F. Kennedy, and their aides had no difficulty recognizing that Hoover's January 8 note about Levison and King had put them all in danger. Once the Bureau had officially notified them that Martin Luther King had a communist adviser, they were in the same position as Harry Truman when he got Hoover's warnings about Harry Dexter White. If they ignored this news, they might face the same fate as Truman in 1947, when Hoover had allied himself with the administration's Republican enemies.

Robert Kennedy's immediate response was to assume that Hoover was right about Levison, but to hope that King did not know about Levison's communist affiliation. Kennedy ordered one of his aides, John Seigenthaler, to warn King in general terms, without naming Levison. White House Special Assistant for Civil Rights Harris Wofford, acting on his own, also warned King, giving him Levison's name this time. Deputy Attorney General Byron White, more observant of the chain of command, asked the FBI whether King should be warned about Levison. Hoover replied that to do so would "definitely endanger our informant ['Solo'] and the national security." Hoover added in a note for internal Bureau consumption that "King is no good anyway. Under no circumstances should our informant be endangered."

Then in February 1962 the Bureau learned that King's Southern Christian Leadership Conference had hired Jack O'Dell on Levison's recommendation for the SCLC's New York office. The FBI believed, on much better evidence than it had on Levison, that O'Dell was currently a communist, in fact a member of the Communist Party's National Committee, though O'Dell consistently refused to confirm, deny, or answer questions about whether he was a Party member. He had been a member of the National Maritime Union, generally considered Party-dominated, and had been expelled in a purge of members considered communists. O'Dell's hiring seemed to confirm the Bureau's suspicion that Levison was working to increase communist influence on King, and so, with Robert Kennedy's approval, on March 20 the Bureau placed a tap on Levison's phone. On his own authority, as was then department practice, Hoover had already placed a microphone in Levison's office. On May 11, 1962, the Bureau put King's name on the Emergency Detention list, which meant that he was to be arrested during a national emergency.

On the basis of the Levison-O'Dell-King connection, the Bureau opened a full-scale investigation on October 23, 1962, for the purpose of determining the extent of communist infiltration of the SCLC. Now the Bureau had a pretext for wiretap and microphone surveillance of King's office.

The investigation of King took on added urgency on November 18, 1962, when King said he agreed with a report of the Southern Regional Council that "there is a considerable amount of distrust among Albany [Georgia] Negroes for local members of the Federal Bureau of Investigation . . . FBI men appear to Albany Negroes as vaguely-interested observers of injustice, who diffidently write down complaints and do no more." King complained that "one of the great problems we face with the FBI in the south is that the agents are white Southerners who have been influenced by the mores of the community. To maintain their status, they have to be friendly with the local police and people who are promoting segregation."

Hoover was furious, and tasked his deputy Cartha DeLoach (who had taken over the retired Lou Nichols's job of handling "grief" for Hoover), with calling King to tell him that four out of five Albany staffers were in fact northerners. DeLoach was supposed to "straighten him out," as the Bureau would say.

King was away from his Atlanta office when DeLoach called, so he left a message for King, but King was notoriously inattentive to such matters. When King never got back to DeLoach, the latter took this as a willful insult to himself and the Bureau, and, furthermore, an admission that King had known his charges were false. DeLoach told his boss, Assistant to the Director John Mohr, that King "obviously does not desire to be given the truth. The fact that he is a vicious liar is amply demonstrated in the fact he constantly associates with and takes instructions from Stanley Levison who is a hidden member of the Communist Party." From this point on the Bureau treated King not only as a communist, but as hostile to the Bureau, which was even worse.

In June 1963 the Kennedy administration was pressing Congress for a new civil rights law. A communism-in-the-civil-rights-movement scandal would have ended any chances of its passage. Robert Kennedy and Burke Marshall, the assistant attorney general in charge of the Civil Rights Division, again urged King to break with Levison. On June 22 the president himself took King into the Rose Garden. Comparing the situation to the Profumo scandal that had destroyed Prime Minister Harold Macmillan's government in London, Kennedy told King that if he did not end his relationship with Levison and O'Dell, the Kennedy administration and the civil rights movement might all be destroyed.

Meanwhile the Bureau was already leaking stories about the SCLC-King-O'Dell relationship to any Southern papers looking for ways to smear the civil rights movement. Governors George Wallace of Alabama and Ross Barnett of Mississippi testified at hearings on the civil rights bill that King was a communist and that the civil rights movement was communist-controlled. The rumors swirling around Washington about King's communist connections terrified liberal members of Congress. They begged the administration for reassurance about King. The Kennedys gave them a carefully crafted written denial that King was a communist or communist-controlled, but distributed it with a confidential oral briefing on the Levison relationship.

Robert Kennedy was now so concerned that he gave serious consideration on July 17, 1963, to wiretapping King. He changed his mind when King finally promised the administration on July 23 that he would break completely with Levison and O'Dell.

But at this critical juncture in the Bureau's battle with King, none other than William C. Sullivan called into question its underlying rationale. On August 23, 1963, while still probing the Martin Luther King–Stanley Levison–Jack O'Dell relationship, and while Hoover was being briefed on communist plans to take part in the upcoming August 28 March on Washington, Sullivan gave Hoover a sixty-seven-page brief on the Party's campaign to infiltrate the civil rights movement. Sullivan concluded, "There has been an obvious failure of the Communist Party of the United States to appreciably infiltrate, influence, or control large numbers of American Negroes in this country."

Hoover was baffled. Sullivan's latest memo contradicted two years of reports he had been sending Hoover about King's close relationships with communists. Hoover fired the report back at Sullivan, with the handwritten comment that "this memo reminds me vividly of those I received when Castro took over Cuba. You contended then that Castro and his cohorts were not communists and not influenced by communists. Time alone proved you wrong. I for one can't ignore the memos re [deletion, presumably Levison and O'Dell] as having only an infinitesimal effect on the efforts to exploit the American Negro by the Communists."

Sullivan gave his account of this controversy after he left the Bureau in 1971. It was affected by his break with Hoover, so has to be weighed carefully. His testimony before a Senate committee in November 1975, and his memoirs, published after his death in 1977, reveal a deeply troubled man, prone to exaggerating his misdeeds to make his contrition more impressive. There is no reason, though, to doubt his statement that his August 23 report provoked an unprecedented crisis within the top ranks of the FBI: "This [memorandum] set me at odds with Hoover. . . . A few months went by before he would speak to me. Everything was conducted by exchange of written communications. It was evident that we had to change our ways or we would all be out on the street."

Now, whenever Domestic Intelligence sent Hoover a report on King and Levison (or, for that matter, on any communist activities), Hoover would ridicule it with comments like his "just infinitesimal!" that he scribbled on a report on communist plans for the August 28 March on Washington, or his comment, "I assume CP functionary claims are all frivolous," which he added to a report on communist plans for follow-up rallies after the march. Sullivan was caught in a trap: He had programmed his division to produce an unending flow of reports on the danger posed by communist activities, and these hardly made sense in light of his August 23 brief.

On August 30, Sullivan wrote an abject apology to Hoover that retracted everything he had said the week before:

The director is correct. We were completely wrong about believing the evidence was not sufficient to determine some years ago that Fidel Castro was not a communist or under communist influence. On investigating and writing about communism and the American Negro, we had better remember this and profit by the lesson it should teach us.

Personally, I believe in the light of King's powerful demagogic speech yesterday [the "I have a dream" speech] he stands head and shoulders above all other Negro leaders put together when it comes to influencing great masses of Negroes. We must mark him now, if we have not done so before, as the most dangerous Negro of the future in this nation from the standpoint of communism, the Negro, and national security.

It may be unrealistic to limit ourselves as we have been doing to legalistic proofs or definitely conclusive evidence that would stand up in testimony in court or before Congressional Committees that the Communist Party, USA, does wield substantial influence over Negroes which one day could become decisive.

We greatly regret that the memorandum did not measure up to what the director has a right to expect from our analysis.

Sullivan followed this memo with a recommendation on September 16 for "increased coverage of communist influence on the Negro," and he proposed something new: "We are stressing the urgent need for imaginative and aggressive tactics to be utilized through our Counterintelligence Program—these designed to neutralize or disrupt the Party's activities in the Negro field." Stripped of terms of art, Sullivan was proposing unleashing the COINTELPRO techniques on Martin Luther King.

Hoover wasn't buying. He wrote Sullivan that "I can't understand how you can so agilely switch your thinking and evaluation. Just a few weeks ago you contended that the Communist influence in the racial movement was ineffective and infinitesimal. This—notwithstanding many memos of specific instances of infiltration. Now you want to load down the Field with more coverage in spite of your recent memo depreciating C.P. influence in racial movement. I don't intend to waste time and money until you can make up your minds what the situation really is."

While Sullivan vacillated, Hoover wrote Tolson: "I have certainly been misled by previous memos which clearly showed communist penetration of the racial movement. The attached is contradictory of all that. We are wasting manpower and money investigating CP effort in racial matter if the attached is correct."

Hoover seems to have been demanding the truth from Sullivan, not trying to maneuver him into a predetermined position. Throughout his career Hoover drew his confidence from having the facts on his side when he sallied forth into political controversy. The Bureau's position had always been that the communists were continually attempting, but failing, to gain influence over American blacks; that position had provided the context within which Hoover had interpreted connections between civil rights and communism whenever they were discovered.

But at this critical moment in the history of the civil rights movement, when Hoover was asking some probing and skeptical questions, he was betrayed by Sullivan, who readily admitted later that he was being knowingly dishonest: "Here again we had to engage in a lot of nonsense which we ourselves really did not believe in. We either had to do this or we would be finished." But Hoover's whole career shows that he was first and foremost a serious person. He did not want nonsense; he wanted the facts.

After he retracted his August 23 memorandum, Sullivan tried to prove by action the strength of his latest set of convictions. From September 1963 on, Sullivan became the motive force behind the Bureau's aggressive campaign to discredit King within the government, to disrupt and neutralize his movement, and to destroy him professionally and personally. For the rest of his FBI career Sullivan seems to have been trying to redeem himself for his brief burst of independence by becoming ever more vicious in his attacks on King and other American dissenters.

William Sullivan's decision to swallow his principles and misrepresent his convictions about the danger of communism in America in 1963 had drastic consequences for American society. The ease with which he abandoned his convictions on that critical matter may have come from countless smaller compromises he and other FBI officials had had to make to survive over the years in Hoover's FBI. A prudent dissimulation in minor matters was the hidden cost of survival in the regulation-ridden FBI of the 1960s. Hoover's system of leadership was turning his men into liars, and so eventually Hoover became a man who had to rely on liars for advice.

Sullivan's dishonesty, of course, does not excuse Hoover. He had created a system in which, finally, advancement came to opportunists like Sullivan who had learned persuasive ways of giving Hoover back his own prejudices and opinions disguised as independent, objective thinking. Hoover's iron discipline had turned the Bureau into an echo chamber resounding with Hoover's passions and phobias. The assistants he depended on for information fed him reports designed to anticipate and reinforce his predictable opinions. Partly this was because Hoover was increasingly loath to accept information that challenged his priorities and the policy of his Bureau. And it was also the result of how the Bureau now worked, a system in which everything depended on Hoover and in which his subordinates were too intimidated to correct his misconceptions. For that situation Hoover had only himself to blame.

Sullivan finally received Hoover's approval for an intensified campaign against King on October 1, 1963. The Bureau would now use those "imaginative and aggressive tactics" that it had developed against Soviet agents and Party members, but now directed against law-abiding American citizens.

Hoover reported to Robert Kennedy that King had failed to make good on his pledge to break off relations with Levison and O'Dell, and so, on October 10, Kennedy told Hoover that he could go ahead and tap the phones in King's Atlanta home and SCLC office. These taps were soon producing a mass of incriminating evidence—incriminating not in that they buttressed the communist-control theory, but in that they provided Hoover with information about King's sexual behavior hard to reconcile with his role as a religious leader and moral spokesman.

On December 23, Sullivan chaired a nine-hour brainstorming conference in Washington that produced a list of twenty-one suggested operations against King. Sullivan reported to Hoover that the conference had developed plans to gather "information concerning King's personal activities . . . in order that we

may consider using this information at an opportune time in a counterintelligence move to discredit him." An April letter from Hoover to special agents in
charge in the field used these very words to instruct agents to redouble their efforts against King, and to use their media contacts against him.

Sullivan and Hoover were now working in tandem. Sullivan, frantic to
prove his reliability, had the Domestic Intelligence Division working fever-
ishly to supply Hoover with three types of information sure to infuriate the director: King's criticism of Hoover and the FBI, his contacts with communists
(still Levison and O'Dell), and King's self-indulgent extramarital sexual activities.

Hoover grew ever more frustrated at his inability to use this material to discredit King, and so he now gravitated toward the one man who *would* take action against King, and that was Sullivan. Not only was Sullivan ingratiating
himself to Hoover when he harassed King, but he was also giving Hoover the
best possible proof that he, Sullivan, believed in the truth and significance of
the King material the Domestic Intelligence Division was producing. The conspiracy against King was a glue in an unhealthy bond between Hoover and Sullivan that lasted until almost the end of Hoover's life.

On October 15, 1963, Sullivan gave Hoover a monograph on "Communism
and the Negro Movement—a Current Analysis," which Sullivan's superior, Assistant to the Director Alan Belmont, characterized as a "personal attack on
Martin Luther King." Belmont predicted it would "startle" Robert Kennedy "in
view of his past association with King."

In fact the report not only startled but angered Kennedy, especially when he
heard that the Pentagon was using the FBI report to justify its own opposition
to the civil rights movement. He ordered Hoover to retrieve all copies. But this
abortive smear was just the beginning of an unrelenting assault that Sullivan
(with Hoover's approval) would now begin to organize and coordinate against
King.

A week after Sullivan's December conference, *Time* magazine named King
its "Man of the Year" for 1963. Hoover was furious: "They had to dig deep in the
garbage to come up with this one." Sullivan had the answer: The Bureau would
groom a successor to King. Once the Bureau had managed to persuade the
country that King was "a fraud, demagogue and moral scoundrel," Sullivan
proposed, "much confusion will reign, particularly among the Negro people."
Therefore the Bureau should build up another black leader (Sullivan's nominee
was New York attorney Samuel R. Pierce Jr.) to take King's place. Hoover approved, and added, "I am glad to see that 'light' has finally, though dismally delayed, come to the Domestic Intelligence Division. I struggled for months to get

over the fact that the communists were taking over the racial movement, but our experts here couldn't or wouldn't see it."

Microphone surveillance of King's hotel rooms was now producing reels of tape documenting what the Bureau called "entertainment": sounds of King partying, drinking, and having sex. Now Hoover had another reason for hating King. "King is a 'tom cat,' " Hoover wrote on one memo, "with obsessive degenerate sexual urges." One tape had King in a hilarious mood describing the sexual accomplishments of his friends, mixing sexual and religious allusions, and telling a joke about the sex life of John F. Kennedy that involved Mrs. Kennedy and the presidential funeral. Convinced that this would persuade President Lyndon Johnson and Attorney General Robert Kennedy that King was "one of the most reprehensible . . . individuals on the American scene today," Hoover sent copies of the report to Robert Kennedy and President Johnson.

In March 1964 the conflict between Hoover and King moved into the public arena when Hoover's January testimony before the House Appropriations Committee was released. Hoover had told the committee, chaired by the segregationist Howard Smith of Virginia, that "Communist influence does exist in the Negro movement." King, concerned that Hoover's remarks provided support for "the salacious claims of southern racists and the extreme right-wing elements," challenged the Bureau to come forward with hard evidence. King added, "I think it was very unfortunate that such a great man as Mr. Hoover allowed himself to aid and abet the racists and the rightists in our nation by alleging that you have Communist infiltration in the movement."

Throughout 1964 the Bureau sent derogatory reports on King to the White House, to universities planning to award King honorary degrees, and to religious organizations. When King received an appointment to meet with the pope, the Bureau contacted New York's Cardinal Spellman (a close ally of Hoover's) to see if he could "ensure that the Pope is not placed in an embarrassing position through any contact with King." When the pope met with King anyway, Hoover found the meeting "astounding" and said "I am amazed that the Pope gave an audience to such a [censored]."

When King was chosen for the Nobel Peace Prize on October 14, 1964, the Bureau briefed such notables as Ralph Bunche, Adlai Stevenson, Vice President Hubert Humphrey, Nelson Rockefeller, and the American ambassadors to England and Sweden: anyone who might come into contact with King. Hoover sent Humphrey a copy of the Bureau's catalog of smears ("Martin Luther King, Jr.: His Personal Conduct") along with a personal letter from Hoover. The Nobel Prize seemed to drive Hoover into a frenzy. He wrote on one memo that King should have gotten the "top alley cat" prize instead.

Hoover had always been able to find influential allies to spearhead his attacks on his enemies. Now the establishment—and this included some southerners—had too much invested in King as a symbol of nonviolent social change to indulge Hoover. Frustrated beyond endurance, Hoover finally came out in the open with his attacks on King.

The occasion was a press conference Hoover gave on November 18, 1964, for a group of women reporters led by veteran journalist Sarah McLendon. Hoover recited all his complaints against King. He charged that King had accused the Bureau of being insensitive to blacks because it had a large proportion of southern-born agents in the South, while actually 70 percent were northerners. He capped his bill of particulars against King with the highly quotable claim that King was "the most notorious liar in the country" and "one of the lowest characters in the country."

Hoover's public outburst before the women reporters may have made Sullivan think that he, too, better take direct action against King. And so he began planning the tape and the threatening note.

Hoover's "notorious liar" attack made headlines across the country. King released a statement suggesting that Hoover had "faltered under the awesome burden, complexities and responsibilities of his office." He wrote Hoover that "I was appalled and surprised at your reported statement maligning my integrity. What motivated such an irresponsible accusation is a mystery to me," and he demanded a meeting.

On December 1, 1964, in the presence of DeLoach and several of King's associates, King and Hoover met in Hoover's Washington offices. Afterward the two sides disagreed on what had happened. DeLoach claims King spent the fifty-five minutes of the meeting effusively praising the director and retracting any criticism of the Bureau. King's aide Andrew Young remembers the meeting as a brief and formal exchange of greetings followed by a fifty-five minute monologue by Hoover on the accomplishments of the FBI. Young even remembers that Hoover was "disarming" and congratulated King on winning the Nobel Prize. For his part, Hoover bragged afterward about how he had lectured King, and he always claimed, "I never addressed him as Reverend or Doctor."

After the meeting the public controversy died down, and the Bureau's quick arrest of the murderers of three civil rights workers in Philadelphia, Mississippi, may have reassured King and his aides that the FBI really was finally enforcing the law against white terror. But behind the scenes, the Bureau's campaign to destroy King went on. And the package to King was already in the mail.

■ ■ ■

And so it had come to this. After decades of basking in public acclaim for its exploits of the thirties, its accomplishments on the home front during the Second World War, and its spectacular investigations of Soviet atomic espionage, how did the FBI sink to these depths of sending anonymous threats to one of the great figures of American history? How did J. Edgar Hoover, now sixty-nine years old, after forty years as FBI director, come to have as his most trusted lieutenant such a man as William C. Sullivan, capable of such recklessness, such malice, such evil?

Could the FBI's precipitous decline into an aging relic, secretly conspiring to block the changes sweeping the country in the 1960s, have been avoided? Probably only if Hoover had taken Attorney General Brownell's advice and retired when he turned sixty-five in 1960.

Hoover's FBI was so tightly ruled by its director, his system of internal controls was so efficient and complete, that Hoover ultimately has to be held responsible for all the policy decisions and for most operational decisions as well during his tenure. In his own mind, however, Hoover saw his management of the Bureau as dependent on the informed, independent, and professional judgment of his executives. After hearing their advice, of course, he reserved the right to make the final decision, and then he would insist on universal acceptance of the policy. But he always thought he could rely on his executives for honest, impartial advice.

By the 1960s, however, the tight discipline Hoover maintained over his subordinates and his insistence on total loyalty and conformity within the ranks made it unlikely that an independent thinker would reach the top ranks of the Bureau. And so when Hoover thought that in William Sullivan he had a man of integrity and intelligence on whose judgment he could rely, a man who could chart the Bureau's course through the shifting currents of American radical politics, he was mistaken. Near the end of his life Hoover admitted that "the greatest mistake I ever made was to promote Sullivan."

At the beginning of Hoover's career, A. Mitchell Palmer had relied on *him* for the research, the analysis, and the strategy for the 1919–1920 antiradical drive. Now, forty years later, Hoover found himself, like Palmer, relying on an ambitious, younger aide to lead the Bureau in yet another campaign against a resurgent radical movement, and it was a movement as incomprehensible to Hoover as communism must have been to Palmer in 1919.

There was absolutely no precedent for Hoover's tolerating Sullivan's sort of independence in a subordinate. Sullivan seemed to cast a spell over Hoover; some FBI colleagues saw a father-son bond between them. Hoover's practice was to call his agents "Mister." When they reached the executive level he dropped the "Mister" and simply called them by their last name. Tolson he called "Clyde," of course. Louis Nichols was "Nick." After Nichols left the Bureau in 1959 the only man Hoover ever again called by a nickname or first name was "Bill" Sullivan.

In Sullivan, Hoover seems to have seen a younger version of himself. Hoover encouraged Sullivan to conceive imaginative tactics against radicalism that recalled Hoover's own creative period four decades earlier as organizer of the department's Radical Division.

Like Hoover, Sullivan had a talent for turning existing laws to purposes unforeseen by their framers. Hoover had made use of the deportation statutes to cripple American radicalism. Sullivan adapted the techniques the Bureau developed against Nazi agents during the war and against Soviet agents during the early Cold War and used these to fight domestic radicals. As head of the Research Section of the Domestic Intelligence Division in the fifties, he prepared the monograph that served as the plan for COINTELPRO. While coordinating COINTELPRO-CPUSA in Washington, Sullivan became the greatest expert on communism the Bureau ever had—except for Hoover himself. Sullivan was in a position to analyze every meeting, every phone call, every conversation within the Party leadership; he was even able to influence Party decisions by advising FBI informants which faction to back in Party struggles. The opportunities for Bureau control of Party policy were so tempting that in late 1956 FBI headquarters had to counsel the field against getting too involved, for fear that the Bureau-backed faction might lose and be purged from the Party. William Sullivan was the FBI official most responsible for the Bureau's shift after 1963 from preparations for an "internal security emergency" (primarily utilizing the Emergency Detention Act of 1950) to the containment of domestic unrest.

In 1961 Sullivan was promoted to head of Division Five with the rank of assistant director. It was while Sullivan headed Division Five that the COINTELPRO operations were expanded beyond the Communist Party to include the Socialist Workers Party in 1961, the Ku Klux Klan in 1964, the black nationalists in 1967. Finally, in 1968 he added the New Left to COINTELPRO's targets.

During the thirties, forties, and fifties the FBI had been the embodiment of American values of progressive science, patriotic defense, and popular justice. Now in the sixties the FBI, under Hoover, was deliberately and defiantly separating itself from the changing cultural aspirations and developments of the nation at large. This generational gap was starting to seem preposterous to some of the public and even to some agents. Hoover's refusal to alter the FBI's grooming habits, his insistence on rules that included Bureau investigation of agents' fiancées, and prohibitions on attending nightclubs without one's wife, in the context of the early sixties betrayed an insulation from the general liberalization of American forms and norms. For the first time both critics and defenders of the Bureau began to notice the gap between the FBI and the world outside. Out of favor with the Kennedy administration and its constituency, the Bureau clung to the values of older members of Middle America, Southern whites, rich conservative Texans, and traditionalists frightened of change.

Other factors besides the separation of the Bureau from the main currents of American society were eroding Bureau morale. In the late fifties and sixties an FBI career was becoming less of a plum for a young lawyer. The Bureau still paid better—much better than the Secret Service, better than Justice Department lawyers of equivalent seniority, one grade above the pay for Ph.D.'s in the CIA (all testimony to Hoover's clout with Congress). Yet the opportunities for lawyers in private practice were even greater. The chief financial attraction of the Bureau for agents was actually something of a prison, because of the retirement program. Agents could retire with one-third pay after twenty years, two thirds after thirty years. The result was again to reinforce the absolute conformity of agents and their obedience to any whim of Hoover's so as not to jeopardize their pensions, since Hoover retained the right to dismiss agents without appeal. (The Bureau was exempt from civil service regulations, though veterans could appeal to a grievance board outside the Bureau.)

The closed, highly disciplined Bureau, permeated with Hoover's inflexible presence, ran counter to the expectations and habits of most college graduates in the sixties. The result was that the Bureau began to have trouble recruiting new agents. In the fall of 1960 there were three occasions when new agents' classes had to be postponed for lack of applicants. Without broadcasting the fact, the Bureau began to recruit nonlawyers as agents. At the beginning of the sixties, 61 out of 349 agent recruits were from the Bureau's clerical workers, many of whom had gone to work for the Bureau out of high school and so were presold and preindoctrinated in the Bureau's ways, called by its critics "Bureauthink." This inbreeding was one reason why some critics charged the Bureau had become a "secret society." Later the Bureau was forced to accept any recruits with a college degree (with three years of relevant business or investigative experience). Realizing the effect this could have on the Bureau's elite reputation, the field offices were warned that "there should be no publicity nor public announcement" of the change.

Robert Kennedy, lean, energetic, aggressive, ready to break the rules to obtain his objectives whether against organized crime or in civil rights, and the Irish mafia of assistants he brought to the Justice Department with him represented the antithesis of Hoover and his agents, who were still wearing hats in the hatless sixties, still wearing dark suits and ties while the attorney general was customarily photographed in shirtsleeves with rolled-up cuffs and his tie down comfortably at half mast. But William C. Sullivan let Hoover believe he had his own mad Irishman, just as aggressive, energetic, and combative as the New Frontiersmen.

Hoover's preoccupation with defending America against attacks on tradition made him let opportunities for law enforcement leadership slip away. The country was undergoing a radical increase in the crime rate—in reality the first real crime wave of Hoover's career (the media crime wave of the thirties had not been reflected in the crime statistics). While Hoover continued to fulminate against the "beastly punks" coddled by "muddle-headed sentimentalists," President Kennedy established the President's Committee on Juvenile Delinquency and Youth Crime in May 1961, with Robert Kennedy as chairman. Robert Kennedy and the committee's executive director, David Hackett (an old prep school friend), were impressed by the "opportunity theory" of Lloyd E. Ohlin and Richard A. Cloward. In their study *Delinquency and Opportunity* (1960), Ohlin and Cloward explained crime as the result of social barriers to the middle-class ambitions of the poor. Hackett and Kennedy were convinced that delinquency was a "cover word" for poverty; that, in turn, was a cover word for racial discrimination. The Juvenile Delinquency Act of September 1961 was based on Ohlin and Cloward's theories, and Ohlin was made head of the Office of Juvenile Delinquency, established under the act.

The gap between the Kennedy approach to juvenile delinquency and Hoover's was another sign of the cultural gulf between them. To Hoover, middle-class values were American values, and the solution to crime was the indoctrination of the young in the mores of the middle class: home, school, and church. To the Kennedys, from the perspective of their aristocratic family background and their cosmopolitan experience, the middle class's own racial prejudices and status distinctions produced the deprivations that led to crime. By the 1960s Hoover's ideas were so far removed from the activist philosophy of the Kennedy Justice Department that the notion of having the FBI play the crime prevention role it had in the thirties and forties was probably unimaginable to Hoover and Kennedy alike.

The Bureau's descent into secret, illegal means of harassing what it considered threats to the nation began slowly during the Kennedy administration, accelerated rapidly under Johnson, and then terminated abruptly halfway through Nixon's first administration. But while the most notable instance of secret and criminal FBI activities under Kennedy was its harassment of Martin Luther King Jr., the Bureau's resistance to the Kennedys' law enforcement agenda was also a factor in pushing the Bureau in the direction of secret operations: After all, for the sake of internal morale, it had to be doing something.

Hoover's response to demands that the FBI take an aggressive part in the Justice Department's effort to protect civil rights demonstrators was to insist that the FBI was strictly an investigative force, and peacekeeping was not its job. It could only investigate crimes after they had been committed. The sight of FBI agents standing by taking notes and pictures for use in future investigations while demonstrators and even federal officers (marshals and Justice Department personnel) were being violently attacked infuriated Robert Kennedy's aides. But Kennedy realized that Hoover could not be budged, and his strategy with Hoover, in *Nation* editor Victor Navasky's judgment, was to "avoid confrontation over anything but great issues of policy."

Hoover first resisted, but finally, and grudgingly, enlisted in Robert Kennedy's war on organized crime. Robert Kennedy came to the Justice Department with a reputation as an expert on the mob. Ever since the late 1950s, Hoover had been trying to fatten up the Bureau's files on the mob, but without compromising the FBI's autonomy by joining any interagency anticrime strike forces. He relied in large part on microphone surveillance ("bugs," or in FBI parlance, MISURs) for this intelligence gathering. The employment of microphones, under long-standing Bureau policy, was done without notifying the attorney general and required only Hoover's approval. Kennedy came to the Justice Department with the idea of setting up a National Crime Commission to combat organized crime. Faced with Hoover's adamant opposition to any such venture, he had to abandon the proposal. Without Hoover's support, it would have been politically and practically futile.

Because of Hoover's initial lack of enthusiasm for organized crime investigations, Kennedy relied on the Organized Crime and Racketeering Section of the Criminal Division (under Edwyn Silberling) rather than the FBI to coordinate information about the mob. He organized a team of twenty lawyers to press the investigation of Jimmy Hoffa and the Teamsters; this was the so-called "Get-Hoffa" squad under former FBI man Walter Sheridan.

By the end of 1961, finally, Hoover gave in and made organized crime an FBI priority, with Courtney Evans's Special Investigations Division spearheading the organized crime effort. Hoover's explanation of his change of heart was that until the September 1961 antiracket laws (steered through Congress by Robert Kennedy) "the FBI had very little jurisdiction in the field of organized crime." Arthur Schlesinger calls this excuse a "transparent fraud," but Hoover probably was pointing in the direction of his genuine rationale. True, Hoover could have found jurisdiction before, had he wanted to, but until September 1961 he could not be sure of the overwhelming public and political support for the sensitive and often unrewarding (in the statistical sense dear to Hoover) area of organized crime. Kennedy's success in getting the new crime laws passed meant that Hoover now had a mandate, not just from the politically weak administration, but from the people he had to please, his supporters in Congress.

The fact was that Kennedy's success in getting congressional approval for anticrime bills in September 1961, Joseph Valachi's 1963 testimony before the McClellan Committee in the Senate, and Hoover's competitive instincts now combined to make Hoover fully commit the Bureau to organized crime investigations for the first time. William Hundley, who had headed Attorney General William Rogers's Organized Crime Section and had stayed on as a special assistant under Kennedy, said "Bobby got them [the FBI] interested in organized crime." Kennedy counted it as one of his accomplishments that "for the first time the FBI changed their whole concept of crime in the United States."

The Kennedy administration's success was less complete than it seemed. The only effective techniques for combating the mob—wiretaps and microphones—were illegal and not admissible in court. That meant that the Bureau was forced to keep what it was doing secret from the Justice Department and Congress as it began to gather the intelligence it needed against the mob. It could not risk cooperating with interagency task forces for fear of having its illegal techniques exposed. Not until 1968 would the Bureau gain legal authority to employ "Title III" wiretaps and use the results in court; not until 1970 would it gain the innovative RICO legislation that has been its most effective tool against organized crime, and in both cases it would take a new director and several years of trial and error to acquire the experience to use these new tools effectively.

■ ■ ■

The Kennedy assassination was potentially a disaster for the FBI if the full record of the Bureau's bungled surveillance of Lee Harvey Oswald were to be revealed. While Hoover defended the FBI publicly, and fiercely rebuffed all criticism by the Warren Commission or anyone else, he fretted that the Bureau's record in neglecting the evident threat posed by Lee Harvey Oswald before the assassination was so miserable that it had, as he scribbled on an internal report on the case, "resulted in forever destroying the Bureau as the top-level investigative organization." For months after the assassination he seems to have been able to relieve his anger and disappointment only by heaping additional punishments on any agent connected to the case. Once again, the Bureau was living a double life: one public, the other a secret life known only to the insiders of an increasingly secret society.

The FBI began its Oswald security file on October 31, 1959, shortly after his defection to the Soviet Union. The FBI's initial investigation concluded that there was no important security leak, even though Oswald might have gained knowledge of U-2 operations while stationed in Japan as a Marine. Hoover also suggested in a letter to the State Department that Oswald's identity might be used by the Russians to slip an impostor back into the United States.

After his return from Russia in June 1962, Oswald was interviewed by the Bureau. After a second interview, his case was closed on August 20, 1962, even though the field agents in Fort Worth, Texas, found him hostile and evasive. In September 1962, shortly before the missile crisis of October, the Bureau learned that Oswald had subscribed to the Communist Party's newspaper, *The Worker*, which should have raised suspicions about his claim that he was disenchanted with communism. The subscription should also have qualified Oswald for the Emergency Detention list, and therefore for increased surveillance, but the agents neglected to follow through.

It was not until the next year that Special Agent James Hosty of the Dallas field office, who had been assigned the Marina Oswald file, finally noticed the *Worker* subscription and recommended reopening the Oswald case. This was approved on March 26, 1963. The next month the New York office learned that Oswald had joined the Fair Play for Cuba Committee and had been passing out pro-Castro material in Dallas. This information was not reported to Dallas until the end of June, and was not sent to Washington until September.

In August, Oswald moved to New Orleans, a hotbed of anti-Castro activity. On August 1, 1963, the FBI seized a ton of dynamite and other weapons anti-Castroites had stockpiled nearby. While Oswald was in New Orleans he tried to join an anti-Castro group on August 7 and was arrested when he got into a fight with a member of that group who had spotted him passing out pro-Castro material. Evidently Oswald, out of sympathy for Castro, had been trying to infiltrate the anti-Castro group, and that also should have interested the Bureau. Shortly after this Oswald requested another interview with the FBI; once again he misrepresented his politics and political activities. Later that month Oswald took part in a radio debate during which he defended Castro and called himself a Marxist.

The most obvious danger signal missed by the Bureau was when Oswald traveled from New Orleans to Mexico City in September and met with a diplomat at the Soviet Embassy. In fact the diplomat belonged to a KGB unit the Bureau believed was responsible for assassination and sabotage assignments. While in Mexico, Oswald also attempted to meet Cuban officials for a trip to Havana. The report on Oswald's visit to Mexico City was still sitting on a desk in Washington on November 22.

In early November the Dallas office learned that Oswald had returned to that city and was working at the Texas School Book Depository. Agent Hosty interviewed Oswald's wife, who seemed nervous. Evidently angered by the Bureau's approach to his wife, Oswald tried to see Hosty at his Bureau office. Hosty was out, so Oswald left him a note, probably a threat to blow up the FBI field office and the Dallas Police Department if Hosty did not stop bothering Marina. Nobody knows for sure, because two days after the assassination, Hosty said he was ordered to destroy the note by his supervisor, and that's what he did.

As soon as word of the assassination reached Washington, the Bureau began assembling a preliminary report for President Johnson. From the outset, the Bureau's leads pointed it toward its eventual conclusion that Oswald was the lone assassin. But there were other facts than the evidence propelling the Bureau toward that same conclusion, and they have fueled endless but false speculation—certainty in some quarters—that the Bureau covered up the existence of a much broader conspiracy to kill the president.

Oswald seems to have acted out of a personal desire to do what he thought Castro would have wanted him to do. Neither the FBI nor any other investigators were able to obtain any evidence that Oswald had been ordered to kill Kennedy either by the Cubans or the Soviets, and yet that was the obvious direction public opinion might have moved in unless all leads from Oswald to anyone else were snipped off. Behind this rush to provide support for the conclusion that Oswald was the lone assassin was another motive: fear on the part of the White House of the public reaction if any of the circumstantial evidence linking Castro to the assassination were to become known. This is not to say that any responsible officials really thought Castro was actually responsible, but there was so much seeming plausibility to a chain of events connecting Havana to Dallas that the White House had to fear uncontrollable demands for revenge against Castro. The agreement that had ended the Cuban missile crisis of October 1962 guaranteed that the United States would not attack Cuba, so a renewed conflict with Cuba would certainly have led to a new confrontation with the Soviet Union whose outcome could not be foreseen.

The Bureau was quickly made aware of the administration's hope that any speculation about a wider conspiracy be choked off. In a phone conversation with Johnson aide Walter Jenkins, Hoover said "the thing I am most concerned about, and so is Mr. [Deputy Attorney General Nicholas] Katzenbach, is having something issued so we can convince the public that Oswald is the real assassin." Katzenbach was even more specific: "Speculation about Oswald's motivation ought to be cut off, and we should have some basis for rebutting thought that this was a Communist conspiracy or (as the Iron Curtain press is saying) a right-wing conspiracy to blame it on the Communists." On December 9, 1963, soon after the Warren Commission was named, Katzenbach wrote each member asking them to issue a press release stating that the FBI report said that Oswald was the lone assassin.

For his own part, Hoover quickly concluded that the FBI's handling of the case was so deficient that the only way for the Bureau to minimize criticism, since it could probably not escape it completely, was to fix all blame for the assassination on Lee Harvey Oswald, unassisted by any other conspirators who might have (1) tied the killing to prior CIA plots or (2) raised the question of why the FBI was unaware of a widespread plot. It is somewhat ironic that theories about a right-wing conspiracy also served the Bureau's cause, since they helped excuse the Bureau for not having paid enough attention to left-wing extremists like Oswald. Everyone had a reason for keeping the investigation focused exclusively on Oswald. This was one reason Hoover assigned the Bureau's work for the Warren Commission to his General Investigative Division, rather than the Domestic Intelligence Division, which had handled the Oswald security file. Despite the Bureau's awareness of CIA involvement in assassination attempts, the FBI did not investigate possible Cuban government or exile involvement and there were no interviews of Cuban informants.

Thus there certainly was a Bureau cover-up in the assassination investigation, but the purpose was to divert attention away from its own deficiencies. Hoover himself regarded the Warren Commission as a potential adversary, its very existence a threat because it might expose those failures, and so the Bureau's main concern during the investigation it conducted for the commission was to protect its own reputation and avoid criticism.

The internal investigation Hoover ordered while the Warren Commission probe was still under way contained a devastating analysis of FBI deficiencies: The report concluded that "Oswald should have been on the Security Index; his wife should have been interviewed before the assassination, and investigation intensified—not held in abeyance—after Oswald contacted Soviet Embassy in Mexico."

Hoover's immediate reaction was to punish everyone connected to the Oswald file. The Inspection Division warned Hoover that this might prove embarrassing because the Warren Commission might subpoena agents who would then have to say they had been punished for their handling of the case. This would surely be interpreted as an admission that the FBI had been deficient. Hoover disagreed, saying, "in any event such gross incompetency cannot be overlooked nor administrative action postponed." On December 10 he sent out seventeen censures (including one to William C. Sullivan) for "shortcomings in connection with the investigation of Oswald prior to the assassination."

Hoover was particularly critical of his agents for not putting Oswald on the Security Index (the old Emergency Detention list) to be picked up if war broke out. When the FBI officials who studied the case came back with the conclusion that under the prevailing criteria Oswald had not qualified for the list, Hoover replied "they were worse than mistaken. Certainly no one in full possession of all his faculties can claim Oswald didn't fall within this criteria."

The Bureau's top executives seemed to regard the FBI's failures in the Oswald case as strictly a public relations problem. A month after the release of the Warren Commission report (it came out September 24, 1964), Hoover deputy Cartha DeLoach reported to the Executive Conference that the Bureau had been damaged by the report, but said it could be repaired with a combination of expanded press relations and investigative achievement; they should adopt Hoover's maxim that "nothing is more devastating to a smear than an offensive of real accomplishment." Hoover was unpersuaded. He said sadly that "the FBI will never live down this smear which could have been so easily avoided if there had been proper supervision and initiative."

Hoover knew that the FBI's failures in its handling of the Oswald security file made it even more important after the assassination to keep the new president happy. Hoover liked Lyndon Baines Johnson; he knew him well. He vastly preferred Johnson to the Kennedys. But he also knew that his reputation and that of his Bureau now depended on absolute subservience to Lyndon Johnson, who was going to make the final decision as to whether any heads should roll for the security debacle in Dallas.

■ ■ ■

The greatest and most lasting achievement of Lyndon Johnson's presidency was to turn the country against the white violence that had kept blacks terrorized, poor, and politically powerless in the South since the end of Reconstruction. Johnson used all of his prodigious political skills to enact a program of new laws and energized law enforcement that broke the back of legally tolerated terrorism in the South. John Doar, who led the Civil Rights Division's prosecutions of civil rights cases in the South, said that originally "the Bureau was ill-prepared for its predicament," but that in 1964, "when a deep-seated change came upon America, a change brought about by many individuals, groups and forces, the Bureau changed as well." Ramsey Clark gives credit to Johnson himself for turning the Bureau around. "I think Mr. Johnson showed that he could do more with Mr. Hoover than anybody who'd ever tried. Getting Mr. Hoover to go down to Jackson, Mississippi, to open that FBI office was quite a feat. I wouldn't have bet much on being able to talk him into doing it, but he did."

The main reason for this change was presidential leadership. Johnson was able to thrust Hoover into the same kind of moral and political drama that Franklin Roosevelt and Homer Cummings had orchestrated in the thirties, and Johnson followed the same script: He interpreted atrocious crimes as declarations of war against the nation and its national government. He drafted new laws to arm the FBI in a new crusade against crime, and then committed the FBI to destroy those who had defied the authority of the national government. Johnson's clear, total, and passionate commitment to civil rights had never been so clearly demonstrated in any previous president. Hoover had always suspected before that he would be abandoned by his superiors if he committed the Bureau to fruitless investigations of white terror against blacks. Now, backed by Johnson's aggressive support, the Bureau was finally willing to commit itself to the civil rights battle.

The Bureau's successes in solving the bombings and killings in Mississippi in 1964 and 1965 were spectacular indeed, but they represented another step by the Bureau into secret and illegal harassment and destruction of its enemies, who now also happened to be the targets of Johnson administration and Justice Department policies.

The Johnson administration's declaration of war against the Ku Klux Klan in 1964 followed almost to the letter Homer Cummings's classic script for the Kansas City Massacre in 1933. On June 22, 1964, three young civil rights workers—Michael Schwerner, James Chaney, and Andrew Goodman—disappeared near Philadelphia, Mississippi. This was two days after Senate passage of the Civil Rights Act that Lyndon Johnson had called John F. Kennedy's legacy. Attorney General Robert Kennedy ordered Hoover to treat the disappearance as a kidnapping and to dispatch his agents to the scene. The next day agents from

New Orleans arrived in Philadelphia, because there was no FBI field office in Mississippi. That same day Johnson also dispatched a fact-finding team led by former CIA director Allen Dulles to Mississippi. Before leaving, Dulles conferred with Hoover and Kennedy, and then interviewed Mississippi Governor Paul Johnson and the head of the Mississippi Highway Patrol. He returned to Washington with a recommendation that the FBI significantly increase its presence in the state. In the midst of all this President Johnson signed the new civil rights law on July 2 which banned racial, religious, and gender discrimination in employment and accommodation. It also empowered the attorney general to initiate private suits to force desegregation, terminated federal funding of discriminatory state or local agencies, and extended the life of the U.S. Civil Rights Commission.

On July 19 Hoover flew to Jackson, Mississippi, to open the new FBI office, and to announce he was committing 153 agents to the investigation. In July 1964 the FBI held a national law enforcement conference on civil rights. That same month headquarters sent outlines of civil rights lectures for agents to use when speaking before law enforcement and civic groups.

The next year another racial murder shocked the country, and Johnson again turned to Hoover and the Bureau. On March 7, 1965, Sheriff Jim Clark of Selma, Alabama, and his police attacked civil rights marchers with tear gas and clubs. A week later, Johnson went before a joint session of Congress to introduce the Voting Rights Act of 1965, ending his speech with his historic quotation of Martin Luther King's "We Shall Overcome." On March 21, King and Ralph Bunche, both winners of the Nobel Peace Prize, led a four-day march from Selma to Montgomery, ending with a speech by King on March 25. That night the Ku Klux Klan shot and killed Mrs. Viola Liuzzo, a civil rights volunteer from Detroit who was driving marchers from Montgomery back to Selma. The Bureau solved the crime in eight hours because riding in the car of the Klansmen who killed Liuzzo was an FBI informant. Johnson went on national television with Hoover standing by his side to announce that "our honored public servant" had captured the murderers. "I cannot express myself too strongly in praising Mr. Hoover and the men of the FBI for their prompt and expeditious performance in handling this investigation. It is in keeping with the dedicated approach that this organization has shown throughout the turbulent era of civil rights controversies." Despite the Bureau's brilliant work, the presence of the FBI informant, Gary Thomas Rowe, in the murder car provoked a sharp but unfair controversy about whether a criminal informant (not an agent) had the duty of preventing a crime as well as reporting on it.

Johnson's television appearance with Hoover may have done more than anything else to turn the country against the Klan and racist terror. Johnson would not have been as effective if he had not had Hoover by his side: not only because of the FBI's reputation for effective investigations, which was fully justified in this case, but because of Hoover's immense prestige as a symbol of serious federal commitment to a cause. Thus Johnson could use the FBI to demonstrate presidential outrage over a great moral issue and to dramatize the importance of new legislation, in this case the Voting Rights Act, which he signed on August 6.

But Hoover's inability to see a moral issue in the civil rights struggle made him try to steer an even course between black protest and white backlash. He claimed that "the Federal Bureau of Investigation has been the target of both extremes in the civil rights issue and I believe this shows the FBI has followed the proper course in its handling of this most delicate issue." He denounced attempts to use the FBI to protect demonstrators: "the FBI will continue to . . . stay within the bounds of its authorized jurisdiction regardless of pressure groups which seek to use the FBI to attain their own selfish aims to the detriment of our people as a whole."

The Bureau was able to solve the Liuzzo murder so quickly because the year before, as part of the upheaval that sent Hoover to Jackson, the FBI had begun to fight the Klan in a new way.

In June 1964, Attorney General Robert Kennedy got a report from a team of Justice Department lawyers he had sent south to study the problem of the Klan. Civil Rights Division head Burke Marshall recommended using the same Bureau techniques against the Klan that had been so successful against the Communist Party. Kennedy liked the idea and wrote Johnson, "Consideration should be given by the Federal Bureau of Investigation to new measures. . . . The techniques followed in the use of specially trained special assignment agents in the infiltration of Communist groups should be of value. If you approve, it might be desirable to take up with the Bureau the possibility of developing a similar effort to meet this problem."

In late July 1964 the Bureau moved responsibility for the Klan and other "hate groups" from the General Investigative Division to William C. Sullivan's Domestic Intelligence Division (where it had been prior to 1958). Within a year the Bureau had 2,000 informants in the Klan, which meant that 20 percent of the total was reporting to the Bureau. FBI informants had leadership positions in seven of the fourteen Klan groups, headed one state Klan, and even created a splinter Klan group under FBI direction. In short order Sullivan's division was providing the Justice Department with complete intelligence on the Klan for use in the legal battle against white terror.

But Sullivan went far beyond intelligence gathering. In September 1964, Hoover accepted his recommendation to create a "White Hate" COINTEL-PRO. For the first time the Bureau's counterintelligence techniques of harassment and disruption were being directed against groups that did not have, even tangentially or theoretically, any connection to foreign intelligence or an international revolutionary movement.

COINTELPRO–WHITE HATE operations disrupted Klan meetings, sowed dissension within local Klans, circulated rumors, both true and false, about the morals of Klan leaders, supplied material on Klan activities and membership to the media, and made use of "overt" investigations (having groups of agents openly follow a Klansman around the clock, noting all of his activities).

Always the realist, Hoover had sound reasons to adopt a counterintelligence rather than a law enforcement approach against the Klan. His experience in bringing civil rights cases before white juries had been profoundly discouraging; his greatest success in this area had come in the late twenties when he had used a morals charge to discredit the head of the Klan. He had ample justification to believe that the indirect approach of disruption promised greater success than investigations, indictments, and trials.

Hoover's rapport with Johnson and the director's distrust of the Justice Department made him prefer operations he could conduct in total independence from the department. Since the COINTELPRO operations did not have to produce criminal cases for the department to prosecute, Hoover could avoid cooperation with or interference by Justice. COINTELPRO could also proceed without involving Southern law enforcement officers, not antagonizing those valuable Bureau contacts.

In the opinion of the agents themselves and of outside observers, the Klan COINTELPRO was outstandingly successful. One section chief said, "I think it was one of the most effective programs I have ever seen the Bureau handle as far as any group is concerned." Attorney General Katzenbach also approved of the program: "The central point . . . is that some Klan members in those states, using the Klan as a vehicle, were engaged in repeated acts of criminal violence. It had nothing to do with preaching a social point of view: it had to do with proven acts of violence. The investigation by the FBI was hard, tough, and outstandingly successful . . . I authorized them. In the same circumstances I would do so again today."

Nevertheless, the White Hate COINTELPRO started the Bureau down a slippery path without its traditional compass, Hoover's preoccupation with the Communist Party. There were those within the Bureau who traced the FBI's later difficulties to this "substantial enlargement" of the Domestic Intelligence

Division's responsibilities. For the first time an American government agency was formally engaged in punishing crime, not by the due process of law but by methods characteristic of the shadow world of spies and counterspies.

Hoover's attack on the Ku Klux Klan was the first in a series of steps that by the end of the Johnson administration would have the FBI taking "the law into its own hands, conducting a sophisticated vigilante operation against domestic enemies," not only against communists and Klansmen but against black radicals and antiwar activists.

. . .

But even as the Bureau slipped deeper and deeper into secret operations against its enemies, concealed even from the rest of the Justice Department, it began to abandon many of the intelligence-gathering techniques it had used with confidential approval of the president or the attorney general. In time, this refusal to place its extralegal investigative tools at the disposal of Johnson and Nixon became a source of tension between the Bureau and the White House.

In the years before 1968, when federal wiretapping (with judicial warrants) became legal, Hoover had relied strictly on presidential authority delegated to the attorney general for Bureau wiretaps, and he used a blanket authorization from Brownell for microphone surveillance. He had also felt he could count on support from the president and attorney general if he got caught. But in the Katzenbach-Clark Justice Department, Hoover felt he would not be supported if he ran into trouble over illegal electronic surveillance. He became certain of this on March 30, 1965, when Attorney General Katzenbach ordered the Bureau to seek his approval for all wiretaps and microphone surveillances. Congressional tolerance for sensitive techniques was also eroding. Early in 1965, Senator Edward V. Long of Missouri began an investigation of government invasions of privacy. Hoover knew it was time to eliminate this danger to the Bureau.

On September 14, 1965, Hoover notified Katzenbach that he was severely restricting the use of many sensitive techniques, and was eliminating the use of wireless surveillance devices (bugs). About this time Hoover also ended trash covers (searches of garbage), mail covers (records of addresses and recipients of mail), and break-ins. In restricting electronic surveillance, Hoover went beyond Robert Kennedy (who was an enthusiastic advocate of wiretapping as a law enforcement technique) and Nicholas Katzenbach (who permitted strictly limited use of electronic surveillance). In fact, Hoover went almost as far as Attorney General Ramsey Clark, who was absolutely opposed to these techniques except in national security cases, and who refused to use the legal procedures for court-authorized wiretapping provided by the 1968 Crime Control Act.

Hoover was more willing than many in the Bureau to give up these surreptitious techniques because he had always seen them as more symbolic than essential. If the public demanded them as evidence of a commitment to serious law enforcement or counterespionage, he was ready to oblige. If the public recoiled from them as signs of an oppressive government, he was ready to oblige again. During Senator Long's investigation Hoover wrote: "I don't see what all the excitement is about. I would have no hesitance in discontinuing all techniques—technical coverage [i.e., wiretapping], microphones, trash covers, mail covers, etc. While it might handicap us I doubt they are as valuable as some believe and none warrant FBI being used to justify them." In fact they were and are valuable and essential in the Bureau's most important investigations, such as high-level political corruption, organized crime, and white-collar economic crime. But of course, the Bureau wasn't doing much about those kinds of crimes, and it would be years before it did.

Another reason for Hoover's caution was that a nervous Congress was showing signs of finally wanting to assert some control over the Bureau. Hoover had to work hard to defeat Eugene McCarthy's attempt in 1966 to give the Senate's CIA oversight committee authority over the FBI as well. Another signal was that the 1968 crime bill provided that FBI directors after Hoover be appointed by the president and approved by the Senate.

As the Justice Department responded to national concern about crime with new and ambitious programs of federal assistance to local law enforcement, Hoover's Bureau was refusing to provide the leadership the country had a right to expect. Hoover's reluctance to share authority meant that there was little place for the FBI in the new initiatives. This meant a diminishment of the Bureau's impact on law enforcement as rivals like the Law Enforcement Assistance Administration increased in importance. The FBI played no role in major federal anticrime initiatives like the District of Columbia Crime Bill of 1967 or the major crime legislation to come out of the Johnson administration, the Omnibus Crime Control and Safe Streets Act (June 1968). Nor did the FBI provide leadership in Justice Department efforts against juvenile delinquency or crimes against small business.

As cries of "Burn, baby, burn" rang out in the summer nights of the 1960s, law and order emerged as a burning political issue, and the issue was largely defined by a controversy between Hoover and the Justice Department over the most effective strategy for dealing with the crime wave. Attorneys General Nicholas Katzenbach and Ramsey Clark held that crime was best fought through a war on poverty. Hoover insisted that the permissiveness behind such theories was the real cause of crime. Against public demands for tough gestures against criminals, meaning black urban criminals, the Justice Department argued accurately but, as it turned out, unconvincingly, that crime statistics were unreliable, that homicide rates were down, and that the crime the public most feared, black violence against whites, was one of the rarest of criminal acts. Hoover's rebuttal was more persuasive because he told the public what it wanted to believe, that it was within the power of the government to curb crime by getting tough, and that Supreme Court–mandated and Justice Department–encouraged permissiveness had caused the crime wave.

One of the most important clashes between Hoover and Johnson's Attorneys General Katzenbach and Clark was over the proper response to urban riots. Hoover wanted to use undercover intelligence; the Justice Department wanted negotiation and open contacts with protesters. Hoover looked upon the rioters and their leaders as subversives trying to overthrow the government and destroy society. The Justice Department saw them as the products of unjust social conditions, and thought that the most effective countermeasures would be political reform and social change. The FBI set up undercover programs to harass and disrupt protest movements, and drew up lists of targets for covert action like its Rabble Rouser and Agitator indexes. The Justice Department set up the Community Relations Service.

Once again, it was William C. Sullivan who provided Hoover with the means of waging his own covert war against black unrest by appiying the disruptive tactics of COINTELPROs against black radicalism. The decision to launch a counterintelligence attack on the "black nationalist" movement was preceded by two years of requests from Johnson for action against black rioters. Ever since the first black ghetto riots of the summer of 1964, Lyndon Johnson had been pressing Hoover for intelligence on urban disorders so that he could plan his responses in advance. He also hoped for proof that the riots were part of a plot, hopefully directed by communists—information that could discredit the rioters. Unfortunately, Hoover could never give Johnson exactly what the president wanted. But on August 25, 1967, Hoover did approve Sullivan's proposal for a COINTELPRO directed against "black nationalist, hate-type organizations."

Hoover's orders to his agents announcing the new COINTELPRO followed the form and even the very words of the authorization for the Klan COINTELPRO. The field was advised to "insure the targeted group is disrupted, ridiculed, or discredited through the publicity and not merely publicized. Consideration should be given to techniques to preclude violence-prone or rabble-rouser leaders of these hate groups from spreading their philosophy publicly or through various mass communication media." Hoover advised agents that "many individuals currently active in black nationalist organizations have backgrounds of immorality, subversive activity, and criminal records," so he ordered that such information should be collected for use in counterintelligence operations. King and the Southern Christian Leadership Conference were on the list of targets. The SCLC was listed from the outset, King himself in February 1968.

The following spring Hoover told agents that "for maximum effectiveness . . . and to prevent wasted effort," he was setting "long-range goals" for the black nationalist COINTELPRO.

1. Prevent the coalition of militant black nationalist groups. In unity there is strength; a truism that is no less valid for all its triteness. An effective coalition of black nationalist groups might be the first step toward a real "Mau Mau" in America, the beginning of a true black revolution.

2. Prevent the rise of a "messiah" who could unify and electrify the militant black nationalist movement. Malcolm X might have been such a "messiah;" he is the martyr of this movement today. Martin Luther King, Stokely Carmichael, and Elijah Muhammad all aspire to this position. Elijah Muhammad is less of a threat because of his age. King could be a very real contender . . . should he abandon his supposed "obedience" to "white liberal doctrines." Carmichael has the necessary charisma to be a real threat in this way.

The Bureau launched 360 disruptive operations against "black hate" groups. Rumors were planted in the media about Elijah Muhammad's sexual conduct, and the IRS was alerted to possible tax fraud by Muhammad. The Bureau gave the media stories portraying the Poor People's March on Washington in 1968 as dominated by violence-prone radicals. In November 1968, COINTELPRO–BLACK HATE was specifically directed against the Black Panther Party, a black radical, sometimes violent organization led by Bobby Seale, Fred Hampton, and Eldridge Cleaver. The Bureau tried to incite confrontations between the Panthers and their militant rivals within the black radical movement. Although it is impossible to prove conclusively that the Bureau was responsible for specific acts of violence, a later Senate investigative committee concluded that "the chief investigative branch of the Federal Government, which was charged by law with investigating crimes and preventing criminal conduct, itself engaged in lawless tactics and responded to deep-seated social problems by fomenting violence and unrest."

For instance, in one of many operations the Bureau encouraged local police to mount against the Panthers between 1969 and 1971, on December 4, 1969, Chicago police raided a house used by the Black Panthers, and killed Illinois Panther chairman Hampton and Peoria chairman Mark Clark. Hampton's bodyguard was an FBI informant, and he had given the Bureau tips and a diagram of the house.

Hoover did not target only the Panthers but anyone who supported them. He authorized operations against what he saw as the 1970s version of the "Parlor Pinks" of 1919: the celebrities who raised money for the Panthers. Early in 1970, Hoover visited President Nixon to crow that he was going to accuse composer Leonard Bernstein and bandleader Peter Duchin of supporting the Panthers. But one of the celebrities caught in the Bureau's attack on the Panthers' Hollywood supporters was an unstable young screen actress named Jean Seberg. The results were tragic.

In April 1970, Seberg was in the fourth month of a pregnancy. The Bureau decided to make her an object lesson to anyone else who might be thinking of supporting the Panthers. Agent Richard Wallace Held telegraphed Washington: "Bureau permission is requested to publicize the pregnancy of Jean Seberg, well-known white movie actress, . . . by advising Hollywood 'Gossip-Columnists' in the Los Angeles area of the situation. It is felt the possible publication of 'Seberg's plight' could cause her embarrassment and serve to cheapen her image with the general public. It is proposed the following letter from a fictitious person be sent to local columnists:"

> *I was just thinking about you and remembered I still owe you a favor. So—I was in Paris last week and ran into Jean Seberg, who was heavy with baby. I thought she and Romain [Romain Gary, Seberg's estranged husband] had gotten together again, but she confided that the child belonged to [deleted] of the Black Panthers, one [deleted]. The dear girl is getting around.*

Headquarters gave its approval, but ordered a two-month delay until the pregnancy was obvious so as not to compromise a phone tap the Bureau was maintaining on the Panther headquarters in Los Angeles. On May 19, 1970, gossip columnist Joyce Haber published an item about the Seberg pregnancy in the *Los Angeles Times*. The story did not use Seberg's name, but gave enough details to make her identity obvious. Haber did not get the tip directly from the FBI, but it is likely that the Bureau was the original source. That same day Hoover circulated a memorandum on Seberg's support of the Panthers to John Ehrlichman, Nixon's domestic policy adviser, Attorney General John Mitchell, and Deputy Attorney General Richard Kleindienst.

Other papers began to print stories referring to the possibility that Seberg was carrying a black baby. Shortly before the baby was due, she tried to kill herself with an overdose of sleeping pills. The baby was born prematurely and died two days later. Seberg never recovered. In 1976, she was notified by the Justice Department that she had been a target of a COINTELPRO operation. That knowledge hastened her emotional deterioration, and three years later she took her own life. Her ex-husband, who had tried to help her through the crisis by claiming he was the dead baby's father, killed himself not long afterward.

The Bureau was now carrying on a public war against the Ku Klux Klan, as well as a clandestine war against black radicalism. In the course of expanding COINTELPRO from an attack on a legally (but ambiguously) proscribed group like the Communist Party to a violence-prone group like the Klan to protest groups like the SCLC and the Student Nonviolent Coordinating Committee, Hoover had become increasingly willing to act without any legal sanction for his actions and to attack those he viewed as America's enemies, whether or not he had any traditional law enforcement or national security justification. In the past Hoover had been able to wage his cultural wars in the open, supported by grassroots approval and powerful political allies. Now the consensus supporting the traditional middle-class values Hoover had always defended was eroding. There was no longer the cement of anticommunism to hold together the coalition of allies like HUAC and the Senate Internal Security Subcommittee who had fought his battles for him before. Now he could no longer count on the support of the Justice Department against challenges to the status quo. Nor could Hoover have easily reversed course. Having encouraged Sullivan to expand COINTELPRO, Hoover and Sullivan were now equal partners. For either to have slackened might have raised doubts in the other's mind about his loyalty and reliability. The FBI's fall from grace was gathering speed and momentum.

The final expansion of counterintelligence techniques during the sixties was the Bureau's covert war against the New Left. In launching this COINTELPRO Hoover now completely abandoned the guidelines that had provided direction to his antisubversive campaigns from 1919 until the sixties: that to qualify for the full attention of the FBI, there had to be some connection, no matter how tenuous, between the American target and the international revolutionary movement. Hoover continued to study the Old Left's attempts to forge an alliance with the New Left (perhaps he hoped as much as the old communists that the effort would succeed; it would have made his job so much easier), but he admitted that what he was now attacking was "a new style in conspiracy—conspiracy that is extremely subtle and devious and hence difficult to understand

. . . a conspiracy reflected by questionable moods and attitudes, by unrestrained individualism, by nonconformism in dress and speech, even by obscene language, rather than by formal membership in specific organizations."

The seeds for the new COINTELPRO were planted on April 27, 1965, when presidential adviser McGeorge Bundy asked Hoover for any information he might have on any communist role in the antiwar demonstrations. The next day Hoover met with Johnson at the White House. Johnson told him

> that he was quite concerned over the anti-Vietnam situation that has developed in this country and he appreciated particularly the material that we sent him yesterday containing clippings from various columnists in the country who had attributed the agitation in this country to the communists as there was no doubt in his mind but that they were behind the disturbances that have already occurred. [The CIA had] stated that their intelligence showed that the Chinese and North Vietnamese believe that by intensifying the agitation in this country, particularly on the college campus levels, it would so confuse and divide the Americans that our troops in South Vietnam would have to be withdrawn in order to preserve order here and it would enable North Vietnam to move in at once.

Hoover realized that he could not possibly provide Johnson with the proof he wanted that a foreign conspiracy was the cause of the antiwar movement any more than he had been able to show him a communist conspiracy was behind the ghetto riots. He would do what he could, however, to turn the Students for a Democratic Society (SDS) into a communist front by calling it one, as if saying so would make it so. When he returned to the Bureau, Hoover ordered his aides to prepare a memo for Johnson

> containing what we know about the Students for a Democratic Society. While I realize we may not be able to technically state that it is an actual communist organization, certainly we do know there are communists in it. . . . What I want to get to the President is the background with emphasis upon the communist influence therein so that he will know exactly what the picture is. . . . I believe we should intensify through all field offices the instructions to endeavor to penetrate the Students for a Democratic Society so that we will have proper informant coverage similar to what we have in the Ku Klux Klan and the Communist Party itself.

The FBI did come up with one useful quote by Communist Party leader Gus Hall that the SDS was an organization the Party has "going for us." (Hoover would almost never mention SDS without including the quote as a tag line.) But despite the lack of any indication that the SDS was communist-controlled, the rapid growth of the organization from 10,000 in October 1965 to 80,000 in November 1968 and its militant rhetoric made it an irresistible target for the FBI's campaign against the antiwar movement. By coincidence, the SDS was just about the size of the Communist Party when Hoover attacked it in 1919 and 1947.

Hoover had no use for the SDS's political beliefs, of course, but he was even more revolted by the fact that "its members dress in beatnik style," which he rightly interpreted as a gesture of contempt for authority. The New Left, Hoover told parents, had "unloosed disrespect for the law, contempt for our institutions of free government, and disdain for spiritual and moral values." It was a "new-style subversion that is erupting in civil disobedience and encouraging young people to mock the law. If the infection continues to spread, the foundations of our republic will be seriously jeopardized." He called the DuBois Club a communist-backed campus organization, "new blood for the vampire of international communism," and said that it worked "together with other so-called 'New Left' organizations such as the Students for a Democratic Society . . . in furtherance of the aims and objectives of the Communist Party throughout the nation."

Hoover's relentless warnings about communist influence in the antiwar movement—in January 1966 he said the Party had an "ever-increasing role in generating opposition to the United States position in Vietnam"—were designed to raise doubts about the patriotism of the antiwar protesters. In his 1967 appearance before the House Appropriations Committee, Hoover told the congressmen,

> I do not believe that everybody who is opposed to the foreign policy in Vietnam is necessarily a Communist. That, of course, would be ridiculous as a charge, but there are many gullible people who are against the policy in Vietnam as a result of the propaganda put out by some college professors who are naive [,] and some students lacking in maturity and objectivity are constantly agitating and carrying on demonstrations in some of our largest universities.

In March 1966, Johnson asked Hoover to "constantly keep abreast" of contacts between foreign officials and "Senators and Congressmen and any citizen of a prominent nature." In December 1967, Attorney General Ramsey Clark set up an Interdivisional Information Unit with Cartha DeLoach at its head to coordinate intelligence on the antiwar movement. It was renamed the Interdivisional Intelligence Unit, and finally it was replaced in 1971 by the Intelligence Evaluation Committee with Hoover in charge.

Hoover's surveillance of the antiwar movement was originally to give the government advance warning of demonstrations. In itself this was intrusive and chilling, but after 1968 the Bureau went even more on the offensive to disrupt and discredit opposition to the war. As campus demonstrations increased (from 400 in the 1966–1967 school year to 3,400 in 1967–1968), the Bureau began to contemplate taking action to combat campus unrest.

It was the takeover of Columbia University in the spring of 1968 by antiwar students led by the SDS that finally made Sullivan and Hoover decide to expand COINTELPRO to target campus radicalism. Charles Brennan, the Sullivan subordinate who designed the New Left COINTELPRO, later said that the program was a response to "a tremendous amount of pressure from the White House" to do something about the "overall problem" of the "thousands of bombings, the arsons, the disruption, the disorder. Our academic communities were being totally disrupted, and I think that a vast majority of American people were subjecting the representatives of Congress and . . . the White House staff and other people in Government to a great deal of pressure, as to why these things were taking place and why something wasn't being done."

The FBI's campaign against the New Left abandoned any pretext of being intended to lead to the prosecution of crimes or the prevention of violence. Its purpose was, purely and simply, to combat political beliefs by discrediting those who held them. A directive on May 23, 1968, informed special agents in charge that the purposes of the new COINTELPRO were to "counter widespread charges of police brutality that invariably arise following student-police encounters," to collect evidence on the "scurrilous and depraved nature of many of the characters, activities, habits, and living conditions representative of New Left adherents," to "show the value of college administrators and school officials taking a firm stand," and to expose "whether and to what extent faculty members rendered aid and encouragement" to the antiwar movement. "Every avenue of possible embarrassment must be vigorously and enthusiastically explored. It cannot be expected that information of this type will be easily obtained, and an imaginative approach by your personnel is imperative to its success." In July agents were encouraged to send anonymous letters about students' behavior to parents, neighbors, and employers; agents should send articles from student newspapers showing the "depravity" of the New Left ("use of narcotics and free sex") to parents.

Between 1968 and 1971, when the COINTELPROs were terminated, the FBI directed 291 operations against the New Left, the majority of them aimed at preventing speech against the war or disrupting antiwar organizations and demonstrators. As the Bureau departed from the original wartime premise of the Emergency Detention Act as the rationale for lists of "dangerous" individuals, the classifications became so loose that the numbers got out of hand. First there was the Rabble Rouser Index in August 1967, then the Agitator Index, then in January 1968 the Key Activist Index. All were justified as modifications of the old Security Index. There was even a Key Activist photo album for ready reference.

The Bureau was now engaged in a secret battle to put down a vast rebellion of draft-age America against the war in Vietnam. What a spectacle it would have been, except that the Bureau kept the spectacle out of sight: a seventy-three-year-old Hoover (in 1968), with 6,590 agents at his command, trying to turn back a grassroots movement that at its peak was regularly able to assemble crowds of hundreds of thousands. Only confidence bred of Hoover's earlier successes against the Old Left and the Klan, fanned to a fever pitch by William Sullivan's enthusiasm, could have encouraged him to embark on a venture so reckless, so irresponsible, and, finally, so futile.

Hoover's great drives against the communists in 1919 and 1947, and against the gangsters of the thirties, had their undercover aspects, some of which would not comfortably stand the light of day, but they were not essentially secret operations. Their covert components were part of highly publicized campaigns toward goals supported by the overwhelming majority of the public, the legal establishment, and the government elite. If the FBI's earlier secret operations were exposed, as they sometimes were, they would not and did not very much damage the Bureau because there was really no secret in general about what the Bureau was doing. But with the COINTELPROs of the 1960s, the public knew nothing, as opposed to the targets, who did know about what the Bureau was doing. And even though the public may have had no great affection for black radicals or antiwar protesters, there would have been hell to pay if they had known that the FBI had taken it upon itself to disrupt, damage, and discredit citizens who had broken no laws while exercising their constitutional rights. By the late 1960s the Bureau was living in the shadows. Dragged into the light of day, it would shrivel and die.

■ ■ ■

The expansion of COINTELPRO was not nearly enough for Richard Nixon. When he took office in 1969 he pressed the Bureau to lead a unified intelligence community (the CIA, military intelligence, the National Security Agency) to gather information on the opposition inside and outside the government to the administration's foreign policy. William Sullivan was eager for the Bureau to take on these exciting (for Hoover, too exciting) responsibilities, but the old director resisted. His refusal touched off an unprecedented rebellion against Hoover's leadership at the Bureau as well as a confrontation between Hoover and Nixon, who came as close as any president ever would to firing the by-now-seemingly-eternal director of the FBI.

Nixon's men later blamed Watergate and the ruin of the Nixon administration on Hoover, even though Hoover died six weeks before the June 17, 1972, burglary. It was only because Hoover had blocked the administration's plans to reorganize the official domestic intelligence network, they said, that in 1971 the White House had to organize its own team of investigators, the White House "Plumbers," to stop news leaks. That created a job opening for G. Gordon Liddy, and Liddy went on to sell John Mitchell and the Committee for the Re-election of the President (CREEP) on the plan to bug the Democratic National Committee. If Hoover had been a better team player, they complained, the Nixon administration never would have recruited men with such a penchant for "black bag jobs" and Waterbuggery.

The Bureau's COINTELPRO operations against the New Left, ambitious though they were, fell far short of the coordinated assault against his enemies that Nixon wanted. He dreamed of something on the scale of the campaign the Bureau had mounted for Franklin D. Roosevelt in the thirties against the gangsters and against critics of preparedness. Hoover refused, fearing that the methods he had employed under previous presidents would destroy the Bureau if they came to light under current conditions. Hoover had come to recognize that the Bureau's survival depended on keeping its secrets, and it was becoming impossible to keep those secrets secret any longer.

Soon after taking office, Nixon began to be tormented by news leaks about his confidential plans for the war. There were twenty-one serious leaks during the first five months of his term, forty-five in all during the first year. He turned to Hoover. Hoover told him there were three possibilities: "to conduct background checks on those suspected as possible sources of leaked information, to have them tailed, or to place wiretaps on their telephones." Nixon claims that Hoover told him that tapping was the "only" effective way to track down the leakers, and that he had been given such assignments by every president since Roosevelt. Hoover probably had in mind the provision that permitted him to carry out intelligence investigations for the State Department because Nixon ordered that "when leaks occurred [Secretary of State Henry] Kissinger would supply Hoover with the names of individuals who had had access to the leaked materials and whom he had any cause to suspect. I authorized Hoover to take the necessary steps—including wiretapping—to investigate the leaks and find the leakers." Nixon wanted to catch the leakers, but for Hoover it was far more important not to get caught himself.

Hoover's search for the source of the leaks was done on the clearest of presidential authority, and the current understanding of the law was that the president had constitutional authority to order national defense wiretaps. The Supreme Court would eventually rule that the president did not possess such authority in the Keith decision (*U.S. v. Sinclair*), but that would not be until 1972. Hoover now decided it was too dangerous for the Bureau simply to rely on oral authorization from the president, and so while he ordered an immediate wiretap on Kissinger aide Morton Halperin, he requested and received written authorizations from Attorney General John Mitchell for all the remaining taps, including on Kissinger himself.

Hoover by now was so worried about the danger of being exposed that, besides making sure that he had written authorization for the Kissinger wiretaps, he had them segregated from the rest of the Bureau's operations. He gave the wiretaps to William C. Sullivan as a personal assignment, ordered that there be no duplicates of the logs, and kept the original logs and all other records outside the FBI files, at first in his own office and later in Sullivan's. The reports on the taps were not indexed and filed, and so the names of persons overheard were not entered in the department's ELSUR (electronic surveillance) index, used by the department to determine if any of its cases had been contaminated by unrelated wiretaps. Some of the taps remained in place for almost two years, in the case of Morton Halperin until February 10, 1971, when he was working on the campaign staff of Edmund Muskie.

Hoover became so nervous about carrying out sensitive political investigations for the Nixon administration that he finally refused a direct order from the White House to investigate one of the leaks that were vexing the president. In June 1969, Nixon had H. R. Haldeman ask the FBI to tap columnist Joseph Kraft's home after Kraft had written that Nixon's recent Vietnam peace proposals were unlikely to succeed. Nixon suspected Kraft was in touch with the administration's enemies, perhaps even with the North Vietnamese. Hoover refused, so Nixon had Haldeman use his own private investigator, Jack Caulfield, one of the White House "Plumbers," to install the tap. Nixon did persuade Hoover to have Kraft followed to Paris, where Kraft was meeting with North Vietnamese officials. Again Hoover had William Sullivan handle the job personally, and Sullivan used French police to tap Kraft's Paris hotel room. Evidently Hoover felt this shifted blame sufficiently away from the Bureau. In November 1969, probably in response to a White House request, Hoover asked

Mitchell for written authorization to tap Kraft's home in Washington, but the authorization was never signed and the tap never installed.

Hoover had concluded the day had passed when the Bureau could use illegal techniques in intelligence investigations relying only on presidential authorization. He explained to Richard Helms of the CIA that

> *there is widespread concern by the American people regarding the possible misuse of this type of coverage. Moreover, various legal considerations must be borne in mind, including the impact such coverage may have on our numerous prosecutive responsibilities. The FBI's effectiveness has always depended in large measure on our capacity to retain the full confidence of the American people. The use of any investigative techniques which infringe on traditional rights of privacy must therefore be scrutinized most carefully.*

Finally Nixon grew so frustrated with the Bureau's refusal to provide him with the domestic intelligence he thought he needed that he decided to reorganize the entire intelligence establishment through the so-called "Huston Plan." This pushed Hoover closer to a break with a president than he had ever come since the tense days of the Truman administration. The Huston Plan also brought into the open the tension that was mounting between William Sullivan, who wanted to make COINTELPRO a model for the FBI's domestic intelligence operations, and a Hoover who was growing increasingly aware of the danger that exposure of these covert operations posed to the Bureau.

Out of fear of such exposure Hoover began to cut off Bureau contacts with all other intelligence agencies, fearing that they might leak word of sensitive Bureau operations. Hoover ended regular liaison with the CIA because the CIA would not give Hoover the name of an FBI agent who had provided the agency with Bureau information without Hoover's permission. Other agencies within the intelligence community protested, and so Hoover ended liaison with all of them except the White House itself. Hoover also informed the other intelligence agencies that he would not carry out any electronic surveillance for them on his own authority, as he had in the past, but would refer the requests to the attorney general for approval. That effectively halted FBI assistance to the other intelligence agencies, since they would not go on record requesting permission for illegal investigations.

With his intelligence community dysfunctional and in disarray, Nixon called the directors of his intelligence agencies to the White House on June 5, 1970: Hoover, Richard Helms of the CIA, General Donald V. Bennett of the Defense Department, and Admiral Noel Gayler of the National Security Agency.

He gave them a dressing down, saying they were disorganized, inefficient, and unproductive. He wanted them to reorganize themselves into a single, streamlined unit that could keep him informed on domestic unrest. He wanted a report on what they would do: Hoover was to be the chairman, and the staff was to be directed by the White House's Tom Charles Huston, who had already mobilized the Internal Revenue Service against the administration's enemies. On an earlier assignment collecting information about foreign involvement in campus disturbances, Huston had struck up a friendship with William C. Sullivan.

Over the next two weeks Huston's staff hammered out a proposal that recommended a permanent interagency committee on intelligence. The committee would "evaluate intelligence, coordinate operations, prepare ongoing threat assessments on domestic protest, and develop new policies." For Huston and Sullivan this was the most important part of the proposal. The report presented the president with a range of choices he might make on sensitive surveillance techniques (mail opening, burglaries, electronic surveillance, and the use of on-campus informants). His options ranged from removing all restrictions to keeping them under the present Hoover-inspired limitations. If the president went in the direction suggested by Sullivan and Huston, there would have been, in effect, a new domestic intelligence agency, with Huston running it from the White House and Sullivan, operating under him, carrying out its investigations from within the Bureau.

Hoover finally saw the staff report shortly before June 23. He said he would not sign it. It would have to be redrafted to remove the most extreme options (removal of restrictions on surveillance) and the recommendation for the interagency committee. Hoover told Sullivan he was no longer willing to "accept the sole responsibility." If someone "higher than myself" approved a surveillance, "then I will carry out their decision . . . But I'm not going to accept the responsibility myself anymore, even though I've done it for many years." Sullivan suggested that rather than forcing the other agencies to rewrite a report they had already approved, Hoover should attach his objections as footnotes, and that is what he did. On electronic surveillance, Hoover wrote: "The FBI does not wish to change its present procedure of selective coverage on major internal security threats as it believes this coverage is adequate at this time. The FBI would not oppose other agencies seeking authority of the Attorney General for coverage required by them and thereafter instituting such coverage themselves." On mail coverage he wrote: "The FBI is opposed to implementing any covert mail coverage because it is clearly illegal and is likely that, if done, information would leak out of the Post Office to the press and serious damage would be done to the intelligence community." On black-bag jobs his footnote ran: "The FBI is opposed to surreptitious entry." And so on down the list of techniques: "The FBI is opposed to removing any present controls and restrictions relating to the development of campus sources. To do so would severely jeopardize its investigations and could result in leaks to the press which would be damaging and which could result in charges that investigative agencies are interfering with academic freedom." He pointed out that accepting the proposal to use military undercover agents in domestic intelligence "would be in violation of the Delimitations Agreement."

The Huston Plan's most important recommendation, by far, was that the president create a new command structure to coordinate domestic intelligence gathering. The report complained that there was currently no "correlation of operational activities in the domestic field." This seemed to be a veiled suggestion that the new intelligence committee might conduct disruptive counterintelligence operations along the lines of COINTELPRO. Huston proposed that the intelligence committee, with members representing the various agencies, have a chair appointed by the president to "coordinate intelligence originating with this committee in the same manner as Dr. Henry Kissinger, Assistant to the President, coordinates foreign intelligence on behalf of the President."

Hoover rejected this out of hand: "The FBI is opposed to the creation of a permanent committee for the purpose of providing evaluations of domestic intelligence." He offered only to have the FBI prepare "periodic domestic intelligence estimates" that would have been little more than the reports he submitted anyway each year to the House Appropriations Committee.

Huston had scheduled a signing ceremony for June 25. The other agencies got their first sight of Hoover's footnotes on June 23; the representatives of the NSA and the Pentagon called Huston immediately to protest. Huston pacified them with assurances that the proposal would go through despite Hoover's objections. Neither Huston nor Sullivan seemed too concerned either, one participant remembered. The attitude seemed to be: "What the White House wanted, the White House would get."

But when the agency heads assembled on June 25, instead of simply having them sign the report, as they expected, Hoover insisted on reading the entire forty-three-page report. As he finished each page he would ask: "Does anyone have any comment on Page 1?" Then he would repeat the same question to each member. Each time he came to Huston, he would get his name wrong. "Any comments, Mr. Hoffman? Any comments, Mr. Hutchinson?" and so on. This was no sudden and uncharacteristic bout of forgetfulness, since Hoover's memory was still sharp as a tack. He was determined to humiliate this twenty-nine-year-old who had been sent to crack the whip over the old men of American intelligence. At one point, Sullivan remembered, "I saw Dick Helms, who was sitting on Hoover's right, lean back in his chair and wink behind the director's back at Tom Huston." After a while Gayler and Bennett got fed up and began quarreling about Hoover's footnotes. Helms restored order. Hoover finished a hurried reading, and the four chiefs signed the document.

Hoover was appalled a few days later when he got a memo from Huston announcing that Nixon had accepted the most extreme recommendations of the plan, that Hoover would be chairman of the new domestic intelligence committee, and that Huston would be the "personal representative to the President" for domestic intelligence. Hoover objected at once, realizing that he was being asked to take enormous risks by authorizing the illegal activities of other agencies. "This ad hoc committee is going out of business just as soon as the report is finished," he said. "Then when we start to put these programs into effect, where am I going to go to get backup? Where am I going to get approval? That puts the whole thing on my shoulders."

Taking DeLoach with him, Hoover rushed to Attorney General John Mitchell's office to warn that the plan was far too dangerous and that it put the president in the position of approving, though indirectly, illegal activities. Mitchell went to the president with Hoover's warnings that "the possibility of public exposure was too great to justify the risks" and told Nixon that he agreed with Hoover. Nixon now realized that "if Hoover had decided not to cooperate it would matter little what I had decided or approved. Even if I issued a direct order to him, while he would undoubtedly carry it out, he would soon see to it that I had cause to reverse myself. There was even the remote possibility that he would resign in protest." The plan was to go into effect on August 1, but on July 28 Nixon withdrew his approval. All copies of the plan were rounded up. The public did not learn anything about the Huston Plan until John Dean's testimony during Watergate.

Hoover's rejection of the Huston Plan has to be viewed in the light of what he was willing to do to the radicals of the late sixties and early seventies as long as he had total and sole control over the operations. The fact is that he *was* harassing the antiwar movement, he *was* battling black militants, and he *was* directing his black nationalist and New Left COINTELPROs against precisely the organizations Huston cited as making the plan necessary.

Hoover was not willing to participate in the dangerous operations urged on him by Nixon unless they were part of a comprehensive plan drafted in response to public demands in a real crisis. He was not willing to move unless he could absolutely count on the support of the president and the public. In the absence of such public and political backing, what Nixon was asking was far too dangerous unless it could be kept secret, and by now Hoover knew that no secrets were ever really safe in Washington. Hoover had learned during the twenties how easily the FBI could be destroyed if it were misused, and he was not going to intentionally ruin his life's work. Unintentionally, in ways not yet apparent, he already had.

But out of the ashes of the Huston fiasco William C. Sullivan rose as the strongman of the FBI, Hoover's heir-apparent. DeLoach, who had earlier announced his intention to resign to join PepsiCo, finally left in July 1970. Hoover then elevated Sullivan to the rank vacated by DeLoach, assistant to the director, the number three position behind Tolson and Hoover.

■ ■ ■

The FBI's power to conduct secret operations depended on its absolute freedom from any inquiry into its internal operations. On the night of March 8, 1971, that changed forever. A group calling itself the Citizens' Commission to Investigate the FBI broke into the FBI resident agency (an outpost, usually small, of a larger "field office") at Media, Pennsylvania. The burglars were never caught; the Bureau was convinced they were supporters of the Catholic East Coast Conspiracy to Save Lives, whose leaders had recently been indicted for conspiring to blow up the capital power system and to kidnap Henry Kissinger. But the Bureau could not gather enough evidence to prosecute them for the break-in, and the case has remained unsolved.

The Bureau had expected someone would try something like the Media burglary, and so had begun to equip its offices with new security systems to defend itself. The Media office, however, had not yet transferred its sensitive files to the new safe. On the morning of March 9 the Media agents discovered their files dealing with domestic security were missing. The Bureau braced itself for the worst.

It was not long in coming. On March 22, Senator George McGovern and Representative Parren Mitchell of Maryland received photocopies of the files, but both refused to have anything to do with the stolen materials and turned the documents over to the Bureau. At the end of the month, however, an eighty-two-page extract of the documents was published by the New Left journal *WIN*.

The documents revealed a wide range of FBI domestic surveillance activities. They revealed a wiretap on the Philadelphia, Pennsylvania, office of the Black Panthers, as well as surveillance of the SDS and other New Left movement groups. The files also showed the FBI had been getting reports on demonstrations from the Philadelphia police. There was a memo from the registrar at Swarthmore College on Congressman Henry Reuss's daughter, who was active in the antiwar movement. The files also revealed surveillance of the Jewish Defense League, the Ku Klux Klan, and the National Black Economic Development Conference. The raid, an FBI official later said, was "the turning point in the FBI image." Release of the files, he said, helped the New Left justify as well founded its "paranoid fear of the FBI, which it hysterically equated with the Soviet secret police." Hoover reacted furiously to the raid. He had the Bureau's top investigators on the case for months, and closed 100 out of 536 resident agencies because they were too vulnerable to attack.

The Bureau might have simply ridden out the storm over the Media documents without any great damage if one of the documents had not carried the caption "COINTELPRO–New Left." It recommended interviewing students in order to "enhance the paranoia endemic in these circles and will further serve to get the point across there is an FBI agent behind every mailbox." Not for another year did anyone pick up that clue about COINTELPRO, but the FBI knew COINTELPRO was now compromised. On March 20, 1972, NBC News correspondent Carl Stern demanded documents dealing with COINTELPRO–NEW LEFT under the Freedom of Information Act. Denied his request, Stern sued, and on December 6, 1973, he received the documents.

Bureau secrecy was now under general attack. On April 24, Representative Hale Boggs accused Hoover of tapping congressional phones and infiltrating college campuses. He asked Mitchell to fire Hoover. "When the FBI adopts the tactics of the Soviet Union and Hitler's Gestapo," Boggs said, "it's time for the Director no longer to be the Director." Hoover assured the attorney general there had been no congressional wiretaps since 1924, and recalled for him the Bureau's standing orders that when a subject being trailed entered the grounds of the Capitol, the surveillance was dropped. Hoover then called congressional leaders to assure them that the Bureau simply did not investigate Congress. (That is, the FBI never investigated them for merely violating the law. If they criticized the Bureau, they were fair game.)

The secrecy protecting COINTELPRO operations had not yet been pierced, but the handwriting was on the wall. The Domestic Intelligence Division's chief told Hoover that "although successful over the years, it is felt that COINTEL-PRO should now be discontinued for security reasons because of their sensitivity." Hoover no longer could be confident that knowledge of these operations could be contained within the Bureau, and so, on April 28, 1971, he formally terminated COINTELPRO operations, which had been the foundation of the Bureau's domestic security operations since 1956. Hoover said there could still be counterintelligence operations but only in "exceptional instances," and he said such requests had to be submitted on an individual basis. The end of the formal COINTELPROs did not totally eliminate all counterintelligence operations, and congressional investigators were later able to find a few individual cases even after April 1971.

Termination of COINTELPRO put the Domestic Intelligence Division, Sullivan's power base, just about out of business. COINTELPRO had been William Sullivan's ticket to the top—it was no secret that Sullivan had his eye on Hoover's job—and now that ticket was canceled. Indeed, if COINTELPRO blew up in Hoover's face, Sullivan was the likely fall guy. Sullivan began picking quarrels with Hoover at the executive conference, and went out of his way to make public statements calculated to incense the old man. If there was anything rational by this time in Sullivan's actions, it must have been a delusion that the White House thought so well of Sullivan that if Hoover fired him, the president might turn around and fire Hoover. On October 12, 1970, Sullivan made a speech before the United Press International in which he downgraded the importance of the Communist Party-USA. At the executive conference he denounced Hoover's decision, which he himself had originally supported, to expand the Legal Attaché (Legat) program overseas.

But Hoover, when he had to, could be sly and resourceful, and he knew how to marshal his forces before he attacked. On July 1, 1971, he promoted Mark Felt, head of the Inspection Division, to a newly created number three position in the Bureau as Tolson's assistant, with the title deputy associate director, telling him, "I need someone who can control Sullivan."

If Sullivan was trying to force the administration to choose between him and Hoover, his strategy failed miserably. On August 28, Sullivan wrote Hoover a four-page letter (with a copy to Mitchell) that Sullivan himself aptly characterized as "intemperate." He accused Hoover of running the Bureau contrary to the president's best interests, and went through a litany of his personal grievances against Hoover. He accused Hoover of building a Bureau filled with yes men who were afraid to think or speak for themselves. He rehashed what had become a major point of contention with Hoover, a speech in which Sullivan had said that the Communist Party was almost defunct in the United States. He also stoked that running dispute with Hoover over the expansion of Legats overseas. Sullivan's memo did not warn Hoover that "there was only one way out" for him, but in many other respects it resembled Sullivan's letter to Martin Luther King.

That was enough for Hoover, and on September 3, 1971, he ordered Sullivan to "submit your application for retirement after taking the annual leave to which you are entitled." Hoover named Alex Rosen to Sullivan's job of assistant to the director. On September 9, Hoover removed Sullivan's protégé Charles Brennan as head of the Domestic Intelligence Division and shunted him off to a meaningless position. Hoover spent his first meeting with Brennan's replacement going over "the restraints and curbs which had to be applied to the operations of the Domestic Intelligence Division."

Sullivan returned from his forced vacation the last week of September 1971. The locks had been changed on his door, Rosen was in his office, and a search was going on for the Kissinger tapes Sullivan had been keeping. On October 6, Sullivan finally resigned. When he removed his personal effects, he left behind his autographed picture of J. Edgar Hoover. Mark Felt remembers that Sullivan seemed "edgy" the last day because he was not permitted to get into his file cabinets, and that is where a copy of the suicide letter to Martin Luther King was later found. As Sullivan prepared to leave the building, Felt accused him of being a Judas, and Sullivan challenged him to a fight. "He was like a little banty rooster, and I think he really would have fought me had I accepted his challenge, although I am half again his height."

Sullivan's strategy of provoking the administration to fire Hoover nearly worked, but only after Sullivan had gotten himself fired first. In October 1971, John Ehrlichman told Nixon that Hoover "had become an embarrassment." Ehrlichman gave the president what Nixon called a "brilliantly argued memorandum written . . . by G. Gordon Liddy, a member of the White House staff and a former FBI agent. The memorandum analyzed in detail the complex situation presented by Hoover's long tenure as Director and concluded with a strong recommendation that he should resign." The Sullivan revolt made Nixon think that the Bureau's morale was sagging and what "had once been Hoover's source of strength—his discipline and his pride—were now seen as temperament and ego." He also recalled Sullivan's charges that "Hoover was trapped in outdated notions of the communist threat and was not moving with flexibility against the new violence-prone radicals." Arguing against firing Hoover was Mitchell, who said that it might involve a public confrontation and pointed out that despite all the criticism, "Hoover still had very substantial support in the country and in Congress. To millions of Americans J. Edgar Hoover was still a folk hero." But in October 1971, Nixon decided that Hoover had to go.

The occasion was to be a breakfast meeting with the president. When Hoover appeared for his scheduled execution, Nixon found him as "alert, articulate and decisive" as he had ever seen him. It seemed to him that Hoover was trying to demonstrate that his mental and physical abilities were as vigorous as ever. After consoling Hoover about a conference at Princeton to investigate the

FBI (it met on October 29 and 30), Nixon pointed out "as gently and subtly as I could" that the attacks were only going to get worse in the future. He told Hoover it would be tragic if he had to leave while under attack instead of with the chorus of tribute and gratitude Nixon implied he could arrange. But Hoover was having none of it. He stated his loyalty to Nixon, saying, "More than anything else, I want to see you re-elected in 1972. If you feel that my staying on as head of the Bureau hurts your chances for re-election, just let me know. As far as these present attacks are concerned and the ones that are planned for the future, they don't make any difference to me. I think you know that the tougher the attacks get, the tougher I get." Nixon saw that if he wanted Hoover's resignation he would have to ask for it. Nixon decided not to: "My personal feeling played a part in my decision, but equally important was my conclusion that Hoover's resignation before the election would raise more political problems than it would solve."

■ ■ ■

At the end of 1971 Hoover had successfully withstood challenges from within and without the Bureau. With Mark Felt as his right-hand man, he had once again established firm control over the FBI. He had ended the COINTELPRO operations that posed the greatest danger to himself and the Bureau, and he had resisted all calls to become involved in any reckless new ventures. There were still occasional neighborly phone calls from Nixon, but he had set the Bureau's dealings with the White House once again on a correct and formal basis.

■ ■ ■

The seventy-seven-year-old Hoover put in a full day of work on May 1, 1972. Several times he conferred with Deputy Associate Director Mark Felt, sometimes in Hoover's office and sometimes over the intercom. As usual, Hoover asked Felt for a summary of the day's news events, as well as routine questions about the stream of office paperwork. Briefing Hoover about these details had once been Tolson's job, but Felt had taken over most of Tolson's duties. Felt remembers that Hoover was "alert, forceful, typically aggressive, and, so far as I could tell, completely normal in every respect."

Congress had designated May 1 "Law Day," and the Bureau released a message to the law enforcement community that criticized the protesters who had been the targets of the recently ended COINTELPRO operations, denouncing "extremists of all stripes in our society [who] ceaselessly attempt to discredit the rule of law as being biased and oppressive." As usual, Hoover stayed at his desk and left the office shortly before six, the signal that the executive staff could leave for the day.

The next morning, his maid Annie Fields went upstairs and knocked on Hoover's door. No answer. She pushed it open. Hoover was lying on the floor in his pajamas. She panicked and ran downstairs. James Crawford, the gardener, came up and felt for Hoover's pulse. He was dead.

■ ■ ■

Hoover's death did not mark the end of the Hoover era for the FBI. Far from it. During his lifetime, Hoover *was* the FBI. For many Americans, he still is, a legacy the Bureau has not yet been able to escape.

Beyond this, there are lessons to be learned from the Hoover era. Until they are learned, we will not be able to protect ourselves against domestic threats to our security.

Only the Bureau has the resources to gather information about danger at home, whether domestic, like the Ku Klux Klan, or foreign, like al Qaeda. But like all intelligence agencies, the Bureau can fall captive to its own ideology and information-gathering methods. If the president cannot evaluate information from the Bureau against information from other independent sources, he too can become a prisoner of the Bureau's agenda. Both John F. Kennedy and Lyndon Johnson were misled by the Bureau's wrongheaded insistence on the threat of domestic communism. Franklin Roosevelt's example should have been better known: He cast about for multiple sources of information, and pitted investigators like Hoover and Martin Dies against each other to cross-check their reliability, often finding both wanting.

The Bureau's COINTELPRO operations have become, in our conventional wisdom, "case closed" proof of the illegitimacy of *any* domestic intelligence gathering. That was the obvious conclusion, but the wrong one, as obvious conclusions often are. In almost all the COINTELPRO operations, the targets did deserve watching: The Communist Party, though not violent, was a petri dish for spies; the Ku Klux Klan was clearly a violent terrorist organization; the Black Panthers were certainly violence prone; the New Left was a broad movement that ranged from pacifist organizations to those capable of robberies, bombings, kidnappings, and murders. Only the Socialist Workers Party was demonstrably nonviolent, but it swam in a sea of violence-prone revolutionary groups.

Where the Bureau went astray was in its *misuse* of domestic intelligence to fuel campaigns of personal destruction—some authorized by presidents and attorneys general, others solely by Sullivan and Hoover. The lesson should be that the Bureau has the obligation to gather intelligence whenever there is reasonable suspicion that a group may be capable of violence, but that such investigations must be strictly supervised by the Department of Justice. This oversight, however, must not be such that it chills the Bureau's ardor for investigations, or convinces it that the danger it faces from its critics outweighs any threat from the nation's enemies. And of course, any use of the intelligence the Bureau gathers must only be in the courtroom, and must never violate the ancient principle of *nulla poena sine lege,* no punishment without trial.

Hoover turned his FBI into a replica of the America he had known during the happy days of his youth. That was part of the problem with Hoover's Bureau. An FBI that had the diversity—particularly at the leadership level—of the America it was investigating would have been far less likely to go astray as it did during Hoover's late years. The wreckage Hoover left at his death was proof that not letting the Bureau change with the times, keeping the Bureau closed to anyone except middle-class white males, was not only unproductive but self-destructive. But Hoover was right in insisting on high standards for agents. In the rush to diversify, the Bureau would later go to the equally destructive extreme of tolerating so much diversity in conduct, behavior, and ethics that it would be impossible to weed out misfits who would eventually betray the Bureau to the Soviets.

Hoover refused to trim the Bureau's law enforcement philosophy to fit changing fashion in criminology which saw the "roots of crime" in poverty, not personal choice. This was not totally misguided: Such theories have a way of swinging back from right to left over time. Nevertheless, Hoover clearly was exceeding his authority when he insisted that FBI law enforcement doctrine conform to his philosophy rather than to the policies of his political superiors. Crime fighting in this country may always be politicized, which is a bad thing, but it does not help if the Department of Justice and the FBI are pitted against each other at opposite sides of the philosophical debate over the causes of crime and the purposes of law enforcement, as they were during the Kennedy and Johnson administrations. It is the duty of presidents and attorneys general to fire subordinates who obstruct the programs they are ordered to carry out. Hoover should have retired in 1960. Or he should have been fired shortly thereafter. The refusal of Kennedy and Johnson to do so does not etch for either a profile in courage.

The FBI's effort to conceal its failures in the Kennedy assassination case is an object lesson in how *not* to deal with the errors that inevitably come to light in high-profile, politically explosive cases. In trying to conceal the mistakes of field agents and supervisors who should have been keeping closer track of Lee

Harvey Oswald, the Bureau kept vital information out of the Warren Commission report. As this information dribbled out over the years, Bureau secrecy contributed to the widespread suspicion that there had been a comprehensive cover-up of the guilt of unknown conspirators. A mature Bureau, government, and public ought to realize that any complex investigation will produce blunders, and without an immediate and thorough airing of them the public's confidence in its government cannot survive.

Hoover has received anomalous and undeserved credit as a civil libertarian for scuttling Nixon's Huston Plan to coordinate domestic intelligence: Hoover actually vetoed the plan not out of any concern for civil liberties, but out of a well-founded fear that the Bureau would be blamed when the enterprise ran aground. But even though Nixon's motives for trying to coordinate domestic intelligence may have been somewhat unholy, coordination was needed then and is still needed now.

Once again we drew the wrong conclusions. We decided that because Nixon probably would have misused any coordination of domestic intelligence, any such coordination was then and always wrong and always to be resisted. But the uncoordinated and inefficient system for gathering intelligence that survived the failure of the Huston Plan would become a growing threat to national security, leaving the country essentially unprotected against a new threat of terror. Nixon's motives may have been less than pure, but the need for coordinating domestic intelligence should have gotten serious consideration, not instant dismissal, which is all it got until 9/11.

For many of us, Hoover's sins have rendered the Bureau forever suspect; its every act is viewed as somehow connected to Hoover's sinister plot against civil liberties. Hoover turned the FBI into a symbol of government repression, and to this day a reflexive opposition to the FBI symbolizes for many of us our commitment to civil liberties. Neither we, nor the Bureau, it seems, have ever been able to move on.

EIGHT

A Haunted Bureau (1972–1978)

J. EDGAR HOOVER was finally gone, years after he should have left for his own sake and the sake of his Bureau. But to the end Hoover had the power to terrify his foes and keep them at bay. That power died with him, while his enemies survived, grim and unforgiving. And the Bureau was now more vulnerable than anyone knew. Secrets long buried would not stay buried much longer, and when they surfaced hatred of the FBI, long confined to the far left fringes of politics, would become a new and powerful force in American life.

Before the seventies were over, Hoover's successor would be driven from office in disgrace for destroying evidence during the Watergate scandal. The secrets of COINTELPRO would be laid bare in excruciating detail and would, unfairly but understandably, come to symbolize the FBI of the Hoover era. The G-man hero, an American icon for decades, would become a popular entertainment villain, the face of a government in conspiracy against its citizens' liberties. FBI agents would be ambushed and executed in the dust of a South Dakota Indian reservation, their convicted killer hailed as a defender of his people. The same FBI that had won fame capturing kidnappers in the thirties would now appeal in vain for help during the Patricia Hearst kidnapping, and no one, out of the scores, even hundreds who knew where she was, trusted the FBI enough to step forward. The Bureau would now become something to be resisted and reviled, a scapegoat for the nation's sins of Vietnam and Watergate, while the FBI's enemies would swell in strength and numbers with each passing year.

. . .

The search for the secrets that were—supposedly—the source of Hoover's power began before his body was in the ground. The afternoon after Hoover's death, Assistant Attorney General L. Patrick Gray visited the office of Assistant to the Director John Mohr. Mohr was working on the arrangements for the funeral. After an exchange of sentiments appropriate to the circumstances, Mohr indicated to Gray that he was busy. Gray, who had been sent by the White House, blurted out, "Where are the secret files?" Mohr responded that there were no secret files. Gray asked again, and when he got the same reply, he went away.

Mohr knew what Gray was after, but he decided to put a technical construction on the word "secret," interpreting it as a legal security classification. By that definition he was right. But he knew that the files Gray was after certainly did exist, though they would not exist many days longer.

Hoover's "secret" files were already being spirited out of Hoover's office by Hoover's secretary, Helen Gandy, and delivered to Hoover's house. There she and Clyde Tolson went through them, destroyed many, and delivered the remainder back to the Bureau to be merged into the regular FBI files.

Historian Athan Theoharis, who has managed to decrypt many of Hoover's file-keeping finagles, has demonstrated that Hoover had three sets of files qualifying as his "secret files" according to the popular understanding of the term: his Official and Confidential Files, his Personal and Confidential Files, and finally a third set of files, regular Bureau files, which were kept under lock and key in Hoover's office. (There were some sensitive files kept in Tolson's and Louis Nichols's offices that also fall into the "secret" category.)

The Official and Confidential Files (O&C), which still exist, many of them having been released under Freedom of Information Act (FOIA) requests, consisted of 164 folders of material, much of it derogatory, on famous or prominent individuals, including several presidents, a first lady, and many high-ranking national officials. In a memo found among these files, Hoover described the O&C files as containing "various and sundry items believed inadvisable to be included in the general files of the Bureau." He went on to say that this material, to be "of value," had to be indexed and filed, presumably so that Hoover could have instant access to it for his own purposes. In general, the material in the O&C files contained information about Hoover's enemies that would be valuable when casting aspersions on their character or loyalty. Thus there is a great deal of material on President John F. Kennedy's sex life, before and during his time in the White House. There is information about an alleged affair between Eleanor Roosevelt and Joseph Lash. And there are many allegations about individuals whose names have been censored out in copies released by the Bureau. While there are no clearly documented cases showing that these files were ever overtly used for the purpose of intimidating Hoover's enemies, such material is even more potent if it is never used, as long as its existence is suspected, as was always the case with Hoover's files.

The second group of secret files in Hoover's office was his Personal and Confidential Files. These files were destroyed by Helen Gandy and Tolson after Hoover's death. Later Gandy testified to Congress that they dealt strictly with Hoover's personal correspondence, but Theoharis argues that Gandy's explanation is not accurate. For some reason not known, in 1971 Hoover and Gandy began to go through the P&C file looking for materials that should be in the O&C file, but they got no further than the letter *C*. One of the files transferred at that time was a memo setting forth the Bureau's very confidential procedures for keeping track of illegal "black bag jobs." Another contained Hoover's orders to implement a "Do Not File" system to conceal other illegal Bureau investigative techniques. Theoharis concludes that the P&C file, in addition to holding Hoover's personal records, was the repository for "documents that, if exposed to public attention, would definitely have jeopardized his tenure as Director and blackened the reputation of the Bureau." That is, it contained evidence of illegal Bureau activities.

The third category of secret files consisted of regular Bureau files that Hoover kept close at hand because they "were highly confidential Bureau information." These files were put back in the Bureau's central files after Hoover's death, and so their contents are unknown.

The sheer bulk of these secret files of Hoover's may be judged from a Justice Department report that found Gandy had removed some thirty-five cabinet drawers of files from Hoover's office to his home. There she and Tolson reviewed them, sending just about all of the material from the P&C files to the Washington field office (then in the Old Post Office) to be shredded, while many of the O&C files went back to the Bureau.

Eventually, though not immediately, most of this O&C material and much of the sensitive information about celebrities in the regular FBI files would trickle out in response to FOIA requests or lawsuits from journalists, political activists, or historians. In the quarter century since Hoover's death a staple of U.S. journalism has been new revelations about the files Hoover kept on show business celebrities, cultural figures, political leaders, and other prominent Americans. Some of these came from the O&C files, but many more came from case files or, very often, files opened on individuals for activities that might have qualified the person for internment in case of hostilities with the Soviet Union.

The "secret files" were a bomb with a long fuse that would not detonate for a while after Hoover's death. But there was another, more immediate threat to the Bureau's reputation. Reporter Carl Stern's appeal to the Bureau under the Freedom of Information Act for the release of documents bearing the caption COINTELPRO–NEW LEFT was working its way through the legal system. His requests and subsequent lawsuit would not be resolved for two more years; the threat of their release terrified the Bureau.

■ ■ ■

These sins of J. Edgar Hoover would lie buried a little while longer, but even without them the FBI's reputation would quickly begin to collapse. The demolition began under his immediate successor, a decent, well-meaning, but all-too-obedient Navy man named L. Patrick Gray III.

Upon Hoover's death, Clyde Tolson became acting director. For several days he would sign—or rather have signed for him by several surrogates, one of them Hoover's chauffeur—the flood of papers requiring the director's signature. But almost as soon as President Nixon heard that Hoover was dead, he decided to name as Hoover's successor that same assistant attorney general who had called on John Mohr.

L. Patrick Gray, born in St. Louis, Missouri, on July 18, 1916, was a 1940 graduate of the Naval Academy. He served in the Navy during World War II, then graduated from J. Edgar Hoover's old school, George Washington University Law School, then passed the Washington, D.C., bar exam in 1949. He was recalled to active duty during the Korean War and stayed in the Navy until his retirement in 1960, rising to the rank of captain and serving as military assistant to the chairman of the Joint Chiefs of Staff.

After leaving the Navy, Gray worked for Nixon in his 1968 presidential campaign and was rewarded with an appointment as assistant attorney general in charge of the Civil Division in the Justice Department. Nixon intended to make Gray the deputy attorney general in 1972, but withdrew the nomination when he named Gray acting director of the FBI.

Gray's reception from the FBI's top executives when he took charge was none too friendly. Some of these men had hoped to succeed Hoover in the top job, so they resented an outsider who snatched the brass ring. But there may have been more to their coldness than that. In his last years Hoover, always self-indulgent in taking advantage of the perquisites of his office, had begun to treat the Bureau like a personal serving staff, expecting it to take care of all of life's little inconveniences, from landscaping his garden to remodeling his house to keeping his television fired up. The other top executives realized that their boss's freeloading would provide cover for their own, and began to call on the Bureau for the same kinds of services. And so, like the embezzling bank teller who cannot afford to take a holiday, Hoover's top assistants may have dreaded an outsider coming on board who might inconveniently catch on to their abuses of position.

To compensate for his lack of rapport with the headquarters brass, Gray cultivated the street agents, and tried to visit all of the field offices in the scant year he was director. He made it to fifty-eight, all except Honolulu. He also relaxed Hoover's outmoded rules on clothing and grooming, permitting agents to have hair fashionably over their ears, wear colored shirts, and put on sport jackets. These reforms were overdue, but they had the unforeseen consequence of eventually breeding an official lack of curiosity about the private behavior of agents. In an intelligence organization, private behavior sometimes offers the only clue that an agent may be going over to the other side. And so the Bureau would, some two decades later, ignore warning signals in the behavior of traitor agents like Earl Pitts and Robert Hanssen that all but shouted they were up to no good. Although most agents still brushed their hair, shined their shoes, and tied their ties the FBI way, a "don't ask, don't tell" ethic made room for agents who should have been looked at more closely.

Gray also accelerated the hiring of minority and female agents. On the day Hoover died there were 61 black agents and 59 Hispanics, and they were there only because of the prodding of Robert Kennedy. There were as yet no female agents. Due to Gray's initiatives, five years later the numbers had improved to 185 black agents, 173 Hispanics, and 147 women.

Gray ran the Bureau, for the most part, through Mark Felt, whom Gray gave the rank of acting associate director. Gray also had three special assistants who could issue orders in Gray's name: David D. Kinley handled the Bureau's administrative side, took care of press relations, and moved the Bureau away from the old Hoover worldview in which the only thing that mattered was whether a person was a friend or enemy of the FBI; Daniel M. Armstrong kept his eye on the Bureau's investigative work; the third special assistant, Barbara L. Herwig, took charge of the Bureau's efforts to recruit women, and tried to make sure that they were treated fairly.

Gray's most important reform was to set up a policy analysis unit to study Bureau goals and priorities: the Office of Planning and Evaluation (OPE). He also abolished Hoover's Crime Records Division, the Bureau's public relations arm, delegating many of its functions to other divisions and moving the press and congressional relations into his own office. But before Gray's reforms could prove themselves, he was drawn into the quicksand of Watergate. The scandal would destroy him after less than a year on the job, under circumstances devastating to the Bureau.

The Watergate burglary of June 17, 1972, was the work of that White House unit created to do the dirty work Hoover refused. The burglary team for the Watergate operation included two ex–FBI agents, James W. McCord Jr. and G. Gordon Liddy. The FBI was called immediately to investigate the break-in. The Bureau would later maintain that it conducted a no-holds-barred investigation, and as far as the investigating agents were concerned, that was true. But Gray himself, consciously or unconsciously, allowed himself to be manipulated by presidential aides intent on containing and controlling the investigation. This began when Gray initially acceded to a White House request that the FBI stay away from Watergate because its investigation might endanger CIA sources. Gray reversed himself only after Mark Felt and Assistant Director in Charge of Criminal Investigations Charles Bates insisted on getting confirmation from the CIA that this was true, and the agency declined to provide it.

Gray also gave preferential treatment to Nixon administration officials who were interviewed by the Bureau during the investigation. He allowed them to be accompanied by their lawyers, contrary to FBI practice. He let Nixon's counsel, John W. Dean III, sit in on FBI interviews with fourteen White House aides, and even let Dean see the raw "302" forms, the actual interview forms agents use when they question suspects and witnesses. Gray's excuse was that Dean was passing along requests from the president, so he had no alternative but to do whatever Dean asked. But Attorney General Kleindienst and Assistant Attorney General Henry F. Petersen had both been approached by Dean with the same requests for the 302s, and both refused (Gray did not know this). And in fact Gray did seem to realize how irregular Dean's requests were, since he would meet with Dean in parks and other outdoor locations, and he made Dean come to the Bureau himself to pick up FBI documents rather than have them sent to the White House by Bureau messenger. In all, Gray passed on to Dean about half of the interviews conducted in the Watergate case. Soon some in the Bureau began to suspect that Gray was obstructing justice in the Watergate investigation, so FBI officials and agents may have begun leaking information about the case to the press and Congress.

Gray's Senate confirmation hearings began on February 28, 1973, and lasted for three weeks. The senators were interested in exploring all the Bureau's alleged shortcomings, but they concentrated on the FBI's handling of the Watergate case. Gray did not seem to know he was in trouble. He freely admitted he had shared FBI documents with John Dean, then offered to share them with the senators too if that would make them happy. The questioning started to get brutal, and the White House began to lose confidence in Gray when he suggested Dean had probably lied to the FBI. The committee was split on whether to send Gray's name to the full Senate, and recessed without concluding its deliberations. Gray then asked the president to withdraw his nomination.

But Gray would not get off so easily. A week and a half after the Watergate burglary, Gray had been called to the White House to see John Dean and John Ehrlichman in the latter's office. They gave Gray two manila envelopes from Watergate burglar E. Howard Hunt's desk, and told Gray these envelopes contained "political dynamite" that "should not see the light of day." In the envelopes were documents Hunt had forged to implicate John F. Kennedy in the assassination of President Ngo Dinh Diem of South Vietnam.

During the nomination hearings the senators had come close to asking Gray about the Hunt documents, but had never gotten to the question. On April 15, 1973, Gray learned that John Dean had begun to cooperate with the prosecutors. Gray went to Connecticut senator Lowell Weicker, who was sponsoring Gray's nomination, and told Weicker he had torn up the documents without reading them, then put them in a Bureau burn bag. Weicker told Gray he would have to resign. After some initial resistance, he did, on April 17, 1973.

Gray had not told Weicker the whole truth. He had actually taken the documents home to Connecticut in June 1972, read them, and then hid them in his shirt drawer. Sometime after Christmas of that year he burned them with the Christmas trash. Gray now faced indictment for perjury and obstruction of justice, and began to cooperate with the Watergate investigators.

It doesn't get much worse than that. The top law enforcement official in the country had destroyed evidence essential to a case being investigated by the Bureau, because the politically powerful subjects of the investigation had asked him to. L. Patrick Gray is remembered today, when he is at all, for having personally destroyed key evidence in a political corruption investigation of the White House and, like William Burns so many years before, for obstructing justice to help cover up a political scandal at the highest level of American government.

■ ■ ■

To succeed Gray, Nixon named William Ruckelshaus, administrator of the Environmental Protection Agency and former attorney general of Indiana, as acting director of the Bureau. (Ruckelshaus had told the president that he was not interested in a permanent appointment.) He was a graduate of Princeton University and Harvard Law School and an army veteran. Before taking over the

Bureau, he had held Gray's old job as assistant attorney general in charge of the Justice Department's Civil Division.

Ruckelshaus showed up for work on Monday, April 30. It was to be a rough day. Attorney General Richard Kleindienst had just announced his resignation because of his involvement with White House officials implicated in the Watergate scandal. Then when Ruckelshaus reached his desk he found on it a copy of a telegram the men who would be working for him had sent to the president:

> *Mister President, this message, by unanimous adoption, is from the acting associate director, all assistant directors, and all special agents in charge of FBI field offices throughout the United States. The hallmarks of fidelity, bravery and integrity and of dedication to constitutional principles of equal justice and preservation of the rights of all citizens have made the FBI a revered institution of our national life. J. Edgar Hoover's precepts of careful selection of agent personnel among highly qualified candidates, rigorous training, firm discipline and promotion solely on merit have developed within the FBI law enforcement leaders of professional stature respected world-wide. In the search for a nominee for the FBI directorship, we urge consideration to the highly qualified professionals with impeccable credentials of integrity within the organization itself. . . . We do not suggest there are not many other highly qualified leaders of proven integrity, but at this critical time it is essential that the FBI not flounder or lose direction in its service to the nation because of lack of law enforcement expertise or of other qualities essential to the FBI directorship. None of us seek personal gain—there is a vast reservoir of qualified executives within the FBI's officialdom from which a nominee could be selected. We are moved to address you thusly, because of our devotion to our sworn duty to the people of the nation, because of our love for this great institution and because we have seen no indication of consideration of FBI officials, among whom there is an inherent nonpartisanship and a deep reverence to the call of duty to all the people of our nation. Respectfully, All FBI Officials.*

His leadership team had also sent copies to the press.

Ruckelshaus served only seventy days, until a permanent director was chosen. It was enough time, however, for him to form some impressions of the Bureau at this critical time in its history. The top management of the Bureau had lived or died on Hoover's approval for so long, he said, that when Hoover was no longer there to praise or scold them, they seemed lost. But he also said that he found the Bureau the "finest governmental organization I have ever been associated with. It runs better and is more responsive to the leadership at the top

than any other organization I have ever been associated with." It was so different from the EPA. When he was at the FBI, "all I had to do was hint that I
wanted something done, and it was done. It was almost like running downhill,
for that group. I am not sure they were that eager to respond to me, but I was
the director and they were used to responding to the director all their lives, and
they could not stop."

He also made a shrewd analysis of the difficulties faced by any director of
the FBI:

> *The Director must be able to conceptualize how the FBI fits into our societal
> fabric at any given historical moment. He must recognize the permissible lim-
> its of investigative techniques—what is permissible in wartime or time of ex-
> treme emergency is impermissible when the threat to our country's security is
> minimal—and he must communicate forcefully those limits to FBI Agents.
> Needless to say, this takes an individual of considerable capacity. Furthermore,
> the necessity to America of our major Federal law enforcement agency's not ex-
> ceeding a wise exercise of its power is too important to leave to the judgment of
> one man. There must be effective oversight of all FBI activities. This essential
> review and check should come from both the executive and legislative branches
> of our government. In my opinion neither the legislative nor the executive over-
> sight or check is sufficient today and needs to be strengthened.*

Perhaps the most significant action Ruckelshaus took as director was to fire
Mark Felt at the end of June 1973. Felt, the acting associate director, was lobby-
ing hard for the job at the top, FBI director, and Ruckelshaus suspected that Felt
was leaking information to the press that would reflect well on his own candidacy.

Ruckelshaus also helped in the search for his own successor, which the
Nixon administration turned into another mess for the Bureau by dangling the
directorship before the judge presiding over the trial of Daniel Ellsberg for
leaking the Pentagon Papers to the *New York Times*. According to one theory,
the administration did this to encourage the judge to see things the prosecution's way. The judge apparently resisted any such pressure, declaring a mistrial
because the government was not forthcoming with materials it should have
provided to the defense regarding FBI surveillance. But the fact of the offer had
been made public, once again embarrassing the Bureau.

After doing so much to damage the Bureau, Nixon finally made an excellent
choice for the new director. Clarence Kelley had had a distinguished career in
the FBI before leaving to head the Kansas City, Missouri, police department.

Kelley, a Kansas City native, was born on October 24, 1911, graduated from the University of Kansas, and received his law degree from the University of Kansas City in 1940. He joined the Federal Bureau of Investigation as a special agent on October 7, 1940, and worked in field offices in Huntington, West Virginia; Pittsburgh, Pennsylvania; Des Moines, Iowa; and the FBI Training Center, Quantico, Virginia, as a firearms instructor. He was in the Navy during World War II, then rejoined the Bureau, working in the Kansas City field office and then at the FBI Headquarters in Washington. He was special agent in charge of the Birmingham, Alabama, office in 1957 and then of the Memphis, Tennessee, office in 1960. He retired from the Bureau a year later to become the chief of police in Kansas City.

In FBI history, Clarence Kelley is identified with the slogan, which under him became almost a mantra, "quality over quantity." He wanted the Bureau to focus only on big, important cases, to the applause of forward-thinking FBI executives like future deputy associate director Oliver "Buck" Revell, who agreed that "the Bureau had to continue to change, that quality-over-quantity was the only program that made any sense." But it would make things more complicated administratively in a huge bureaucracy that had to compare people for purposes of advancement, since quality was much harder than quantity to measure statistically.

In pushing for quality over quantity Kelley was trying to set the Bureau back on the road it had abandoned soon after 1908. No FBI director, not even Finch or Bielaski, had wanted to pursue the dangerous political corruption investigations that had led to the creation of the Bureau. And Hoover had departed farthest of all from "quality." All Hoover had seemed to want out of law enforcement from the Bureau was statistics, particularly statistics he could use to show the Bureau was taking in more money in terms of fines and recovered property than it was costing Congress to support it. The easiest way to achieve those statistics was by recovering cars after interstate thefts. In many cases, all the Bureau had to do was take one phone call from the police in the state that recovered the car, and then place another call to the police in the state from which it was stolen to send someone over to pick it up. That phone call produced the Blue Book value of the "recovered" car that could be added to the money the Bureau had made for the government that year.

That was the Hoover regime at its most absurd, in which a systemic emphasis on high-volume case management for each agent meant that an agent who handled dozens of the meaningless cases and solved a great number of them was considered a rising star. An agent who worked on one difficult case for a long time, however, would have some explaining to do. The Hoover system decreed that quality cases—public corruption, white-collar crime, organized crime—took too much time and money to be justified, except, of course, in Hoover's favorite areas of foreign counterintelligence and domestic surveillance.

Kelley liked to cite one public corruption case as the milestone marking the shift from quantity to quality, "the end of one era and the beginning of another." Public corruption was one category of "quality" cases that was strictly off limits under Hoover. The reason was, Kelley recalled, that "J. Edgar Hoover had discovered that congressional support for his programs was tough enough to come by without making people mad. And the surest way to make politicians mad at you was to put their friends in jail. Worse yet was this looking too closely at their own affairs. Bad business, investigating politicians. Don't do it."

Hoover had bragged about this hands-off policy to Congress, claiming that it proved his reverence for the separation of powers. Congress applauded the policy ostensibly for the same reason, but of course, if the FBI was not investigating crooked congressmen and senators, no one was, which was just the way some of them liked it. Congress had used the same argument when William Burns investigated it during the Washington land-fraud investigation. And so, Kelley reported, "for years the FBI's unwritten policy had been unswerving: no involvement in local politics or politicians."

■ ■ ■

The case began with rumors that any construction firm in Oklahoma that wanted to do business with the state had to make a large kickback directly to the governor, David Hall, who was known to be in financial difficulties. Two agents in the Oklahoma City field office, Paul A. Baresel and Travis W. Muirhead, looked into these rumors, wrote up a summary of their investigation, and sent it to Washington. They already had permission to proceed with the investigation from the U.S. attorney in Oklahoma City, pending permission from FBI Headquarters.

The supervisor at headquarters who reviewed Oklahoma's request quickly responded. "Running true to form," the supervisor telephoned Oklahoma City Special Agent in Charge Wilburn K. DeBruler and ordered him to shut down the investigation and to report within ten days that it had been closed. DeBruler called the supervisor (whom he outranked). He told him he had heard that the new director had ordered the Bureau to concentrate on important cases, and this was certainly one of them:

All the evidence here suggests that this could be an extremely important case. It warrants full FBI attention. And if I understand what the new director is telling us, the FBI should pursue this matter to its conclusion. Until somebody else tells me to leave this one alone, we are going to continue the investigation of Governor Hall.

The next day DeBruler got a telephone call from the assistant director in charge of the Criminal Investigative Division and was told "in no uncertain terms, to shut down the case: The FBI would not get involved in a case regarding the governor of Oklahoma." DeBruler was furious. "Outranked and overruled," Kelley said, DeBruler "could see that the case was following an all-too-familiar pattern. An FBI field man found a hot one; FBI-Washington felt the matter was too controversial." DeBruler had run into one of Hoover's most inflexible policies. Even though Hoover was gone, Hoover-trained supervisors were determined to follow Hoover's orders to the letter.

It was unheard of for a mere field agent, even a SAC, to try to talk to the director. Kelley himself could recall only one instance in his entire time with the FBI when a field agent called the director, and that had been when an agent called Hoover to tell him JFK had been shot. Nevertheless, DeBruler decided to risk his career and call Kelley directly. When he tried to put his call through, he was informed that a call to the director would be "ill-advised." Nevertheless he tried and kept on trying, although his first calls were intercepted and sidetracked by assistant directors. He finally got through and outlined the case to Kelley, complaining that he was getting "enormous resistance within the Bureau." Kelley told him to go ahead. DeBruler then said something that amused Kelley: "Thank you sir. I think this is one of your high-priority cases. If I am right, it's real quality, Mr. Director."

The investigation sent the governor to jail for three years and dismantled a pervasive scheme of corruption in the state. Recognizing the historic nature of the case, Kelley said that it was "probably the first in which the Bureau had deliberately entered into a high-priority investigation of that nature with full force." For the first time since the land-fraud cases, the FBI had deliberately decided to investigate one of the crimes against the United States that the Bureau was founded to fight.

Kelley's nearly five years as director were a personal ordeal because of the terminal cancer of his wife, Ruby, who generally was too weak to leave her doctors in Kansas City. For much of his term Kelley had to commute back to Missouri on weekends. His tenure also became a professional ordeal, as the skeletons J. Edgar Hoover thought he had buried began to rise from their graves in the FBI files. Carl Stern's request for documents relating to COIN-TELPRO–NEW LEFT had been turned down by Attorney General Richard G. Kleindienst and so Stern sued in the Federal court of the District of Columbia. He wanted a copy of the orders that authorized the COINTELPROs, dated May 10, 1968, and the order from headquarters to the field that canceled all COIN-TELPROs, dated April 28, 1971.

Kelley's argument against releasing the COINTELPRO files was that law enforcement and intelligence gathering depended on a "reliable system of confidential informants . . . without that network, law enforcement in a free society would grind to a halt," and so "confidential information must remain confidential. . . . A free society like ours, peopled with human beings that are imperfect, indeed often criminal, must take the necessary steps to protect itself. The COINTELPROs, despite some disturbing 'improvisational' characteristics, were designed by the FBI to protect the stability of our nation, and to promote its general welfare through an unfortunately secret battle with those who would promote anarchy and violence." Nevertheless, faced with a court order, on July 6, 1973, the Bureau had no choice but to turn over the documents to the court, and on December 6, 1973, Judge Barrington D. Parker handed them over to Stern.

The day before the documents were released, Kelley sent a memo to all special agents in charge warning that they soon could expect inquiries about FBI violations of civil liberties. The day after the release, Kelley issued a statement energetically defending the programs, stressing "that at a time of national crisis the government would have been derelict in its duty had it not taken every legal measure to protect the fabric of society."

Stern wasn't finished. On December 7 he demanded the FBI give him

> *Whatever documents authorized and defined the programs Cointelpro-Espionage; Cointelpro–Disruption of White Hate Groups; Cointelpro–Communist Party, USA; Cointelpro–Black Extremists; Socialist Workers Party–Disruption Program. Whatever documents directed changes in the programs. Whatever documents authorized a counterintelligence action of any kind after 4/28/71.*

Kelley told Stern that the requested documents were exempt from the Freedom of Information Act because they were confidential records of investigations. Stern then appealed Kelley's decision to Attorney General William B. Saxbe. On March 6, 1974, Saxbe handed over "part but not all" of the requested documents to Stern and to CBS reporter Fred Graham; the batch included one

COINTELPRO document on white hate groups, two on black extremists, one on the Socialist Workers Party, three general memos on counterintelligence, and several additional documents. At the same time, in response to a request from President Gerald Ford for a report on COINTELPRO, Saxbe appointed a committee chaired by Assistant Attorney General Henry Petersen to review all FBI COINTELPRO documents. Meanwhile the subcommittee on constitutional rights of the Senate Judiciary Committee under Senator Sam Ervin also demanded the COINTELPRO documents, but agreed to Kelley's request that they be discussed in executive session. Soon the comptroller general of the United States and the House Judiciary Committee also wanted to know about COINTELPRO.

The Petersen Committee submitted its report to Saxbe on May 21, 1974, and in October Saxbe told Kelley he had decided to release Petersen's report to the public. Kelley told Saxbe that full disclosure would permanently affect the ability of the FBI to do its job:

> *The most critical issue of all was not who knew and approved of COINTELPRO practices, but what harm a full public disclosure would do at this time. Full disclosure would doubtless affect the overall operations of the FBI. Not only would it undermine our credibility with the American people, but such disclosure might well result in an inability to develop and use informants. Speaking of informants, a number of good, innocent citizens who had been associated with COINTELPROs in the past would now suffer undue hardships—if their involvement were to become public knowledge.*

Kelley knew the release of the COINTELPRO documents would be a disaster for the Bureau, and he realized, "I was in a tight spot." In an effort to minimize the damage, he told the press that "the FBI's intent was to prevent dangerous acts against individuals, organizations, and institutions, public and private, across the United States. FBI employees in these programs had acted in good faith and within the bounds of what was expected of them by the president, the attorney general, Congress, and, I believe, the majority of the American people." He pointed out that the U.S. Capitol had been bombed, as well as other locations across the country; there had been riots that had nearly destroyed entire American cities; and the country had been terrorized by killings, kidnappings, and assassinations. Kelley, for the sake of morale, had to defend COINTELPRO and his agents, but the Bureau's rapidly swelling legions of critics seized on Kelley's remarks as proof that the Bureau was unashamedly unreformable and could never be trusted if it could not admit that something obviously as bad as COINTELPRO was wrong.

The worst of the COINTELPROs *were* simply indefensible, no matter how hard Kelley tried to excuse them, but he did have a point. COINTELPRO *was* a dangerous abuse of something that was one of the FBI's most serious responsibilities—gathering domestic intelligence about potentially violent groups, a duty the Bureau had to protect the nation from terrorist attacks. But as COINTELPRO was dissected in gory and painful detail, it would be hard to keep the public's condemnation of COINTELPRO from extending to a general condemnation—even a general prohibition—of all domestic intelligence gathering, no matter how dangerous the group under investigation might be. Within a few years the Bureau would in fact be criticized for intelligence investigations even of very violent extremist organizations—the Weather Underground, for one. L. Patrick Gray, along with Mark Felt and Deputy Associate Director Edward Miller, were all indicted for authorizing illegal break-ins of the homes of relatives of the Weather Underground. Felt and Miller were convicted but later pardoned by President Reagan. Charges against Gray were dropped. As an inevitable consequence, the Bureau would begin to shy away from all domestic intelligence work, and individual agents would avoid such assignments like the plague. Not a few analysts who have seen a "risk-aversive" culture as the cause of the Bureau's 9/11 failures have traced that aversion to the Watergate-era investigations of the Bureau that used the undeniable abuses of COINTELPRO to attack any and all investigations of groups that had not yet committed any crime, and to declare that such investigations were themselves crimes, for which the FBI had to be punished, individually and collectively.

On November 18, 1974, Saxbe released a heavily edited version of the Petersen report, along with what was intended to be his own defense of the Bureau. During the period 1965–1971, he said, there had been 3,247 COINTELPROs proposed, 2,370 of which were implemented. In only 1 percent, Saxbe claimed, could it be "even argued" that the FBI had acted "improperly or illegally." But in a statement that would seem like treason to FBI personnel, he affirmed that those 1 percent "must be considered to be abhorrent in a free society such as ours."

Kelley vowed to Congress that COINTELPRO would never be repeated. He challenged Congress to provide the Bureau with a charter to define and authorize its domestic intelligence-gathering operations. He would have to return again and again as still more counterintelligence programs turned up—each one hopefully described as absolutely the last that would surface.

Hoover had always warned that the FBI had been created by the efforts of thousands, while the reckless act of one man could destroy it. As in the Sibylline oracles of old, that man had turned out to be himself.

• • •

In Kelley's recollections of events, Saxbe's release of the Petersen report led directly to the creation of the Senate select committee on intelligence activities in January 1975 that would demolish what was left of the public's respect for the Bureau. Kelley's memory was not accurate on this point, since the committee was actually formed to investigate misdeeds by the CIA. But the most sensational findings and reports of that Senate committee dealt with COINTELPRO and attached a devastating significance to FBI abuses that were, in the Petersen report, treated as essentially aberrations in the otherwise laudable history of the Bureau.

What was permanently devastating to the Bureau, however, was not the Senate's revelation (once again) of COINTELPRO, bad though that was, but the manner in which the congressional investigators made COINTELPRO into the central exhibit in a brief that purported to prove that the Bureau was, in effect, a permanent conspiracy against dissent in the United States. This was not so much a conclusion as an assumption, but with the existence of that conspiracy as a working hypothesis, every individual abuse, whether titanic or trivial, whether actual or aborted, took on dire significance as further proof that the FBI had been from the start at war with civil liberty. Each was another nail in the Bureau's coffin. Without the confidence of the American people, which these investigations were destroying, the Bureau would soon find itself unable to solve important cases because of pervasive suspicions throughout the country about its motives.

To make matters worse, the congressional investigations of the FBI proceeded in an atmosphere made electric by the media's obsessive fascination with the fact of *secrecy* itself. In the wake of Watergate, the very existence of a government secret now became evidence of the impulse to conspire against the public. The fact that the Bureau had any secrets at all was enough to convince many that the Bureau itself constituted a conspiracy against the rights of Americans.

The Senate Select Committee to Study Government Operations with Respect to Intelligence Activities was created in January 1975, chaired by Frank Church of Idaho. The House followed suit with a committee led by Lucien Nedzi of Michigan, soon replaced by Otis Pike of New York. Their hearings became a feast for conspiracy theorists. Sessions on the Huston Plan, for instance, hardly thought it worth mentioning that the plan had never been adopted. Nor did the hearings deign to consider whether there might not have been a need for some kind of unification of the intelligence-gathering agencies. Today, in fact, the country is still searching for a way to accomplish the same unification of domestic security agencies that Nixon, for admittedly nefarious purposes, had attempted with the Huston Plan.

The Church Committee staff's *Final Report* completed the destruction of the Bureau's reputation by turning its once glorious history into a plot against the republic. The *Final Report* contained a detailed staff study of COINTEL-PRO, subtitled "The FBI's Covert Action Programs Against American Citizens." It had a devastating and detailed account of the Bureau's harassment of Dr. Martin Luther King Jr., and its campaign against the Black Panther Party. There were also condemnatory studies of the Bureau's use of informants in domestic intelligence investigations, "black bag" break-ins and microphone surveillance, mail-opening programs, and, finally, a report on the Huston Plan. To put this all in historical context, the report included a devastating narrative of FBI domestic intelligence investigations from the Bureau's earliest years that raised doubts about whether the FBI ever had legal authority to do *anything* except investigate federal crimes.

As the staff laid out the sorry chronological record of FBI abuses of civil liberties, it felt free, perhaps even obliged, to offer an interpretation of why the Bureau had strayed. The FBI's transgressions simply did not make sense to the staff without what it described as an "unexpressed major premise." According to the staff, "The unexpressed major premise of the programs was that a law enforcement agency has the duty to do whatever is necessary to combat perceived threats to the existing social and political order." And again, "The unexpressed major premise of much of COINTELPRO is that the Bureau has a role in maintaining the existing social order, and that its efforts should be aimed toward combating those who threaten that order."

The "unexpressed major premise" theory raised the prosaic record of FBI abuses to the level of epic evil, turning FBI history into a conscious campaign against civil liberty in America. A charge so serious should have been supported by documentary evidence that the FBI had actually and consciously acted in pursuit of such a goal. Such evidence did not exist, although by the peculiar logic of the conspiracy theorist, its very absence suggested the conspiracy's skill at hiding its hand. The Senate staff's "unexpressed major premise" here seems to have been one it carried with it into the hearing rooms.

But the day was past when the FBI was going to get fair treatment from Congress, the media, or the public, whatever the merits of its case. And so the

Senate staff felt free to argue, without much fear of rebuttal, that the historical record supported charges that had been leveled against the Bureau since (at the latest) 1919: "The Bureau's self-imposed role as protector of the existing political and social order blurred the line between targeting criminal activity and constitutionally protected acts and advocacy."

The most dramatic testimony came from former assistant director William C. Sullivan, who seemed to be trying to redeem himself through a ritual of self-flagellation. He told the senators that in Hoover's FBI, domestic intelligence was "a rough, tough dirty business, and dangerous. It was dangerous at times. No holds were barred. . . . We have used [these techniques] against Soviet agents. They have used [them] against us. . . . [The same methods were] brought home against any organizations against which we were targeted. We did not differentiate."

Borrowing a phrase from a published excerpt of the COINTELPRO papers (*COINTELPRO: The FBI's Secret War on Political Freedom*), the staff concluded that the Bureau had been waging "a secret war against those citizens it considers threats to the established order." It demanded a "combination of legislative prohibition and Departmental control" to "guarantee that COINTELPRO will not happen again."

The Church Committee undercut its thesis of an FBI war against civil liberties when it conceded that the Bureau was forced to adapt to changing times without any guidance from above, while its political superiors were demanding information and action:

> *The policy assumptions behind FBI domestic intelligence were established in the 1930s and 1940s and became unquestioned dogma as the years went by. In the 1960s, new and unexpected events occurred which did not fit these established concepts. There was no longer a consensus among Americans as to the nature of government's proper response to homegrown dissidents who might engage in violence as a form of political protest, to racist groups using force to deprive others of their civil rights, to civil disorders growing out of minority frustrations, or to large-scale protest demonstrations. Presidents and Attorneys General turned to the FBI for intelligence about these matters without adequate controls.*

That led to an alternative conclusion that, rather than the "unexpressed major premise" of a war against civil liberty, the Bureau's record was one of "confusion and mistakes" and of chaotic social conditions that had "called into question some of the fundamental assumptions underlying the FBI intelligence programs of the previous three decades." That is, the Bureau was confused by events and did not really know what it was doing. That is pretty close to what an FBI official said in explanation of COINTELPRO, that something like it was almost inevitable, given the apparent collapse of social order in the late sixties and early seventies and an FBI that was used to taking charge in times of crisis: "The FBI's counterintelligence program came up because . . . if you have anything in the FBI you have an action-oriented group of people who see something happening and want to do something."

The committee used COINTELPRO to support a sweeping condemnation of *all* domestic intelligence investigations, advancing something like a Heisenberg uncertainty principle of intelligence gathering, that merely observing something has an impact on what is being observed: "The ordinary means of collecting information inevitably has an adverse impact on the rights of individuals." With that as another "unexpressed major premise," FBI critics could claim the Bureau was doing something wrong whenever it put itself in a position to know anything about anybody.

The legislative goal of the Church Committee was a charter for the FBI that would strictly limit its intelligence operations. That never happened, perhaps because the FBI's opponents preferred to keep FBI abuses as a political issue rather than do anything about them. There were, however, two important consequences for the Bureau directly traceable to the 1975–1976 congressional investigations. Congress established oversight committees for intelligence (the Senate in 1976, the House in 1977) to supervise the FBI (and the CIA). Then it passed the Foreign Intelligence Surveillance Act in 1978, which created a mechanism for providing the Bureau with judicial warrants for gathering intelligence on groups affiliated with foreign governments, but which assumed that strictly domestic terrorism should be handled in an *ex post facto* fashion, investigating crimes after they occurred rather than preventing them.

In an effort at damage control, Kelley tried to claim that the final report of the Church Committee had brought the COINTELPRO controversy to a satisfactory conclusion, and that on balance it was "overwhelmingly inconclusive." Trying to shore up the FBI's shattered morale, he offered a not entirely unpersuasive defense of COINTELPRO, which, he said, raised "an interesting philosophical question: Can we conduct an effective counter subversive effort in our country without endangering our constitutional liberties in the process?" He said that the Bureau's record, examined fairly, showed we could. "The preponderance of historical evidence and the ultimate results suggest that, by and large, what the Bureau did was right for the time and, without question, in the best interests of the United States. Constitutional liberties were not trampled.

Though abuse may have existed, I believe it was minimal. And though minimal, it was not illegal in any instance." (In fact, a Justice Department investigation had determined that no prosecutable charges should be brought against the Bureau or its agents.) There may have been something to Kelley's argument, but it was too late. The public had already reached its own verdict on the FBI and COINTELPRO: guilty.

After 1975 the image in American popular culture of the FBI (and the CIA as well) would be of a secret government at war with American democracy, assassinating national and world leaders, blackmailing enemies in pursuit of malign bureaucratic power or an equally evil agenda of world domination.

■ ■ ■

The Justice Department had to respond to demands that the FBI be subjected to some kind of house arrest after the Church Committee report, and so, on March 10, 1976, Attorney General Edward Levi established rules for FBI noncriminal domestic investigations. According to what would be known as the "Levi Guidelines," the FBI could launch "preliminary investigations" when it had "allegations or other information that an individual or group may be engaged in activities which involve or will involve the violation of federal law." Preliminary investigations could last only ninety days and were restricted to determining whether the allegations had a basis in fact; investigative techniques were severely restricted, limited to reviews of the files and public records and interviews. To continue the surveillance, the FBI needed approval for a "full investigation" that required "specific and articulable facts giving reason to believe that an individual or group is or may be engaged in activities which involve or will involve the use of force or violence and which involve or will involve the violation of federal law." Such investigations required approval from the Justice Department and had to be reviewed after 180 days, and at least once a year the Justice Department had to "determine in writing whether continued investigation is warranted." Full investigations could use informants, wiretaps, and mail covers.

Kelley reorganized the Bureau's investigative divisions in response to the Church Committee's investigations. He transferred responsibility for domestic radical and terrorist groups from the Intelligence Division (Division Five) to the General Investigative Division (Division Six) because the latter "operated under more restrictive guidelines." The result was a reduction of domestic intelligence investigations from twenty-two thousand to four thousand. Internal subversion was also shifted to Division Six, "including attempts to overthrow the United States government." Kelley explained that the "express purpose of this was so that such cases would "be managed like all other criminal cases in that division," since Division Six investigated only actual violations rather than "spying" on persons "merely suspected of planning to break the law." The Intelligence Division would retain responsibility only for espionage and terrorist cases involving foreign governments or groups.

Buck Revell later explained that the abolition of the Intelligence Division's Domestic Security Section and transfer of its functions to the Terrorism Section of Division Six "was intended to neutralize the effect of the political actions and beliefs of a group, so that the political motive of a particular crime became irrelevant in the new criteria that determined whether an investigation was warranted. All that mattered now was whether a crime had been committed, or whether there was evidence of a continuing conspiracy to commit crimes."

A quarter of a century later, the congressional inquiry into the 9/11 attacks found that FBI agents and officials traced the Bureau's risk-aversive culture, so evident in its timid surveillance of potential Islamic terrorists in this country, back to the the Church Committee hearings. Buck Revell also thought that the "reforms" enacted in the wake of the Church Committee had contributed to the Bureau's failure to stop 9/11. The rules laid down then, he said, "require the FBI to have their eyes closed and their ears plugged up and look the other way" unless they had evidence that a crime "has been or is about to be committed."

As the FBI's reputation collapsed under the relentless exposure of Hoover's secrets, so did its heroic image in popular culture. When I began writing about the FBI years ago, J. Edgar Hoover's *Masters of Deceit* was what got me started. I found it fascinating that this legendary lawman had put together a book that used references to "Dracula" and "Frankenstein" to describe "masters of deceit," that is, foreign and American communists. My first book looked at how the FBI had dug itself so deeply into American popular culture, and how popular culture's image of the G-man had, in turn, shaped the Bureau's own image of itself and what it should be doing. The G-man hero that had emerged from the thirties—James Cagney chasing the Dillinger gang—enlarged and glamorized even more by the Bureau's exploits during World War II and the Cold War, had fueled the Bureau's public image for decades.

Then it all came crashing down.

On December 22, 1975, just as the Church Committee finished its hearings, *Time* magazine ran a cover story, "The Truth About Hoover." *Time*'s story marked the replacement of one mythic "truth"—the infallible and omniscient director who had, basically, saved the nation single-handedly from gangsters, Nazi spies, communism, and God knows what else, substituting for it another mythic "truth," Hoover the master blackmailer with a file on everybody, capable of every evil. *Time*'s story announced that "the legend is crumbling. There had always been a few blemishes ... but now, under congressional and journalistic scrutiny ... a darker picture is coming into view." That "picture": a Hoover who was a racist, a martinet, a tyrant, and had "trampled on the rights of citizens;" that COINTELPRO was a campaign to repress citizens who were simply trying "to express grievances against their government." *Time* was offering its readers as the "truth" an image of the FBI that had long been the intellectual and emotional sustenance of the American left, one familiar to longtime readers of *The Nation* and the exposés of Fred J. Cook and ex-agent William Turner: that it was a secret conspiracy against truth, justice, and of course the American way. The truth about the FBI was no longer its celebrated cases, but rather its failures and abuses of power. To prove it, *Time* went down the list of the Bureau's most famous gangster and espionage cases, jeering at each one as overblown or unproven. And just two year earlier, when Hoover died, *Time* had eulogized him as "one of the greats."

Popular opinion was moving in the same direction. Television's *The FBI* had been broadcasting the adventures of Inspector Erskine (Efrem Zimbalist Jr.) since 1965, and its moralizing, squeaky clean, nonviolent, open and aboveboard FBI was no longer what the public wanted. The show went off the air in September 1977.

After Watergate, the public looked to the press, not the FBI, for the truth about things that mattered. After Hoover's death, the public that had once swallowed anything Hoover's publicists cooked up would now just as readily believe any new revelations that fit the now regnant stereotype of the FBI as an American Gestapo bent on exterminating constitutional liberties.

The FBI's fall reflected a more general collapse in Americans' trust in their government. The decline of the Bureau's reputation was not only a symbol of that collapse, it was one useful, even essential, to anyone whose political beliefs or aspirations rested on a general distrust of government, who now had an insatiable appetite for bad news about the FBI. Just as Hoover's FBI kept attacking his enemies long after he was dead and they had forgotten why they were supposed to hate, for example, Melvin Purvis, FBI "critics" now kept pursuing the Bureau long after Hoover's original sins had faded into the fog of popular forgetfulness. Attacking the FBI now just seemed a good thing to do, whatever the occasion.

To see the crisis that broke the bond between the public and the Bureau as a cultural revolution is only to follow the lead of the major actors on both sides of the struggles of the Nixon era, all of whom interpreted the clash in cultural terms, as a test of strength between contrasting systems of values and outlooks. One mind-set saw the Cold War as a struggle between an aggressive Soviet Union and a United States defending the nations of the free world against it. The far left, on the other hand, had always seen the Cold War as an American-led conspiracy against the legitimate aspirations of oppressed people throughout the world, and believed that it was the United States that was aggressive and expansive. Hoover and the FBI, as primary supporters of the orthodox interpretation of the domestic Cold War, were bound to suffer the consequences when that orthodox view was discarded, as it was by many after Vietnam and Watergate.

And even liberals who were not willing to throw out the basic tenets of anti-communism and anti-Stalinism as the price of rejecting the war and Nixon had long agreed with the far left on one thing at least, that J. Edgar Hoover and Richard Nixon were largely responsible for everything liberals loathed as Mc-Carthyism writ large. And so while the far left and the liberal left disagreed on so much else in their analysis of why we were in Vietnam, they all could agree on one thing, and that was that J. Edgar Hoover and the FBI were no good no matter how you looked at them.

In *Breach of Faith,* his analysis of Watergate, Theodore H. White wrote that "all great political conflicts everywhere are underlain by a struggle of culture, as men begin to see their places in the world differently, as their 'consciousness' is 'raised' to new perceptions and indignations." J. Edgar Hoover and the G-men were heroes of that old order, they were legends, and so if one mythology was being replaced by another, that revolution could be signaled by toppling the G-man legend. And so it was toppled. And Hoover's fall, like Nixon's, seemed to prove that the counterculture's alienated analysis of American politics had been right all along. Nixon's resignation and the demonization of the FBI suddenly made the counterculture's worldview respectable and, even more important for opinion- and taste-makers, stylish. So ever since 1975 nearly all portrayals of the FBI in the media, whether documentary or fictional, tapped into a quasi-paranoid suspicion of government that had once been confined to the counterculture or the political fringes, but now was thoroughly mainstream.

■ ■ ■

A year after Hoover's death the FBI found itself being forced to play its new role of cultural villain in a drama staged on a remote Indian reservation called Pine Ridge on the High Plains of South Dakota. The FBI's involvement in Pine Ridge and other Indian reservations goes back to an 1875 law, the Seven Major

Crimes Act, which made murder, manslaughter, rape, assault, arson, burglary, and larceny on Indian reservations federal offenses. In fact, until the New Deal expansion of the FBI's jurisdiction, crimes on Indian reservations were almost the only crimes against persons or property specifically assigned to the FBI. That was an historical anomaly that thrust it into situations where it was resented by a local Indian population that nevertheless depended on it to preserve law and order when the local tribal authorities proved unwilling or incompetent to control crimes committed by reservation Indians.

FBI agents had been active on Indian reservations from the Bureau's earliest days. One of J. Edgar Hoover's favorite cases, one that he regularly dangled before tame journalists looking for colorful FBI adventures, was the Osage Indian case of 1923, in which a wealthy Fairfax, Oklahoma, banker named William K. Hale had begun murdering the richest of the oil-rich Indians one by one, funneling their estates toward the Indian wife of Hale's nephew. The Osage Indian Council appealed to the Justice Department to end the reign of terror, and a team of Bureau agents was dispatched to Oklahoma. The case appealed to Hoover, and to the producers of the Jimmy Stewart film *The FBI Story*, because the Bureau's informants, actually local detectives, operated undercover. There was a cattle buyer, an insurance salesman, an oil prospector, and an Indian herb doctor. Hoover liked to show off the letter the tribe sent to Washington after the case was closed: "sincere gratitude for the splendid work done in the matter of the investigating and bringing to justice the parties charged with the murders of . . . members of the Osage Tribe of Indians."

The events that drew the FBI to its tragedy on Pine Ridge can be traced back to 1890, when about 350 Sioux—120 men and 230 women and children—under Chief Big Foot gathered on December 28 to surrender their weapons to the Seventh Cavalry, George Armstrong Custer's old outfit. They were assembled at Wounded Knee, South Dakota, on the southern edge of the Pine Ridge Sioux Reservation. As the soldiers attempted to search the Indians' robes for weapons, an Indian pulled out a rifle from beneath his blanket and fired, and within moments both sides were blazing away at point-blank range. Artillery pieces poured explosive shells into the tepees, and the Indians began to flee, pursued by the cavalry. Thirty-one soldiers were killed, along with around 300 Indian victims.

So the Pine Ridge Reservation, the second largest in area in the country, with fifteen thousand residents, could not have been better chosen by a malign providence for a confrontation between a radicalized Indian movement and an FBI that events were typecasting as the symbol of repressive government.

In 1972, the Pine Ridge tribal government was in the hands of a thirty-eight-year-old mixed-breed plumber named Dick Wilson. As was often the case on the reservations, the political lines were drawn between the traditionalists, who resisted assimilation, and the "progressives," who embraced the values of American society. Generally speaking, the traditionalists were predominantly full-blooded Indians, the progressives of mixed blood. In this context, Dick Wilson, who wore denim pants and work shirts and sported a crew cut, was a progressive, though to the outside world his flag-waving, American Legion–style patriotism, his support from the John Birch Society, and his penchant for Red-smearing the opposition as communists rendered the label of progressive something of a contradiction.

Coming to the aid of the traditionalist Indians who opposed Wilson were members, and soon the national leadership, of a radical Indian rights group called the American Indian Movement (AIM). AIM was founded in Minneapolis in July 1968, with Dennis Banks and Clyde Bellecourt, both reservation-raised Minnesota Chippewas, among its organizers. AIM attracted its first members from Indian ghettos in cities like Minneapolis, San Francisco, and Denver. Russell Means, an Oglala Sioux from Porcupine, South Dakota, headed the second AIM chapter in Cleveland. Means had a genius for publicity. He had dreamed up the Thanksgiving Day 1970 capture of the *Mayflower II,* helped take over Mount Rushmore in June 1971, and grabbed headlines with a lawsuit against baseball's Cleveland Indians for their emblem of Chief Wahoo.

On Tuesday evening, February 27, 1973, a thirteen-car caravan of Indians left Calico Hall in the town of Pine Ridge and passed by the heavily fortified Bureau of Indian Affairs (BIA) headquarters, followed by BIA police, FBI special agents, and U.S. deputy marshals. At about eight in the evening the Indians, followed by the FBI, BIA, and marshals, arrived at the little village of Wounded Knee—a Catholic church, an Episcopal church, a trading post, museum, and post office, along with a few residences. The FBI agents and marshals heard the sounds of shotgun fire from somewhere within the village. Special Agent in Charge (Minneapolis) Joseph Trimbach decided to establish roadblocks on the four roads leading into it. And so began a siege that would last until May 8, and would be (to that date) the longest standoff in FBI history.

The Indians' takeover of Wounded Knee started the same day as the beleaguered L. Patrick Gray's confirmation hearings in the Senate. Still hoping to be confirmed, he desperately hoped to avoid a bloodbath or anything close to it, and the Indians knew it, which strengthened their bargaining position. And his increasingly precarious grip on his office, which came to a pathetic conclusion when he admitted destroying some of the "White House horror files," did nothing for the morale of his men on the front lines in Wounded Knee.

Moreover, President Nixon, who would have to make the ultimate policy decisions, was busy covering up his involvement in Watergate, and delegated authority to an aide, Ken Cole. On the scene, Special Assistant to the Attorney General Ralph Erickson set up a chain of command over the Bureau, the marshals, and the BIA, but the situation tended to be dominated by Wayne Colburn, head of the U.S. Marshals Service, who favored aggressive use of firepower and, although commanding an organization with less direct responsibility than the FBI, personally outranked the FBI officials on the scene.

Maintaining the siege were 116 FBI agents and 100 marshals. Special Agents in Charge (SACs) from Milwaukee and Oklahoma City were sent to back up the relatively inexperienced Trimbach. Another complication was Dick Wilson, who was eager to unleash his tribal police on the AIM occupiers. He claimed he had eight hundred men armed and ready to go, perhaps an exaggeration, but the AIM takeover was certainly opposed by large numbers of the reservation Indians.

On March 11, FBI Special Agent Curtis Fitzgerald was shot in the hand by fire from a passing van. Trimbach and the other SACs demanded that the Army be called to put down the insurrection. At this point Gray relieved Trimbach and sent him back to Minneapolis. Attorney General Richard Kleindienst ordered the FBI to back off: "The FBI should cut back on its efforts to obtain evidence; ease off investigative efforts substantially, even to the point of not making efforts at this time to obtain evidence as we have in the past, and the FBI should concentrate on intelligence work." The Justice Department was quite unhappy with the performance of Trimbach and the Bureau: "It stemmed from Trimbach's perception of his role as an enforcer of the law rather than a referee of political issues." Headquarters now realized, too late, that the Bureau faced a massive public relations problem at Wounded Knee, something Trimbach and others on the scene did not seem to fully comprehend. Trimbach was replaced by the legendary Ray Moore, who immediately pulled the Bureau out of any further negotiations or press relations, explaining that to continue either might hamper the Bureau at subsequent trials.

Washington rejected Moore's appeal for a military solution to the impasse, and for the next month the standoff continued as agreements were hammered out and rejected, the federal blockade tightened and loosened, while the AIM occupiers attracted more and more support, national and international, particularly from church groups and the left. Dozens of radical groups pledged support for the Indians, while the *Berkeley Barb* predicted that Wounded Knee would take the place of the Vietnam War as a source of unity for the left.

At the end of March, Associate Director Mark Felt urged Gray to pull all FBI agents from Wounded Knee since the situation "has deteriorated beyond our control."

The standoff finally ended when, according to terms negotiated in Washington, the Indians were allowed to leave the demolished village on May 8, 1973, with no retribution except the arrest of those with outstanding warrants, leaving the Bureau licking its wounds. The Wounded Knee cemetery gained another grave, adorned with ribbons like those from the 1890 battle. It holds the body of Buddy Lamont, the lone AIM casualty of the standoff, marked with the inscription, "2500 came in '73, 1 remains."

The FBI tried afterward to learn a lesson from Wounded Knee. Overall, the official FBI review questioned Trimbach's initial decision to establish what would soon harden into a siege. The Indians later reported that they had, somewhat naively perhaps, assumed that they would confront the owners of the trading post and museum, with whom they had some grudges, make their point, and leave. It might have been better, despite the sounds of gunfire, to back off and investigate later under conditions more favorable to the Bureau.

The FBI review focused on two problem areas. The first was the lack of unified authority. The Bureau complained that officials such as the head of the marshal service and the senior Justice official on the scene "would fly back to Washington, D.C., presumably for conferences and would return with a new policy of which FBIHQ was not aware. The military did not realize in many cases that they were there to assist and not direct the FBI." The report quoted SAC Richard G. Held of Chicago that for the FBI "to have any success at Wounded Knee it would be necessary to withdraw the 'political types' and make it an FBI operation under FBI direction and leadership." He went on to say that it was the "constant vacillation of instructions and policy which was devastating." All the SACs "recommended should we in the future become involved in another situation similar to Wounded Knee where Special Agent personnel are deployed that the entire operation be under the direction of FBI officials and when law enforcement personnel from other agencies are involved it should be clearly understood the FBI is in the decision making role." And it was "the consensus of opinion among the headquarters supervisors that no Government official who is not a trained law enforcement officer be permitted to direct a law enforcement operation the magnitude of Wounded Knee."

The report urged Kelley to meet with the attorney general and tell him that in future confrontations the FBI would *insist upon taking charge from the outset and will not countenance any inter-ference on an operational basis with respect to our actions. They should under-stand the FBI due to its long years of experience and training is able to make law enforcement decisions without over-reacting to protect the general public, its Special Agent personnel, and the violators of the law. The AG [Attorney General] and DAG [Deputy Attorney General] should be advised it is our broad policy in such instances as this to "get in and get out as quickly as possi-ble" with complete regard for the safety of all concerned. The FBI furthermore would seize control quickly and take a definite, aggressive stand where neces-sary. It should be clearly stated that the FBI does not desire to become involved in any political situations and definitely not participate in any discussions where it is obviously political in nature.*

The FBI's analysis of what went wrong at Wounded Knee was wildly off the mark. Perhaps Kelley sensed that his executives had missed the point, since he declined to pass their recommendations to the attorney general.

At Wounded Knee the Bureau found itself at the center of a situation that was nothing if not political. The takeover of the little community was a politi-cal act, performed for political purposes, and it succeeded beyond the wildest dreams of the participants, who initially thought they would take over the post, issue a statement, and then drift away.

Yet in its analysis the Bureau went into a brain lock, falling back on Hoover's old scapegoat, "political interference." If only the politicians had left the Bureau alone, FBI thinking went, the Bureau could have resolved the standoff just as it had solved its great cases in the thirties, presumably with some machine-gun justice.

But the real reason the standoff turned out so badly for the Bureau was not too much, but too little, political interference. If a political confrontation like Wounded Knee was going to be resolved in any way satisfactory to the government (but under the circumstances, there probably was no possible satisfactory resolution), it was going to be through direct involvement of the political leaders who could make decisions about the activists' demands: the president, the attorney general, and the secretary of the interior. And in fact the standoff was finally settled through the direct intervention of top-level politicians like Senator George McGovern, Secretary of the Interior Rogers B. Morton, Morton's Assistant Secretary for Indian Affairs Marvin Franklin, and the government's lead negotiator, Assistant U.S. Attorney General Kent Frizzell.

With the country in turmoil over Watergate and the ultimate decisions being made by a discredited president and FBI director, there was no way the government could have seized the moral high ground in this confrontation, even though the AIM activists were breaking more laws by the hour. It was, in the final analysis, a lose-lose situation for the government and the Bureau. Nevertheless, the takeover became totally unwinnable for the government the minute Trimbach and the Bureau decided to treat it strictly as a law enforcement situation, to be handled according to the standard FBI procedures of isolate, contain, then negotiate, in preparation for an assault if necessary. The interference from Washington that so rankled the FBI supervisors was probably all that kept the Bureau from escalating the siege into a massacre, particularly after Special Agent Fitzgerald was wounded.

The lesson for the Bureau *should* have been that whenever the politics of a case completely overwhelms its law enforcement aspects, as at Wounded Knee, the Bureau must insist on strategic and even tactical direction from their political superiors. Trying to transform a political into a criminal situation is, was, and always will be a recipe for disaster. Agree with him or not, Hoover had always realized this, and when faced with a political confrontation, he confronted it politically himself. He would attack the Rosenbergs not for their crime (espionage), but for their motives (communism).

The Bureau not only failed to learn anything from the debacle at Wounded Knee, it spent the next two years trying, by sheer force of numbers, to rewrite the occupation retroactively into a simple matter of law enforcement, to be solved through more and more law enforcement.

After the takeover, law and order broke down completely on Pine Ridge. Dick Wilson's Guardians of the Oglala Nation militia (pejoratively referred to by their initials, GOONS) and their traditionalist enemies were killing each other day and night; AIM went on a murderous hunt for FBI informants in its ranks; there was an epidemic of arson (nothing from before the takeover still stands at Wounded Knee today, and throughout the reservation almost all its historic buildings have been burned down or are at risk of being torched). And there are still the pervasive unemployment, alcoholism, and despair that long preceded the troubles of the seventies and are, if anything, worse today.

In the aftermath of Wounded Knee, AIM's leaders and members were fleeing federal warrants for their role in the takeover and other crimes. Many of them went to ground on the reservation. The FBI responded by flooding Pine Ridge with agents, a response that would lead, in June 1975, to one of the great tragedies in Bureau history.

■ ■ ■

A few miles southeast of the South Dakota town of Oglala, on the way to Wounded Knee on the Pine Ridge Indian Reservation, a dirt road turns off to the west. It runs a few hundred yards past a compound of small wooden buildings owned by a Lakota Sioux school principal named Calvin Jumping Bull, and then slopes down to a grassy pasture. Nothing marks that patch of grass, weeds, and thorns as anything out of the ordinary.

To the south and west of the pasture are dense woods, while above the pasture, on top of a low hill, a small house overlooks it. Near the top of the hill, between the house and the pasture, are several overgrown depressions, abandoned foundations and root cellars. A car in the pasture, should it come under attack, would be totally exposed to gunfire from the house and the buildings that once stood on the foundations, not more than five hundred feet away. Anyone behind the car could come under fire from at least one of the strong points on the hill. An attempt to gain the cover of the woods would mean crossing a dozen yards of open field, in the crossfire, before reaching the trees.

Just a few minutes before noon on June 26, 1975, two FBI special agents, Jack Coler, in a white and tan 1972 Chevrolet Biscayne, and Ron Williams, in a 1972 green Rambler, were brought to a halt in that pasture by heavy gunfire from Indians on the ridge above them and in the underbrush below. Coler and Williams carried only their service revolvers and a shotgun. A .308-caliber rifle was locked in the Biscayne's trunk, per Bureau regulations. They were pinned down by crossfire from semiautomatic rifles and an AR-15 assault weapon, as well as an assortment of high-powered hunting rifles.

Williams was hit almost immediately. Coler managed to open the trunk and retrieve the rifle, but as he got off his first shot, a bullet went through the trunk lid and ripped into his arm, almost taking it off. Williams managed to reach Coler to try to apply a makeshift tourniquet torn from his shirt. He then tried to signal to the attackers that they were giving up. They had gotten off five shots. Their cars had taken 125 hits.

As they crouched behind the car, probably shouting that they had surrendered, a gunman with an AR-15, perhaps accompanied by one or two others, approached. Williams suddenly realized what was about to happen, and raised his hand to push away the muzzle of the AR-15 just as it was fired. The bullet ripped off three of his fingers and smashed into his face, killing him. Coler was probably unconscious when the gunman dispatched him with shots to the head and throat. Then the gunman, or one of his accomplices, stripped the two dead agents of their weapons and took Coler's green FBI field jacket.

Coler and Williams were two of the many agents detailed around Pine Ridge after Wounded Knee, and were looking for a Pine Ridge Indian named

Jimmy Eagle, who was being sought for robbing two local white residents. The agents had gotten a tip that Jimmy Eagle's Jeep might have been spotted on the Jumping Bull compound. It turned out that the vehicle was not Jimmy Eagle's. It belonged to Leonard Peltier, who would become the prime suspect in their murders. According to a statement made by Peltier when he was eventually arrested in Canada, he had assumed that the FBI agents at Jumping Bull were looking for him, since there was a warrant out for him involving an assault on a policeman in Milwaukee.

I was once in FBI headquarters when word arrived that an agent had come under fire. In a moment an electric shock ran through the Bureau—agents, secretaries, clerks, all with their attention riveted on the danger one of their own was facing. When an agent is killed a wave of emotion sweeps across the entire FBI, and, until the case is solved, it is an obsession. Once the bullet-torn bodies of Williams and Coler were discovered, what became known as RESMURS, the reservation murders, became the Bureau's highest priority. There were soon some two hundred agents working the case. They were in a mood described as vengeful, while Calvin Jumping Bull was quoted by author Peter Matthiessen as saying that the Bureau of Indian Affairs police and the FBI "had planned this all along, planned to raid the place [and] it backfired. I hate to say this, but I think that [Coler and Williams] deserve what they got." When I talked to Jumping Bull twenty-five years later, he had not changed his mind.

The Bureau collected overwhelming evidence that Peltier was one of Williams and Coler's killers and probably had pulled the trigger. The rearview mirror of the vehicle the agents had followed had one of Peltier's prints, which they identified from his booking in Milwaukee. A woman who lived at Jumping Bull, Angie Long Visitor, testified she knew the names of three of the Indians she saw shooting at the agents, and one of them was Peltier. Another prime suspect in the shooting, Bob Robideau, was caught on the Kansas Turnpike with the AR-15 murder weapon and Coler's rifle. The third, Dino Butler, was captured with Williams's pistol. After Peltier escaped from a shootout in Oregon, Coler's pistol was found in a paper bag bearing one of Peltier's thumbprints.

Before Peltier was captured and extradited from Canada, Butler and Robideau went on trial. Defended by William Kunstler, they were acquitted in a trial that Kunstler turned into a protest against the mistreatment of the Indians by the U.S. government.

When Peltier went on trial in March 1977 the judge refused to permit his lawyers to turn the jury's vote into a referendum on the plight of the Indians. The proceedings dealt with the deaths of the two agents, not the history of the conflict between America and its Indians. The government was able to present Angie Long Visitor and two other Indians who said they had seen Peltier approach the two wounded agents just before the killing. There was also testimony from a Canadian Mountie who said Peltier had remarked, when he was captured, "They were shot when they came to a house to serve a warrant on me." This time the jury found Peltier guilty of first-degree murder in both killings.

FBI agents everywhere were outraged that three men had walked down that slope to execute Coler and Williams, and only one had been convicted. The two others had escaped justice, agents thought, because the judge had let the case turn into a trial of the FBI for its role in the history of America's treatment of the Indians. The jury, finally, had to vote to acquit or else seem to approve of that entire history.

Worse was to come. In March 1983, Peter Matthiessen, one of the country's finest novelists, published *In the Spirit of Crazy Horse*, which charged, first, that the FBI had "ruthlessly" pursued Leonard Peltier in the RESMURS case as part of an ongoing conspiracy to destroy the American Indian Movement (AIM), and second, that the FBI had suborned perjury, manufactured evidence, and finally framed Leonard Peltier for a crime he did not commit.

The book is gracefully written and, to a reader swept up by Matthiessen's outrage at the history of American injustice toward the Indian, persuasive. Under less indulgent analysis, the book breaks down as detail after detail of Matthiessen's evidence turns out to be not quite what he says, and he shows a perhaps willful misunderstanding of the convincing ballistics evidence that linked Peltier to the murder scene. In a *New York Times* review of *Crazy Horse*, attorney Alan Dershowitz picked apart Matthiessen's arguments, writing that he was

> *utterly unconvincing—indeed embarrassingly sophomoric—when he pleads the legal innocence of individual Indian criminals. . . .*
>
> *Mr. Matthiessen not only fails to convince; he inadvertently makes a strong case for Mr. Peltier's guilt. Invoking the clichés of the radical left, Mr. Matthiessen takes at face value nearly every conspiratorial claim of the movement, no matter how unfounded or preposterous. Every car crash, every unexplained death, every unrelated arrest fits into the seamless web of deceit he seems to feel was woven by the F.B.I. and its cohorts.*

Nevertheless, the effect of Matthiessen's book was to help turn the Peltier case into an international cause. Even overseas there are groups in near-perpetual mobilization to denounce Peltier's imprisonment and to demand his release. Then in 1991, Matthiessen provided CBS's *60 Minutes* with an amazing interview with a "Mr. X" who claimed to have been the actual killer. Peltier claimed that he had known it had been Mr. X all along, but "we all took an oath that we would never betray anyone, so for me—or for anyone else—to expose him would have been an act of treason. I wouldn't even ask him to come forward now—and I hope he doesn't come forward—because they still wouldn't let me go, and it would just mean he'd go to prison too." The interview was taped by Oliver Stone, and Matthiessen used it as an epilogue to the reissue of his book in 1991. Unfortunately for Matthiessen, his surprise witness was exposed several years later by one of the two acquitted suspects. Dino Butler said that the entire Mr. X. story had been concocted at a California meeting of Peltier supporters, that they had concluded they would not use the Mr. X story, since it was a lie. Afterward the Mr. X story had nevertheless been passed on to Oliver Stone.

Inconvenient revelations like these or others, like the 2004 conviction of an AIM member for the death of another AIM supporter, a supposed FBI informant who said she had heard Leonard Peltier boast of killing the agents, have not discouraged those who insist that the real issue is the FBI's war against the Indians' just cause. That is the position of Peltier's sympathizers around the world, who regularly petition for his release. Amnesty International, Desmond Tutu, an archbishop of Canterbury, and more than fifty congressmen have called for his release. His name has been submitted to the Nobel Prize committee for the peace prize. In 1994, FBI Director Louis Freeh was forced to take a public stand against efforts to persuade President Clinton to commute Peltier's sentence. The fact that Clinton had even considered a pardon for a person convicted of murdering FBI agents indicated to many in the Bureau that their lives meant nothing at all to the country anymore, and that killing an FBI agent could be excused, even approved, by Bureau-hating politicians if they calculated it to be to their political advantage.

· · ·

On February 4, 1974, Patricia Campbell Hearst, a nineteen-year-old junior at the University of California, Berkeley, returned home after a full day of classes, turned off the burglar alarm system, and went to bed for a nap. Her fiancé, Steven Weed, got home at 6:30. They watched *Mission: Impossible* on TV, and then cleared the kitchen table for a few hours of study before bed. Just past nine o'clock the doorbell rang.

Steven Weed opened the front door. A young woman babbled a confused story of having been in an accident. She wanted to come in and use the phone. The next moment two men, one white and one black, rushed into the house and the girl produced a pistol. One of the men tied Patty's hands behind her back, blindfolded and gagged her. The other beat Steve into submission. Patty managed to spit out the gag and scream, but was knocked semiconscious with a blow from the stock of a carbine and rushed out of the house.

After they had bound and blindfolded her and put her in a padded closet with a radio playing loud soul music, her captors identified themselves. The leader said he was General Field Marshal Cin (for "Cinque Mtume") of the Symbionese Liberation Army (SLA). Patty recalled this was the group that had just murdered Marcus Foster, the first black superintendent of schools in Oakland. Patty had been "arrested," she was told, because she was the daughter of Randolph Hearst of the newspaper family, "a corporate enemy of the people."

For two months Patty was kept blindfolded in that closet. When she left for the toilet or a bath, she was watched. Her captors told her there were detachments of the SLA all over the country allied with other bands of militant radicals. Maybe it was true, she began to believe: "maybe all the radicals in the Bay Area or even throughout California had banded together in some wild scheme to take over the country." They tried to plant and nurture a fear of the FBI in Patty: The FBI, she was told, was engaged in a massive manhunt for her, and when they attacked, she would be the first to die. The FBI "always came in with guns blazing at revolutionaries." Cinque told her about radicals the FBI had killed, that "the FBI would just as soon kill me as them," and then would "blame the SLA for my death and further discredit revolutionaries throughout the country." If the FBI did not kill her when they assaulted the safe house, the SLA promised to put a bullet through her head.

Day after day Hearst was harangued. She was told that her father was a member of the "Committee of Forty," a "super-secret, high-level group of big businessmen, corporate executives and millionaires like the Rockefellers who were all part of the CIA and it was they and the CIA who told the President of the United States what to do. It was they who really ran the country." On the fifth day, General Field Marshal Cinque entered her closet and began to read a ransom message that she had to then repeat, sentence by sentence, into a tape recorder: that she was not being forced to make her statement, that she was being treated well, and that she was captured in retaliation for the capture of two SLA members who were in San Quentin Prison for the assassination of Foster. "I am here because I am a member of a ruling class family," she had to say. The tape was released with a demand that Patty's father distribute seventy dollars in food to every poor person in California.

As Patty grew physically weaker and emotionally traumatized, the intensity of the group's warnings about the FBI increased.

Not a day passed, I believe, without some mention of the possibility of an FBI raid. They never failed to explain that the FBI would want to kill me in order to discredit the SLA and all revolutionary movements. The SLA wanted me alive so it could negotiate for food for the poor people; but the FBI and the corporate-military dictatorship wanted me dead. It was a battle for the minds of the people and public opinion. If the FBI shot and killed me, they asked, how could the SLA ever convince anyone that it was the FBI and not the SLA who had killed me? Strange as that reasoning may seem now, I believed it at the time. I knew they believed it. When it came to fear of the FBI, there was a ring of truth in their voices. Every few days there was a full-scale combat drill in preparation for the anticipated arrival of the FBI.

I had lived in fear of the SLA for so long now that fear of the FBI came easily to me. I knew nothing about the organization, except for fictional accounts on television, and the SLA comrades were well versed on shoot-outs. They told me story after story of the FBI storming radical hideouts, shooting through doors, killing everyone inside, asking no questions. The FBI could kill with impunity. They had a license to kill. And they would shoot and kill in order to wipe out radical movements in the country. . . . Then I would surely die in the cross fire.

Cinque "was convinced that the FBI had super-listening devices by which they could tune in on this house from a car parked in the vicinity." When Randolph Hearst hired a psychic to provide clues on the SLA's whereabouts, they ordered Patty to empty her head of thoughts that might let the psychic guide the FBI to their hideout. She believed them "when they said that if the FBI, with all their vaunted expertise, traced the SLA to this hideout, there would be a gun battle, without surrender, until we were all dead. They talked about this imaginary shoot-out incessantly and my paranoia over the FBI finding us was beginning to match theirs."

In her next tape-recorded communiqué she read a script that blamed the FBI for the deadlock in negotiations: "I realize now that it's the FBI who wants to murder me. Only the FBI and certain people in the government stand to gain anything by my death." She also told her parents that she had now been issued a 12-gauge riot shotgun.

Finally Cinque told her that she had a choice, to join or be released and go home. Hearst immediately reasoned that it was a test, and that if she gave the wrong answer she would die. "I want to join you," she said. Cinque then gave her the task of "persuading" each of the other members of the SLA to let her join. She was summoned to a council meeting, still blindfolded, and asked a series of questions, ending, "Are you ready to renounce your past and become a guerrilla soldier in the Symbionese Liberation Army?" Yes, she replied, and Cinque announced that now, after fifty-seven days in the closet, she could take her blindfold off. "You are now a guerrilla fighter and a soldier in the Symbionese Liberation Army."

On April 4, the SLA released a communiqué that Patty was now Tania and had joined the SLA. Eleven days later, on April 15, the SLA, with Patty Hearst holding an M-1 carbine, robbed the Hibernia Bank in the Sunset section of San Francisco. She was supposed to station herself in front of the bank camera and recite a political speech she had rehearsed, but with her "comrades" rushing about waving weapons and screaming, all she could remember was "This is Tania . . . Patricia Hearst." It was enough.

It was a national sensation; not only that Hearst had seemingly renounced her family and joined the SLA, but that the FBI had been hunting them for two months and they could still pull off such a daring robbery.

The FBI was humiliated. A reporter asked Kelley, "Why is it in this particular kidnapping, the Hearst affair, the FBI seems to be so powerless?" The California attorney general scolded the police and the FBI for being too "timid" out of concern for the heiress. U.S. Attorney General William B. Saxbe charged that Hearst was "not a reluctant participant" and that she and the SLA were common criminals. FBI Director Clarence Kelley and Charles Bates, the San Francisco special agent in charge leading the investigation, refused to blame the victim, and said only that Hearst was wanted in connection with the bank robbery and that it would be up to a jury to decide the nature of her involvement.

There were now wanted posters of Hearst in every post office, while the photo of Tania with beret and carbine in front of the SLA flag had become a counterculture icon, with the text, "We Love You Tania."

Deciding that San Francisco was too hot, Cinque led his army to Los Angeles, where they established new safe houses. Under the delusion that there was support for the SLA in the black community, Cinque began to brag about his exploits to try to recruit new members from among the neighbors. The Los Angeles police located their hideout on May 15, 1974, surrounded it, and then, after a gun battle, set it ablaze with tear gas grenades. All perished except for Hearst and Emily and Bill Harris, who had been out robbing a sporting goods store.

The Harrises and Patty then headed back to San Francisco. They rented another safe house, then tried to dun their former radical friends for money, before they finally struck pay dirt with Kathleen Soliah, a former SLA associate whom Hearst thought had been "too flaky" to be taken underground with the rest. Soliah introduced them to Jack Scott, a self-styled sports activist who had spirited a Revolutionary Army terrorist wanted for bombings in Berkeley, Wendy Yoshimura, to the East Coast. Scott informed them that he was a modern "Harriet Tubman, who had run an underground railroad to smuggle black slaves out of the South to the North during the days of the Civil War. He was running a similar underground railroad now for radical and revolutionary fugitives." Scott then ferried Hearst and the Harrises, one by one, across the country to a Pennsylvania farmhouse they shared with Yoshimura, then to another farm in Jeffersonville, New York.

At the end of the summer the Harrises, Hearst, and Yoshimura decided to return west and make Sacramento their base. There they joined Kathy Soliah, her brother and sister, and their friend Jim Kilgore, who were working as hippie painting contractors. There were two new recruits, radical Mike Bortin and his girlfriend Seanna. Hearst found the new situation much more to her liking: The Soliahs "were nice, normal revolutionaries," while she was fairly sure the Harrises were nuts.

The reconstituted SLA began robbing banks again, first the Guild Savings and Loan in Sacramento on February 25, 1975, and then the Crocker National Bank branch in Carmichael, California. During the Crocker robbery Emily Harris panicked and shot and killed Myrna Lee Opsahl, a forty-two-year-old mother of four. "It really doesn't matter," said Harris. "She was a bourgeois pig anyway."

The group moved back to San Francisco. On August 7, 1975, they blew up a police car. A bomb under a second car was a dud. On August 13 they blew up another police car and issued a communiqué, claiming responsibility in the name of the New World Liberation Front. On August 20 they blew up two cars at the Marin County Civic Center.

On May 9, FBI Director Clarence Kelley had admitted in a news conference that he was "stumped" by the Hearst case. He had taken to walking into the offices of his assistant directors, saying, "We've got to catch Patty Hearst. We've got to end this."

The Bureau was devoting enormous resources to the case, but to no avail. The FBI was using, according to Kelley, police dogs, terrorist experts, kidnapping experts, and even a psychic, along with the psychic's psychiatrist, who interpreted the psychic's "babblings." By the end of the case the Bureau would have spent more than five million dollars, and the field office in charge of the case, San Francisco, had interviewed more than 27,000 possible sources. Not until the middle of March did the FBI get a real break in the case. Jack Scott's brother Walter returned from an overseas trip, and became angry when he learned that Scott had involved himself (and their parents, as drivers) with the SLA, so he went to the FBI. He provided the address of the Pennsylvania farmhouse where Hearst and the Harrises had hidden out the previous summer. The SLA and Hearst had not been at the house for six months, but dogs picked up Hearst's scent, and in what would prove a major break, agents found a fingerprint of Wendy Yoshimura, not yet known to be connected to the case.

At the San Francisco office a rookie agent was given the routine job of rechecking the Yoshimura file for new leads. He learned that Yoshimura's boyfriend, William Brandt, was serving a prison term for the same bombing that had gotten Yoshimura indicted. He had the inspired idea of checking the logbook for Brandt's visitors, and one turned out to be Kathy Soliah. That got the Bureau interested in Soliah, her brother Steve, and their sister Josephine.

On August 18, 1975, Special Agent Curtis Holt visited the Soliahs' parents, Martin and Elise Soliah, in Palmdale, California. Martin Soliah told the agent that his son and daughters had sworn to him that they were not involved with the SLA. All their father would tell the Bureau was that the children were working at house painting in the San Francisco area. The Bureau began checking on houses that were being painted, and soon Special Agents Jason Moulton and Ray Campos managed to locate the Soliahs' current job.

Within an hour the agents were following Kathy and Josephine Soliah, who led them to the Morse Street apartment where it turned out Hearst was staying. The next day Steven Soliah led the agents following him from the Morse Street apartment to the Harrises' hideout, and the agents then followed Bill Harris to confirm his identity. The following day the agents let the Harrises tire themselves jogging, then surrounded and captured them, but when they returned to the Harrises' house, where they thought they would find Patty, it was empty.

Special Agents Tom Padden and Jason Moulton, along with San Francisco detectives Tim Casey and Larry Pasero, decided to check out the Soliah house on Morse Street. They crept up the back stairs, and Padden looked through the open top of a Dutch door. He spotted Yoshimura, and shouted "FBI and police. Freeze!" Patty fled to the bedroom when Padden yelled. He grabbed her and said, "Aren't you glad it's over?" But she just looked at him and said nothing. As Patty was taken into the federal building, she smiled and gave a clenched-fist salute.

■ ■ ■

Why had it taken the Bureau so long to solve the Hearst case? Kelley asked himself that question again and again. "How did that extremely radical, dangerously unbalanced group succeed in evading a nationwide FBI search for nineteen months, and in thwarting the efforts of thousands of FBI agents and police officers to find them? How did they avoid recognition by millions of Americans?" Kelley had a simple answer: "There were no informants. Absolutely no leads reached the Bureau from those fringe elements in our society who knew, really knew, where the various SLA hideouts were located. None." For the nineteen months Hearst was with the SLA, her captors' security procedures were inept, their personal behavior was reckless, they even "cold called" potential recruits to try to get them to join their preposterous revolutionary army. For all those months their whereabouts were always known to dozens, even hundreds, of others. And yet the counterculture's distrust of the FBI was so profound that no one from that community came forward with information on what was clearly, even from the perspective of the radical left, a dangerous, anarchic, and murderous gang.

The fact is that, for lack of informants, the Hearst case had been no closer to solution after a year and a half than at the start. Bill and Emily Harris, Wendy Yoshimura, and Patty Hearst might have eluded capture longer, perhaps much longer (Kathy Soliah hid from the Bureau until June 1999, twenty-five years later), if Walter Scott had not made his way to a police station, worried that his brother had gotten their parents involved in criminal activity. And so the tip came from someone outside the "fringe elements," motivated not by any particular distaste for the SLA or its crimes but out of concern for his parents, perhaps fortified by a natural sibling rivalry with his brother and a few, perhaps more than a few, drinks.

The real question is *why* were there no informants. Once the Bureau got its tip from Walter Scott, and just that one tip, it was able to apply its institutional resources and the individual brilliance of its agents—because it took a gifted detective to think of checking Yoshimura's boyfriend's prison logs—and quickly break the case. Throughout the history of the Bureau, throughout the entire history of law enforcement, that is how cases have always been solved.

But a professional law enforcement agency at the top of its game does not wait for walk-in informants like Walter Scott to solve its cases. It moves into the community in advance to develop informants so it will have sources when there is something it needs to know. But growing numbers of Americans were now so fearful of the Bureau they would not cooperate with it in any way. In some circles that refusal was absolute, and extended even to matters of life and death. And so the Bureau had lost its ability to function throughout large segments of the population.

Worse, there were signs that the toxic distrust of the Bureau was no longer confined to the counterculture but had, to a certain extent, infected the public at large. Patty Hearst was no radical before she was kidnapped, but the SLA nevertheless had no difficulty persuading her that the FBI was a murderously fascist organization that would kill all of them if it got the chance. Hearst was able to discern when the SLA's fear about the Bureau verged into insanity (when, for example, the SLA told her to empty her head of all thoughts about their locations so that Bureau psychics could not trace her thought waves), but the rest of the SLA's paranoia about the Bureau resonated with her. She probably had been hearing things like that about the Bureau for a long time.

But it was not just that the FBI would find it difficult to gather intelligence about what was happening in radical America. It was no longer even trying. Under Gray and Kelley the Bureau was ending surveillance of domestic political groups as fast as it could. The Bureau would now get its information about extremist America only during the course of criminal investigations, and given the climate of the times, no one was about to launch such investigations without plenty of support from the top, and that was rarely forthcoming. The Bureau would eventually grow so out of touch with what was going on among potentially dangerous groups—and in its political correctness would actually pride itself on not knowing things its critics thought it ought not to know—that after 9/11 a frustrated Richard Clarke, chief terrorism adviser during the Clinton and Bush administrations, would testify that "I know how this is going to sound, but I have to say it: I didn't think the FBI would know whether or not there was anything going on in the United States."

Kelley had hoped the Hearst arrests would restore the FBI's morale and reputation, but his good news had to compete with new revelations about the Bureau's bungling of Oswald's surveillance before the JFK assassination. Kelley probably realized that the Hearst case concealed an awful truth about the Bureau: The FBI no longer knew anything about what was happening in violence-prone extremist groups, and it no longer had the capacity or will to learn anything about them. Kelley lamented that "over a period of nineteen months, our agents studied and shadowed the wide-ranging network of sympathizers related in some way to the SLA. These individuals, all of whom were close to the SLA or were part of it, provided assistance or sanctuary to its members." Despite the Bureau's efforts, the useful information gathered from these potential sources "was, of course, nil." The Bureau had been able to penetrate neither the SLA nor the much vaster network of sympathizers who supported it. "We always did try to get people in—informants and that kind of thing. But this was a very tight revolutionary group . . . and we never did it. It frightens me to think that we do have revolutionary groups that are so dedicated."

■ ■ ■

Kelley finally became a victim himself of the personal indulgence and petty corruption that had spread through the top ranks of the Bureau during Hoover's last years.

For a long time J. Edgar Hoover (and Clyde Tolson) had freeloaded at the expense of their rich friends. Within the Bureau, Hoover helped himself to whatever perks came his way, and after a while nearly every requirement of his personal life found itself satisfied and indulged by the Bureau—his personal transportation, odd jobs around the house as well as major remodeling, his gardening—much of it handled by the carpenters and other craftsmen in the Exhibits Section of the Bureau. (When on official assignment they built mock-ups necessary for courtroom presentations of evidence.)

This abuse came to light when the Pike House Select Committee investigating the intelligence agencies notified the Justice Department it had learned that top officials in the Bureau were improperly profiting from a sweetheart deal with a Washington company called U.S. Recording, which supplied surveillance equipment to the Bureau. This all started when Hoover decided not to go through regular advertising and bidding procedures for the equipment out of concern that the public or the media might learn about the Bureau's electronic surveillance activities if the purchases were put out to bid. Hoover decided that U.S. Recording would be the only source used by the Bureau, and all the divisions of the Bureau were notified to that effect.

The Justice Department turned the investigation over to Michael E. Shaheen Jr., who headed the department's Office of Professional Responsibility. Shaheen appointed John M. Dowd and Craig A. Starr to conduct the actual investigation with a team of thirty FBI agents. In November 1976, Dowd and Starr reported that the head of U.S. Recording had a close personal relationship with John Mohr, the number three man under Hoover, and with Kelley's top assistant, Associate Director Nicholas Callahan. The report concluded that U.S. Recording was billing the Bureau unconscionably high markups and implied that this was due to Mohr and Callahan's relationships with the company's management. Although they had not profited in a financial way, they had gotten many small gifts and trips from the company.

But during their investigation Dowd and Starr stumbled on something that would blow apart the old guard leadership of the Bureau, and would drag Kelley down with them. The break came when a carpenter in the Exhibits Section of the crime lab called John Dowd and said he would talk to Dowd if the attorney general protected him from retribution. "He said he had been keeping an insurance policy for forty years."

When Attorney General Edward Levi gave the carpenter a letter promising him immunity, he turned over detailed records of work he had done at the homes of FBI officials, including Hoover, Tolson, and Hoover's secretary Helen Gandy. The records also detailed other gifts and services, like keeping Gandy's car filled with gas and changing her tires. These three were long gone, but there were also records showing that Hoover's top brass kept cashing in after Hoover died. Cartha DeLoach had had the FBI craftsmen build him a bar, a bathroom cabinet, and lawn chairs. (DeLoach, perhaps not wanting to give Hoover a hold over him, had had the men do the work on their own time and had paid for their materials.)

John Mohr had been getting his car taken care of by Bureau employees, who had washed it, waxed it, and taken it to garages for repair. Mohr also had free electrical work done on his house, had his TVs repaired, and had a birdhouse constructed for his home. Some work was still being done even after his June 1972 retirement. The five-year statute of limitations had expired on Mohr, but the head of the Exhibits Section, John P. Dunphy, agreed to a plea bargain in exchange for testimony. Also implicated were Ivan W. Conrad, head of the Laboratory Division, who had appropriated FBI electronic equipment for his own use, and Nicholas Callahan, who had had fences built at his beach house and a fence and shelves installed at his home in Washington.

And so, for a couple of shelves and some fences, the second most powerful man in the Bureau lost his job. Callahan was fired on orders from the Justice Department, and was replaced by Richard Held as Kelley's associate director. Buck Revell, who was the special agent in charge of Oklahoma City, was brought in as Held's right-hand man, launching his career as one of the most important FBI officials of the late 1970s and 1980s.

Kelley was also drawn into the scandal. He was working himself ragged running the Bureau and commuting back to Kansas City, where his wife was terminally ill. (She died in November 1975.) During this time of stress for Kelley, Nicholas Callahan had had a set of curtain valances installed in Kelley's apartment by the Exhibits Section. (Kelley did much of his work at home and had complained about lack of privacy.) Kelley had not requested the valances, and when he saw them he did not like them—so the Exhibits Section rebuilt them.

The Radio Engineering Section also installed two television sets in Kelley's apartment.

Hoover may have permitted his top associates to skim some cream from the government to protect himself from their using his freeloading against him. Callahan may have been trying to do the same thing to Kelley, although that is only conjecture. When Kelley learned that he was being investigated he paid for the valances and had the Bureau take the televisions back.

John Dowd urged that Kelley be fired. Michael Shaheen disagreed: "Kelley did not ask for valances. His wife was dying of cancer. Kelley was unaware of who picked up the costs." Levi's final report mildly criticized Kelley, but also noted that Kelley had not known about the first installation of the valances, had reimbursed the Bureau for the goods and services, and had helped the investigation and implemented reforms to prevent any recurrence. It was a penny-ante scandal, and yet it was exactly the kind of scandal that costs people their jobs and even sends them to jail, since such cases are so easy to prove. More subtle but far more serious forms of public corruption, such as providing special government access to campaign contributors, seldom cost anyone their jobs.

By post–Watergate/Church Committee standards, Hoover and his top aides would have been removed for corruption. As Buck Revell observed, "things that were somewhat taken for granted back then would be prosecuted today." Dowd even called Hoover's career "the greatest shakedown in United States history going on behind the badge," which betrays a certain ignorance of some of the other great shakedowns in American police history.

When presidential candidate Jimmy Carter heard about the FBI scandals he vowed he would appoint a new FBI director if elected. Revell called it "heartrending to witness," and felt that Kelley was being unfairly punished both by those who wanted him to pay for the sins of Hoover and those in the FBI hierarchy angry at him for de-Hooverizing the Bureau. The decision to replace Kelley, Revell said, "sounded wholesome, above reproach. But it wasn't. Not only was it a morally flawed decision, the unseating of Clarence Kelley had an insidious, albeit unintended side effect" in that it rendered meaningless the ten-year term that had been provided for FBI directors. Attorney General Griffin Bell prevailed on Carter to hold off for a year to permit Kelley to accrue a pension; Kelley submitted his resignation on February 15, 1978.

Kelley's forced resignation over a curtain for his apartment—there were *no* other allegations against him—was a travesty of justice. It was not really President Jimmy Carter's fault: He had made a snap decision during the heat of an election campaign on what he mistakenly thought was reliable information, and then felt he could not backtrack on what had become, in effect, an election promise. Despite Carter's misreading of the situation, there was really nothing wrong with Kelley's integrity. He had been dragged down into a pit dug during the exhumations of the FBI's past.

The poisonous atmosphere of distrust that swirled outside the Bureau had now penetrated the Justice Department and the Bureau itself. The Justice Department now reflexively distrusted the Bureau and its director, so petty infractions that should have been handled administratively with a reprimand now set a relentless legal machinery in motion against offending agents. Within the Bureau, agents' distrust of each other and perhaps even institutional self-loathing had agents and officials settling scores with accusations of unethical behavior. In the new order of things these were immediately taken out of the hands of the Bureau, and handed over to independent investigators who had to justify their positions, sometimes by turning minor misdeeds into career-ending crimes.

Kelley was also caught up in the clash between Hoover loyalists and FBI reformers, marked for destruction because he threatened the old way of doing things in the Hoover-era Bureau. He had irritated the old guard by insisting that Gray's and Ruckelshaus's policies on increasing agent diversity be continued. When Kelley left, the number of black agents had risen to 185 (out of 7,931), 173 were Hispanic, and 147 were women. On many occasions Kelley had learned how dangerous it could be to hint that the old FBI had been less than perfect. He gave a college commencement speech in May 1976 in which he said, innocuously enough, that some of the FBI's activities under Hoover had been "clearly wrong and quite indefensible. We most certainly must never allow them to be repeated," and that "the FBI should never again have the unique position that permitted improper activity without accountability." Many ex-agents were outraged. The Society of Former Agents sent Kelley a quote from the old Elbert Hubbard plaque that Hoover used to hang in every Bureau office:

If you work for a man, in heaven's name work for him; speak well of him and stand by the institution he represents . . . if you [criticize the institution], the first high wind that comes along will blow you away, and probably you will never know why.

Under Kelley the FBI took its first tentative steps toward once again investigating the high-level political corruption that first created a need for the Bureau. But at the same time, the Bureau was losing its ability to counter other dangerous threats to the nation. The combination of its unpopularity and its inability to protect its secrets—including the identities of its confidential informants—meant it could no longer gather the intelligence needed to combat violent political groups like the Symbionese Liberation Army or solve cases like the Hearst kidnapping. At Wounded Knee the Bureau found itself thrust into the role of a hated occupying army in hostile terrain. The lack of public sympathy for the murder of its agents on the Pine Ridge reservation reinforced the Bureau's sense of being isolated and defenseless. Realizing that it had no hope of gaining cooperation from those it was trying to protect, it began to think the answer lay in the aggressive use of overwhelming force to resolve crises that, if they could be resolved at all, could only be resolved politically.

. . .

There now seemed no bottom to the hatred of the Bureau, a hatred that had now spread from the Old Left to the entire antiwar community. After the dismal end of the Vietnam War in 1975, the values of that antiwar community came to be shared by much of mainstream America, and one of those convictions was that the FBI was presumptively suspect in everything it did. Enemies of the Bureau were now a large enough constituency for politicians to have to take it into account, and so there were political payoffs in discrediting the FBI and making sure it stayed discredited. As they say, the Bureau's enemies hated it, and its friends didn't exactly like it either.

After decades of being glorified by popular culture, the Bureau found itself demonized in popular entertainment: The popular culture image of the G-man had once opened all doors to the FBI; now they were slammed in its face. Only unwavering support from the president, the attorney general, and Congress could have restored public confidence in the Bureau, but even had they wanted to help, the FBI was too hot and supporting it too dangerous for any practical politician to contemplate. And so many politicians found that there were too many easy points to be scored off the Bureau even to be tempted to help it through its troubles.

The battering the FBI endured during the decade after Hoover's death in 1972 made it virtually impossible for the Bureau to function effectively. The congressional investigations of the mid-seventies had convinced the public that the Bureau could not be allowed to gather domestic political intelligence, so it had no alternative but to stop gathering it. Within a few years the FBI had forgotten how to gather it, even if the Bureau had wanted to, which it most decidedly did not, and so it began a desperate search for an apolitical role that would give it safe haven from political assaults against which it was defenseless. The FBI yearned to be allowed to occupy itself solely with simple crimes against persons and property, even though that meant abdicating its responsibility for the most serious crimes against the United States, those crimes in which, as an FBI official later put it, if the Bureau failed, the nation would fall. And so, abandoned by politicians and the public, the Bureau swiftly became incapable of protecting the public against the real threats to its security.

The Bureau's search for a role in American life free of political conflict could lead it—carried to its logical conclusion—into irrelevance. The FBI's true task, detecting and prosecuting the most serious crimes against the United States, necessarily immerses it in controversy. Protecting the nation against such crimes means investigating groups and individuals whose wealth, political power, and ethnic or ideological associations mean trouble for the Bureau, especially when the Bureau is simply gathering the preliminary intelligence it needs to detect—or better yet, prevent—attacks on the nation. The kinds of crimes that only the FBI can investigate are of their very nature political.

But an uncontroversial, apolitical FBI is no solution. It is probably the Bureau's fate—when it is living up to its responsibilities—never to be able to escape political controversy. When the Bureau is not doing anything controversial, it is also probably not doing much of anything at all to protect the country against "crimes against the United States."

NINE

Exorcising the Ghosts (1978–1993)

ETWEEN September 1976 and July 1981, the FBI developed an intense interest in the activities of a jewel thief named Donnie Brasco. Brasco was a connected guy, in Mafia lingo, an associate of Benjamin "Lefty Guns" Ruggiero, a soldier in a crew headed by Dominick "Sonny Black" Napolitano, the top captain of the Bonanno Mafia crime family of New York.

Ruggiero and Napolitano had been assigning Brasco jobs that demanded discretion, intelligence, and creativity. Brasco had engineered an alliance for them between the Bonannos and the Milwaukee branch of the Mafia in a mutually profitable vending machine racket. He had also gotten Napolitano permission from the Florida Mafia to move into nightclubs and loan-sharking in that state.

Brasco's dream was to move up from the status of a connected, or "half-ass," wiseguy to become a made guy—that is, an initiated member of the Mafia—not just because it represented an opportunity to engage in more lucrative activity, but because of the vastly greater prestige accorded to a full-fledged wiseguy, at least by those who respected that sort of thing.

In 1981, Brasco began getting signals that he was on the verge of getting made. He had been ordered to "clip" a cocaine-addicted Mafia member, and a murder, or "making your bones," was the last step before getting made. "I was so close to getting made and becoming a real wiseguy that I could taste it," Brasco said. "As a made guy I would have enormous clout as [Sonny Black's] emissary. I would be able to sit down with anybody. As a wiseguy, I would be Sonny's partner. Sonny could have used me almost like an ambassador, an intermediary with other families." Only one thing stood in the way of Brasco becoming a made member of the Mafia. It was that Donnie Brasco was actually FBI Special Agent Joseph D. Pistone.

The FBI had never had an agent go undercover as deeply or as long, or into so much danger, as Joe Pistone did between 1977 and 1981. The FBI had had some enormously productive undercover informants before—Jackie Presser, president of the mobbed-up Teamsters Union, Herbert Philbrick, the "communist for the FBI," and "Solo," the brothers Jack and Morris Childs, the American Communist Party's liaisons with the Kremlin—but they had all been informants, not sworn agents.

J. Edgar Hoover, in fact, almost never allowed agents to go undercover except briefly and in exceptional circumstances. It wasn't sufficiently productive in terms of statistical accomplishments, and he may have feared it would corrupt some of his agents.

In Pistone's case, neither fear would have been justified. Pistone's testimony, in conjunction with evidence secured through wiretaps and bugs, led to more than one hundred convictions of Mafia leaders and soldiers, including the 1985 "Pizza Connection Case," which broke the conspiracy between the Sicilian and American Mafia to distribute heroin, and the 1986 "Commission Case" trial in New York, which led to the imprisonment of the leaders of all five New York crime families. And Pistone's undercover work, which he narrated in his memoir, *Donnie Brasco,* was turned into one of the best of all FBI movies. He was, in the words of his boss in the New York field office, "the FBI's most accomplished and heroic undercover agent in history. Period." And incorruptible—unless a professional pride that made him furious when the Bureau pulled him out of the mob before he could achieve detective immortality by being "made" could be held against him.

The Bureau's victories over the Mafia in the 1980s raise the question of why it took the FBI so long. As early as 1911 the Bureau had gone into battle against one form of organized crime, interstate and international prostitution rings. It would have been legally possible, though perhaps politically difficult, for the Bureau to have maintained that interstate organized crime had always been within its jurisdiction, certainly since the expansion of FBI authority in 1934. J. Edgar Hoover is widely regarded as having claimed, however, that there was no such thing as a Mafia, although what he actually said was that there was no national crime organization; he knew full well there was a Mafia. But since the days of Courtney Ryley Cooper, Hoover's vision of the Bureau's role in the law enforcement community depended on maintaining the position that all crime was local. Even when a nationwide criminal syndicate was exposed by the 1957 arrests of crime bosses from around the country in Apalachin, New York,

Hoover could have made the same argument, except that the public had concluded otherwise. Just because local crime bosses got together occasionally to iron out differences did not mean that there was in fact a single group governing organized crime across the nation.

Why did J. Edgar Hoover so resolutely keep the FBI out of organized crime investigations? One explanation, offered by Hoover biographer Anthony Summers, is that Hoover was being blackmailed by the mob, which had secured evidence of Hoover's homosexuality. But just as Summers's allegations about Hoover's supposed transvestism fall apart under any serious analysis, so do his theories that the mob had some sort of hold over Hoover. When Hoover was finally ordered to fight organized crime by a president, John F. Kennedy, and an attorney general, Robert F. Kennedy, whose demonstrated commitment meant he could count on their support, he threw himself into the fight, even though the Bureau did not yet have the legal authority to use wiretaps and bugs, the only effective tools in such investigations. (He used them anyway.)

Hoover had other reasons to resist pressure to combat organized crime before the Kennedy administration. Until the 1960s organized crime enjoyed political protection on the local, state, and even national level. Organized crime investigations are long and difficult, and if political influence is brought to bear early on to end them, there isn't usually enough evidence yet to keep the investigation going. But the collapse of big-city political machines in the sixties meant the mob had far less political clout than in Hoover's day.

Jules Bonavolonta coordinated all the New York field office's organized crime investigations while Pistone was undercover. Bonavolonta credits the Bureau's turnaround to a group of young Vietnam-veteran agents who, he claims, were not about to lose another war, and were looking for one that they could win. That may be so, although many of the key agents investigating the New York mob turn out not to have been veterans.

The single most important reason for the FBI's success against the mob in the 1980s, in the opinion of Bonavolonta and others, was the influence of one particular individual. This was Robert Blakey, a law professor who served in the Organized Crime Section of the Justice Department and then on the legal staff of the Senate Subcommittee on Criminal Laws and Procedures. Blakey was regarded as the country's top authority on the Mafia, and in 1968 was one of the authors of the Omnibus Crime Control and Safe Streets Act. He drafted the key component of that act, which finally gave the Bureau the one tool it needed to investigate the mob: a wiretap whose findings would be admissible in court. Under Title III of the act, the Bureau could apply to a federal judge for a warrant to place a wiretap or a bug for a limited period of time, provided the Bureau could persuade the judge that there was a reasonable cause to suspect a crime was being committed. Within the law enforcement community such bugs and wiretaps were referred to as "Title IIIs."

But it was another law Blakey had authored, the Racketeer Influenced and Corrupt Organizations Act of 1970, universally known as RICO, that for the first time gave Jules Bonavolonta and the Bureau an effective strategy for dismantling the mob, rather than just picking off a few soldiers every now and then. The key provision of the RICO Act made it unlawful

> for any person employed by or associated with any enterprise engaged in, or the activities of which affect, interstate or foreign commerce, to conduct or partici- pate, directly or indirectly, in the conduct of such enterprise's affairs through a pattern of racketeering activity or collection of unlawful debts.

RICO allowed federal prosecutors to use a pattern of criminal acts (the so-called predicate acts—two are needed over a ten-year period) to establish that an association of individuals is a criminal enterprise. Those managing the enterprise are then subject to extremely heavy criminal and civil penalties, even if it cannot be proven that they themselves committed any criminal acts.

Bonavolonta learned about the possibilities opened up by RICO at a semi- nar at Cornell that Blakey gave for Bonavolonta and fellow agent Jim Kossler in 1980. They heard Blakey tell them that

> a comprehensive and successful preemptive strike aimed directly at the heart of La Cosa Nostra is the only viable strategy for dealing with this cancer that has existed in American society for more than seventy years. Such an attack can only be implemented through the strategic use of wiretaps and bugs—and RICO.

This had the force of a revelation to Bonavolonta and Kossler. And Bonavo- lonta responded with an appropriately reverent "Holy shit!" The two agents stayed with Blakey for three days mastering the entire esoteric "criminal enter- prise" doctrine (which in print would seem too complex for any but the most philosophic legal minds to comprehend, yet jury after jury has had no trouble fitting the Mafia into its rubrics). Then they rushed back to New York to put the theory into practice and, propelled by Bonavolonta's enthusiastic leadership, Blakey's RICO transformed the FBI.

Before RICO, the Bureau would pull a wiretap as soon as it learned of a crime, and would seek prosecution of the individual responsible. Now the Bureau could act strategically. It would gather evidence against the entire crime family, with the goal of bringing the godfathers themselves to justice for the crimes committed by their subordinates.

From the time Joe Pistone went undercover in 1977 until John Gotti, the "Teflon Don," was finally convicted on April 2, 1992, the Bureau—armed with new investigative techniques, new prosecutive strategies, and new attitudes in the street and in Washington—brought down the entire New York Mafia, with all the leaders of all the five families either in prison or dead, themselves victims of mob violence (the Commission Case), and then the Bureau destroyed an alliance between the Sicilian and American Mafias to import heroin into the United States (the Pizza Connection Case).

Bonavolonta's Mafia cases mobilized some 350 FBI agents and 100 New York City police. He had, Bonavolonta recalled,

> *on the front lines in New York—and the memories will never fade because I have never experienced anything like it before or since—a team of agents, police officers, supervisors and prosecutors who were possessed of a sense of mission like nothing you have ever seen. What we were about was doing good work—and doing good: We thought of ourselves, corny as it may seem now, as the good guys. For most of us, I don't think we have ever felt, before or since, as energized, as bulletproof, as destined, as we did when we were turning the corner in our war against the Cosa Nostra.*

The first shot in the Bureau's RICO war against organized crime was *United States v. Napolitano et al.,* which used the evidence gathered by Joe Pistone to accuse his old associates in the Bonanno family, Sonny Black Napolitano and the rest of his crew, of operating a criminal enterprise. (Before he could stand trial, Sonny Black would be murdered in 1981 for having been gulled by Pistone. The prosecutors who won that case were Assistant U.S. Attorneys Barbara Jones and Louis Freeh, the latter the future FBI director.) For the first time, the Bureau had shifted its focus from investigating individual criminals, prosecuting each as soon as it had enough to make a case, and instead had patiently assembled the evidence needed to understand and dismantle an entire criminal organization.

The RICO strategy having been tested and proven, the Bureau then launched a comprehensive investigation of all five of New York's Mafia families. The Bureau's best source was a bug placed in the home of Paul Castellano, head of the Gambino crime family, which led, among other things, to an extraordinary set of photographs of a meeting of the "Commission" made up of the heads of the five families. Bonavolonta assigned the job of preparing the case for court to special agents Charlotte Lang and Pat Marshall, the latter regarded by Bonavolonta as a genius in developing and pumping informants. At the start of the investigation its strongest advocate in Washington was Rudolph Giuliani, then associate attorney general in Washington (the number three position in the Justice Department). Giuliani then moved to New York to take over as United States attorney for the Southern District. He planned to argue the case himself, but when he began the political corruption and Wall Street insider-trading prosecutions that would launch his political career, he handed the Mafia cases to Michael Chertoff as lead prosecutor. Chertoff obtained convictions of the heads of the five families and their top associates on November 19, 1986, and they were then sentenced to a hundred years apiece in prison.

Shortly after Joe Pistone was pulled out of undercover in July 1981, organized crime agents in the New York field office began noticing some unusual interlopers associating with members of the New York Mafia. Investigation revealed that the newcomers were members of the Sicilian Mafia, and that they had combined first with the Gambino and then the Bonanno crime families to import heroin and distribute it from behind fronts established as pizza parlors (hence the "Pizza Connection").

The Pizza Connection investigation moved the Bureau into a new era of law enforcement cooperation. Investigations in New York were run by teams of FBI agents, New York City police, and agents of the Drug Enforcement Agency. It also required the highest level of cooperation between American and Italian investigators, with assistance from French, Spanish, and South American law enforcement agencies. Louis Freeh, who emerged as a superstar prosecutor during the Pizza Connection trial, personally created the alliance between American and Italian anti-Mafia investigators. He also developed a close personal friendship with Judge Giovanni Falcone, the head of Italy's anti-Mafia task force (later murdered by the Mafia, and now memorialized in a garden at the FBI Academy). At the climax of the investigation Freeh and the FBI were working with law enforcement agencies from ten different countries. Freeh argued the case himself in a trial that began on September 30, 1985, and ran until March 2, 1987. Up to that time it was the longest trial in the history of federal courts. It was also one of the most complex, requiring spider webs of charts mapping the routes of money and drugs between the United States and Europe and South America; it was also one of the most innovative: Freeh hired professional actors to dramatize the reading of wiretap transcripts; they became known as the "Pizza Players," and until ordered to stop, added show biz flair to the proceedings by reciting their lines in heavy stage Italian accents and wearing costumes of Mafia chic: black suits, black shirts, and red ties.

There seems to be a law that every solution in time becomes a new problem, sometimes worse than the first. The Bureau's success against the New York Mafia raised the bar of what was expected from field offices in organized crime investigations. But there was only one Joe Pistone. Lacking a Pistone of their own, field offices substituted "Top Echelon" or "TE" informants, and recruitment of TEs became a measure of an agent's success, a reversion to the old quantity-over-quality ethic of the Hoover years. In Boston, for example, the FBI was drawn into an unholy alliance with its TEs in the Irish mob. Before it was over, the TEs' handlers were drawn into criminal and murderous conspiracies with their informants, even setting up rival mobsters for elimination by the Bureau's informants.

■ ■ ■

The Bureau's move against the mob was first launched by Clarence Kelley and then encouraged by William Webster, who was appointed by President Carter after Kelley's forced resignation. William H. Webster was born on March 6, 1924, in St. Louis, Missouri, and graduated from Amherst College in 1947 after serving as a naval lieutenant during World War II. He got a law degree from Washington University Law School in St. Louis in 1949, and was called back to Navy duty during the Korean War. He practiced law in St. Louis from 1949 to 1959, then was appointed United States attorney for the Eastern District of Missouri in 1960. Webster was named a judge of the United States District Court for the Eastern District of Missouri in 1970 and then served in the United States Court of Appeals for the Eighth Circuit from 1973 until President Carter named him director of the Bureau in 1978.

■ ■ ■

If the Bureau had traditionally erred in criminal investigations by ignoring (before RICO) the forest for the trees, in foreign counterintelligence the FBI's faults had tended to run in the opposite direction, focusing on the Big Picture rather than the shrubs and bushes of espionage—that is, the Bureau had always been more concerned about learning the goals and methods of Soviet-bloc espionage than prosecuting individual spies. And as a result the Bureau often had to explain how the apocalyptic threat it claimed to see in the secret world of Soviet espionage could produce such a small number of convictions.

That all changed during the Webster-Reagan years: A surge of counterespi-

onage reached such a peak in 1985, when the Bureau uncovered so many com-
munist-bloc spies (in all, twenty-six Americans were arrested) that it became
known as "The Year of the Spy." The breakthrough was the defection of Vitaly
Yurchenko, head of the KGB's First Department of the First Chief Directorate,
responsible for North American Operations. Yurchenko defected on August 1,
1985, and then, after revealing the identities of two American spies for the Soviets, redefected on November 2, claiming that he had been drugged by the
CIA. There is still a debate today in intelligence circles as to whether Yurchenko
was a true defector who changed his mind or a "dangle" sent to the West to
spread disinformation.

The first of the Soviet agents given up by Yurchenko was National Security
Agency analyst Ronald W. Pelton, who, upon investigation, was found to have
sold the Soviets many of the United States' most important communications
secrets and is now serving three life terms.

The second case was a major embarrassment for the Bureau. This was the
spy Yurchenko called "Robert," who proved to be Edward Lee Howard, a
trained CIA operative who had been kicked out of the agency in 1983 for failing
a polygraph on the eve of an assignment to Moscow. His firing left Howard,
who could be a heavy drinker, with a grudge against the CIA and a memory
stuffed with CIA tradecraft.

Soon after he was fired, Howard went to the Soviet Consulate in Washington and offered himself to the KGB. A year later he all but confessed to the CIA,
but said he had only considered entering the consulate. This startling news, that
a vengeful ex-CIA agent had admitted thinking about going over to the KGB,
should have been reported to the FBI. It was not, and the CIA's informants in
Russia began to disappear.

Yurchenko provided enough details about "Robert" in 1985 for the CIA to
identify him instantly, but the agency, obviously embarrassed, delayed relaying
the information to the Bureau, giving Howard time to meet with his Soviet
control in Vienna.

On August 10, the CIA finally sent the Bureau Howard's name and address
in New Mexico. The Bureau's surveillance was obvious to Howard, who had
been trained in the same techniques. He hired a lawyer and notified the Bureau
that he was ready to cooperate. Actually, he was ready to escape.

Howard prepared a dummy, known as a "jib," a jack-in-the-box in the surveillance trade. At about four o'clock in the afternoon, on Saturday, September
21, Howard sat in the passenger seat of his family's red Oldsmobile. His wife,
Mary, was in the driver's seat, the dummy hidden between them. Howard

ducked out of the car. The dummy was put in his place. The FBI lookout never saw them.

This breakdown in surveillance has exposed the Bureau to criticism and ridicule ever since. The agent in the van was working his first assignment, and claimed that he could not see because of the glare of the desert sun. The Bureau thought the excuse was lame, and it cost the rookie his job.

By the time the FBI figured out Howard was gone, he was already more than halfway across the Atlantic, eventually popping up nine months later in Moscow. Howard had been trained by the CIA to elude surveillance by exactly the same techniques he employed in his escape. He had been trained, in fact, to elude the FBI, whose agents had played the roles of pursuers in the training exercises. In his training he had succeeded in escaping from the FBI, and that was one of the reasons he had been hired by the CIA. Who is to say that, even if the FBI had performed at its best, he would not have eluded them anyway?

While the FBI has had to live with the embarrassment of Howard's escape, the Senate Intelligence Committee concluded that the key failure had been that "CIA security officials failed to alert and involve the FBI in a timely fashion." The senators pointed out that it was obvious that the FBI should be notified whenever an employee is dismissed from the CIA who might possess "motivations for espionage." Remedies, however, were still years away.

Another of the Bureau's spy cases of the eighties exposed one of the deepest mines of Soviet espionage in the history of the Cold War.

The Bureau's first lead was a call from Barbara Walker, ex-wife of a former sailor named John Walker. Her information led the Bureau to believe there might be a major espionage ring within the Navy. Special Agent Robert W. Hunter of the Norfolk, Virginia, office took the case in February 1985, installed wiretaps, and began surveillance.

The Bureau learned that a ring headed by Walker had been selling military secrets to the Soviets since 1967, that is, for nearly twenty years. Walker recruited his friend Jerry Whitworth, who supervised communications at the electronic surveillance outpost on Diego Garcia Island, and later handled all communications on the aircraft carrier *Constellation*, with full access to all cryptographic material. Walker's son Michael, then serving aboard the *Nimitz*, was delivering secret documents from the ship's burn bags to his father. Walker's brother Arthur, a former naval officer at Groton, Connecticut, was also involved.

Two months into the case, phone conversations between Walker and family members made Hunter suspect Walker might be dropping off material for his handler the weekend of May 18, 1985. Hunter surrounded Walker's house in Norfolk, and set up full surveillance: six cars and a spotter plane.

After seeing nothing for two days, at 12:10 P.M. on Sunday the plane spotted Walker in his car: "He's on the move," the pilot radioed Hunter. A short time later the spotter plane reported that Walker was driving evasively, heading toward Washington.

Following a car in a major city is so difficult that the Bureau reinforced Hunter's group with agents from the Washington field office, bringing the total surveillance unit to forty-one agents in twenty vehicles, one of the largest in the history of the Bureau. But when Walker moved out of Washington into rural Maryland, the car surveillance risked being too obtrusive, and was pulled back. They would rely on the plane. Then the plane lost contact. The automobile surveillance was sent back into the field, but it was too late. They had lost him. Back in the command post at the Washington field office the Norfolk agents "went ballistic about how the hell a little office like Norfolk could follow John Walker for over three hours and then the 'real agents' from Washington field lose him inside of an hour."

They sent the plane back into the air, and at 7:45 the pilot spotted Walker's van. The automobile surveillance resumed the chase. Agents saw Walker place a 7-Up can by the side of the road. Counterintelligence agents knew that had to be a signal to the KGB that a "dead drop" (where Walker had left his documents) was "loaded," and so they ordered that it be left undisturbed. Through a miscommunication, however, an agent bagged the can for evidence. Shortly after, a car with Soviet diplomatic plates was spotted cruising past the signal site looking for the can. The car was registered to the third secretary at the Soviet Embassy, Aleksei Gavrilovich Tkachenko, a known KGB operative. Three days later Tkachenko and his family unceremoniously fled to Moscow.

Walker continued driving and, with the FBI watching from a distance, stopped under a large oak tree. Then he drove off. As soon as he had disappeared, an FBI team flooded the area. An hour later, Special Agent Bruce K. Brahe II spotted a grocery bag in tall grass near a utility pole. He grabbed it, shouted "I've got it," and raced back to his squad. It was stuffed with classified documents from Michael Walker's ship, the aircraft carrier *Nimitz*. It was the first time in FBI history that a spy had been tracked to a dead drop.

Back at his motel, John Walker was alarmed. After leaving the documents by the utility pole, he had gone to another dead drop where his money should have been left, but there was none. When he had gone back to retrieve the documents, they and the 7-Up can were both gone. Had the FBI been watching? Or had there been a mix-up with the dead-drop procedure? That had happened before. At 3:30 A.M. his phone rang. It was the front desk. His van had been sideswiped. Would he come down to take a look? He knew that was an old detective trick, but he had to know. He opened the door and stepped out, pistol in hand. There was Special Agent Robert Hunter with Special Agent James L. Koluch, wearing bulletproof vests and armed with revolvers. Walker dropped his gun.

Four hours later, Walker's brother Arthur was picked up for questioning. An hour later, FBI agents visited Jerry Whitworth in Davis, California, questioned him, searched his trailer, and put him under surveillance. In two weeks he, too, was arrested for espionage. On the other side of the world, Robert's son Michael was arrested aboard the *Nimitz* in the port of Haifa.

The materials the Walker ring sold the Soviets had enabled them to decipher almost all coded messages sent by the Navy for over a decade (according to Yurchenko, "one million messages"). Walker had also sold the Soviets the Navy's retaliation plans in the event of war as well as the locations of the under-sea microphones used by the Navy to track Soviet subs. During his interrogation, he could not even remember all he had given the Soviets. "I'll tell you this. If it was within my grasp, you can color it gone. Because it's gone."

After John Walker's testimony against him, Jerry Whitworth was sentenced to 365 years in prison without possibility of parole. Arthur received life. John got two life terms plus one hundred years; under sentencing guidelines he would be eligible for parole in ten years, but the sentencing judge promised to recommend to the board that Walker never be freed. His son Michael, for whom Walker had traded his testimony in exchange for a lighter sentence, got concurrent twenty-five-year terms with eligibility for parole after ten years. Special Agent Robert Hunter got a letter of commendation.

• • •

Worse was to come. In 1985, just a month before Robert Hunter broke up the Walker family spy ring, a Central Intelligence Agency analyst named Aldrich H. Ames walked through the gates of the Soviet Embassy in Washington. He passed an envelope to the guard at the reception desk addressed to "Stanislav Androsov," the KGB *rezident*, that is, the head of Soviet intelligence and espionage at the embassy. Inside that envelope were the names of two CIA sources in the KGB, which would be known only to someone strategically placed in the CIA. Ames included a CIA organization chart with his own position highlighted in the CIA's Soviet/East Europe Division's counterintelligence group, with access to the names of all the CIA's Soviet assets. Last, but certainly not least to Ames, there was a request for $50,000. Three weeks later Ames was summoned to a secure room deep in the recesses of the Soviet Embassy. He was handed a bundle of used currency totaling $50,000.

Thus began the career of the most murderous spy in American history. Over the next eight years Ames handed the Soviets the names of almost all the United States' informants in Soviet intelligence agencies, resulting in the execution—in some cases the torture deaths—of at least ten. The information he sold to the Soviets completely dismantled American penetration of Soviet intelligence during the final years of the Cold War. It was, the chief of the Washington field office said, "the most important U.S. espionage case the FBI has ever had."

Neither the CIA nor the FBI knew about Ames's defection, but they both knew something was wrong when, beginning in 1985, almost all their assets in the KGB, known now as the SVR, disappeared. Among the earliest disappearances were two of the Bureau's most prized informants, Valery Martinov and Sergei Motorin. They had been recruited by COURTSHIP, a joint Bureau-agency operation (begun in 1980) to turn KGB operatives into double agents. Altogether, five of the CIA's informants in the KGB went silent during the second half of 1985. Even more devastating was the loss of Dimitri Fedorovich Polyakov (TOPHAT), a general in the GRU (Soviet military intelligence), who since 1961 had been furnishing the CIA with an astounding haul of almost every important aspect of Soviet intelligence.

In October 1986, alarmed by the disappearance of Martinov and Motorin, the Bureau set up a task force, code-named ANLACE, six investigators under Soviet analyst Tim Caruso. By early 1987 ANLACE had learned about the magnitude of the CIA's loss, but reached a dead end on the loss of Martinov and Motorin. ANLACE was disbanded, and after December 1988 FBI-CIA conferences on the matter ended. The CIA's special task force also gave up, and would not look into the situation again for three years.

In November 1989 a CIA analyst, Diana Worthen, made a social visit to Ames's home in Arlington, Virginia (purchased for $540,000 in cash), and was astounded at the wealth on display there. (Ames by this time had gotten almost $2 million from the Soviets.) The CIA launched a probe of Ames's finances, and unearthed more evidence of spending out of all proportion to his income (then in the neighborhood of $60,000). Yet the agency decided that there must surely be an innocent explanation and looked no further.

Finally, in April 1991, a thoroughly frustrated CIA investigator, Paul Redmond, went to the FBI. He met with Tim Caruso, and for the first time the FBI learned how bad the situation in Moscow had become. A new task force was set up. It was called the Special Investigations Unit, consisting of the CIA's SKY-LIGHT team of investigators and the FBI's PLAYACTOR squad.

Late in August they had identified twenty-nine prime suspects, and Ames was one of them. On November 12, 1991, the investigators interviewed Ames, and followed up with a full review of the CIA's records on him. That uncovered a July 1986 FBI request to the CIA for an explanation of Ames's visits to the Soviet Embassy (which the FBI had under surveillance). The CIA had promised to follow up, but never had.

With the CIA and the FBI working together, the evidence began to fall into place. The Bureau located its surveillance records of Ames's unreported visits to the Soviet Embassy. The CIA studied Ames's bank deposits. The dates matched. Each time Ames visited the embassy, his bank account received an almost immediate infusion of cash. Then, in January 1993, a KGB informant was able to supply the Bureau not with Ames's identity but with his code name, and with the fact that the mole had met with his handlers in Bogotá and Rome. That fit Ames like a glove. The FBI had its mole. On May 24, 1993, Robert "Bear" Bryant, then special agent in charge of the Bureau's Washington field office, called Les Wiser, a supervisory special agent, to his office on the eleventh floor of the old Buzzard Point building. Wiser, then thirty-eight years old, had served as both prosecutor and defense counsel for the Navy's judge advocate general before joining the Bureau. At that moment he was running one of the field office's twenty-two counterintelligence squads, his group focusing on espionage from nontraditional countries (that is, from outside the former communist bloc). Bryant told Wiser the case was his and code-named it NIGHTMOVER. Wiser's job was to get evidence on Ames that would hold up in court. He decided to use a trash cover (to go through Ames's garbage) and to use the Bureau's Special Surveillance Group (non-agent surveillance specialists trained to blend into any environment).

> *I got together with some people I'd worked with over the years. . . . But I wasn't going to just drive into the neighborhood and get the trash. I had asked for a neighborhood survey. These houses cost $400,000–$500,000 apiece: not just the kind of neighborhood you just cruise in and steal something, I wouldn't think. . . . I then said . . . "go out and practice. I want you to practice how you are going to do this. I don't want the first time you execute this to be on the run." So they . . . got it down to where . . . it would be eleven seconds. I think that's pretty good. . . . And we went out and did the trash cover.*

But Bryant became worried that the entire investigation might be compromised if neighbors—late at night when the windows are open, air conditioners go off, and the streets become silent—had seen or heard the agents messing around with Ames's garbage. And so at the end of August he ordered Wiser to discontinue the trash cover.

A few weeks later Wiser's agents followed Ames on what seemed to them to be a tour of his dead drops, though they could not spot the signals Ames was looking for. They already knew the names of some of the drops, but they didn't know where they were. On the other hand, there was a standard routine followed by all spy agencies, Russians and Americans included. A signal site was paired with a specific dead drop. If a spy placed a chalk mark on a signal site, for instance a mailbox on Garfield Terrace, which Ames and the Russians knew as code name ROSE, it meant he would leave a package at GROUND, a site under a bridge at Pinehurst Parkway and Beech Drive. When the Soviets "unloaded" the site, that is, picked up the package, they would erase the chalk mark so that Ames would know they had gotten it. There was one set of signals and dead drops for traffic from Ames to the Soviets, another for deliveries from the Soviets to Ames.

But after a couple of bad days when the agents lost track of Ames, Wiser played a hunch that they ought to take another look at Ames's garbage.

Now we had stopped the trash cover when [Ames escaped surveillance] . . . Right after that I thought this would be a good opportunity to resume the trash cover so I told [Special Agent] Mike Anderson [in my squad] I wanted the trash cover done on Wednesday night. Mike said to me, "Bear [Bryant] said not to do that." I said, "Damn don't tell anybody. This one is on me, so if it goes bad, we didn't talk about it" so nobody . . . [would know] I didn't have permission. . . . I wanted to move the case along and clearly I felt that we had suffered a yardage loss and I wanted to do something.

I got a call at four or five in the morning . . . that they had had this great success. They found this note in the trash. And it was only [a Post-It note]. That is all it is. And this note was ripped into all these pieces, I think about nine.

What they found were the first and second drafts of a note to Ames's handlers saying that he wanted to meet the Soviets in Bogotá for some money, with instructions on how they should confirm that the Bogotá trip was on. Wiser said, in an understatement, Ames's putting that note in the garbage "was a mistake."

On the 6th [of October] we do another trash cover. In that trash cover we get a typewriter ribbon out of it. . . . We got the ribbon out and sent it to the lab. They couldn't help us. They did later on when they figured out this was an important case. And we wanted to read the ribbon. It's sort of backwards, so we sent somebody over [to get] the mirror off [secretary] Diane Johnson's wall . . . and we got some take up reels . . . and so took turns, somebody would feed, somebody would wind it and somebody would hold the mirror and read, and Linda Williams, the secretary, would type it up. So we read the thing and that's how we did it. And at one point we paused and I said, "You know in the movie this will be some huge computer," because I had some vision of the [movie] Red Dragon and they carry toilet paper he had written on and they get it down to the lab and overnight they get it back . . . It was just so funny. This high-tech FBI [and] we're standing there with a mirror reading this thing.

The ribbon had the imprint of a five-page letter to the Russians discussing classified material.

It would have been nice to see them meet. That would have been good. We didn't see that but what we saw was good enough. We got back and had to think about how we were going to wrap this thing up. We thought we wanted to catch him in a drop. But at this point they changed the way they did business at the CIA with computers. Until this time [Ames] could only collect paper documents. That limited the type of material you could pass. It also enabled us to go in and see what kind of stuff was sitting there [so] we had a pretty good idea of what he was giving up. But in December he had four disks with all kinds of stuff in it and we couldn't let that stuff go.

He was arrested on February 21, 1994, and within two months [he was sentenced] to life without parole. This was the maximum sentence under the law. He couldn't get more than that. Since then Congress fixed the statute to provide for the death penalty. If you think about it . . . under the sentencing guidelines, he just has to plead guilty and he doesn't get life. It was a wonderful result and the reason we got that was the leverage we had with Rosario [his wife]. We bargained down Rosario to sixty-three months in order to get this result, [the life sentence] and the debriefings. We got the maximum sentence. We got money back—we sent over a check to the Crime Victims Assistance Fund for $540,000 because we seized about $600,000 worth of property. We got all that plus the debriefings. And we still got sixty-three months for Rosario.

The Ames case, painfully prolonged by failures of communication between the CIA and the Bureau, highlighted a fundamental problem of American counterintelligence: The primary target of foreign espionage, the CIA, was by culture and tradition unwilling to cooperate with the FBI, which had had the statutory responsibility to coordinate all counterintelligence operations since an executive order in 1981, and which had far and away the greater expertise in the ways of Soviet espionage in this country.

The spy cases that had been unfolding since 1985 exposed obvious deficiencies in American counterintelligence. Most serious, of course, was the lack of cooperation between the American intelligence agencies, first and foremost between the CIA and the FBI, but also between the Bureau and the military counterespionage services.

■ ■ ■

Relations between the Bureau and the agency had been bad from the outset, ever since J. Edgar Hoover had worked behind the scenes to scuttle "Wild Bill" Donovan's plan for the OSS to take over all American intelligence after World War II. According to legend, at least, the hostility between the two intelligence services was exacerbated by class and ethnic differences—the FBI used to refer to the Yale-dominated CIA by the old OSS nickname, "Oh So Social," while the agency sneered at the Bureau as "Fordham Bronx Irish."

In 1970 there was a complete rupture in relations between the two agencies. The president of the University of Colorado, Joseph Smiley, was worried because one of his history professors, Thomas Riha, had disappeared. The CIA's campus contact told Smiley that Riha was fine and was dealing with some marital difficulties. Smiley's CIA source said he had gotten the information from an FBI agent. Smiley had been sworn to secrecy, but let it slip that government sources had assured him of Riha's safety. The Denver field office suspected one of its agents had been Smiley's informant. The CIA then confessed it had been Smiley's source, and that the information had come from an FBI agent in Boulder. In Washington, Sam Papich, the liaison between the Bureau and the agency, demanded from the CIA the name of the agent. The CIA in Boulder refused to divulge the FBI agent's name, and CIA Director Richard Helms backed him up. In retaliation, Hoover ordered the liaison between the Colorado offices of the Bureau and the agency be terminated, and the Washington liaison be ended as well: "any contact with CIA in the future [is] to be by letter only." Sam Papich protested that cooperation between the two agencies was essential to national security, but Hoover said, "Helms forgets that it is a two way street." On March 2, 1970, Hoover sent a coded teletype to all FBI offices, "Immediately discontinue all contact with the local CIA office."

President Nixon tried to force a rapprochement between the agency and the Bureau with the Huston Plan, but that had, of course, been scuttled by a nervous Hoover, who was habitually suspicious of cooperation with the CIA or other agencies, because it triggered his reflexive conviction that the underlying issue in any counterespionage case was to prevent other agencies from encroaching on FBI turf.

Nixon tried again. On December 3, 1970, he established an Intelligence

Evaluation Committee in the Justice Department under Assistant Attorney General Robert Mardian. When Hoover balked, that too went nowhere. "We've got enough damn coordination in government now, too much in fact," Hoover is supposed to have said.

When Clarence Kelley took over at the FBI, he and CIA Director William Colby established a personal relationship, and tried to put cooperation back on track. Kelley appointed William Cregar, who had once been Sam Papich's assistant, as formal CIA liaison. A former agent recalled that "under Bill Cregar, we had a number of cases we ran together, or shared information on—black areas I still can't talk about—where I didn't see any essential distinction between the two outfits. We were working as one team." Cregar also instituted exchanges between the training facilities at Quantico and Langley, Virginia, with agents from the CIA and FBI attending both agencies' counterintelligence classes. In still another effort to force FBI-CIA coordination, President Gerald Ford established a National Foreign Intelligence Board chaired by the director of Central Intelligence, with a representative of the FBI director as a member. The goal of cooperation was dealt a major blow, however, when Clarence Kelley, who had been briefed on the CIA's JENNIFER project to raise a sunken Soviet submarine from the bottom of the Pacific, told Los Angeles Police Chief Ed Davis about it, and Davis leaked it to the *Los Angeles Times,* angering the CIA.

Coordination suffered another setback in 1975. A defector from the Russian navy, Nicholas Shadrin, who was being handled by the FBI, was sent to Vienna to allow a CIA mole in the KGB, Igor Kochnov, to "recruit" Shadrin as a double (triple?) agent. When Shadrin was kidnapped and killed by the KGB, the FBI blamed the agency for not briefing it fully on the dangers of having Shadrin meet Korchnov, since some in the agency suspected Korchnov was still loyal to the Soviets. The Bureau also blamed the CIA for not having run a secure and properly supervised operation, since the CIA agent handling Shadrin in Vienna had just been exposed as an agent, and so she was not available at her emergency number when Shadrin vanished.

During the Carter administration, the so-called "spy wars" caused more hard feelings between the Bureau and the agency. William Webster and Attorney General Griffin Bell wanted to increase public awareness about the magnitude of the Soviet espionage threat: There were about 800 Soviet bloc agents working in the U.S., and the FBI had fewer than 200 counterintelligence agents watching them. The FBI and the Justice Department proposed arresting and prosecuting Soviet agents not protected by diplomatic immunity as soon as they recruited an American, and expelling KGB agents under diplomatic cover whenever they were detected engaging in espionage. The CIA protested that this would touch off retaliatory expulsions from the Soviet Union, which proved to be the case. The FBI tricked two KGB agents into buying submarine secrets from an FBI dangle. When Webster had them prosecuted (and convicted), this did indeed set off a spy war, which ended only when the two Soviets were traded for American agents the Soviets had seized as hostages. The Bureau also annoyed the agency in 1978 when it insisted that the agency give it a copy of a surveillance satellite manual that former CIA officer William Kampiles had sold to the Soviets to use as evidence in Kampiles's trial. The agency was embarrassed by the discovery that fourteen more copies had disappeared, and it did not want this publicly known. It took an order from President Carter to force the CIA to disgorge the manual. During the Kampiles trial, the CIA made the astounding claim that a Carter executive order prohibited the CIA from investigating (or requesting that the FBI investigate) Americans, even its own agents, unless it had evidence they had committed a crime. CIA Director Stansfield Turner explained the CIA's inability to prevent its ranks from being infiltrated by saying, "We pay a price for respecting the rights of our citizens, and therefore must accept that our counterintelligence efforts will never be as effective as the KGB's." The CIA was now using its devotion to civil liberties to excuse its failures. In a few years the FBI would follow suit.

In April 1988, Webster, now at the CIA, set up a new Counterintelligence Center (CIC) at Langley headquarters. One FBI agent was assigned full time to the center. Webster and his successor at the FBI, William Sessions, signed a memorandum of understanding that year pledging the agency would brief the Bureau about Central Intelligence cases "in a timely fashion." Cooperation broke down again, however, in late 1993, when the CIA stopped informing the Bureau about terrorism leads, and when he took over the Bureau, Louis Freeh withdrew the Bureau's agents from the CIC in Langley.

■ ■ ■

The FBI's organized crime units by now had become experts in recognizing patterns of criminality that pointed to the existence of criminal conspiracies. The Bureau's foreign counterintelligence agencies had always done the same thing as they uprooted entire espionage networks. This was a model that begged to be applied to domestic and international terrorism. But it was not.

Instead, FBI terrorist investigations remained bound in the same case-file mentality that had doomed to irrelevance earlier Bureau investigations of organized crime. Bureau counterterrorism investigators pressed for quick convictions to reassure the public that the threat of terrorism was under control. They seemed to have come to share the same belief as many Bureau critics, that terrorism was less of a problem than the public's *fear* of terrorism, and that an arrest and a conviction of a few individuals could lay the fear to rest—and of course the Bureau had a long history orchestrating such rituals. But the greater problem was that the emerging threat of terrorism in the early 1990s—despite the Bureau's preference for focusing on right-wing movements—was Islamic extremism. Any comprehensive effort to gather intelligence about the threat from those quarters in the United States would have laid the Bureau open to charges from the only enemy it really feared these days—suspicious civil libertarians—that it was engaged in ethnic profiling. Moreover, an investigation of the Islamic community within which fundamentalist extremists operated would have plunged the Bureau into conflict with the black community, since Islam was attracting ever growing numbers of African-Americans. That was another battle the Bureau no longer had any taste for fighting.

And so, while the rest of the Bureau was adopting sophisticated, comprehensive strategies to combat organized crime and espionage, in counterterrorism the Bureau not only resisted the trend, but dug into its past to revive an old FBI tradition thought to have been long discarded: "machine-gun criminology." While the Bureau paid lip service to the idea of fighting terrorism with the skull work of intelligence gathering, risk assessment, and analysis, it actually began to commit its resources to a more glamorous and muscular brand of counterterrorism: It organized its own army for fighting terrorists, on the disastrous assumption that the terrorist threat of the future would send the Bureau into combat with entrenched terrorists holding hostages to extract concessions from the government.

Many countries had a head start on the FBI organizing what would become known as special forces or assault teams. After the Black September attacks on the 1972 Munich Olympics, Germany created its GSG-9 assault team (*Grenzschutzgruppe 9*, or Border Protection Group 9). The Israelis had the commando unit that liberated the Air France plane bound for Tel Aviv and hijacked to Entebbe, Uganda. France formed its GIGN *(Groupement d'Intervention de la Gendarmerie Nationale)*. The British had its 22nd Regiment of the Special Air Service.

In the United States the first counterterror assault team was the First Special Forces Operational Detachment–Delta, created by Charles Beckwith in 1978. Beckwith, who had trained with the British Special Air Service, modeled Delta Force on the British SAS and set up joint training sessions with them in England and at Fort Bragg, North Carolina. In August 1980 the Navy established SEAL Team Six under Richard Marcinko—who now prospers as the author of a series of SEAL thriller novels—as its own counterterrorism assault unit.

Until 1983 the FBI's plan was to use the military, specifically Delta Force, to deal with major hostage incidents. The military itself, however, began to develop misgivings when their FBI counterparts pointed out there would be grand jury investigations of any deaths, even of the terrorists. The military would also have to provide depositions, and their weapons would be seized as evidence after the rescue. The Delta Force would also be subject to civil lawsuits for injuries or damages, even to suspects.

The idea of the FBI developing an assault team of its own was born at a legendary demonstration Delta Force and the SEALs staged for William Webster at Fort Bragg. After watching the commandos race through a hostage-taking exercise, Webster had a chance to talk to the Delta and SEAL team members and examine their equipment. It was all very impressive, but one thing puzzled Webster. According to the story, which Webster says may even be approximately accurate, Webster commented to Major General Richard Scholtes, commander of the Joint Special Operations Command, "I don't see any handcuffs." Scholtes replied, "We're not taking any prisoners, it's not our job. It's just two shots right in the middle of the forehead."

At that moment Webster decided that if assault teams were going to operate on American soil, they had better be American law enforcement officers with an idea of what the Constitution required for a legal arrest.

Webster named Danny O. Coulson to train and lead the new force, to be called the Hostage Rescue Team (HRT). It was a difficult assignment because, according to his aide, John B. Hotis, Webster didn't "want a bunch of colonels sitting around Quantico sharpening their bayonets. He wants them to think and act like FBI agents. The problem is, how do we insure that they don't become commandos, that they remain FBI agents?" When Buck Revell formally handed the assignment to Coulson, he said, "We've got to keep this thing in proper perspective. You're not to re-create Delta. You have to remember this is an FBI deal." But Webster also told Coulson, "I expect the FBI to have the best counterterrorist team in the world. We're the best and we should have the best."

That was Coulson's goal, too. In the end, though, the two goals, to have the best counterterrorist force in the world and to make sure they remained FBI agents, would not be easy to bridge.

Part of the problem was the nature of the FBI agent, who lives for competitive challenges. As soon as word of the HRT got out, Coulson was flooded with applications from the best of the best of the Bureau. Before Coulson had his first man, the HRT had taken on the image of being the Bureau's best, its elite, its Green Berets or Airborne. Whatever it was, it was going to be the role model for the rest of the FBI and its face to the public.

Coulson had 150 volunteers to put through the first selection process, finally choosing fifty of the best. They had to pass grueling tests of their physical strength, judgment, and willingness to risk their lives for the survival of their team and the hostages. The physical focus was on upper-body strength, because Coulson had learned from the other counterterrorist groups that the most difficult part of the job was getting to the scene, and that could involve "climbing, jumping, swimming, running, crawling, walking, or fast-roping out of helicopters. All these required extraordinary upper-body strength." As a consequence there has never been a female "operator," as HRT members are called, except in such support roles as handling logistics or piloting aircraft.

The HRT is organized into squads of snipers and operators. The snipers advance to forward positions, locate the "Tangos" and relay their observations to the rest of the team, then protect the operators as they move into position for the assault. The assault demands the skills of close-quarter battle: fast and furious movements into danger, using rapid fire to kill the targets while avoiding injury to the hostages.

The fundamental difference between a law enforcement SWAT (Special Weapons and Tactics) team and an assault team is that a SWAT team moves into position for an arrest slowly and quietly, peering around corners with mirrors, for instance. The assault team moves in with extreme speed, noise, and violence, which is why it almost always uses flash-bang grenades, intended to deafen, blind, and stun the targets.

The HRT was unveiled just before the Los Angeles Olympics in 1984. The press was invited to watch a close-order battle exercise to free hostages from the shooting house in Quantico (one of the hostages was Buck Revell). Needless to say, the press was entranced, and the HRT had taken its first step to becoming a new and glamorous image for the FBI, just as machine-gun-wielding gang-busters had been the public face of the Bureau in the 1930s.

After the 1984 Olympics passed without a hitch, the HRT settled back once again into its training routine. Coulson felt his men were going stale, doing nothing but training and demonstrating their skills. One went to Coulson and complained, "We need jobs. We didn't come on this team just to train." In September 1984, Coulson offered the HRT to the resident agent in Coeur d'Alene, Idaho, where the Bureau was trying to arrest a white supremacist named Robert Matthews, whose Order was targeting national leaders for assassination as the start of a war to create an Aryan nation in the Northwest.

Coulson had a hard time convincing Revell to let him send the HRT to Idaho, telling him, "Our guys need to work. If you don't use us, we'll become just like Delta. Not enough work. Every counterterrorism leader in the world has to struggle to find jobs for their people, especially at first."

Revell remembers it differently, that Coulson had been in touch with the Seattle field office, and it was the field office special agent in charge, Al Whittaker, who asked Revell to send the HRT to help him. At first only a small detachment of the HRT was sent to Idaho, but after Matthews escaped a firefight with agents of the Portland field office and fled to Whidbey Island in Puget Sound, Revell sent Coulson and half the HRT, twenty-five operators and snipers, to assist the local agents.

Matthews was holed up in a cedar chalet protected by a cliff and thick fir trees. There were soon bad feelings between the HRT and Whittaker, who at first refused to let the HRT snipers set up positions near the chalet, fearing that they would be spotted. Negotiations with Matthews were going nowhere, and it seemed Matthews was determined to go down fighting to inspire his movement.

Fresh SWAT operators from the Los Angeles and San Francisco field offices then arrived to relieve the Seattle SWAT team. According to Coulson, he and Whittaker decided that the HRT was no longer needed, and so the team headed back to Whidbey Naval Air Station to wait for their C-130 transport to take them back to Quantico. While they were waiting for the planes, Coulson reported, Whittaker had his men shoot tear gas into the building, but Matthews had a gas mask, and so the gas did not bother him. Instead he began to fire accurately at the SWAT teams. Whittaker summoned Coulson back and asked him to secure the perimeter around the cabin. Then one of the agents shot a lighting flare into the cabin to help the SWAT team spot Matthews. The cabin caught on fire and burned to the ground, Matthews along with it.

In April 1985 the HRT was deployed to resolve another standoff with another white supremacist group, this one in Arkansas. A member of Matthews's Order had shot two Missouri state troopers, then retreated to a fortified compound belonging to the Covenant, Sword, and Arm of the Lord (CSA) paramilitary group on Bull Shoals Lake in Arkansas. The CSA had .50-caliber weapons, hand grenades, and an armored personnel carrier. There were 200 in the compound, and 150 law enforcement officers surrounding it. Upon arrival, the HRT first secured the scene and set up a command structure among the local, state, and federal law enforcement agencies on the scene. Standard Bureau policy is for only the negotiation team to talk to the suspects; the idea is for the negotiator to play for time by having to refer the target's requests back to his superior. Coulson thought the CSA leaders were so rank-conscious they would be flattered if they were allowed to speak directly to a commander. It turned out Coulson's instincts here were on the money, and the result was a peaceful surrender with no loss of life.

When Coulson left the HRT to become the assistant special agent in charge in the Washington field office in April 1986, he was succeeded by David W. "Woody" Johnson, a Marine Vietnam veteran who had foreign counterintelligence experience. Johnson's HRT handled the Marielito prison riots, when criminals deported from Cuba, housed in federal penitentiaries, rioted after they learned they were going to be sent back to Castro. They first took over the Oakdale, Louisiana, federal detention center, and then the federal penitentiary in Atlanta. The HRT handled the Oakdale riot. For Atlanta, Coulson had to cobble together another unit of FBI SWAT teams from around the country, reinforced by SWAT teams from other federal agencies.

In the HRT the Bureau had something that was irresistibly glamorous and awesomely effective. The Bureau also had, as events would prove, a tiger by the tail. The HRT let the Bureau go into battle and win just about anywhere against just about anybody. And so it began to go into battle when there were other—less violent—ways of solving dangerous crimes and resolving dangerous situations. For example, Ruby Ridge.

Ruby Ridge began as the U.S. Marshals Service's mess. Randy Weaver, his wife Vicki, their two children Sammy and Sara, and their adopted son Kevin Harris had settled on a remote hilltop, Ruby Ridge, near Bonners Ferry in northwest Idaho. They tried to create a self-sufficient refuge according to the doctrines of the Christian Identity movement, which saw the Anglo-Saxon race as the true Chosen People of the Bible, besieged by a Zionist-controlled government ("jack-booted thugs in black helicopters," i.e., the FBI). They awaited the apocalypse predicted by William Pierce (writing as Andrew MacDonald) in *The Turner Diaries,* in which the final conflagration involves the destruction of the Hoover FBI headquarters in Washington by a Christian Identity army. The Bureau of Alcohol, Tobacco, and Firearms (ATF), which was investigating illegal traffic in guns by right-wing extremists, had an informant go to Weaver and ask him to shorten two shotguns illegally, whereupon the ATF arrested him on January 17, 1991. Released on bond, Weaver retreated to his mountaintop cabin and refused to show up for court appearances.

That brought the U.S. Marshals Service into the case. They were reconnoitering Weaver's property on August 21, 1992, when Sammy Weaver's dog started barking at the marshals. The Weaver boy and Kevin Harris, both armed, went out to investigate. What happened next has never been satisfactorily explained, but there was a gunfight that left U.S. Marshal William F. Degan, Sammy Weaver, and the dog all dead.

The FBI has jurisdiction over crimes against federal agents, and so the Hostage Rescue Team was dispatched to Idaho. The HRT was told by the U.S. marshals, who may have been in a state of panic, that Weaver was the most dangerous fugitive the FBI would ever face. An employee at a ski resort used as a rear base by the HRT told me that some of the HRT operators seemed to have buck fever, that is, to be in a state of high pre-battle excitement. Back in Washington, Danny Coulson remembered something that the founder of Delta Force had told him: "Son, don't be afraid that your superiors will give you what appears to be an impossible mission. You and your boys will figure out a way to do it. Your greatest fear should be that you will be given a failed tactical mission from another unit. You will forever be tarred with the brush of their failure."

HRT commander Richard Rogers led his team into positions blocking the three approaches to the Weaver cabin, the fourth being a steep cliff. The plan was that after they had secured the perimeter, a negotiator would approach the cabin in an armored personnel carrier to inform the Weavers of the warrants for their arrests, and would leave a field telephone so that they could commence negotiations.

Around dusk, snipers dug shallow shooting pits concealed from the cabin by fallen logs. It was sleeting when a Bureau helicopter appeared overhead. Weaver, Sara, and Harris burst through the door brandishing rifles. Since they appeared to be on the verge of shooting at the helicopter, one of the snipers, Lon Horiuchi, took a shot at Weaver, wounding him. Despite his wound, Weaver ran back toward the cabin, followed by his daughter and Harris. Horiuchi feared that they would continue to fire at the helicopter from inside the building, and so he shot again just as Harris ran through the door.

It was ten days before Weaver surrendered. Horiuchi learned only then that his second shot had passed through the door, killing Vicki Weaver, who had been holding the door open with one arm and holding her baby, Elisheba, in her other. The same shot wounded Kevin Harris.

To many in Idaho, the HRT's killing of Vicki Weaver seemed proof that *The Turner Diaries'* apocalyptic vision of a murderous federal government sending killer troops from the FBI to round up citizens for exercising their Second Amendment rights had come to pass. It could be argued that once Randy Weaver was charged with violating the laws prohibiting the production of sawed-off shotguns, it was his duty to surrender and defend himself in court, and not, in effect, to challenge the federal authorities to come and get him. On the other hand, time is always on the side of the government. There would have always been opportunities for the authorities to arrest Weaver during one of his many trips to the outside world for supplies. The U.S. marshals surely erred in forcing the issue by trying to approach Weaver's cabin. The FBI erred by deciding that Ruby Ridge was made to order for the HRT. But perhaps the first error was for the FBI to have a Hostage Rescue Team at all.

On April 12, 1993, Weaver—defended by the flamboyant Gerry Spence—and Harris were tried on federal charges ranging from illegal weapons possession to the murder of a federal officer (William Degan). After a two-month trial in the federal court in Boise, Idaho, Kevin Harris was acquitted of all charges, and Randy Weaver of all but two—failure to appear in court and violating the terms of his bail after his original arrest on weapons charges—but he was acquitted of the weapons charges themselves. The *New York Times* called the verdict "a strong rebuke of the government's use of force during an armed siege."

Public feeling in Idaho ran strongly against the Bureau. Horiuchi was indicted in state court for killing Vicki Weaver, but the state charges were dismissed and referred to a federal court. There they remained until 2001, when a federal panel ruled that Horiuchi could be tried in state court; but a new Idaho prosecutor dismissed the manslaughter charges, finally ending Horiuchi's ordeal. Weaver received a $3.1 million settlement of his wrongful death lawsuit for the killing of his wife and son.

The problem with the HRT was that it was *too* good. Its operators were the cream of the agency: athletic, smart, and brave, able to solve almost any kind of tactical problem under fire. And like the HRT, which was in some ways now the model for the Bureau, the Bureau was also, if anything, becoming too good when it came to guns and guts, but it lacked the subtle political and cultural knowledge needed to deal with a changing American society and world. Given the intelligence of the HRT, their commanders, and for that matter their superiors at headquarters, it sounds harsh to say that the HRT was a sign that in counterterrorism, the Bureau was becoming all brawn and no brains. Brains in counterterrorism consists of collecting intelligence about potential threats, analyzing it, and then "thinking outside the box" about how those threats might actually be realized. By glamorizing the HRT, the Bureau was reverting to a latter-day version of the gangbuster ethos that had been its trademark during the thirties—its ticket to popular culture fame and fortune. The Bureau seemed to be straining to achieve the rock-'em-sock-'em apolitical heroism that had won over depression America. That old-time agent Robert Lamphere was thinking along these lines when he complained to me, "I don't see why the FBI has to have an army. We're supposed to be detectives."

• • •

The FBI director's term is ten years, and William Webster's was about to expire in 1988. He wanted to get out of government and practice law, but that would have to wait. When the Iran-Contra affair swept over the Reagan administration in 1986, William Casey, director of Central Intelligence, was at the center of the scandal. Casey tried to tough it out, but he was dying from terminal brain cancer. He resigned in January 1987, and died a few days later.

The CIA was in shambles, and needed leadership, fast. The logical choice to succeed Casey was Robert Gates, the acting director (and Casey's former deputy director), but he had been accused, unfairly as it turned out, of being involved in Iran-Contra, and so was considered unconfirmable. (Gates would later be named to the post by George Bush, serving from 1991 to 1993.)

That left the administration desperate to get someone over to the CIA who was qualified to run the agency, and, just as important, could get confirmed. Buck Revell, among many others, suggested Webster. When Reagan told Webster he needed him, he agreed to take the job. He resigned his FBI directorship on May 25, 1987, and the next day was sworn in as director of Central Intelligence, where he served until August 31, 1991.

The Bureau was still taking such a beating over the constant revelations from the Hoover years (Webster said he spent much of his time dealing with those messes) that the White House had a hard time getting anyone to take Webster's old job. It was particularly hard now that a federal judge seemed the best choice after the Bureau's happy experience with Webster, which meant the candidate had to give up his lifetime judicial tenure. John Otto, the executive assistant director for Law Enforcement Services, ran the Bureau as acting director for three months until a judge was located who would take the job. He was William Sessions, chief judge of the Federal District Court for Western Texas. Sessions took the oath on November 2, 1987.

Top Bureau officials desperately wanted the new director to succeed, but from the beginning they noticed a strange disconnect between Sessions and his job. He seemed to see the position as largely ceremonial. He accepted nearly every invitation to speak and continuously junketed around the country—particularly back to Texas—to attend meetings that seemed trivial to his executives. They thought it looked amateurish for Sessions always to be wearing his gold FBI badge on his shirt, something real agents rarely did. He tried to ingratiate himself by displaying his ignorance about the Bureau; he liked to say how surprised he had been to learn that the Bureau did counterespionage. This was perhaps an attempt to connect with his audiences, except that it would have been a remarkably uninformed American who had never heard that the FBI sometimes chased spies. And Americans do expect their FBI directors to know a little bit about their job.

Another problem was Sessions's wife. Some agents and officials thought she acted, in effect, as co-director of the Bureau. Alice Sessions responded that the top officials were simply misogynistic, which may have been true, describing their attitude as "we aren't used to having a wife involved in the FBI and we don't intend to." She further antagonized the agents by letting it drop that she thought the trouble was that none of the other directors had had wives, or at least healthy wives. Agents who had served under Clarence Kelley resented this, because they had sympathized with him as he nursed his dying wife in Kansas City. William Webster's wife was highly regarded by the Bureau, and she too had died while he was director.

Bureau officials were convinced that Sessions bounced important personnel decisions off Alice, and that her dislikes could ruin their careers. It was widely believed that Sessions's decision to name W. Douglas Gow associate deputy director for investigations over William Baker, whom many thought more qualified, was based on his wife's low opinion of Baker. She called herself Sessions's "eyes and ears" at the Bureau, and said she got useful information for her husband from secretaries in the elevator. She also made known her opinion that the FBI was filled with incompetents: "In the bureau the saying is 'mess-up, move up.' . . . This has come to me as Bureau-ese. The other big thing you'll hear is everybody covers ass." She said Bureau officials were not "well educated or intellectually bright, but they are cunning." She complained that headquarters was hostile to her from the start, and she suspected her enemies there were tapping her phones and planting bugs in her bedroom. She saw slights where none were intended, and resented it when subordinates got social invitations that did not go to her or her husband. (Both were teetotalers, which might have had something to do with it.)

Shortly after Sessions took over, Attorney General William P. Barr had to rebuke him for taking his wife on FBI planes to visit family and friends, a violation of government regulations. Agents complained that Alice Sessions had security guards park her car under the Hoover headquarters building when she went shopping. She created the appearance of trying to steer an expensive security contract for their house to Dan Munford, husband of Sarah Munford, Sessions's personal assistant. (The Bureau refused to award the contract, citing the high cost, lack of competitive bidding, and Dan Munford's close relationship with the director's assistant.) She demanded a special pass at headquarters that allowed her to bring in visitors without signing them in, and then often forgot the pass and demanded to be waved in with her friends.

The impression that Sessions was dominated by the women in his life was reinforced by the activities of Sarah Munford, the personal assistant he brought with him from Texas. According to agents that journalist Ronald Kessler interviewed, Munford did not seem up to her responsibilities, and blamed her mistakes on the agents in Sessions's personal detail. Like Alice Sessions, she too received special treatment, sometimes in trivial ways that were nevertheless hot buttons to agents: She continued to register her car in Texas after she had moved to Virginia, which might seem like a small matter, but reregistering was an inconvenient and expensive obligation for agents when they relocated. It was one of the many inconveniences endured by the oft-transferred agents, who resented it when Sessions exempted his assistant from the regulation. She had also tried to use her FBI credentials to get out of a traffic ticket in Texas, without being disciplined by Sessions even though the matter was serious enough to later get her fired. She developed a reputation for blaming agents around her when she made mistakes. Soon almost no one at the Bureau would deal with her, which made it almost impossible for her to get anything done for Sessions.

Sessions liked to portray himself as a stickler for regulations, which made his actual laxity regarding himself, his wife, and his assistant infuriating to his subordinates. Kessler heard from agents that when these infractions were brought to his attention, "Sessions turned a deaf ear, allowing Munford and his wife to do as they pleased, displaying an arrogance that conflicted with his image as a fair-minded, objective individual and making a mockery of the FBI's program of policing itself." Early on, Buck Revell, then executive associate director for operations, had to reprimand Sessions for using his Bureau limo and driver to pick up the director's father at the airport. It was an offense that would have automatically earned a thirty-day suspension for any agent or official. Revell warned Sessions that such laxity had tainted Kelley's reputation—and in effect had gotten him fired—and that Hoover would have gone to jail for the way he enriched himself from his position, if he had the bad luck to live a decade longer.

Soon after Sessions took over, a controversy over domestic surveillance seemed to reveal that the Bureau was still targeting citizens for special attention because of their political beliefs. The dispute actually proved that no surveillance of any domestic political group by the Bureau would any longer be regarded as legitimate, and that any group investigated by the FBI could thereby claim victim status for itself and, by a strange logic, legitimacy for its cause.

CISPES, Citizens in Solidarity with the People of El Salvador, was an American group that opposed the Reagan administration's support for anticommunist regimes in El Salvador and other Central American countries. Since the group was providing moral and vocal (though nothing in the way of material) support to the guerrilla insurgency in El Salvador, the Bureau began to look into it, beginning with a criminal investigation in September 1981 that went nowhere. Then the Intelligence Division submitted a request in March 1983 to the Justice Department's Office of Intelligence Policy Review for permission to investigate the group. This was approved for three months, and then the case was closed. After a series of bombings in Washington that suggested possible links between the bombers and CISPES, the investigation was reopened and assigned to the Criminal Investigation Division.

Earlier that summer an informant had walked into the Dallas field office and said he knew all about terrorism in El Salvador and the activities of Salvadorans in the United States. The informant, a Salvadoran immigrant named Frank Varelli, and his FBI handler, Special Agent Daniel Flanagan, seemed to have an unholy influence on each other, with ruinous consequences for the Bureau. The Bureau needed information on CISPES, and Varelli could supply seemingly authentic but actually fabricated accounts of CISPES support for the insurgent movement in El Salvador. By the time headquarters became fully aware of what was happening, the CISPES investigation had "taken on a life of its own," and was being actively pursued by twelve offices across the country, even though there was no real evidence of criminal activity or contact with terrorist organizations by CISPES beyond uncorroborated statements by Varelli. Buck Revell reviewed the case and launched an investigation of Flanagan, which revealed that Flanagan had been pocketing payments meant for Varelli. He was fired, and his supervisor in Dallas was transferred. Revell ordered the case closed on June 18, 1985.

Early in Sessions's term, in January 1988, a Freedom of Information Act request brought the CISPES investigation to light. Opponents of the Reagan administration's Central American policies claimed it proved the administration had unleashed the FBI to harass and suppress its enemies. It did not seem to matter that the Bureau had, on its own, terminated the CISPES probe after discovering abuses of FBI procedures and had punished the agent responsible, who was forced to resign.

The Bureau's own review concluded that the Bureau had sufficient cause to begin the investigation, and that the Bureau had broken no laws in the course of it. But instead of defending the Bureau, Sessions apologized profusely for CISPES to the Senate Intelligence Committee. His weak defense—that the investigation had been properly predicated and that no laws had been broken—were offered as a *sotto voce* afterthought. Agents and Bureau officials were unnerved by Sessions's apologies, knowing the paralyzing impact they would have on future counterterrorism investigations. As Buck Revell wrote, "For political gain, many in Congress often (and wrongly) lambasted the FBI, [and so] the Bureau could not afford to habitually apologize for mistakes it hadn't made, and crimes it hadn't committed."

The House Judiciary Committee's 1988 inquiry into CISPES falsely accused the FBI of burglarizing CISPES offices. Congress demanded scapegoats and Sessions provided them. In 1985, Revell had wanted to bring criminal charges against Flanagan as the only person who had actually broken the law as well as Bureau regulations in the CISPES matter, but the Justice Department and the U.S. attorneys all declined. Now punishments Revell considered unfair were dealt out to Flanagan's Dallas supervisor, his headquarters supervisor, the assistant special agent in charge in Dallas, and the chief of the counterterrorism section of Division Six. As Revell put it, "And so the Bureau leadership under Director Sessions proceeded onto the battlefield to bayonet its wounded." After CISPES, Sessions was becoming known around the Bureau as Director "Concessions." In contrast, former director William Webster offered a spirited defense of the Bureau's record on civil liberties: Since Hoover, he said, "there has not been a single proven case of a violation of constitutional rights. You always have people claiming it. It costs ten dollars to file a lawsuit. But there hasn't been a single one."

From a post-9/11 perspective, the eagerness of Congress and the media to punish the Bureau for crimes against CISPES it had not committed persuaded the Bureau to abandon any capability for dealing with domestic or foreign terrorism. Looking back at the CISPES affair, Buck Revell predicted that "the long term damage incurred by the Bureau through rumor and innuendo would have tragic consequences." The Bureau basically decided that all counterterrorism investigations were taboo, and were to be avoided at all costs by agents with any concern for their careers:

> *The Counter-Terrorism Section was effectively neutralized. After all of the removals and censures, we practically had to order people to work on counterterrorism investigations. People were always going to criticize what you were doing or not doing, fraught as it was with peril. Agents would be only too happy*

to work noncontroversial cases, such as bank robberies and kidnappings. To work counterterrorism was to become a target for the wildest and cruelest of accusations a law enforcement officer could possibly endure.

Revell also noted that the CISPES controversy became justification for keeping the restrictive Levi guidelines in place until passage of the Patriot Act (these guidelines were slightly modified in 1983 by Attorney General William French Smith, but were essentially unchanged). Buck Revell thought,

Perhaps more damaging was the continuation of laws and guidelines that would keep law enforcement from investigating groups directly espousing violence and supporting terrorist groups before they were known to have broken specific laws. Even in an age of weapons of mass destruction, where chemical and biological weapons and high-order explosives are easy to come by, law enforcement has to sit on its hands. Even though there's plenty that can be done without violating the civil rights of citizens, nothing is done. And if we wait until there is blood in the streets, the blood will be running in rivers, not streams.

■ ■ ■

By the end of the first Bush administration, Attorney General Barr had become so disgusted by Sessions's failure to provide the Bureau with leadership that he wanted the president to fire Sessions for incompetence. He thought Sessions was concerned about nothing except attending the right parties, while Sessions's analysis of events and recommendations seemed bizarre. When Barr asked Sessions for Bureau proposals for dealing with the Rodney King riots in Los Angeles, Sessions suggested sending in the Hostage Rescue Team, a response that seemed ridiculous when an entire city was in chaos.

Before Barr could act, the controversy over the abuse of authority and privilege by Sessions, his wife, and Sarah Munford, which had been largely confined to the upper reaches of the department and the Bureau, became public knowledge, and dealt another blow to what was left of the Bureau's reputation.

Sessions brought his final humiliation on himself. He had given *Washington Post* reporter Ronald Kessler unprecedented access to the Bureau: Sessions and his wife gave lengthy interviews to Kessler, and Sessions ordered agents and supervisors to make themselves available. (It is a violation of Bureau regulations for Bureau personnel to talk to anyone about Bureau business without authorization; the charge is "unauthorized disclosure.") Before long Kessler began to hear about the bitterness in the Bureau over the behavior of the Sessionses and Sarah Munford. Kessler put the charges against William and Alice Sessions and Sarah Munford into a ten-page, single-spaced letter, and handed it to the Bureau's public relations office on June 24, 1992, asking that it be delivered to the director for comment. The letter, unknown to Kessler, was also turned over to the Bureau's Office of Professional Responsibility (OPR), as was required by Bureau regulations of any allegations against Bureau personnel. Since in this case the charges concerned their director, the Bureau OPR turned the letter over to the Justice Department's OPR. Kessler later learned that a second, anonymous letter written by an unknown agent went to the attorney general a day later, dealing with many of the same abuses.

Once the investigation of Sessions began, his supporters began leaking information to the press to discredit the probe, claiming that the Bush administration was trying to block an FBI investigation of Italian bank loans to Saddam Hussein, an embarrassment to the Bush administration since it revealed the White House's support for Hussein before the first Gulf War. Sessions's enemies, perhaps in the Bureau, leaked misinformation that criminal charges were being considered against Sessions for falsely claiming exemption from the District of Columbia income tax. The charges against Sessions became public in an October 11, 1992, ABC-TV report by Sam Donaldson, and President Bush's opponents—the election was less than a month away—were happy to portray the Sessions affair as a plot against a reformist director by the administration and old "Hooverites." Alice Sessions claimed her husband was being framed, and that he was "waking up out of a stupor, realizing he's been had," a remark that hardened opinion against her and her husband within the Bureau. Sessions also did himself no good by flying with his wife to Atlantic City for a Bolshoi Ballet performance on the FBI Saberliner, the ticket paid for by a gambling casino. It made him seem, under the circumstances, reckless and defiant.

After the OPR issued its report, Sarah Munford was fired for making personal long-distance phone calls from her office, for failing to register her car in Virginia, and for using her FBI credentials to avoid a traffic ticket. Her attorneys said she was "an unfortunate pawn in what appears to be a high-stakes battle over the future direction and leadership of the FBI."

The OPR report concluded that the charges against Sessions were so serious that they should be forwarded to President Bush for his decision on whether Sessions should be removed. Attorney General Barr wrote to Sessions that, "Given that you are a former U.S. attorney and federal judge, and that you are currently director of the premier federal law enforcement agency, I must conclude that there is no excuse for your conduct."

Sessions and his wife still charged that they were being railroaded to derail the Bureau's investigation into the Italian bank scandal. Sessions also claimed that old-line FBI officials wanted to block his program for the affirmative-action hiring of minorities.

Back in Texas, where he was special agent in charge of the Dallas office, Buck Revell put out a statement:

From what I have read, these are very serious allegations. No Federal official, much less the Director of the FBI, should abuse ethical standards in the conduct of his official duties or in his personal affairs. Director Sessions has served our Nation honorably and well in a number of high-level positions over the past twenty years and he is entitled to defend himself on these charges. If he cannot show our new President that he has conducted himself in an ethical and honorable fashion, then he should resign for the good of the Bureau and our Country.

Revell followed this up with a private letter to Sessions:

In my opinion your conduct and demeanor has been below the standards required of the Director of the Federal Bureau of Investigation. I must ask you to do the right thing for the Bureau and your country. Resign while you still have some semblance of dignity and before you do further harm to an agency that you have professed to honor and respect.

The OPR report was released to the public on the day of President Bill Clinton's inauguration, January 20, 1993. Its 161 pages documented Sessions's ethical and legal failings and poor judgment. The *New York Times* called it "a seemingly endless record of chiseling and expense account padding."

But the first World Trade Center bombing on February 26, 1993, and a burgeoning crisis at the Branch Davidian compound near Waco, Texas, made it impossible for Clinton to fire Sessions as quickly as he might have liked. The new president was also having trouble getting an attorney general installed (his first two nominees ran afoul of rules governing the pay and benefits of household employees), and so no one was really in charge at the Justice Department until Janet Reno was confirmed on March 12, 1993. In the meantime, although Sessions's days were numbered, he was kept on to maintain some semblance of order at the department and the Bureau.

. . .

The delay in firing Sessions was a factor in one of the worst and bloodiest debacles in FBI history.

On the morning of April 19, 1993, eighty-five members of David Koresh's Mount Carmel religious community, among them twenty-five children, were huddled inside a rambling, asymmetrical complex of buildings on the outskirts of Waco. They were armed with an arsenal of handguns and shoulder weapons. A light plane buzzed overhead.

Surrounding the Mount Carmel compound were seven hundred government agents: the FBI Hostage Rescue Team, SWAT teams from neighboring Bureau offices, agents from the Bureau of Alcohol, Tobacco, and Firearms (ATF), Texas state troopers, the Texas National Guard, Texas Rangers, and observers from the Delta Force. They were supported by HRT operators in nine Bradley Fighting Vehicles, two M1A1 Abrams tanks, and five M278 combat engineering vehicles. Helicopters were ready in backup locations. Three miles away, but within sight, nearly a thousand print and broadcast reporters and technicians watched. CNN was transmitting live around the world. In Washington, leaders of the Justice Department and the FBI gathered in the Bureau's Strategic Information and Operations Center (SIOC). With them was Danny Coulson, founder of the Hostage Rescue Team, which was on the front lines of the government forces. The field commander was Special Agent in Charge Jeff Jamar from San Antonio, backed up by SACs Bob Ricks from Oklahoma City, Dick Swensen from New Orleans, and Dick Schwein from El Paso.

At 6:02 A.M. two of the M278s with HRT drivers moved up to the living quarters of the compound, knocked out the windows, and sprayed the interior with tear gas. Gunfire from the compound sprayed the M278s. According to plan, the HRT moved the Bradley tanks in, punched holes in the walls with their booms, and then fired in "ferret rounds" of tear gas to suppress the gunfire by making the compound uninhabitable. When the gunfire did not stop, the M278s broke more holes in the walls and sent in more gas. Back in Washington, Janet Reno left the SIOC at 10:00 A.M. to make a speech. At 11:30 the Bureau got a new supply of gas grenades, and fired them into the building, the last at about 11:40 A.M.

Twenty-seven minutes later, at 12:07 P.M., the Bureau's spotter plane picked up infrared indications of fire at three locations. Flames began spreading throughout the buildings. In a matter of minutes, fanned by enormous drafts coming through the gaping holes in the walls, the interior was an inferno. Seventy-five people would die in that fire, including twenty-five children under age fifteen. Among the dead were two fetuses, born spontaneously after their mothers died. A few of the bodies, including David Koresh's, showed that they had died by gunshot wounds, some self-inflicted. The rest had burned to death. In Washington, Janet Reno announced, "I made the decision. I'm accountable, the buck stops with me." Bill Clinton called her the next day and told her "That-a-girl." Later he told the press, "I do not think the United States government is responsible for the fact that a bunch of religious fanatics decided to kill themselves."

Waco was the bloodiest day in the history of American law enforcement, no matter how it is measured. It was the most violent action directed by the American government against Americans since 120 died at Wounded Knee in 1890.

The day of the tragedy, Sessions said, "I had hoped to report that today's careful and humane efforts by the FBI and ATF agents to bring the Branch Davidians out of their compound had resulted in a peaceful resolution of the standoff. Instead, we are faced with destruction and death. However, I have no question that our plan was correct and was conducted with professionalism." Sessions's successor, Louis Freeh, also defended the Bureau: "I am quite satisfied with the operational aspects, planning aspects, chain-of-command aspects and leadership aspects of that operation. . . . I will take whatever actions—mostly positive actions—that are included in the recommendations [of the Justice Department's review]. I do not contemplate any disciplinary actions." But at the Treasury Department, almost the entire command structure of the ATF was fired or disciplined for its performance at Waco.

There had been a religious community at Mount Carmel since 1957, made up of a group of Seventh-Day Adventists known as Branch Davidians (derived from, though not affiliated with, the national Adventist Church). In 1981 the twenty-two-year-old Vernon Wayne Howell, product of a turbulent and abusive Houston home, a talented would-be rock musician and a lifelong Adventist, came to Mount Carmel. By 1985, displaying a dazzling command of the Bible (particularly Revelation) and an ability to explain biblical arcana to followers whose minds were consumed by a hunger for biblical knowledge, he had taken over the community and revealed that he was a reincarnation of Christ. He took the name David Koresh.

The Bureau of Alcohol, Tobacco, and Firearms began an investigation of Koresh for possible firearms violations in January 1992. Specifically, the ATF suspected that Koresh possessed unregistered automatic weapons and hand grenades, based on recent purchases of more than one hundred rifles, grenade casings, and black powder. In 1993 the ATF began undercover investigations to secure probable cause for search warrants, and on February 25, 1993, the warrants were signed by a local magistrate. On February 28, having assembled the largest contingent of agents in the history of the ATF, and ignoring warnings from its own undercover informant that security had been compromised and Koresh knew what was coming, seventy-six ATF agents launched the first attack on Mount Carmel, supported in the air by three National Guard helicopters.

Nothing went right. The helicopters were hit by small-arms fire and had to withdraw. As they closed in, agents were caught in the open. Four agents were killed, twenty-eight wounded. Within the compound five Branch Davidians died, and many others wounded, including Koresh, who was shot in the wrist and the stomach.

The ATF may have been looking for a splashy, headline-grabbing spectacle that would help its leaders survive a recent series of sex discrimination and harassment cases in its ranks when they appeared at an upcoming Senate Appropriations Committee hearing. The ATF had sent advance teams of PR specialists to Waco, and alerted the media that they had "something big going down" in Waco. In a *60 Minutes* investigation afterwards, Mike Wallace reported that "almost all the agents we talked to said that they believe the initial attack on that cult in Waco was a publicity stunt—the main goal of which was to improve ATF's tarnished image."

After the failed ATF assault, the siege dragged on for fifty-one days, punctuated by moments when hopes rose for a peaceful resolution, only to be deflated when Koresh, who was subject to periods of divine inspiration, was ordered by supernatural authority to retract his promises and continue working on his magnum opus, a definitive decryption of the Seven Seals of the Book of Revelation.

After the ATF fiasco, the FBI took over, since the Bureau had jurisdiction in cases involving the killing of federal law enforcement officers. Jeff Jamar, the FBI field commander, would try to apply the standard FBI doctrine of "isolate, contain, negotiate." He was later criticized for having the negotiators and the tactical commanders report to him separately (known in command terminology as "stove-piping"), instead of letting them coordinate their efforts and present him with their joint recommendations, as is now Bureau doctrine. The result was that the negotiators' efforts to establish a rapport with Koresh were undercut by the intimidating maneuvers of the tactical units.

On April 7, more than a month into the standoff, FBI Assistant Director Larry Potts and Deputy Director Floyd Clarke visited Waco to confer with

Jamar. They concluded that the war of nerves was wearing more on the FBI than on Koresh, who might actually be rallying the spirits of himself and his followers. The Hostage Rescue Team was becoming fatigued, particularly the snipers, who had been manning their positions for a month without relief. Foul conditions inside the compound were creating a hazardous situation for the children. Something had to be done "to move Koresh off the dime."

On April 12, Sessions, Clarke, and Potts explained the FBI's plan to resolve the standoff to Attorney General Reno, who was just one month on the job. They were going to inject tear gas (using combat engineering vehicles) into the compound, section by section, gradually constricting the space that the defenders could inhabit, until there would be nothing for them to do but leave. Reno asked how the gas would affect the children, pregnant women, and older people in the compound. She also wanted to get the reaction of the military to the plan. On April 14 military experts on tear gas told her that the gas would not permanently injure anyone and could not cause a fire. She considered the plan for two more days, and then (accounts differ) either rejected it or deferred a decision. She demanded a written report from the Bureau on the entire situation, including its justification for tear gas. Then on Saturday, April 17, evidently moved by Sessions's statement that there was child abuse in the compound, she gave her approval to the FBI plan, which now called for the gas to be progressively injected over a period of forty-eight hours, so that the tactics could be modified in light of developments. One contingency in the plan evidently did not register clearly with Reno: If the Bureau's vehicles came under fire, the remaining vehicles would rapidly introduce gas into the entire compound in all all-out chemical assault.

The day before the HRT moved in with their tanks and tear gas, Koresh had shouted, "If you don't know what you're doing, this could be the worst day in law enforcement history." He was right.

As the FBI's full contingent of tanks began shooting tear gas in as fast as supplies permitted, the FBI commanders on the scene must have believed they were now committed to playing out their hand regardless of the consequences, that there was no turning back. But, as with a plane diving to earth in a death spiral, the disaster at Waco was not the result of one bad decision, but of a chain of decisions, none of them unambiguously bad, but each clearly marginal enough to be questionable. Each FBI decision limited the options for the next. Each decision made sense in terms of those that preceded it, but wrenched out of the chain, the final decision to send in the tanks was so reckless as to raise suspicions that somehow the FBI had collectively lost its mind. To jog his commanders out of disastrous decision loops, General George Marshall used to prod them to "forget about the cheese; get out of the trap." There came a time in the decision-making process at Waco when the FBI was so concerned with the cheese—arresting Koresh, getting the children out of the compound—that it could no longer see that the only sane decision was a 180 degree turn back from the barricades.

The ATF barely survived the investigations of the disaster, and nearly its entire top command was replaced. Janet Reno's immediate acceptance of responsibility for Waco, however, proved magical in deflecting any immediate serious consequences at the department or the Bureau.

A House inquiry into Waco degenerated into a partisan brawl, revealing an interesting but temporary realignment of the two political parties. Since the original ATF complaint against Koresh involved illegal gun trafficking, Democrats, currying favor with their gun control constituents, defended the FBI, the ATF, and their new attorney general. Charles Schumer, then a congressman from Brooklyn, charged that the investigation into the Waco disaster was a National Rifle Association plot to discredit gun control. Conversely, Republicans beholden to the gun lobby found themselves in the temporary position of criticizing the FBI, their logic being the flip side of the same argument.

The lesson the FBI may have carried away from the congressional hearings was that it really had nothing to fear when it attacked right-wing domestic extremists, since its actions—and its mistakes—would be excused by liberals and Democrats, while in the long run conservatives and Republicans were going to support the Bureau no matter what. And so the Bureau made right-wing extremist groups the almost exclusive focus of its domestic intelligence operations, even though the first World Trade Center bombing on February 26, 1993, should have been a wake-up call that Islamic extremists represented the graver threat, despite the Oklahoma City bombing of April 19, 1995. And that bombing can in some ways be traced back to Waco, since Timothy McVeigh made a pilgrimage to the site of the Branch Davidian compound before planning his own attack. He set off the explosion on the April 19 anniversary of the FBI assault at Waco, and regarded as prophetic *The Turner Diaries,* which accused the FBI of being the agent for a gun-confiscating ZOG (Zionist Occupation Government) regime.

The FBI reviewed its performance after Waco, but decided no changes were called for except some tinkering with command and control to ensure more coordination between negotiators and tactical units. The HRT *did* respond to criticism that it should have known more about Koresh's religious beliefs by attending seminars at Princeton to familiarize itself with the biblical doctrine of the Apocalypse, in case they had to deal with more David Koreshes in the future. They should have read the Koran.

But the Bureau gave no real thought to whether it (or for that matter the ATF) should ever have had an "army," that is, the HRT, in the first place, or if, now that it had one, it should so regularly be deployed in situations so far removed from its original scenario: rescuing hostages (passengers) from an explosive environment (such as a jet plane) held by violent, perhaps suicidal captors (like Islamic terrorists). But once the Bureau had acquired a resource like the HRT, it *was* going to be deployed, and, given the aggressive, can-do spirit of the HRT, it would look for chances to be deployed, and would always be volunteering for dangerous assignments other agencies (and other Bureau units) would be glad to hand over. That may have been the first link in the chain of bad decisions. Without an HRT, the Bureau would have been forced to rely on patience and intelligence. And how bad would that have been?

But in a mind set unhappily reminiscent of the Vietnam-era military, the Bureau decided that the problem at Waco had been that there were not enough negotiators and that the HRT was not big enough for the job, since agent fatigue and lack of HRT replacement personnel had created a sense of urgency that the standoff had to be brought to a conclusion. So the decision was made to double the size of the HRT and to hire more negotiators.

■ ■ ■

Sessions's weak leadership at the Bureau during Waco contributed to the tragedy: His decisions during the crisis inspired no confidence, particularly, his offer to go to Waco himself to take charge of the negotiations "Texan to Texan" style. This seemed a grandstand play to save his job, and was overruled by the attorney general. Most of his decision-making authority was ceded to Larry Potts, Doug Gow, Floyd Clarke, and Danny Coulson at headquarters. A stronger director might have questioned the decision, largely influenced by Reno's concern for the children within the compound, to launch the disastrous tear-gas and tank assault on the compound. As Buck Revell said afterward, although Reno properly and courageously took responsibility for the fatal decision, "we all knew that the FBI should have given her better advice. We should have had a better plan. We should have taken into account the possibility of mass suicide, and we should have been prepared for fire."

The Waco standoff complicated the matter of getting rid of Sessions. The Clinton White House thought it important that the president not make the decision, since the purpose of the director's ten-year term was to keep presidents from politicizing the Bureau through close control of the directorship. Clinton staffers also suspected the motives of anyone in the Bush Justice Department, so they were skeptical about the OPR report on Sessions. They had taken the bait, as Sessions had expected they would, when he charged that "Hooverites" were trying to block his affirmative-action policies. The new administration also knew how devastating Waco had been to FBI morale, and so they worried that firing Sessions might look like they were scapegoating the Bureau for Waco when it had been their own attorney general who had given the order to attack.

Finally, on Saturday, July 17, 1993, Reno told Sessions that Clinton would fire him if he did not quit by Monday. While leaving the meeting Sessions tripped on the sidewalk and broke his elbow. After a visit to the hospital, he met reporters that evening to tell them that he would refuse to resign as "a matter of principle." And so on Monday, July 19, Clinton announced that he had phoned Sessions that morning to tell him that he was out and Floyd Clarke was now acting director.

TEN

Louis Freeh's FBI
(1993–September 11, 2001)

SHORTLY BEFORE 8 A.M., Monday, January 25, 1993. A driver got out of a car across from the CIA traffic waiting to pass through the security gates guarding the agency's Langley, Virginia, headquarters. He was carrying an AK-47.

Senator Robert Smith of New Hampshire was on his way to the Capitol that morning: "I was about 50 feet from the gunman, maybe less. He walked between those two rows of cars that were lined up going into the CIA and coolly and methodically, with no emotion, no expression and no words, simply fired at point-blank range into the windows, at these people. It was a pretty horrifying experience." Frank Darling of the CIA was shot in the shoulder. He pushed his wife down into the passenger-side foot well. When the firing stopped, she lifted her head to see if it was safe, and found herself staring into the eyes of the gunman. His next shot missed her but blew away most of Darling's head and splattered her with his skull and brains. Lansing Bennett of the CIA lay dead of gunshot wounds in another car. Three other drivers were wounded. As survivors fled in panic, the gunman returned to his car and drove off. No one remembered his license plate number.

That morning, Special Agent Brad Garrett, a forty-five-year-old ex-Marine, was at his desk in the FBI's Washington field office. His supervisor in C-4, the Violent Crimes Squad, took the call and ordered Garrett to find out what had happened.

"When I got there a little after 8:30," Garrett recalled, "I realized it was not inside the CIA . . . the supervisor that covered crimes on government reservations was thrilled because it was not his case."

It would be Garrett's case. He located the Fairfax County detectives already on the scene and began helping them identify witnesses, direct medevac crews, and hold off the news camera crews—"if there was one, there were thirty." When he finally got back to his desk, he asked himself, "What do we have here?"

What he had was certainly a "crime against the United States," though it was, technically, not a federal crime. But if ever a crime was an attack against the entire nation, this one was. It was an attack on an agency seen throughout the world, for better or worse, as a symbol of the United States of America.

Seven months later, on September 1, 1993, Louis Freeh would be sworn in as FBI director. During Freeh's first five years the FBI would track the Langley gunman around the world. When Brad Garrett finally caught up with him, it would be on the Afghanistan-Pakistan border, and would demonstrate how the FBI could now bring those guilty of crimes against the United States to justice, no matter how far they might flee. But the drama of the Bureau successes of the 1990s against individual terrorists, like Garrett's capture of the CIA Headquarters killer, would divert attention, even among those most knowledgeable about the Bureau, from a fatal deterioration of FBI capabilities. The decline, in some respects, had started in the earliest days of the Bureau. It had been gathering force since Hoover's death, but the worst of the collapse took place on Louis Freeh's watch. By the time Freeh left in the summer of 2001, the Bureau would no longer be capable of protecting America against the greatest "crime against the United States" in our history, the attacks of 9/11.

■ ■ ■

Garrett started his investigation with some routine police work.

The obvious [thing] was where it happened. So you've got one motive, probably, that someone has something directed against the CIA. We looked at disgruntled employees that had been fired. We could still be looking at those today. There were so many, you know, wacky folks out there, present and past. The only linkage seemed to be, somebody had targeted the CIA.

In a nine-week period we processed something like five thousand leads. Ten or so agents, and about the same number of Fairfax detectives. The way we set it up was, we were in a room . . . about twenty hours a day. Myself and the lead detective pretty much lived together. They fed everything to us.

In the latter part of January we get a call from a gun store in Chantilly, Virginia. So we went out and found out that this guy, whose name turned out to be Mir Aimal Kansi, had purchased an AR-15, which is a semiautomatic M-16, and a couple of handguns and a bunch of ammunition previously. He came back on the 22nd of January [Friday] and exchanged the AR-15 for an AK-47. Said he had a problem, it was jamming. So he [takes that one] and of course we have the shooting on Monday.

We go to the address and find that there is another Pakistani that lives at that address whose name is Zahid Mir. A few days before, Zahid had filed a missing person report on Kansi.

Garrett asked Zahid about January 25, and Zahid said

"Well, I really don't know anything, but Kansi had made a statement to me a week to ten days before the shooting that he was fed up with U.S. policies particularly in Moslem countries . . . and that these were upsetting to him and that he was going to go do something quite big."

Zahid gave Garrett permission to search the room. They pushed back a couch and "lo and behold," there was an AK-47 under the couch in a green plastic trash bag.

Garrett obtained a warrant and found ammunition, clothes that matched the shooter's, and passport photos. On Kansi's jacket and shoes, they found glass from the victims' windshields. They also found his fingerprints on shell casings at the scene.

On February 9, Garrett and the Fairfax County detective obtained tandem federal and state warrants for capital murder and unlawful flight. But where was their man?

Afterward Garrett learned from Kansi that he never thought he would get away from the shooting. He imagined it pretty much as a suicide mission. After he drove away, he stopped in a community park a couple of miles away and waited two hours to see what would happen. Then he bought a McDonald's hamburger and returned home. Later that afternoon, he visited a combination market and travel agency run by a Pakistani. He found he could get a ticket to Pakistan but it would not be ready until the next day.

He spent the night at a Day's Inn in Herndon. The next day the travel agent drove him to National Airport, where he caught a plane to JFK in New York and from there to Karachi. His kinsmen in his native city of Quetta, near the Afghan border, were surprised to see him. He was supposed to be in the United States. "Oh," he said, he "had gotten tired of America." By the time Garrett figured out who he was, Kansi was half a world away.

A few days later, when CNN ran Kansi's picture in Pakistan and reported that he was wanted for the CIA murders, he disappeared across the border into

Afghanistan. According to Kansi, he spent the next four and a half years in Afghanistan and never returned to Quetta until he was captured.

Soon after the warrants were issued, Garrett began visiting Pakistan. From February 1993 until June 1997, he kept traveling there, first with other agents and then,

It's pretty much just me. Sometimes I took another agent with me, and sometimes I didn't. I would wind up working with the Legat [since there was no FBI legal attaché in Pakistan, Garrett worked with one from Bangkok]. I figured out that in the four and a half years we worked this case until we caught him, I was in Pakistan a year and a half.

He knew in February 1993 [we were after him] because we were in country. At that point the Pakistanis were putting in the paper every day what we were doing, that agents are flying to so-and-so. He knew from the get-go that people were roaming around Pakistan looking for him. He told me that when Ramzi Yousef got caught in February of 1995, he got real concerned we might catch him because of the lengths we went to catch Ramzi. [Ramzi Yousef, wanted for the World Trade Center bombing in 1993, was captured in Pakistan and then turned over to Garrett to be brought back to the United States.]

The other problem was there are a lot of Pakistanis that don't care for us and particularly don't care for the CIA because the Afghan-Russian war really culturally mixed that place up. So the concern was that when we gave information to the Pakis it would go either directly to him or to his family. So we were trying to work around that because we had no authority to do anything law enforcement–wise in Pakistan. [But] over the years we had developed some relationships with some particular Pakistanis in the government that we could sort of semi-trust.

We ended up getting a piece of information in the late April, early May, time frame in 1997. There are Bureau assets, and agency [CIA] assets and DEA assets. Then the other category is nobody's informant. People just calling. And that's how this lead comes to us. It's a call-in.

On June 4, at 7 A.M., Tom Pickard, then assistant director in charge of the FBI's Washington field office, later the assistant director in charge of criminal investigations, deputy director, and finally acting director, huddled with the chief of the field office's Criminal Investigative Division, Special Agent in Charge Jimmy C. Carter.

Carter called his wife at 11:30 that same morning and told her that he was leaving, and couldn't say where or for how long. "Truth was, I had no idea when I was going to be back, or where exactly I'd be going."

Five hours later Carter and Garrett boarded a commercial plane for a twenty-two-hour flight to Islamabad. In Islamabad, Carter and Garrett were joined by an FBI Legat and four "operators" from the Quantico Hostage Rescue Team. On June 6, President Clinton was told about the mission, and the next day gave his approval. As the operation progressed, Clinton would be kept briefed, sometimes several times a day.

In Pakistan, Garrett and the other agents

practiced how we were going to get into this place and who was going to do what. You still have that discomfort: you are armed; you do have on body armor but you really haven't any backup.

We rolled into this location in Pakistan near the Afghan border, and it's four o'clock in the morning and we thought there will be nobody up in this little bitty place. It looked like something out of The Good, the Bad, and the Ugly, *one of those spaghetti westerns, those little towns that Clint Eastwood used to ride into. So we go in there, and there were like three hundred people in the street, because it was so hot that time of the year people worked in the early morning and stopped at noon. We thought, how are we going to work around this?*

Plus, the intel people said you won't have any trouble getting in the hotel. It's not locked. So we drive down in a smoked-up vehicle. We're dressed in Pakistani garb with weapons and body armor underneath.

While Carter and two of the Hostage Rescue Team operators waited at the car, Garrett, the Legat, and the other two HRT operators approached the hotel. The door was locked. "So here we are, standing outside, the four of us, the four horsemen in the dark." Finally a security guard let them in, and they climbed to the third floor. Garrett recalls, "We were able to use a ruse to get Kansi to crack the door. When he cracked it, we kicked it," in what Jimmy Carter described as "a tactical move performed with a great deal of velocity." In an instant, they had Kansi on the floor.

The first guy in was an HRT guy and he jumped him and it turned out to be quite a tussle. Kansi kept screaming and I kept telling him to shut up. We wound up gagging him. At one point I said, "If you'll quit screaming, we'll take the gag off." I said, "What's your name?" and he said, "Fuck you." I actually said, "Thank you [because now] I know that you speak English."

One of Garrett's worries had been that they might be grabbing the wrong guy. The person on the floor, if he was Kansi, had gained a lot of weight and had a beard and a mustache. There was not much resemblance. "The Legat and I looked at each other and said, 'Holy shit. Is this the right guy?' " Garrett finger-printed him, and it checked out; they knew they had him.

"There was a contingent of people outside who were waiting for us and for-tunately, they were still there. The other people who were with us—and it's sen-sitive to say who they were—were adamant that his face be covered. So he was bagged." The people on the street could see that a man was being marched out of the hotel with his hands cuffed behind his back, and a bag over his head. No-body paid any attention.

We get him outside and I put him in the back of the 4x4. He said, "Are you going to take me back to America and execute me." I thought for a minute and I said, "Well . . . it's a long way off . . . but that is a possibility." We drive to an aircraft and then fly a short distance back to Islamabad.

They had snatched him fairly easily, but it would take days of negotiations be-fore they could leave the country with him. These talks were "as high as you could go. I know that they had to get the prime minister of Pakistan involved." There were reports that it took pressure from the White House to "clear the way."

Seven months later, in a Virginia courtroom, Kansi was sentenced to death for two counts of capital murder. He was executed on November 14, 2002. It was, Jimmy C. Carter said later, just another "fugitive investigation [of the kind] we do every day over here. Only it happened to be nine thousand miles away."

. . .

The Kansi case was an amazing demonstration of what the FBI could do in the 1990s: It could go anywhere in the world, arrest terrorists who had attacked Americans in the United States or overseas, bring them back to face American justice—and have the cases stand up in court.

But after 9/11, critics of the Bureau would say that was not enough, that the FBI should also have been gathering intelligence so that it could prevent terror attacks, not just punish terrorists after the fact. The ultimate question of the

9/11 failure, then, is why the FBI was doing this (indictments, arrests, and trials) instead of that (prevention).

The explanation involves both internalities—historic tendencies of the Bureau to do, let us say, this thing instead of that thing—and externalities—factors outside the Bureau's control.

The most important internal factor was that for the past quarter century the FBI had been taught, with the subtlety of a two-by-four to the head, that the only law enforcement we Americans would tolerate from it would be after the fact. Louis Freeh would hail it as a virtue that the Bureau would turn a blind eye to suspicious groups rather than encroach on their civil liberties. There were almost no conceivable circumstances under which we would allow the FBI to investigate political or ethnic groups to see if they might be planning acts of terror or anything else. Those who know the history of the Bureau will perhaps sympathize with FBI agents and directors who could draw no other conclusion from the punishment we had dealt the Bureau since the death of Hoover.

The most important of the externalities was that law enforcement had become the nation's de facto counterterrorism policy by the early 1990s. The Joint Inquiry into the 9/11 attacks found that

> *in the absence of a more comprehensive strategy, the United States defaulted to relying on law enforcement, at home and abroad, as the leading instrument in the fight against al-Qa'ida. The perpetrators of the 1993 World Trade Center bombing and the plot against New York City landmarks, several conspirators in the 1998 embassy bombings, and several members that planned Millennium attacks were all prosecuted. This emphasis on prosecution continued a trend begun in the 1980s when Congress and President Reagan gave the FBI an important role in countering international terrorism, including attacks overseas.*

The policymakers who testified in the post-9/11 inquiries all said that the country had not deliberately chosen such a strategy, but had drifted into it—and they all agreed that military and diplomatic efforts were the only really effective response to terror, particularly when the terrorists had a safe base in a hostile nation like Afghanistan. (Actually, bin Laden's hold on Afghanistan was so secure that some said that it was a question of a terrorist network supporting a state rather than one of state-supported terrorism.)

But because neither American public opinion nor world opinion would have tolerated the all-out military and diplomatic efforts that could have eliminated the threat of the Middle Eastern terror networks, American policy came to rely by default on law enforcement, that is, on the FBI.

Even the FBI was uneasy about this policy, and that is clear from the post-9/11 comments by the agents and officials who had to implement it. One FBI agent scoffed at the strategy of using the Bureau to take the lead in countering al Qaeda, noting that all the FBI can do is arrest and prosecute. It cannot shut down training camps in hostile countries. He noted that the strategy is "like telling the FBI after Pearl Harbor 'to go to Tokyo and arrest the Emperor.' " In his opinion, a military solution had always been necessary because "[t]he Southern District doesn't have any cruise missiles."

One early sign of the shift in counterterrorism policy toward law enforcement was a series of laws passed, beginning in the mid-1980s. These gave the Bureau new jurisdiction to act overseas in pursuit of terror suspects; they eventually gave the Bureau the lead role over rival agencies in both counterterrorism and foreign counterintelligence.

Brad Garrett's arrest of Ramzi Yousef and Mir Aimal Kansi in Pakistan would not have been possible without these new legal instruments giving the FBI jurisdiction over acts of terrorism committed against Americans anywhere in the world. The 1984 Hostage Taking Act and the Anti-Terrorism Act of 1986 made terrorism against Americans, wherever committed, a federal crime under the jurisdiction of the FBI, and set up a reward program that can range up to $7 million for information that leads to the arrest of terrorists or the prevention of terrorist acts. The Antiterrorism and Effective Death Penalty Act of 1996 not only raised the penalties for acts of terrorism, but also broadened the definition of terrorism, and authorized increased funding to federal agencies, including the FBI, for the prevention and investigation of terrorism. Presidential Decision Directive 39 (1995) set in motion the integration of "the roles of all pertinent federal [counterterrorism] agencies in a comprehensive, proactive program, with the FBI as the 'lead' investigative agency," while PDD 62 of May 1998 created mechanisms for coordinating all government antiterrorist activities and established the Office of the National Coordinator for Security, Infrastructure Protection and Counter-Terrorism.

Operationally, in 1995 the FBI established its own Counterterrorism Center staffed with personnel from twenty federal agencies, and in 1999 the Bureau established five Rapid Deployment Teams capable of responding to multiple incidents.

During the 1990s the Bureau also finally became the undisputed lead agency in foreign counterintelligence, ending its long-standing rivalry with the CIA over spy hunting. In March 1994, the National Security Council (NSC) reviewed FBI-CIA conflicts in a study of the Aldrich Ames case, and recommended a new national Counterintelligence Center headed by the FBI, and said the CIA's investigations office should be headed by an FBI agent. A Senate select committee decided that Ames would have been caught much earlier if the agency had lived up to the Sessions-Webster accord of 1988. In 1994, Senator Dennis DeConcini drew up a Counterintelligence and Security Enhancement Act that would have turned over all counterintelligence to the FBI. The NSC proposed an NSC-based National Counterintelligence Policy Board, and a National Counterintelligence Center to implement policy, and, of course, handed the CIA's counterintelligence investigations to the FBI.

Presidential Decision Directive 24 on May 4, 1994, put these reforms into effect, pointing to the counterintelligence failure in the Ames case as the reason for the changes. The directive

1. Created a National Counterintelligence Policy Board to report to the president through the national security adviser. The board consists of one representative each from the CIA, the FBI, the departments of State, Defense, and Justice, from the military department's counterintelligence component, and from the National Security Council. The chair is nominated by the director of Central Intelligence for a term of two years, rotating between the CIA, FBI, and Defense.

2. Set up a National Counterintelligence Operations Board under the Policy Board, with senior counterintelligence representatives from the CIA, FBI, Defense, military counterintelligence components, National Security Agency, State, Justice, and the chief of the National Counterintelligence Center.

3. Established a National Counterintelligence Center. Initially the head was a senior FBI official with a military counterintelligence component executive as deputy. After that the chief would rotate between the FBI, Defense, and CIA, except that whenever the FBI does not hold the position of chief, it will hold the position of deputy chief.

4. Stated that the chief of the CIA's Counterintelligence Center Counterespionage Group will be permanently staffed by a senior executive from the FBI.

5. Ordered CIA counterintelligence officers to permanently staff and manage positions in the FBI's National Security Division and field offices.

Provision four was the key, since the rest replicated the previous ten years' efforts to set up machinery to ensure coordination between the FBI and CIA. Having an FBI executive run the CIA's own counterintelligence investigations virtually ceded the territory to the FBI whenever there was a conflict between the Bureau and the agency. But as events would prove, this table-of-organization chart integration of the FBI, the CIA, and other agencies did not overcome a far more intractable barrier to effective coordination between the government's counterterrorism forces: legal decisions and departmental policies that effectively precluded any real cooperation between the CIA and the FBI where it counted, during the actual investigations of real terror networks.

These reforms greatly expanded the authority of an FBI that had already greatly expanded its capabilities overseas, ever since it became clear to a few visionary Bureau officials that the greatest future threats would come from outside U.S. borders. Just as in the 1930s the great challenge to law enforcement had been interstate crime, the crime challenge in the future would be international. The Bureau had risen to its first challenge in 1933 and 1934, and its successes had made it the undisputed leader of American law enforcement for the rest of the century. How the FBI responded to the challenge of international crime, Bureau leaders believed, would define its new place in America—and around the globe.

The future would bring, the FBI was sure, investigations that would make the famous cases of the thirties look like child's play. Instead of a gangster with protection from a crooked city police department and a crooked mayor, the Bureau faced criminal gangs protected by national governments, such as the mafias that seemed the most powerful force in the disintegrating Soviet empire. In some countries there were criminal organizations so deeply entwined with legitimate businesses that entire economies could fall if the criminal organizations were destroyed. There were now gangs that violated American laws yet conformed to the laws in their countries of convenience.

■ ■ ■

The key figure in the internationalization of the Bureau was Buck Revell, the deputy director under William Webster and William Sessions.

When Revell was in the Inspection Division in 1972 and 1973, his final assignment was a tour through Asia to evaluate the Bureau's Legal Attachés in Tokyo, Manila, Hong Kong, and Singapore. There he learned to appreciate the vital role on-the-scene representation played in gaining foreign police cooperation with FBI investigations. When Revell was named assistant director in charge of the Criminal Investigations Division in June 1980, he reviewed the division's programs and concluded that

> *the level and intensity of international crime was significantly increasing. Whether it was organized crime, international frauds, fugitives, or terrorist organizations, there were strong indications that the United States was going to face a growing threat from abroad.*

And yet, except for the Legat program, the FBI presence abroad was minimal. The FBI had joined Interpol in 1938, but German domination prevented any real FBI participation in the organization. During the Cold War, the role of communists in Interpol led Hoover to pull the Bureau out completely in 1950. After Hoover's death there were cautious efforts in the Bureau to rethink its role in Interpol, and in 1974, Associate Director Nicholas Callahan attended Interpol's annual conference in Cannes. Foreign police officials used to ask Revell why the Bureau was not a member, and he "simply didn't have a good answer." In the fall of 1980, Revell sent his assistant, Dana Caro, to the General Assembly of Interpol in Manila as an observer. Caro reported that the organization was inefficient and corrupt, but that the Bureau should join it and work to reform it. In 1982, Revell pushed to have the FBI formally rejoin Interpol. That year he went himself to the regional conference in Lima, Peru, where he lobbied to have Interpol change its policy that terrorism was a political issue, and therefore outside Interpol's jurisdiction. (Revell denounced the excuse he heard there that "one man's terrorist is another man's freedom fighter.") Within a year Revell succeeded in having Interpol agree to facilitate investigations of international terrorism. The FBI also helped engineer an audit of the Interpol secretariat, which led to the new chief's being chosen from Scotland Yard.

Revell also worked to emphasize the "international" in the International Association of Chiefs of Police (IACP), and he joined its Advisory Committee for International Affairs in 1979. This alone was a telling shift of FBI priorities: During J. Edgar Hoover's regime, the official who held a position comparable to Revell's, Cartha DeLoach, chaired the Americanism Committee of the American Legion, which managed its anticommunism programs. Revell also worked to recruit leading American and foreign police officials to join the IACP's Committee on Terrorism. And so, Revell said, "with the FBI's relationship with Interpol fully established, and the new IACP recognition of terrorism as a significant interagency issue, we were in an excellent position to carry out our duties in this critical area."

The first deployment of FBI agents overseas in response to acts of terrorism against American citizens was the investigation of the October 23, 1983, bombing of the Marine barracks (241 Marines killed) in Beirut, Lebanon. In June 1985, President Reagan established the Vice President's Task Force on Terrorism, with FBI Director William Webster a member and Revell on the Senior Review Group that made recommendations for action to the task force members. He proposed increasing the FBI's international law enforcement liaison with the European Union's antiterrorism groups. When William Webster promoted Revell to executive assistant director for investigations (the number two spot in the Bureau) in June 1985, it was with a mandate to study FBI operations at the international level. Revell then moved the Legat program out of the Intelligence Division and into a separate office that would work with the Criminal Investigative Division and the Training Division, thus ending the Legats' primary emphasis on counterintelligence.

In the late 1980s the Bureau began to show how Revell's efforts had expanded its global reach. The first of these cases was in September 1987. A squad of FBI agents led by Revell captured Fawaz Younis, who had hijacked and blown up a Royal Jordanian jet in Beirut with three Americans aboard, and later hijacked a TWA jet. Revell and his squad lured Younis to a yacht just off the coast of Cyprus. Two female agents waved invitingly to Younis as he came aboard. The waiters who offered Younis a drink just before they threw him down on the deck and cuffed him were also agents. Younis is now serving a thirty-year sentence in a federal prison in Kansas.

A dozen years later more than five hundred FBI personnel poured into Tanzania and Kenya in 1999 to investigate the Dar es Salaam and Nairobi U.S. Embassy bombings. Within hours FBI Legal Attachés stationed in South Africa had arrived on the scene. The Bureau negotiated a cooperative investigation with local authorities that resulted in identification of Osama bin Laden as the ringleader of the conspiracy, and the return to the United States of two individuals suspected of actually detonating the bombs.

■ ■ ■

Freeh, a director with wide experience in international law enforcement, vastly deepened and broadened the Bureau's partnerships with foreign police and security agencies. In the long run, this will be Louis Freeh's most valuable contribution to the war on terror.

When Louis Freeh was sworn in on September 1, 1993, he arrived with a uniquely appropriate experience that made him see the value of Revell's internationalization of the Bureau. Forty-three years old when he was sworn in,

Freeh brought to the directorship experience as an FBI street agent from 1975 until 1981, and ten years (1981–1991) as a prosecutor in Rudy Giuliani's high-powered U.S. attorney's office for Southern New York (Manhattan)—Giuliani, among others, recommended Freeh for the directorship—and then two years as a federal judge in Manhattan.

Reared in North Bergen, New Jersey, in a Catholic German-Italian family, son of a real estate salesman, the young Louis Freeh had been a Catholic altar boy before Rutgers (Phi Beta Kappa, 1971) and Rutgers Law School (1974). In 1975, after a year on New Jersey Senator Clifford Case's staff, he joined the FBI as a special agent, assigned to the Bureau's Manhattan field office.

For his next five years in the Bureau, Freeh worked on the "UNIRAC" (UNIon RACketeering) investigation of the Mafia-dominated East Coast long-shoremen's union. Freeh went undercover as "Luigi," an out-of-work attorney, and hung around the Shelton Health Club on Brooklyn's Boerum Place, where "Big Mike" Clemente of the Genovese family received his payoffs from shipping companies. Later Clemente spotted his old friend Luigi in the courtroom at his arraignment. He had his lawyers tell the prosecutors, "Let the kid go. He had nothing to do with it." (Freeh said the comment made him "three inches tall.") UNIRAC led to 125 convictions, most notably of Tony Scotto, the politically and socially connected boss of the Brooklyn longshoremen's union, whose trial featured a parade of prominent New Yorkers, including former governor Hugh Carey, as character witnesses.

Freeh made a name for himself as thoroughly familiar with applying the RICO Act to organized crime investigations, and in 1980 he was transferred to Washington headquarters to work in the Labor Racketeering Unit of the Organized Crime Section of Division Six. After ten months of what he recalls as frustrating bureaucratic warfare, Freeh resigned for a position as assistant U.S. attorney in New York, where he remained for the next ten years. There Freeh was the lead prosecutor under Rudy Giuliani in the seventeen-month-long Pizza Connection trial. The case was a landmark in the Bureau's war against the mob; it also had a decisive influence on Freeh's theory of law enforcement. During the investigation there was unparalleled cooperation between American, Italian, French, Swiss, and Spanish law enforcement. Freeh became convinced that teamwork between international law enforcement agencies would be the key to success in top-level law enforcement, since the greatest current challenges in the field of organized crime were from criminal gangs that crossed international boundaries, in their own corrupt version of globalization.

Freeh's other high-profile case at the U.S. attorney's office was the December 16, 1989, mail bomb assassination of Federal Appeals Court Judge Robert S. Vance in Birmingham, Alabama, which was followed by three more mail bombs, one of which killed civil rights attorney Robbie Robinson in Savannah. All told, three separate field offices were involved in the case along with five U.S. attorney's offices. Buck Revell, at that time executive assistant director for investigations, appointed Larry Potts, a deputy assistant director in Division Six, to be inspector in charge of the case, now called VANPAC. In view of the difficulties of coordinating the large number of U.S. attorneys involved, Potts had the Justice Department appoint a special prosecutor, and with the blessing of Rudy Giuliani, Freeh got the case in May 1990, bringing as his assistant Howard Shapiro, also from the U.S. attorney's office in New York.

Freeh agreed with the FBI laboratory's Tom Thurman that the bomber was Walter Leroy Moody Jr., who had been found guilty of the accidental bombing of his wife seventeen years earlier. A bug planted in Moody's house overheard Moody mumble, "Now you've killed two . . . now you can't pull another bombing." Freeh got Moody indicted on November 7, 1990, for killing Vance and Robinson. After a trial in St. Paul, Minnesota, that consisted largely of expert testimony by Thurman, Moody was convicted of the murders and sentenced to seven life terms plus four hundred years. Thurman was promoted to head the lab's Explosive Unit and Bomb Data Center, while Potts was named the assistant director of Division Six. Shortly after the verdict, in July 1991, Freeh was named to the federal bench in New York and awarded the Attorney General's Award for Distinguished Service. Two years later, on July 20, 1993, President Clinton nominated Freeh to be FBI director. He was confirmed September 1.

■ ■ ■

One of J. Edgar Hoover's most effective strategies for coordinating the American law enforcement community had been to offer local police officials—the rising-star administrators—advanced training at the FBI Academy at Quantico. The National Academy's eleven-week courses had become an important credential qualifying local police officials for promotion.

The FBI had always trained a few foreign police officials. Freeh's FBI vastly expanded its outreach to foreign law enforcement. The Legats comb through their country's police forces to identify officers with the leadership potential to have an impact on that country's law enforcement and then nominate them for training at Quantico.

Foreign police officials—generally about twenty per year—are now part of the regular National Academy eleven-week mid-level program for American police executives. The first was Superintendent Torleiv Vikla of the Royal Norwegian Ministry of Justice and Police. The academy is accredited by and affiliated with the University of Virginia, which maintains a full-time representative at Quantico for consultation by students and staff. Foreign police officers receive a certificate in criminal justice education from the university and become members of the FBI National Academy Associates. This now numbers more than 25,000 members, with its own newsletter and programs intended to maintain contacts between the graduates and the Bureau. The visiting officers receive the same training in management science, behavioral science, law, education, communication, forensic science, and health and fitness as their American counterparts. The thousands of officials from 106 countries who have gone through the National Academy sessions and joined the National Academy Associates, make up a global resource the Bureau can call on when it needs assistance anywhere in the world.

The most remarkable instance of the Bureau's internationalization under Freeh was its International Law Enforcement Academy in Budapest, Hungary. The American and Hungarian governments are full partners in running the academy. Canada, Great Britain, Ireland, Italy, Germany, and Russia have also contributed instructors, while the European Union and the Council of Europe have joined in its development and operation. The core program is an eight-week personal and professional development course, five sessions a year, with fifty mid-level police officials each session. The first session began on April 25, 1995, and on June 26 of that year thirty-three police officers from Hungary, Poland, and the Czech Republic completed their training. The next class came from Latvia, Romania, and Hungary. Since then students have come from the entire former Soviet bloc: Albania, Armenia, Azerbaijan, Belarus, Croatia, the Czech Republic, Estonia, Georgia, Hungary, Kazakhstan, Kyrgyzstan, Latvia, Lithuania, Moldova, Poland, Romania, Russia, Slovakia, Slovenia, Tajikistan, Turkmenistan, Ukraine and Uzbekistan. In all these countries there are now police officials with personal and professional links to the FBI they formed at the Budapest academy. Thousands more are trained at one- and two-week regional sessions, an average of some 1,500 in the last few years, although for some years totals ran much higher, as many as 3,843. There are now FBI-trained officials from Eastern Europe, across Russia, and the countries of Central Asia. Similar programs are in place or planned in Asia, Latin America, and Africa, and the Bureau also serves on the faculty of the academy run by the Drug Enforcement Administration in Bangkok.

The FBI could now see farther than ever. It could go farther than ever, and wherever it went, it had foreign law enforcement and security colleagues eager to cooperate—after all, they had all gone to school together at Quantico.

But any leads the FBI got overseas that led back to the United States went nowhere. The FBI no longer knew what was going on in extremist communities at home, and it no longer had any way of finding out. The Bureau no longer had any domestic surveillance to speak of. Overseas, it had an eye that never slept. At home, it had blinded itself.

■ ■ ■

It was not that the FBI was unaware of its dangerous vulnerability. Under Louis Freeh the Bureau underwent an unprecedented self-study to produce a strategic plan that clearly identified the inadequacies of its domestic intelligence gathering.

Strategic plans had been required of federal government agencies since the Government Performance and Results Act in 1993. But the FBI's strategic plan, a seven-month effort by the Bureau's Strategic Planning Office under Deputy Director Bear Bryant in 1998, started as a routine exercise and shifted to a discovery that, while as presently constituted the Bureau might be able to fulfill its current tasks, without radical changes it would become less and less able to meet the demands of the new century. As a result, the five-year plan would read like a charter for a radical reshaping of the FBI.

The 64-page strategic plan, said its author, Bear Bryant, represented a conceptual break from the FBI's past.

"We set up Tier One, Two, and Three priorities in the strategic plan."

The first tier was national security issues, counterintelligence and counterterrorism, and economic security. "If we have an attack of fraud on the insurance companies of the United States," said Revell, "it doesn't sound like a big deal, but if your pension funds go under in the United States, it is a big deal."

The second tier focused on organized crime and public corruption, as well as "the protection of civil rights and civil liberties of the citizen."

The third tier was "crimes against persons and property." Where once these had been the Bureau's most famous and popular cases, now they would be "small potatoes."

The concept, Revell said, was that "the special agents in charge are under the contract [to adhere to the Three Tier priorities]. I look at how their time is being spent in the field office. The assistant directors from the Criminal Division and from the National Security Division . . . go on the spring briefings with the SACs and we will grade them on how they've done on these contracts. . . . There's some grousing about it but sometimes you march, you know, and so basically if New York is way out of line on some issue we are going to get after them."

The strategic plan was a management tool intended to bring the allocation of Bureau resources in line with Bureau priorities and, in particular, to wean the Bureau away from the low-level crimes against persons and property that had always, no matter what the emergency, been what kept the Bureau busy. And that was a hard thing to do: Even after 9/11, the FBI was still getting around 40 percent of its convictions in the Tier Three category of bank robberies, bank regulation violations, and bank fraud.

Despite pressure from the strategic plan to cut down on Tier Three investigations, under Freeh the Bureau did what it has always done when a category of serious "crimes against the United States"—in this instance, preventing acts of terrorism through domestic surveillance—would get it in trouble. It ran away from trouble, and busied itself instead with crimes against persons and property, precisely the Tier Three crimes the Bureau was now supposed to avoid. It came up with impressive-sounding projects like the Safe Streets programs targeting youth gangs, the Safe Trails program targeting violent crimes and gangs on Indian reservations, the famous Innocent Images program to trap Internet pedophiles. It expanded its services to local police: instant identification of guns, license plates, and, at enormous expense and with great difficulty, an instant fingerprint identification service—most of which should probably have been shunted off to strictly technical agencies, since there is no reason to have special agents performing routine noninvestigative tasks.

In another Tier One category of serious crime, major financial fraud, the Bureau showed that same tendency to look for the easy way out when it ran into politically powerful opposition to an investigation. In the Bureau's price-fixing case against the food giant Archer Daniels Midland, the Bureau and the Justice Department showed every sign of wanting to jettison the case when ADM's high-powered law firm said it had reason to suspect the two agents from Decatur and Springfield, Illinois, who broke the case were involved in the informant's wrongdoing. (These charges were found to be groundless by the Bureau and the Justice Department.) In the end the case was carried through to a successful conclusion, but along with the convictions of the ADM executives, the Bureau and the department had the informant put away for as long as the price fixers. It was as though the Bureau and the department were sending a message to potential whistle-blowers that it really didn't want these troublesome cases, and that if you got them involved in one, you were going to pay.

It just may be that the Bureau has become too big to specialize only in important cases. It would be an unpromising move to increase the size of the Supreme Court from nine to, say, 11,000 judges, about the size of the FBI, on the theory that if nine justices can do a good job, 11,000 will do a truly swell job.

Before long, just to keep busy, those 11,000 supreme court justices would be supervising real estate closings, arbitrating spite fence disputes in trailer parks, umpiring Little League games, and starring on Supreme Court *Judge Judy* television shows.

If the Bureau is going to give its full attention to the most important crimes against the United States, it should have just the number of agents needed for those cases, and no more. Otherwise it will be unable to resist the temptation to start doing anything that looks easy, won't get it into trouble, and will give it a good press. Its ordinary work will become its normal routine; important cases will become exceptional, to be avoided and then abandoned as soon as possible—because they can only get the Bureau into trouble and because they distract the Bureau from the Tier Three cases that would, and have, become its bread and butter.

But setting that aside, Revell's strategic plan clearly placed counterterrorism within the highest category of a Tier One priority. And it recognized that to do the job the Bureau needed top-flight ("world-class" was the phrase) domestic intelligence and the Bureau did not have it. In other words, the Bureau was unequipped to do the job that it, the president, and the country all regarded as its most important task.

And why did the FBI no longer have any domestic intelligence by the 1990s?

You know the answer: The entire prior history of the FBI had risen up to block any more domestic surveillance. From the earliest days of the Bureau's national security responsibilities before World War I, its domestic surveillance had been creating enemies for the FBI and, ever since, its spying on Americans had done nothing for it but make more enemies. Opposition to FBI domestic surveillance had become a reliable touchstone of American political orthodoxy. When J. Edgar Hoover's COINTELPRO abuses were exposed in the mid-seventies, the Bureau's enemies were able to say with conviction and plausibility that they had been right all along—that the Bureau had manufactured the fear of communism for the purpose of trampling on the civil liberties of dissenters. There never had been a subversive threat in the United States, these critics had long said; there had never been any threat except the Bureau's own covert war on the rights of Americans. By the 1990s the rest of us had begun to agree.

In the post-Hoover era, the Bureau had learned that it was damned no matter what it did in domestic surveillance. Whenever it was learned that the Bureau had kept an eye on anyone who had not yet committed a crime, a hue and cry would be raised, attacks against which the Bureau no longer had any defense. When Bureau officials like Felt and Miller narrowly escaped jail for surveilling a murderous group like the Weather Underground, or when the Bureau was humiliated over a program like CISPES which it had exposed and halted on its own, it learned that the domestic intelligence game was finished. We Americans did not want any more domestic surveillance by the FBI. Period.

By the time Freeh arrived at the Bureau, the prohibitions against domestic intelligence had begun to be codified into Justice Department and Bureau policy. Based on interpretations of court rulings later discovered to have been needlessly (in a legal sense) restrictive, the Justice Department erected the infamous "wall" between criminal and intelligence investigations that made it impossible for one to communicate with the other within the Bureau. This was encapsulated in the memo from Deputy Attorney General Jamie Gorelick that Attorney General Ashcroft introduced at the 9/11 Commission hearings. That Gorelick memo set up a wall of separation between criminal and intelligence investigations. As Gorelick admitted, it went beyond what she believed the law required, so that the Bureau and the department could avoid giving even the appearance of engaging in improper domestic surveillance:

Although the counterintelligence investigation may result in the incidental collection of information relevant to possible future criminal prosecutions, the primary purpose of the counterintelligence investigation will be to collect foreign counterintelligence information. Because the counterintelligence investigation will involve the use of surveillance techniques authorized under the Foreign Intelligence Surveillance Act (FISA) against targets that, in some instances, had been subject to surveillance under Title III, and because it will involve some of the same sources and targets as the criminal investigation, we believe that it is prudent to establish a set of instructions that will clearly separate the counterintelligence investigation from the more limited, but continued, criminal investigations. These procedures, which go beyond what is legally required, will prevent any risk of creating an unwarranted appearance that FISA is being used to avoid procedural safeguards which would apply in a criminal investigation.

The "wall" paralyzed any effective efforts to learn before the fact what potentially violent groups might be planning. Because the existence of a criminal investigation would prevent intelligence investigators from getting a FISA warrant, criminal investigations of suspicious groups tended to be vetoed by headquarters. And because an intelligence investigation could contaminate a criminal case, that too might be discouraged. In the worst-case scenario, the two fears would add up to no investigation at all.

Bureau planners recognized this. Revell's strategic plan found that "FBI intelligence taken as a whole is inadequate to the task of the future. The FBI will not succeed . . . unless it also has a world-class intelligence capability. . . . To succeed, the FBI must have an intelligence operation that can 1) identify emerging national security threats and crime patterns; 2) determine associations and relationships among individuals and groups engaged in criminal, terrorist, or counterintelligence activities in order to develop effective multijurisdictional investigations and program initiatives; and 3) provide real-time information in support of terrorist, criminal, and counterintelligence investigations."

The plan found that "human source information, the lifeblood for FBI intelligence, has not only not kept pace with the demands posed by new investigative areas, but in some programs the number of human sources has declined." It complained about the low skill levels of intelligence analysts and the abysmal condition of the Bureau's electronic database equipment and systems.

But the report then came down to earth with the admission that "well-settled constitutional protections and more recent policy decisions restrict the FBI's ability to seek the information on which useful intelligence depends." The Bureau recognized that it had to have domestic intelligence if it was going to fight terrorism, but it had concluded that effective domestic intelligence was legally impossible, given the current interpretations of the law and internal regulations that governed its intelligence activities. It could not do what it had to do because the courts and department lawyers would not let it.

According to the rules in effect on 9/11, unless the Bureau was able to find evidence that a foreign government was behind a group suspected of planning an act of terrorism, it would have to convince Bureau lawyers that the group was planning an imminent act of violence, since the definition of terrorism used by the Justice Department (until 1996) was for "the unlawful use of force or violence against persons or property to intimidate or coerce a government, the civilian population, or any segment thereof, in furtherance of political or social objectives." This was superseded by the Antiterrorism and Effective Death Penalty Act of April 24, 1996, which defined terrorism as

> *an offense that . . . is calculated to influence or affect the conduct of government by intimidation or coercion, or to retaliate against government conduct; and is in violation of at least one of a number of general offenses including destruction of an aircraft, arson, assassination, kidnapping, conspiracy to injure*

the property of a foreign government, and destruction of communications fa-
cilities.

The Bureau could be confident domestic surveillance was legal only if a group had committed or was committing an act of violence. Trying to forestall acts of terrorism, Freeh felt, would lead back to Hoover's justification for surveilling any and all political organizations. And so Freeh said approvingly, in his intro- duction to the strategic plan, "With respect to core values, it is important to note that a large part of the FBI mission is inherently reactive and rightly so."

A reconceived Hostage Rescue Team was central to the Freeh FBI's strategy against terror. After its Sessions-era disasters, the HRT had rethought its mis- sion, and had become part of CIRG, the Critical Incident Response Group, a Bureau think tank for counterterrorism. The HRT was just as muscular as ever, but now saw its primary mission as taking charge of the crime scene after a ter- rorist attack to preserve evidence and prepare it for trial.

The HRT had studied Ruby Ridge, Waco, and the Freemen standoff (a heav- ily armed group of tax resisters in Jordan, Montana, who held out against a Bu- reau siege for nearly three months), and thought they had learned from these cases. Neil Gallagher, Freeh's assistant director in charge of the National Secu- rity Division, said that

> *From the Freemen case, we learned patience. We had the bigger army, we could*
> *have gone in anytime and won, but if we had gone in that would have been the*
> *end of the FBI. But we persevered and we won. It was the high point of FBI pro-*
> *fessionalism. We had enormous pressure to go in fast. But, we had control from*
> *the outset.*
>
> *From Waco we learned to measure tactical approaches versus other solu-*
> *tions. In any barricade situation there will be SWAT teams. But now there is a*
> *different relationship between the decision to use force to resolve the situation*
> *and the decision to wait it out. If we had gone in at Jordan the FBI would have*
> *been destroyed. I can give another example. When I was the SAC in New Or-*
> *leans we had a barricade situation north of Shreveport and we walked away—*
> *we would resolve it another day in another way. You have to build into the*
> *command structure a method for dealing with crises.*

The Bureau's new and cautious strategy for dealing with standoffs was dubbed "Weaver fever," a recognition of the Bureau's determination never to repeat its errors at Ruby Ridge.

As the brains now as well as the brawn of Bureau strategy for responding to terror attacks, the HRT gave the Bureau the capacity for responding to an emergency, such as the embassy attacks in Africa, quickly and with a massive FBI presence following them after they had established a beachhead.

The new HRT-CIRG fit in with Freeh's strategy of pouring Bureau resources into investigations of terror attacks abroad. But this ability came at a cost. The resources the FBI had to devote to any one of its overseas terrorism cases—the African embassy bombings, Khobar Towers in Saudi Arabia, or the USS *Cole*—were immense, and so these resources were drawn away from intelligence gathering and attack prevention. As former FBI Assistant Director for Counterterrorism Dale Watson explained, "Special Agents in Charge of FBI field offices focused more on convicting than on disrupting."

Overseas crime investigations represented a return to a classic FBI strategy for calming the public when it became alarmed over vague threats to its security. Under Hoover, the Bureau rose to fame and power by taking symbolic action against symbolic enemies. In the past, however, whether the enemy was Jack Johnson, the IWW, the 1930s gangsters, the Nazi Underground, or the CPUSA, there never really was, at least in the apocalyptic terms used by FBI publicity, any truly dangerous threat. Since the threat was essentially symbolic, so too could be the response.

So the Bureau in the 1990s was still always looking for the big play, the big arrest, the big trial, the big conviction that could convince the country that it could relax, the Bureau was taking care of things. But the terrorist threat of the 1990s was unlike any of the great fears that had swept the country before. It was real. It could not be solved with a stroke of public relations. And even recognizing the Bureau's great accomplishments in actually identifying and in some cases capturing terrorists who had attacked Americans, it was nothing but a symbolic victory to indict bin Laden for the attacks on the *Cole* or the African embassies. What was needed was not symbolism but real surveillance that could protect the homeland against bin Laden's network.

The HRT was the most impressive, the most able group of the FBI, so it exemplified in the most dramatic way what was wrong with the Bureau's counterterror strategy in the 1990s: The HRT was strictly reactive, but it was so good at reacting that it allowed Freeh to commit an enormous amount of the Bureau's resources to solving difficult overseas terrorism cases where there were no ACLU watchdogs. These efforts would have been better devoted to a creative analysis of bin Laden's activities in this country—but the country had effectively forced the Bureau to halt any such surveillance. The FBI's strategy against terror was to arrest terrorists after they had attacked. The FBI was getting better and better at doing that, and the HRT was the best of all, but after 9/11 arresting them turned out to have really been beside the point.

Freeh's Bureau felt constrained to wait until almost the last moment in a terrorism case, and then race against time. According to Neil Gallagher, the Bureau under Freeh could initiate surveillance only when there was "reasonable indication of intent of criminal activity." This had to involve not merely "rhetoric but overt activity." For example,

> there was a case in the Far West, a group of individuals that made known their hatred of homosexuals and blacks and that they would like to kill some. They began exploring ways and training to carry them out. They began to build and detonate small devices. At this point a source was introduced. They began to identify locations and to plan. Finally, when they began to transport the devices, they were arrested.

Gallagher described other efforts the Freeh Bureau made to keep domestic surveillance on the right side of, not exactly the law, since the law is open to interpretation, but on the right side of its critics, which is a difficult, if not a losing, proposition. Take the American Indian Movement, which has been involved in more than a few acts of violence, ranging from simple assaults to premeditated murder. Gallagher would say, "There should not be an investigation of every aspect of an organization just because one aspect shows intent to commit criminal acts." In other words, only the individuals within an organization who intend to commit a crime should be investigated; the entire organization cannot be targeted only because of a behavior of its members, even though the situation begged for en expansion of RICO to terror.

> Another example: There is a Church . . . in Illinois that advocates criminal acts. In fact, the attorney general has said that it should be and is being investigated. But there are other unusual churches similar to it that should not be investigated just because of the similarity. Are violent people using that church as a pulpit, or does it consist only of violent people?

■ ■ ■

Domestic surveillance was a hot potato for the Bureau, and hedging it about with limitations and restrictions was hardly going to cool it off. Bureau reorganizations since Hoover's time had tried to defuse domestic surveillance by moving it where it could do the least harm. The assumption behind the constant shuffling of domestic surveillance from one division to another was that the only way the Bureau could stay out of trouble in domestic surveillance was not to do it. That is why when I asked Gallagher two years before 9/11 what he was doing about terrorism, I got this answer: "We aren't violating anybody's civil liberties."

The only way the Bureau's strategic planners could imagine a revival of domestic intelligence was a plain impossibility: "The development of an appreciation for intelligence will undoubtedly require a significant culture change for FBI managers." This blithe talk of a culture change at the Bureau overlooked the basic facts of "cultural" life. The FBI can no more create its own culture independent of the rest of the government and the rest of society than Rhode Island can create its own climate independent of Massachusetts, New York, and Connecticut. An organization like the FBI does not develop its own culture in isolation from the rest of society. It either has it forced upon it or it absorbs it, and with the Bureau both had happened. After Hoover's death we forced an anti-intelligence culture on it, and then over the years the Bureau, out of necessity, began to absorb the politically correct dogmas that were the intellectual underpinnings of the prohibition against domestic intelligence gathering. The Bureau couldn't have created a culture of domestic intelligence if it wanted to. And because it had internalized the values of those of us who criticized it, it didn't want to any more.

Toward the end of his directorship Freeh tried to bring domestic intelligence back to life inoffensively through a synergy between international organized crime investigations and foreign counterintelligence. Throughout the Hoover era, domestic surveillance of political groups was handled by Division Five, known in the forties and fifties as, in turn, the General Intelligence Division, the National Defense Division, the Security Division, the Domestic Intelligence Division (with two branches, Espionage and Research), and Internal Security and Liaison. Clarence Kelley transferred domestic intelligence investigations to the General Investigative Division, "where they would be managed like all other criminal cases in that division." He then designated Division Five the Intelligence Division, which was restricted to foreign counterintelligence. In October 1993, Louis Freeh put domestic intelligence back in Division Five, now renamed the National Security Division, tasked to deal with espionage and terrorism, both domestic and, increasingly, international.

On June 26, 1999, Freeh split Division Five into separate divisions, one investigating espionage, the other terrorism. The proposal grew out of a government-wide review of counterintelligence operations that included the FBI, CIA, and Defense Department. FBI officials suggested that there "was a sense that as the battle against terrorism became more important, counterespionage operations were given less priority." According to Gallagher, the idea was that "Counterintelligence will remain Division Five. Criminal Investigation will remain Division Six. There was some sentiment for aligning them [Antiterrorism and Counterintelligence] together, but divisions Four and Seven already had their stationery printed."

There would be a new unit called the Investigative Services Division. Freeh's idea, Gallagher said, was "to bring the analytical expertise of the Soviet-bloc-counterintelligence people to bear on Soviet organized crime, and [likewise] to pull together all forms of information through the use of computers. The result will be a new multidimensional capability for the Bureau." But all the shuffling of the organizational chart did nothing to revive domestic intelligence.

■ ■ ■

Any real proposal to revive domestic intelligence would have set off protests by Bureau critics, some of whom firmly believed that there never had been any real threat that justified domestic surveillance by the FBI, not then and probably never; that domestic surveillance by the Bureau always had been part of a larger program to use the Red smear to stifle dissent, crush reform, and keep workers and minorities powerless. The only real threat to the country, many felt, was covert surveillance by the FBI.

This view of the Bureau was particularly prevalent in the media and in entertainment. The existence of an FBI file on a celebrity—Elvis Presley, Frank Sinatra, John Lennon—released through a Freedom of Information Act request, no matter what it revealed (often nothing), meant that the FBI had been doing things it shouldn't and had to be watched to keep it from doing again.

With very few exceptions, such as Jodie Foster in *The Silence of the Lambs,* the image of the FBI in popular entertainment was still of a repressive organization equally at war with idealist agents and with the country's civil liberties. Even a movie about an FBI success, like *Donnie Brasco,* created drama by portraying Joe Pistone as a round peg in a square FBI hole, with the Bureau conspiring to crush his creativity and crusading spirit.

And so Louis Freeh was playing the cards we dealt him. Our image of the Bureau was still that it was Hoover's FBI, that is, the Church Committee's image of the FBI as COINTELPRO writ large, a deathless Dracula, unchanging and terrible, stalking through the years hungry for the civil liberties and the blood of new victims. Despite the passage of time, that image had never changed, and if anything, had gotten more dire and dismal, as popular entertainment turned the FBI into a venomous snake pit of plots against the public and against the occasional heroic agent, as in television's *The X-Files.* Guides on the FBI tour in the 1990s said the first question they got usually was, "Where are the X-Files?"

Freeh faced a popular culture that seized on every lapse by the Bureau as confirming its image of an FBI congenitally in conspiracy against civil liberties. Even worse, the FBI's successes were ignored because they did not fit the paranoid stereotype of that Bureau of plots and conspiracies.

And so Freeh tried to project an alternative image of the FBI as an organization *primarily* dedicated to civil liberties, even at the cost of not getting a conviction. It was as though he were single-handedly trying to change the popular image of the Bureau from *The X-Files* formula to the formula of programs like *Law and Order* (which premiered in 1990) and *NYPD Blue* (1993), whose preternaturally idealistic cops and lawyers spend so much time debating subtleties of constitutional and ethical conundrums that the jury's verdict is little more than a usually ironic afterthought. Popular culture had seen a paradigm shift from the old brutal, repressive police formula of the 1960s and 1970s to a new breed of saintly cops and idealistic lawyers. The FBI was still trapped in the old paradigm, and Freeh was doing everything he could to set it free. Freeh could see that television's new breed of civil libertarian cops had a good thing going, and he wanted the FBI to have a piece of it.

So what was an FBI director to do?

If the G-man could no longer spy on America, then the G-man would inspire America. Louis Freeh's substitute for an FBI domestic intelligence program was a program of FBI ethics. In Louis Freeh's FBI there was no escape from the director's moral earnestness. In the past, directors' reports had simply listed the Bureau's accomplishments and set new priorities, with a pro forma preface affirming that, in the opinion of the director and the Bureau, crime was a bad thing. By contrast, majestically, and perhaps a bit menacingly, Freeh even prefaced his first five-year report with a verse from Scripture:

> *He who walks in the way of integrity*
> *shall be in my service.*
> *No one who practices deceit*
> *can hold a post in my court.*
> *No one who speaks falsely*
> *can be among my advisors.*

> —PSALM 101

In Freeh's new model ethical FBI, the Hooverian maxim "Don't Embarrass the Bureau" was turned into an ethical categorical imperative and infused with earnest moral content. Under Freeh almost every FBI publication or website paid tribute to the credo of Freeh's ethical G-man, the FBI "core values." These were

> *rigorous obedience to the Constitution of the United States; respect for the dig-nity of all those we protect; compassion; fairness; and uncompromising per-sonal and institutional integrity. . . . Observance of these core values is our guarantee of excellence and propriety in performing the FBI's national security and criminal investigative functions.*

The post-9/11 inquiries might have pointed to some of Freeh's core values as providing a blueprint for FBI failures in its surveillance of the 9/11 plotters:

> *Rigorous obedience to constitutional principles ensures that individually and institutionally we always remember that constitutional guarantees are more important than the outcome of any single interview, search for evidence, or in-vestigation.*

This sentiment conformed, of course, to the self-congratulatory American legal maxim that it is better to let a hundred guilty men go free than to punish an innocent man. In the post-9/11 world, we are starting to question whether it is better to let a hundred terrorists go free than to incarcerate one who may have just been in the wrong place at the wrong time. But Freeh was writing in another time and, to all intents and purposes, in another country.

There was nothing wrong with Freeh's core values:

> *Respect for the dignity of all whom we protect reminds us to wield law enforce-ment powers with restraint and to recognize the natural human tendency to be corrupted by power and to become callous in its exercise. Fairness and compassion ensure that we treat everyone with the highest regard for consti-tutional, civil and human rights. Personal and institutional integrity reinforce each other and are owed to the Nation in exchange for the sacred trust and great authority conferred upon us. We who enforce the law must not merely obey it. We have an obligation to set a moral example which those whom we protect can follow. Because the FBI's success in accomplishing its mis-sion is directly related to the support and cooperation of those whom we pro-tect, these core values are the fiber which holds together the vitality of our institution.*

Nothing was wrong with the core values, that is, if the FBI were also conducting effective intelligence investigations of suspected terrorists while it kept these values in mind. But it was not. In practice, the core values became an excuse for shying away from investigations that might be questioned on ethical grounds. And so agents had a new worry—whether in the course of an investigation they might do something that could be construed as unethical—which in Freeh's Bureau was worse than criminal.

Freeh liked to impress on his agents and on the public that ethics—defined not only as moral behavior but also as strict adherence to constitutional standards—was the Bureau's first priority, and he would point to the Holocaust as the almost inevitable result of any deviation from this standard:

> *Compliance with the highest ethical standards is essential for all law enforcement officers because history's darkest lesson teaches us what happens when the law is subject to the most horrifying misuse by police. The place was Nazi Germany and the time was the 1930s. The Nazi terror began not by breaking the law but by using the law, as the Holocaust Memorial so graphically shows us.*
>
> *Hitler persuaded the German president to invoke a section of the German constitution that in effect suspended all civil liberties, thus permitting warrantless searches and seizure of property without due process. These emergency decrees became the legal basis for the concentration camps in which millions of innocent persons perished.*
>
> *The decrees were initially carried out not by the Gestapo but by the regular civilian police in many cases. This is a lesson that no one should forget. Democracy depends on law enforcement to protect the rights of all citizens and to rescue them from harm. When police fail in this great responsibility, suffering and death follow. This lesson must be foremost in the minds of all in the FBI.*
>
> *The FBI is determined that the grim meaning of the Holocaust will not be forgotten by its special agents.*

Nowhere was Freeh's image of the moral G-man more apparent than in the ethical training of new agents during his era as director. The FBI trains its recruits on the Marine Corps base at Quantico, Virginia, the gates tightly secured by fatigue-clad Marine guards who shout "Sirs" and "Ma'ams" where civilians would use periods or exclamation points. At any one time there are twelve hundred staff and students at the academy, including new agents and local and foreign police.

The centerpiece of Louis Freeh's new model FBI was the new agents' ethics class. To be sure none of them missed its significance, they took ethics at the beginning and end of their training. In the Freeh years, the syllabus began with ethics, and then covered legal matters, forensic science, interviewing, informant development, communications, white collar crime, drug investigations, organized crime, behavioral science, and computer skills: 645 hours of classroom training. While the new agents were being introduced to the latest developments in law enforcement, they were surrounded by reminders of the past: Every day they passed through the Bureau's Hall of Honor, inscribed with the names of the forty-six agents who have died on the job, from Edwin C. Shanahan, the first agent to be killed in the line of duty (1925), Raymond J. Caffrey, killed in the Kansas City Massacre that touched off the FBI's gangbusting wars of the thirties, the famous agents killed during the Dillinger gang manhunt of 1934, W. Carter Baum, Herman E. Hollis, and Samuel P. Cowley, to the sobering number of agents killed in recent years, seven in the decade of the nineties alone. They walked by the Bureau's meditation garden with its statue of Judge Giovanni Falcone, the Bureau's Italian ally during the great Mafia cases of the 1980s, who had visited Quantico for international councils of war against organized crime, before he was assassinated by the Mafia in Sicily.

Freeh almost never missed a Quantico graduation. He would arrive hours before the ceremony for a picture with the new agent and his family. Freeh gave the graduation address, recalling his own cases as agent and as prosecutor: the Pizza Connection and the mail bombing of Federal Judge Vance. He would list the places they would be sent in a few days, from Atlanta to Saudi Arabia. If a baby started wailing, Freeh would ask the mother or father to stay in the auditorium with the infant, to make the point that they too were part of the Bureau, and that their spouse's success would depend on their family's support. He would tell them that in coping with the stress of the job, "nothing is more important than your family." In many ways the image of Freeh's FBI agent was similar to the domestic G-man of Hoover in the 1950s, when the agent as dutiful family man was the director's answer to the threat of communism. As the culture of personal relationships and sensitivity swept America during the 1990s, Louis Freeh's G-man became as sensitive as the next guy, unless the next guy was Phil Donahue or Doctor Phil.

He would assure the new agents that the Bureau was not resting on its past, but was planning new and better facilities like the new lab just completed at Quantico—this during the scandals at the old lab in the Hoover building.

Then he got to his real message: how the reputation of the FBI was the key to their success. No one has to help you, he would tell them, except out of respect for the FBI, and agents should not take this respect for granted. Even the slightest breach of the Bureau's reputation for integrity would make it impossible for them to succeed.

The most important award presented to a member of the graduating class was the FBI Award, given by the new agents to the classmate who best exemplified "the moral high ground." Their sixteen-hour course in "Ethics in Law Enforcement" was taught by an agent with a doctorate in philosophy, who led students through the ethical foundations of the Constitution and the Declaration of Independence, with an overview of the philosophies of Thomas Jefferson, John Locke, and Immanuel Kant. They studied the nature of corruption, as in the bad, who act in "direct opposition to Kant's categorical imperative"; the meat eaters, who try to extract the maximum profit from their job; the grazers, who steal when they have the chance; the self-controlled, "who do the right thing, but resent the higher standard to which they are held"; and, finally, the truly excellent. What the Bureau wanted were "individuals who respect, even love honesty. Truly incorruptible." They were given a simple set of ethical signals, "the Book, the Bell, and the Candle" (a variation on the old movie title), to warn when an officer is confronting a potentially unethical situation. "The Book"—Is your conduct legal? "The Bell"—Does an internal alarm go off that this doesn't feel right? "The Candle"—What would the person you most respect [your mom?] think if this came to light?

Agents discussed three classic law enforcement dilemmas: honesty versus loyalty; truth versus justice; and due process versus crime control. The instructor warned them about "noble cause corruption," which justified brutal, immoral, or illegal means to a worthy goal (*Dirty Harry*). The instructor contrasted what he called "dog loyalty," that is, loyalty to one's friends, with "cat loyalty," loyalty to the house and its rules, principles, and morality. "Remember that your highest loyalty must be to the Constitution. We are striving to make the FBI an organization where there is no conflict between loyalty to its members and loyalty to the rules of the Bureau and the Constitution."

Students learned about Freeh's "Bright Line Policy": "Agents will not lie, cheat, or steal or tolerate those who do." The penalty was immediate dismissal. The Bright Line included a draconian prohibition on any use of alcohol while on duty, and since an agent must be available for duty twenty-four hours a day, that effectively meant no drinking at all. The only exception was when an agent was assigned to undercover work.

Then student agents worked through ethical scenarios, many of them involving a new agent who sees a senior agent doing something illegal. The trainee is asked to imagine the consequences of not turning his partner in; he finally finds himself used as a bargaining chip as his partner tries to negotiate a deal during a corruption investigation. It probably isn't the first time he has broken the law. Sooner or later he will be caught—and now he has something he can use against you.

■ ■ ■

From the beginning, Freeh's management style rubbed his headquarters executives the wrong way, and while it made him popular with field agents, the media, and Congress, it was ultimately responsible for a series of failures in high-profile FBI cases. Perhaps his management style stemmed from his having to rely on the same executives who had turned on and toppled his predecessor. Buck Revell, now the Dallas special agent in charge, probably the best-known FBI official after Sessions, had gone public with a call for Sessions to resign. When the next controversy hit the Bureau and the blame game began, would they be any more loyal to Freeh than they had been to Sessions? Moreover, the Bureau was still reeling from the Waco and Ruby Ridge debacles. Public confidence in the Bureau's competence could not have been lower, while Freeh's executives seemed more intent on covering up their mistakes than offering credible explanations for what had gone wrong in Texas and Idaho.

Whether Freeh did not trust the subordinates he inherited, or whether he felt that a house cleaning was needed to restore confidence in the Bureau after Ruby Ridge and Waco, he brought in his own management team, largely from New York. He installed his VANPAC assistant Howard Shapiro as chief counsel, and made Justice Department attorney Bob Bucknam his chief of staff, equal in rank to the deputy director (David G. Binney). He all but dispensed with Executive Conference meetings, and eliminated the two associate deputy director positions, thus placing himself one level closer to the assistant directors in charge of the headquarters divisions. He abolished forty-nine management positions at headquarters and began moving agents out of headquarters, the first batch of 150 to the Washington and Baltimore field offices, another 450 out into the field over the next year. He renamed the Intelligence Division the National Security Division to acknowledge the growing importance of counterterrorism. He moved the Technical Services Division into a new Information Resources Division, with responsibilities for the Bureau's electronic surveillance. The Administrative Services Division was split into a Finance Division and a Personnel Division. He abolished Sessions's Total Quality Management Program, a business school technique for improving performance, and removed that program's supervisor, Assistant Director G. Norman Christensen, from his position after Christensen defended TQM at one of the first Executive Conference meetings.

Freeh's shakeup of headquarters aroused deep and long-lasting resentment among senior officials: For some it meant an immediate end to their careers; for others, opening up key technical slots to non-agent employees narrowed possibilities for promotions. Gripes from inside and outside the Bureau would periodically make trouble for the new director, but they were balanced by his popularity among the rank and file. Freeh made it his business to visit all of the Bureau's field offices. After brief meetings with the special agent in charge, he would have meetings with the field agents alone that often turned into gripe sessions, sometimes followed by the transfer of the SAC. Freeh often showed up at Quantico to jog with the trainees and tried to choose first assignments that would not disrupt their families. Freeh began enforcing the mandatory retirement age of fifty-seven for FBI agents and officials (though with a few widely resented waivers for special cases). Very shortly the top echelon of the FBI had a vigorous and youthful cast, one that shared the director's own almost fanatical devotion to physical fitness.

What many, including Buck Revell, sensed as Freeh's disdain for the hierarchy he inherited was publicly demonstrated when Freeh censured and suspended the highly admired assistant director in charge of the New York field office, James Fox, for having technically violated his guidelines forbidding agents from commenting on cases under investigation. (Fox had denied that the FBI had had advance warning of the World Trade Center bombing, and had added that the Bureau would have certainly stopped the attack if there had been any such information.) A few years later, James Fox's funeral at an East Side church in New York took on the atmosphere of an anti-Freeh rally, with the deposed William Sessions one of the principal eulogists and Freeh conspicuously absent.

■ ■ ■

Louis Freeh's FBI was a strange place, with a radical disconnect between impressive appearances and disastrous performances. Until 9/11, it was impossible to tell which represented the real FBI. Despite some notable accomplishments like the return of Kansi from Pakistan and the quick solution of the Oklahoma City federal building bombing, the Freeh years provided a numbingly depressing series of mistakes and scandals, along with high-profile cases (like the UNABOMB and the Atlanta Olympics bombing) that dragged on for years unsolved.

During Clinton's first administration, the Bureau was attacked by Republicans for Waco and Ruby Ridge. Freeh refused to defend the Bureau's record during those two crises, because, in the view of one of his agents, "these problems had not happened on Freeh's watch." Freeh's refusal to defend the Bureau's performance—and worse, to his agents—his criticism of it, left unrebutted the right-wing extremist stereotype of the Bureau as "jack-booted thugs."

Freeh's Bureau was dogged by controversy over whether the Bureau had been responsible for any of the Davidians' gunshot deaths and, more critically, whether Bureau grenades could have caused the fire.

On the first question, the Bureau position was that it had not fired a single gunshot during the assault, and that was the truth: Bureau procedures require agents to account for every expended round of ammunition. The rigor of these procedures makes it almost impossible for a shot to be fired without its becoming a matter of Bureau record and, in cases like this, public record as well. Right-wing critics of the Bureau pointed to images on the Bureau's own spotter plane videotape that seemed to indicate muzzle flashes from within the Bureau's armored vehicles, but scientific analysis established that these were reflections of sunlight.

The Bureau also denied that its tear-gas grenades could have caused the fires that consumed the compound, and again it was telling the truth, but it created the impression of a cover-up by employing language that was technically true but was not the whole story. The gas the HRT had injected into the buildings was certainly inert, but when suspended in the air it *could* act as an accelerant for fires and explosions, although not start them. The compound was filled with open sources of flame because the FBI had shut down electrical service and the Davidians were using gas mantle Coleman lanterns throughout the building. There were also cans of kerosene and gasoline in the compound, and the impact of gas grenades on them theoretically could have started a fire. But photographic evidence showed three separate fires starting almost simultaneously at widely separated locations, which is not consistent with those scenarios.

The FBI also said it used no explosive grenades at all. It actually *had* used two military-type explosive (M651) pyrotechnic ("flash-bang") grenades. This false statement came about because Freeh would not let Bureau SACs conduct the customary post-operation examination of the fiasco. Since Waco had happened before he came aboard, he might have felt that anything he did might implicate him in the mess. The result was that only one SAC knew that the Bureau had fired flash-bang grenades into a concrete structure away from the main building, and he was not interviewed (They are often, even usually, employed by the HRT during assaults.) But since they were fired between 8:30 and 9:30 in the morning, some two to three hours before the fire, which was certainly started by Koresh, probably deliberately, and since they were inserted far from the buildings that caught fire, the Bureau testified that no grenades that could have caused the fire were used. That was true, but when it was discovered, six years later, that pyrotechnic grenades *had* been used, it sounded as though the Bureau had covered up the possibility that it had started the fires that had killed Koresh and his followers. One SAC said that the reason the Bureau set itself up for this embarrassment was that "Louis Freeh decided he did not want Waco to touch him."

When lawyers for the Davidian plaintiffs' wrongful death suit discovered that the Bureau had used a type of grenade that it had always denied, the impact was devastating. Why conceal something unless it was incriminating? That was the reaction the plaintiffs hoped for, and which they got. There was such consternation at the Justice Department that Janet Reno had federal marshals invade FBI headquarters to seize the Bureau's spotter plane videotapes that proved the rounds had been ordered and used, and then she appointed a special investigator, former Senator John Danforth, to reinvestigate Waco in the light of the revelations.

In the end, the Danforth Commission, while not uncritical of the Bureau, concluded that the FBI's original explanation of the fires and the "gunshot" flashes was correct, and that its statements about the explosive grenades, while misleading, were basically true. In combination with many credible reports that the Davidians had planned suicides on previous occasions, and had discussed suicide in the event of an assault, the evidence still strongly supported the Bureau's position that the fires were set from within and that the gunshots in the complex occurred during a mass suicide.

The Bureau's reluctance to lay its cards on the table immediately after Waco was an accelerant that fueled paranoia through the far right. As one of the consultants to the Justice Department's 1993 investigation pointed out,

> *People like the militia have a whole bunch of crazy ideas. However, they have two pieces of truth in all the craziness. One is "Look at what happened at Waco. And the government hid its mistakes and concealed its misdeeds." And the other piece of truth is that the Bureau of Alcohol, Tobacco, and Firearms made this attack on Waco because Koresh's followers had guns. And the militias have guns. So the militias have these two kernels of truth in all their craziness about*

our government: Waco, and the fear that the government will come after them because they have guns.

It would have been hard for anyone to make the Ruby Ridge disaster worse for the Bureau than it was, but Louis Freeh could not have done better if he had been trying. Freeh did fight hard to protect Lon Horiuchi from federal and state prosecution for killing Vicki Weaver, but he and the Bureau bungled the rest of its handling of the tragedy. First, during the preliminary stages of the federal murder trial against Randy Weaver for the death of U.S. Marshal William F. Degan, it was learned that a headquarters official, Michael Kahoe, had destroyed all copies of an internal inquiry into the case that faulted the Bureau. Kahoe was convicted of obstructing justice and served eighteen months in prison.

Freeh had nothing to do with Kahoe, but his fingerprints were all over the Bureau's handling of another serious issue in the case. This was a set of highly irregular, even unconstitutional, "rules of engagement" that had been approved for the HRT at Ruby Ridge by the assistant director in charge in the Criminal Investigative Division, Larry Potts. Instead of the Bureau's normal rules of engagement, which restrict the use of deadly force to situations where the agent or another person is at risk of serious injury, Potts approved rules that said deadly force "can and should" be employed against any armed adults at Ruby Ridge.

These rules were immediately recognized as improper by members of the HRT, and there is no evidence any of them regarded themselves as permitted to do anything not authorized by the Bureau's standard rules. Both of Horiuchi's shots fell within the old guidelines, since it was his judgment that unless he stopped the Weavers and Harris, they would begin shooting at the Bureau helicopter.

But an internal examination of the "can and should" rules led to severe disciplinary action against agents all along the chain of command, except for Potts, who received only a letter of censure. Potts, you recall, had formed a close relationship with Freeh when they both worked on the Judge Robert Vance murder case, where Potts was the lead investigator. When one of the agents, the field commander at Ruby Ridge, protested that his punishment was unfair since Potts was being treated so leniently, the FBI's general counsel, Howard Shapiro, who had also worked with Freeh on the Vance investigation, dismissed the complaint as baseless and added that bringing such charges could be destructive to the Bureau.

Freeh then added insult to injury—at least in the eyes of field agents—by promoting Potts (in May 1995) to the position of deputy director of the Bureau, thus making him second in command, despite a warning by Jamie Gorelick, the deputy attorney general, that Potts was still under investigation for Ruby Ridge. Two months later, facing strong criticism, Freeh had to cancel Potts's promotion, and when the Justice Department's inquiry into Ruby Ridge criticized Potts, Freeh suspended him while the investigation dragged on for more than two years until Potts retired.

Reporter and author Ronald Kessler, who had written two *Washington Post* pieces charging Freeh with mismanaging the Bureau, has argued convincingly that in both Waco and Ruby Ridge the Bureau was guilty of nothing more than understandable (under the circumstances) mistakes compounded by bad luck, but also that Freeh refused to let his subordinates defend the Bureau while he himself sided with those who criticized its actions. It was devastating to Bureau morale when Freeh appeared before a Senate inquiry into Ruby Ridge on October 20, 1995, to say that the Bureau's performance during the standoff at Ruby Ridge, Idaho, and in its aftermath was "terribly flawed." Freeh went on to say of Horiuchi's conduct, "I am not saying that I approve of it, I am not trying to justify it. I am not saying I would have taken it. . . . I am certainly not saying that in a future similar set of circumstances, FBI agents or law enforcement officers should take such a shot." The *Washington Post* called Freeh's testimony an "extraordinary public confession of errors by an FBI director."

It is disheartening to men and women being sent in harm's way when they realize that they are going to be abandoned if there is trouble by superiors trying to protect their careers from the contamination of failure. In the heat of battle, mistakes will be made, but when agents make errors as opposed to intentionally illegal acts, they *have* to be backed up by their superiors, or agents will no longer take the risks necessary for success. Under Freeh, agents and supervisors were learning that if things went wrong, they were on their own.

Freeh also habitually micromanaged high-profile cases. This was a factor in three of the Bureau's most notorious fiascos of the nineties. Freeh injected himself into the middle of the Bureau's investigation of the April 19, 1995, bombing of the Alfred P. Murrah Federal Building in Oklahoma City. Almost immediately after the explosion, Special Agent Jim Norman managed to use a truck axle's vehicle identification number to locate the Ryder agency that had rented the truck to the bomber. The owners gave an FBI artist enough of a description for a motel owner in Junction City, Oklahoma, to recognize the suspect from the sketch, and give the Bureau the name of the suspect, Timothy McVeigh, and his address, a Michigan farm owned by James and Terry Nichols. Agents established that James Nichols had purchased the sort of farm materials —fertilizer and fuel oil—that FBI experts had concluded were the ingredients in the bomb. A check on McVeigh through the Bureau's National Crime Information Center discovered that he had been arrested right after the bombing for driving without a license and carrying a concealed pistol, and was still locked up. The FBI ordered the police in Perry, Oklahoma, to hold onto McVeigh, who was due for a bail hearing almost at that moment. They had their man.

But now Freeh insisted, over the objections of the case agents and the Detroit special agent in charge, that James Nichols be arrested and charged with conspiracy, overruling the agents on the scene who warned that they had no evidence connecting James Nichols to the bombing, and that the potential bomb-making materials he had purchased were commonly used on many farms. Nichols was released after spending a month in jail despite having, in the words of a federal judge, no "connection, no evidence other than friendship for being charged." Freeh had marred a brilliant example of detective work by the FBI by what Bureau critics could charge was another instance of FBI "overzealousness."

Freeh personally turned the FBI's investigation of the July 27, 1996, bombing of the Centennial Olympic Park in Atlanta during the Olympics into another mess for the Bureau.

Richard Jewell was a security guard hired to protect an AT&T light and sound tower at the Olympic Park who had told police he had seen a suspicious-looking object shortly before the explosion. Then he appeared on television news to tell how he had helped the police clear out the park after the bombing. In these circumstances the FBI and most other police agencies investigate amateur "first-responders," since arsonists, for instance, sometimes start blazes just so they can live out their fantasies of becoming a hero. And so the FBI was certainly interested in learning more about Jewell, and was doing so when the *Atlanta Journal-Constitution* broke a story that Jewell was a suspect.

The FBI agents on the scene, realizing that their chances for an informal—and possibly more informative—interview with Jewell were slipping away, asked him to come to the Atlanta field office. Their pretext was that they were making a training film about how to interview a "first-responder"—they told him he would be a "superstar." Jewell liked the idea, and sat for an interview that lasted over an hour and a quarter. At this point Freeh called up the Atlanta special agent in charge, David "Woody" Johnson, who was in his office with SAC Barry Mawn and U.S. Attorney Kent B. Alexander. When Freeh, back in Washington, learned that Jewell was being questioned at the field office, he insisted that Jewell be read his *Miranda* warning. The SACs and the U.S. attorney protested that it was not necessary and would change the dynamics of a productive interview—that the *Miranda* warning was required only if the suspect was in custody or was going to be arrested, and this was not the case. Bear Bryant back at headquarters also protested that the warning was not needed and would impede the investigation. Woody Johnson relayed Freeh's order to the agents interviewing Jewell, but they tried to salvage the interview by telling Jewell that the *Miranda* warning was being read to him just to make the training film seem more realistic. When they asked Jewell to sign the warning, however, he decided that things were getting too real and he asked to call his attorney. End of interview. Later Freeh directed the search of Jewell's home by issuing a running series of orders over his cell phone.

Without Freeh's intervention, it is very likely that the informal interview would have eliminated Jewell as a suspect. Instead, it became a three-month ordeal for Jewell, who was hounded mercilessly by the media. It turned out he was guilty of nothing at all except trying to help at a disaster and having a vague similarity to an FBI profiler's conjectures about possible personality traits of the bomber. FBI officials were disgusted with Freeh's interference. A Justice Department official said that "Freeh acted like a young, inexperienced agent"; an FBI director should "select the right people, ask the right questions, and let them do their job." A former Atlanta SAC said that "it was inappropriate for Louis to run that operation. He did that on major incidents. You can't do that because you don't have all the information you need."

Defending himself, Freeh chose precisely the same words to justify his intervention that investigators of the FBI's 9/11 failure would use to characterize what had kept the FBI from pursuing its leads on the hijackers: Freeh said he had ordered the warning "in an excess of caution." It was the Bureau's "excess of caution" that the Joint Inquiry into the 9/11 attacks blamed for the FBI's failure to follow up on the leads in Phoenix and Minneapolis that might have exposed the 9/11 plot.

The Wen Ho Lee espionage case at Los Alamos, New Mexico, was another investigation botched by Freeh. He turned what should have been approached as a counterintelligence inquiry—not necessarily aimed at a prosecution—into a premature criminal investigation that finally, when it collapsed, left unclear what the scientist was guilty of, although he certainly was guilty of something.

Wen Ho Lee was a Chinese-born mechanical engineer in the Los Alamos National Laboratory section that developed new models of nuclear bombs. The FBI became interested in Lee when he called another Chinese scientist who was suspected of spying for China and offered to help find out who had informed on him. When the FBI talked to Lee, he denied at first having talked to the scientist at all, and then, when confronted with proof of the contact, came up with an implausible explanation. It was also suspicious that Lee did not always report his trips to China as required by Los Alamos regulations, and when he did report them, he never mentioned any attempts by Chinese security agents to recruit him as a spy, although when other Chinese-American scientists visited China, they almost always reported such efforts.

Eventually the laboratory itself became suspicious of Lee and pulled him off sensitive research. In 1999 the FBI finally gave Lee a polygraph. When he was asked whether he had given the Chinese information on the nation's most advanced nuclear bomb, the W-88, the polygraph indicated that he was lying when he said no. When the FBI searched Lee's office computer they found that he had downloaded 430,000 pages of documents and had taken the files home, and that after he failed the polygraph he had started deleting the files. The *New York Times* got hold of the story and wrote it up as a major espionage case. Republicans in Congress demanded to know why the Bureau was dragging its feet in charging Lee. Then Freeh became personally involved, and unleashed a brigade of agents to interview everyone who knew the scientist.

It is always difficult to get evidence of espionage that will stand up in court. It usually takes a confession, or catching the spy in the act of transmitting classified information, which almost never happens. In Chinese espionage cases, contacts between the spies and their handlers always take place in China, out of sight of the FBI.

Nevertheless, even though the Bureau still had no evidence likely to persuade a jury, Freeh made a play for congressional approval by having Lee indicted on fifty-nine counts of seeking to "injure the United States or . . . to secure an advantage to any foreign nation," a charge carrying a life sentence. A former Justice Department official who had worked espionage cases with the Bureau complained that "because Freeh did not have the evidence for a classic espionage case, he painted this as a devastating case and tried to cover up the lack of evidence by bringing a fifty-nine-count indictment citing vague and unsupportable charges."

Lee was in solitary confinement under twenty-four-hour surveillance for nine months. During preliminary hearings an FBI agent was found to have testified falsely on one aspect of the case against Lee. Although the agent claimed it was an honest mistake, the judge lashed out at the Bureau, and said that the court had been "led astray by the executive branch of our government" and that Lee's jailing "embarrassed our entire nation and each of us who is a citizen of it."

There is no doubt that Lee had mishandled classified documents, and should have been fired for that. He was fired for that, and he was found guilty of that, but of nothing more. And whether he did more may never be known because when the case went to trial, that was the only evidence the Bureau had. In the end the FBI stood indicted in the media and in public opinion for persecuting what looked to be an innocent man. In that sense, Lee was exonerated, though under close examination it still looks like Lee was up to something, but God knows what.

The entire record of FBI failures under Freeh need not be recounted in full and depressing detail. There were Frederick Whitehurst's charges that the FBI laboratories were "shading" evidence. Freeh made things worse by punishing the whistle-blower, Whitehurst. It later developed that although the Bureau's lab procedures were certainly not up to the highest professional standards, the laboratory's agents had done nothing illegal and no cases had actually been contaminated by false or shaded testimony. This could have been established by an impartial investigation that would have left the reputation of the FBI laboratory intact, instead of destroying it. Far worse, after the nightmare of Special Agent Earl Pitts's betrayal of the Bureau to the Soviet Union, the FBI discovered that another of its own, Robert Hanssen, had been spying for the Russians since 1979, and over the course of his career handed the Russians the identities of all the CIA's most important spies in the Soviet Union. Many of them were executed.

Freeh's management style certainly left much to be desired, but in some ways that style was forced upon him. When he took over the Bureau he could not rely on the loyalty of executives who had risen up against William Sessions and might rise against him. Their most deadly weapon against Sessions had been leaks to the media, not just about Sessions's personal misdeeds, but also about his mismanagement of the Bureau. And mismanagement by a boss is always in the eye of the beholder, if the beholder is the boss' subordinate. So Freeh went to self-destructive extremes to keep his executives from going to the media behind his back by forbidding them to talk to the press at all.

Then, too, his executives had done almost nothing except botch cases for him. He could be forgiven for believing he had better get his hand in every important case, since he would have to take the rap when his men screwed it up.

And finally, it must have seemed to him that the press, Congress, and the rest of the country were always just looking for a chance to bash the Bureau every time it made a mistake, since the Bureau had been a national punching bag as long as he could remember.

Despite his problems, Freeh turned out to be a magician with Congress, the public, and, for the most part, the press. Almost everyone was entranced by

Freeh, except for journalist Ronald Kessler, the same Ronald Kessler who was instrumental in Sessions's downfall and was now a voice in the wilderness crying that Freeh's leadership was destroying the Bureau once again. I was entranced by Freeh myself. It was refreshing to see Headquarters, the Quantico academy, and the field offices all staffed with energetic, enthusiastic, and creative people with no reluctance to criticize the old Bureau, eager to celebrate the ethics and ideals of Freeh's new FBI. It was an FBI that talked—perhaps too much—about how the protection of a suspect's constitutional rights was a higher priority than merely getting their man. If Hoover's FBI had used cases to demonstrate how crime must always fall before the FBI formula of organization and science, Freeh's FBI seemed to want to make its cases prove the Bureau's commitment to a higher standard, and to turn each case into a demonstration of just how ethical it could be.

Doubtless Freeh was sincere in his convictions, but they also did him no harm with the new liberal establishment. Freeh was appointed by President Clinton, a liberal Democrat at a time when Democrats were in control of Congress, and he made a great show of sharing the administration's preference for individual civil liberties over efficient crime control, when it came to a choice between the two. He naturally enjoyed the party's support, and he was attacked by Republicans early in his tenure for giving the appearance, though probably inadvertently, of doing political favors for the White House. Freeh's general counsel, Howard Shapiro, gave the White House an advance copy of *Unlimited Access*, a sensationalistic book by an ex-agent that attacked the competence and even the patriotism of the Clinton White House staff and the first lady. And, most likely because of clerical bungling, the Bureau also furnished the White House with information from its files on a list of former Bush administration officials obviously compiled for political purposes.

When Republicans in Congress attacked Freeh and the FBI for Waco and Ruby Ridge, Democrats defended him and the Bureau, since Freeh's enemies were their enemies. At both Ruby Ridge and Waco, the Bureau had pursued right-wing extremists who were convenient political targets for the Democrats, and who, Democrats tried to claim, were birds of a feather with Newt Gingrich and other Republican conservatives. And whenever Freeh admitted the Bureau had bungled, he always did so in a way that put him on the moral high ground of civil liberties, condemning any abuse of rights by his agents, no matter what extenuating circumstances there might be. The first Clinton administration saw Freeh as one of their own, valiantly trying to rein in the sinister culture of the Hoover-era FBI that liberals loved to hate. Freeh's emphasis on ethics, integrity, and civil liberties in the training and discipline of his agents played well with liberals leery of what they had always seen as the congenital authoritarianism of the Bureau.

When the Republicans captured Congress in the 1996 elections, Freeh did an about-face and aligned himself with Clinton's Republican enemies. When Janet Reno refused to appoint an independent counsel to investigate charges of illegal fund-raising by the Clinton campaign, the press got hold of a memo Freeh had written to Reno that took issue with her decision and implied that the Justice Department was too politicized to be trusted with the investigation. It was generally believed that the memo, which Reno had refused to give to Congress on the basis of executive privilege, was leaked by someone on Freeh's staff. During the height of the Whitewater-Lewinsky scandal, Freeh went out of his way to praise Independent Counsel Kenneth Starr, and even attended a reception in Starr's honor. Now the Republicans adored him; Democrats seethed.

This all makes Freeh seem a master Machiavellian intriguer, edging magnetically toward the stronger pole of political power. There may have been some of that in Freeh, but all evidence is that he came by his convictions honestly—that they derived from his deepest beliefs about what the FBI had to do to reflect well on itself (and on him) in the confusing cultural climate of the 1990s.

Hoover had always sought political independence for himself and his Bureau, particularly after FDR's death. Freeh sought it too, essentially breaking off his relationship with the Clinton White House shortly after the 1996 election. This may have been because the Republicans now controlled Congress, and so had to be placated. And then it might have been due to real fear that the corruption scandals of the administration, particularly the involvement of Chinese donors in the president's and vice president's fund-raising for the 1996 campaign, might drag Freeh down as Watergate had dragged down L. Patrick Gray. After the Monica Lewinsky scandal broke in 1998, Freeh's distancing of himself from the White House may also have been motivated by his personal distaste for Clinton's sexual dalliances.

In any case, during the last four years of the Clinton administration Louis Freeh was essentially on his own, with no political direction, no strategic direction from outside as to what the Bureau should be doing. The breakdown in the relationship between the White House and the Bureau certainly contributed to the Bureau's failure to do anything to overcome the hostility in the country to domestic surveillance. Throughout Bureau history, it has taken powerful backing from the president and the attorney general to persuade the FBI to depart from policies that brought it acclaim and refuge from the political storms; that is, by devoting itself to the routine solution of routine crimes when they come to the attention of the public. Perhaps nothing could have been done in the best of circumstances to rebuild the Bureau's domestic surveillance capabilities, but in a climate of open hostility between the director and the president, no one even tried.

For several years there had been rumors that Freeh, who was carrying a hefty mortgage on his home and was facing college expenses for his six sons, was financially hard-pressed on his salary of $141,300 and would have to move to a private sector job—perhaps at MBNA headquarters in Wilmington, Delaware, which was becoming a haven for former high FBI officials from the New York field office. On May 1, 2001, with the FBI still reeling from the morale-shattering news that Headquarters Soviet analyst Robert Hanssen had been selling counterintelligence secrets to the Russians for more than two decades, Louis Freeh announced his retirement, effective the next month.

Now that he was a short-timer with little political clout, Freeh's enemies no longer had to worry about him. They could let him have it. And they did.

Journalist Ron Kessler, who had helped drive William Sessions out of his seventh-floor office at the Hoover Building, got in a few last kicks, as did Buck Revell and some of the other high-ranking ex-officials Freeh had gotten rid of when he took over.

The FBI did not give Freeh a particularly good send-off. A week after Freeh's announcement, the Bureau admitted to Oklahoma City bomber Timothy McVeigh's lawyers that it had failed to turn over around three thousand pages of documents, violating an unusual judicial order to turn over *all* investigation materials to the defense. (Usually such orders are limited and specify what types of documents have to be turned over.) A furious Attorney General John Ashcroft had to delay McVeigh's execution until the defense could go over the documents. Four days later the Bureau discovered seven more documents in its Baltimore office, then announced that it was going to have to search all its field offices, and could give no assurance that even then it would manage to locate every last piece of paper in the McVeigh case.

As Freeh's last day in office approached, the media ran retrospectives of his stewardship, and they were not very complimentary. Most omitted any mention of the Bureau's successes during the past eight years. They listed as the key events a series of failures: the mishandling of the Wen Ho Lee case, and the Bureau's tardy admission that it had used grenades of the flash-bang variety, which, it was again pointed out, seemingly contradicted its long-standing assertion that it had not used any devices that could have caused the Waco fire. Other stories recounted the leak of Freeh's memo to Janet Reno recommending an independent counsel be appointed to investigate possible illegal contributions from the Chinese to Vice President Al Gore during the 1996 presidential campaign. There were accounts of Freeh's personal involvement in the bungled interrogation of Richard Jewell for the Centennial Olympic Park bombing in Atlanta, and the FBI's subsequent failure to catch anti-abortion bomber Eric Robert Rudolph, who the Bureau finally decided was the actual bomber and who was eventually caught by a North Carolina police officer in May 2003.

The problem, some claimed, was Freeh's failure as an administrator. According to Senator Charles E. Grassley, Republican from Iowa and a regular critic of the FBI, "Freeh tried to some extent, but he was not able to change the cowboy culture inside the FBI," and so the next director "is going to have to be someone who understands that this culture has to change and who is committed to changing it." Senator Arlen Specter, Republican of Pennsylvania, who had led investigations of Waco and Ruby Ridge, gave credit to Freeh for trying to fix the management problems at the FBI, but said that he had failed. "He's been rushing and rushing around trying to plug holes in the dike, but it has been impossible to keep all the water out."

The more charitable Clinton officials agreed. One said, "Whether he was unable or unwilling, Freeh did not expend the political capital necessary to change the Bureau's institutional culture." Michael R. Bromwich, who as Justice Department inspector general had investigated the lapses at the Bureau's crime laboratories, also argued that the Bureau, rather than being the "centralized paramilitary organization" of public perception, was really "a series of fiefdoms" that refuse to cooperate and coordinate, and "no one can explain why the culture doesn't change."

But that's easy. The FBI's culture was simply its adaptation to the culture of the Justice Department, Congress, and the entire country, a culture deeply opposed to effective law enforcement and of course to any domestic surveillance at all. For the Bureau's culture to change, the rest of the country's culture would have to change as well—as it did (how permanently remains to be seen) after 9/11.

After Freeh left the FBI on June 25, 2001, things got much worse. The Democrats, who had long resented his obvious contempt for Bill Clinton, had a chance to get in their licks, if for no other reason than to send a message to future FBI directors that they had better be more evenhanded in their treatment of the opposite party.

The Senate Judiciary Committee, chaired by Senator Patrick Leahy, Democrat of Vermont, learned that the FBI's and Justice Department's Office of Professional Responsibility had recommended in 1999 that two senior FBI officials be suspended and Freeh and another agent be censured for their handling of the internal FBI investigations of the Ruby Ridge disaster. The Justice Department's OPR report had faulted Freeh for placing a 1994 investigation in the hands of a friend of a target of the probe, then–Assistant Director Larry Potts. When the 1994 report was rejected by the Justice Department, Freeh assigned a second investigation in 1995 to a friend of Deputy Assistant Director Danny O. Coulson, who was also a target. When the 1995 report singled out the on-site commander, Eugene F. Glenn, Glenn protested, and so the FBI's Office of Professional Responsibility launched its own investigation that same year.

The FBI's OPR completed its inquiry in 1999 and recommended that Freeh be censured, and this was seconded by the Justice Department's Office of Professional Responsibility. The grounds for their recommendation were not released, but the grounds may well have been Freeh's assigning the two investigations to agents with personal relationships with prospective targets. Yet on January 3, 2001, Assistant Attorney General Stephen R. Colgate refused to censure Freeh, arguing, among other considerations, that since the FBI director was a presidential appointee, his judgments were not subject to Bureau or departmental discipline. Leahy blasted Colgate's decision, and characterized Freeh's handling of the Ruby Ridge investigations as a "textbook example of [FBI] abuses. It appears from this that the 'good old boy' network has been able to persist at the FBI. It serves to protect some senior FBI executives from the same scrutiny and discipline applied to rank-and-file agents. . . . This double standard is unfair and demoralizing." And the FBI agents who prepared the 1999 report called Colgate's refusal to censure Freeh "outrageous" and a "whitewash." A bitter valedictory for a director who had made raising the ethical standards of the Bureau one of his primary objectives.

Once again, Congress and the press were demanding a new director be chosen for his potential to undo the sins of his predecessor, to be the anti-Freeh, one who would use the reputed failures of the Freeh years as the blueprint for his or her own reforms. It seemed to be the consensus that these failures lay chiefly in the area of managerial discipline and computerization. When Robert Mueller's name surfaced as a possible nominee to replace Freeh, the Bush administration's public relations machine touted his prior success in tightening up the previously slack U.S. attorney's offices he had headed.

Mueller was sworn in as FBI director on September 4, 2001. A week later, the reputation of Louis Freeh's FBI lay in smoke and rubble.

■ ■ ■

Who was responsible for the intelligence failure of 9/11? Well, we all were. The FBI did not turn itself into a risk-aversive Bureau because it wanted to be that way. It did not turn into an FBI that paraded its political correctness as an all-purpose excuse for not doing its job because that was the kind of Bureau it wanted to be.

You can't protect a country that doesn't want to be protected. And for at least a quarter century, we sent every signal to the FBI that we did not want to be protected, and we punished the FBI whenever it tried to protect us.

We told the FBI what we wanted it to be: an FBI that never violated anyone's civil liberties. We punished the FBI every time it did anything that even looked like a violation of civil liberties. In the end, we got the FBI we wanted—an FBI that didn't violate anybody's civil liberties and didn't do much else.

Even with a perfect FBI and a perfect director—and the FBI during the 1990s was far from perfect—the United States was in no mood to permit the kind of domestic surveillance that would have been the only way the Bureau could have reacted quickly and efficiently enough to block the 9/11 plot. Instead, we trained the FBI to second-guess itself and never to do anything that would let us rake it over the coals once again.

No one who has tried to understand the history of the FBI could join in the general assault on Louis Freeh and the Bureau for not turning itself loose on terrorism suspects in the United States. Everything history teaches us about the Bureau shows that if Freeh had even hinted at reviving domestic surveillance before 9/11, he would have been hounded from office for bringing back the FBI of J. Edgar Hoover.

It can never be known whether, despite the FBI's failures during the summer of 2001, the 9/11 attacks could have been foreseen and therefore prevented, but those fatal failures by the FBI could easily have been foreseen by anyone familiar with the Bureau's history. And behind the FBI's failures were failures by the rest of us.

We all must share the blame for encouraging the FBI to blind itself to the realities of terrorists and terror networks. The history of the FBI teaches one of history's oldest lessons, and that is that everything has consequences. If the Bureau is repeatedly attacked for its every mistake, it will soon learn that the only infallible strategy for escaping mistakes and punishment is to do nothing. If you beat a dog every time it barks, do not be surprised when it lets a thief into the house. The price we paid for beating the Bureau for barking was a Bureau that would not bark.

Freeh is attacked now (by some who did nothing but praise him when they worked for him—and does that say more about them or him?) for a stubborn, perhaps quixotic attachment to the notion that the rule of law should replace brute force in the affairs of men and of nations. How bad is that? There are worse things to believe. As was said of Woodrow Wilson, the real problem with Freeh may have been "that he was a man of principle and was ahead of his time."

For almost all of our history America has stood for the rule of law at home and abroad. It is almost inevitable that the country will return to that ideal once again when the shock of 9/11 has receded somewhat deeper into the past. But a realist would say, "Don't hold your breath."

End or Mend?

SINCE 9/11 the FBI has been fighting for its life. And maybe living on borrowed time.

As the enormity of its 9/11 failure emerged, there were demands that the Bureau be divested of its intelligence responsibilities, that they be handed over to an as-yet-undefined new agency. The model most frequently mentioned was Great Britain's MI5, the domestic version of MI6, the foreign intelligence agency of James Bond fame.

Threats to the Bureau used to come from the left. But now those old enemies seemed content, possibly feeling that in Louis Freeh's civil libertarian FBI they had about as good an FBI as they were likely to get. Now the danger came from the right, from conservatives furious that, despite the vast sums of money showered on the Bureau during the 1990s, the FBI had failed to carry out its repeated promises to reform itself to fight terror.

As the 9/11 Commission met in 2004, it dropped clues that a new intelligence agency to replace the FBI might be one of its recommendations. But its final report merely called for the creation of a National Counterterrorism Center to be staffed by agents from the FBI and the rest of the intelligence community, along with the appointment of a national intelligence director to oversee all fifteen agencies of the intelligence community, the FBI included—recommendations immediately endorsed, with slight modifications, by President Bush. But the basic question of whether the FBI should continue to function as both a law enforcement and an intelligence agency will not go away.

■ ■ ■

Now, as in 1917, responsibility for national security investigations carries with it the status of the nation's premier investigative agency. Losing control of domestic intelligence would sound the death knell to the Bureau's reputation for being the best—the source of its institutional pride and *esprit de corps*.

Avoiding such a fate has clearly been on FBI Director Robert Mueller's mind ever since the attacks of 9/11. He has studied the emerging results of official inquiries into the reasons for the Bureau's failure, and has tailored his reforms of the Bureau to meet, point by point, the indictment of its performance by the Joint Inquiry and the National Commission.

Mueller has seen the solution—and the FBI's salvation—as "transforming the Bureau into an intelligence agency" by "reformulating our personnel and administrative procedures to instill within our workforce an expertise in the processes and objectives of intelligence work." This transformation is radically different from the reforms the Bureau attempted under Louis Freeh. At that time there was some reshuffling of the organizational chart, and Freeh set up an Investigative Services Division staffed, supposedly, with broad-gauged intelligence analysts, but the 9/11 inquiry found that these analysts, instead of devoting themselves to "connecting the dots" in the big picture of terrorism, were instead regularly drafted to work with ongoing investigations, criminal as well as terror or counterintelligence, that could produce convictions. Hobbled by completely dysfunctional communications systems, the Bureau had really continued with business as usual, and that business was putting together criminal cases. The tyranny of the case file still ruled—the mentality that Senator Richard Shelby of the Joint Inquiry pointed to as proof that "policemen make poor intelligence analysts." In other words, a good cop could never be a great spy.

Whether the Bureau survives as the nation's premier investigative agency will depend on whether Mueller can convince the White House, Congress, and the country that his FBI, reborn as an intelligence agency, can do the job better than a new agency designed from birth to do nothing but gather intelligence on terror and espionage threats to the United States.

Mueller has tried to transform the Bureau both from the top down and the bottom up. In Washington there is a new Office of Intelligence that Mueller proposes be upgraded to a "Directorate of Intelligence," "a service within a service" with "broad and clear authority over intelligence-related functions." There is a College of Analytical Studies at Quantico, modeled on the CIA's Sherman Kent School, to raise the standard of intelligence analysis. There are new twenty-four-hour counterterror "watchtowers" to scan the horizon for terror threats, investigate them, and present the raw and analyzed "product" to policymakers.

Far more important, the transformation has also been from the bottom up. "We are making," Mueller says, "intelligence-based training a part of FBI agents' and support employees' careers from their first day on the job to their last." New agents are hired on the basis of their qualifications for intelligence work; their training has been revamped to introduce them early on to intelligence gathering. A new evaluation system for agents and supervisors centers on terror-related intelligence gathering and threat prevention, rather than on the traditional measures of arrests and convictions. The current workforce of executives, agents, and support personnel has been extensively retrained and re-indoctrinated in carrying out intelligence cases, and a "back to basics" program has stressed the importance of developing informants in communities likely to be used as havens by terrorists and their cells.

The FBI today is a lot less brawn and a lot more brains. In the key document describing the new Bureau, the FBI's *Report to the National Commission*, Mueller does not once mention the Hostage Rescue Team. The new face of the Bureau is the analyst, the translator, the computer expert, the special agent re-trained as an intelligence specialist. The *G* in "G-man" now stands for "geek."

Training for new agents at Quantico now includes 110 hours of instruction in intelligence-related activities rather than the previous 55 hours. The curriculum is designed to demonstrate how intelligence and criminal investigative techniques can work in tandem, emphasizing human sources and cooperation with other agencies. New courses reflecting the focus on intelligence have been added to the curriculum:

- FBI intelligence mandates and authorities
- Overview of the intelligence cycle
- Introduction to the U.S. intelligence community
- Intelligence reporting and dissemination
- FBI intelligence requirements and the collection management process
- Role of intelligence analysts
- Validating human sources

Significantly, Mueller's *Report* does not mention ethics, except in reference to civil liberties. The agents' first assignments, which under Freeh had been chosen with an eye to the agents' morale and family stability, have been structured to make sure that each agent, in addition to gaining a broad-based familiarity with the Bureau's law enforcement procedures, works from the beginning on intelligence cases and projects.

For advanced training of agents later in their careers, there is the new College of Analytical Studies. A degree from that College will be required before agents are given an Intelligence and Counterterrorism/Counterintelligence skill designation that will be required for advancement. The Bureau also pays the tuition for further advanced study at leading universities.

■ ■ ■

Mueller echoes the *Joint Inquiry Report* critique of the Bureau by pointing to two specific issues widely seen as responsible for the Bureau's 9/11 failures, but he claims that they have been almost completely resolved. First were the restrictive legal and regulatory barriers that kept the Bureau's intelligence agents and criminal investigators from working together or even talking to each other, and kept the Bureau from freely sharing information in either direction with its so-called partners in the intelligence community. This "wall" was dismantled by the Patriot Act. As a symbol of its passing, the two separate case files that would be opened in a terror investigation, one intelligence, the other criminal, have been merged into one, the same file number shared by both sets of investigators, its contents available to both.

Second, the dysfunctional computer system that the Bureau could not fix or replace during the Freeh years, in part because of a lack of real interest at the top, has been replaced by a web-based system with wide- and local-area-network file sharing, all in a familiar Windows point-and-click environment. The Bureau is rapidly shifting to a paperless environment, where agents will work in virtual case files so their findings can be transmitted instantly to analysts looking for broader indications of terrorist activity. The Bureau is shifting its files and records from the field offices and headquarters to a central database "warehouse" (a server), so that once information has been completely scanned into electronic records, everything the Bureau knows will be available for instant and regular analysis by hundreds of new analysts and translators.

The Bureau's system of prioritization has also been rethought. In the three-tier system of the Freeh era, terror, espionage, and large-scale financial fraud were at the top, and crimes against persons and property at the bottom. Mueller complained that this system allowed field offices and supervisors too much flexibility within each tier. Priorities are now listed in the order in which they must be addressed, and every executive and agent must run through the priorities in descending order, not expending any resources on lower priorities until the higher have been satisfied. The priorities now begin with counterterrorism:

1. Protect the United States from terrorist attack. "Every FBI manager, Special Agent, and support employee understands that the prevention of terrorist attacks is the FBI's overriding priority and that every terrorism-related lead must be addressed. Counterterrorism is the top

priority in the allocation of funding, personnel, physical space, and resources, as well as in hiring and training. No matter their program assignment, all FBI field, operational, and support personnel stand ready to assist in our counterterrorism efforts."

2. Protect the United States against foreign intelligence operations and espionage. This consists of "1) preventing hostile groups and countries from acquiring technology to produce weapons of mass destruction; 2) preventing the compromise of personnel, information, technology, and economic interests vital to our national security; and 3) producing intelligence on the plans and intentions of our adversaries."

3. Protect the United States against cyber-based attacks and high-technology crimes. "The FBI is the only government entity with the wide-ranging jurisdiction, technical resources, personnel, and network of relationships necessary to address the threat from multi-jurisdictional cyber crimes and cyber terrorism."

4. Combat public corruption at all levels. "The FBI has extensive experience investigating public corruption. Our public corruption investigations focus on all levels of government (local, state, and federal) and address all types of judicial, legislative, regulatory, and law enforcement corruption."

5. Protect civil rights. "The FBI is the federal agency with responsibility for investigating allegations of federal civil rights violations and abuses. In pursuit of this mission, the FBI investigates allegations of brutality and related misconduct by law enforcement officers as well as hate crimes. Recently, our civil rights program has focused particularly on hate crime cases related to Muslim, Sikh, and Arab-American communities that suffered threats and attacks in the aftermath of September 11, 2001, and Operation Iraqi Freedom."

6. Combat transnational and national criminal organizations and enterprises. "As the world grows smaller and investigations become more international, the FBI increasingly uses its expertise and relationships with foreign counterparts to dismantle or disrupt those major criminal enterprises that are responsible for cross-border criminal activity."

7. Combat major white-collar crime. "During the past two years, we have dedicated scores of agents to the investigation of corporate scandals

involving Enron, WorldCom, and others, and focused our criminal analytical capabilities on major health care fraud and bank fraud threats. At the same time, we are scaling back our investigations into smaller bank frauds and embezzlements that are ably handled by other agencies and our state and municipal partners."

8. Combat significant violent crime. "Most violent crime in the U.S. is investigated and prosecuted by state or municipal authorities. While federal statutes give the FBI jurisdiction over many types of violent crime, we . . . concentrate our efforts on those criminal targets—such as organized criminal enterprises and violent narcotics gangs—that pose a significant threat to our society. We participate in the fight against violent crime wherever we bring something special to the mix, whether it is special capabilities, resources, or our jurisdiction to enforce applicable federal statutes."

9. Support federal, state, municipal, and international partners.

10. Upgrade technology to successfully perform the FBI's mission.

■ ■ ■

Freeh's failure to do many of the same things promised by Mueller created a certain degree of skepticism about the Bureau's willingness (or ability) to change. Some, particularly Senator Shelby of the Joint Inquiry, believe it simply cannot. But there are signs that this time the Bureau really has changed. Mueller's reforms are meant to penetrate into the agent culture of the Bureau in a way the Freeh reforms never contemplated, except in the area of agent ethics. I myself was skeptical. I had been enormously impressed by the creativity and talent at the Freeh FBI, all engaged in continually improving the Bureau's performance. Was I simply fooled then, and likely to be fooled again?

I don't think so. The problem with the Freeh Bureau was that its creativity was unfocused. The Freeh Bureau seemed to have turned every agent loose to come up with imaginative reasons why his program was vital to the Bureau's mission and should never be cut. Under Freeh, the Bureau had come to resemble one of those 1970s conglomerates that sold everything from soda to jet planes, and that had never been subjected to a discipline, like that of the Boston Consulting Group, of distinguishing the cash cows in its operation from the stars and the dogs. And in the public sector, the cash cows tend to subsidize the dogs forever, since hardly anything in government, no matter how useless, is ever really put to rest.

There is a story about a British artillery officer in the First World War who wondered why one of the soldiers assigned to each motorized gun stood there with nothing to do. He asked an old-timer if he could shed any light on the problem, and was told, "Why, he's there to hold the horses." In the Bureau, as in any government operation, there are plenty of people who are still holding the horses, doing jobs that have long been obsolete, like investigating bank robberies, that Congress and private interests just won't let the Bureau get rid of. In an outfit as creative as the Bureau, the old dogs are always learning impressive new tricks, but they are still dogs.

The Bureau's new priorities provide a guide to shedding nonessential tasks—defined as jobs that can be done by local or state authorities—if Congress approves. Yet further reductions in size and responsibilities are still needed. Cyber crime should be spun off to a dedicated cyber crime force outside the Bureau. And the Bureau needs to be slimmed down to reflect its more disciplined focus, although Mueller claims he needs the excess staff to give the Bureau a "surge" capacity to throw overwhelming numbers of agents into an emergency. On the other hand, white-collar crime—top-level financial fraud—should be moved back closer to the top of the list, since Enron-class debacles do as much damage to the economy as any terror attack. Preventing crimes of that magnitude should be given priority equal to detecting and prosecuting them.

No matter how well the Bureau transforms itself into an "intelligence agency," however, a new agency totally dedicated to intelligence work, starting from scratch, would probably do an even better job of developing structures and procedures for gathering intelligence and could more easily equip itself with state-of-the-art technology. For one thing, it would not be held back by the Bureau's need to integrate old data, equipment, and personnel with the new. The question is, then, whether the Bureau brings anything extra to the table that a new agency could not.

It certainly does, which amounts to a powerful argument for keeping domestic intelligence within the Bureau. Proponents of a new MI5 contend that separating the intelligence and investigative functions from counterterror will allow each to do what it does best: the FBI to arrest terrorists and bring them to trial, the new MI5 to gather intelligence in order to forestall attacks. But on the fundamental question of the relationship between intelligence and criminal investigations, Mueller persuasively argues that, far from hindering each other, they are actually complementary. "By definition," Mueller says, "investigations of international terrorism are both 'intelligence' and 'criminal' investigations."

Mirroring the dual nature of a counterterror investigation are the Bureau's twin capabilities. Mueller points out that

The Bureau is designed, and has always operated, as both a law enforcement and an intelligence agency. It has the dual mission: 1) to investigate and arrest perpetrators of completed crimes (the law enforcement mission)*; and 2) to collect intelligence that will help prevent future crimes and assist policy makers in their decision making* (the intelligence mission). *History has shown that we are most effective in protecting the U.S. when we perform these two missions in tandem.*

Before 9/11, Mueller argues, the "Wall" kept the Bureau from taking advantage of the complementarity of intelligence and criminal investigations, but now the Patriot Act lets the Bureau do what it should always have been doing. And as sworn law officers with the power of arrest and experience in preparing cases for trial, FBI agents working on intelligence/criminal terrorist investigations can wait until a strategic moment to decide whether to arrest and prosecute or to maintain surveillance. Separating the intelligence from the criminal investigation would remove that flexibility. And given the complexity and rigor of the due process demanded by American courts for the collection of evidence and testimony, it is unlikely that any cases deriving from purely intelligence investigations would ever stand up in court.

There is another compelling reason for keeping intelligence on domestic terror threats within the FBI. An effective campaign against terror requires comprehensive cooperation between local, state, and foreign law enforcement and intelligence agencies, as well as with the public. The FBI has spent decades building relationships at all these levels. Its field offices and resident agencies have always had maintaining liaison with local and state authorities, as well as with district and United States attorneys, as part of their job. These relationships cannot be duplicated easily, if at all, by a new agency, since they are based not on a few cold calls or letters of introduction, but on a long history of cooperatively solving cases, resolving common problems, and rendering mutual assistance.

One of Louis Freeh's most valuable contributions was his expansion of the Bureau overseas. There are now forty-seven legal attaché offices abroad, a significant number of the new ones in Muslim countries, and more are constantly being opened. Freeh also provided the Bureau with the resources to nurture its contacts with foreign law enforcement and intelligence agencies, contacts that depend on slow-maturing cop-to-cop relationships: There are the FBI's training academies abroad, its training sessions for foreign police and intelligence agents at Quantico, and its contributions to foreign-U.S. intelligence and law enforcement task forces. Disturbing these relationships would be folly.

The *esprit de corps* of an elite agency is another asset not readily duplicated.

Any new intelligence force would have to cherry-pick the FBI's best intelligence agents, analysts, and translators, leaving behind a demoralized Bureau that would still be needed in the fight against terrorism on the criminal side. And there would be no real assurance that the new agency would be able to develop quickly or ever the high level of discipline and resolve that took the Bureau nearly a hundred years to achieve.

But even as the FBI under Mueller becomes a new Bureau, it will still be the old Bureau as well. That need not be a reason to discard it, if the Bureau can learn from its past. Its history, with its traditions and pride, may be one of the best reasons for continuing to rely on the FBI. Great institutions—and the FBI is a great institution—do not come about all that often. When you have one, you had better hang onto it. You will probably not be able to put one together again.

All of this—the synergy between intelligence and criminal investigations, the Bureau's web of law enforcement and intelligence relationships from the local to the global level, and the added performance obtainable only from an elite agency—will become even more vital if the focus of the war on terror shifts back from military force to law enforcement, as, I think, is inevitable.

It *was* necessary to use military force to destroy al Qaeda's secure base of operations in Afghanistan. Given bin Laden's control of the Kabul Taliban regime, nothing except military action could have accomplished it. But since that regime was toppled, almost all the important successes against terror at home and abroad have come from law enforcement. The continued reliance on military force after Afghanistan has probably hampered the campaign against terror. The aftermath of the Iraq war only underscores the need to return once again to the rule of law against terror, backed by diplomacy and military force if necessary.

The rule of law, which has been the enduring goal of the United States in world affairs for a century, can function only if the world's strongest country supports it, instead of discarding it when convenient. For much of the world that is the message of Iraq. It may be that we will look back at our reliance on law enforcement against terror during the 1990s as flawed not in principle but in execution, because it was not backed up by a credible threat of force. Judging by the past, once the recriminations over Iraq are over, the United States will once again turn to law enforcement—as well as prevention—as its primary tool in the fight against terror. And when that happens, we might have to put a broken-up FBI back together again, since once again collection of evidence, indictments, arrests, and trials will become essential to the fight against terror. Taking intelligence gathering away from the FBI would then be seen as a mistake that set back the fight against terror in ways not easily remedied. It might even have been a fatal mistake.

Some have said that the Bureau should keep its domestic intelligence functions, but within a stand-alone division inside the FBI. But that is essentially what the Bureau has created under Mueller, with its Office (and perhaps Directorate) for Intelligence. But because the "stand-alone" unit is housed within a comprehensive law-enforcement agency, there is, as Mueller points out, "the flexibility to move seamlessly from intelligence gathering to disruption at a moment's notice." That is, if you are a terrorist, the FBI can investigate you, arrest you, or kill you. It's your call.

■ ■ ■

Effective domestic intelligence and effective law enforcement, as the history of the FBI demonstrates, depend on the public's confidence in the investigating agency, whether the Bureau or a new agency. Repairing that trust—which does not exist today—is even more important to the war on terror than which particular agency, old or new, is chosen to lead the fight.

That trust cannot be created by the intelligence agency itself. It can be sustained by the agency's rigorous obedience to the law, or lost if the agency becomes lawless, but it can be created only by the national leadership of the country—the White House and the Department of Justice. They have to convince Americans that domestic intelligence is not being used for partisan or ideological purposes or to advance an agenda hostile to civil liberties.

Needless to say, that confidence has not been restored by George W. Bush or his attorney general, John Ashcroft. The manner in which they rammed the Patriot Act through Congress further eroded confidence in domestic surveillance, no matter who is chosen to conduct it. And to the extent that the Patriot Act destroyed confidence in the government's motives for investigating terror at home, it may have hindered the war on terror, no matter how valuable some of its measures might have been.

In fact, some of the most important parts of the Patriot Act—removing the "wall" between criminal and intelligence investigations, and ending the prohibition against sharing information from grand jury investigations with other intelligence agencies—could have been accomplished without its passage. Vigorous lawyering probably could have stripped away the barriers set up by a decade of what Senator Shelby called "timorous" lawyering by the Justice Department and FBI. In addition to being divisive, the Patriot Act may not have even been necessary.

The FBI, to a degree unlikely in any new agency, is highly disciplined and eminently "leadable." What it needs is constant leadership and direction from the president, which it has almost never gotten throughout its history. It needs to have its nose pointed constantly and forcefully toward the prey the country wants it to hunt, or else it will wander off to bark up trees at squirrels.

But the best domestic surveillance agency in the world will not be able to do its job until the country—led by a president and an attorney general it trusts— resolves its conflicted feelings about having a government agency poking around in areas that inevitably bump up against the exercise of First Amendment rights. Any effective intelligence agency will necessarily have to look into matters that turn out to be quite innocent as it tries to stay informed about matters not so innocent.

Developing the public confidence necessary for the success of whatever agency is conducting intelligence investigations will depend also on a new willingness in the media and the political opposition not to politicize every move by an investigative agency, and not to turn inevitable errors by intelligence gatherers into partisan arguments against domestic surveillance altogether, as if a case of malpractice were reason enough to outlaw medicine. A lot to ask, but without that kind of restraint, there can be no effective intelligence against terror. By now, however, it is probably a lost cause to ask the political opposition, the media, or the public to trust Attorney General Ashcroft. Despite whatever good he has done in refocusing the FBI, his failure to create any unified support for the domestic aspects of the war on terror suggests that his departure will be necessary before anything can be done to build the public support needed before any intelligence agency, the FBI or its successor, can do its job.

Collecting domestic intelligence—that is, intelligence about terrorist threats in the United States, whether domestic or foreign—has never been a real threat to civil liberties. Misuse of that intelligence, or fear of its misuse, has. The FBI or any new agency will inevitably make mistakes; that's why there are erasers on the ends of pencils. What has to be feared—and prevented—is the misuse of domestic intelligence for partisan purposes—the patterns of abuse that took hold under Hoover. That danger can be prevented by strict adherence to the current system of congressional oversight. Congress has to keep itself informed on what the intelligence agency is investigating and why. Furthermore, that information, stripped of anything that would compromise ongoing investigations, has to be immediately relayed to the public to prevent the suspicions of conspiracy that flare up whenever domestic surveillance is hedged about with secrecy.

There has developed in this country by now a long-standing hostility to domestic surveillance in particular, to government national security policies in general, and, ultimately, to America's role in the world. This hostility seizes on any and all Bureau misdeeds, real or in some cases imaginary, to validate its position. That hostility is not going to go away. Any new agency will inevitably take over that particular Bureau role in American popular culture. We cannot expect to wipe the slate clean by setting up a new domestic intelligence service.

I remember an FBI supervisor pointing at a Manhattan-phonebook-size book of Bureau rules, and telling me that every regulation in there was the result of "some agent fucking up." A new agency will start with a slim book of regulations, but its own fuck-ups will bulk it up in a hurry, especially since a new agency will not have the FBI's institutional memory of what can happen to it if it gets on the wrong side of the Bill of Rights.

I once asked a Japanese criminologist about the difference between law enforcement in Japan and in America. In Japan, he replied, crime is not politicized; in America, it is. In a country that wants to be protected against terror, domestic surveillance cannot be politicized either. Yet, judging by the disproportionate and indiscriminate protest over the Patriot Act, we may be farther away from that ideal than we were before 9/11. It would be easy to blame this on our leaders, or on the FBI, and they are certainly not blameless. The fault, however, is in ourselves.

What should we choose—the FBI we know, or something else, some new agency whose chief virtue is that we know nothing about it? The FBI has changed enough to deserve a second chance.

But have we?

NOTES

Chapter 1

4 he was staying at a bin Laden guesthouse in Pakistan: This summary follows the account in the most authoritative study of 9/11 to date, the *Joint Inquiry into Intelligence Community Activities Before and After the Terrorist Attacks of September 11, 2001,* report of The U.S. Senate Select Committee on Intelligence and U.S. House Permanent Select Committee on Intelligence Together with Additional Views, December 2002, 107th Cong., 2nd Sess. S. Rept. No. 107-351, H. Rept. No. 107–792 (hereafter referred to as *Joint Inquiry Report*). Other valuable studies include *The 9/11 Commission Report* (2004), John Miller and Michael Stone with Chris Mitchell, *The Cell: Inside the 9/11 Plot and Why the FBI and CIA Failed to Stop It* (New York: Hyperion, 2002), Bill Gertz, *Breakdown: How America's Intelligence Failures Led to September 11* (Washington, DC: Regnery, 2002), and Gerald Posner, *Why America Slept: The Failure to Prevent 9/11* (New York: Random House, 2003).

4 "conspiracy to attack defense installations of the United States": *Joint Inquiry Report,* p. 135. (Downloaded versions of the *Joint Inquiry Report* will vary as to pagination. I have adopted the pagination from the original printed report.)

4 working that case like a street agent: Elsa Walsh, "Louis Freeh's Last Case," *The New Yorker,* May 14, 2001, pp. 68–79.

5 "attacks with little or no warning": From a "Chronology" in the *Joint Inquiry Report.*

5 "spectacular and traumatic" attack on the country: *Joint Inquiry Report,* pp. 209, 212.

5 "Attack will occur with little or no warning!": *Joint Inquiry Report,* p. 216.

6 no credible information of an imminent attack *within* the United States: *Joint Inquiry Report,* p. 217.

7 seeking to attend flight schools: *Joint Inquiry Report,* pp. 343–44.

7 eight of the suspected al Qaeda sympathizers to the CIA: Gertz, *Breakdown,* p. 84.

7 prominent al Qaeda figures: *Joint Inquiry Report,* p. 351.

9 "the knowledge that he would have needed . . .": *Joint Inquiry Report,* pp. 334–35.

10 "this type of aircraft—that is it": *Joint Inquiry Report,* p. 339.

10 a full-fledged member: CNN, 8/8/2003, report on court proceedings of January 20, 2002.

10 the pilot of a fifth plane, targeting the White House: As stated in Moussaoui's federal indictment, *United States of America vs. Zacarias Moussaoui,* U.S. District Court for the Eastern District of Virginia, Alexandria Division, December 2001 term, http://www.fas.org/irp/world/para/docs/mous_indict.html.

10 fought for al Qaeda in Chechnya: *Joint Inquiry Report,* p. 341; Moussaoui federal indictment.

10 a Muslim fighter killed in Bosnia: *Los Angeles Times,* December 31, 2001.

11 reported to al Qaeda on their progress: Miller and Stone, *The Cell,* p. 277.

12 proved to have been the hijackers: Miller and Stone, *The Cell,* p. 295.

12 to go over the final details: *Las Vegas Review Journal,* October 26, 2001.

12 "raised profiling issues": *Joint Inquiry Report,* p. 344.

13 infiltrated by al Qaeda moles: Coleen Rowley to Robert Mueller, memorandum, May 21, 2002.

14 "traveling from Europe to the U.S.": *Joint Inquiry Report,* p. 337.

14 except through headquarters: Rowley to Mueller.

15 just before the hijacking: See *Joint Inquiry Report,* pp. 159–77.

16 "the threat of terrorism in the United States is low": Quoted in Mark Riebling, "Freeh at Last, the Former FBI Director Uncovers (and Defends) the Agency's pre-9/11 Incompetence," *National Review,* October 17, 2002, http://www.nationalreview.com/comment/comment-riebling101702.asp.

16 "elsewhere in the country": Rowley to Mueller.

16 indicted, if not sooner: Rowley to Mueller.

16 "the FBI from embarrassment": Rowley to Mueller.

19 "damn to your heart's content": *Time,* Dec. 22, 2002.

19 its classified report to Congress:
The Senate members were:

> Bob Graham, D. - Florida, Chairman
> Richard C. Shelby, R. - Alabama, Vice Chairman
> Carl Levin, Michigan
> Jon Kyl, Arizona
> John D. Rockefeller, West Virginia
> James M. Inhofe, Oklahoma
> Dianne Feinstein, California
> Orrin Hatch, Utah
> Ron Wyden, Oregon
> Pat Roberts, Kansas
> Richard J. Durbin, Illinois
> Mike DeWine, Ohio
> Evan Bayh, Indiana
> Fred Thompson, Tennessee
> John Edwards, North Carolina
> Richard Lugar, Indiana
> Barbara Mikulski, Maryland

The House side included:

> Porter J. Goss, R. - Florida, Chairman
> Nancy Pelosi, D. - California, ranking Democrat
> Doug Bereuter, Nebraska
> Sanford D. Bishop, Georgia
> Michael N. Castle, Delaware
> Jane Harman, California
> Sherwood L. Boehlert, New York
> Gary A. Condit, California
> Jim Gibbons, Nevada
> Tim Roemer, Indiana
> Ray LaHood, Illinois
> Silvestre Reyes, Texas
> Randy "Duke" Cunningham, California

Leonard L. Boswell, Iowa
Peter Hoekstra, Michigan
Collin C. Peterson, Minnesota
Richard Burr, North Carolina
Bud Cramer, Alabama
Saxby Chambliss, Georgia
Terry Everett, Alabama

20 a new agency: "September 11 and the Imperative of Reform in the U.S. Intelligence Community, Additional Views of Senator Richard C. Shelby, Vice-Chairman, Senate Select Committee on Intelligence," December 10, 2002. Shelby's personal report is in the "Additional Views of Members" section of the *Joint Inquiry Report,* separately paginated, at the end of the report.

24 a culture of "Risk Aversion": *Joint Inquiry Report,* "Additional Views, Senator John Kyl, Senator Pat Roberts."

26 "we don't do it at all": *Joint Inquiry,* transcript of hearing, October 8, 2002, http://www.thememoryhole.org/911/hearings/911hearing-trans-oct08.htm. For a caustic comment on Freeh's testimony, see Riebling, "Freeh at Last."

26 young Middle Eastern Islamic radicals: Gertz, *Breakdown,* p. 86.

Chapter 2

28 strawberry farms in Township 11-7: Township 11 South, Range 7 East.

29 a John A. Benson and an F. A. Hyde: Lincoln Steffens, "The Taming of the West, Discovery of the Land Fraud System" and "A Detective Story," *American Magazine,* Sept. 1907, p. 491.

29 he said, was revenge: John Messing, "Public Lands, Politics, and Progressives: The Oregon Land Fraud Trials, 1903–1910," *Pacific Historical Review,* XXXV (1966), p. 39.

30 state and federal land offices: Steffens, "Detective Story," p. 495.

30 as Richards had expected he would: Steffens, "Detective Story," p. 493.

30 burning his daybooks and other files: Messing, "Oregon Land Fraud Trials," p. 40.

30 moonlighting as McKinley's mistress: Messing, "Oregon Land Fraud Trials," p. 43.

32 his best man, Special Agent William J. Burns: Burns was lionized for his part in the exposé in Lincoln Steffens, "The Making of a Fighter," *American Magazine,* Aug. 1907, and "The Taming of the West," *American Magazine,* May–Oct. 1907. When Don Whitehead, who wrote his history of the FBI under Hoover's direction, discusses the investigation of the land fraud, he does not name Burns, but refers to him only as a former "Secret Service agent"; on the other hand, he does name Larry Richey, one of Hoover's patrons and friends, as one of the "outstanding" investigators on the case. When the Taft administration, quarreling with Roosevelt over conservation policy, sought to discredit the land-fraud investigation, it charged Burns with jury tampering. Discussing this, Whitehead not only names Burns—identifying him only as "a detective"—but claims Burns was "guilty of actions far worse than the crimes charged to the prosecuted" (p. 18). Burns's biographer claims that the charges against Burns were "thoroughly discredited" (Gene Caesar, *Incredible Detective: The Biography of William J. Burns* [Englewood Cliffs, NJ: Prentice Hall, 1968], p. 6). In this instance Whitehead seems to have been manipulated into supporting the Hoover line that everybody connected to the old (pre-Hoover) Bureau was corrupt. Don Whitehead, *The FBI Story* (New York: Random House, 1956), p. 18.

32 "Corrupt to the very core": Caesar, *Incredible Detective,* p. 107.

34 how high and mighty they might be: Steffens, "The Taming of the West," p. 503.

35 accepted the offer: Steffens, "The Taming of the West," p. 585.

36 "land thieves of Oregon": Steffens, "Detective Story," p. 589.

36 "he is protecting somebody": Steffens, "Detective Story," p. 594.

36 the matter of the 11-7 strawberry fields: Jerry A. O'Callaghan, "Senator Mitchell and the Oregon Land Frauds, 1905," *Pacific Historical Review,* XXI (1952), p. 258.

36 to end the investigation: Messing, "Oregon Land Fraud Trials," p. 50.

37 they were quickly approved: Steffens, "Detective Story," p. 600; Messing, "Oregon Land Fraud Trials," p. 51; Caesar, *Incredible Detective,* p. 119; O'Callaghan, "Senator Mitchell and the Oregon Land Frauds," p. 257.

38 approval of Hall's political allies: Steffens, "Detective Story," p. 599.

38 while the verdict was still under appeal: After three hard-fought trials Congressman Williamson was convicted of land fraud on September 28, 1905. On February 8, 1908, John Hall would be convicted for his part in another land-fraud conspiracy.

40 his compensation of $1,500 a year: Homer Cummings, "The Nation's Law Office," in *Selected Papers of Homer Cummings,* Carl Brent Swisher, ed. (1939; rpt. New York: Da Capo, 1972), p. 4.

40 "the laws will execute themselves": Joseph Story, *Life and Letters* (1851), I, p. 244.

40 our own neighbors to the north: Charles Reith, *The Blind Eye of History* (1952; rpt. Montclair, NJ: Patterson Smith, 1975), p. 2.

41 justify the means: This was the point of the debate during Washington's first administration over the establishment of a national bank, with Hamilton's argument for a "loose" construction of the Constitution prevailing over Jefferson's "strict" construction.

42 public land swindlers: The Secret Service did not begin protecting the president until 1894, and then only informally and part time. Presidential protection did not become the service's formal responsibility until 1901, after the assassination of McKinley, and was not funded by Congress until 1906. Secret Service website, Secret Service history.

42 the Department of Justice came into being: 16 Stat. 162; Cummings, "Nation's Law Office," p. 225.

43 "for no other purpose whatever": *Congressional Record* (Feb. 11, 1909), p. 2182.

44 the Justice Department's semiofficial bureau of investigation: Harry and Bonaro Overstreet, *The FBI in Our Open Society* (New York: Norton, 1969), p. 15.

44 "Father was killed by the Pinkerton men": Frank Morn, *"The Eye That Never Sleeps," A History of the Pinkerton National Detective Agency* (Bloomington: Indiana University Press, 1982), p. 103.

44 which supplied strikebreakers and industrial guards: Morn, *"The Eye That Never Sleeps,"* p. 107.

45 Justice could concentrate on the prosecutions: Overstreet, *The FBI in Our Open Society,* p. 15.

45 their superb legal defense teams: Overstreet, *The FBI in Our Open Society,* p. 16.

46 "deeper than any law now upon the statute books": Overstreet, *The FBI in Our Open Society,* p. 17.

46 technical violation of congressional prohibitions: Overstreet, *The FBI in Our Open Society,* p. 15.

46 former policemen or railroad claims agents: Willard B. Gatewood, *Theodore Roosevelt and the Art of Controversy* (Baton Rouge: University of Louisiana Press, 1970), p. 241.

46 "a central pool of detective manpower": Overstreet, *The FBI in Our Open Society,* p. 15.

47 "the prosecution of the violators": Inquiry Pursuant to Resolution Authorizing Investigation of Secret Service," *Senate Report,* 60th Cong., 2nd sess., No. 970, p. 5.

48 the Constitution's system of checks and balances: A few years later, during World War I, these same conservatives would applaud far more extensive expansion of executive power

through investigations of political radicals and labor unionists. It was all, a cynic might say, a question of whose political ox was being gored.

48 "organization for the investigation of suspected offenses": *Attorney General's Report*, 1906, p. 7.

48 replacing corrupt politics with rational, scientific solutions to social problems: *Century Magazine*, March 1910, has an article on Attorney General Bonaparte. See also Joseph Bucklin Bishop, *Charles Joseph Bonaparte, His Life and Public Services* (New York: Scribner, 1922).

48 as soon as it could be arranged: This discussion follows Overstreet, *The FBI in Our Open Society*, pp. 17–18.

49 "is assuredly not fully equipped for its work": *Attorney General's Report*, 1907, pp. 9–10.

49 "he is no longer a Government employee": *Congressional Record* (May 1, 1908), p. 5555.

49 to police the entire government: *Congressional Record* (May 1, 1908), p. 5555.

50 the government would be "absolutely defenseless": Mr. Fitzgerald, *Congressional Record* (May 1, 1908), p. 5560.

52 his own bureau of investigation in the Justice Department: This and the preceding comments during the debates are in *Congressional Record*, 60th Cong., 2nd sess., House 2757, 5554 and passim.

52 "in or under said Secret Service Division": *Congressional Record*, 60th Cong., 2nd sess., 5554. See also Gatewood, "The Secret Service Controversy," *Roosevelt and the Art of Controversy*, Chapter VIII.

53 assigned to the land-fraud cases: Special Agent Charles Appel, *History of the Bureau of Investigation*, November 18, 1930, an internal memorandum evidently prepared for the director and for the Bureau's press office, now in the files of the FBI Office of Congressional and Public Affairs, p. 2.

53 undetected and unprosecuted: There were also about fifty investigators assigned to naturalization cases, but these do not figure in the organization of the Bureau. In 1909 naturalization investigations were transferred to the Department of Commerce and Labor.

53 "The Senators are duly warned": *New York Times*, May 6, 1908, quoted in Overstreet, *The FBI in Our Open Society*, p. 25.

53 to be "Chief Examiner": The general agent, Cecil Clay, had died, and his assistant, Robert V. LaDow, was appointed superintendent of prisons and prisoners.

53 who had not worked for the Secret Service: Finch to J. D. Harris, July 3, 1908, Bureau of Investigation files, National Archives.

53 commissioned them special agents of the Justice Department: According to Walter S. Bowen and Harry Edward Neal, *The United States Secret Service* (New York: Chilton, 1960), p. 83, there were only eight: George M. Kennoch, Irving Sauter, George Kraft, Louis P. Elsmere, Charles Dolan, Frank Wallace, Edward Chaims, and Edward J. Brennan. But by February 6 several more of the Secret Service agents who had worked on the land-fraud cases were in the Bureau: Eberstein, DeBelle, John C. Wallis, Robert D. Hobbs.

53 the department's force of twelve examiners: Names of agents appearing in early files include Allred, Donnella, Dolan, Bryon, Melrose, Eberstein (evidently a SAC in Chicago), Charles C. Wall, Hobbs, Crim; three hired on July 28, Byron, Craft, and Meetz (with Meetz soon fired); five agents at the New York office—Wall, Craft, DeBelle, Kennoch, Sauter (SAC); in Chicago, Dolan and Eberstein, Byron and Hobbs, and Brennan, Barnes, Baley, Chaims, Clyatt, Church, Chapson, etc. See *Memo for the Attorney General, Showing Status of Work of Special Agents Employed Under the Supervision of the Chief Examiner*, 1/20/1909, Records of the Federal Bureau of Investigation, RG 65, NARA.

54 "at the head of the force therein organized": Gatewood, *Roosevelt and the Art of Controversy*, p. 281. Wilkie's son, in his memoirs, also mentions his father's expectation that he

would lead the new force. Don Wilkie, *American Secret Service Agent* (New York: Frederick A. Stokes, 1934), pp. 68–69.

54 Chief Examiner Stanley Finch: *Report of the Attorney General*, 1909, p. 9. Although a matter of no great significance, historians have noticed that, earlier in July, Finch spoke of hiring nine former Secret Service agents and one new investigator whose background he did not describe, for a total of ten new agents. (For example, see Finch to Bielaski, July 3, 1908, Letters sent by the Chief Examiner, 1907–1911, Records of the Federal Bureau of Investigation, Vol. II, Box 1, RG 65, NARA.) It is likely that the discrepancy between Finch's tally of ten new employees and the attorney general's count of nine is due to one Agent Meredith's having declined his appointment to the Justice Department (after it was proffered) because he had already accepted a position in the Immigration Department. Additionally, there was a fairly rapid turnover of agents during the Bureau's first few months as Finch discovered their suitability (or lack of same) for the work he assigned them. Finch to Bonaparte, August 13, 1908, Records of The Federal Bureau of Investigation, Vol. II, Box I, RG 65, NARA. Throughout the first six months of the Bureau's existence, the total number of special agents varied between 29 and 35. "Statement Showing the Number of Special Agents Employed . . . ," Records of the Federal Bureau of Investigation, Administrative Reports on Cases, 1908–1911, Vol. I, Box 1, RG 65, NARA.

54 the exception of bank examinations: Banking was also handed over to Finch later that year, and he assembled a small group of accountants for that purpose.

54 festivity down to the present day: Charles Appel, *History of the Bureau of Investigation*, FBI, Office of Congressional Affairs, November 18, 1930. Don Whitehead's authorized *The FBI Story* (New York: Random House, 1956), p. 21, slightly mischaracterizes this order by stating that it created an investigative agency in the Justice Department.

55 "criminals in any branch of the public service": Overstreet, *The FBI in Our Open Society*, p. 28.

55 *except* those committed by members of Congress: Overstreet, *The FBI in Our Open Society*, p. 28.

55 "like shall never be seen again": *Congressional Record* (Feb. 25, 1909), p. 3133.

56 "vanity, arrogance and imperial egotism": *Congressional Record* (Feb. 25, 1909), p. 3133.

56 "the House of Representatives and of the Senate": *Congressional Record*, House (Jan. 8, 1909), p. 660. This was John Sharp Williams of Mississippi.

56 the frauds uncovered by the Secret Service: Gatewood, *Roosevelt and the Art of Controversy*, p. 268.

57 "their different departments": *Congressional Record* (Feb. 25, 1909), pp. 3133.

57 responsible to nobody but himself: *Congressional Record* (Feb. 25, 1909), p. 3135.

57 "But he did not know it": *Congressional Record* (Feb. 25, 1909), p. 3135.

58 "as future needs demand it": *Congressional Record*, Senate (Feb. 11, 1909), p. 2183.

59 "a specific appropriation is not otherwise made": *Congressional Record*, Senate (Feb. 11, 1909), p. 2191.

59 [Applause]: *Congressional Record*, House (Feb. 25, 1909), p. 3127.

59 Roosevelt must have loved that: *Congressional Record*, House (Feb. 25, 1909), p. 3128.

60 no small reason for his defeat: Gatewood, *Roosevelt and the Art of Controversy*, p. 286.

60 insulting reference to criminals in Congress: Gatewood, *Roosevelt and the Art of Controversy*, p. 237.

60 on K Street in northwest Washington: Susan Rosenfeld, "Buildings and Physical Plant," in Athan Theoharis et al., *The FBI: A Comprehensive Reference Guide* (Phoenix: Oryx Press, 1999), p. 246.

60 by each of his thirty-six agents: It is difficult to ascertain the names of all of this first class of agents, because there were, even before the force went into operation, several dis-

missals, resignations, and replacements. The following names appear on the earliest rosters:

Allred
Baley
Barnes
Brennan   (probably from the Secret Service)
Byron
Chaims   (probably from the Secret Service)
Chapson
Church
Clyatt
Craft, G.C.   (probably from the Secret Service)
Craft, P.P.
Dannenberg
DeBelle   (probably from the Secret Service)
DeSaules
Donaghy
Dolan   (probably from the Secret Service)
Donnella
Eberstein   (probably from the Secret Service)
Elsmere   (probably from the Secret Service)
Green
Hall
Harper
Hobbs   (probably from the Secret Service)
Hope
Jentzer
Kennoch   (probably from the Secret Service)
Kraft   (probably from the Secret Service, but may be the same as G. C. Craft)
Kron
Lamoreaux
Martin
Melrose
Mountjoy
Poulin
Sauter   (probably from the Secret Service)
Seibel
Smith
Tucker
Vann
Wallace   (probably from the Secret Service)
Wallis   (probably from the Secret Service)
Watt

60 as few coded terms as possible: See Agent G. Scarborough to Finch, May–June 1905, Reports of Special Agent J. W. Green, Correspondence with Special Agents, Records of the FBI, RG 65, NARA.

Chapter 3

62 "the signal victory of Jack Johnson": Randy Roberts, *Papa Jack: Jack Johnson and the Era of White Hopes* (New York: The Free Press, 1983), p. 55.

62 "The White Man must be rescued": Roberts, *Papa Jack,* p. 68.

63 "he will be a leader among men": Roberts, *Papa Jack,* p. 66. The discussion of Johnson during the case largely follows Roberts.

64 had been law since 1875: Alien Prostitution Importation Act, ch. 141, 18 Stat. 477 (1875) (codified as amended at 18 U.S.C. && 1328 (1982) International Agreement for the Suppression of the White Slave Traffic, May 18, 1904, 35 Stat. 426, 1 L.N.T.S. 83. See Nora V. Demleitner, "Forced Prostitution: Naming an International Offense," 18 *Fordham International Law Journal,* 163, November 1994; Michael Conant, "Federalism, the Mann Act, and the Imperative to Decriminalize Prostitution," 5 *Cornell Journal of Law and Public Policy,* 99, Winter 1996; Marlene D. Beckman, "Note: The White Slave Traffic Act: The Historical Impact of a Criminal Law on Women," 72, *Georgetown Law Journal,* 1111, Feb. 1984.

64 the treaty had already been ratified: Beckman, "Note: The White Slave Traffic Act," International Agreement for the Repression of the Trade in White Women, June 15, 1908, 35 Stat. 1979, T.S. No. 496.

65 "Help me—I am held captive as a slave": Beckman, "Note: The White Slave Traffic Act."

65 "the so-called 'white-slave traffic' ": Frederick K. Grittner, *White Slavery: Myth, Ideology and American Laws* (New York: Garland Publishing Company, 1990), p. 95.

65 "the great army of prostitutes": Grittner, *White Slavery,* p. 96.

65 signed into law by President Taft: Beckman, "Note: The White Slave Traffic Act." White Slave Traffic Act, ch. 395, 36 Stat. 825 (1910) (codified as amended at 18 U.S.C. &&2421–2424 (1982).

65 petition drives backed Finch's efforts: David J. Langum, *Crossing Over the Line: Legislating Morality and the Mann Act* (Chicago: University of Chicago Press, 1982), p. 7.

65 "the general supervision of the Commissioner": Homer Cummings and Carl McFarland, *Federal Justice* (New York: Macmillan, 1937), pp. 381–82.

65 40 regular agents in the Bureau: Langum, *Crossing Over the Line;* Grittner, *White Slavery,* p. 97.

65 "an important place in the detective world": Max Lowenthal, *The Federal Bureau of Investigation* (New York: William Sloane, 1950), p. 13.

66 field offices across the country: Langum, *Crossing Over the Line,* p. 49.

66 Finch added two more, in California and Texas: Susan Rosenfeld, "Organization and Day to Day Activities," in Athan Theoharis et al., *The FBI: A Comprehensive Reference Guide* (Phoenix: Oryx Press, 1999), p. 207. This was after Bonaparte had originally stopped Finch's plans for the New York and Chicago offices. Rosenfeld, "Organization and Day to Day Activities," p. 236.

66 arrests under the pertinent state laws: Grittner, *White Slavery,* p. 97.

66 "the act was primarily directed": Roberts, *Papa Jack,* p. 145.

66 did involve commercialized traffic in sex: Roberts, *Papa Jack,* p. 145.

67 "evils to be reached by [the] white slave act": Roberts, *Papa Jack,* p. 146.

68 "against the peace and dignity of the United States": Roberts, *Papa Jack,* p. 153.

68 "blot on our civilization": Roberts, *Papa Jack,* p. 158.

69 "strongly prejudiced against Negroes": Roberts, *Papa Jack,* p. 170.

69 "penniless and happy": Roberts, *Papa Jack,* p. 178.

70 "and therefore a real threat": Roberts, *Papa Jack,* p. 152.

71 "a certain number of small ones": Overstreet, *The FBI in Our Open Society* p. 227.

71 than had the Roosevelt administration: See, for example, Finch to U.S. Attorney in Virginia, requesting reports on all Standard Oil suits, 10/6/09.

71 wealthy enough to make trouble: In Finch's report on the Bureau's first seven months of operations, and in other reports, he said his agents had investigated, in addition to many antitrust, land frauds, and peonage cases, such matters as the following:

> Breaking and entering railway cars in interstate shipment
> Holding up a train
> National Bank Act
> Bankruptcy frauds
> Bribery of jurors
> Charges against U.S. officials
> Chinese smuggling cases
> Copyright laws
> Counterfeiting cases investigated incidentally in connection with other
>   investigations
> Customs cases
> Forgery
> Internal Revenue cases
> Libel
> Lotteries
> Miscellaneous, such as investigation of a fire on the site of a post office, and a claim
>   for the support of prisoners in Alaska
> Murder and other crimes on government reservations and in connection with
>   government officials and informants
> Neutrality laws (along Mexican border)
> Pardon of prisoners
> Perjury
> Post Office fraud cases
> Crimes on the high seas
> Service of subpoenas

Finch to Bonaparte, "Statement Showing the Number of Special Agents Employed by the Department of Justice . . . During the Period from July 1, 1908 to January 31, 1909," Records of the Federal Bureau of Investigation, RG 65, NARA. See also a somewhat different analysis of Finch's reports in Appel, *History of the Bureau of Investigation*, p. 4, in which Appel comes up with a count of twenty-five categories of crimes being investigated at this time.

72 two hundred rounds of smokeless cartridges: J. W. Green to Finch, Sept. 23, 1908, Correspondence with Special Agents, 1908–1912, Records of the FBI, RG 65, NARA.

72 called Chief Finch a "King Detective": *Boston Globe,* July 3, 1910, quoted in Cummings, *Federal Justice,* p. 381.

73 "perpetrated on the American public": "Is White Slavery Nothing More than a Myth?," 55 *Current Opinion,* 348 (1913). Cited in Beckman, "Note: The White Slave Traffic Act."

73 "a new witchcraft mania": "Popular Gullibility as Exhibited in the New White Slavery Hysteria," 56 *Current Opinion,* 129 (1914). Cited in Beckman, "Note: The White Slave Traffic Act."

73 the "over advertised" white slave: "Is White Slavery Nothing More than a Myth?," 55 *Current Opinion,* 348 (1913). Cited in Beckman, "Note: The White Slave Traffic Act."

73 over precisely nothing: For example, the "Massachusetts Commission," *Report of the*

Commission for the Investigation of the White Slave Traffic, So Called, February 1914 (Boston: Wright and Potter Printing Company, State Printers, 1914).

73 abolished the Justice Department's White Slave Commission that Finch had led: He went into private business, and in later years he moved in and out of government. Between 1922 and 1925 he served in the antitrust division of the Justice Department. In 1931 he moved back into the Justice Department as an inspector in the Bureau of Prisons, and in 1935 was appointed an audit clerk for the department. And finally he became, in January 1940, the chief examiner for the federal courts, the same job he had held before taking over the Bureau in 1908. He retired later that year and died in 1951. Susan Rosenfeld, "Biographies," in Theoharis, *The FBI: A Comprehensive Reference Guide*, p. 326.

73 But it had: A. Bruce Bielaski, "The United States Fighting White Slavery," *Light* (Nov.–Dec. 1915), p. 56.

75 not only were immoral but were federal crimes: 242 US 470 (1917); Grittner, *White Slavery*, p. 141.

75 "the act was primarily directed": Grittner, *White Slavery*, p. 97.

76 "widely varied social status": Don Wilkie, *American Secret Service Agent* (New York: Frederick L. Stokes, 1939), pp. 16–17.

76 roll up that Montreal ring: Rhodri Jeffreys-Jones, *Cloak and Dollar: A History of American Secret Intelligence* (New Haven: Yale University Press, 2002), pp. 4–7.

77 Ciudad Juarez and El Paso, Texas: This generally follows Wilkie, *American Secret Service Agent*, ch. 14.

78 "they can rely upon the Secret Service": Wilkie, *American Secret Service Agent*, p. 174.

79 investigating violations of the neutrality laws: Joan Jensen, *The Price of Vigilance* (Chicago: Rand McNally, 1968), p. 13.

79 an illegal conspiracy in restraint of trade: Jensen, *The Price of Vigilance*, p. 13.

79 the job belonged to Justice: Quoted in Jensen, *The Price of Vigilance*, p. 13.

80 to gather evidence to expose their activities: Walter S. Bowen and Harry Edward Neal, *The United States Secret Service* (Philadelphia: Chilton, 1960), p. 85.

80 unwilling to defend the country: Jensen, *The Price of Vigilance*, p. 14.

80 if so requested by the State Department: Jensen, *The Price of Vigilance*, p. 15.

81 "the lost territory in Texas, New Mexico and Arizona": Jeffreys-Jones, *Cloak and Dollar*, pp. 5–9.

81 most likely a Secret Service agent: Barbara Tuchman, *The Zimmerman Telegram* (New York: Dell, 1965), p. 173.

82 German spies who were, it was feared, everywhere: Jensen, *The Price of Vigilance*, pp. 26–27.

82 "the intercepted note of the German minister to Mexico City is eloquent evidence": Jensen, *The Price of Vigilance*, p. 31.

82 "ancient lineage and experience was sufficient license to catch spies": Jensen, *The Price of Vigilance*, p. 16.

83 interned only two to three thousand: Jensen, *The Price of Vigilance*, p. 166.

83 construed as interfering with the war effort: These were expanded and augmented in April 1918 by the Sabotage Act and in May 1918 by the Sedition Act.

83 "weaken the arm of the American Government": "America Infested with German Spies," *Literary Digest*, Oct. 6, 1917, p. 9.

83 "America Infested with German Spies": "America Infested with German Spies," p. 9.

83 German spies were "everywhere": "America Infested with German Spies," p. 9.

83 firing squads for spies and "plotters": This and the previous two quotes are from Jensen, *The Price of Vigilance*, pp. 99–100.

84 "a few prompt trials and a few quick hangings": This and the previous two quotes are from Jensen, *The Price of Vigilance*, pp. 106, 108.

84 a war zone, and should be so declared: Jensen, *The Price of Vigilance*, p. 113.

84 gets the girl: This and the previous quote are from Jensen, *The Price of Vigilance*, p. 224.

84 to the Bureau for investigation and arrests: Jensen, *The Price of Vigilance*, p. 118.

85 "to supplant the investigation services of the Department of Justice throughout the country": Jensen, *The Price of Vigilance*, p. 124.

85 the other to American Military Intelligence: Jensen, *The Price of Vigilance*, p. 119.

85 the Army to take over espionage investigations and prosecutions: This and the previous quote are from Jensen, *The Price of Vigilance*, pp. 120, 225.

85 spying in China for Germany: Frank J. Rafalko (ed.), *A Counterintelligence Reader: American Revolution to World War II*, ch. 3, National Counterintelligence Center website, http://www.fas.org/irp/ops/ci/docs/ci1/ch3a.htm.

87 "as may be required from time to time": Jensen, *The Price of Vigilance*, p. 22.

87 "for the protection of public property, etc.": Jensen, *The Price of Vigilance*, pp. 24–25.

87 Germans in America were plotting espionage and sabotage: Jensen, *The Price of Vigilance*, p. 31.

87 The day passed without incident, and no organized protests: Jensen, *The Price of Vigilance*, p. 46.

88 "report to the authorities every suspicious circumstance and disloyal remark or conversation coming to their notice": Jensen, *The Price of Vigilance*, p. 143.

88 claiming that his resources now numbered 400,000: This and the preceding quote are from Jensen, *The Price of Vigilance*, pp. 114, 185.

89 "Others are 'free lances' commissioned to follow strangers of whom they have suspicions": All quotes are from "German Plotters Fear Him," *Literary Digest*, Sept. 29, 1917, pp. 62, 64.

89 "Auxiliary to the Justice Department," on their badges: This and the preceding three quotes are from Jensen, *The Price of Vigilance*, pp. 24, 52, 129, 137.

89 to the draft boards or to special agents of the Bureau: Jensen, *The Price of Vigilance*, pp. 190–91.

90 that his orders would have any impact: Jensen, *The Price of Vigilance*, pp. 191, 223.

90 was working hard to recruit more agents for the local APL: Jensen, *The Price of Vigilance*, p. 197.

90 the logistics for the giant raid: Jensen, *The Price of Vigilance*, p. 199.

90 the fourth great draft registration, held on September 12: Jensen, *The Price of Vigilance*, p. 213.

91 and only half resulted in convictions: Jensen, *The Price of Vigilance*, pp. 169, 172.

91 "It is the historic mission of the working class to do away with capitalism": William Preston, Jr., *Aliens and Dissenters* (1963; rpt. New York: Harper Torchbooks, 1966), pp. 39–40.

92 "crime, sabotage or other methods of violence": Preston, *Aliens and Dissenters*, p. 48.

92 "we will fight against you, not for you": Preston, *Aliens and Dissenters*, pp. 60, 61, 89.

93 an employer's reply: Preston, *Aliens and Dissenters*, p. 105.

93 across the New Mexico border: Jensen, *The Price of Vigilance*, p. 63.

94 arrests against the IWW: Jensen, *The Price of Vigilance*, p. 128.

94 to collect information on them: Jensen, *The Price of Vigilance*, p. 64.

95 he could not afford to offend the APL since he depended on their help: Jensen, *The Price of Vigilance*, pp. 75, 77.

95 "the IWW was crushed and has never revived": Richard Gid Powers, *Secrecy and Power: The Life of J. Edgar Hoover* (New York: The Free Press, 1987), p. 295.

95 provided evidence against her: Jensen, *The Price of Vigilance*, p. 100.

96 agents with legal or linguistic qualifications: Jensen, *The Price of Vigilance*, pp. 89, 94, 102.

96 "what the enemy is doing abroad": Jensen, *The Price of Vigilance*, p. 98.

96 began to absent himself from the meetings: Jensen, *The Price of Vigilance*, pp. 103–104.

97 did continue to get reports from the APL: Jensen, *The Price of Vigilance*, pp. 231, 233, 252.

97 and to fifteen by the first of the year: Jensen, *The Price of Vigilance*, pp. 246, 247.

97 to give the public a feeling of security: Jensen, *The Price of Vigilance*, p. 251.

Chapter 4

102 German plot against America and its allies: Lloyd C. Gardner, *Safe for Democracy: The Anglo-American Response to Revolution, 1913–1923* (New York: Oxford University Press, 1987), p. 195. George F. Kennan, "The Sisson Documents," *Journal of Modern History* 28 (June 1956), pp. 130–54.

103 "multitudes of radical workers throughout the world": Debs: *The Liberator* (May 1919), quoted in Theodore Draper, *The Roots of American Communism* (New York: Viking, 1957), p. 110. Haywood: in Robert K. Murray, *Red Scare: A Study in National Hysteria, 1919–1920* (1964; rpt. Minneapolis: University of Minnesota Press, 1955), p. 30. Goldman: Candace Falk, *Love, Anarchy, and Emma Goldman* (New York: Holt, Rinehart and Winston, 1964), pp. 262–287. Reed: John Reed, *Ten Days that Shook the World* (1919; rpt. New York: International Publishers, 1967); Robert A. Rosenstone, *Romantic Revolutionary: A Biography of John Reed* (1975; rpt. New York: Vintage, 1981), pp. 320–46; Bertram D. Wolfe, *Strange Communists I Have Known* (1965; rpt. New York: Stein and Day, 1982). Muste: Ralph Lord Roy, *Communism and the Churches* (New York: Harcourt Brace, 1960), pp. 15, 17, 47, 49, 64–65.

103 would soon connect Russia to a communist Europe: See Stanley W. Page, *Lenin and World Revolution* (New York: New York University Press, 1959), p. 109.

103 workers' wartime gains by rolling back wages: Murray, *Red Scare*, pp. 63, 65.

103 sent to Ellis Island in New York to await deportation: William Preston, *Aliens and Dissenters* (Cambridge, MA: Harvard University Press, 1963), p. 206.

104 a communist regime took over in Hungary under Béla Kun: Page, *Lenin and World Revolution*, p. 124; U.S. House, Committee on Rules, *Attorney General A. Mitchell Palmer on Charges Made Against Department of Justice by Louis F. Post and Others*, 66th Cong., 2nd sess., June 1, 1920, p. 386; William Henry Chamberlain, *The Russian Revolution* (1935; rpt. New York: Grosset & Dunlap, 1965), Vol. II, p. 378.

104 "to stop this sort of thing in the United States": *Charges of Illegal Practices of the Department of Justice*, Senate Judiciary Subcommittee Hearings, 66th Cong., 3rd sess., Jan. 16–March 3, 1921, p. 580.

105 as revenge for the government's repression of anarchists during the war: See Richard Gid Powers, *Not Without Honor: The History of American Anticommunism* (New York: The Free Press, 1995), p. 22; and Paul Avrich, *Sacco and Vanzetti: The Anarchist Background* (Princeton: Princeton University Press, 1991), pp. 156–57.

105 "destroy the government at one fell swoop": Stanley Coben, *A. Mitchell Palmer: Politician* (New York: Columbia University Press, 1963), pp. 207, 211; Murray, *Red Scare*, p. 80; *New York Times*, June 4, 1919; *Washington Post*, June 19, 1919.

106 Flynn's assistant director (or "Chief"): *New York Times*, June 4, 1919; Murray, *Red Scare*, p. 80.

106 $500,000 to investigate the bombings: Murray, *Red Scare*, p. 81.

107 United States Supreme Court Justice Harold Burton: The following biographical material is from Richard Gid Powers, *Secrecy and Power: The Life of J. Edgar Hoover* (New York: The Free Press, 1987), pp. 5–35.

108 just about what was needed to replace his father's income: Powers, *Secrecy and Power*, pp. 35–43.

109 processing arrested alien enemies for internment or parole: Powers, *Secrecy and Power,* pp. 46–55.

109 for policing the home front: Powers, *Secrecy and Power,* pp. 48–55.

109 to Bureau agents in Burke's or Flynn's name: Powers, *Secrecy and Power,* p. 67.

111 "shall be deemed guilty of promoting sedition": U.S. Senate, *Investigation Activities of the Department of Justice, Letter from the Attorney General.* Transmitting in Response to a Senate Resolution of October 17, 1919, a Report on the Activities of the Bureau of Investigation of the Department of Justice against Persons Advising Anarchy, Sedition, and the Forcible Overthrow of the Government, 66th Cong., 1st sess., Nov. 15, 1919, p. 14.

111 "under legislation of that nature which may hereafter be enacted": *Investigation Activities of the Department of Justice,* pp. 30, 31.

111 "no officers other than a secretary-treasurer": *Investigation Activities of the Department of Justice,* p. 32.

111 "by the use of propaganda": Section 6, Federal Penal Code of 1910; Coben, *A. Mitchell Palmer,* p. 217; *Attorney General A. Mitchell Palmer on Charges,* p. 166.

112 the tsarist regime in Russia rather than the American government: Powers, *Secrecy and Power,* pp. 75–76; Louis F. Post, *The Deportations Deliriums of Nineteen-Twenty: A Personal Narrative of an Historic Official Experience* (1923; rpt. New York: Da Capo Press, 1970), p. 23. According to an undercover agent working for Ohio governor (and future presidential nominee) James M. Cox (see attachment to Cox to Palmer, Nov. 13, 1919, DJ File 2035577-3 1/2, RG 60, National Archives), Trotsky had founded the group in 1906 when he was living on New York's Lower East Side.

112 before being transferred to a federal prison: Powers, *Secrecy and Power,* pp. 78, 79; Coben, *A. Mitchell Palmer,* pp. 20–22 (Coben cites the *New York Times* and *New York World* for Nov. 8, 1919); a photograph of the damage was reprinted in R. G. Brown et al., *Report Upon the Illegal Practices of the United States Department of Justice* (Washington, DC: National Popular Government League, 1920; rpt. New York: Arno, 1969), p. 17; Murray, *Red Scare,* p. 197; Brown, *Illegal Practices of the Department of Justice,* p. 11.

113 awaiting final processing for deportation: Powers, *Secrecy and Power,* pp. 78–79; see also Sowers to Palmer, Nov. 14, 1919, DJ File 203557-8, RG60, NA; Palmer's reply was in *Investigations Activities of the Department of Justice;* Shorr to Palmer, November 13, 1919, cited in Coben, *A. Mitchell Palmer,* p. 221.

113 admitted he was an alien. No problem there: Hoover to Creighton, Aug. 23, 1919, DJ File 186233-13 sec. 3, and Hoover to Caminetti, Sept. 15, 1919, DJ File 186233-13-200, RG 60, NA; see Powers, *Secrecy and Power,* pp. 80–81.

113 "the legal way of deportation": The story is in *National Magazine,* March 1925, in a scrapbook in the Hoover Memorabilia Collection, RG 65, NA, and also in a scrapbook in the FBI OCPA.

113 as specified in the deportation order: *New York Times,* Nov. 30, 1919, p. 30, and Dec. 9, 1919, p. 19; Hoover to Caffrey, Dec. 5, 1919, DJ File 186233-13-224, RG 60, NA; Post, *Deportations Delirium,* p. 18; unidentified New York newspaper, Dec. 9, 1919, Hoover Memorabilia Collection, RG 65, NA. For a letter of Hoover's indicating that he was present at the hearing on December 9, see Hoover to Carter, Dec. 13, 1919, DJ File, 202600-65-2, RG 60, NA.

114 "just as often as is necessary to rid the country of dangerous radicals": *New York Tribune,* Dec. 22, 1919, Hoover Memorabilia Collection, RG 65, NA.

114 were forced out of the Party for espousing violence: *Attorney General A. Mitchell Palmer on Charges,* p. 364; Don Whitehead, *The F.B.I. Story* (New York: Random House, 1956), p. 44; Draper, *Roots of American Communism,* p. 158.

114 "not propose to 'capture' the bourgeois political state but to conquer and destroy it": *Attorney General A. Mitchell Palmer on Charges,* p. 323.

115 John Reed, Ben Gitlow, and William Bross Lloyd: Powers, *Secrecy and Power,* p. 96.

115 along with a list of forty-seven names for warrants: Powers, *Secrecy and Power,* p. 102.

116 Bureau agents to prepare for raids to take place January 2: Caminetti to Hoover, Dec. 24, 1919, DJ File 205492-10, 15, RG 60, NA; Hoover to Chief Clerk, Jan. 2, 1920, DJ File 205492, RG 50, NA; Coben, *A. Mitchell Palmer,* p. 224; Powers, *Secrecy and Power,* pp. 102–104.

116 they sent 291 memos to Caminetti with 2,705 requests for warrants: For Hoover's and Baughman's warrant requests, see DJ File 205492, passim, RG 60, NA.

117 Hoover's briefs on the two parties: Murray, *Red Scare,* p. 218.

117 "It gives you the creeps a little": The GID Bulletin is on Reels 16-18 of *U.S. Military Intelligence Reports: Surveillance of Radicals in the United States, 1917–1924* (Frederick, MD: University Publications, 1984); *Attorney General A. Mitchell Palmer on Charges,* p. 155.

117 "the ways and means of preventing international collapse": *A. Mitchell Palmer on Charges,* pp. 221, 238, 239, 244.

118 arrests of IWW members, five hundred at a clip: Hoover to Burke, Feb. 21, 1920, DJ File 186701-14, RG60, NA.

118 "a dragnet raid would be detrimental": Hoover to Burke, Feb. 21, 1920, DJ File 186701-14, RG 60, NA.

118 for belonging to the Communist Party: *New York American,* Jan. 22, 1920; *Scrapbook,* Hoover Memorabilia Collection, RG 65, NA; Powers, *Secrecy and Power,* p. 113.

118 "more than 500 were ordered by me": Post, *Deportations Delirium,* pp. 152, 155, 167.

119 to help the United States attorney present the case: *Boston Post,* April 14, 1920, in *Scrapbook,* Hoover Memorabilia Collection, RG 65, NA.

119 the seriousness of the revolutionary threat: Coben, *A. Mitchell Palmer,* p. 235.

119 including the sedition bill: Powers, *Secrecy and Power,* p. 119.

120 repression of the American left: Powers, *Not Without Honor,* pp. 32, 33. R. G. Brown et al., *Report Upon the Illegal Practices of the United States Department of Justice* (Washington, DC: National Popular Government League, 1920; rpt. New York: Arno Press, 1969); William A. Donahue, *The Politics of the American Civil Liberties Union* (New Brunswick, NJ: Transaction Publishers, 1985).

120 "*Left Wing" Communism: An Infantile Disorder:* Albert S. Lindemann, *The Red Years: European Socialism versus Bolshevism, 1919–1921* (Berkeley: University of California Press, 1974), p. 132.

120 membership of the two communist parties: Draper, *Roots of American Communism,* p. 275.

120 hopes for a global revolution: Irving Howe and Lewis Coser, *The American Communist Party* (New York: Praeger, 1962), pp. 91–93.

121 communist plots supported by Moscow gold: Powers, *Not Without Honor,* pp. 41–42.

121 "the Assistant Secretary of Labor in canceling the warrants": Hoover to Palmer, May 5, 1920, DJ File 209264-3? and May 27, 1920, DJ File 209264, RG 60, NA.

122 "I want to stand between Harding and them": Francis Russell, *The Shadow of Blooming Grove: Warren G. Harding and His Times* (New York: McGraw-Hill, 1968), p. 449.

122 vouched for his honesty as attorney general: Russell, *The Shadow of Blooming Grove,* pp. 512–16.

123 British shenanigans for the Germans: Russell, *The Shadow of Blooming Grove,* p. 516; Gene Caesar, *Incredible Detective: The Biography of William J. Burns* (Englewood Cliffs, NJ: Prentice Hall, 1968), pp. 198–204 passim.

124 "whiskey was the desired commodity": J. Edgar Hoover, *Persons in Hiding* (Boston: Little, Brown, 1938), pp. 264–65.

124 "Means presents little that is high minded": Hoover, *Persons in Hiding,* pp. 266–67.

125 railroad workers as well as miners: Russell, *The Shadow of Blooming Grove,* p. 541.

125 "sustain the right of the men to work": Russell, *The Shadow of Blooming Grove,* p. 546.

125 "to leave or enter the service of the railroad companies": Russell, *The Shadow of Blooming Grove,* p. 547.

126 "he was specifically forbidden to prosecute": Russell, *The Shadow of Blooming Grove,* p. 548.

126 National Council for the Protection of the Foreign Born: Powers, *Not Without Honor,* p. 74.

127 failing to investigate corruption in the administration: Russell, *The Shadow of Blooming Grove,* p. 617.

128 "Daugherty's agents could not be trusted": Walter S. Bowen and Harry Edward Neal, *The United States Secret Service* (Philadelphia: Chilton, 1960), p. 97.

128 "submit all reports via registered mail": Bowen and Neal, *The United States Secret Service,* p. 99.

128 acting director of the Bureau of Investigation: Powers, *Secrecy and Power,* pp. 142–43.

129 greeted with approval in some circles: Powers, *Secrecy and Power,* p. 152.

129 "Whoever could picture an 'Old Sleuth' doing that?": *National Magazine,* March 1925, and *Pittsburgh Press,* Jan. 27, 1925, both in *Scrapbook,* Hoover Memorabilia Collection, RG 65, NA; "A New Kind of Government Sleuth in Washington," *Literary Digest,* Jan. 24, 1925, Research Unit, OCPA.

131 "conduct as is forbidden by the laws of the United States": According to Hoover's version of events, it was he who suggested these guidelines to Stone (Whitehead, *The F.B.I. Story,* p. 67). See also Ralph de Toledano, *J. Edgar Hoover, the Man in His Time* (New Rochelle, NY: Arlington House, 1973), p. 72. There is no way of definitively establishing the provenance of the guidelines. One of the conditions was that the staff of the Bureau would be reduced as far "as is consistent with the proper performance of its duties." This hardly sounds like a condition *any* bureaucrat would set as his price for accepting a job. For the guidelines, see Stone to Hoover, May 13, 1924, quoted in Alpheus Thomas Mason, *Harlan Fiske Stone, Pillar of the Law* (New York: Viking, 1954), p. 151.

131 antilabor and antiradical behavior: Baldwin to Stone, Aug. 6, 1924, JEH Personnel File, FBI File 67-561, FOIA Reading Room, FBI.

131 under Lyndon Johnson and Richard Nixon: For a discussion of the extent of the Bureau's political investigations during the Coolidge and Hoover administrations, see Powers, *Secrecy and Power,* pp. 161–68.

132 "discontinued for the best interests of the service": Whitehead, *The F.B.I. Story,* pp. 68–69.

132 field offices would reach an historic low of 22: For details see the annual reports of the attorney general, portions of which are quoted in de Toledano, *J. Edgar Hoover,* pp. 89–91. See also Baker to Powers, April 11, 1985, memo on Bureau personnel statistics; Hoover to Attorney General, Feb. 6, 1933, "Justice Department Accomplishments," Taylor-Gates Collection, Herbert Hoover Library. Because of ambiguities due to differences in year-end dates of reporting years, and confusion between agents and nonagent personnel, Bureau personnel statistics vary between good sources. See, for example, Athan G. Theoharis et al., *The FBI: A Comprehensive Reference Guide* (Phoenix: Oryx Press, 1999), pp. 4–5.

133 "all must fall, including the power of crime": For a discussion of Hoover's role as a symbol of police professionalism, see Nathan Douthit, "Police Professionalism and the War Against Crime in the United States, 1920s–1930s," in G. L. Mosse, *Police Forces in History* (Beverly Hills, CA: Sage, 1974).

134 Appel was the entire staff: David Fisher, *Hard Evidence: How Detectives Inside the FBI's Sci-Crime Lab Have Helped Solve America's Toughest Cases* (New York: Dell, 1995), p. 9.

134 This was revised in 1929 and again in July 1930: Powers, *Secrecy and Power,* pp. 153–54. See also an account of a revolt by an agent who felt that Hoover's emphasis on rules and regulations was destroying the Bureau's efficiency as an investigative organization: Powers, *Secrecy and Power,* p. 154; Bayless to Mapes, March 26, 1929, "Justice-FBI, 1929," Presidential Papers, Cabinet Officers Series, Herbert Hoover Library.

135 founded in 1893, and given its present name in 1902: This was followed by the National Probation Association in 1907 and the American Institute of Criminal Law and Criminology in 1909.

135 Central Bureau of Identification: Thomas J. Deakin, *Police Professionalism: The Renaissance of American Law Enforcement* (Springfield, IL: Charles C. Thomas, 1988), p. 37.

136 moved to the Justice Department: Deakin, *Police Professionalism,* p. 67.

136 employing a full-time criminologist: Deakin, *Police Professionalism,* pp. 89–104. See also August Vollmer's *The Police and Modern Society* (1936; rpt. Montclair, NJ: Patterson Smith, 1976).

Chapter 5

141 "We got the Dillingers and the Machine Gun Kellys": Powers interview with Louis B. Nichols, June 26, 1975.

142 "Who doesn't?": John Cobler, *Capone* (New York: Putnam, 1971), p. 314. See also Richard Gid Powers, *G-Men: Hoover's FBI in American Popular Culture* (Carbondale, IL: Southern Illinois University Press, 1983), ch. 1.

143 "wider and still wider areas of life": Quoted in "Gangland's Challenge to Our Civilization," *Literary Digest* 107 (Oct. 25, 1930), p. 8; see Powers, *G-Men,* p. 7.

143 "it is a problem we all must face": Powers, *G-Men,* p. 16.

144 not to expect much from new federal laws: *New York Times,* March 7, 1932, p. 11; see Powers, *G-Men,* p. 11.

144 "the sovereignty and the standing of state government": *Literary Digest* 107 (Dec. 6, 1930), p. 7; see Powers, *G-Men,* p. 24.

144 "then organized into a national body": *New York Times,* March 3, 1932, p. 8; see Powers, *G-Men,* p. 11.

144 "to flourish and destroy all": *Literary Digest* 113 (May 28, 1932), p. 7; see Powers, *G-Men,* p. 11.

145 "the fear of Uncle Sam": *New York Times,* March 4, 1932, p. 9; see Powers, *G-Men,* p. 12.

147 if Cummings kept the two Bureaus separate: Ralph de Toledano, *J. Edgar Hoover, The Man in His Time* (New Rochelle, NY: Arlington House, 1973), p. 101; Don Whitehead, *The FBI Story* (New York: Random House, 1956), p. 91; Richard Gid Powers, *Secrecy and Power: The Life of J. Edgar Hoover* (New York: The Free Press, 1987), p. 183.

147 with a war against crime: *New York Times,* June 18, 1933, pp. 1, 8; see Powers, *Secrecy and Power,* pp. 183–84. The FBI's version of the massacre has recently been called into question by Robert Unger, *The Union Station Massacre* (Kansas City: Andrews McMeel, 1997), who argues, convincingly, that the agents were the victims of friendly fire. He also argues, less convincingly, that the FBI used false evidence in the ensuing trial.

148 second-in-command, John S. Hurley: Powers, *Secrecy and Power,* pp. 184–85; *New York Times,* July 30, 1933, p. 2; *Attorney General's Report,* 1934, p. 133.

148 when Urschel was kidnapped: For a detailed account of the case, see John Toland, *The Dillinger Days* (New York: Random House, 1963), pp. 82–102.

150 how FBI agents got their name as well as their man: *New York Times,* Sept. 12, 1933, p. 3. In the early accounts of the story, the APO gave credit for the capture to the Memphis detectives. The *Washington Star*'s rewrites made Hoover's special agent in charge, William

Rorer, the hero of the case (*New York Journal,* Sept. 26, 1933, p. 1, and *Washington Star,* Sept. 26, 1933, p. 1). The *Star's* rewrite of the AP story said that Rorer was carrying out "Hoover's plan" and that the key to the capture was a planeload of agents from around the country who had converged on Memphis when the Bureau learned of the Kellys' whereabouts. See Powers, *Secrecy and Power,* p. 188, and FBI website. Kelly and his wife both got life sentences for the kidnapping.

150 and got a two-year sentence: This account is based on Toland, *The Dillinger Days.* See also Robert Cromie and Joseph Pinkson, *Dillinger: A Short and Violent Life* (New York: McGraw-Hill, 1962); Powers, *G-Men,* ch. 7.

153 "make another Dillinger impossible": *New York Times,* April 24, 1943, p. 1; April 25, 1933, p. 3; May 24, 1933, p. 2; Powers, *Secrecy and Power,* p. 190.

153 "facing machine gun fire in the pursuit of gangsters": *New York Times,* May 19, 1934, p. 1.

154 "I'll get Baby Face Nelson": *New York Evening Journal,* Nov. 28, 1934, pp. 1, 2; Powers, *Secrecy and Power,* p. 195.

155 "Purvis was a figurehead": Louis B. Nichols, quoted in Ovid Demaris, *The Director* (New York: Harpers Magazine Press, 1975), p. 71. See also Powers, *G-Men,* p. 131.

157 "the G-men never give up the hunt": Powers, *G-Men,* p. 134.

157 "American Justice in 'getting his man' ": Courtney Ryley Cooper, "Getting the Jump on Crime," *American Magazine* 116 (Aug. 1933), p. 25; see Powers, *Secrecy and Power,* p. 198.

158 "The view is idiotic": Courtney Ryley Cooper, *Ten Thousand Public Enemies* (New York: Blue Ribbon Books, 1935), p. 46.

160 "they could continue to do what they wished": Murray Schumach, *The Face on the Cutting Room Floor* (New York: William Morrow, 1964), p. 20.

160 "something acceptable to men and women": *Commonweal* 20 (May 18, 1934), p. 58.

161 "revenge in modern times shall not be justified": Olga Martin, *Hollywood's Movie Commandments* (New York: H. W. Wilson, 1937), p. 120.

161 "The cards are stacked against you": Quotes are from the soundtracks of films in the collection of the Library of Congress.

162 "in my opinion, highly effective": Martin, *Hollywood's Movie Commandments,* p. 113; Powers, *G-Men,* p. 70.

162 "to applaud the efforts of the police": O. W. Wilson, "Police Administration," in *Municipal Year Book* (Chicago: International City Management Association, 1936), pp. 82–83; Powers, *G-Men,* p. 72.

163 extermination at the hands of Hoover's FBI: Quoted in Martin, *Hollywood's Movie Commandments,* pp. 134–35.

163 Hoover in high wrath: *Time,* Aug. 8, 1949, p. 15.

164 " 'Put the cuffs on him boys,' I said": Hoover's account is in J. Edgar Hoover, *Persons in Hiding* (Boston: Little, Brown, 1938), and in Frederick L. Collins, *The F.B.I. in Peace and War* (New York: Putnam, 1943), pp. 86–87. This quote is in Collins, p. 287.

165 25 G-MEN LED BY HOOVER CAPTURE BANDIT ON WEST 102ND STREET: *New York Times,* Dec. 15, 1936, p. 1.

165 and electrocuted him in 1944: de Toledano, *J. Edgar Hoover,* p. 145.

166 "apathy, selfishness or indulgence": J. Edgar Hoover, "Patriotism and the War Against Crime," Speech to the DAR, May 23, 1936; see Powers, *Secrecy and Power,* p. 212.

167 in 1933 to 1,141 in 1938: Athan G. Theoharis et al., *The FBI: A Comprehensive Reference Guide* (Phoenix: Oryx Press, 1999), p. 4.

167 in violation of the espionage laws: Whitehead, *The FBI Story,* pp. 161, 162; Hoover to Cowley, May 10, 1934, Senate Select Committee, *Final Report,* Book III, p. 25. See also Kenneth O'Reilly, "A New Deal for the FBI: The Roosevelt Administration, Crime Control, and National Security," *Journal of American History* 69 (Dec. 1982), pp. 638–58.

168 "political life of the country as a whole": Hoover memos, Aug. 24, 25, 1934, Senate Select Committee, *Final Report,* Book III, p. 395.

168 "investigate the cock-suckers": Whitehead, *The F.B.I. Story,* p. 158; de Toledano, *J. Edgar Hoover,* p. 152; Senate Select Committee, *Final Report,* Book III, pp. 395, 396.

169 "individuals having some ulterior motive": Hoover to Cummings, Oct. 10, 1938, enclosed with Cummings to FDR, Oct. 20, 1938, in Senate Select Committee, *Final Report,* Book III, p. 398; see Powers, *Secrecy and Power,* p. 230.

169 "a severe grilling by the FBI": *New York Journal American,* Feb. 22, 1938, p. 3; Feb. 28, 1938, p. 1.

170 "greatest peacetime spy ring in history": *New York Journal American,* May 9, 1938, p. 4; May 12, 1938, pp. 1, 2; June 20, 1938, p. 1. The report was entitled "Investigation . . . Nazi Training Camps in the United States," Dec. 31, 1937, cited in Kenneth O'Reilly, *Hoover and the Un-Americans* (Philadelphia: Temple University Press, 1983), p. 307. The lead agent in the case, Leon Turrou, made the mistake of capitalizing on the case by contracting to write a series of newspaper articles on it for the *New York Post,* and was promptly drummed out of the Bureau by Hoover. Eventually Turrou's articles were collected in book form in *The Nazi Spy Conspiracy in America* (New York: Random House, 1939), which was turned into a powerful film, *The Confessions of a Nazi Spy,* starring Edward G. Robinson as the FBI agent.

170 the Western Hemisphere, including Hawaii: Cummings to FDR, with Hoover memo, Oct. 20, 1938, Senate Select Committee, *Final Report,* Book III, p. 399, with other important Hoover memos, pp. 399–402.

171 "subversive activities and violations of the neutrality laws": Statement of the President, Sept. 6, 1939, Senate Select Committee, *Final Report,* Book III, p. 404; see Powers, *Secrecy and Power,* p. 232.

171 to defer to the FBI: Theoharis, *The FBI,* p. 17.

172 that roster of potential detainees: Powers, *Secrecy and Power,* p. 233.

173 "the declaration of a national emergency": Theoharis, *The FBI,* p. 17.

173 "some degree of amnesty at least is being extended in Spain": Whitehead, *The F.B.I. Story,* p. 176.

174 Hoover was off the hook: Powers, *Secrecy and Power,* p. 234.

174 as far as possible, to aliens: FDR to Jackson, May 21, 1940, Senate Select Committee, *Final Report,* Book III, p. 279.

175 "you've been caught with your pants down": Francis Biddle, *In Brief Authority* (Garden City: Doubleday, 1967), pp. 164, 166.

175 "altogether humane qualities": Hoover to FDR, June 18, 1940, President's Personal Files, FDR Library.

175 bypassing the attorney general in both directions: Theoharis, *The FBI,* p. 19.

176 "Stalin's agents and spies": Hoover to Watson, March 7, 1940, Official File 10-B, FBI Numbered Report 46, FDR Library. See Powers, *Secrecy and Power,* p. 238.

176 a hunt for red spies, was counterproductive: For Chambers's charges see Berle's notes in Adolf Berle Papers, U.S. Committee on Un-American Activities, FDR Library, as well as discussions in Allen Weinstein, *Perjury: The Hiss-Chambers Case* (New York: Knopf, 1978), and de Toledano, *J. Edgar Hoover,* p. 222. This is a conclusion vigorously disputed by Athan Theoharis in his *Chasing Spies: How the FBI Failed in Counterintelligence but Promoted the Politics of McCarthyism in the Cold War Years* (Chicago: Dee, 2002).

177 the spy who had stolen the blueprints: Joseph E. Persico, *Roosevelt's Secret War: FDR and World War II Espionage* (New York: Random House, 2001), p. 37.

177 "German intelligence in the United States overnight": Persico, *Roosevelt's Secret War,* p. 115.

177 he was not in charge of naval intelligence: Ted Morgan, *FDR* (New York: Simon & Schuster, 1985), p. 621.

178 the Office of naval Intelligence just before the attack: Hoover to Early, Dec. 12, 1941, Stephen Early papers, FBI, FDR Library.

178 "not acted upon by the Military authorities": Hoover to Early, Dec. 12, 1941.

179 and certainly to the Japanese: Gordon W. Prange, *Pearl Harbor: The Verdict of History* (New York: McGraw-Hill, 1986), p. 239. Powers, *Secrecy and Power,* p. 242; see also *New York Times,* Feb. 17, 1946, p. 15.

180 "to oust Hoover from his seat of tremendous power": John O'Donnell, *Washington Times Herald,* circa Dec. 29, 1941, following Hoover to Early, Dec. 29, 1941, Stephen Early Papers, FBI, FDR Library.

181 the FCC chief had refused on the basis of "existing statutes": Hoover to Watson, Jan. 5, 1942, Official File 10-B, FBI Numbered Report 1097, FDR Library.

182 the real threat to their commands: Powers, *Secrecy and Power,* p. 245.

182 one bound for New York, the other for Florida: This follows Ronald Kessler, *Bureau: The Secret History of the FBI* (New York: St. Martin's Press, 2002), pp. 65–69, and Persico, *Roosevelt's Secret War,* pp. 198–205.

184 "a great piece of work" whose story had never been told: This is from a letter Berle wrote to Hoover, Sept. 17, 1946, Adolf Berle Papers, "H," FDR Library. Also see Whitehead, *The F.B.I. Story,* p. 210. This account follows Leslie B. Rout Jr. and John F. Bratzel, *The Shadow War: German Espionage and American Counterespionage in Latin America During World War II* (Frederick, MD: University Publications, 1986).

185 chief of the Bureau's Washington field office: Whitehead, *The F.B.I. Story,* pp. 224, 347.

186 "report them to the FBI and then say nothing more": Hoover, "Problems of Law Enforcement," speech to the International Association of Chiefs of Police, Oct. 10, 1939, *Vital Speeches,* Nov. 1, 1939, pp. 54–57. See also Hoover, "Our Future," Notre Dame Graduation, May 10, 1942, OCPA, FBI; Hoover, "An American's Privilege," Annual Banquet of the Holland Society of New York, Nov. 9, 1942, OCPA, FBI.

186 "Hoover's motives to be that simple": Whitehead, *The F.B.I. Story,* p. 208. Hoover's quest for publicity puzzled his British counterespionage partners, since they came out of a tradition that kept secret operations secret. The British claimed that "he lived by publicity," whereas they themselves "avoided publicity at all costs. Inevitably the FBI got the credit." The FBI "handled some information with reckless disregard for consequences. By trumpeting successes, they tipped off the enemy." William Stevenson, *A Man Called Intrepid* (New York: Harcourt Brace, 1976), pp. 374, 269.

186 that lit the way was "Public Cooperation": J. Edgar Hoover, "Stamping Out the Spies," *American Magazine* (Jan. 1940), p. 83.

186 "humane agents of the F.B.I.": The film (*The House on 92nd Street*) was directed by Hoover's favorite producer, Louis de Rochemont. Quotes are from the press release for *The FBI Front,* New York Public Library of the Performing Arts.

187 or that might in the future: Carlos Clarens, "Hooverville West: The Hollywood G-Man, 1934–45," *Film Comment* (May-June 1977), pp. 10–16. The Bureau endorsed a 1949 reissue of *G-Man,* this time with the FBI seal right after the Warner logo.

187 the first few months after Pearl Harbor: Whitehead, *The F.B.I. Story,* p. 193.

188 police officers who had participated in these conferences: Whitehead, *The F.B.I. Story,* p. 209; Hoover to Watson, May 9, 1941, and Watson to Hoover, May 13, 1941, Official File 10-B, FBI Numbered Report 766, FDR Library. FDR had Watson tell Hoover, "Keep up the good work, boy!"

188 informants in nearly four thousand industrial plants: Whitehead, *The F.B.I. Story,* p. 207. This left Hoover open to charges that the Bureau was once again engaged in labor spying.

See reports on General Motors and Allis Chalmers, both Hoover to Watson, May 15, 1941, FBI Numbered Report 776, and May 17, 1941, FBI Numbered Report 778. Also Hoover to Watson, Nov. 15, 1940, FBI Numbered Report 460; Hoover to Hopkins, July 18, 1942, FBI Numbered Report 2216A, all Official File 10-B. Rowe to FDR, June 26, 1941, President's Secretary's File, Justice Department, all FDR Library.

188 whatever security issues worried them were under control: Hoover to Hopkins, June 30, 1942, Hopkins Papers, FBI Charts, FDR Library. Whitehead, *The F.B.I. Story*, pp. 208–209. Athan Theoharis, "The FBI and the American Legion Contact Program, 1940–1966," *Political Science Quarterly* (Summer 1985), pp. 271–86. Microfilms of FBI files of the program are reproduced in *The FBI American Legion Contact Program*, Athan Theoharis, ed. (Wilmington, DE: Scholarly Resources). See Belmont to Baumgardner, June 22, 1960, FBI File 66-9330-389; Hoover to Tamm and Clegg, Nov. 18, 1940, FBI File 66-9330-2. The number of contacts is from Theoharis, "American Legion Contact Program," p. 278.

188 while its support staff increased from 1,199 to 8,305: Theoharis, *The FBI*, p. 4.

189 countered with a show of his own: While they were still friends Collins wrote of Hoover, "Of course the men love him. They know he is a hard taskmaster. They feel from time to time the weight of his heavy hand, the impact of his rigid standards of efficiency; they find themselves staggering sometimes under his everlasting drive. But they know he works harder than any of them, and dares as much. They plead with him not to expose himself to the dangers he insists on sharing with them, and if you want to know what they think of him as a man, and a gentleman—well all you have to do is to get out your Bible and plagiarize the Beatitudes" (Collins, *The FBI in Peace and War*, p. 290). Louis Nichols called Collins "a free-wheeler out to make money. The Bureau was very unhappy at the inaccuracy and sensationalism of his show" (Nichols interview with author, June 26, 1975).

Chapter 6

193 during the perilous first years of the Cold War: The following is based on my interview with Robert Lamphere, November 5, 1999, and Robert L. Lamphere and Tom Schachtman, *The FBI-KGB War: A Special Agent's Story* (New York: Random House, 1986), p. 25.

194 Nunn May himself was convicted of espionage: Lamphere, *The FBI-KGB War*, pp. 32–34; Kathryn S. Olmsted, *Red Spy Queen: A Biography of Elizabeth Bentley* (Chapel Hill: University of North Carolina Press, 2002), p. 92.

194 Stettinius's assistant secretaries was a Soviet spy: Hoover to Connolly, September 12, 1945, reprinted in Robert Louis Benson and Michael Warner, eds., *Venona* (Washington, DC: National Security Agency, CIA, 1996), p. 61.

195 "hit gold on this one": Olmsted phone interview with Special Agent Don Jardine, July 13, 2001, in Olmsted, *Red Spy Queen*, p. 100.

195 rolling up the Bentley network: Olmsted, *Red Spy Queen*, p. 105. Allen Weinstein and Alexander Vassiliev, *The Haunted Wood: Soviet Espionage in America, The Stalin Era* (New York: Random House, 1999), pp. 104, 105.

195 "as sophisticated as the enemy": Lamphere, *The FBI-KGB War*, p. 27.

195 "a means of doing so": Lamphere, *The FBI-KGB War*, p. 78.

195 "KGB operations in the United States": Lamphere, *The FBI-KGB War*, p. 79.

197 "who had fashioned the Russian A-Bomb": Lamphere, *The FBI-KGB War*, p. 133.

197 a spy among the British scientists at the project: Lamphere, *The FBI-KGB War*, p. 134.

198 Fuchs confessed: On January 24, 1950, Fuchs confessed to atomic espionage. On March 1, 1950, Fuchs was sentenced to fourteen years in prison.

198 "but will later readily identify a better photo": Lamphere, *The FBI-KGB War*, p. 143.

199 "the name of Raymond—Klaus Fuchs—26th May, 1950": Lamphere, *The FBI-KGB War,* p. 151.

199 "during the war years and immediately thereafter": Lamphere, *The FBI-KGB War,* p. 160.

199 "which information I later gave to JOHN": Lamphere, *The FBI-KGB War,* p. 177.

201 "since the summer of 1948 were now fulfilled": Lamphere, *The FBI-KGB War,* p. 207.

201 discouraged the Bureau from investigating Soviet espionage rings is "pure speculation": Athan Theoharis, *Chasing Spies: How the FBI Failed in Counterintelligence But Promoted the Politics of McCarthyism in the Cold War Years* (Chicago: Ivan R. Dee, 2002), p. 36. Theoharis is referring to my conclusions in Richard Gid Powers, *Secrecy and Power: The Life of J. Edgar Hoover* (New York: Free Press, 1987).

201 "without first obtaining [the Secretary of State's] approval": Theoharis quotes this conversation from Blind Memo, April 1, 1944, appended to Hoover to Attorney General, memorandum, undated, both in Francis Biddle Papers, FBI, FDR Library, which seems to undermine his thesis, Theoharis, *Chasing Spies,* p. 52.

202 "towards a citizen spy system. Not for me": Robert Ferrell, ed., *Dear Bess: Letters from Harry to Bess Truman, 1910–1959* (New York: Norton, 1983), p. 55, quoted in Anthony Summers, *Official and Confidential: The Secret Life of J. Edgar Hoover* (New York: Putnam, 1993), p. 166.

202 "Pres. Feels very down, afraid of 'Gestapo' ": George Elsey note, May 2, 1947, George Elsey Papers, Harry S. Truman Library (HSTL), quoted in Summers, *Official and Confidential,* p. 161.

202 while he was in the Justice Department: Herbert Brownell, interview with author, May 6, 1986.

202 his natural allies and constituents: For the reports on Truman's criticism of Hoover, see the news clippings from the *Washington Times Herald,* Feb. 4 and Feb. 7, 1942, in "Pearl Harbor," Nichols Official and Confidential File, FBI. Truman says Biddle offered to resign. Biddle says he was fired. See Harry S. Truman, *Memoirs* (Garden City, NY: Doubleday, 1955), vol. I, p. 325. For Hoover's attitude toward Biddle, see Tom Clark's remarks in Ovid Demaris, *The Director* (New York: Harpers Magazine Press, 1975), p. 133. For the report that Hoover intimidated Clark, see Pat Collins's interview in Demaris, *The Director,* p. 135.

203 "which represents the great majority of American Communists": Hoover, "The Reconversion of Law Enforcement," Speech to IACP, Dec. 10, 1945, OCPA.

204 to buy strategic equipment from the United States: Hoover to Vaughan, Jan. 4, 1946, Subject File FBI P, President's Secretary's File, HSTL. For the Easter crisis memo, see Hoover to Attorney General, Subject File Communist, President's Secretary's File, HSTL. For the uprisings in France, see Hoover to Vaughan, Feb. 15, 1946, Subject File FBI H, President's Secretary's File, HSTL. For more war warnings, see Hoover to Attorney General, Oct. 12, 1946, Subject File FBI S, President's Secretary's File, HSTL; Hoover to Vaughan, 3/25/46, PSF 60; Hoover to Attorney General, June 20, 1946; Hoover to Vaughan, July 30, 1946; Hoover to Allen, Sept. 10, 1946, all Subject File FBI Communist, HSTL.

204 war between the United States and Russia: Hoover to Allen, Feb. 24, 1947, Subject File FBI N; Hoover to Vaughan, Aug. 21, 1947, President's Secretary's File, HSTL.

204 Molotov was now probably in charge: Irving Howe and Lewis Coser, *The American Communist Party* (New York: Praeger, 1962), pp. 437–49. The report about Stalin's demise is in Hoover to Vaughan, Nov. 19, 1945, Subject File FBI S, President's Secretary's File, HSTL.

204 Soviet diplomats and their families: Hoover to Vaughan, Oct. 6, 1947, Subject File FBI N, President's Secretary's File, HSTL.

205 to the White House before 9/11: National Commission on Terrorist Attacks, *Intelligence Policy, Staff Report* #7.

205 OSS searches of the magazine's offices: In 1950 there were two inquiries into sensational charges that the Justice Department had fixed the case: one by a Senate panel under Millard Tydings, and another by a New York grand jury. Those suspicions have recently been proven to have been correct. For a balanced and detailed treatment of the case, see Earl Latham, *The Communist Controversy in Washington* (Cambridge, MA: Harvard, 1966), pp. 203–16. Also see *The Nation*, June 17, 1950. Harvey Klehr and Ronald Radosh, "Anatomy of a Fix," *New Republic*, April 21, 1986, traces the methods used by the influential Washington lawyer Tommy Corcoran to have charges against John Stuart Service dropped; they surmise the motive for the Justice Department's reluctance to prosecute the case was to avoid providing opponents of Chiang Kai-shek a forum for publicizing the failures of the administration's China policy. For Hoover's resentment of Clark and the Justice Department, see Nichols to Hoover, Feb. 24, 1955, FBI File 94-3-4-317-366, in which Nichols says it would not be "in good taste to express our real feelings on Tom Clark," and Hoover to Tolson et al., May 31, 1950, "Jaffe II," Nichols O & C, FBI. While Radosh thinks Hoover acquiesced in the cover-up to avoid revealing the wiretaps he was maintaining on Thomas Corcoran at Truman's request, Lou Nichols informed Peyton Ford on May 29, 1950, that while the Bureau did not want to admit the wiretapping, it was prepared to do so "and point out we were ordered to do this." Given Hoover's dislike of Truman and Clark, he probably would not have minded revealing that he had been tapping one of Truman's enemies on orders from the White House. Nichols to file, May 29, 1950, "Jaffe I," Nichols O & C, FBI. See also Harvey Klehr and Ronald Radosh, *The Amerasia Case: Prelude to McCarthyism* (Chapel Hill: University of North Carolina Press, 1996).

206 "former member of the Communist underground organization": Hoover to Allen, May 29, 1946, Subject File FBI Atomic Bomb, President's Secretary's Files, HSTL.

207 published by the Chamber of Commerce: Later Cronin became assistant secretary of the Social Action Department of the National Catholic Welfare Council, was a liaison between Nixon and the FBI during the Hiss case, and was the chief speechwriter for Vice President Nixon in the fifties. Joshua B. Freeman and Steve Rosswurm, "The Education of an Anti-Communist: Father John F. Cronin and the Baltimore Labor Movement," *Labor History* 33 (Spring 1992), p. 218. Steve Rosswurm, "The Catholic Church and the Left-Led Unions: Labor Priests, Labor Schools, and the ACTU," in Steve Rosswurm (ed.), *The CIO's Left-Led Unions* (New Brunswick, NJ: Rutgers University Press, 1992).

207 problems of unprecedented complexity for the Bureau: Comments by the Church Committee staff that "detention . . . solely on the basis of race was exactly what the . . . Program was designed to prevent" are irrelevant. In the conflict with the Soviet Union that Hoover foresaw, the use of ethnic categories would not have been possible. U.S. Senate, Select Committee to Study Government Operations with Respect to Intelligence Activities, *Final Report, Supplementary Detailed Staff Reports on Intelligence Activities*, Book III, 94th Cong., 2nd. sess., Report 94-755, Serial 13133-5, p. 417.

208 additional authority should be sought from Congress: The Security Index, Hoover told Clark, included "known members of the Communist Party, USA; strongly suspected members of the Communist Party; and persons who have given evidence through their activities, utterances and affiliations of their adherence to the aims and objectives of the party and the Soviet Union." Ladd to Hoover, Feb. 27, 1946, Hoover to AG, March 8, 1946, Hoover to AG, Sept. 5, 1946, cited in Senate Select Committee, *Final Report*, Book III, p. 430, 8.

208 "in the event of extensive arrests of Communists": Ladd to Hoover, Feb. 27, 1946, in Senate Select Committee, *Final Report*, Book III, p. 430.

208 "A Communist for the FBI": For an exhaustive description of the development of this ef-

fort to influence public opinion through the media, see Kenneth O'Reilly, *Hoover and the Un-Americans* (Philadelphia: Temple, 1983), pp. 75–100 and passim.

209 "the preservation of the American way of life": David Caute, *The Great Fear: The Anti-Communist Purge Under Truman and Eisenhower* (New York: Simon & Schuster, 1978), p. 26. Robert Justin Goldstein, *Political Repression in America* (Cambridge, MA: Schenckman/Two Continents, 1978), p. 295.

209 direct government policy, or control the economy: Goldstein, *Political Repression in America*, p. 295, who also cites Peter H. Irons, "American Business and the Origins of McCarthyism: The Cold War Crusade of the United States Chamber of Commerce," in Robert Griffith and Athan Theoharis, eds., *The Specter: Original Essays on the Cold War and the Origins of McCarthyism* (New York: New Viewpoints, 1974), pp. 72–89.

209 A. Devitt Vanech, whom Hoover had nominated: See Senate Select Committee, *Final Report*, Book III, pp. 431–35.

209 the FBI be allowed to keep its files confidential: Director to Vanech, Jan. 3, 1947, Loyalty report of the Temporary Commission, Vanech Papers, HSTL; Minutes, Temporary Commission, Jan. 17, 1947, Stephen Spingarn Papers, President's Temporary Commission, HSTL; Clark to Vanech, memorandum, Feb. 14, 1947, HST Papers, OF 252-1, HSTL, reprinted in Athan Theoharis, *The Truman Presidency: The Origins of the Imperial Presidency and the National Security State* (Stanfordville, NY: Coleman, 1979), pp. 253–56.

210 whether to call on the FBI: Hoover to Clark, March 19, 1947, FBI Loyalty, Vanech Papers, HSTL. Memo for the Files, Stephen Spingarn, Feb. 20, 1947, Spingarn Papers, President's Temporary Commission, HSTL, cited in Theoharis, *The Truman Presidency*, p. 256. What later became known as the Attorney General's List was part of the Loyalty Program. The program called on the Attorney General to "designate . . . totalitarian, fascist, communist, or subversive" organizations. "Membership in, affiliation with, or sympathetic association with" any such organization would constitute reason for removal from federal employment or cause a person to be barred from employment. In April 1947 Hoover advised Clark that the department should "bring up to date its material on the illegal status of the Communist Party" and also update the antiquated list originally drawn up by Biddle for use in Hatch Act and Smith Act prosecutions. The new Attorney General's List, based on suggestions from Hoover, was released in December 1947. By March 1948 it contained 87 organizations, and by November 1950, 197. The Attorney General's List served as one of the most effective weapons of HUAC, the Loyalty Board, and private Red-hunters. It was used as well by the Truman administration to intimidate groups opposed to its new foreign policy of communist containment and confrontation. Executive Order 9835, March 21, 1947, Charles Murphy Files, HSTL, reprinted in Theoharis, *The Truman Presidency*: pp. 257–61. O'Reilly, *Hoover and the Un-Americans*, p. 117. Goldstein, *Political Repression in America*, p. 311.

210 on the loyalty issue: Roosevelt had always been able to limit the damage caused by HUAC's forerunner, the Dies Committee, but Truman did not have FDR's ability to overawe congressmen, and, more important, the Dies Committee had been a Democratic committee. In 1947, HUAC was controlled by Republicans who smelled presidential blood in the water in November 1947 and were going into a feeding frenzy in anticipation of 1948. The new chairman was Republican J. Parnell Thomas of New Jersey, but the brains and energy were supplied by that rising star in the anticommunist firmament, Richard M. Nixon, the young congressman from California.

210 a statement on communism for his testimony: O'Reilly, *Hoover and the Un-Americans*, p. 116.

211 "sinister figures engaged in un-American activities": Latham, *The Communist Contro-

versy, pp. 373–93. All quotes are from Hoover's testimony before HUAC, reprinted in the *Congressional Record*, Appendix, March 28, 1947, pp. A1409–A1412.

212 "subversive employees of the Federal government": Hoover to Attorney General, March 31, 1947, Loyalty Commission, Vanech Papers, HSTL.

213 "It's dangerous": Senate Select Committee, *Final Report*, Book III, p. 434.

213 "the one responsible Federal official most directly concerned with Communism and Communists": *Newsweek*, June 9, 1947, p. 30.

214 "aliens and citizens of the dangerous category": Ladd to Hoover, Jan. 22, 1948; Hoover told the Attorney General that in his opinion Congress would "readily" pass this legislation, Hoover to AG, Jan. 27, 1948, both in Senate Select Committee, *Final Report*, Book III, p. 439.

214 intent on avoiding the mistakes that had defeated him before: Michal R. Belknap, *Cold War Political Justice: The Smith Act, the Communist Party, and American Civil Liberties* (Westport, CT: Greenwood, 1977), p. 46; for a "review" of the FBI's treatment of communist theory and organization, see Gilbert Green, *Cold War Fugitive* (New York: International Publishers, 1984), p. 25. Green, one of the eleven convicted at the Foley Square trial, comments that "Like the man whose sole interest in literature was to search for erotic passages, the FBI historians had combed through the many works of Marx, Engels, and Lenin, and the often turgid writings of lesser Marxists or self-styled Marxists for every mention of violence or forceful overthrow. Yet, significantly, they could not cite a single case of the advocacy or use of violence on the part of Communists in the United States" (p. 25).

215 a New York federal grand jury looking into subversion: For the stops and starts of Clark's hesitant policy here, see Ronald Radosh and Joyce Milton, *The Rosenberg File: A Search for the Truth* (New York: Holt, 1983), p. 83, and Belknap, *Cold War Political Justice*, p. 48. Hoover based his proposal on a recommendation from the head of the Bureau's Intelligence Division that the Bureau "work earnestly to urge prosecution of important officials and functionaries of the Communist Party [under the Smith Act]. . . . Prosecution of Party officials and responsible functionaries would, in turn, result in a judicial precedent being set that the Communist Party as an organization is illegal; that it advocates the overthrow of the government by force and violence; and finally that the patriotism of Communists is not directed towards the United States but towards the Soviet Union and world Communism." See Hoover to Attorney General, Jan. 27, 1948, Ladd to Hoover, Jan. 22, 1948, Senate Select Committee, *Final Report*, Book III, p. 439.

215 the remaining seven were arrested over the next two weeks: The indictment stated that the twelve had conspired with each other and others to "organize as the Communist Party of the United States, a society, group and assembly of persons who reach and advocate the overthrow and destruction of the Government of the United States by force and violence, and knowingly and willfully to advocate and teach the duty and necessity of overthrowing and destroying the Government of the United States by force, which said acts are prohibited by . . . the Smith Act." Belknap, *Cold War Political Justice*, pp. 48, 51.

216 false accusations that Party leader Louis Fraina was an informer: See Theodore Draper, *The Roots of American Communism* (New York: Viking, 1957), pp. 227–32.

216 "coverage which this Bureau must maintain in the internal security field": Belknap, *Cold War Political Justice*, p. 156.

217 Alger Hiss and his brother Donald were undercover communists: Allen Weinstein, *Perjury: The Hiss-Chambers Case* (New York: Knopf, 1978), pp. 351, 340–41. Chambers first talked to Adolph Berle in the State Department in 1939, and had incorrectly assumed that Berle had passed the information along to the FBI. Actually the FBI did not get Berle's memo until 1943.

217 "any accusations as he lacked direct proof": Quoted in Weinstein, *Perjury,* p. 357.

217 why he left the State Department on December 10: Weinstein, *Perjury,* pp. 357, 359, 365–67. There is a resemblance between the Hoover-Truman arrangement regarding Hiss and Truman's erroneous recollections of another deal he thought he had worked out to handle the Harry Dexter White case. Truman, speaking carelessly, may have confused the two cases.

218 "We've been had! We're ruined!": Weinstein, *Perjury,* p. 15.

219 "leaving him only a puppet to be manipulated at will": J. Edgar Hoover, "The Crime of the Century: The Case of the Atom Bomb Spies," *Reader's Digest,* May 1951, pp. 149, 150, 168.

219 one of American politics' most powerful figures: Max Lowenthal, *The Federal Bureau of Investigation* (New York: Sloan, 1950). For the story of White House interest and involvement in Lowenthal's project, see George M. Elsey Oral History, p. 461, OH 128, HSTL. In Lowenthal to Hopkins, May 14, 1950, OF 10-B, HSTL, Lowenthal asks for White House help in getting early copies of the FBI Law Enforcement Bulletins from the rare book rooms of the Library of Congress. Although Elsey tried to claim that Truman did not agree with Lowenthal about the Bureau ("The President was just tolerant, shrugged his shoulder, tended to laugh it off and say, 'Oh, Max is that way'"), Truman wrote Lowenthal to congratulate him for his "wonderful service to the country" and that he "got a great kick out of reading . . . [the] manuscript and making notes on the margin." However, Truman kept his satisfaction to himself; when asked about the book at a press conference he said he had not read it. Elsey Oral History, HSTL. Truman to Lowenthal, June 17, 1950, President's Personal Files—Max Lowenthal, Truman to Lowenthal, June 6/22/50, President's Secretary's Files-General (Max Lowenthal), HSTL, cited in O'Reilly, *Hoover and the Un-Americans,* p. 140.

220 The head of the society sent a copy to Truman: Dick to HST, Jan. 22, 1951, OF 10-B, HSTL. For a general account of the Bureau reaction to Lowenthal's book, see "The FBI Reviews a Book," *The Nation,* June 27, 1951.

220 utterly discredited the Red hunt as an exercise in irrationality: Ken Hechler, *Working with Truman* (New York: Putnam, 1982), pp. 185–88. Truman, *Memoirs,* vol. II, pp. 272–73. "Witch Hunting and Hysteria," Internal Security File Vol. III, Spingarn Papers, HSTL. There was, the study contended, a relatively permanent undercurrent of "hate and intolerance" in America. Periodically this surfaced as an outburst of intolerance against new objects of popular hysteria. Truman was reassured to learn that after each of these periods, "the common sense of the American people soon began to tire of the alarms" of the extremists as they had "more serious things to think about." Truman, *Memoirs,* vol. II, pp. 272–73.

221 "no morals except those which further the world revolution directed by Moscow": Hoover before Senate Internal Security Subcommittee, Nov. 17, 1953, quoted almost in entirety in Ralph de Toledano, *J. Edgar Hoover: The Man in His Time* (New Rochelle, NY: Arlington House, 1973), p. 248.

222 he was working for men who were serious: The two Truman-era cases that had particularly frustrated Hoover were the administration's refusal to push the prosecution of the Amerasia case and the Justice Department's willingness to furnish the court with raw and embarrassing FBI files during Judith Coplon's espionage trial in 1949. Hoover also felt that Truman had him in mind when he harped on civil liberties at a time when he should have been stressing law enforcement; one instance was when he warned Tom Clark against "prosecuting officers becoming persecuting officers." Truman, *Memoirs,* vol. I, p. 325.

222 "he would have the complete support of my office": Dwight D. Eisenhower, *Mandate for Change, 1953–1956* (Garden City, NY: Doubleday, 1963), p. 90.

222 the most effective way of accomplishing that: During the summer of 1953, Arthur Sulzberger of the *New York Times* said Eisenhower should come up with an objective test to determine loyalty. Eisenhower had Brownell turn the idea over to Hoover. Eisenhower was too shrewd to imagine that there was anything to this bizarre brainstorm, but he turned it into a small gesture of his regard for the director's expertise. (Eisenhower to Brownell, Brownell 1952–1955, Administrative Series, Papers as President of the United States, Dwight D. Eisenhower Library [DDEL].)

222 any of his previous superiors in the Justice Department: Louis Nichols had helped Brownell during the 1948 presidential campaign that Brownell managed for Thomas Dewey. Hoover maintained one direct line to the White House by virtue of his chairmanship of the Interdepartmental Intelligence Committee (IIC), established by the National Security Council in 1949. This let Hoover report directly to the White House liaison of the National Security Council, bypassing the attorney general, so he could provide the White House with the same kind of unevaluated intelligence he had sent earlier to Larry Richey, Steve Early, Harry Hopkins, Harry Vaughan, and George Allen. This situation continued until President Kennedy put his attorney general, Robert Kennedy, in charge of the IIC. (U.S. Senate, Select Committee to Study Government Relations with Respect to Intelligence Activities, *Final Report, Supplementary Detailed Staff Reports on Intelligence Activities,* Book III, 94th Cong., 2nd sess., Report 94-755, Serial 13133-5, p. 458.) Demaris, *The Director,* p. 148. Hoover to Rogers, Jan. 3, 1953, April 10, 1956, April 11, 1956, May 3, 1956, Jan. 3, 1957, April 3, 1958, June 27, 1958, Nov. 7, 1958, June 17, 1959; Rogers to Hoover, Dec. 9, 1954, Dec. 21, 1954; FBI Correspondence to and from Mr. Hoover, Rogers Papers, DDEL. By the end of the administration Eisenhower was sending Hoover "Dear Edgar" letters. See Eisenhower to Hoover, March 28, 1960, FBI, Confidential File, White House Central Files, DDEL, requesting an informal evaluation of a sermon Eisenhower objected to.

222 Rogers assured Hoover: Rogers informed Hoover that if these employees had been hired, "there might well have resulted serious prejudice to the best interests of the United States, and, at the very least, there would certainly have resulted acute embarrassment to the President." Rogers to Hoover, Dec. 21, 1953, FBI Correspondence to and from Mr. Hoover, Rogers Papers, DDEL.

223 security officers in each department: This summary follows Herbert S. Parmet, *Eisenhower and the American Crusades* (New York: Macmillan, 1972), p. 256. See also Athan Theoharis, *Spying on Americans* (Philadelphia: Temple, 1978), pp. 208, 210. The Eisenhower Loyalty Program was Executive Order 10450 of April 27, 1953. Stephen E. Ambrose, *Eisenhower, The President* (New York: Simon & Schuster, 1984), p. 46.

223 any proof of disloyalty: Ambrose, *Eisenhower, The President,* p. 64. David M. Oshinsky, *A Conspiracy So Immense: The World of Joe McCarthy* (New York: Free Press, 1983), p. 146. Parmet, *Eisenhower,* p. 343.

224 White's "spying activities for the Soviet Government": Oshinsky, *A Conspiracy So Immense,* p. 147.

224 this would help the FBI with its investigation: Truman may have been confusing the White and the Hiss cases. In the Hiss case there was an understanding to let Hiss continue with the State Department while the investigation proceeded.

224 "used very bad judgment": Quoted by de Toledano, *J. Edgar Hoover,* p. 256.

224 to use the FBI to give him "sensational competition": Parmet, *Eisenhower,* p. 335.

225 Jim Juliana, as chief investigator: Matthews's charges were in the July 1953 issue of *American Mercury.* Oshinsky, *A Conspiracy So Immense,* p. 57, gives the rundown on McCarthy's staff.

225 his assistant, later his wife, Jean Kerr: Oshinsky, *A Conspiracy So Immense,* p. 117.

225 "victim of the most extremely vicious criticism that can be made": Quoted in I. F. Stone, "The J. Edgar Hoover–McCarthy Axis, Sept. 5, 1953," in I. F. Stone, *The Haunted Fifties* (New York: Vintage, 1969), p. 23–24.

225 the lifeblood of Washington's anticommunist establishment: Oshinsky, *A Conspiracy So Immense*, pp. 257, 117, 321. In November 1953, when Senator Karl Mundt casually told a Utah dinner audience that the Bureau leaked information about communists to Congress, Hoover had Mundt deny that this was true and that he had even made the statement.

226 "a carbon copy of precisely nothing": Oshinsky, *A Conspiracy So Immense*, p. 430.

228 "provide all persons combating communism with a handy reference": Hoover to Jackson, 9/18/56, enclosing "Communist Press, USA, Statements Directed Against American Society," September–December 1919, DDEL, 121.

228 Finally, there was Hoover's live-in maid, Annie Fields: Sullivan to Hoover, Oct. 6, 1971, in William C. Sullivan, *The Bureau: My Thirty Years in Hoover's FBI* (New York: Norton, 1979), pp. 268–69.

229 by implication, without effective black leadership: Just about all the reports Hoover ever made on black organizations called attention to the potential for communist infiltration.

229 hardly distinguishable from a communist cell meeting: "The Communist Party and the Negro," Feb. 1953, Office of the Special Assistant for National Security Affairs (SANSA), White House Office, DDEL. Hoover to Anderson, Oct. 6, 1955, FBI S(1), SANSA White House Office; Hoover to Anderson, Mar. 6, 1957, FBI O-R(1), SANSA, White House Office, DDEL.

229 By the fifties this had become fixed Bureau policy: Hoover complained that "while it is incumbent to the effective working of democracy that the perpetrators of such offenses [lynchings] should be apprehended and prosecuted for their crimes," he pointed out to his superiors that "under the present circumstances it appears that the work of the Department and the Bureau is completely ineffective both as a deterrent and as a punitive force." Later he told the Attorney General that "an increasingly large number of people are taking a critical attitude toward the Department because of its failure to 'get results' in these cases" and so "I feel it is a mistake for the Department and the Bureau to enter these mob violence cases unless and until there is some showing of a Federal violation." (Director to AG, Sept. 12, 1946, FBI File 66-6200-44-?; Director to AG, Sept. 17, 1946, FBI File 66-6200-44-?; Untitled, March 5, 1947, FBI File 66-6200-44-?).

230 "over which this Bureau has investigative jurisdiction": Bureau Bulletin #66, Series 1947, Nov. 6, 1947, FBI File 66-6200-44-?; SAC Letter #144, Series 1947, Nov. 12, 1947, FBI File 66-6200-44-?; Untitled, Oct. 29, 1952, FBI File 66-6200-44-?.

230 "opinions by Agents cannot be disassociated from their official status": SAC Letter #55-59, Sept. 20, 1955, FBI File 66-6200-44; "The FBI and Civil Rights," Sept. 1955, "Based on a memorandum from W. C. Sullivan to Mr. A. H. Belmont," in FBI File 66-6200-44.

231 "the FBI was to conduct no investigation": Monitor Radio Program, Dec. 5, 1955, DJ File 144-012, cited by Scott Rafferty, *Federal Protection of Civil Rights Against Acts of Violence* (unpublished Princeton B.A. thesis, 1976), pp. 36–37, John F. Kennedy Library (JFKL).

231 until Lyndon B. Johnson's administration: "The challenge for America in 1960," John Doar wrote in 1975, "was the destruction of the caste system itself. At the outset, few men had fully perceived this fact." (John Doar and Dorothy Landsberg, "The Performance of the FBI in Investigating Violations of Federal Laws Protecting the Right to Vote—1960–1967," in Senate, Select Committee to Study Government Operations with Respect to Intelligence Activities, *Hearings,* Vol. 6, FBI, 94th Cong., 1st sess., p. 948.)

232 to keep out of each other's bailiwicks: Fred J. Cook, *The FBI Nobody Knows* (New York: Macmillan, 1964), p. 227. For rumors of an implicit agreement between the FBI and or-

ganized crime to stay out of each other's way, see George Allen interview in Demaris, *The Director*, p. 23; also Hank Messick, *John Edgar Hoover: An Inquiry into the Life and Times of John Edgar Hoover and His Relationship to the Continuing Partnership of Crime, Business and Politics* (New York: David McKay, 1972). To say that this thesis is dubious is to put it mildly.

232 "with other agencies that were or might become rivals": James Q. Wilson, *The Investigators: Managing FBI and Narcotics Agents* (New York: Basic Books, 1978), p. 170. Wilson adds, "In my view it is the desire for autonomy, and not for large budgets, new powers, or additional employees, that is the dominant motive of public executives" (p. 165).

233 "kicking and screaming" into organized crime investigations: Demaris, *The Director*, p. 150.

233 only four to organized crime: Cook, *The FBI Nobody Knows*, p. 229. Arthur M. Schlesinger, *Robert Kennedy and His Times* (Boston: Houghton Mifflin, 1978), p. 264. It should be noted, however, that the agents assigned to communism in New York also had to handle Soviet and Eastern bloc espionage agents under UN diplomatic cover, an enormous job.

233 something along the lines of nationwide organized crime actually did exist: Cook, *The FBI Nobody Knows*, p. 230. Sanford J. Ungar, *FBI* (Boston: Atlantic Monthly Press, 1976), pp. 392–93. For an account of the struggle within the Bureau to get Hoover to change the Bureau line on the Mafia's nonexistence, see also Sullivan, *The Bureau*, p. 121.

234 members of the Mafia's "national commission": For the Brownell memo see Attorney General to Director, May 20, 1954, Senate Select Committee, *Final Report*, Book III, p. 297. For Brownell's clarification, interview with author, May 6, 1986.

234 summaries of "Communist Party Activities": Hoover to Cutler, Mar. 18, 1953, Staff Files, SANSA, DDEL. The FBI Series of the Office of the Special Assistant for National Security Affairs at the Eisenhower Library contains some sixty titles, some consisting of more than one volume. See Powers, *Secrecy and Power*, pp. 565–66.

234 "public complacency toward the threat of subversion": Goldstein, *Political Repression in America*, p. 402; Belknap, *Cold War Political Justice*, p. 261, quoting Hoover's 1958 annual report.

234 before the department would prosecute them: Senate Select Committee, *Final Report*, Book III, p. 449.

234 domestic security program needed an overhaul: In *Yates*, Justice Harlan ruled that a Smith Act conviction was valid only when it was proven that what was advocated was not a mere "abstract doctrine of forcible overthrow" but "action to that end, by the use of language reasonable and ordinarily calculated to incite persons to that end." There must be advocacy of doctrine and not simply advocacy of action. This effectively ended Smith Act prosecutions under the "advocacy" clause. In 1961 the Court's *Scales* decision made convictions under the membership clause become equally unlikely. Like Secretary of Labor Wilson and Louis Post long before, the Supreme Court held that a person was liable only for "knowing" participation in a proscribed organization, not merely for passive membership. Alfred Kelly et al., *The American Constitution* (New York: Norton, 1993), p. 596.

235 "The people are sick and tired of witch hunts": Hoover to Seaton, June 26, 1957, FBI, Seaton Papers, DDEL.

235 the actual number of COINTELPRO operations: Select Committee, *Final Report*, Book III, pp. 15, 17. John Crewdson, "Seeing Red," *Sunday: The Chicago Tribune Magazine*, March 2, 1986, p. 10. Former Chicago Special Agent Wesley Swearington says that although the Bureau admitted to 238 burglaries from the end of World II until official termination of the technique in 1966, he personally participated in more than 500—and this was only one agent in one city, Chicago.

236 having the informants expelled from the Party: Belmont to Boardman, Aug. 28, 1956, Senate Select Committee, Hearings, FBI, Vol. 6, pp. 21, 372–76. Director to SAC, Chicago, Nov. 23, 1956, FBI File 100-3-104-? (COINTELPRO-CPUSA file).

236 fear of getting caught: Senate Select Committee, *Final Report,* Book III, pp. 45, 58, 33–61. (The accusation of homosexuality was never made, since the agents withdrew their request for permission to proceed when they learned that the individual stopped working for the Party.) Frank J. Donner, *The Age of Surveillance* (New York: Knopf, 1980), p. 187. Donner also gives an account of the case of William Albertson, a communist leader whose life was destroyed by an FBI plot to frame him as an FBI spy (pp. 192–94).

236 going the way of the buffalo hunters: Belknap, *Cold War Political Justice,* pp. 190, 197; Peter L. Steinberg, *The Great "Red Menace": United States Prosecution of American Communists, 1947–1952* (Westport, CT: Greenwood, 1984), p. 281.

236 Most were approved by Hoover himself: Senate Select Committee, *Final Report,* Book III, p. 62.

237 passing the first civil rights laws since Reconstruction: The Church Committee in 1975 was frankly puzzled about why "a law enforcement agency" transformed itself "into a law violator." One agent said, "At this time [the mid-1950s] there was a general philosophy, too, the general attitude of the public at this time was you did not have to worry about Communism because the FBI would take care of it. Leave it to the FBI. I hardly knew an agent who would ever go to a social affair or something, if he were introduced as FBI, the comment would be, 'we feel very good because we know you are handling the threat.' We were handling the threat with what directives and statutes were available. There did not seem to be any strong interest of anybody to give us stronger or better defined statutes." (Senate Select Committee, *Final Report,* Book III, p. 10.) The Church Committee distrusted the Bureau's explanation that it had been frustration with the Supreme Court's weakening of the Smith Act as a weapon that had led to COINTELPRO. The committee concluded that Hoover had turned the FBI into an organization so attuned to the fight against communism that the Supreme Court had left it nowhere legally to go. One agent explained, "The FBI's counterintelligence program came up because there was a point— if you have anything in the FBI you have an action-oriented group of people who see something happening and want to do something to take its place" (*Final Report,* p. 11). Interview, Brownell, May 6, 1986.

237 "size has little relation to the importance of the CP's mission": Hoover to Cutler, Jan. 16, 1958, forwarding "Real Meaning of 'Peaceful Co-existence,' " FBI O-R(1), Staff Files, SANSA, DDEL. This study was abstracted by Robert Cutler's assistant for his information. Hoover to Gray, Oct. 23, 1958, FBI C(4), Staff Files, SANSA, DDEL.

237 "it will then proceed inflexibly toward its final goal": Walter Goodman, *The Committee: The Extraordinary Career of the House Committee on Un-American Activities* (New York: Farrar, Straus, 1968), p. 417.

238 the "subversive" in American reform movements: Hoover to Cutler, June 11, 1957, enclosing "The Communist Party and Social Reform," FBI Series, Staff Files, SANSA, DDEL.

238 his characteristic patterns of speech and thought: A team of five agents in the Research Section put together what Sullivan called "a serious study of communism." The project was then taken over by Lou Nichols, who gave it to Fern Stukenbroeker, one of the writers in his Crime Records Division, to add anecdotal and human interest material. Finally, according to Nichols, he himself "did the finished writing with the help of another chap." This "other chap" was probably the William I. Nichols of *This Week:* There are two plugs for that magazine in *Masters,* one for an article by Hoover, another for a piece in which ex-Vice President Henry Wallace apologized for associating with communists when he

ran for the presidency in 1948 on the Progressive Party ticket (Sullivan, *The Bureau,* p. 91; Demaris, *The Director,* pp. 90–91). There exists a handwritten speech by Hoover in OCPA, FBI, dated Dec. 10, 1956. His style and that of his ghostwriters' were so similar it is impossible to tell that speech from one written by one of his agent writers in the Crime Records Division.

239 *This Week* magazine editor William I. Nichols, and the FBI Recreation Fund: Demaris, *The Director,* pp. 90, 13–20.

240 Lou Nichols and the Crime Records Division: Kenneth O'Reilly and Athan G. Theoharis, "The FBI, the Congress, and McCarthyism," in Athan G. Theoharis, ed., *Beyond the Hiss Case: The FBI, Congress and the Cold War* (Philadelphia: Temple, 1982), p. 373. Whitehead also wrote *Attack on Terror: The FBI Against the Ku Klux Klan in Mississippi* (New York: Funk & Wagnalls, 1970).

240 "you don't edit Don Whitehead": Louis B. Nichols, interview with author, June 26, 1975.

240 "No more. No less": Whitehead, *The F.B.I. Story,* pp. 323, 328.

241 "it was the story of the FBI": Mervyn LeRoy, quoted in Demaris, *The Director,* p. 68.

242 in group orgies, are demonstrably false: Athan G. Theoharis, *J. Edgar Hoover, Sex and Crime: An Historical Antidote* (Chicago: Ivan Dee, 1995), refuting Summers, *Official and Confidential.*

242 Hoover thanked him for the advice, and ignored it: Brownell interview with author, May 6, 1986.

Chapter 7

246 "filthy fraudulent self is bared to the nation": After Sullivan left the Bureau, a copy was found in his files which Sullivan claimed was a "plant" by his enemies. Sullivan later said he could not recall ever having seen the letter, but that it was "possible" he had something to do with it but could not remember. U.S. Senate, Select Committee to Study Governmental Operations with Respect to Intelligence, *Final Report, Supplementary Detailed Staff Reports on Intelligence Activities,* Book III, "Dr. Martin Luther King, Jr., A Case Study," Senate, 94th Cong., 2nd sess., Report No. 94-755, p. 160. Almost all who have looked into the matter, myself included, conclude that Sullivan himself was the author.

246 mail it from the Miami Post Office: David J. Garrow, *The FBI and Martin Luther King, Jr.: From "Solo" to Memphis* (New York: Norton, 1981), pp. 125–26.

246 "They are out to get me, harass me, break my spirit": Garrow, *The FBI and Martin Luther King, Jr.,* pp. 133–34.

247 the Party's finances in the late forties and early fifties: Garrow, *The FBI and Martin Luther King, Jr.,* p. 40.

247 a persecution that continued even after King's assassination: Garrow, *The FBI and Martin Luther King, Jr.,* p. 41. The other principal source for this discussion is Senate Select Committee, Final Report, Book III, pp. 79–184. The FBI's source was one of the Bureau's most trusted informants on the Party, code-named "Solo."

248 Hoover had allied himself with the administration's Republican enemies: Both Victor Navasky, *Kennedy Justice* (New York: Atheneum, 1971), p. 152, and Arthur M. Schlesinger, Jr., *Robert F. Kennedy and His Times* (Boston: Houghton Mifflin, 1978), p. 359, point out the possible connection between the White case and the Kennedys' response to the allegations about King.

248 "should our informant be endangered": See Garrow, *The FBI and Martin Luther King, Jr.,* p. 45.

248 expelled in a purge of members considered communists: See an article based on a 2003

interview with O'Dell in *The Peak,* Simon Fraser University student newspaper, March 3, 2003, http://www.peak.sfu.ca/the-peak/2003-1/issue9/fe-odell.html.

249 "people who are promoting segregation": See Garrow, *The FBI and Martin Luther King, Jr.,* p. 55.

249 as the Bureau would say: See Executive Committee to Director, Nov. 22, 1955, FBI File, 66-6200-?, in Max Rafferty papers, John F. Kennedy Library (JFKL). Garrow, *FBI and Martin Luther King, Jr.,* p. 56. The fact that Hoover and DeLoach tried to approach King means that they had not yet written him off as hopeless, since there are many memos in which Hoover orders his men not to waste their time trying to straighten someone out once Hoover has decided the person is his enemy.

249 hostile to the Bureau, which was even worse: Garrow, *FBI and Martin Luther King,* Jr., p. 59.

250 "large numbers of American Negroes in this country": Senate Select Committee, *Final Report,* Book III, p. 106.

250 "on the efforts to exploit the American Negro by the Communists": Hoover note on memo from Baumgardner to Sullivan, Aug. 23, 1963, Senate Select Committee, *Final Report,* Book III, pp. 105–106.

251 "or we would all be out on the street": Arthur M. Schlesinger, Jr., who knew Sullivan long before Sullivan left the Bureau, told me he did not hear Sullivan criticize Hoover in conversations with him before Sullivan was fired in 1971; the change in attitude afterward was marked. Arthur M. Schlesinger, Jr., telephone interview with author, June 4, 1986; Sullivan testimony, Nov. 1, 1975, in Senate Select Committee, *Final Report,* Book III, p. 107.

251 in light of his August 23 brief: Hoover comments on Baumgartner to Sullivan, Aug. 26, 1963, and Baumgartner to Sullivan, Aug. 29, 1963, Senate Select Committee, *Final Report,* Book III, p. 107.

251 "what the director has a right to expect from our analysis": Sullivan to Belmont, Aug. 30, 1963, Senate Select Committee, *Final Report,* Book III, p. 108.

252 "disrupt the Party's activities in the Negro field": Director, FBI, to SAC, Oct. 1, 1963, in Senate Select Committee, *Final Report,* Book III, p. 111.

252 the COINTELPRO techniques on Martin Luther King: Baumgartner to Sullivan, Sept. 16, 1963, Senate Select Committee, *Final Report,* Book III, p. 108.

252 "make up your minds what the situation really is": Hoover's marginal notes on Baumgartner to Sullivan, Sept. 16, 1963, in Senate Select Committee, *Final Report,* Book III, p. 109.

252 "We are wasting manpower and money investigating CP effort in racial matter if the attached is correct": Hoover marginal note on memorandum from Tolson to Hoover, Sept. 18, 1963, Senate Select Committee, *Final Report,* Book III, p. 109.

252 and to destroy him professionally and personally: The Church Committee characterized Sullivan's testimony as "only one side of the story." It raised the possibility that Sullivan had been trying to maneuver Hoover into supporting increased domestic intelligence programs. The third and most likely possibility, ignored by the Church Committee, is that Hoover really wanted to know the truth, since he was going to have to defend his position against media cross-examination. Senate Select Committee, *Final Report,* Book III, p. 111.

254 to use their media contacts against him: Baumgardner to Sullivan, Sept. 16, 1963. This intensification was announced to the field in a memorandum, Hoover to SACs, Oct. 1, 1963. Sullivan to Belmont, Dec. 24, 1963; Hoover to Atlanta Field Office, April 1, 1964, Senate Select Committee, *Final Report,* Book III, pp. 108, 111, 134.

254 to organize and coordinate against King: See Senate Select Committee, *Final Report,* Book III, pp. 131–32; Garrow, *FBI and Martin Luther King, Jr.,* pp. 74–75.

255 "but our experts here couldn't or wouldn't see it": Hoover note on UPI Press Release, Dec. 29, 1963; Sullivan to Belmont, Jan. 8, 1964, Senate Select Committee, *Final Report,* Book III, pp. 135, 136. See Garrow, *FBI and Martin Luther King, Jr.,* pp. 101–50, for a thorough discussion of these FBI plots.

255 Hoover sent copies of the report to Robert Kennedy and President Johnson: Garrow, *The FBI and Martin Luther King, Jr.,* pp. 107–109.

255 "Communist infiltration in the movement": Garrow, *The FBI and Martin Luther King, Jr.,* p. 114.

255 "I am amazed that the Pope gave an audience to such a [censored]": Baumgardner to Sullivan, Aug. 31, 1964, Hoover's note on UPI Release, Sept. 8, 1964, and *New York Herald Tribune,* Sept. 19, 1964, Senate Select Committee, *Final Report,* Book III, p. 143. For a full description of the Hoover-Spellman relationship, see John Cooney, *The American Pope* (New York: Times Books, 1984). The two men were strikingly similar in age, appearance, political and religious beliefs, organizational skills, closeness to their mothers, even in the persisting rumors of their homosexuality.

256 "one of the lowest characters in the country": DeLoach to Mohr, Nov. 11, 1964, p. 6, Senate Select Committee, *Final Report,* Book III, p. 157.

256 he demanded a meeting: *New York Times,* Nov. 11, 1964, in Senate Select Committee, *Final Report,* Book III, p. 157.

256 "I never addressed him as Reverend or Doctor": Senate Select Committee, *Final Report,* Book III, pp. 163–66. Hoover, "Off the record remarks," informal reception for editors of Georgia and Michigan newspapers, April 16, 1965.

256 enforcing the law against white terror: Senate Select Committee, *Final Report,* Book III, p. 167.

257 "the greatest mistake I ever made was to promote Sullivan": Mark Felt, *The FBI Pyramid: From the Inside* (New York: Putnam, 1979), p. 142.

257 as communism must have been to Palmer in 1919: Sullivan was born in 1912 on a farm near Bolton, Massachusetts. He got a degree in education from American University and taught school in Bolton. He then worked for the Internal Revenue Service in Boston before joining the FBI in August 1941. He worked in counterintelligence during the war, until he became ill while on a special assignment in Spain and was transferred to the Domestic Security Division in Washington, where he spent the rest of his career. See William C. Sullivan with Bill Brown, *The Bureau: My Thirty Years in Hoover's FBI* (New York: Norton, 1979), passim, esp. 14–46. Obituary, *New York Times,* Nov. 10, 1977, p. D13; Sanford Ungar, *FBI* (Boston: Atlantic Monthly, 1975), pp. 295–312; Ovid Demaris, *The Director: An Oral Biography of J. Edgar Hoover* (New York: Harper's Magazine Press, 1975), pp. 76–97, passim.

258 called by a nickname or first name was "Bill" Sullivan: Felt, *The FBI Pyramid,* p. 111.

258 might lose and be purged from the Party: Sullivan to Belmont, Oct. 9, 1956, FBI File 100-3-104, sec. 2; Director to SAC, Chicago, Nov. 23, 1956, all in Rafferty Papers, JFKL.

259 traditionalists frightened of change: William L. O'Neill, *Coming Apart: An Informal History of America in the 1960s* (New York: Quadrangle, 1971), p. 46.

259 veterans could appeal to a grievance board outside the Bureau: William W. Turner, *Hoover's FBI, The Men and the Myth* (New York: Dell, 1971), pp. 292, 241–42.

259 "no publicity nor public announcement" of the change: Turner, *Hoover's FBI,* p. 243. The "secret society" model is from Navasky, *Kennedy Justice,* p. 15 *passim.*

260 the Office of Juvenile Delinquency established under the act: Hoover quotation is from

January 1961 issue of the *FBI Law Enforcement Bulletin,* quoted in Schlesinger, *Robert F. Kennedy,* p. 409. The discussion of the Juvenile Delinquency Act also follows Schlesinger, p. 411.

260 unimaginable to Hoover and Kennedy alike: Schlesinger, *Robert F. Kennedy,* p. 413.

261 "anything but great issues of policy": Navasky, *Kennedy Justice,* p. 100.

261 "Get-Hoffa" squad under former FBI man Walter Sheridan: Schlesinger, *Robert F. Kennedy,* p. 269; Navasky, *Kennedy Justice,* p. 26.

262 supporters in Congress: Schlesinger, *Robert F. Kennedy,* p. 264.

262 "their whole concept of crime in the United States": Navasky, *Kennedy Justice,* p. 81; Schlesinger, *Robert F. Kennedy,* p. 269.

263 "the Bureau as the top-level investigative organization": Hoover, note on Belmont to Tolson, Oct. 1, 1964, Senate Select Committee, *Final Report,* Book V, "Assassination of JFK," pp. 52–55.

263 but the agents neglected to follow through: Senate Select Committee, *Final Report,* Book V, p. 89.

263 and was not sent to Washington until September: For Hosty's account, see James P. Hosty Jr., *Assignment Oswald* (New York: Arcade, 1996).

263 passing out pro-Castro material: Hosty, *Assignment Oswald,* p. 47.

264 still sitting on a desk in Washington on November 22: Senate Select Committee, *Final Report,* Book V, p. 92.

264 and that's what he did: Hosty, *Assignment Oswald,* pp. 59–61.

265 Oswald was the lone assassin: Hoover to Johnson, Nov. 23, 1963, preliminary report; Katzenbach to Moyers, Nov. 26, 1963, Senate Select Committee, *Final Report,* Book V, p. 23.

265 protect its own reputation and avoid criticism: Hoover to Belmont, Dec. 10, 1963, Senate Select Committee, *Final Report,* Book V, p. 23. See also p. 5. The Church Committee later thought it was obvious that Hoover's great concern was possible criticism of the Bureau's handling of Oswald's security case (p. 47).

266 "the investigation of Oswald prior to the assassination": William C. Sullivan said that the reason Hoover was in such a rush to discipline the agents was that, if the Warren Commission did break through his defenses, he could show that he had cracked down on the offenders. Sullivan, *The Bureau,* p. 52.

266 "Oswald didn't fall within this criteria": Hoover's note on DeLoach to Mohr, Oct. 6, 1964, Senate Select Committee, *Final Report,* Book V, p. 57.

266 if there had been proper supervision and initiative: In Hoover's jargon, "smear" simply meant criticism of the Bureau, true or false. Hoover's note on DeLoach to Mohr, Oct. 6, 1964, Senate Select Committee, *Final Report,* Book V, p. 57.

267 "on being able to talk him into doing it, but he did": John Doar and Dorothy Landsberg, "Performance of the FBI in Investigating Violations of Federal Laws Protecting the Right to Vote—1960–1967," in Senate Select Committee on Intelligence Activities, *Hearings,* Vol. 6, "FBI," [94th Cong., 1st sess., 1975], p. 950. Ramsey Clark interview, Demaris, *The Director,* p. 232.

268 speaking before law enforcement and civic groups: Hoover to Jenkins, July 17, 1964, FG 135-6, WHCF, Lyndon Baines Johnson Library (LBJL).

268 preventing a crime as well as reporting on it: Statement by the president, March 26, 1965, Appointment File Back-up, LBJL. See also Hoover to Tolson, March 26, 1965, FBI File, 67-9524, Tolson Personnel File, FBI, in which Hoover told Katzenbach that he had an informant in the car, had the houses of the suspects under surveillance, and wanted to move fast so they didn't get away. Sullivan was in Selma directing the investigation.

269 "to the detriment of our people as a whole": Hoover, "Our Heritage of Greatness," speech to Pennsylvania Society, Dec. 12, 1964, OCPA; Hoover, "Time for Decision," speech at Sword of Loyola Awards Dinner, Chicago, Nov. 24, 1964, OCPA.

269 "possibility of developing a similar effort to meet this problem": Doar and Landsberg, Performance of the FBI, Senate Select Committee, *Hearings*, Vol. 6, p. 985. See also *Final Report*, Book III, pp. 471–75.

269 the legal battle against white terror: Senate Select Committee, *Final Report*, Book III, p. 471. Robert J. Goldstein, *Political Repression in Modern America* (Cambridge, MA: Schenckman/Two Centuries, 1978), p. 445.

270 follow a Klansman around the clock, noting all of his activities: Hoover to SACs, Sept. 2, 1964, Hoover to SACs, Oct. 12, 1964, Senate Select Committee, *Hearings*, vol. 6, pp. 377–82.

270 "In the same circumstances I would do so again today": George C. Moore testimony, Nov. 3, 1975, p. 31, Senate Select Committee, *Final Report*, Book III, pp. 18, 19. Katzenbach testimony, *Hearings*, Vol. 6, p. 219.

271 against black radicals and antiwar activists: Senate Select Committee, *Final Report*, Book III, p. 27.

271 time to eliminate this danger to the Bureau: See Watson to LBJ, Nov. 30, 1965, JL, WHCF; "Wiretaps," Administrative History, Department of Justice, Vol. III, LBJL. "Warrantless FBI Electronic Surveillance," Senate Select Committee, *Final Report*, Book III, pp. 271–351, esp. 285, 310.

271 (records of addressees and recipients of mail), and break-ins: Hoover to Katzenbach, Sept. 14, 1965, Senate Select Committee, *Final Report*, Book III, p. 287; Athan Theoharis, *Spying on Americans* (Philadelphia: Temple, 1978), p. 113. In 1964, Hoover also ended mail covers and trash covers. Goldstein, *Political Repression in Modern America*, p. 443. Johnson's order banning wiretaps was drafted by Katzenbach on April 8, 1965, to take effect July 1 (White to Moyers, April 10, 1965, Katzenbach to LBJ, April 8, 1965, Busby to Moyers, April 20, 1965, Justice Department, Moyers File, LBJL). Hoover ended mail covers on Sept. 29, 1965; he ended surreptitious entries on July 19, 1966 (Sullivan to De-Loach, July 19, 1966, p. 3, Senate Select Committee, *Final Report*, Book III, p. 365).

272 "none warrant FBI being used to justify them": Belmont to Tolson, Feb. 27, 1965, Senate Select Committee, *Final Report*, Book III, p. 670.

272 directors after Hoover be appointed by the president and approved by the Senate: Public Law 90–351, June 1968.

272 crimes against small business: Daniel J. Freed, "Proposed District of Columbia Crime Control Program," Oct. 12, 1967; see Gaither: Crime-General, and Crime General—Juvenile Delinquency, Presidential Task Forces, Gaither Papers, LBJL.

273 permissiveness that caused the crime wave: Richard Harris, *Justice: The Crisis of Law, Order, and Freedom in America* (1969; rpt. New York: Avon, 1970), p. 56. Nicholas Katzenbach later said that one of the reasons he left the Justice Department was that he found it so unpleasant working with Hoover. (Senate Select Committee, *Hearings*, Vol. 6, p. 202.)

273 Hoover could never give Johnson exactly what the president wanted: Hoover to Tolson et al., July 25, 1967, July 25, 1967, Hoover, Memorandum for Personal Files, July 31, 1967, FBI File 67-9524, Tolson Personnel File.

273 a COINTELPRO directed against "black nationalist, hate-type organizations": Senate Select Committee, *Final Report*, Book III, p. 179.

274 The SCLC was listed from the outset, King himself in February 1968: Hoover to SAC Albany, Aug. 25, 1967, Senate Select Committee, *Hearings*, Vol. 6, p. 383; *Final Report*, Book III, pp. 3, 20, 21, 180.

274 "has the necessary charisma to be a real threat in this way": Hoover to SACs, March 4,

1968, Senate Select Committee, *Final Report,* Book III, p. 180; *Hearings,* Vol. 6, pp. 387–90.

274 "fomenting violence and unrest": Senate Select Committee, *Final Report,* Book III, p. 189.

275 against the Panthers from 1969 until 1971: Ungar, *FBI,* p. 466: "It is fair to say that the FBI was shopping around for a law enforcement unit that was willing to conduct a raid that it, the Bureau, wanted to see carried out, but had no legal pretext for staging it on its own."

275 The results were tragic: John Ehrlichman, *Witness to Power* (New York: Simon & Schuster, 1982), p. 164. For a thorough account of the Seberg case, see David Richards, *Played Out: The Jean Seberg Story* (New York: Playboy, 1981).

275 thinking of supporting the Panthers: Richards, *Played Out,* p. 237.

275 "The dear girl is getting around": Richards, *Played Out,* p. 238.

275 and Deputy Attorney General Richard Kleindienst: It has not been established whether the source of Haber's article was in fact the Bureau, but it seems very likely. Richards, *Played Out,* p. 240.

277 "membership in specific organizations": Hoover, "Turbulence on Campus," *PTA Magazine,* Feb. 1966, p. 4.

277 "it would enable North Vietnam to move in at once": Hoover memo, April 28, 1965, Senate Select Committee, *Final Report,* Book III, p. 485.

277 "the Ku Klux Klan and the Communist Party itself": Hoover memo, April 28, 1965, Select Committee, *Final Report,* Book III, p. 485. Goldstein, *Political Repression in Modern America,* p. 449. The resulting intelligence-gathering effort was called the VIDEM (Vietnam Demonstration) program, and it disseminated intelligence about demonstrations to the White House and other interested government agencies. SAC letter, March 26, 1968, Senate Select Committee, *Final Report,* Book III, pp. 488, 491.

278 when Hoover attacked it in 1919 and 1947: Goldstein, *Political Repression in Modern America,* p. 430. See also FBI Director's Report, 1968, p. 56, FBI Narrative History, Documentary Supplement, LBJL.

278 "objectives of the Communist Party throughout the nation": Hoover, "Turbulence on Campus," p. 4. Goldstein, *Political Repression in Modern America,* p. 438.

278 "demonstrations in some of our largest universities": The Bureau also continued its practice of placing material in the hands of friendly journalists like Walter Trohan of the *Chicago Tribune,* to "expose" the communist influence in the antiwar movement. Goldstein, *Political Repression in Modern America,* p. 438. DeLoach to LBJ, July 10, 1967, FG 135-6, WHCF, LBJL. Hoover, Statement to House Appropriations Committee, 1967, p. 93, FBI Narrative History, Documentary Supplement, LBJL.

279 the Intelligence Evaluation Committee with Hoover in charge: Goldstein, *Political Repression in Modern America,* p. 449.

279 "why something wasn't being done": Charles D. Brennan testimony, Sept. 25, 1975, Senate Select Committee, *Final Report,* Book III, p. 524.

279 New Left ("use of narcotics and free sex") to parents: Headquarters to SAC, May 23, 1968, Senate Select Committee, *Final Report,* Book III, p. 24. Headquarters to SACs, July 6, 1968, *Final Report,* Book III, p. 89.

280 a Key Activist photo album for ready reference: Senate Select Committee, *Final Report,* Book III, p. 511. Goldstein, *Political Repression in Modern America,* pp. 452–53. Senate Select Committee, *Hearings,* Vol. 6, p. 371, and, for examples of COINTELPRO–NEW LEFT operations, pp. 812–13; Senate Select Committee, *Final Report,* Book III, pp. 88–89.

281 for "black bag jobs" and Waterbuggery: That is Tom Charles Huston's theory, paraphrased in Demaris, *The Director,* p. 251.

281 secrets secret any longer: Hoover's aide, John Mohr, said "he knew that this stuff was bad if it became public knowledge"; after Watergate, Mohr added, "obviously everybody

in the world would say he was right" (John Mohr interview, Demaris, *The Director,* p. 311).

281 forty-five in all during the first year: Richard Nixon, *RN: The Memoirs of Richard Nixon* (New York: Grosset & Dunlap, 1987), p. 386.

282 "to investigate the leaks and find the leakers": Nixon, *Memoirs,* p. 387. Nixon's assertion that wiretapping was urged on him by Hoover has to be taken with a grain of salt in light of Hoover's subsequent near panic over its danger.

282 all the remaining taps, including on Kissinger himself: The memos from Hoover to Mitchell requesting authority, bearing Mitchell's signature, are in U.S. House, Select Committee on Intelligence, U.S. Domestic Agencies and Activities: Domestic Intelligence Programs, *Hearings,* Part 3, 94th Cong., 1st sess., pp. 1208–20. Mitchell later denied having signed the memos, but offered no convincing alternative explanation for the existence of the signed authorizations.

282 working on the campaign staff of Edmund Muskie: Haig deposition, *Halperin v. Kissinger,* Civ. No. 1187-73 (D.D.C.), Oct. 25, 1974, pp. 9–10, in Senate Select Committee, *Final Report,* Book III, p. 325.

283 and the tap never installed: "Unfortunately none of these wiretaps turned up any proof linking anyone in the government to a specific national security leak": Nixon, *Memoirs,* p. 389; Senate Select Committee, *Final Report,* Book III, pp. 323, 336.

283 "must therefore be scrutinized most carefully": Hoover to Helms, March 31, 1970, U.S. Senate, Select Committee to Study Governmental Operations with Respect to Intelligence Activities, *Hearings,* "Huston Plan," Vol. 2, 94th Cong., 1st. sess., Sept. 23, 24, 25, 1975, pp. 354–56.

283 the tense days of the Truman administration: Nixon, *Memoirs,* p. 471.

283 go on record requesting permission for illegal investigations: Nixon, *Memoirs,* p. 472.

284 struck up a friendship with William C. Sullivan: Theodore White, *Breach of Faith: The Fall of Richard Nixon* (New York: Atheneum, 1975), p. 133; Theoharis, *Spying on Americans,* pp. 16–17; Nixon, *Memoirs,* p. 473.

284 should attach his objections as footnotes, and that is what he did: This follows the account of the Church Committee staff, and Hoover's reaction is related by Sullivan, who was, by the time he testified before the Church Committee (Nov. 1, 1975), trying to discredit Hoover (Senate Select Committee, *Final Report,* Book III, p. 942).

285 "What the White House wanted, the White House would get": Willard interview, Senate Select Committee, *Final Report,* Book III, p. 944.

286 the four chiefs signed the document: Sullivan interview, Senate Select Committee, *Final Report,* Book III, p. 945. Sullivan, *The Bureau,* p. 214.

286 "That puts the whole thing on my shoulders": Sullivan says that when Hoover learned Nixon had approved the plan in spite of his objections, he "went through the ceiling." "That hippie [his nickname for the somewhat long-haired Huston] is behind this," he began. "I've had this kind of responsibility for years, and I just won't take it any more. I'll only accept the recommendations outlined in this draft if the President orders me to. And I'll only carry them out if someone else—the President, the attorney general—takes the responsibility" (Senate Select Committee, *Final Report,* Book III, p. 956; Sullivan, *The Bureau,* p. 211; Sullivan interview in Demaris, *The Director,* p. 312). Arthur Schlesinger, *Imperial Presidency* (Boston: Houghton Mifflin, 1973), p. 274: "It may well be that he did not care all that much about civil liberties, but he did care supremely about the professional reputation of the FBI." Sullivan thought Hoover's real objection was to the degree of interagency cooperation the plan envisioned and the call for periodic review of intelligence operations (Sullivan, *The Bureau,* p. 212).

286 approving, though indirectly, illegal activities: Hoover told Mitchell that "despite my

clear-cut and specific opposition to the lifting of the various investigative restraints referred to above and to the creation of a permanent interagency committee on domestic intelligence, the FBI is prepared to implement the instructions of the White House at your direction. Of course we would continue to seek your [Mitchell's] specific authorization, where appropriate, to utilize the various sensitive investigative techniques involved in individual cases" (Hoover to Mitchell, July 25, 1970, Senate Select Committee, *Final Report,* Book III, p. 957).

286 until John Dean's testimony during Watergate: Senate Select Committee, *Final Report,* Book III, p. 956. Nixon, *Memoirs,* pp. 474–75.

287 the number three position behind Tolson and Hoover: There is some confusion as to when Sullivan actually assumed his new position. Sullivan later said he replaced DeLoach in June, but DeLoach was still active in the fight against the Huston Plan at the Bureau in July. For memos showing how Sullivan protected himself with both sides by posing as promoter or foe of the plan depending on the audience, see Senate Select Committee, *Final Report,* Book III, pp. 965–66.

287 to blow up the capital power system and to kidnap Henry Kissinger: On April 5, 1972, two of the eight Catholic activists (Philip Berrigan and Elizabeth McAlister) were convicted of lesser charges (smuggling letters out of a prison) and the rest acquitted. Harrisburg [PA] Defense Committee Records, 1970–1973, Swarthmore College Peace Collection; Athan G. Theoharis et al., *The FBI: A Comprehensive Reference Guide* (Phoenix: Oryx, 1999), p. 78.

287 the New Left journal *WIN:* Felt, *The FBI Pyramid,* p. 93. See also Cathy Perkus, ed., *COINTELPRO: The FBI's Secret War on Political Freedom* (New York: Monad, 1975).

288 National Black Economic Development Conference: Ungar, *FBI,* p. 139.

288 "hysterically equated with the Soviet secret police": Felt, *The FBI Pyramid,* pp. 88, 98.

288 and on December 6, 1973, received the documents: Theoharis, *The FBI,* pp. 126–27.

288 they were fair game: Hoover to Tolson et al., April 6, 1971, five memos, record phone calls from Kleindienst, Hugh Scott, and Haldeman. Edmund Muskie and Senator Gaylord Nelson of Wisconsin denouncing FBI director Hoover for having agents at Earth Day activities. Muskie charged that there were some forty to sixty reports covering Earth Day demonstrations. Hoover said fifty offices did report on fifty-seven rallies; but in all but four cases the FBI simply picked up information from outside sources and passed it to Washington. Hoover to Tolson et al., April 15, 1971, FBI File 67-9524, Tolson File, FBI. Nelson called for a special committee to investigate the FBI. (The motion died, and was reintroduced in 1973, 1974, and 1975. The Senate Select Committee was finally established in May 1976.)

289 individual cases even after April 1971: Theoharis, *Spying on Americans,* p. 150. Letter from FBI Headquarters to all SACs, April 28, 1971, in Senate Select Committee, *Final Report,* Book III, p. 3.

289 to expand the Legal Attaché (Legat) program overseas: Felt interview, Demaris, *The Director,* p. 271; Executive Conference Memorandum, June 2, 1971, Senate Select Committee, *Final Report,* Book III, p. 539.

289 "I need someone who can control Sullivan": Felt, *The FBI Pyramid,* p. 133.

289 the expansion of Legats overseas: Sullivan, *The Bureau,* pp. 242–425.

290 "the operations of the Domestic Intelligence Division": See Sullivan, *The Bureau,* p. 244; Felt, *The FBI Pyramid,* pp. 138, 140.

290 "I am half again his height": Felt, *The FBI Pyramid,* p. 140, 141.

290 "To millions of Americans J. Edgar Hoover was still a folk hero": Ehrlichman, *Witness to Power,* p. 166. According to DeLoach, Nixon wanted to get Hoover out of the Bureau by making him a figurehead "Director Emeritus," and Kleindienst recommended this to

Nixon (Kleindienst interview in Demaris, *The Director,* p. 244). Nixon, *Memoirs,* pp. 596, 597.

290 a breakfast meeting with the president: Ehrlichman, *Witness to Power,* p. 166.

291 "would raise more political problems than it would solve": Nixon, *Memoirs,* pp. 598–99.

292 executive staff could leave for the day: Hoover, "Message from the Director," May 1, 1972, reprinted in Senate, *Memorial Tributes,* p. 14. Felt somewhat improves Hoover's actual schedule by saying that Hoover customarily worked until 6:30 or 7 in the evening. De-Loach and one of Hoover's neighbors say that he usually left earlier. Judging by the time he usually got home, he normally left shortly before 6. For the report that Hoover was leaving for work later and returning earlier, see *Washington Star,* May 7, 1972, and De-Loach, interview with author, March 10, 1975.

Chapter 8

296 they would not exist many days longer: A Curt Gentry, *J. Edgar Hoover, The Man and the Secrets* (New York: Norton, 1991), p. 36.

296 which were kept under lock and key in Hoover's office: Athan G. Theoharis and John Stuart Cox, *The Boss: J. Edgar Hoover and the Great American Inquisition* (Philadelphia: Temple University Press, 1988), p. 329.

297 always the case with Hoover's files: Theoharis and Cox, *The Boss,* p. 332.

297 illegal Bureau activities: Theoharis and Cox, *The Boss,* p. 330. See also Ronald Kessler, *The Bureau: The Secret History of the FBI* (New York: St. Martin's Press, 2002), p. 169.

297 "highly confidential Bureau information": Helen Gandy, quoted in Theoharis and Cox, *The Boss,* p. 329.

297 while many of the O&C files went back to the Bureau: Theoharis and Cox, *The Boss,* p. 329, citing Senate Select Committee on Intelligence Activities, *Hearings,* Vol. 6, "FBI" (94th Cong., 1st sess., 1975), pp. 351–56; House Subcommittee on Government Information, *Hearings on Inquiry into Destruction of Former FBI Director Hoover's Files and FBI Record Keeping* (94th Cong., 1st sess., 1975), p. 101.

298 the threat of their release terrified the Bureau: Clarence M. Kelley and James Kirkpatrick Davis, *Kelley: The Story of an FBI Director* (Kansas City: Andrews, McMeel & Parker, 1987), p. 183.

298 he named Gray acting director of the FBI: FBI website.

299 173 Hispanics, and 147 women: Kessler, *The Bureau,* p. 196.

299 tried to make sure that they were treated fairly: Sanford J. Ungar, *FBI* (Boston: Atlantic Monthly, 1975), pp. 511–12.

299 moving the press and congressional relations into his own office: Ungar, *FBI,* p. 523.

300 about the case to the press and Congress: It is Edward J. Epstein's thesis that the Deep Throat Woodward and Bernstein cited as their main source was in fact a series of leaks, including raw 302 reports, from FBI agents in revolt against L. Patrick Gray. *Commentary,* June 1974.

301 "should not see the light of day": Ungar, *FBI,* p. 532.

301 cooperate with the Watergate investigators: Gray was indicted along with Mark Felt and Edward Miller for authorizing illegal break-ins of the homes of relatives of the Weather Underground. Felt and Miller were convicted, and pardoned by Ronald Reagan. Charges against Gray were dropped. *New York Times,* Dec. 1, 1983, p. A19.

301 he was not interested in a permanent appointment: Ungar, *FBI,* p. 542.

302 in charge of the Justice Department's Civil Division: William Doyle Ruckelshaus served as acting director of the FBI between April and July 1973. Born in Indianapolis, Indiana, on July 24, 1932, he graduated cum laude from Princeton University in 1957 with a B.A.

In 1960, Harvard University awarded him a J.D. and Mr. Ruckelshaus entered private law practice in Indiana. After serving in a number of state offices, Mr. Ruckelshaus was appointed to the U.S. Department of Justice and, in 1970, became the first administrator of the new Environmental Protection Agency (EPA). He served in the EPA until his appointment as acting director of the Bureau. After Director Kelley was confirmed, Mr. Ruckelshaus returned to private practice. In 1983 he returned to Washington as the fifth administrator of the EPA and served there until 1985. FBI website.

302 White House officials implicated in the Watergate scandal: Ungar, *FBI*, p. 544.

302 "Respectfully, All FBI Officials": Ungar, *FBI*, p. 545.

303 "I have ever been associated with": Ungar, *FBI*, p. 548.

303 "and they could not stop": Ungar, *FBI*, p. 548.

303 "check is sufficient today and needs to be strengthened": Commencement Address, Ohio State University, June 8, 1973, quoted in Ungar, *FBI*, p. 560.

303 that would reflect well on his own candidacy: Ungar, *FBI*, p. 557.

304 "quality-over-quantity was the only program that made any sense": Oliver "Buck" Revell and Dwight Williams, *A G-Man's Journal* (New York: Pocket Books, 1998), p. 149.

305 "Bad business, investigating politicians. Don't do it": Kelley, *Kelley, The Story of an FBI Director*, p. 298.

305 "no involvement in local politics or politicians": Kelley, *Kelley, The Story of an FBI Director*, p. 298.

306 "the investigation of Governor Hall": Kelley, *Kelley, The Story of an FBI Director*, p. 300.

306 "If I am right, it's real quality, Mr. Director": Kelley, *Kelley, The Story of an FBI Director*, p. 302.

306 "a high-priority investigation of that nature with full force": Kelley, *Kelley, The Story of an FBI Director*, p. 303.

307 canceled all COINTELPROs, dated April 28, 1971: Kelley, *Kelley, The Story of an FBI Director*, pp. 175, 176.

307 "who would promote anarchy and violence": Kelley, *Kelley, The Story of an FBI Director*, p. 176–77.

307 handed them over to Stern: Kelley, *Kelley, The Story of an FBI Director*, p. 177.

307 "protect the fabric of society": Kelley, *Kelley, The Story of an FBI Director*, p. 177.

307 "action of any kind after 4/28/71": Kelley, *Kelley, The Story of an FBI Director*, p. 179.

308 also wanted to know about COINTELPRO: Kelley, *Kelley, The Story of an FBI Director*, p. 178.

308 "if their involvement were to become public knowledge": Kelley, *Kelley, The Story of an FBI Director*, p. 183.

309 Charges against Gray were dropped: *New York Times*, Dec. 1, 1983, p. A19.

309 "a free society such as ours": Kelley, *Kelley, The Story of an FBI Director*, pp. 184–85.

311 legal authority to do *anything* except investigate federal crimes: Book III of the *Final Report* contained individual detailed staff reports on COINTELPRO (subtitled "The FBI's Covert Action Programs Against American Citizens"), pp. 3–77; the "Dr. Martin Luther King, Jr., Case Study," pp. 79–184; "The FBI's Covert Action Program to Destroy the Black Panther Party," pp. 185–223; "The Use of Informants in FBI Domestic Intelligence Investigations," pp. 227–70; "Warrantless FBI Electronic Surveillance," pp. 271–351; "Warrantless Surreptitious Entries: FBI 'Black Bag' Break-ins and Microphone Surveillance," pp. 353–71; a very important study, "The Development of FBI Domestic Intelligence Investigations," pp. 373–558; "Domestic CIA and FBI Mail Opening Programs," pp. 559–677; "National Security, Civil Liberties, and the Collection of Intelligence: A Report on the Huston Plan," pp. 921–86; as well as reports on several other government agencies.

311 "threats to the existing social and political order": Senate Select Committee, *Final Report,* Book III, p. 3.

311 "combating those who threaten that order": Senate Select Committee, *Final Report,* Book III, p. 7.

312 "constitutionally protected acts and advocacy": Senate Select Committee, *Final Report,* Book III, p. 28.

312 "We did not differentiate": William C. Sullivan testimony, Nov. 1, 1975, pp. 97–98, quoted in Senate Select Committee, *Final Report,* Book III, p. 7.

312 excerpt of the COINTELPRO papers: Cathy Perkus, ed., *COINTELPRO: The FBI's Secret War on Political Freedom* (New York: Monad, 1975). The Senate *Report* was released in April 1976.

312 to "guarantee that COINTELPRO will not happen again": Senate Select Committee, *Final Report,* Book III, p. 77.

312 "intelligence programs of the previous three decades": Senate Select Committee, *Final Report,* Book III, p. 377.

313 "want to do something": Senate Select Committee, *Final Report,* Book III, p. 11.

313 "an adverse impact on the rights of individuals": Senate Select Committee, *Final Report,* Book III, p. 377.

314 "it was not illegal in any instance": Kelley, *Kelley, The Story of an FBI Director,* pp. 189–90.

314 Full investigations could use informants, wiretaps, and mail covers: Athan Theoharis, "A Brief History of the FBI's Role and Powers," in Theoharis, ed., *The FBI: A Comprehensive Reference Guide* (Phoenix: Oryx, 1999), p. 38. The quotes are from the Levi guidelines. Tony G. Poveda, "The Traditions and Culture of the FBI," in *The FBI: A Comprehensive Reference Guide,* p. 195.

314 from twenty-two thousand to four thousand: Kelley, *Kelley, The Story of an FBI Director,* p. 153.

315 involving foreign governments or groups: Kelley, *Kelley, The Story of an FBI Director,* p. 153.

315 "evidence of a continuing conspiracy to commit crimes": Revell, *A G-Man's Journal,* p. 127.

315 "has been or is about to be committed": "Terror Threat Renews Debate over Investigation Restrictions," Associated Press, Nov. 30, 2001. See also Revell statements in Bill Gertz, *Breakdown* (Washington, DC: Regnery, 2002), pp. 94–95.

318 larceny on Indian reservations federal offenses: Rolland Dewing, *Wounded Knee II* (Chadron, NE: Great Plains Network, 1995), p. 6. Later (1948, 1949, 1952) this became known as the Ten Major Crimes Act with the addition of kidnapping, robbery, and a variety of sex crimes. Currently it is included in 18 USC 1153 (2003).

318 "members of the Osage Tribe of Indians": Don Whitehead, *The FBI Story* (New York: Random House, 1956), pp. 113–18.

318 around 300 Indian victims: This follows Dewing, *Wounded Knee II,* pp. 7–10.

318 turning into a symbol of repressive government: Dewing, *Wounded Knee II,* p. 38.

319 Indians for their emblem of Chief Wahoo: Dewing, *Wounded Knee II,* pp. 21, 26.

319 on the four roads leading into it: Gebhardt to O'Connell, The Use of Special Agents of the FBI in a Paramilitary Law Enforcement Operation in the Indian Country, Apr. 24, 1975, FBI File 100-462483-49.

320 large numbers of the reservation Indians: Dewing, *Wounded Knee II,* p. 70.

320 might hamper the Bureau at subsequent trials: Dewing, *Wounded Knee II,* pp. 83, 85.

320 a source of unity for the left: Dewing, *Wounded Knee II,* p. 93. On March 21 the entire *Dick Cavett Show* was devoted to Wounded Knee, with seven of the leading activists appearing to explain their position.

321 the situation "has deteriorated beyond our control": Dewing, *Wounded Knee II*, p. 98.

321 "the magnitude of Wounded Knee": Dewing, *Wounded Knee II*, p. 5.

325 assault on a policeman in Milwaukee: Scott Anderson, "The Martyrdom of Leonard Peltier," *Outside*, July 1995, p. 15, http://outside.away.com/magazine/0795/7f__leo1.html.

326 "was woven by the F.B.I. and its cohorts": Alan Dershowitz, "Agents and Indians" (review of Peter Matthiessen, *In the Spirit of Crazy Horse*), *New York Times Book Review*, March 6, 1983, p. 1.

327 Afterward the Mr. X story had nonetheless been passed on to Oliver Stone: Anderson, "The Martyrdom of Leonard Peltier."

327 Peltier boast of killing the agents: Heidi Bell Grease, "Wife of AIM Leader says Leonard Peltier Admitted Killing FBI Agents," *Rapid City Journal*, April 12, 2004.

327 Nobel Prize committee for the peace prize: Anderson, "The Martyrdom of Leonard Peltier," p. 15.

328 a bullet through her head: Patty Hearst, *Patty Hearst, Her Own Story* (originally published as *Every Secret Thing*) (1982; rpt. New York: Avon, 1988), pp. 44, 55. See also HEARNAP FBI file #7-15200.

329 "Then I would surely die in the cross fire": *Patty Hearst, Her Own Story*, p. 90.

329 "my paranoia over the FBI finding us was beginning to match theirs": *Patty Hearst, Her Own Story*, pp. 75, 91.

329 a 12-gauge riot shotgun: *Patty Hearst, Her Own Story*, p. 100.

330 "soldier in the Symbionese Liberation Army": *Patty Hearst, Her Own Story*, p. 109.

330 "This is Tania . . . Patricia Hearst." It was enough: *Patty Hearst, Her Own Story*, p. 161.

330 "the FBI seems to be so powerless?": Kelley, *Kelley, The Story of an FBI Director*, p. 201.

330 the nature of her involvement: *Patty Hearst, Her Own Story*, p. 170.

331 "radical and revolutionary fugitives": *Patty Hearst, Her Own Story*, p. 286.

331 two cars at the Marin County Civic Center: *Patty Hearst, Her Own Story*, pp. 361–80.

331 "We've got to end this": *New York Times*, May 10, 1974, p. 42.

332 more than 27,000 possible sources: Kelley, *Kelley, The Story of an FBI Director*, pp. 206, 219.

332 to be connected to the case: *Patty Hearst, Her Own Story*, p. 349.

332 her brother Steve, and their sister Josephine: "The Story of Patty," *Newsweek*, Sept. 29, 1975, p. 20ff.

332 a clenched-fist salute: *Newsweek*, Sept. 29, 1975, p. 20ff.

333 "the various SLA hideouts were located. None": Kelley, *Kelley, The Story of an FBI Director*, pp. 219–20.

333 a few, perhaps more than a few, drinks: http://www.claykeck.com/patty/capture.htm. "Hearst Figure Tells of Offer to Deliver Heiress," *New York Times*, Aug. 14, 1975, p. 42.

334 "anything going on in the United States": Quoted in Philip Shenon, "9/11 Panel Plans Hard Questions for the FBI and the Justice Department," *New York Times*, April 6, 2004.

335 "It frightens me to think that we do have revolutionary groups that are so dedicated": Kelley, *Kelley, The Story of an FBI Director*, p. 217; *New York Times*, May 10, 1974, p. 42; *Newsweek*, Sept. 29, 1975, p. 20ff.

335 presentations of evidence: Among the home improvements were a front portico and a rear deck, a fishpond with water pump and lights and shelves; they also painted his house and installed an artificial turf lawn, a garden fence, a flagstone court, and sidewalks. They set his clocks, repaired his wallpaper, and did his taxes. Moreover, the lavish presents given to the director were built by Bureau craftspeople on government time. *Masters of Deceit* was written by agents in the Crime Records Division, but Hoover pocketed a good part of the take. Kessler, *The Bureau*, p. 192.

335 many small gifts and trips from the company: Kessler, *The Bureau,* pp. 190–91; Revell, *A G-Man's Journal,* pp. 114–15.
336 "insurance policy for forty years": Kessler, *The Bureau,* p. 191.
336 had paid for their materials: Kessler, *The Bureau,* p. 192.
336 at his home in Washington: Kessler, *The Bureau,* p. 192.
337 had the Bureau take the televisions back: Kessler, *The Bureau,* p. 193.
337 seldom cost anyone their jobs: Kessler, *The Bureau,* p. 193.
337 "would be prosecuted today": Kessler, *The Bureau,* pp. 192–93.
337 Kelley submitted his resignation on February 15, 1978: Revell, *A G-Man's Journal,* pp. 122, 123, 127.
338 173 were Hispanic, and 147 were women: Kessler, *The Bureau,* p. 196.

Chapter 9

341 "an intermediary with other families": Joe Pistone with Richard Woodley, *Donnie Brasco* (1987; rpt. New York: Signet, 1989), p. 378.
342 "heroic undercover agent in history. Period": Jules Bonavolonta with Brian Duffy, *The Good Guys: How We Turned the FBI 'Round and Finally Broke the Mob* (New York: Simon & Schuster, 1999), p. 230. But just as Melvin Purvis was later hounded out of the Bureau, Pistone resigned in disgust, like Robert Lamphere, when he was assigned to Dallas and set down behind a wiretap to monitor it like a rookie agent (p. 231).
343 had secured evidence of Hoover's homosexuality: Anthony Summers, *Official and Confidential: The Secret Life of J. Edgar Hoover* (New York: Putnam, 1993), p. 245 and passim; for a thorough discussion and dismantling of Summers's thesis, see Athan G. Theoharis, *J. Edgar Hoover, Sex, and Crime: An Historical Antidote* (Chicago: Ivan Dee, 1995).
344 "pattern of racketeering activity or collection of unlawful debts": Bonavolonta, *The Good Guys,* p. 83. See also http://www.ricoact.com/ricoact/nutshell.asp.
344 "Holy shit!": Bonavolonta, *The Good Guys,* pp. 83–84.
345 "in our war against the Cosa Nostra": Bonavolonta, *The Good Guys,* p. 271.
346 the heads of the five families: Bonavolonta, *The Good Guys,* p. 160.
346 a hundred years apiece in prison: Bonavolonta, *The Good Guys,* p. 269.
347 black suits, black shirts, and red ties: Ralph Blumenthal, *Last Days of the Sicilians* (New York: Crown Publishing, 1988), pp. xvi, 357.
347 elimination by the Bureau's informants: See Dick Lehr and Gerard O'Neill, *Black Mass: The Irish Mob, The FBI and A Devil's Deal* (New York: Public Affairs, 2000). See also Ralph Ranalli, *Deadly Alliance: The FBI's Secret Partnership with the Mob* (New York: Harper Torch, 2001).
348 in all, twenty-six Americans were arrested: Mark Riebling, *Wedge: The Secret War Between the FBI and the CIA* (New York: Knopf, 1994), p. 362.
349 popping up nine months later in Moscow: David Wise, *The Spy Who Got Away* (New York: Random House, 1988), pp. 223–25.
349 "motivations for espionage": Wise, *The Spy Who Got Away,* p. 243.
350 six cars and a spotter plane: Robert Hunter and Lynn Dean Hunter, *Spy Hunter: Inside the FBI Investigation of the Walker Espionage Case* (Annapolis, MD: U.S. Naval Institute Press, 1999), p. 49.
350 "the 'real agents' from Washington field lose him inside of an hour": Hunter, *Spy Hunter,* p. 53.
350 and raced back to his squad: Hunter, *Spy Hunter,* p. 59.
351 bulletproof vests and armed with revolvers: This account closely follows Pete Early, *Family of Spies* (New York: Bantam, 1988), pp. 320–27.

351 "Because it's gone": Hunter, *Spy Hunter,* p. 207.

351 Last, but certainly not least to Ames, there was a request for $50,000: Peter Maas, *Killer Spy* (New York: Warner, 1995), pp. 50–58.

352 "the most important U.S. espionage case the FBI has ever had": Maas, *Killer Spy,* p. 162.

352 FBI-CIA conferences on the matter ended: Michael R. Bromwich, Justice Department Inspector General, "A Review of the FBI's Performance in Uncovering the Espionage Activities of Aldrich Hazen Ames, Unclassified Executive Summary," p. 4.

352 would not look into the situation again for three years: Tim Weiner, David Johnston, and Neil A. Lewis, *Betrayal: The Story of Aldrich Ames, an American Spy* (Rockland, MA: Wheeler Large Print Books, 1995), p. 150.

355 "And we still got sixty-three months for Rosario": Les Wiser, interview with author, October 13, 1999.

356 "any contact with CIA in the future [is] to be by letter only": Riebling, *Wedge,* p. 254.

356 "Immediately discontinue all contact with the local CIA office": Riebling, *Wedge,* p. 255.

357 that too went nowhere: Riebling, *Wedge,* p. 289.

357 "too much in fact," Hoover is supposed to have said: Riebling, *Wedge,* p. 284.

357 Davis leaked it to the *Los Angeles Times:* Riebling, *Wedge,* pp. 317, 318, 326, 321–23.

357 she was not available at her emergency number when Shadrin vanished: Riebling, *Wedge,* pp. 328–29.

358 "will never be as effective as the KGB's": Riebling, *Wedge,* pp. 334–36.

358 brief the Bureau about Central Intelligence cases "in a timely fashion": Riebling, *Wedge,* p. 395. Also discussed in James Adams, *Sellout: Aldrich Ames: The Spy Who Broke the CIA* (New York: Penguin, 1996), p. 152.

358 agents from the CIC in Langley: Riebling, *Wedge,* p. 441.

359 hijacked to Entebbe, Uganda: The Israeli force was commanded by Col. Jonathan Netanyahu, brother of the future Israeli prime minister. Colonel Netanyahu was the only member of the strike force killed.

360 to deal with major hostage incidents: Oliver "Buck" Revell and Dwight Williams, *A G-Man's Journal* (New York: Pocket Books, 1998), p. 214.

360 injuries or damages, even to suspects: Danny O. Coulson and Elaine Shannon, *No Heroes: Inside the FBI's Secret Counter-Terror Force* (New York: Pocket Books, 1999), p. 137.

360 "It's just two shots right in the middle of the forehead": Roger Nisely, interview with author; William Webster, interview with author.

360 "that they remain FBI agents?": Coulson, *No Heroes,* p. 140.

360 "You have to remember this is an FBI deal": Coulson, *No Heroes,* p. 146.

360 "We're the best and we should have the best": Coulson, *No Heroes,* p. 148.

361 logistics or piloting aircraft: For an inside look at the HRT, see Christopher Whitcomb, *Cold Zero* (Boston: Little, Brown, 2001).

361 the Los Angeles Olympics in 1984: Revell, *A G-Man's Journal,* p. 214.

362 "to find jobs for their people, especially at first": Coulson, *No Heroes,* p. 197.

362 Matthews along with it: Coulson, *No Heroes,* p. 206. Afterward Revell determined that Coulson's version was not exactly true. Revell claims that Coulson and Whittaker had a disagreement over tactics, and Coulson withdrew his men rather than participate in what he felt was a fatally flawed plan to extricate Matthews. Revell determined that Coulson had been right in opposing Whittaker's plans, but that he should not have withdrawn the HRT without orders from Washington. Revell, *A G-Man's Journal,* p. 218.

363 peaceful surrender with no loss of life: Revell, *A G-Man's Journal,* pp. 220–21.

364 "the brush of their failure": Coulson, *No Heroes,* p. 399.

365 "use of force during an armed siege": Quoted in Alan W. Bock, *Ambush at Ruby Ridge* (New York: Berkley, 1996), p. 227.

366 "We're supposed to be detectives": Robert Lamphere, interview with author, November 5, 1999.

366 he was dying from terminal brain cancer: Revell, *A G-Man's Journal*, p. 259.

367 "having a wife involved in the FBI and we don't intend to": Revell, *A G-Man's Journal*, p. 281; Ronald Kessler, *The FBI* (1993; rpt. New York: Pocket Books, 1994), p. 469.

367 "everybody covers ass": Kessler, *The FBI*, p. 469.

367 might have had something to do with it: Kessler, *The FBI*, p. 467.

367 a violation of government regulations: Kessler, *The FBI*, p. 471.

368 demanded to be waved in with her friends: Kessler, *The FBI*, pp. 473–75.

368 to get anything done for Sessions: Revell, *A G-Man's Journal*, p. 281; Kessler, *The FBI*, pp. 456–57, 477, 480–82.

368 "a mockery of the FBI's program of policing itself": Kessler, *The FBI*, p. 485.

368 the bad luck to live a decade longer: Revell, *A G-Man's Journal*, p. 282.

369 payments meant for Varelli: Revell, *A G-Man's Journal*, p. 293; Kessler, *The FBI*, p. 182.

369 his supervisor in Dallas was transferred: Revell, *A G-Man's Journal*, pp. 292–94.

370 "crimes it hadn't committed": Revell, *A G-Man's Journal*, p. 297.

370 "proceeded onto the battlefield to bayonet its wounded": Revell, *A G-Man's Journal*, p. 296.

370 Director "Concessions": Revell, *A G-Man's Journal*, p. 298.

370 "But there hasn't been a single one": Kessler, *The FBI*, p. 521.

371 "the blood will be running in rivers, not streams": Revell, *A G-Man's Journal*, pp. 296–97.

372 and old "Hooverites": Kessler, *The FBI*, p. 489.

372 under the circumstances, reckless and defiant: Kessler, *The FBI*, pp. 492–93.

372 "future direction and leadership of the FBI": Kessler, *The FBI*, p. 491.

373 "there is no excuse for your conduct": Kessler, *The FBI*, p. 497.

373 "an agency that you have professed to honor and respect": Revell, *A G-Man's Journal*, pp. 419–20.

374 one of the worst and deadliest debacles in FBI history: The key documents on Waco are U.S. Department of Justice, *Report on the Events at Waco, Texas, February 28 to April 19, 1993*; U.S. Department of the Treasury, Report of the Bureau of Alcohol, Tobacco, and Firearms, *Investigation of Vernon Wayne Howell also known as David Koresh*, September 1993; U.S. House of Representatives, *Events Surrounding the Branch Davidians Standoff in Waco, Texas*, Hearings before the Committee on the Judiciary, U.S. House of Representatives, 103rd Cong., 1st sess., April 28, 1993; Subcommittee on Crime of the Committee on the Judiciary and the Subcommittee on National Security, International Affairs, and Criminal Justice of the Committee on Government Reform and Oversight, *Joint Hearings on Activities of Federal Law Enforcement Agencies Toward the Branch Davidians*, 104th Cong., 1st sess., July 19–August 1, 1995; Committee on Government Reform and Oversight in conjunction with the Committee on the Judiciary, *Investigation into the Activities of Federal Law Enforcement Agencies Toward the Branch Davidians*, Report 104–179, 104th Cong., 1st sess.

374 observers from the Delta Force: David B. Kopel and Paul H. Blackman, in *No More Wacos* (Amherst, NY: Prometheus, 1997), p. 140, say there were 668 FBI personnel, 136 agents or support personnel from the Bureau of Alcohol, Tobacco, and Firearms, 15 from the Army, 131 Texas state troopers, 13 members of the Texas National Guard, and 31 Texas Rangers; they must mean at one time or another. Dick J. Reavis, *The Ashes of Waco* (New York: Simon & Schuster, 1995), p. 263, puts it at 720 total, with 250 FBI and 140 ATF— and nearly 1,000 from the media.

374 Helicopters were ready in backup locations: Kopel and Blackman, *No More Wacos*, p. 135.

374 Dick Schwein from El Paso: Coulson, *No Heroes*, p. 431.

374 the last at about 11:40 A.M.: Coulson, *No Heroes,* pp. 450–53.

375 "I made the decision. I'm accountable, the buck stops with me": *Dallas Morning News,* April 20, 1986.

375 "a bunch of religious fanatics decided to kill themselves": Kopel and Blackman, *No More Wacos,* p. 204.

375 since 120 died at Wounded Knee in 1890: If fine distinctions are appropriate in comparing catastrophes like Wounded Knee and Waco, it might be pointed out that the Indians were not American citizens, and that the cavalry and the Sioux were at war, since Wounded Knee developed out of an attempt to disarm the Indians as called for in the terms of surrender—so hostilities remained in effect when the shooting began that day.

375 "was conducted with professionalism": *Dallas Morning News,* April 20, 1986.

375 the entire command structure of the ATF was fired or disciplined for its performance at Waco: *Dallas Morning News,* Oct. 1, 1993. It should be noted that for the five ATF officials who were suspended, two on the scene and three in Washington, the charge was that they ignored evidence that their raid should have been stopped (because it had been compromised) and they lied to cover up the failure. In addition, ATF Director Stephen Higgins announced his resignation and was immediately replaced.

376 the warrants were signed by a local magistrate: Kopel and Blackman, *No More Wacos,* p. 64.

376 Senate Appropriations Committee hearing: Kopel and Blackman, *No More Wacos,* p. 48.

376 "to improve ATF's tarnished image": Kopel and Blackman, *No More Wacos,* p. 48.

376 the intimidating maneuvers of the tactical units: Coulson, *No Heroes,* p. 435.

377 "to move Koresh off the dime": Coulson, *No Heroes,* p. 445.

377 rejected it or deferred a decision: Coulson, *No Heroes,* p. 447.

377 "this could be the worst day in law enforcement history": Coulson, *No Heroes,* p. 448.

378 *The Turner Diaries:* By "Andrew MacDonald" (William L. Pierce) (North Carolina: The National Alliance, 1978).

378 more David Koreshes in the future: Roger Nisely, interview with author.

379 and to hire more negotiators: Waco *Tribune-Herald,* Feb. 27, 1994, p. 10, reporting on the Oct. 8, 1993, Justice Department report by Deputy Attorney General Philip Heymann.

379 tear-gas and tank assault on the compound: Revell, *A G-Man's Journal,* p. 427.

379 "we should have been prepared for fire": Revell, *A G-Man's Journal,* p. 428.

380 look like they were scapegoating the Bureau for Waco: Kessler, *The Bureau,* p. 515.

380 "a matter of principle": Kessler, *The Bureau,* p. 518.

Chapter 10

381 "It was a pretty horrifying experience": B. Drummond Ayres Jr., "Gunman Kills 2 Near CIA Entrance," *New York Times,* January 26, 1993.

382 "They fed everything to us": Special Agent Brad Garrett, author interview, Washington field office, FBI, Aug. 11, 1999.

383 "and of course we have the shooting on Monday": The fugitive warrants and the initial arrest stories spelled the suspect's name "Kansi." Later news stories tended to use another spelling, "Kasi," favored by the suspect. Here I use "Kansi," the pronunciation and spelling used by Garrett and the rest of the Bureau.

385 a twenty-two-hour flight to Islamabad: Pierre Thomas and Robert Suro, "Going Global to Get Their Man," *Washington Post,* June 19, 1997, p. 1.

385 Clinton would be kept briefed, sometimes several times a day: Thomas and Suro, "Going Global to Get Their Man," p. 1.

385 "this location in Pakistan near the Afghan border": Neither Garrett nor the Bureau would

comment to me officially on the location of the capture or the countries that aided the Bureau in the operation, but news accounts based on well-informed sources (presumably within the Bureau or the CIA) have said that the capture took place in Afghanistan, which would mean that government officials, police, and the military in both countries presumably were involved in the operation. On Feb. 4, 1999, in a statement to the Senate Appropriations Committee, Freeh confirmed that Kansi was "rendered" from Afghanistan. See "The Threat to the United States Posed by Terrorists," a Statement for the Record Before the Senate Committee on Appropriations, Feb. 4, 1999.

385 "a tactical move performed with a great deal of velocity": Special Agent in Charge Jimmy C. Carter, author interview, April 30, 1999.

386 pressure from the White House to "clear the way": Thomas and Suro, "Going Global," p. 1. According to *Time* magazine both Clinton and Madeleine Albright telephoned Prime Minister Nawaz Sharif to gain his approval of the operation. Reported in *Atlanta Constitution,* June 23, 1997, p. 1.

387 encroach on their civil liberties: "Keeping Tomorrow Safe," draft FBI Strategic Plan, 1998–2003, May 8, 1998, p. 2.

387 "including attacks overseas": *Joint Inquiry Report,* p. 234.

387 rather than one of state-supported terrorism: "The government never intended law enforcement to be the only, or even the principal strategy against terror," and yet "covert action and military force had little impact before 9/11." *Joint Inquiry Report,* p. 235.

388 "[t]he Southern District doesn't have any cruise missiles": *Joint Inquiry Report,* p. 236.

388 the FBI as the "lead" investigative agency: Jim McGee, "The Rise of the FBI," *Washington Post* (July 10, 1997), p. W10 ff.

389 handed the CIA's counterintelligence investigations to the FBI: Mark Riebling, *Wedge: The Secret War Between the FBI and the CIA* (New York: Knopf, 1994), p. 449.

390 whenever there was a conflict between the Bureau and the agency: Presidential Decision Directive 24, May 4, 1994.

391 "to face a growing threat from abroad": Oliver "Buck" Revell, *A G-Man's Journal* (New York: Pocket Books, 1998), pp. 87, 173.

391 pull the Bureau out completely: Revell, *A G-Man's Journal,* p. 173.

391 Callahan attended Interpol's annual conference in Cannes, France: Sanford J. Ungar, *FBI* (Boston: Little, Brown, 1975), p. 244.

391 "one man's terrorist is another man's freedom fighter": Revell, *A G-Man's Journal,* pp. 173, 243.

391 "an excellent position to carry out our duties in this critical area": Revell, *A G-Man's Journal,* p. 245.

392 thus ending the Legats' primary emphasis on counterintelligence: Revell, *A G-Man's Journal,* pp. 246, 248.

393 former governor Hugh Carey, as character witnesses: Robert Draper, "The Freeh World," *George,* Oct.–Nov. 1995, p. 191; Bruce Porter, "Facing Facts at the FBI," *New York Times Magazine,* Nov. 2, 1997, p. 56.

394 Howard Shapiro, also from the U.S. attorney's office in New York: Revell, *A G-Man's Journal,* p. 343.

394 the Attorney General's Award for Distinguished Service: John F. Kelly and Phillip K. Wearne, *Tainting Evidence: Inside the Scandals at the FBI Crime Lab* (New York: The Free Press, 1998), pp. 95–127. Kelly and Wearne are skeptical of the case against Moody. Suspicion arose in some minds that the importance of VANPAC in Freeh's career, and the importance of Tom Thurman and the lab's evidence in obtaining that conviction, might have had some bearing on Freeh's resistance when whistle-blower Frederic Whitehurst

charged that Thurman and the lab had a habit of shading evidence to suit the prosecution when they testified.

394 Royal Norwegian Ministry of Justice and Police: *The Investigator,* Dec. 1995–Jan. 1996, p. 1.

395 totals ran much higher, as many as 3,843: FBI release, International Training and Assistance Unit II Training Division, as of February 15, 1999; *The Investigator,* Dec. 1995–Jan. 1996, pp. 2–3.

396 represented a conceptual break from the FBI's past: Robert "Bear" Bryant, author interview, April 13, 1999.

399 "would apply in a criminal investigation": Jamie Gorelick to Mary Jo White, Louis Freeh, et al., March 4, 1995.

400 "criminal, and counterintelligence investigations": "Keeping Tomorrow Safe," p. 30.

400 database equipment and systems: "Keeping Tomorrow Safe," p. 31.

400 "on which useful intelligence depends": "Keeping Tomorrow Safe," p. 14.

400 "in furtherance of political or social objectives": Susan Rosenfeld, "Organization and Day-to-Day Activities," in Athan Theoharis, ed., *The FBI: A Comprehensive Reference Guide* (Phoenix: Oryx, 1999), p. 226.

401 "the property of a foreign government, and destruction of communications facilities": Public Law 104–132, quoted by Rosenfeld, "Organization and Day-to-Day Activities," p. 226.

401 "inherently reactive and rightly so": Strategic Plan, p. 2.

401 "a method for dealing with crises": Neil Gallagher, author interview, JEH-FBIH, August 5, 1999.

402 "more on convicting than on disrupting": *Joint Inquiry Report,* p. 236.

403 "when they began to transport the devices, they were arrested": Neil Gallagher interview.

403 "or does it consist only of violent people?": Neil Gallagher interview.

404 "a significant culture change for FBI managers": Strategic Plan, p. 33.

404 "all other criminal cases in that division": Clarence Kelley, *Kelley: The Story of an FBI Director* (Kansas City: Andrews, McMeel and Parker, 1987), p. 189.

404 restricted to foreign counterintelligence: Rosenfeld, "Organization and Day-to-Day Activities," p. 226.

404 "counterespionage operations were given less priority": David Johnston, "FBI Is Proposing a Special Division for Hunting Spies," *New York Times,* June 26, 1999.

405 "but divisions Four and Seven already had their stationery printed": Neil Gallagher interview.

405 "a new multidimensional capability for the Bureau": Neil Gallagher interview.

406 Psalm 101: Louis J. Freeh, *Ensuring Public Safety and National Security Under the Rule of Law: A Report to the American People on the Work of the FBI 1993–1998* (Washington: FBI, n.d.), p. i.

407 "the fiber which holds together the vitality of our institution": Freeh, *A Report,* inside cover.

408 "the Holocaust will not be forgotten by its special agents": Freeh, *A Report,* p. 14.

410 think if this came to light?: Author visit to FBI Academy ethics class, October 4, 1999.

411 a call for Sessions to resign: Revell, *A G-Man's Journal,* p. 420.

411 450 out into the field over the next year: During his testimony before the 9/11 Commission, Freeh offered a new explanation for the transfers, claiming they were made necessary by a hiring freeze during his first year.

412 one of the first Executive Conference meetings: Ronald Kessler, *The FBI* (1993; rpt. New York: Pocket Books, 1994), p. 528.

413 "had not happened on Freeh's watch": Special Agent in Charge Bob Ricks, quoted in

Ronald Kessler, *The Bureau: The Secret History of the FBI* (New York: St. Martin's Press, 2002), p. 330. See also Kessler, *The Bureau*, p. 317.

413 felt that anything he did might implicate him in the mess: Kessler, *The Bureau*, p. 328.

414 "Louis Freeh decided he did not want Waco to touch him": Kessler, *The Bureau*, p. 329.

414 to reinvestigate Waco in the light of the revelations: *New York Times*, Sept. 9, 1999.

414 during a mass suicide: This was revealed by Danny Coulson in an interview with the *Dallas Morning News*, Aug. 24, 1999.

415 "the government will come after them because they have guns": Paul J. Boyer, "The Children of Waco," *The New Yorker*, May 1, 1995, p. 45.

415 anything not permitted by the Bureau's standard rules: Danny O. Coulson and Elaine Shannon, *No Heroes* (New York: Pocket Books, 1999), pp. 411, 466; Revell, *A G-Man's Journal*, pp. 467–68; Kessler, *The Bureau*, pp. 325, 326.

416 more than two years until Potts retired: Kessler, *The Bureau*, p. 330.

416 an "extraordinary public confession of errors by an FBI director": George Lardner Jr., "Freeh Says FBI Actions at Ruby Ridge Were 'Flawed', " *Washington Post*, Oct. 20, 1995, p. 2.

417 They had their man: Kessler, *The Bureau*, p. 248.

417 another instance of FBI "overzealousness": Kessler, *The Bureau*, pp. 348–50.

418 "you don't have all the information you need": Kessler, *The Bureau*, p. 359.

418 "in an excess of caution": Kessler, *The Bureau*, p. 359.

419 "embarrassed our entire nation and each of us who is a citizen of it": Kessler, *The Bureau*, pp. 371, 372.

422 someone on Freeh's staff: Kessler, *The Bureau*, pp. 319, 320. Kessler quotes Buck Revell: "The Republicans were really starting to come down on Freeh. All of a sudden this memo he wrote to Reno is leaked. It was a typical bureaucratic ploy. But it is not something that happened under Kelley, Webster, or Sessions" (p. 320).

423 former high FBI officials from the New York field office: David A. Vise and Lorraine Adams, "FBI Chief Wants Job in Private Sector," *Washington Post*, April 4, 2000.

423 ex-officials Freeh had gotten rid of when he took over: Ronald Kessler, "Fire Freeh," *Washington Post*, Feb. 27, 2001.

424 caught by a North Carolina police officer in May 2003: "Key Events During Louis Freeh's Role as FBI Director," *Washington Post*, May 16, 2001.

424 "no one can explain why the culture doesn't change": Robert Suro, "FBI 'Culture' Must Change, Critics Say, Freeh Leaving Behind Unfulfilled Goals," *Washington Post*, May 13, 2001.

425 Assistant Attorney General Stephen R. Colgate: George Lardner Jr., "Censure of Freeh Was Secretly Rejected, Review of FBI's Flawed Ruby Ridge Probes Had Prompted Disciplinary Recommendation," *Washington Post*, Aug. 5, 2001, p. A1.

425 refusal to censure Freeh "outrageous" and a "whitewash": Lardner, "Censure of Freeh Was Secretly Rejected," p. 41.

427 "was ahead of his time": Roger K. Larson, M.D., letter to *Woodrow Wilson Quarterly*, Spring 2004, p. 4.

Afterword: End or Mend?

428 will not go away: *Final Report of the National Commission on Terrorist Attacks Upon the United States* (New York: Norton, 2004), pp. 403–406, 407–15; Deb Riechmann, "Bush to Back Creation of Intelligence Czar," *Washington Post*, August 3, 2004.

429 "processes and objectives of intelligence work": FBI, *The FBI's Counterterrorism Program*

Since September 2001, Report to the National Commission on Terrorist Attacks upon the United States, April 14, 2004, p. 37.

429 a good cop could never be a great spy: The Shelby quote is from "September 11 and the Imperative of Reform in the U.S. Intelligence Community, Additional Views of Senator Richard C. Shelby, Vice-Chairman, Senate Select Committee on Intelligence," December 10, 2002, p. 100. Shelby's personal report is in the "Additional Views of Members" section of the *Joint Inquiry Report,* separately paginated, at the end of the report.

429 authority over intelligence-related functions: Testimony of Robert S. Mueller III before the House Appropriations Committee, June 2, 2004.

430 "from their first day on the job to their last": FBI, *Report to the National Commission,* p. 32.

430 Validating human sources: FBI, *Report to the National Commission,* p. 33.

433 perform the FBI's mission: FBI, *Report to the National Commission,* pp. 7–9.

433 believe it simply cannot: Shelby, "Additional Views," p. 121.

433 stars and the dogs: http://www.tutor2u.net/business/strategy/bcg_box.htm.

434 "both 'intelligence' and 'criminal' investigations": FBI, *Report to the National Commission,* p. 23.

435 "these two missions in tandem": FBI, *Report to the National Commission,* p. 23.

437 stand-alone division inside the FBI: Richard A. Clarke, "The Wrong Debate on Terrorism," News of the Week in Review, *New York Times,* April 25, 2004, p. 15. Richard Shelby offers this as an alternative if Congress decides not to set up a new intelligence agency. Shelby, "Additional Views," p. 122.

437 at a moment's notice: Mueller, Testimony, June 2, 2004.

ACKNOWLEDGMENTS

For the FBI (and for me, too) this book began in one age and ended in another: pre- and post-9/11. Having written about the FBI for most of my career, I had developed a fondness for the Bureau, with all its faults, and a respect for the men and women who serve the Bureau and our country bravely, honestly, and creatively. And I had long agreed with the classic FBI historian of the 1950s, Don Whitehead, who concluded that the story of the FBI is the story of America—I would add, for good and ill. The 9/11 attacks came close to destroying my empathy for the institution: Louis Freeh's leadership during the 1990s, which had seemed to guide the Bureau toward a rational and ethical vision of law enforcement, instantly appeared fatally flawed; the blunders that had seemed to me understandable in an institution that was changing so rapidly, were clearly revealed to be indications of a Bureau that had, for reasons vitally important to understand, neglected its main task of protecting the country, while it continued business as usual in ways ever more unfocused as it moved in all directions at once, most of them unrelated to its most serious business. Thus a book that had begun in an effort to describe what the Bureau was doing right instantly became a search for what had gone wrong. And it took me quite a while to return to the essential truth of Don Whitehead's observation of half a century ago—that what the Bureau is doing, right or wrong, is a part of what the country is doing, and so the country must share with the FBI the blame for having failed on 9/11.

Louis Freeh's Bureau opened itself up to me from its highest executives to street agents. This may not be the book they had hoped for, but, as with all my books about the Bureau, it was written without taking any glee in pointing out the Bureau's failures. I am particularly grateful to Neal Schiff and Rex Tomb for their hard work in arranging headquarters and field interviews and tours of Bureau facilities. And to Samuel Baechtel, Warren T. Bamford, Robert "Bear" Bryant, Steven G. Burmeister, Jimmy C. Carter, R. Joe Clark, John Collingwood, Michael DeFeo, James V. DeSarno, Stephen G. Fischer, Kevin Foust, Tom Fuentes, Neil Gallagher, Brad Garrett, John Hall, Les Hazen, Donald M. Kerr,

Patrick J. Kiernan, Tom Knowles, Elizabeth Knowlton, Robert Lamphere, Edward R. Leary, A. Jackson Lowe, John E. Lynch, Jim Margolin, Pat Marshall, Jorge Martinez, Ken Moore, Kenneth E. Neu, Charlie Parsons, Millie Parsons, Frank L. Perry, Thomas J. Pickard, Ernie Porter, Judy Rasmussen, Russell P. Schubert, John E. Shea, Wiley D. Thompson, Mike Vatis, Dale Watson, William Webster, Christopher Whitcomb, Ronald J. Wilcox, Stephen R. Wiley, W. K. Williams, and Les Wiser.

Thanks also to FBI scholars Thomas J. Deakin, Sue Falb, David Garrow, and John Haynes for helping me work through some puzzles, to my colleague Steve Stearns for his helpful comments on the manuscript, and to my editors at Free Press, Edith Lewis for blazing a straight path through a much revised typescript, and Bruce Nichols for keeping this project focused and, even more important, keeping it moving. And to my wife Eileen for reminding me on many occasions that there was a book upstairs to be written.

ILLUSTRATION CREDITS

G-Men: *G-Men,* © 1937 Better Publications, New York
Freeh swearing in: AP/Wide World Photos
Ku Klux Klan: CORBIS
Pinkerton: courtesy of the author
Senator John Mitchell: courtesy of the U.S. Senate Historical Office
Stanley Finch: Library of Congress
Jack Johnson: Library of Congress
Bruce Bielaski: courtesy of the FBI
Application for American Protective League: Joan M. Jensen, *The Price of Vigilance,*
    ©1968 Rand McNally & Company
Attorney General Palmer: AP/Wide World Photos
Hoover at desk: Library of Congress
FBI Story scene: Photofest
Dillinger poster: courtesy of the FBI
Marking the map: courtesy of the FBI
Cagney movie still: Photofest
Nazi saboteurs: Bettmann/CORBIS
Agent Lamphere: Bettmann/CORBIS
The Rosenbergs: Library of Congress
Hoover and McCarthy: National Archives
Anticommunist warning: J. Edgar Hoover, *Masters of Deceit,*
    ©1958 Pocket Books, Inc.
1959 film scene: Photofest
Hoover and Sullivan: William C. Sullivan, *The Bureau:*
    My Thirty Years in Hoover's FBI, W. W. Norton & Company
Martin Luther King Jr.: Library of Congress
Lee Harvey Oswald: CORBIS
Patty Hearst: AP/Wide World Photos
Pine Ridge: AP/World Wide Photos
Time cover: Time Life Pictures/Getty Images
Joe Pistone: Jules Bonavolonta and Brian Duffy, *The Good Guys:*
    How We Turned the FBI 'Round—and Finally Broke the Mob,
    ©1996 Simon & Schuster, Inc.
Fat Tony Salerno: AP/Wide World Photos
ABSCAM: AP/Wide World Photos
Hostage Rescue Team: courtesy of the FBI
Distorted sketch: © David Levine—*New York Review of Books*
Kansi arrest: courtesy of the FBI
CIA mole Ames: AP/Wide World Photos

Mulder and Sculley: Photofest
Waco: AP/Wide World Photos
Ruby Ridge: AP/Wide World Photos
Rowley testimony: AP/Wide World Photos
Mueller swearing in: AP/Wide World Photos

INDEX

ABOUT THE AUTHOR

Richard Gid Powers is a professor of history at CUNY Graduate Center and the College of Staten Island. The author of definitive books on J. Edgar Hoover and American anticommunism, Powers has also written for *The New York Times Book Review* and has been a consultant for the History Channel and PBS. He lives with his wife in Brooklyn and New Orleans.